THE WAR FOR THE SEAS

Historian Evan Mawdsley was Professor of International History at Glasgow University. He is the author of *December 1941*, a *Sunday Telegraph* Book of the Year.

Further praise for *The War for the Seas*:

'This powerfully argued reappraisal establishes command of the sea as the critical issue that shaped and defined the Second World War.' Andrew Lambert, author of *Seapower States*

'Rich in detail on the tactics and technology that mattered, and on the roller-coaster campaigns in the Atlantic and Pacific theatres, Mawdsley provides the first full, integrated account of a truly global dimension to the war.' Richard Overy, author of *The Bombing War*

'The beautifully crafted and deeply researched maritime history of World War II that we have always needed. Few books deserve to be called "definitive" – this is one of them.' Joseph Maiolo, author of *Cry Havoc*

'Will be prized for its concision, clarity and sound judgement, all backed by impeccable scholarship.' Simon Ball, author of *The Bitter Sea*

THE WAR FOR THE SEAS

A MARITIME HISTORY OF WORLD WAR II

EVAN MAWDSLEY

YALE UNIVERSITY PRESS
NEW HAVEN AND LONDON

First published in paperback in 2020

For information about this and other Yale University Press publications, please contact:
U.S. Office: sales.press@yale.edu yalebooks.com
Europe Office: sales@yaleup.co.uk yalebooks.co.uk

Set in Minion Pro Regular by IDSUK (DataConnection) Ltd
Printed in Great Britain by Clays Ltd, Elcograf S.p.A.

Library of Congress Control Number: 2019941052

ISBN 978-0-300-19019-9 (hbk)
ISBN 978-0-300-25488-4 (pbk)

A catalogue record for this book is available from the British Library.

10 9 8 7 6 5 4 3

All freedom . . . depends on freedom of the seas.

President Franklin D. Roosevelt, 27 May 1941

CONTENTS

List of Plates, Maps and Tables *ix*
List of Technical Abbreviations *xiii*

Introduction xxxv

PART I Sea Power and the European War, September 1939–June 1940

1. The Twilight War, September 1939–April 1940 3
2. Norway: A Costly Victory 29
3. The Defence of the British Isles 47
4. The Bitter Fate of the French Navy, 1940–44 64

PART II The British Empire at Bay, June 1940–April 1942

5. The Battle of the Atlantic, Round One, June 1940–December 1941 83
6. The Struggle for the Mediterranean, July 1940–December 1941 111
7. Defending the Motherland: The Embattled Soviet Navy, June 1941–December 1944 135
8. An Undeclared Naval War: The Neutral US and the Axis Threat 154
9. Japan Attacks Britain and America, December 1941–April 1942 170

PART III Global War at Sea, April–December 1942

10. The Pacific in the Balance: From Carrier Raids to Midway 201
11. The South Pacific: The American Offensives at Guadalcanal, the Solomons and New Guinea, August 1942–May 1944 224

12. The Battle of the Atlantic, Round Two, January–December 1942 251
13. Britain and the Beginnings of Amphibious Operations in Europe, March 1941–December 1942 271
14. The Mediterranean: The British Regain the Initiative, January 1942–November 1942 286

PART IV Victory at Sea, January 1943–June 1944

15. The Battle of the Atlantic, Round Three, January 1943–May 1944 307
16. The Mediterranean: The Allies Gain Control, November 1942–August 1944 328
17. The Submarine War in the Pacific and Indian Oceans 350
18. The US Navy's Drive across the Central Pacific, November 1943–June 1944 370

PART V Commanding the Seas, Defeating the Axis, June 1944–August 1945

19. The Invasion of France and the Defeat of the Third Reich 419
20. The Philippines, Okinawa and the Defeat of Imperial Japan 439

Conclusion: The Commanded Sea 475

Endnotes 479
Bibliography 517
Index 533

PLATES, MAPS AND TABLES

PLATES

1 SS *Athenia*. Library and Archives Canada / Clifford M. Johnston fonds / a056817.
2 Type VII U-boat. © Bundesarchiv, Bild-23-63-15.
3 Cruiser *Admiral Hipper*. © Bundesarchiv, Bild 101II-MW-5607-32.
4 Adm. Erich Raeder. © Bundesarchiv, Bild 101II-MO-0726-12A.
5 HMS *Warspite*. © Imperial War Museum (A 9701).
6 Junkers Ju 88. © Bundesarchiv, Bild 101I-418-1840-10.
7 British troops at Dover Dunkirk. © Imperial War Museum (H 1645).
8 Battleship *Dunkerque*. Central Press / Hulton Archive / Getty Images.
9 Battleship *Giulio Cesare*. © Bundesarchiv, Bild 134-C1440.
10 Fairey Swordfish. © Imperial War Museum (A 12871).
11 Lofoten Raid. ©I mperial War Museum (N 397).
12 Troopship *Iosif Stalin*, 1941. © Bundesarchiv, Bild 101II-MN-2787-30.
13 Soviet reinforcements. TASS / Alexei Mezhuyev / Getty Images.
14 Adm. Stark, Pound and King. © Imperial War Museum (A 4980).
15 HMS *Azalea*. © Imperial War Museum (FL 1300).
16 SS *Samuel Chase*. Courtesy of Naval History and Heritage Command (80-G-21433).
17 USS *Reuben James*. Courtesy of Naval History and Heritage Command (NH-6455).
18 Adm. Yamamoto. ullstein bild Dtl. / Getty Images.
19 Battleship *Yamato*. Courtesy of Naval History and Heritage Command (NH 73092).
20 Pearl Harbor. Courtesy of Naval History and Heritage Command (NH-83065).

21 HMS *Prince of Wales*. © Imperial War Museum (A 29068).
22 Battleship *Scharnhorst* and *U 124*. © Bundesarchiv, Bild 101II-MW-4221-03.
23 RAF bombers over Brest. © Imperial War Museum (C 4109).
24 The Battle of Sirte. © Imperial War Museum (A 8166).
25 Butch O'Hare. Courtesy of Naval History and Heritage Command (80-G-457493).
26 Carrier *Hiryū*. Courtesy of Naval History and Heritage Command (USAF-3725).
27 USS *Yorktown*, 4 June 1942. Courtesy of Naval History and Heritage Command (80-G-312018).
28 Japanese A6M/ZEKE fighter. Courtesy of Naval History and Heritage Command (NH 91339).
29 Operation PEDESTAL. © Imperial War Museum (A 11285).
30 Beachhead: Dieppe, 19 August 1942. © Bundesarchiv, Bild 101I-362-2207-22.
31 *Mauritius* and *Queen Mary*. ©Imperial War Museum (A 11322).
32 Convoy PQ.18. © Imperial War Museum (A 12022).
33 Loss of USS *Wasp*. Courtesy of Naval History and Heritage Command (80-G-457818).
34 Battle of Santa Cruz. Courtesy of Naval History and Heritage Command (80-G-20989).
35 Invasion of French North Africa. © Imperial War Museum (A 12732).
36 Admiral Darlan and Allied leaders. Popperfoto / Getty Images
37 Russian convoy. © Imperial War Museum (A 14337).
38 Adm. Dönitz and Albert Speer. © Bundesarchiv, Bild 146III-372.
39 HMS *Biter*. © Imperial War Museum (FL 2164).
40 Escort carrier aircraft attack a U-boat. Courtesy of Naval History and Heritage Command (80-G-68694).
41 Liberator patrol bombers. © Imperial War Museum (CH 18035).
42 Adm. Tovey and Fraser. © Imperial War Museum (A 16484).
43 USS *Custer*. Courtesy of Naval History and Heritage Command (80-G-204846).
44 Sicily invasion. Courtesy of Naval History and Heritage Command (SC 217406).
45 USS *Savannah*. Courtesy of Naval History and Heritage Command (NH-95562).
46 The Italian Fleet under British escort. © Imperial War Museum (A 19859).
47 Adm. Spruance, King and Nimitz. Courtesy of Naval History and Heritage Command (80-G-307861).

48 USS *Trigger*. Courtesy of Naval History and Heritage Command (19-N-83820).
49 Grumman F6F-3 Hellcat. Courtesy of Naval History and Heritage Command (80-G-217624).
50 USS *Essex*. Courtesy of Naval History and Heritage Command (NH-91339).
51 Cruiser *Haguro*. Courtesy of Naval History and Heritage Command (NH-95558).
52 Tarawa. Frederic Lewis / Getty Images.
53 Gen. Eisenhower and Adm. Ramsay. © Imperial War Museum (H 39152).
54 Normandy Beachhead. Courtesy of Naval History and Heritage Command (80-G-45714).
55 The Battle of the Philippine Sea, 18–19 June 1944. Courtesy of Naval History and Heritage Command (80-G-239462).
56 USS *Cahaba*. Courtesy of Naval History and Heritage Command (80-G-K-6112).
57 Leyte Gulf: the Battle off Samar, 25 October 1944. Courtesy of Naval History and Heritage Command (80-G-287505).
58 Kamikaze: Lingayen Gulf, 6 January 1945. Courtesy of Naval History and Heritage Command (NH-79448).
59 Surrender and sea power: USS *Missouri*, 2 September 1945. Courtesy of Naval History and Heritage Command (SC-210628).

MAPS

1. The Norwegian Sea and Scandinavia
2. The English Channel and the North Sea
3. The North Sea and the Baltic
4. The North Atlantic Ocean
5. The Mediterranean and the Black Sea
6. The North Pacific and Japan
7. The Central and South Pacific
8. The Indian Ocean and Southeast Asia
9. The Global Ocean

TABLES

Table 5.1. The Battle of the Atlantic, 1939–41
Table 12.1. The Battle of the Atlantic, 1942

Table 15.1. The Battle of the Atlantic, January 1943–May 1944
Table 15.2. Allied Shipping Losses, June 1943–May 1944
Table 15.3. Troop Movements across the Atlantic (Eastbound), January 1943–June 1944
Table 17.1. Japanese Merchant Ship Losses, 1941–45
Table 17.2. US and Japanese Submarine Forces, 1941–45
Table 17.3. US Submarine Patrols in the Pacific, 1941–45
Table 17.4. Allied Merchant Ship Losses in the Pacific and Indian Oceans, 1941–45
Table 18.1. Aircraft Carriers Operating in the Pacific and Indian Oceans, 1943–45
Table 18.2. Major US Amphibious Operations in the Pacific, 1942–45
Table 19.1. Troop Movements across the Atlantic (Eastbound), June–December 1944
Table 19.2. Allied Divisions Disembarked in France, 1944–45
Table 19.3. The Battle of the Atlantic, June 1944–May 1945

TECHNICAL ABBREVIATIONS

The sixteen points of the compass, occasionally used in the text for greater precision, are (clockwise) N, NNE, NE, ENE, E, ESE, SE, SSE, S, SSW, SW, WSW, W, WNW, NW and NNW.

A-20	Boston/Havoc medium bomber (USAAF)
A6M	Zero/ZEKE carrier fighter (IJN)
AA	anti-aircraft
AAF	(US) Army Air Force
ABDA	Inter-Allied command in SE Asia in early 1942
APA	attack transport (USN)
A/S	anti-submarine
B-17	Fortress heavy bomber (USAAF)
B-24	Liberator heavy bomber (AAF)
B-25	Mitchell medium bomber (USAAF)
B5N	KATE carrier torpedo bomber (IJN)
B6N	JILL carrier torpedo bomber (IJN)
BB	battleship
BEF	British Expeditionary Force (1939–40)
Bf	Messerschmidt/Bayerische Flugzeugwerke (aircraft manufacturer)
BPF	British Pacific Fleet
C3	fast merchant-ship type (US)
CA	heavy cruiser
CAP	combat air patrol
CCS	Combined Chiefs of Staff (British/US)
C-in-C	Commander-in-Chief

CINCPAC	C-in-C, Pacific Fleet (USN)
CL	light cruiser
CNO	Chief of Naval Operations (USN)
CO	Commanding Officer (USN)
COMINCH	Commander-in-Chief, US Fleet
COS	Chiefs of Staff Committee (UK)
CV	aircraft carrier
CVE	escort carrier
CVL	light aircraft carrier
D3A	VAL carrier dive bomber (IJN)
D4Y	JUDY carrier dive bomber (IJN)
DD	destroyer
DE	destroyer escort
DF	direction finding
Do	Dornier (aircraft manufacturer)
DSM	Distinguished Service Medal (US decoration)
DSO	Distinguished Service Order (British decoration)
DUKW	amphibious truck
F4F	Wildcat carrier fighter (US)
F4U	Corsair carrier fighter (US)
F6F	Hellcat carrier fighter (US)
FAA	Fleet Air Arm (UK)
Fw	Focke-Wulf (aircraft manufacturer)
FY	fiscal year
G3M	NELL medium bomber (IJN)
G4M	BETTY medium bomber (IJN)
GM	General Motors
GRT	gross register tons (used for merchant ships)
He	Heinkel (aircraft manufacturer)
HF/DF	high-frequency direction finding
Hs	Henschel (missile manufacturer)
IGHQ	Imperial General Headquarters (Japan)
IJN	Imperial Japanese Navy
JCS	Joint Chiefs of Staff (US)
Ju	Junkers (aircraft manufacturer)
KG	*Kampfgeschwader* (bomber group)
LCI	landing craft, infantry
LCI(L)	landing craft, infantry (large)
LCT	landing craft, tank
LCVP	landing craft, vehicle/tank, personnel

LSI	landing ship, infantry (RN)
LSI(L)	landing ship (large) (RN)
LSM	landing ship (medium)
LST	landing ship, tank
LVT	landing vehicle, tracked
MTB	motor torpedo boat
MV	motor (diesel) vessel
NAG	Naval Air Group (*Kokutai*) (IJN)
NDL	Norddeutscher Lloyd shipping line
NGS	Naval General Staff (IJN)
NI	Netherlands Indies
OKW	Oberkommando der Wehrmacht
PB4Y	Liberator patrol bomber (USN)
PBY	Catalina flying boat (USN)
POA	Pacific Ocean Area (Nimitz command)
PT	patrol torpedo boat (USN)
RN	(British) Royal Navy
SBD	Dauntless carrier dive bomber (US)
shp	shaft horsepower
SKL	Naval War Staff (*Seekriegsleitung*)
SNLF	Special Naval Landing Force (Japanese naval infantry)
SS	steamship
StG	*Stukageschwader* (dive bomber) group
SWPA	South West Pacific Area (MacArthur command)
T5	German acoustic torpedo
TA	traffic analysis
TBF	Avenger torpedo bomber (US)
TF	Task Force
TG	Task Group
USAAF	US Army Air Force
USMC	US Marine Corps
USN	US Navy
VLR	very long range (aircraft)
VMF	*Voenno-morskoi flot* (Navy) (Russia)

Greenland (Dan.)
30°
70°
20°
Arctic Circle
Denmark Strait
Reykjavik
5/40
Hvalfjord
ICELAND
Glorious, 6/40
NORWEGIAN SEA
ATLANTIC OCEAN
Rawalpindi, 11/39
60°
Faeroe Is. (Dan.)
4/40
Shetland Is.
Orkney Is.
Scapa Flow
Loch Ewe
GREAT BRITAIN
Glasgow
Rosyth
NORTH SEA
4/40
Namsos
4/40
4/40
Åndalsnes
Trondheim
4/40
Bergen
Stavanger
4/40
Kristiansand
Oslo
Skagerrak
4/40

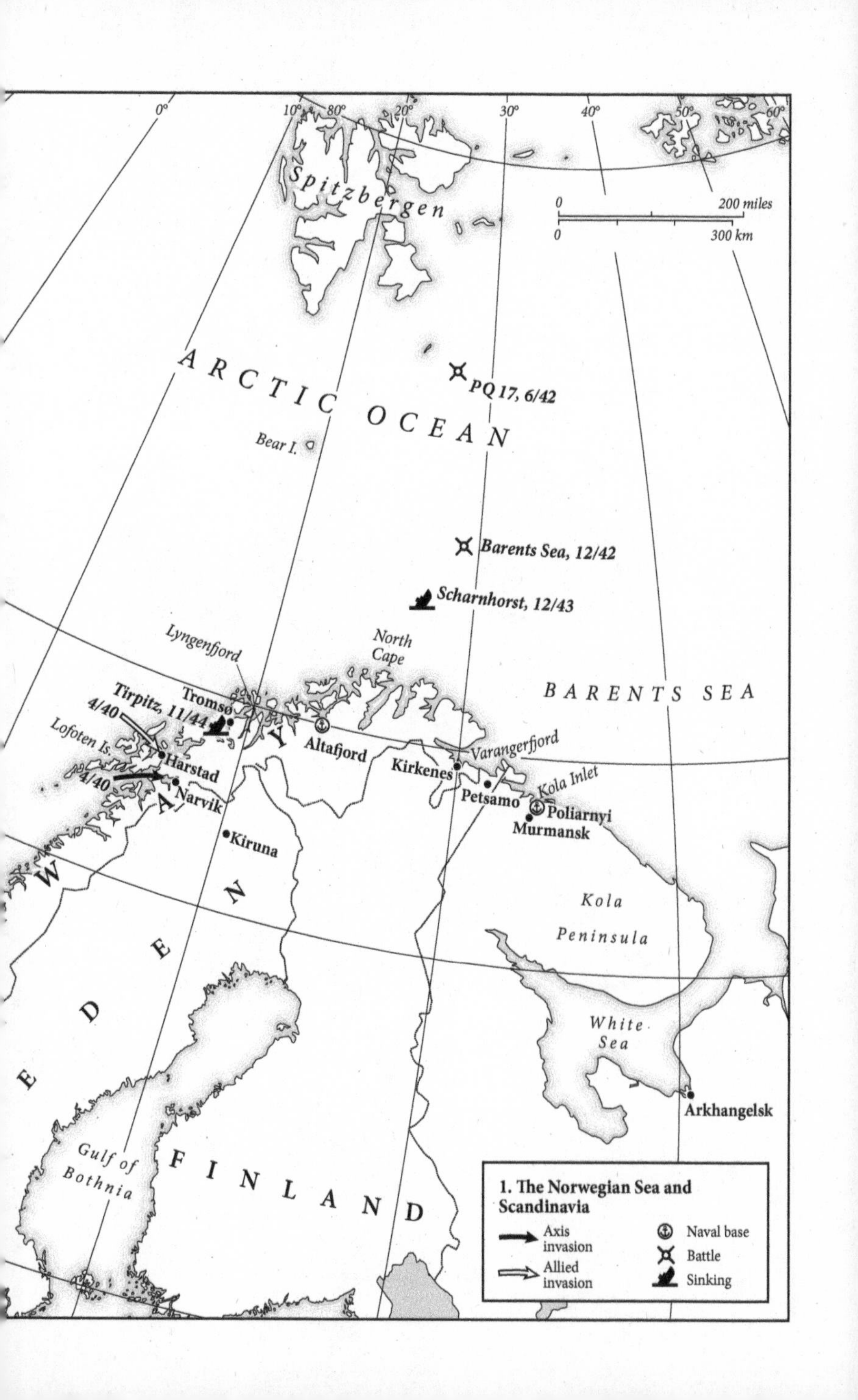
0°
10°
80°
20°
30°
40°
50°
60°
Spitzbergen
0
200 miles
0
300 km
ARCTIC OCEAN
PQ 17, 6/42
Bear I.
Barents Sea, 12/42
Scharnhorst, 12/43
Lyngenfjord
North Cape
BARENTS SEA
Tirpitz, 11/44
Tromsø
4/40
Lofoten Is.
Harstad
4/40
Narvik
Altafjord
Kirkenes
Varangerfjord
Petsamo
Kola Inlet
Poliarnyi
Murmansk
Kiruna
Kola Peninsula
White Sea
Arkhangelsk
Gulf of Bothnia
FINLAND
1. The Norwegian Sea and Scandinavia
Axis invasion
Allied invasion
Naval base
Battle
Sinking

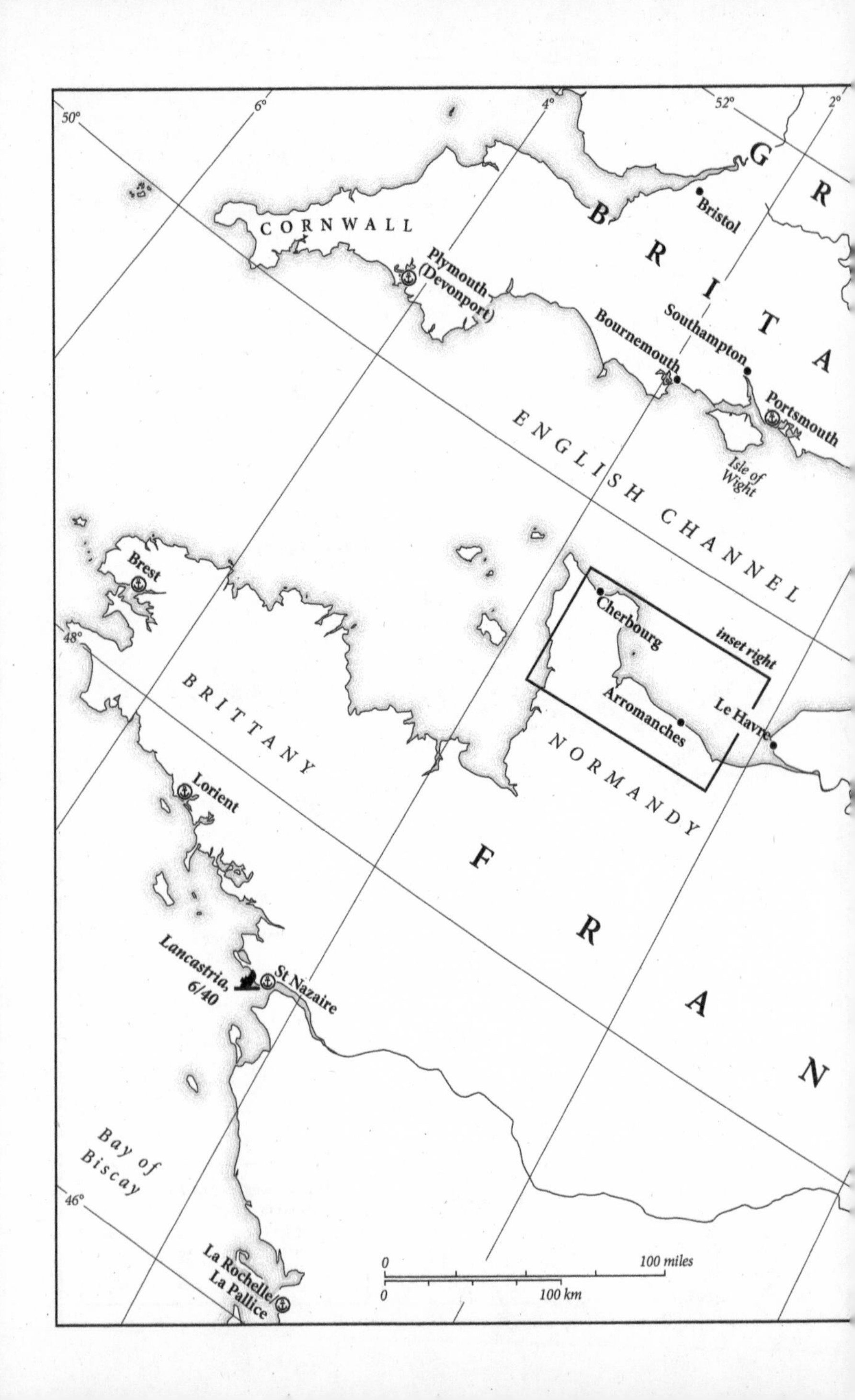
50°
6°
4°
52°
2°
G R
B R I T A
Bristol
CORNWALL
Plymouth (Devonport)
Bournemouth
Southampton
Portsmouth
Isle of Wight
ENGLISH CHANNEL
Brest
48°
BRITTANY
Cherbourg
inset right
Arromanches
Le Havre
NORMANDY
Lorient
F R A N
Lancastria, 6/40
St Nazaire
Bay of Biscay
46°
La Rochelle/ La Pallice
0
100 miles
0
100 km

2. The English Channel and the North Sea
Allied invasion
Naval base
Sinking
0°
2°
54°
4°
6°
EAST ANGLIA
NORTH SEA
London
Harwich
Chatham
Sheerness
KENT
Brighton
Folkestone
Dover
Hastings
Beachy Head
Strait of Dover
Cap Griz-Nez
Calais
PAYS DE CALAIS
Boulogne
Dunkirk
Ostend
Walcheren
Scheldt Estuary
Rotterdam
Amsterdam
NETHERLANDS
Antwerp
Lille
Brussels
BELGIUM
8/42
St Valéry
Dieppe
Rouen
Paris
Normandy landings, 6/44
Cherbourg
English Channel
UTAH
Cotentin Peninsula
OMAHA
GOLD
JUNO
SWORD
Carentan
Arromanches
Bayeux
NORMANDY
St Lô
Caen

60°
0°
4°
8°
12°
56°
52°
NORWAY
Bergen
Stavanger
Oslo
Kristiansand
Skagerrak
NORTH SEA
SWEDEN
Kattegat
DENMARK
Schillig Roads
Flensburg
Kiel
Copenhagen
Karlskrona
Wilhelmshaven
Bremenhaven
Hamburg
Lübeck
Cap Arcona, 5/45
Rostock
Bornholm
BALTIC
Wilhelm Gustloff, 1/45
Gotenhafen/ Gdynia
Danzig
Stettin
GERMANY
Berlin
POLAND

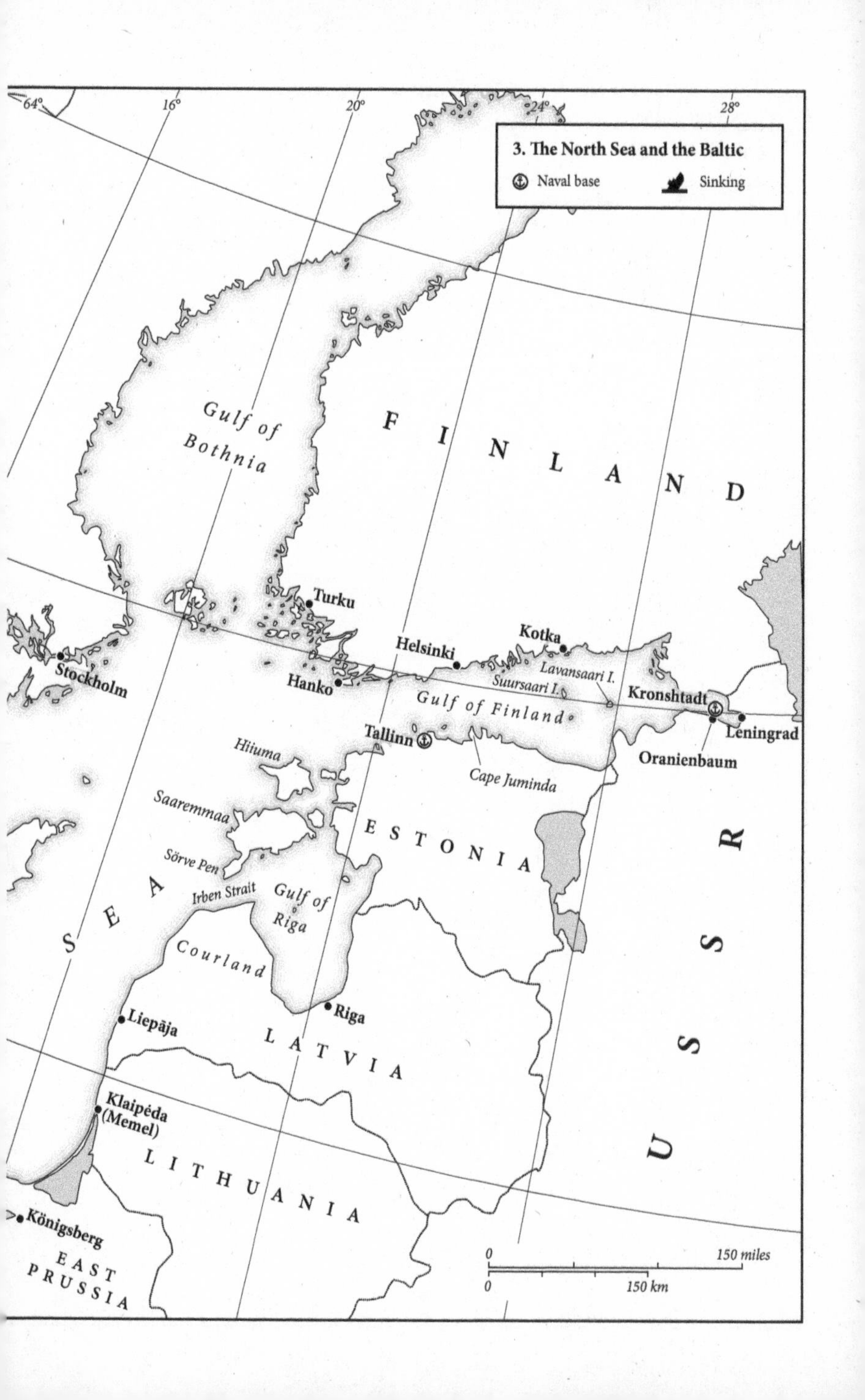
3. The North Sea and the Baltic
Naval base
Sinking
64°
16°
20°
24°
28°
Gulf of Bothnia
FINLAND
Turku
Helsinki
Kotka
Lavansaari I.
Suursaari I.
Kronshtadt
Leningrad
Oranienbaum
Stockholm
Hanko
Gulf of Finland
Tallinn
Hiiuma
Cape Juminda
Saaremmaa
ESTONIA
Sörve Pen
Irben Strait
Gulf of Riga
SEA
Courland
Riga
Liepāja
LATVIA
Klaipėda
(Memel)
LITHUANIA
Königsberg
EAST PRUSSIA
USSR
0
150 miles
0
150 km

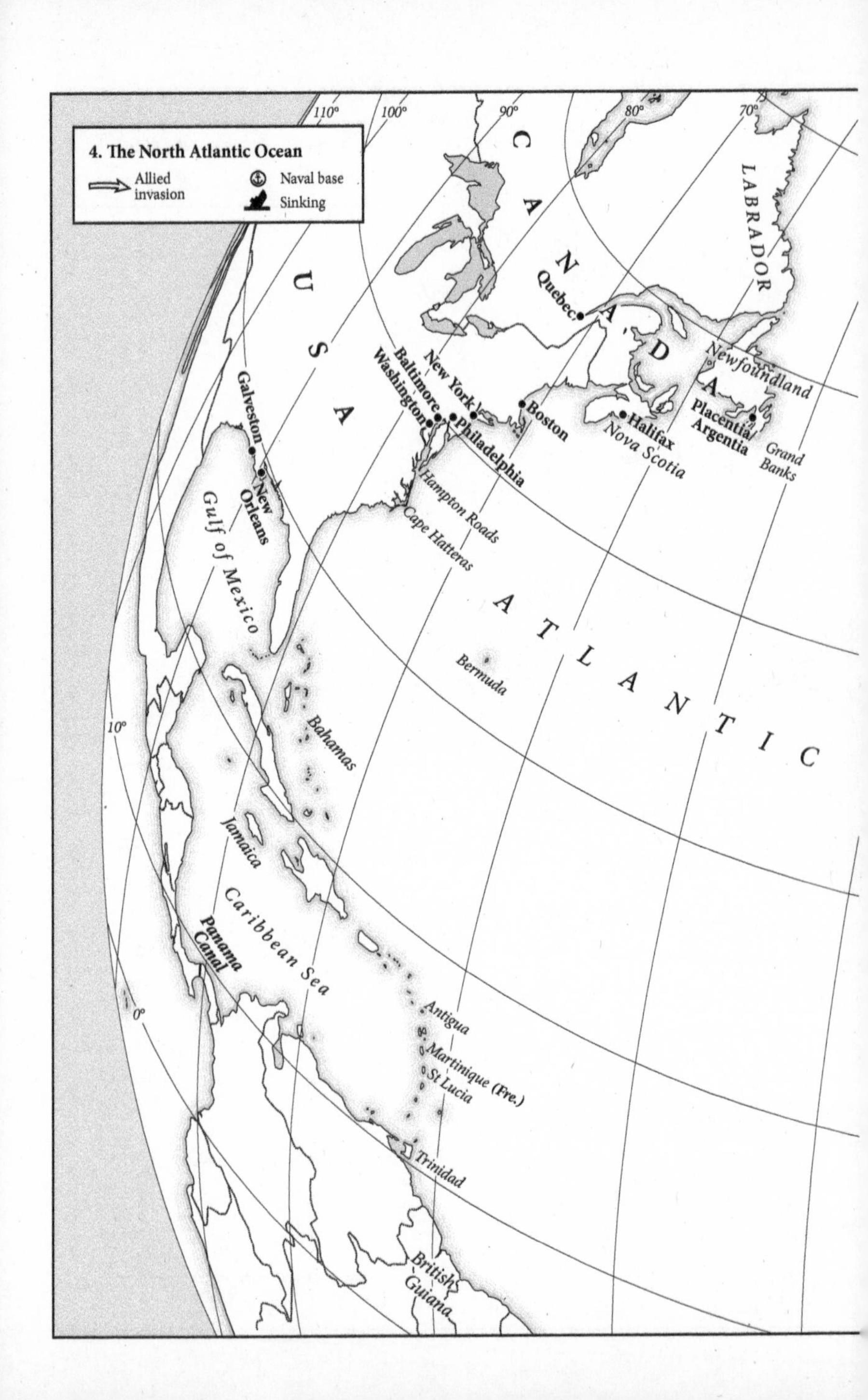

4. The North Atlantic Ocean
Allied invasion
Naval base
Sinking
110°
100°
90°
80°
70°
10°
0°
CANADA
LABRADOR
USA
Quebec
Newfoundland
Placentia
Argentia
Grand Banks
Halifax
Nova Scotia
Boston
New York
Philadelphia
Baltimore
Washington
Hampton Roads
Cape Hatteras
Galveston
New Orleans
Gulf of Mexico
ATLANTIC
Bermuda
Bahamas
Jamaica
Caribbean Sea
Panama Canal
Antigua
Martinique (Fre.)
St Lucia
Trinidad
British Guiana

Greenland
Denmark Strait
Hvalfjord
ICELAND
Hood, 5/41
Trondheim
Scapa Flow
Loch Ewe
Athenia, 9/39
Glasgow
Empress of Britain, 10/40
GREAT BRITAIN
Londonderry
Belfast
Liverpool
Kiel
Wilhelmshaven
Jervis Bay, 11/40
Reuben James, 10/41
Courageous, 9/39
Bismarck, 5/41
Brest
Lorient
St Nazaire
FRANCE
La Rochelle/
La Pallice
Bordeaux
Toulon
SPAIN
PORTUGAL
Lisbon
Azores
(Por.)
OCEAN
Gibraltar
Oran
Mehdia
11/42
Casablanca
Fédala
MOROCCO
Safi
Block Island, 5/44
ALGERIA
Canary Is.
(Spa.)
Cape Verde Is.
(Spa.)
Dakar
Senegal
0
1500 miles
0
1500 km
60°
50°
40°
30°
20°
10°
0°
10°
20°

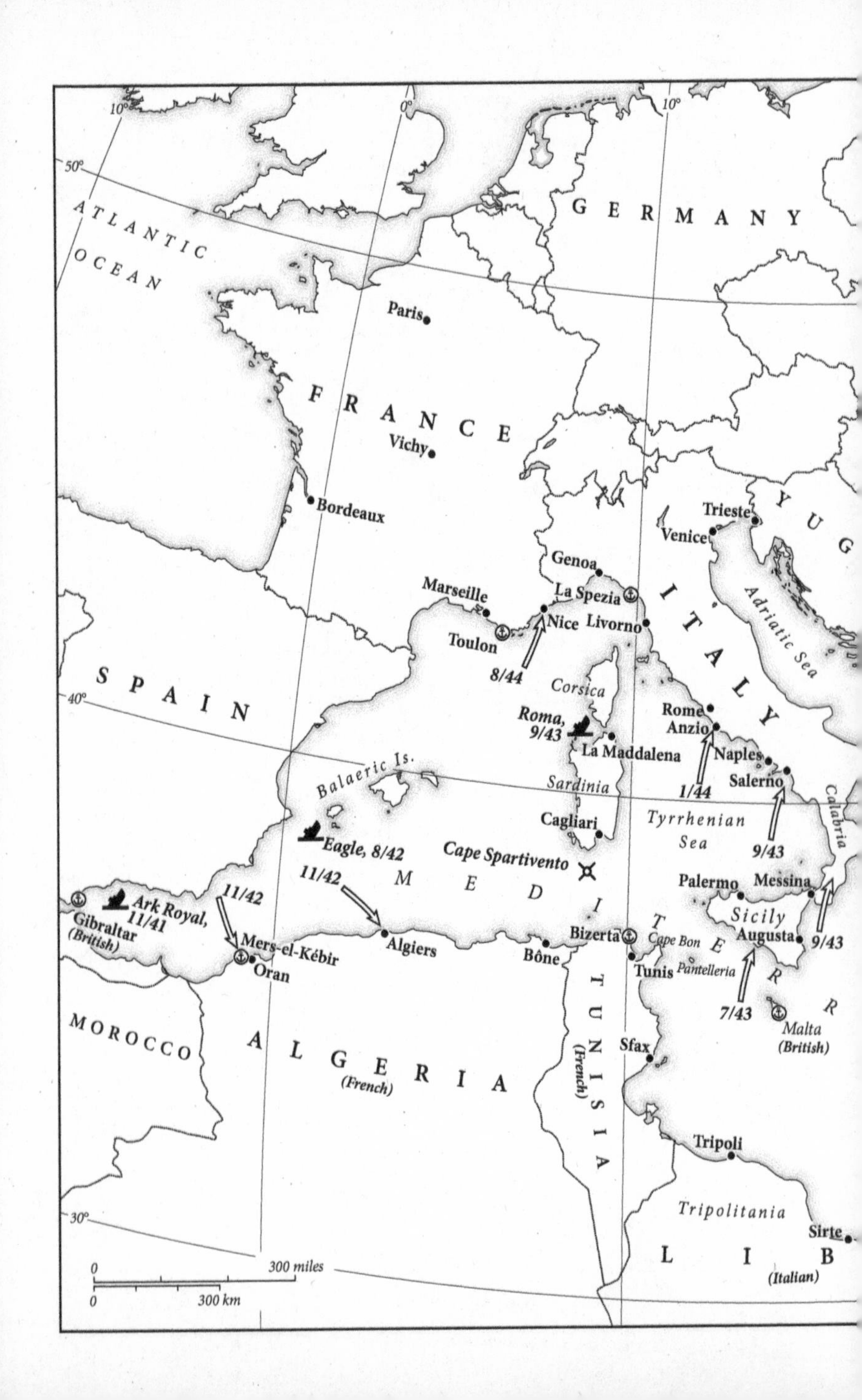
10°
0°
10°
50°
40°
30°
ATLANTIC
OCEAN
GERMANY
Paris
FRANCE
Vichy
Bordeaux
Trieste
Venice
YUG
Genoa
Marseille
La Spezia
Nice
Livorno
Toulon
ITALY
Adriatic Sea
8/44
Corsica
SPAIN
Roma,
9/43
Rome
Anzio
La Maddalena
Naples
Balaeric Is.
Salerno
Sardinia
1/44
Calabria
Tyrrhenian
Sea
Cagliari
Eagle, 8/42
Cape Spartivento
9/43
11/42
MED
Palermo
Messina
Ark Royal,
11/41
11/42
ITER
Sicily
Gibraltar
(British)
Mers-el-Kébir
Algiers
Bône
Bizerta
Cape Bon
Augusta
9/43
Oran
Tunis
Pantelleria
7/43
Malta
(British)
MOROCCO
ALGERIA
(French)
TUNISIA
(French)
Sfax
Tripoli
Tripolitania
Sirte
LIB
(Italian)
0
300 miles
0
300 km

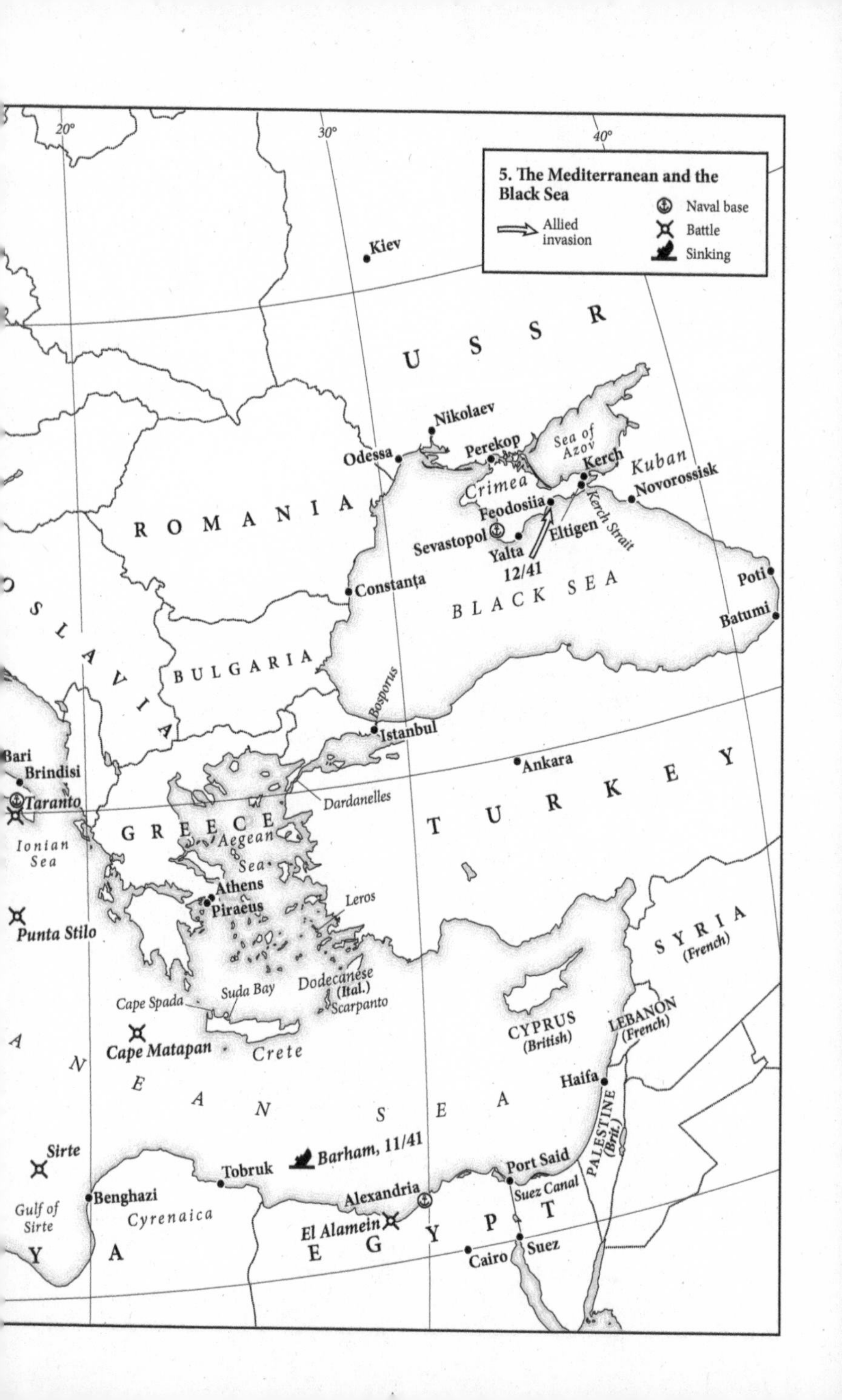
5. The Mediterranean and the Black Sea
Allied invasion
Naval base
Battle
Sinking
20°
30°
40°
Kiev
U S S R
Nikolaev
Odessa
Perekop
Sea of Azov
Kerch
Kuban
Novorossisk
Crimea
Feodosiia
Sevastopol
Eltigen
Kerch Strait
Yalta
12/41
ROMANIA
Constanța
BLACK SEA
Poti
Batumi
BULGARIA
Bosporus
Istanbul
Ankara
TURKEY
Bari
Brindisi
Taranto
Dardanelles
GREECE
Aegean Sea
Ionian Sea
Athens
Piraeus
Leros
Punta Stilo
SYRIA
(French)
Dodecanese
(Ital.)
Scarpanto
Suda Bay
Cape Spada
CYPRUS
(British)
LEBANON
(French)
Cape Matapan
Crete
Haifa
PALESTINE
(Brit.)
Sirte
Barham, 11/41
Tobruk
Port Said
Suez Canal
Benghazi
Alexandria
Gulf of Sirte
Cyrenaica
El Alamein
EGYPT
Suez
Cairo

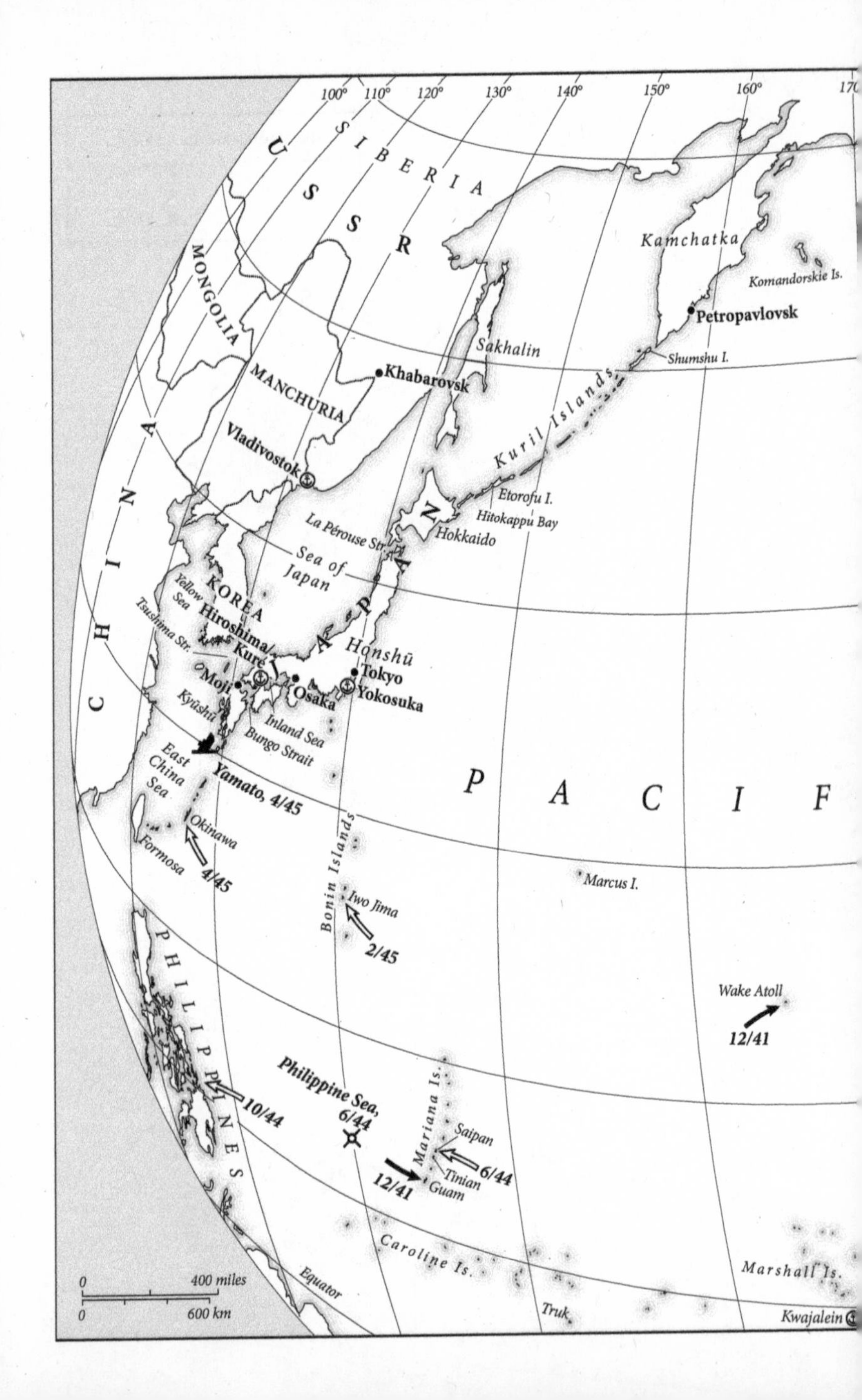

100°
110°
120°
130°
140°
150°
160°
U S S R
S I B E R I A
MONGOLIA
MANCHURIA
C H I N A
KOREA
J A P A N
Kamchatka
Komandorskie Is.
Petropavlovsk
Sakhalin
Shumshu I.
Khabarovsk
Kuril Islands
Vladivostok
Etorofu I.
Hitokappu Bay
La Pérouse Str.
Hokkaido
Sea of Japan
Yellow Sea
Tsushima Str.
Hiroshima/
Kure
Honshū
Tokyo
Moji
Osaka
Yokosuka
Kyūshū
Inland Sea
Bungo Strait
East China Sea
Yamato, 4/45
P A C I F
Okinawa
Formosa
4/45
Bonin Islands
Marcus I.
Iwo Jima
2/45
Wake Atoll
12/41
P H I L I P P I N E S
Philippine Sea, 6/44
10/44
Mariana Is.
Saipan
6/44
Tinian
Guam
12/41
Caroline Is.
Marshall Is.
Truk
Kwajalein
Equator
0
400 miles
0
600 km

180°
170°
60°
160°
150°
140°
130°
50°
US
Bering Sea
Aleutian Islands
Dutch Harbor
5/43
Kiska I.
40°
O C E A N
I C
30°
Midway, 6/42
Midway Atoll
Pearl Harbor
Oahu
Hawaiian Is.
20°
Johnston I.
10°
1/44
0°
6. The North Pacific and Japan
Axis invasion
Allied invasion
Naval base
Battle
Sinking

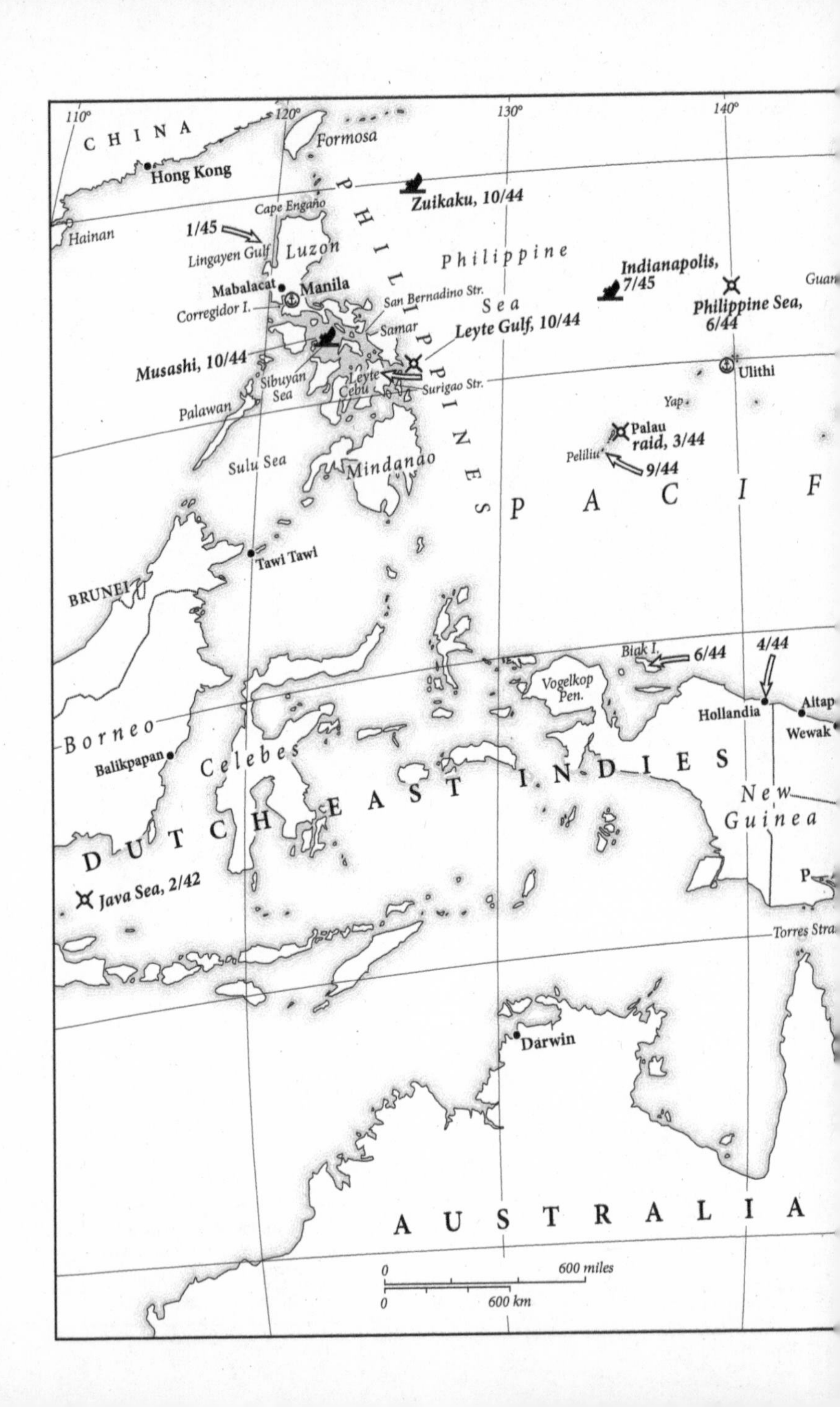
110°
120°
130°
140°
CHINA
Hong Kong
Formosa
Hainan
Zuikaku, 10/44
Cape Engaño
1/45
Lingayen Gulf
Luzon
PHILIPPINES
Philippine Sea
Indianapolis, 7/45
Philippine Sea, 6/44
Guam
Mabalacat
Manila
Corregidor I.
San Bernardino Str.
Samar
Leyte Gulf, 10/44
Musashi, 10/44
Sibuyan Sea
Leyte
Cebu
Surigao Str.
Ulithi
Yap
Palawan
Palau raid, 3/44
Peliliu
9/44
Sulu Sea
Mindanao
PACIF
Tawi Tawi
BRUNEI
Biak I.
6/44
4/44
Vogelkop Pen.
Hollandia
Aitape
Wewak
Borneo
Balikpapan
Celebes
DUTCH EAST INDIES
New Guinea
Java Sea, 2/42
Torres Strait
Darwin
AUSTRALIA
0
600 miles
0
600 km

7. The Central and South Pacific
Axis invasion
Allied invasion
Naval base
Battle
Sinking
150°
160°
170°
180°
20°
10°
0°
10°
20°
Mariana Islands
Saipan
6/44
Tinian
Marshall Islands
Eniwetok I.
Kwajalein
1/44
Majuro
Caroline Islands
Truk raid, 2/44
I C O C E A N
Makin
Tarawa
11/43
Gilbert Islands
Admiralty Islands
Manus I.
Bismarck Sea
New Ireland
Rabaul
1/42
Bismarck Arch.
Cape Gloucester
New Britain
SOLOMON ISLANDS
Bougainville
Eastern Solomons (8/42)
Huon Pen.
Lae
Vitiaz Str.
Empress Augusta Bay
Salamaua
Vella Lavella
U A
Buna
Kolombangara
Santa Cruz, 10/42
New Georgia
5/42
Port Moresby
Milne Bay
Guadalcanal
8/42
Coral Sea, 5/42
Wasp, 9/42
Espiritu Santo
New Hebrides
Fiji
Townsville
Nouvelle Calédonie
Nouméa

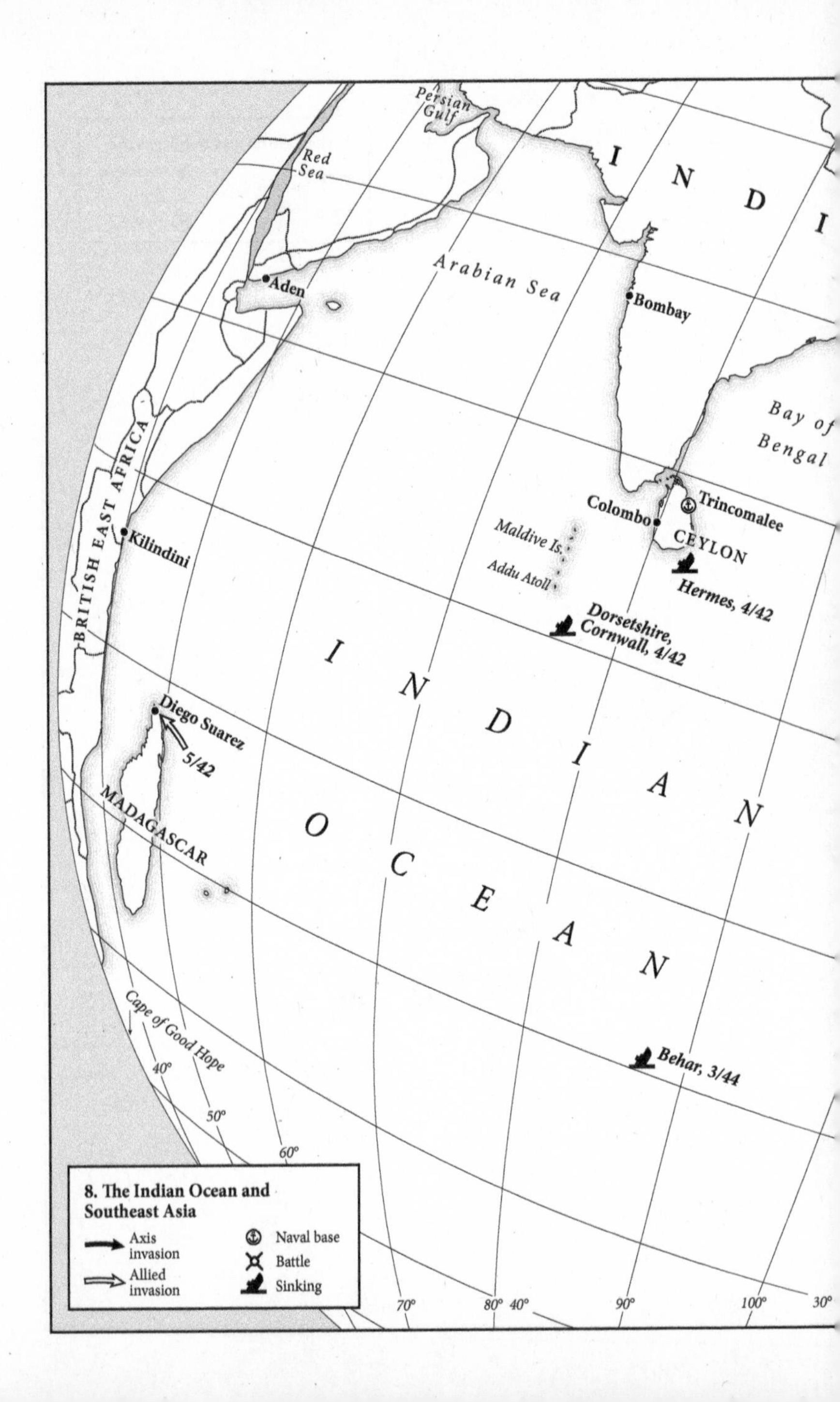

Persian Gulf
Red Sea
INDIA
Arabian Sea
Aden
Bombay
Bay of Bengal
BRITISH EAST AFRICA
Kilindini
Colombo
Trincomalee
CEYLON
Maldive Is.
Addu Atoll
Hermes, 4/42
Dorsetshire, Cornwall, 4/42
INDIAN OCEAN
Diego Suarez
5/42
MADAGASCAR
Cape of Good Hope
Behar, 3/44
40°
50°
60°
70°
80°
40°
90°
100°
30°
8. The Indian Ocean and Southeast Asia
Axis invasion
Allied invasion
Naval base
Battle
Sinking

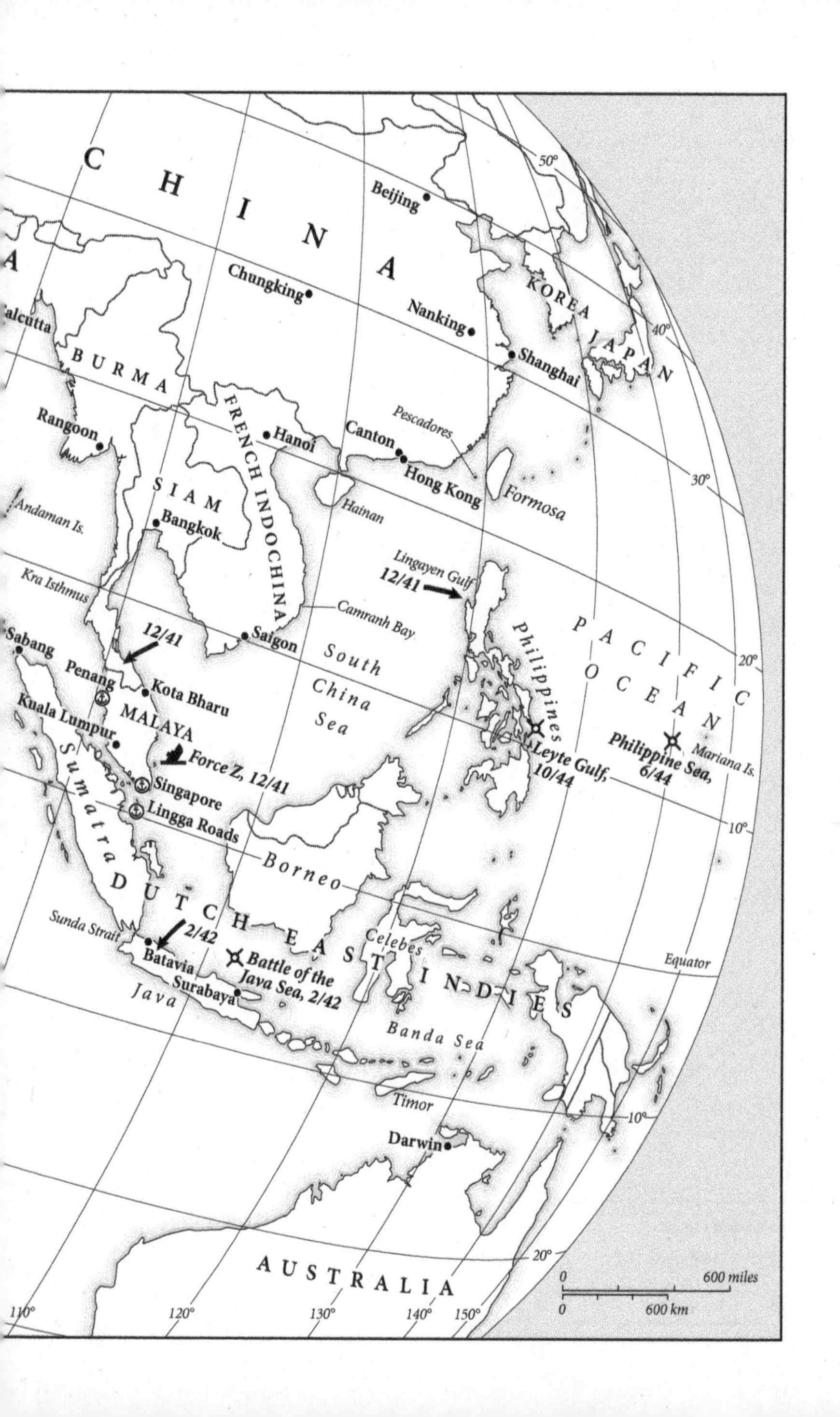

CHINA
Beijing
Chungking
Nanking
Shanghai
KOREA
JAPAN
Calcutta
BURMA
Rangoon
FRENCH INDOCHINA
Hanoi
Canton
Hong Kong
Pescadores
Formosa
Hainan
SIAM
Bangkok
Andaman Is.
Kra Isthmus
Lingayen Gulf
12/41
Camranh Bay
Saigon
12/41
Sabang
Penang
Kota Bharu
MALAYA
Kuala Lumpur
Force Z, 12/41
Singapore
Lingga Roads
South China Sea
Philippines
Leyte Gulf, 10/44
PACIFIC OCEAN
Philippine Sea, 6/44
Mariana Is.
Sumatra
Borneo
DUTCH EAST INDIES
Celebes
Sunda Strait
2/42
Batavia
Battle of the Java Sea, 2/42
Surabaya
Java
Banda Sea
Timor
Darwin
AUSTRALIA
Equator
50°
40°
30°
20°
10°
10°
20°
110°
120°
130°
140°
150°
0
600 miles
0
600 km

9. The Global Ocean

Allied supply lines

Japanese supply lines

Sinkings

Greenland
Iceland
60°
Liverpool
Seattle
Halifax
Marseille
NORTH
San Francisco
AMERICA
New York
Baltimore
Los Angeles
Gibraltar
New Orleans
NORTH
30°
Pearl Harbor
ATLANTIC
Hawaiian Is.
AFRICA
OCEAN
Dakar
Sierra
Leone
Freetown
VENEZUELA
Panama Canal
Equat
Laconia, 9/42
SOUTH
AMERICA
Bora Bora
French Polynesia
Rio di Janeiro
PACIFIC OCEAN
30°
SOUTH
Montevideo
Buenos
Aires
River Plate
Cape Town
Graf Spee, 12/39
ATLANTIC
OCEAN
Cape Horn
60°
180°
150°
120°
90°
60°
30°
0°
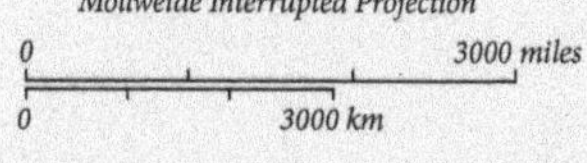
Mollweide Interrupted Projection
0
3000 miles
0
3000 km

INTRODUCTION

On 5 November 1942, Dwight D. Eisenhower arrived at a secret new command centre buried under the British fortress at Gibraltar. The young American general had been put in command of Operation TORCH, the invasion of north-west Africa. It was a colossal expedition, but planning had begun in London only a few months before. 'Ike' was a gifted planner and an astute leader of committees but, thus far, an inexperienced man of war. With him in Gibraltar's Admiralty Tunnel were his staff, including his chief naval commander, the British admiral Andrew Cunningham.

These two men knew the vast scale and significance of what was about to unfold. Three years later, in May 1945, having fought and won history-making battles, Eisenhower wrote a note of thanks to Cunningham. He described 'the hours that you and I spent together in the dripping tunnels of Gibraltar' as the one period in the whole war he would remember longest. 'It was there,' the general avowed, 'that I first understood the indescribable and inescapable strain that comes on one when his part is done – and when the issue rests with fate and the fighting men he has committed to action.'[1]

Under Operation TORCH over 70,000 troops were to be transported across the Atlantic and landed in North Africa, in territory controlled by the pro-Axis government of Vichy France. The invasion was planned for the night of 7/8 November and was divided into two parts: the Atlantic coast of Morocco and Mediterranean coast of Algeria.

The Morocco landing would be undertaken by American troops, who had sailed directly from the US; this was the Western Task Force. The elements of the 'fast' assault convoy, with over thirty transports, had departed from Hampton Roads, Virginia. At sea it met with a powerful US Navy covering force, before following an evasive course east towards Africa.

The landings in Algeria would involve more troops from the US Army than from the British one. The Americans, however, were to be transported from forward bases in the UK in British convoys and escorted by the Royal Navy. These convoys to Algeria were organised as the Central Task Force (for Oran) and the Eastern Task Force (for Algiers). Like the American convoy to Morocco they would have to make long passages through dangerous Atlantic waters, proceeding south from Scotland to Gibraltar. The slower convoys sailed first, in late October, with nearly a hundred transports and over thirty escorts. The first two 'slow' assault convoys stole through the Strait of Gibraltar at night, on 5/6 and 6/7 November. The most important British 'fast' convoy, with the first wave of assault troops for Algeria, had departed the UK on 26 October, with over thirty transports. Admiral Pound, the First Sea Lord, described the British effort to Prime Minister Winston Churchill as 'the most valuable convoys ever to leave these shores', and the same could surely have been said on the American side.[2]

Amphibious or 'combined' operations are highly complex. The initial task of TORCH was to seize working ports, through which an even larger 'expeditionary force' with men and vehicles could later be channelled to fight a full-scale military campaign in northwest Africa. The essential preliminary stage involved putting assault troops ashore over open beaches, and five separate assault areas in Morocco and Algeria were targeted. These forces would then manoeuvre overland to take – from the rear – nearby ports, hopefully in undamaged condition.

On the eve of the TORCH landings Eisenhower, Cunningham and their fellow commanders were hopeful that the approach of the invasion convoys had been kept secret. So many things, however, could go wrong. The vital element of surprise might yet be lost. The weather, especially the autumnal Atlantic swell off Morocco, might swamp landing craft on the invasion beaches. Defending ground forces and coastal artillery might drive off the still untested Allied troops as they came ashore. Air and submarine attacks might rip through the transport fleets standing off the beaches. The French might succeed in holding or sabotaging the main ports, preventing the unloading of vehicles and stores for the Allied 'follow-on' forces. The Germans might have time to rush in their ground and air forces, and the great Allied crusade of liberation would be stalled; worse yet it might be transformed into another Dunkirk evacuation.

Action began, as these events so often did, in the middle of the night. Landing craft were lowered from transport ships shortly before midnight on 7 November. On the Atlantic coast of Morocco the 'lowerings' took place off beaches near Port Lyautey and Casablanca, and at Safi. In the Mediterranean, the landing craft were put into the water near Oran and Algiers. H-Hour, the moment the troops of Operation TORCH would actually begin to come ashore from their landing craft, was set for 1.00 a.m. on Sunday, 8 November.

Fortune smiled on the invaders. The beaches turned out to be undefended; the main obstacles were the rough seas off Morocco and the unknown terrain. Some of the landing craft were poorly constructed; many of the crews were not fully trained. But the few French-manned coastal guns near the beaches remained silent. By about 3.00 a.m. the French commanders in Morocco and Algeria became aware that some kind of military attack was going on, but very little else was clear. They did not grasp the large-scale nature of the action, and indeed they did not even know who was on the other side.

In the early hours of Sunday daring Allied attempts were made to rush the main ports of Oran and Algiers, using only two small warships in each place. The American and British planners believed it was essential to prevent the French from blocking port installations before the main body of troops could arrive overland from the main invasion beaches (10 or 20 miles away). These bold attacks were carried out in darkness, but two hours had passed since the initial beach landings and the defending French warships and shore batteries were now at action stations. The Allied ships were shot up with very heavy loss of life; the worst episode was at Oran harbour, where several hundred very brave men, mostly Americans, were killed aboard the sloop HMS *Hartland*. Despite repeated attempts, the harbour areas were not secured.

This had been a bloody setback, but by dawn on Sunday the bulk of Allied troops were safely ashore on beaches flanking Oran and Algiers; landings had also been successfully accomplished in Morocco. Advance parties dashed inland to seize airfields. As the new day dawned British and American planes from Gibraltar and from aircraft carriers off Morocco and Algeria flew in to neutralise French air bases, and to make them available for Allied air operations.

The response of the local Vichy authorities was unpredictable: would they rally behind the Allied troops as liberators or would they follow the orders of the puppet government in France and offer bitter resistance? Confused, outnumbered and lacking information, local French commanders reacted in different ways. Their Air Force launched only light attacks on the fleet offshore. Their weak Army units only attempted to block movement of invading troops, rather than to fight back. The French Navy, however, mounted counter-attacks, with a cruiser, destroyers and submarines sallying forth from Casablanca and from Oran. Superior American and British naval forces, under the overall command of Admiral Cunningham, dealt quickly with this threat, sinking a number of French ships. To the northeast a powerful British fleet of carriers, battleships and cruisers shielded the Mediterranean part of the TORCH expedition from any action by the Italian Navy or by Vichy ships coming from bases in southern France.

Events now proceeded favourably and quickly. Late on Monday morning the French high command in Algiers accepted a local ceasefire and agreed to co-operate with the Allies. The main invasion force near Oran was able to enter that town on the following day. And the last resistance to the Americans in the Casablanca area ceased on Wednesday morning. The Allies – and Allied sea power – had prevailed; General Eisenhower's main campaign in northwest Africa could proceed.

The grand plan for TORCH incorporated a pipeline of fresh troops and supplies; indeed, reinforcement convoys were already at sea before the main landings. The first American 'follow-on' convoy to Morocco had left New York six days before the first invasion. It reached Casablanca – now securely in Allied hands – on 18 November; a much larger convoy arrived on 1 December. For Algeria a fast British follow-on convoy departed from Scotland eight days before the invasion and reached Gibraltar on the 10th – two days after the first landings. A couple of days later its ships reached Allied-controlled Oran and Algiers.

It is true that northwest Africa had turned out to be a soft target. The French forces defending it were weak; the Allied expedition was strong. But the main feature was the fatally overstretched German position in the west. Spread thinly across Europe at the end of 1942, the *Wehrmacht* (the three German armed services) did not command sufficient ground or air forces to protect or garrison territory supposedly under the control of the Third Reich. Especially telling was the weakness of German 'sea/air' forces. Adolf Hitler had declared in February 1941 that 'wherever Britain touches the continent, we will immediately oppose it, and wherever British ships put to sea, our U-boats and aeroplanes will be deployed against them until the hour of decision comes'.[3] This promise had turned out to be hollow.

The huge transoceanic Allied operation demonstrated the extent to which Britain and the United States now controlled the Atlantic and the western Mediterranean. The *Luftwaffe* (the German Air Force) had no maritime patrol aircraft in North Africa, a weakness which allowed the Allies to achieve complete surprise on 7–8 November. Neither the Germans nor the Italians had an effective bomber force in the western Mediterranean, and no heavy air attacks were made on Allied shipping in the critical first days of the landings. Meanwhile, German surface ships presented no danger to the TORCH convoys; in the course of the previous two years the Royal Navy and RAF had sunk them or forced them out of the North Atlantic. Nor could the German U-boats attack the invasion shipping in any strength, despite Allied 'worst-case' fears that fifty submarines might be engaged.[4] Whatever the successes of German submarines against normal merchant shipping in 1942, the Allies were able to move large numbers of military personnel and their supplies safely across the ocean.

* * *

Writing in the immediate wake of World War II, the eminent British maritime historian and strategic thinker Admiral Sir Herbert Richmond set out a particular definition of 'sea power'. It was 'that form of national strength which enables its possessor to send his armies and commerce across those stretches of sea and ocean which lie between his country or the country of his allies, and those territories to which he needs access in war; and to prevent his enemy from doing the same'. A simpler version dates from a letter the admiral wrote in June 1942: 'Sea power is the power of using the sea for one's own purpose and depriving the enemy of its use'. Looking at the November 1942 invasion of North Africa in the context of four centuries of British maritime history, Richmond concluded that no example 'of the influence of sea power upon military operations . . . is more striking than this'.[5] But, in addition, between 1939 and 1945 Britain and its successive maritime allies – especially the United States – were able on many other occasions to use the sea for their own purposes and to deprive Germany, Italy and Japan of its use. This was a central reason why the Allies emerged victorious from World War II, and why the Axis powers were defeated. This book is about that struggle for the seas and oceans during the war. The structure follows the course of the maritime war from its beginning, with five parts covering the periods of the global conflict as they unfolded.

Part I tells the story of the war in northern Europe between September 1939 and June 1940, as Britain and France fought Germany. The Allies possessed large navies and global empires, while Germany had limited access to the oceans and a small navy. Nevertheless, it was the landlocked power which won a series of stunning victories and gained effective control of western and central Europe. The defeat of France in June 1940 ended this period, but with a stalemate between the British Empire and the Third Reich: neither was able to knock the other out of the war. The British Army was certainly in no position to return to northwestern Europe, but sea power protected the United Kingdom from invasion.

Part II deals with an even more threatening period for the British Empire, July 1940 to April 1942. In maritime terms it was now standing on its own, confronting a range of enemies. Germany made use of new forward naval bases in western France and Norway. Fascist Italy was waging an offensive war on land and sea in the Mediterranean. But for the first year of this period, at least, sea power gave Britain the ability to protect vital supply lines to North America, fight overseas campaigns in North Africa and inflict serious damage on the Axis navies – although at high cost in warships and their crews. The real crisis came in late 1941, in the later part of the period, when Imperial Japan moved from hostile neutral to active enemy, and when the maritime war changed from a European to a global one. It was hugely important that in these months Russia and the United States became allies of Britain – in June and December 1941, respectively – but at first they could contribute little directly to the war at sea. In the case of the US this impotence was unexpected and a result of the stunning surprise attack on Pearl Harbor. Although the Americans lost the Philippines, the heaviest Japanese blow was directed against Britain's empire in Southeast Asia. The Royal Navy suffered the loss of its Eastern Fleet and its base at Singapore, and suddenly the Japanese Navy seemed capable of contesting control of the Indian Ocean.

Part III covers April to December of 1942 – the shortest period but in some ways the most dramatic. These seven months were certainly pivotal, as after the spring of 1942 Axis territorial expansion – in Europe and Asia – reached its limits. A genuinely global maritime war was now going on. For the first time the Axis had a powerful sea-going fleet available, as the Imperial Japanese Navy was far superior to the naval forces of the Germans or the Italians. But, by the summer, hard-fighting task forces of the US Navy were at sea both in the Atlantic and the Pacific. At the battles of the Coral Sea, Midway and Guadalcanal the Americans were able to inflict – at high cost to themselves – decisive defeats on the Japanese Navy. The British, meanwhile, were able to maintain their global shipping network in the face of a strengthened U-boat attack. The production of North American shipyards – the pump primed in 1940–41– meant by the end of 1942 that the tonnage of the Allied merchant fleet was no longer falling. The Allies used their control over the Atlantic and western Mediterranean to mount successful amphibious operations, most notably TORCH. The same was true in the Pacific, with the six-month battle for Guadalcanal.

Part IV takes in the period from January 1943 to June 1944. In these eighteen months the British and Americans *won* the maritime war, a year before the overall final surrender of Germany and Japan. Massive reinforcements in the form of warships, cargo vessels, amphibious shipping and aircraft became available, with the number of ships and aircraft in the US Navy first matching, and then rapidly overtaking, that of their British ally. The maritime Allies together strengthened their control of the global shipping lanes, and won decisive victories in battle. The Italian fleet surrendered to the British in September 1943, and the US Navy won its decisive offensive victory over the Japanese in the Philippine Sea in June 1944. In both the Mediterranean and the Pacific the Allies together demonstrated a mastery of amphibious warfare.

Part V covers the last year of the war (from June 1944 to August 1945) when the Allies *used* their command of the sea to complete the defeat of the Axis. Ground troops in huge numbers were moved across the Atlantic before and after D-Day in Normandy to complete the destruction of the Wehrmacht. The transport of the Allied expeditionary forces into northwestern Europe, especially the 'follow-on' forces of the US Army, was the climax of 'using the seas for one's own purposes' during World War II. At the same time the surrender of Japan was achieved; bases were seized in the western Pacific from which the main islands of the last Axis power could be blockaded and bombarded.

The book will not be a simple 'operational narrative' of all these events. As well as telling the story of the maritime war it will take in a range of important background factors: national naval strategies, capabilities and traditions; the role of individual leaders; rivalry and co-operation between the various military services; overall technical competition and change; the background role of logistics and intelligence. Especially important are the links between land and sea operations, and battles to attack and defend merchant ships. The book stresses throughout the way in which the war for the seas was technologically unlike any previous conflict, especially in the way in which the operations of sea, ground and air forces were interconnected. The historian Paul Kennedy has referred to 'a new hybrid form of power, part air, part sea', and the term 'sea/air' warfare will be used throughout the present book. I prefer 'sea/air' to 'air–sea' as it emphasises the centrality of the sea – and the notion of the fighting above it, on it and under it.[6]

The approach is international. The maritime effort of all the major maritime powers is brought in, including those of the British Empire (especially Britain and Canada), the United States, Japan, Germany, France, Italy and the Soviet Union. The last three states, it must be said, have not received as much attention as they might from British and American historians. Furthermore, the story arcs of the various participant states – and navies – were very different; an extreme example would be the contrast between the United States and France. Watertight divisions cannot, of course, be made between the various periods of the war. The conflict was a global one, and there is a difference between decisive battles fought over two or three days and long campaigns of attrition (like the six-year 'Battle' of the Atlantic). Events cannot be related in strict linear form unless history is reduced to chronology. Some narrative detours are, therefore, necessary, but each chapter does deal with a coherent subject.

* * *

A few words are in order as to how this book about the sea war came about. My previous writing on World War II has been concerned with that most nonmaritime of fighting theatres, the steppes and forests of Russia; this experience had the advantage of giving me a different perspective from that of the expert naval historian. However, my interest in naval history goes back a long way. I was born near Chatham in Kent, where my father had been serving alongside the wartime

Royal Navy. Much of my childhood was spent near New York in a small Long Island town where, in early 1930, the first workshop of the Grumman Aircraft Engineering Company was located; Grumman would eventually design and produce the most important naval aircraft of World War II, built in huge numbers. And my home is now in Glasgow on the Clyde, a river steeped in the history of global maritime trade and the construction of warships and merchantmen.

* * *

Heather McCallum at Yale University Press provided inspiration and long-term support for this project. The patient advice of Marika Lysandrou, my editor at Yale, also proved invaluable. Jacob Blandy provided comprehensive and well-informed advice as copy-editor. I would not pretend to expertise in all the many and distant reaches of the global war for the oceans. In this respect, a number of colleagues, with specialist knowledge much fuller than my own, have kindly taken the time to look over parts of the manuscript. These include Marcus Faulkner, John Gooch, Ilya Grinberg, Steven Kepher, Joseph Maiolo, Phillips O'Brien, Alessio Patalano, Klaus Schmider and Martin Thomas. I would also thank two anonymous readers who provided Yale with their overall comments. Any remaining errors and omissions, of course, remain my own responsibility. Christopher Black kindly helped with Italian translations. Sergei Vinogradov and Christopher Wright have, over the years, provided advice and rare publications on the Soviet Navy. In Glasgow Alan Clements and Michael McAvoy provided welcome encouragement and support. Working with George Franklin and Gjert Lage Dyndal, two outstanding and well-informed graduate students at Glasgow University, taught me much about anti-submarine technology and maritime patrol aircraft. My Glasgow friends and colleagues Ben E. Shepherd and Alexander Marshall offered long-term general encouragement. In addition, the staff at the National Library of Scotland and the University of Glasgow Library were of great help in providing books, articles and inter-library loan material. And, as always, gratitude is due to my wife Gillian for her sustained patience; this vessel has been on the stocks for a long time.

PART I

SEA POWER AND THE EUROPEAN WAR

SEPTEMBER 1939–JUNE 1940

As far as the Navy is concerned, obviously it is in no way very adequately equipped for the great struggle with Great Britain . . .

Admiral Erich Raeder, 3 September 1939

CHAPTER 1

THE TWILIGHT WAR

September 1939–April 1940

THE SINKING OF THE *ATHENIA*, 3 SEPTEMBER 1939

The SS *Athenia* was a substantial vessel, but not one of the great liners; a passenger ship of some 13,500 tons, with accommodation for 1,000 passengers, her speed was 15 knots: the white stripe on her single thin black funnel marked her as one of the ships of the Donaldson Atlantic Line. Completed in 1923, she regularly carried passengers – often emigrants – from the British Isles to Canada. In August 1939 there was a new urgency to get aboard, among those hurrying to escape the outbreak of another European war. The *Athenia* left Glasgow, bound for Montreal, on the evening of 1 September; that day, Germany had invaded Poland. After picking up passengers at Belfast and Liverpool, the liner sailed out into the open Atlantic on the 3rd. A few hours earlier the Prime Minister, Neville Chamberlain, had announced a state of war with Germany.

In the afternoon of the 3rd, south of Rockall, and about 200 miles out into the ocean, the *Athenia* was sighted by a U-boat cruising on the surface. The captain of the *U 30* decided to attack and submerged his boat; no warning was given. At about 7.30 p.m. torpedoes were ordered to be launched. One struck home, and the passengers and most of the crew of the *Athenia* took to the lifeboats. Messages got through to the Admiralty with some delay via Malin Head in County Donegal. 'Important Admiral Rosyth intercept 2207 Jamming near Athenia GFDM 1400 passengers some still aboard Sinking fast bearing 291 approx.' HMS *Electra* arrived with two other destroyers to rescue survivors from the stricken ship: 'Surrounded by wreckage and the inevitable oil slick, she lay at a drunken angle, with the falls of the lowered boats trailing in the water, and giving her an untidy, bedraggled, appearance, accentuating her air of helplessness.'[1] The liner took fourteen hours to go down, and most of the fatalities resulted from the initial torpedo explosion or from poor handling of the lifeboats. Altogether ninety-three passengers (eighty-five of them women and children) and nineteen crew members perished.

The *U 30* was one of eighteen submarines that had been ordered to take position near British waters in late August 1939. One of the first Type VII (medium-sized) submarines commissioned into the new *Kriegsmarine* (Navy) of the Third Reich, the *U 30* had been completed in the autumn of 1936. Her captain was Lieutenant Fritz-Julius Lemp, at twenty-six years old one of the youngest officers to command a U-boat.

Like all other U-boat commanders, Lemp had been instructed to obey the German Navy's prize rules, which followed international law. Merchant ships were supposed to be warned before attack, giving their crews the chance to make for a place of safety. The Nazi government in Berlin was keen – at this stage at least – to limit the scope of the war and to avoid upsetting powerful neutrals like the US. U-boat attacks on merchant ships had political implications; such events had been used in 1917 by the US to justify entry into World War I. In any event Lemp later claimed that he thought the rules did not apply in this case, because he had identified his target as a combatant. She had been acting suspiciously, and he believed she was an 'armed merchant cruiser' (AMC) – a fast merchant ship deployed by the Royal Navy as an 'auxiliary cruiser'. Lemp only realised on listening in to the BBC that he had sunk a passenger ship performing her normal activities. He compounded his blunder by failing to report to base.

German naval headquarters must have guessed what had happened. On 4 September it put out a secret alert forbidding submarine attacks on passenger ships, even in convoy. Meanwhile the authorities in Berlin denied any involvement. When the *U 30* eventually returned to Wilhelmshaven three weeks later, the senior officer, U-boats, a commodore named Karl Dönitz, stood on the quayside to meet her. Lemp requested a private word and admitted what had happened. The commodore immediately put him on a plane to Berlin to explain himself to higher authorities. Dönitz – according to a statement made at the 1946 Nuremberg trial – punished Lemp on his return by confining him to his quarters, but he did not authorise a court martial. His view was that the young captain had made a genuine mistake in the confusion of 'battle'. He accepted the view of his superiors that open action against Lemp would be embarrassing. Dönitz's staff entered a report in the war diary of the U-boat command which mentioned two other merchant ships sunk by the *U 30* (in both cases in accordance with prize rules), but not the *Athenia*; a replacement page for 3 September was crudely inserted in the *U 30*'s logbook.

The captain of the U-boat thus escaped any real punishment. Not only was Lemp not court martialled for disobeying orders, but the Navy awarded him the Iron Cross (2nd Class) in late September, and promoted him to the rank of lieutenant commander (*Kapitänleutnant*). The *U 30* carried out further patrols under his command; Lemp turned out to be just the sort of aggressive submarine commander the Kriegsmarine (and other navies) craved. In November 1939 he damaged the British battleship *Barham* north of Ireland with a torpedo; the following year he was awarded the Wehrmacht's highest military medal, the Knight's Cross (*Ritterkreuz*).

The official German version was a lie. There is no evidence that the *Athenia* was zig-zagging or that she was blacked out – it was not yet dark as she approached the *U 30*. She may have been somewhat off the main shipping route; the captain of the *Athenia* refused to reveal his course to the British civilian inquiry, as he had been 'under secret naval instructions'. While the *Athenia* was a plausible armed merchant cruiser (her Donaldson Atlantic Line sister ship, the SS *Letitia*, served in this role from November), at the start of September Britain did not yet have any AMCs in commission.

Lemp later took command of the new *U 110*. This submarine was attacked by British warships south of Iceland during her second patrol, in May 1941, and forced to surface. The crew failed to scuttle the badly damaged boat, and a British boarding party salvaged the Enigma cypher machine and confidential code papers; the capture greatly aided the later interception of German radio signals. Lieutenant Commander Lemp was drowned.

THE KRIEGSMARINE: THE NEW GERMAN NAVY

On 3 September 1939, the same day that Lieutenant Lemp sank the *Athenia*, his ultimate superior in the German Navy drafted a pessimistic and bitter memorandum. 'Today', wrote Admiral Erich Raeder, 'the war against France and England broke out, the war, according to the Führer's previous assertions, we had no need to expect before about 1944.' Raeder outlined the fleet of ships that might have been available in 1944–45, a fleet with which Germany – along with its allies – could have defeated the Royal Navy and isolated the United Kingdom; 'the prospect . . . of bringing about the final solution [*sic*] of the British problem would have been good.' Today, however, the situation was very different:

> As far as the Navy is concerned, obviously it is in no way very adequately equipped for the great struggle with Great Britain . . . It is true that in the short period since 1935 . . . it has built up a well-trained, suitably organised submarine arm . . . the submarine arm is still much too weak, however, to have any decisive effect on the war. The surface forces, moreover, are so inferior in number and strength to those of the British Fleet that, even at full strength, they can do no more than show that they know how to die gallantly and thus are willing to create the foundations of later reconstruction.[2]

Admiral Raeder was the central figure in the Kriegsmarine in the first half of the war. When the fighting began he was sixty-three years of age, the oldest member of Hitler's military high command. He had already been head of the Navy for eleven years, having taken over five years before Hitler and the Nazis came to power. He would serve on until the start of 1943.

Raeder had entered the Imperial Navy in 1894 and progressed rapidly. From 1912 until 1917 he was on the staff of Admiral von Hipper, who commanded the battle-cruiser force. In this capacity he took part in the battles of Dogger Bank (1915) and Jutland (1916), and in 1917 he became Hipper's chief of staff. In 1918–19 he suffered the treble shock of mass naval mutiny, the abdication of the Kaiser and the surrender of the best ships of the fleet to the British.

Raeder's career prospered in the small post-war *Reichsmarine*; he reached flag rank in 1922. His involvement in the unsuccessful right-wing Kapp Putsch of 1920 briefly sidetracked him into work on the official history of the German Navy during the war. Significantly – for his future strategy – Raeder wrote the volumes on oceanic 'cruiser warfare' (*Kreuzerkrieg*) against Allied merchant ships. By the middle of the 1920s he was given a mainstream post, and in 1928 he was brought in to take overall command of the German Navy; he received the title Commander-in-Chief, Navy (*Oberbefehlshaber der Marine*, or *OBdM*), in 1935. Like much of the military elite, the admiral had welcomed the coming to power of Hitler and the Nazis in 1933. From January 1937 he wore on his uniform the Golden Party Badge, with the initials 'A.H.' stamped on its reverse. He shared many of the attitudes and aspirations of the new rulers of Germany. But while the rebirth of a strong Germany was important to him, even more essential was the creation of a powerful navy.

In 1934 the German naval high command moved into a striking ten-storey modernist office block, Shell-Haus, on Berlin's Tirpitz Embankment. Admiral Raeder continued the development of a new navy, with France and Poland as its most likely opponents. He was not a blinkered conservative in terms of naval doctrine, nor was he prepared to confine his operations to coastal defence. Having seen the woeful experience of the German High Seas Fleet (*Hochseeflotte*), which festered in port for most of the 1914–18 war, he became an advocate of offensive operations; these were to be carried out both in the North Sea and in the Atlantic and the Mediterranean. A powerful force of cruisers would deny potential enemies the use of their oceanic shipping routes. Not surprisingly, in view of the success of Germany's submarine campaign in World War I, he also supported the development of the U-boat force. When the Nazi government began to release funds for comprehensive rearmament he proved an effective participant in inter-service competition; he made the Navy's case effectively, in the face of a powerful Army and a rapidly growing Air Force. In particular, he carefully cultivated a relationship with Adolf Hitler.

Hitler, for his part, is sometimes accused of not 'understanding' sea power, but that is not a very meaningful criticism. He had a broader perspective than that of simple navalism. In his writings and speeches before 1933 he had criticised the overseas colonial ambitions of the Kaiser's Germany, and its development of the High Seas Fleet; these policies, in his view, had fatally antagonised Britain. When he came to power in January 1933 he had not given much thought to the Navy. At his first one-to-one meeting with Admiral Raeder three months later he expressed a lack of interest in the sea, and a desire to stay on good terms with the British. It is clear that he was, then and later, essentially a 'continentalist', and in geopolitical terms that was sensible enough. In the short term he aimed to restore Germany's position in central Europe, settling scores with the French; in the longer term he wanted to control a raw-material base even further east in the Russian steppe. These goals would logically be best served by the Army, which also helped maintain the internal security of the Third Reich. In addition he took a great interest in the development of an air force, a project championed by his close Nazi comrade, Hermann Göring. The overarching reality was that any naval build-up demanded time and long-term planning. Hitler was the opposite of a long-term planner; he was an opportunist, although often a clever – and lucky – one.

Nevertheless, Hitler did want to build up the new Kriegsmarine (as the Reichsmarine was renamed in June 1935), and he provided it with considerable resources. He was aware that whatever his immediate geopolitical objectives some use of the sea would be essential. If the Führer was no expert about what the Navy's ships would do in wartime, he knew they conferred significant international prestige, as well as potentially providing a diplomatic and deterrent advantage. He seems to have got on well with Admiral Raeder and dealt with him – a man thirteen years his senior – with respect. In January 1938 Hitler took over from Field Marshal von Blomberg as head of the Reich Ministry of War, co-ordinating the three armed services: for Raeder, an 'impartial' civilian – Hitler – was preferable to an Army field marshal who favoured his own service at the expense of the Navy. Raeder and Hitler seem to have had only one pre-war falling out, in November 1938, over the shipbuilding programme; the admiral offered his resignation but it was not accepted.

The *Kaiserliche Marine* had been – if only for a decade before 1914 – the second largest navy in the world. But Germany had lost the *Weltkrieg*, and under the terms of the 1919 Treaty of Versailles its fleet had been greatly cut down – with ships forcibly scrapped or surrendered as reparations. Naval personnel were now limited to 15,000 men. The treaty designated a number of warships which would form the new German Navy. Excluding a small reserve, there were six pre-dreadnought battleships (launched in 1902–05), six small cruisers, twelve destroyers and twelve torpedo boats.[3] The treaty also imposed blanket bans on German military aircraft and submarines (although these could to some extent be circumvented).

The treaty did provide for replacements; larger ships could be retired twenty years after their launch date, and smaller ships after fifteen years. There were limits on the size of these replacements. What the French-language terms of the treaty described as a *cuirassé* ('armoured ship') could not exceed a displacement of 10,000 tons; for cruisers the limit was 6,000 tons, and for destroyers 800 tons (this at a time when new battleships of the major fleets displaced 25,000–30,000 tons and destroyers 1,200 tons). Before the Nazi takeover in 1933, German shipyards had completed, as replacements, five light cruisers and a number of small destroyers. Construction had also begun of a new class of 10,000-ton 'armoured ships' (*Panzerschiffe*) – three vessels taking the place of three now over-age pre-dreadnoughts.

For the first two years after coming to power in January 1933, Hitler was concerned with building up his position at home and avoiding intervention by outside powers. He made few foreign policy initiatives and, formally, Germany abided by the terms of the Versailles Treaty. Naval construction, within treaty limits, continued. Panzerschiff 'A' (the *Deutschland*) was completed in April 1933; the *Admiral Scheer* ('B') and the *Admiral Graf Spee* ('C') followed in November 1934 and January 1936.

Meanwhile, the Nazi government began covert preparations for an all-round breakout from the Versailles armaments limits, especially with respect to ground forces and military aviation, but also the Navy. In May 1934 the German dictator agreed that the next two projected Panzerschiffe ('D' and 'E') could be modified beyond the Versailles limits. (This modification was directly in response to the laying down by France of two new fast battleships, the *Dunkerque* and the *Strasbourg*.) In any event, the planned 'replacement' ships would eventually have an official displacement of 26,000 tons, and be 150 feet longer than the 'Deutschland' class Panzerschiffe. Their main armament would be nine rather than six 11-inch guns.[4] The vessels were actually laid down in May 1935, and would be completed as the *Scharnhorst* and the *Gneisenau*. Because of bottlenecks in the German engineering industry, the *Scharnhorst* was equipped with steam turbines manufactured in Switzerland. The first two new 1,625-ton destroyers – more than twice Germany's Versailles limit for destroyer size (800 tons) – were begun in October 1934 and completed in early 1937; by September 1939 a further nineteen destroyers would be commissioned.

In March 1935 Hitler issued a proclamation which openly denounced the disarmament clauses of the sixteen-year-old Versailles Treaty. Most importantly he re-introduced conscription for the German Army, and the existence of the Luftwaffe was admitted at the same time. The other European powers could make no effective response. More remarkable from the naval – and diplomatic – point of view, Germany was able in June 1935 to make an agreement with the British government which permitted the construction of all types of warship. London had long believed that the harsh terms of 1919 were unsustainable and counter-productive. Aware that Hitler's Germany would, in any event, now ignore the treaty, the British attempted damage limitation, at least in terms of naval forces. Without consultation with France, the Anglo-German Naval Agreement was signed, which allowed Germany to build up to 35 per cent of British tonnage in all the various categories of warship: battleships, aircraft carriers, cruisers, destroyers, submarines, etc. The battleship tonnage allowance for Germany was now about the same as the French and Italian battleship allowance specified in the 1922 Washington Naval Treaty; at 175,000 tons, this had been 33 per cent of the British and US totals.[5] Tonnage and armament of these Germans vessels were in effect limited only by the Washington Treaty and the 1930 London Treaty, which applied to all the major navies.

Germany possessed shipyards capable of building large warships, although their facilities required expansion. The most important were the naval dockyards at Wilhelmshaven and Kiel, and the private yards of Blohm & Voss (Hamburg), Deschimag (Bremen) and Germaniawerft (Kiel). By 1936 new warships of all classes were under construction. In July 1935 the *Admiral Hipper*, the first of five planned conventional (8-inch gun) heavy cruisers, notionally of 10,000 tons, had been laid down. Completed in April 1939, she was followed by the *Blücher* and the *Prinz Eugen*.[6] In July 1936 construction began at Hamburg of the first full-sized battleship (ship 'F'), notionally of 35,000 tons, with eight 15-inch guns; she became the famous *Bismarck*. Her final design displacement was 41,700 tons, although this was 'legal' by the time of her launch; in March 1938 the powers formally involved in the naval limitation process had accepted a 45,000-ton limit for battleships. She was followed in the Wilhelmshaven shipyard three months later by the future *Tirpitz* (ship 'G').

Many of these warships would play a role in the naval battles of World War II. In terms of the future history of the war, however, it was submarine development and construction that would be most important. The Reichsmarine had kept abreast of submarine technology in the 1920s, and a German-led design and construction firm in the Netherlands produced a small number of boats for foreign navies. In 1934 fittings and machinery for submarine construction began to be assembled in Germany. The first 250-ton coastal/training boat (Type II), the *U 1*, was commissioned in June 1935; she was followed by two dozen more of this class. Dönitz, then a captain and commander of the first

U-boat flotilla, was influential in developing doctrine. He favoured group attacks, and this led to construction emphasis on a large class of the relatively small (by international standards) '500-ton' Type VII class, the first of which (the *U 27*) was completed in June 1936. The other major wartime class would be the longer-range '720-ton' Type IX; the first boat of this class (the *U 37*) was completed in August 1938.[7]

Naval aviation was, however, a significant weakness. This was partly because of Germany's late start (resulting from the Versailles Treaty), partly because the naval leadership had limited interest in aviation even in the second half of the 1930s, and partly because Hermann Göring and his Luftwaffe wanted control of all military aircraft. A 28,000-ton aircraft carrier, the *Graf Zeppelin*, was laid down in December 1936 and launched in December 1938; problems with her complex 200,000-shp machinery (the largest in any German ship) and the low priority given the project by both the Navy and the Air Force meant that she would never be completed. In early 1939 Raeder made a deal with Göring, who also had great influence as head of the Four-Year Plan for the overall development of the Nazi economy. The big shipbuilding programme, with all its steel and labour requirements, was given the green light, and in exchange the Navy did not demand its own air force.

Much has been made by historians of this shipbuilding programme, the ten-year Z-Plan. Hitler secretly approved it in January 1939, and at the same time gave the Navy a high priority in steel allocation. The Z-Plan had no effect on the reality of World War II. At its core were six planned 55,500-ton diesel-powered battleships armed with eight 16-inch guns. Battleships 'H' and 'J' were laid down in Hamburg and Bremen in the summer of 1939, but they were cancelled as soon as the war began in September. The projected Kriegsmarine was to have included, by 1948, thirteen battleships and battle cruisers, four aircraft carriers, eight heavy cruisers, thirteen light cruisers, twenty-two 6,300-ton 'scout cruisers', sixty-eight destroyers and 249 submarines.[8] The battleship-heavy mix of ship types was indicative of a conservative technical perspective, and it has also been argued that the plan was quite unrealistic in terms of the fuel-oil resources available to Germany at the time.[9] In any event, on 29 April 1939 Hitler denounced the Anglo-German Naval Agreement.

A momentous guarantee had been made to Poland by Britain and France on 31 March 1939, promising support if Polish independence was threatened. The following day, 1 April, was memorable for the Kriegsmarine, as Hitler travelled to Wilhelmshaven to take part in the launching of the battleship *Tirpitz*. (He had also been present at the launch of the *Bismarck* in Hamburg three months earlier.) After the launch of the *Tirpitz* the Führer boarded the nearby *Scharnhorst*. On the battleship's quarterdeck he presided over a ceremony at which Raeder's forty-five years of naval service were celebrated, and he promoted Raeder to the exalted rank of *Grossadmiral.* Hitler expressed the hope that the head of his Navy would continue in his post for a long time to come. The dictator then departed for a three-day North Sea cruise on the newly completed liner *Robert Ley* (sister ship of the ill-fated *Wilhelm Gustloff*).[10]

Navies could not be quickly expanded – the construction of the biggest vessels took a long time. The fact that such ships could be kept in service for twenty or thirty years greatly favoured the traditional naval powers, with their head start. Allied military unpreparedness did not apply to naval forces. In 1939 the Third Reich had two battleships in service, compared to twenty-two for Britain and France. The Kriegsmarine had no aircraft carriers (compared to eight for the Allies), ten cruisers (compared to seventy-two) and twenty-one destroyers (compared to 253). The Navy was even behind in submarines, with only fifty-seven U-boats (compared to 141 Allied submarines).[11]

Raeder was among a handful of senior officers who were privy to Hitler's pre-war diplomatic and military plans. Indeed, he would be one of two dozen senior German leaders tried as major war criminals at Nuremberg in 1946, accused of plotting wars of aggression. (He was one of twelve spared the death penalty; sentenced to life imprisonment, he was released due to ill health in 1955.) He attended with a few other military leaders the meetings of 5 November 1937 and 23 May 1939 at which Hitler laid out his plans for gaining control of Austria, Czechoslovakia and Poland by military means, even at the risk of general war. From May 1938 the Kriegsmarine began seriously to plan for war with Britain, which Hitler now believed would be in the ranks of the likely opponents of the Third Reich. Following the directives of the Wehrmacht high command in the spring of 1939, the Naval War Staff (the *Seekriegsleitung* or SKL) under Admiral Otto Schniewind drafted plans for a naval war against Poland, with contingency plans for dealing with British, French or Russian intervention.

However, as Admiral Raeder implied in his 3 September 1939 memorandum, he had not expected that the Führer's daring diplomatic moves would actually lead to a general war. The possibility of fighting had indeed become more real in April 1939, but Poland might be crushed without external intervention. Moreover, the August pact with Stalin's Russia was an astonishing diplomatic coup. But Hitler – and Raeder – had fatally underestimated the resolve of the British and French governments.

BRITANNIA RULES THE WAVES

When war broke out on 3 September the leaders of the British Royal Navy were certainly more confident than was Admiral Raeder in Germany. Britain still controlled the largest navy and merchant marine in the world, and the Empire provided a global system of naval bases. Her French ally possessed a powerful fleet,[12] and Fascist Italy – contrary to expectations – had remained neutral.

The German and British command systems were different. Admiral Raeder's opposite number (and near contemporary) was Admiral Sir Dudley Pound, the First Sea Lord and Chief of Naval Staff. Pound had taken up his post only two months before the war broke out, following the fatal illness of his predecessor. Like Raeder, he would serve on through the middle of the war, until 1943. Unlike Raeder, Pound possessed extensive active command experience. He had been captain of a dreadnought at the Battle of Jutland, and he was Chief of Staff and then Commander-in-Chief (C-in-C) of the Mediterranean Fleet in the 1930s. As First Sea Lord, he was in an unusual situation compared to the other two British service chiefs (Army and RAF): he had both a day-to-day operational role and an administrative one.

The abilities of this First Sea Lord have aroused much controversy. He was certainly not in good health, and by 1941 showed signs of his age. The historian Correlli Barnett summed him up as a 'hard working plodder of limited intellectual range and interests', and a man with 'a lack of wide strategic grasp and . . . a habit of directing in detail'. The judgement of Arthur Marder was rather different. For that eminent American naval historian, the admiral was reserved and humourless, but he noted that Churchill (as First Lord of the Admiralty and then Prime Minister) was impressed by Pound's 'energy, keen intellect and analytical mind, and mastery of his profession'. Above all, in Marder's view, 'Pound feared neither God, man, nor Winston Churchill'.[13] Even Pound's critics accepted that he proved adept at containing some of the demands of that altogether more dynamic character.

Unlike in Germany, British civilian politicians, above the First Sea Lord, had direct overall responsibility for the Royal Navy. Churchill had been appointed to be First Lord of the Admiralty (in effect Minister of the Navy) by Prime Minister Chamberlain on 3 September. Neither Churchill's predecessor (Lord Stanhope) nor his successor (A.V. Alexander, from 1940 to 1945) was very memorable. Churchill, however, was a powerful and energetic figure with the widest range of ministerial experience, although he had been out of the Cabinet, 'in the wilderness', for ten years. He was knowledgeable about military affairs and took a strong – perhaps damagingly strong – interest in operational details. He had previously served as First Lord from 1911 to 1915, when the Royal Navy was at its greatest power and prestige. He could be counted on to protect its interests; when he took over, the signal 'Winston is back' was transmitted to the fleet. Churchill was destined for even greater things, but when he became Prime Minister in May 1940 he maintained – as Minister of Defence – a very strong influence in naval matters.

The British had a better high command structure than the Germans (and until 1942 a better structure than the Americans). This was partly thanks to their long experience in World War I; furthermore, in comparison with the Americans they had a two-year head start (from September 1939) in World War II. As a parliamentary democracy, decisions were made in Britain with a degree of collective discussion, unlike in Hitler's Germany. The ministerial War Cabinet functioned efficiently, and the Chiefs of Staff Committee (COS), with its network of sub-committees, became increasingly effective. Inter-service rivalry certainly existed, but it was less marked than in other countries.

For the Navy the centre of activities was the Admiralty Building in London's Whitehall, off Trafalgar Square. In 1940 a bomb-proof bunker was added on the side of Horse Guards Parade, jokingly known as 'Lenin's Tomb'. The members of the Board of Admiralty controlled from this complex the various functions of the Navy.

The Royal Navy operated two major fleets in September 1939, the Home Fleet and the Mediterranean Fleet, although there were also a number of overseas stations and shore commands within the United Kingdom itself. Unlike the Germans – and at this stage even the Americans – the Royal Navy had the advantage of a global network of bases and ports. In Britain, the main fleet base was at Scapa Flow in the Orkney Islands, north of Scotland, although it was not well defended at first. There were also bases and headquarters at Portsmouth and Plymouth (Devonport) on the south coast, Chatham in the Thames estuary (the 'Nore'), and Rosyth, near Edinburgh in Scotland.

British rearmament, especially naval rearmament, has aroused decades of controversy among historians. This was the era of the so-called 'Ten-Year Rule', which was ostensibly used as the basis for limiting defence expenditure; introduced in 1919 and confirmed by Winston Churchill (then Chancellor of the Exchequer) in 1928, the policy assumed there would be no major war in that period. It is really hard, however, to accept the view that the Royal Navy slept through or ignored reality in the inter-war years. One eminent historian (Paul Kennedy) describes these as 'years of decay', another (Correlli Barnett) cites 'twenty years of national illusion . . . and neglect'.[14] The reality is that Britain ended World War I in 1918 with much the largest navy in the world. Despite scrapping many ships and accepting nominal parity in capital ships with the US, the Royal Navy remained the best-equipped, most experienced and widely deployed naval force in the world.

The Navy of Britain's twentieth-century sea-power rival, Germany, had essentially been eliminated; the same was true of the Russian Navy, after the 1917 revolution. The new naval arms control treaties also did not have the effect of 'demolition work on British seapower' that historians and navalists sometimes ascribe to them.[15] The 1922 Washington Treaty, already mentioned in the German context, led to British acceptance of parity in capital ships with the expanding US Navy. There was, however, no likelihood of fighting the US, and a strong American Navy was surely in British interests; this had been the case in 1917–18, and would be so again in 1941–45. A naval war with the old enemy across the Channel was also unlikely, but in any event the treaty set the tonnage limit of French capital ships at one-third the British. The same ratio (3:1) applied to the Italians although, even in the early years of Mussolini, Italy did not seem a probable enemy. The only halfway-realistic potential enemy in the 1920s was Japan, which had been a naval ally of Britain from 1902 to 1923. The Japanese capital ship allowance, however, was set at only 60 per cent of the British, and the foreign policy of Tokyo was not yet dangerous.

Britain also had the world's largest shipbuilding industry, and it held that position throughout the 1920s and 1930s, although the industry was weaker in the second decade. There were seven shipyards, all privately owned, which were able to build battleships and – later – fleet aircraft carriers: Vickers-Armstrongs (Tyne) and Swan Hunter in Newcastle, Cammell Laird in Liverpool, Vickers-Armstrongs in Barrow (Cumbria), Fairfield and John Brown on the Clyde, and Harland & Wolff in Belfast. Half a dozen other yards were capable of building cruisers. Only two major warship-building yards closed in the inter-war period, neither of the first rank.[16]

After 1922, in accordance with the Washington Treaty, the Royal Navy did begin to scrap many ships, including a number of modern battleships and battle cruisers scarcely ten years old and armed with 13.5-inch guns. All the same, the Royal Navy was left with the ten most powerful battleships to serve in any navy during World War I, the 'Queen Elizabeth' and 'Revenge' ('R') classes, as well as three battle cruisers. All thirteen ships were armed with 15-inch guns. And although this decade is often depicted as a battleship-building 'holiday', the British Empire, uniquely, was granted an exemption. Its Navy was allowed to design and build two new battleships, armed with 16-inch guns and incorporating the lessons of Jutland; these were the *Nelson* and the *Rodney* (laid down in late 1922 and completed in 1927).

Cruisers were very important to the Royal Navy – defensively, to protect trade, and offensively to enforce blockade. The Royal Navy constructed in the late 1920s, in competition with the US and Japan, a group of thirteen heavy cruisers, with a displacement of 10,000 tons and an armament of eight 8-inch guns; these were known as 'treaty' cruisers, because their specifications were based on the Washington Treaty upper limit. These were named after British counties; the first unit, laid down in October 1924 and completed in January 1928, was HMS *Cumberland*. In 1922 the Royal Navy had possessed fifty-six cruisers. Some fourteen of these had been disposed of as obsolete by 1930; the bulk of the remainder were thirty-five small 'C' and 'D' class cruisers of about 5,000 tons, built during World War I.

The Washington Treaty had not limited the total cruiser tonnage in individual navies. Such a limit, however, was put into place in the London Naval Treaty, signed in April 1930 by Britain, the US and Japan. The British Empire was now allowed fifteen heavy cruisers (these were new ships already in commission) and 192,200 tons of light (6-inch gun) cruisers. The Royal Navy began to dispose of some of its existing light cruisers as they reached the fifteen-year replacement age. In the early 1930s, immediately after the London Treaty, some eleven light cruisers were built. These were armed with eight 6-inch guns in twin turrets. Their displacement of about 7,000 tons was 2,000 tons larger than the 'C' and 'D' class cruisers (built for World War I) which were being replaced, and the new ships were also better suited to oceanic operations.

The state of affairs with regard to destroyers was similar. Britain had built a great number of these vessels during the 1914–18 war to support the Grand Fleet and to escort shipping. There was no need to build new flotillas in the 1920s. In 1922 the British Empire had 197 destroyers (including flotilla leaders), mostly launched in 1915–19; fifty-nine of these had been disposed of by the end of 1930.[17] As with light cruisers, there was a potential problem of 'block obsolescence', too many identical units needing replacement at the same time. After the testing of a couple of experimental vessels in the mid-1920s, replacements began to be built in quantity. HMS *Active* was the first of these standard destroyers, part of a flotilla of eight; she was laid down in July 1928 and commissioned in February 1930. The 1930 London Treaty also set numerical limits on destroyer fleets for Britain, the US and Japan. The British and American limit was 150,000 tons, with individual ships capped at 1,500 tons. The Royal Navy built a flotilla (eight ships) or more a year; until 1937 these were the similar 'A' to 'I' classes. (These were matched by the disposal of seventy-four over-age destroyers in 1931–38.)

In the 1930s, amidst a perfect storm of challenges, the achievement of adequate national defence became more difficult, A severe economic crisis began in 1930–31, leading to two episodes which touched the Royal Navy, the Invergordon Mutiny of 1931 (over naval pay) and the Jarrow March of 1936 (over closure of shipyards). The early 1930s saw Britain and the Royal Navy in a worse position, with the Navy Estimates (the annual budget) dropping to a low of £50.5 million in 1932–33. More important, external threats suddenly became greater, beginning with the Japanese occupation of northeastern China in September 1931, and followed in Europe by the creation of the nationalist Hitler government in Germany in January 1933, and the invasion of Ethiopia by

Italy in October 1935. Unlike in the 1920s, Britain now faced concrete threats, and increased expenditure on armaments had to be reconsidered in a time of straitened economic circumstances.

However, the release of funds by the British government for rearmament in the winter of 1935–36 is less of a break than it is often described as, except in the building of battleships and large aircraft carriers. Even here, the construction of the 22,000-ton carrier *Ark Royal* had begun somewhat earlier, in September 1935. It is true that the laying down of new British capital ships was delayed by the 1930 London Naval Treaty until January 1937. The same treaty permitted the Italians to build replacement vessels, and two 35,000-ton battleships were laid down in Genoa and Trieste in October 1934. The Germans began work on their first (notionally) 35,000-ton ship (the *Bismarck*) in July 1936.[18] (The Americans and Japanese, however, were even later in starting than the British, and did not lay down post-treaty battleships until October and November 1937, respectively.)

In any event, there was a burst of activity in British shipyards in 1937. Two of a new class of battleship, the 35,000-ton *King George V* and *Prince of Wales*, were laid down on 1 January, the day the Washington Treaty quantitative limits expired. They were armed with ten 14-inch guns and capable of 28 knots. Three more of these vessels were laid down before the end of the summer of 1937, as were three 23,000-ton armoured aircraft carriers of the 'Illustrious' class; a fourth carrier began construction in November. What did *not* happen was a jump to a successor battleship class (of more than 35,000 tons), which the Germans, Americans and Japanese all succeeded in making. The projected 'Lion' class was an enlarged 'King George V' class, at 40,750 tons and armed with nine 16-inch guns. The first two were laid down in Liverpool and Newcastle in June and July 1939, but construction effectively ended with the outbreak of war; two more planned vessels were never even begun.[19] On the other hand, the capital ship force was significantly strengthened by full-scale reconstruction (in 1934–40) of three of the older battleships, the *Queen Elizabeth* and her sister ships *Valiant* and *Warspite*, as well as the battle cruiser *Renown*. In addition a fifth armoured carrier was laid down in February 1939.

Meanwhile cruiser construction had been accelerated with the laying down from late 1934 (again, before the winter of 1935–36) of ten large light cruisers of 9,000 to 10,000 tons with twelve 6-inch guns. (These were a response to four similar 'Mogami' class, begun by the Japanese in 1931.) The first of this 'Town' group, the *Southampton*, joined the fleet in March 1937. The 'Towns' were followed on the building slips from the autumn of 1937 by a class of eleven smaller (5,600-ton) 'anti-aircraft cruisers', designed to mount ten dual-purpose 5.25-inch guns.[20]

Construction of destroyers continued, with a new standard single-funnel type, beginning with the 'J' class. The first of these was the *Jervis*, begun in August 1937 and commissioned in May 1939. Alongside these were two flotillas (sixteen ships) of large and heavily-gunned 'Tribal' class destroyers, a response to the Japanese 'Fubuki' class; the first of the class (the *Afridi*) joined the fleet in May 1938. Britain entered the war with 176 destroyers, not many fewer than the number on hand in 1922; there were also thirty-one sloops, multi-purpose ships of nearly destroyer size. The majority of the destroyers were new ships built in the 1930s. The remainder were seventy ships left over from World War I construction, mostly of the 'V' and 'W' type. Although twenty years old, they would prove invaluable as convoy escorts during the Battle of the Atlantic.

The shortcomings of the Royal Navy in the 1920s and 1930s are often exaggerated. There was, however, one critical problem, one which would dog the service through the first three or four years of the coming sea/air war and would only be resolved with extensive help from the United States. This was 'naval' aviation, involving both aircraft operating from carriers and maritime patrol aircraft (flying boats and landplanes) operating from shore bases.[21]

This was a weakness, both in absolute terms and relative to the two other biggest naval powers, the US and Japan. It was in many respects remarkable, as the Royal Navy had pioneered naval aviation during World War I with its Royal Naval Air Service (RNAS). The RNAS brought into operation the first seaplane carrier (1914) and the first aircraft carrier (1917), and by the spring of 1918 it had been operating nearly 3,000 aircraft.

The central long-term problem was an organisational one: the premature creation in April 1918 of the independent Royal Air Force (RAF), merging the RNAS and the Army's Royal Flying Corps. Over more than two decades this structure had a pernicious effect on the capabilities of British armed forces over the sea (and also in combined-arms operations over land).[22] As we will see, in both the US and Japan there was no independent air force, and the Army and Navy were each responsible for their own aircraft and aircrew; in particular, the navies kept control of carrier planes and some shore-based bombers and maritime patrol aircraft. The leaders of the new British RAF in the 1920s and 1930s were preoccupied with their 'independent' role – especially strategic bombing – and greatly exaggerated its war-winning potential. Their doctrine stressed the 'indivisibility of air power', which in their view should be entirely under the control of the Air Ministry.

The senior admirals of the Royal Navy did understand, in general, the significance of aviation. On the other hand, one especially significant long-term effect of the 1918 reorganisation was that no influential group of middle- and senior-ranking officers took shape in the Royal Navy which was able to champion naval aviation; flying was also not an advantageous career path for able junior officers. In the navies of the US and Japan, such men *were* present at various levels, including the top rank, despite the predominant influence of the battleship traditionalists even there. In the Royal Navy, 'big-gun' admirals of the surface navy met less competition in terms of allocation of resources and development of overall naval doctrine and planning.

All the same, the Admiralty did eventually push hard to regain control of the shipboard aircraft of the Fleet Air Arm (FAA).[23] After years of controversy, including a threat of resignation by Admiral Ernle Chatfield, the First Sea Lord, the British government gave in to Admiralty pressure in 1937 and agreed to restore the aircraft and flying personnel of the carriers to the Navy. The takeover process, however, continued through to May 1939, and the government rejected the Admiralty's request for the transfer of the shore-based maritime aircraft and personnel of RAF Coastal Command.

Despite the administrative arrangements for aircraft in the 1920s and 1930s the Admiralty held onto responsibility for the design and construction of ships to carry these planes. Three large aircraft carriers were in the fleet by the end of the 1920s, converted from battle cruisers built for World War I; these were the *Furious*, the *Courageous* and the *Glorious*.[24] As already mentioned, a new large fleet carrier was begun in 1935 (the *Ark Royal*), and the first four 'armoured' fleet carriers in 1937 (the *Illustrious*, the *Victorious*, the *Formidable* and the *Indomitable*). The *Ark Royal* was commissioned in December 1938 and the *Illustrious*, the first of the armoured carriers, would enter operational service in August 1940. These new fleet carriers made up the largest carrier programme anywhere in the world, exceeding those of the US and Japan.[25]

The primary weakness of the British forces for sea/air operations – with hindsight and relative to its rivals – lay not with the ships but with aircraft. The machines on hand were second-rate, and there were too few of them. On the outbreak of war in September 1939 the Royal Navy possessed only 410 aircraft, about half of which were shipborne. In July of that year the US Navy had 2,098 aircraft on hand, including 1,316 combat types. As for the Japanese, even at the end of 1937 their Navy outnumbered the FAA, with 332 carrier planes and 563 shore-based planes.[26] There was also a technical limitation, in that the number of aircraft deployed on each British carrier was low, typically about thirty on the older carriers and only forty-five on the *Ark Royal*, compared to about twice that number aboard contemporary American carriers, which normally carried between seventy-five and eighty aircraft.[27] A consequence of these low numbers was low quality. Ordering small batches of high-performance aircraft meant a very high unit cost. Attempts were made to order multi-purpose aircraft, but these tended to be inadequate in each role.

The quality of existing and projected Royal Navy carrier aircraft was low. Famously, for better or for worse, the Fleet Air Arm of the first years of World War II is remembered for (successful) small-scale attacks by the Fairey Swordfish torpedo bomber, a biplane with an open cockpit and fixed undercarriage, and a maximum speed of about 140 mph. Torpedo bombers were regarded by all three major navies as important, as only they could sink, or at least slow down, heavily armoured capital ships. By 1938 both the Americans and the Japanese had in service monoplane torpedo bombers, with enclosed cockpits and retractable landing gear; the Douglas TBD and the Nakajima B5N (later code-named KATE) were at least 65 mph faster than the Swordfish.

Outmoded torpedo bombers were only the most visible weakness. The Admiralty had accepted, well before the outbreak of the war, the importance of the dive bomber for attacking carriers and smaller warships. Although such an aircraft would have been extremely valuable against the Axis navies (especially in the Mediterranean), the Royal Navy had only procured a small number of Blackburn Skuas, a dual-role fighter-dive bomber. This type carried a 500lb bomb, but was slow and was withdrawn from front-line service in 1941. The most successful dive bomber of the sea/air war in European waters would certainly be the shore-based Junkers Ju 87 Stuka of the Luftwaffe. By the beginning of 1941 the air groups of the American and the Japanese carriers included modern dive bombers, and they would be used extensively in the Pacific war.[28] Torpedo planes and dive bombers could also be used for bombing land targets like airfields and ports, and the small number available in 1939–42 lowered the potential of the Royal Navy's carriers.

Fleet air defence was another vital function of carrier aircraft. The 1930s was a time of very rapid technical change in aviation, and the air forces of potential enemies developed fast all-metal twin-engined bombers. The Heinkel He 111 had a top speed of 270 mph and the Italian Savoia-Marchetti SM.79 a top speed of 285 mph; the new German *Schnellbomber*, the Junkers Ju 88, could reach 315 mph. All three types would have a major sea/air role from 1939–40 onwards. The RAF had developed excellent new single-seat interceptors like the Hawker Hurricane and the Supermarine Spitfire to operate from its land bases, but the situation aboard the Royal Navy carrier force was much less favourable. A small batch of a 'navalised' version of an older RAF fighter was ordered as a stop-gap; this was the Gloster Sea Gladiator, a single-seat biplane.[29] When it ordered new monoplane fighters after 1937, the Admiralty also insisted on a second crew member responsible for over-sea navigation and communications. The maximum speed of the Sea Gladiator was only 260 mph; that of the two-seat Skua was only 225 mph. Such aircraft would have difficulty intercepting modern fast bombers, and they were incapable of effectively engaging modern shore-based fighters like the Messerschmitt Bf 109. Small numbers of these second-rate aircraft were all that the Fleet Air Arm could operate in the first year of the war. It was only in the winter of 1940–41 that a limited quantity of better carrier fighters became available – by acquiring the Grumman G-36 (F4F) from the US, and a navalised version of the Hurricane.[30]

Experience later in the war made it clear that the systems for developing and procuring carrier aircraft (at least from British industry) remained poor; this was in marked contrast to the navies of the US and Japan. Indeed in the course of the whole coming war only two modern purpose-built British-designed carrier planes would enter service.[31]

Carrier aircraft were only the most obvious weakness of British maritime aviation. The RAF had failed before September 1939 to procure an effective shore-based patrol or attack force for operations over the sea. In this respect, however, the British position was not so bad relative to the Americans, or, to a degree, to the Japanese.[32] The patrol aircraft ordered in largest quantity before 1939 was the Avro Anson, which was small, and had short-range and very limited anti-ship and anti-submarine (A/S) abilities. The RAF did develop and procure before the war a big four-engined flying boat, the Short Sunderland, based on the Empire civilian flying boat. However, belated and half-hearted attempts to order twin-engined shore-based torpedo bombers and a medium-sized (twin-engined) flying boat for RAF Coastal Command ended in technical failure.[33] This shortage was only addressed on the eve of the outbreak of war by ordering patrol planes from US manufacturers, the Lockheed Model 14 Hudson and the Consolidated (Model 28) PBY Catalina flying boat, but only the Hudson was available in any numbers in the first period of the war. Fortunately shore-based RAF medium (twin-engined) and heavy (four-engined) bombers would eventually be used in the maritime patrol and A/S role, as well as B-17 Fortress and B-24 Liberator four-engined bombers acquired from the US. This, however, would not take place until 1942.

All this meant that the British had limited ability to use shore-based aircraft for anti-invasion (in Britain in 1940, Malaya in 1941 and Ceylon in 1942) or anti-submarine operations (until 1942). In what would turn out to be a sea/air war this weakness would prove very telling, at least from the spring of 1940.

Despite the shortcomings of naval aviation, the Royal Navy was at the heart of national strategy for most of the 1920s and 1930s. Latterly the RAF budget increased, but only at the end of the 1930s did it surpass that of the Navy. If there was a Cinderella service it was the British Army. When Britain began to accelerate rearmament in 1936 the emphasis was on home defence and imperial defence rather than on a major 'continental commitment'. For better or for worse, only in February 1939 would it become a priority to raise ground forces that could directly support Britain's French ally against Nazi Germany.

The Allies were in some ways militarily unprepared in September 1939, but they were economically more powerful than Germany. Their expectation was that once they had caught up with the armaments programme of the Third Reich they could begin decisive operations. As things turned out, they seriously underestimated the energy and skill of their opponent.

THE FIRST SEA/AIR BATTLES

The fighting on land and in the air in the first six months of the war had little effect on the British and French. The Germans attacked Poland with greatly superior ground and air forces; Warsaw fell on 27 September, bringing an effective end to the fighting. The French made no more than a token offensive effort with their army in the west, although they and the British built up their ground forces. The British Expeditionary Force (BEF) was sent across the Channel in September and October 1939 without interference from the enemy.

A short-lived little naval war took place in the Baltic. The Kriegsmarine actually fired the first shots by German forces, on 1 September. The old battleship *Schleswig-Holstein* bombarded a Polish enclave below Danzig at the mouth of the Vistula; she was one of the six pre-dreadnoughts originally permitted to Germany under the Versailles Treaty and was normally employed as a training ship. Poland's coastline was short, and its navy small. Three of the Polish Navy's four modern destroyers (built in France and Britain in the 1930s) made a dash to the UK (Operation PEKIN) in the last days of peace. The fourth destroyer, the *Wicher*, was sunk by Luftwaffe dive bombers in the Hela naval base on 3 September, along with the large minelayer *Gryf*; they were the first proper warships ever sunk in action by aircraft.

Of five Polish submarines, three were interned in Sweden, and the others made their way to Rosyth in Scotland, the *Orzel* after a particularly adventurous voyage (including a brief internment in Estonia). Twin 14,000-ton, Italian-built ocean liners, pride of the Polish merchant fleet, were safely outside the Baltic when the invasion began. The MV *Pilsudski* was mined off the British coast in November 1939, but the MV *Batory* would have a long career as an Allied troopship. Polish seamen who escaped the Germans played a memorable role in the later fighting; over the course of the six-year war the British supplied them with two (old) light cruisers, six modern destroyers and three submarines.

What Churchill called the 'Twilight War' lasted from September 1939 to May 1940. During this period there were, as far as the British and French were concerned, more developments at sea than on land or in the air. In early September the British re-established the Northern Patrol to cover the exits from the North Sea; this enabled a distant blockade of German ports and guarded against the breakout of enemy warships. A third of the German merchant fleet – some 330 vessels of 1.6 million tons – was caught abroad by the sudden outbreak of a general war in September 1939. Of these, seventy-six broke through the blockade and returned home by April 1940; they included the 52,000-ton Norddeutscher Lloyd liner SS *Bremen*, which had been en route to New York. Some twenty-eight ships were scuttled, including another big NDL liner, the 32,000-ton SS *Columbus* (from Vera Cruz); shadowed by a British destroyer, the *Columbus* was forced to scuttle herself off the Virginia coast in December 1939. Another twenty-six vessels were captured by the Allies, and 160 were marooned in neutral ports outside the Mediterranean.[34]

The main naval fighting in the autumn of 1939 and the following winter was around the British coasts and particularly in the North Sea. Despite the embarrassment of the *Athenia* affair, the U-boat was very quickly re-established as a powerful anti-warship weapon.[35] The first large naval vessel to be lost in the war was HMS *Courageous*, a 22,500-ton aircraft carrier; she was one of three former battle cruisers converted into carriers in the 1920s. The Admiralty had ordered the *Courageous* out from Plymouth in an offensive 'sweep' against U-boats which were threatening the Atlantic Ocean to the west of Ireland and Great Britain. Having detached two of the four destroyers of her escort, the carrier was herself attacked by the *U 29* some 150 miles southwest of Ireland on the evening of 17 September. She was hit by two torpedoes and sank in twenty minutes with many fatalities: 514 officers and men were lost.

The new carrier *Ark Royal*, engaged in a similar offensive sweep northwest of Northern Ireland, had been attacked by the *U 39* three days earlier, but in her case the enemy torpedoes malfunctioned. After these two events the Royal Navy ceased active patrolling with fleet carriers. The U-boat which attacked the *Ark Royal* was quickly counter-attacked and sunk by three destroyers of her escort. The *U 39* was the first of a great many German submarines to be lost; unusually, her crew survived and became the war's first naval POWs.

The other dramatic submarine action in these months was the penetration of the naval base at Scapa Flow in the Orkney Islands by the *U 47*, commanded by Lt Commander Günther Prien. On the night of 13/14 October 1939, Prien was able to manoeuvre his boat through an ill-protected channel to the east of the huge anchorage. Although there were few ships present, due to the current vulnerability of Scapa to air and sea attack, Prien was able to hit the anchored *Royal Oak* with four torpedoes. The battleship suffered a devastating magazine explosion and quickly sank. Some 833 members of her crews were killed, including the admiral commanding the 2nd Battle Squadron. A second battleship, the *Barham*, was hit by a torpedo off the north coast of Scotland at the end of December by Fritz-Julius Lemp's *U 30* (of *Athenia* fame); the big ship would be in dockyard hands for four months.

U-boats also began to lay magnetic mines off the British coast in November; these weapons were activated by the magnetic field of passing ships. The first major victim was the brand-new *Belfast*, which on 21 November was damaged by a mine laid by the *U 21* in the Firth of Forth (near the Rosyth naval base). Structural damage was so severe that the cruiser would not be back in service for two years, until the autumn of 1942. (She is now, of course, a museum ship in London.) Another mine, laid by the *U 52* inside the Loch Ewe fleet anchorage in northwestern Scotland, put the battleship *Nelson* out of action for six months; at the time, in December, she was one of the Royal Navy's two most powerful ships. However, on balance Admiral Raeder's decision to deploy magnetic mines in limited numbers and at such an early stage in the war was a mistake; it enabled the British to develop effective counter-measures.

The Germans despatched destroyers for an active campaign off the English North Sea coast in mid-October, with anti-shipping sweeps and minelaying. Disagreements about the details of these operations led to a shake-up in the German naval command. Wartime operations had been led by two shore-based 'Navy Group Command' headquarters (*Marine gruppen kommandos*), Navy Group Command East covering the Baltic, and Navy Group Command West the North Sea and the Atlantic. The C-in-C of Navy Group Command West was Admiral Alfred Saalwächter, and subordinate to him was the sea-going commander of the battle fleet (*Flottenchef*), Admiral Hermann Böhm. In mid-October Böhm complained about excessive meddling in operational details by Saalwächter (specifically about the use of heavy ships near the British coast). Raeder came down on Saalwächter's side, and the Flottenchef resigned. In any event, destroyer attacks continued throughout the winter of the Twilight War, under a new Flottenchef, Admiral Wilhelm Marschall.

The Germans mounted an unprecedented long-range sortie with the new battleships *Scharnhorst* and *Gneisenau*, commanded by Marschall, at the end of November. On the evening of 23 November they caught the armed merchant cruiser HMS *Rawalpindi* between Iceland and the Faroes. She was a mobilised P&O liner equipped with eight old 6-inch guns and went down after a forty-minute duel; only a few dozen of her crew of nearly 300 survived.

The sea/air warfare in World War II began over the North Sea. During the Twilight War, warships were favoured as bomber targets by both sides, because cities and other civilian objectives were off limits. The RAF mounted small-scale attacks on German North Sea naval bases at the beginning of the war, with little effect and heavy losses. The Luftwaffe, meanwhile, with better aircraft but also with limited numbers, attempted to catch the British fleet at sea and in its bases. Neither side had the special weapons or training required for effective sea/air warfare – such as a sufficient number of long-range torpedo bombers.

The Luftwaffe organised two anti-shipping air groups, *Kampfgeschwader* (KG) 26 and KG 30;[36] they came under a special headquarters, *Fliegerkorps* X (Xth Air Corps). KG 30 was equipped with a few of the new German 'wonder weapon', the high-speed Junkers Ju 88 bomber. On 25–26 September German bombers, Heinkel He 111s and the some of the first operational Ju 88s, attacked elements of the Home Fleet – the battle cruiser *Hood*, the carrier *Ark Royal* and two cruisers – which were sailing in the North Sea, halfway between Scotland and the entrance to the Skagerrak, the strait between Norway and Denmark. The limited effectiveness of high-level bombing against rapidly manoeuvring ships at sea was first demonstrated here, but the Luftwaffe pilots (and German propaganda) claimed to have sunk the *Ark Royal*. A Blackburn Skua, a two-seat fighter-dive bomber from the carrier, shot down a shadowing Dornier Do 18 flying boat, the first ever interception by a carrier aircraft (and the first German aircraft destroyed by the British in the 1939–45 war). In mid-October a small Luftwaffe Ju 88 force made the first air raid on Britain, when they attacked British ships off Rosyth; among the potential targets was the battle cruiser *Hood*. They achieved no damage and the raid commander was shot down. The following day a small raid on Scapa Flow also had no serious results. In February 1940 bombers from KG 26 mistakenly attacked a friendly destroyer flotilla in the North Sea, an action which led to the loss of two German vessels; altogether some 500 German seamen were lost.

Overall the British had in these months mounted a successful blockade line, especially covering the Greenland–Iceland–UK gap. Meanwhile the Allies were able to maintain their merchant shipping, much of it in convoy, with little interference. They were able to carry out long-range troop reinforcements across the sea, the most important being big convoys from Canada to the UK. U-boat activity was limited, especially on the wider oceans, even after a directive (*Weisung* No. 9) issued by Hitler on 29 November 1939 which prioritised attacks on British economic targets. On the other hand, Admiral Raeder and the Naval War Staff showed a greater readiness to use the surface fleet than had been the case in World War I.

THE DESTRUCTION OF THE *ADMIRAL GRAF SPEE*

In the summer of 1939 the leaders of the Kriegsmarine had not been sure whether the Danzig crisis would result in a shooting war with the Poles, let alone whether the British and French would join in. As a contingency plan Admiral Raeder had ordered two major surface ships, the *Deutschland* and

Admiral Graf Spee, secretly to put to sea in mid-August 1939. For the first month of the war the two raiders were held on standby far from the shipping lanes. There was some hope in Berlin that the quick overthrow of Poland might be followed by a return to normal relations with Britain and France, if direct combat was kept to a minimum. When the warships were unleashed in October the *Deutschland* and a supply ship were sent to the North Atlantic. The big raider was not very successful; in the end she only sank two small merchant ships and captured a third, before creeping back to Germany in mid-November. The voyage of the *Admiral Graf Spee*, the *Deutschland*'s sister ship, would turn out to be far more memorable.

Commanded by Captain Hans Langsdorff and supported by the supply ship *Altmark*, the *Admiral Graf Spee* had by the beginning of December cruised for a distance of 18,600 miles, including a run into the Indian Ocean nearly to Madagascar. Some nine enemy merchant ships had been accounted for, without any loss of life. This was the embodiment of Admiral Raeder's Kreuzerkrieg and a sea adventure fit for the pages of Jules Verne. (In the 1956 British film *The Battle of the River Plate* Langsdorff – clean-shaven in real life – was played by the goateed actor Peter Finch, in a performance uncannily similar to Verne's Captain Nemo.)[37] The *Admiral Graf Spee* and her two sisters were indeed remarkable ships. To squeeze maximum firepower into a cruiser hull they had been designed with two main turrets, each mounting three 11-inch guns. They were unusual, too, because they were powered by diesel motors, rather than steam turbines. This gave them an extremely long range and relatively high speed – 26 knots – compared to the older British and French battleships. Langsdorff would, in real life, boast of his ship's capabilities to one of his prisoners: 'Ships of the British Navy which have guns which could sink me are not fast enough to catch me, *and the ships with the speed have not the guns heavy enough*.'[38]

The name *Admiral Graf Spee* also had a connection with Germany's short naval history. Fixed to her massive foremast tower she bore a plate with the word 'Coronel' inscribed upon it. Admiral Maximilian von Spee, the German *Reichsgraf* after whom the ship was named, had commanded a cruiser squadron stationed in the Far East in 1914. His biggest vessels were the armoured cruisers *Scharnhorst* and *Gneisenau* (after which the two famous World War II battleships would be named). Spee achieved the only outright victory of the Kaiser's Navy in a sea battle: he engaged and sank two British cruisers off the Chilean port of Coronel in November 1914. His own squadron was then ambushed by two enemy battle cruisers in the Falkland Islands five weeks later, and nearly all the German ships were sunk. Spee himself went down with his flagship, and his two sons also perished; his daughter would launch the *Admiral Graf Spee* at Wilhelmshaven in 1934.

The question was whether Captain Langsdorff could avoid the fate of Spee. By December 1939 maintenance in a home port for the *Graf Spee* was becoming necessary, and Langsdorff began to make his way home. He had been informed by radio in early December about the general location of the Allied warships that were searching for him – probably on the basis of signals intelligence: he learned there were four cruisers covering the long coast of South America. Langsdorff had been ordered to avoid contact and engagements with enemy warships. He believed, however, that having fulfilled his main commerce-raiding mission, he could now chance a more impressive attack, in a more heavily patrolled area, which might lead to contact with escorting British warships. He knew that one focal area of British shipping – for the important meat and grain trade – would be off the River Plate, the deep estuary between Uruguay and Argentina with its ports of Montevideo and Buenos Aires.

The danger to Langsdorff and the *Admiral Graf Spee* was real. When unknown German surface raiders began to sink and capture British ships in early October 1939 the Allies had formed eight 'hunting groups'. Force G was one of the weakest, with the heavy cruisers *Cumberland* and *Exeter*; the light cruisers *Ajax* and *Achilles* (the latter with a mainly New Zealander crew) were added later. Commodore Henry Harwood, long-time commander of the Royal Navy's South American Division, led Force G. Harwood made a well-educated guess about the intentions of the mysterious surface raider. Based on her previous operations and the location of her last known attack, he anticipated that she would appear off the River Plate in mid-December.

And so contact was made between the two navies on the perfect, clear early morning of 13 December, at 5.52 a.m., about 400 miles ENE of the entrance to the River Plate. Langsdorff's lookouts spotted what they identified as British warships. The German captain did not turn and run, as laid down in the operational instructions of the Naval War Staff; he closed the range to investigate, at 25 knots. He hoped that his powerful guns would so badly damage this enemy that they would not be able to shadow the *Graf Spee*. He also calculated that in such clear weather, and many hours before dusk, shaking off the enemy ships without battle would be impossible. Twenty-five minutes later, at 6.16 a.m., the *Graf Spee* opened fire, at a range of 19,400 yards (about 11 miles).

Harwood – flying his commodore's broad pennant in the light cruiser *Ajax* – had thought through his tactics in advance and informed his captains about them. He continued the Royal Navy tradition of aggressive action: 'My policy – attack at once; day or night.'[39] He intended to divide his force to split the enemy's fire, and that is what happened on the day; the *Ajax* and the *Achilles* kept to their original northeast course, and the *Exeter* turned to the northwest. The cruisers blocked Langsdorff's escape route to the east, the *Exeter* firing torpedoes, and at 6.36 a.m. he turned sharply to the northwest, and then due west.

During the exchange of fire the *Graf Spee* concentrated on the most powerful enemy, the *Exeter*. Within a few minutes she had knocked out the British cruiser's 'B' turret (the second from the bow), and a spray of splinters from the exploding shell injured most of the personnel on the open bridge behind it. The three British ships were also able to achieve hits. Despite her popular appellation of 'pocket battleship', the *Graf Spee* had only the thin armour protection of a cruiser. The 8-inch shells of the *Exeter* penetrated her armoured belt and the 6-inch shells of the *Ajax* and the *Achilles* caused much damage to her superstructure. Langsdorff was superficially injured by shell splinters, and an explosion knocked him to the deck, where he briefly lost consciousness. This may have affected his judgement in the minutes that followed; he shifted fire to the two light cruisers when he might have finished off the *Exeter*.

At 7.10 a.m. Harwood ordered his light cruisers to close the range for a torpedo attack. The damaged *Exeter*, guns out of action but machinery largely undamaged, made smoke and left the action at 7.30; the two light cruisers continued to engage. The *Ajax* and the *Achilles* were able to close the range to 8,000 yards – about 4.5 miles. Although they fired smaller (6-inch) shells, they had a high rate of fire. The *Graf Spee* was frequently changing course, and this and the British cruisers' smoke screen reduced the chances of hitting them.

The guns of the *Ajax* and the *Achilles* inflicted much more damage on the *Graf Spee* than did those of the *Exeter*: the German ship suffered eighteen 6-inch shell hits, and only two 8-inch. The *Ajax* only lost seven men killed, and the *Achilles* four; sixty-one died aboard the *Exeter*. German casualties were also relatively light for a major naval action – thirty-six men were killed and sixty wounded, out of a crew of 1,200. Although his guns and machinery were functioning, Langsdorff had expended half his ammunition. Serious damage to the hull plating forward made the ship unseaworthy for future movement in the winter North Atlantic. Meanwhile hits to the galleys and fuel processing system made it essential to put into a port for repairs. Langsdorff now decided to break off the action and withdraw to the west; he was shadowed on either flank by Harwood with his two remaining cruisers. The time was still only 7.40 a.m. and the bloody part of the battle was over.

During the daylight hours of the 13th the *Admiral Graf Spee* continued towards the coast. Langsdorff took the decision to put into the Uruguayan port of Montevideo, on the north side of the River Plate, to attempt repairs. He dropped anchor in the outer harbour in the middle of the night, seventeen hours after the battle. Langsdorff was in an impossible position. Because his ship was repairing damage he could, under international law, remain in port for more than the normal twenty-four hours, but the longer he stayed the more ships the Royal Navy could bring up. On the day following the battle he believed that the battle cruiser *Renown* and the carrier *Ark Royal* had joined the cruiser force and were already waiting outside the port – one of his officers had erroneously reported a sighting. In fact Harwood had been reinforced only by the heavy cruiser *Cumberland* which had dashed north from the Falklands.

Langsdorff consulted with Berlin about his choice of action: should he allow the *Graf Spee* to be interned, should he scuttle her, or should he re-engage the British? Berlin gave him freedom of action; on the evening of the 17th he took off his men and blew up the ship. He was evidently not prepared to sacrifice his young crew in a pointless and uneven battle, and he had the cruel example of the 1914 Falklands defeat as a warning. Harwood, by now promoted to rear admiral, reported the finale to the Admiralty: 'Navigation lights were now switched on and the squadron steamed past the Whistle Buoy within four miles of the GRAF SPEE. It was now dark, and she was ablaze from end to end, flames reaching as high as the top of her control tower, a magnificent and most cheering sight.'[40]

The mission of the *Admiral Graf Spee* had been ill-conceived. She had caused relatively little damage to British shipping – nine ships totalling about 50,000 tons. Langsdorff made some bad decisions. He decided to operate off the River Plate, and he engaged in a battle with enemy warships on 13 December; both actions disregarded Berlin's instructions. He was acutely aware of these mistakes; a week after he scuttled his ship he shot himself in his Buenos Aires hotel room. More significantly, the fate of Langsdorff's ship demonstrated the fatal weakness of the Kreuzerkrieg concept: with Germany lacking overseas bases, any damage to a raider could be fatal.

CHAPTER 2

NORWAY

A Costly Victory

SURPRISE ATTACK, 9 APRIL 1940

Operation WESER EXERCISE (WESERÜBUNG) was timetabled to erupt at 4.15 a.m. on Tuesday, 9 April 1940. At that moment the German Navy launched simultaneous surprise attacks at six points on the long and jagged coastline of neutral Norway.

The most daring strike was aimed at Narvik. The ore port, small but strategically valuable, lay 140 miles north of the Arctic Circle, and 1,250 miles away from the nearest German naval base. Very early on Tuesday morning a flotilla of ten big German destroyers dashed through the narrow Ofotfjord, which stretches 35 miles from the Norwegian Sea to the port of Narvik itself. These vessels made up about half the destroyer strength of the German Navy; they carried below decks 2,000 mountain troops, commanded by General Eduard Dietl. The advancing force had been detected by Norwegian patrol boats at the entrance to the long fjord.

An hour and a half later, at Narvik itself, the flagship was confronted by two outdated coast-defence ships, the *Eidsvold* and the *Norge*. After a brief parley, during which the Norwegian ships refused to surrender, the German commodore ordered the launch of torpedoes. One of the old ships was literally blown out of the water, killing nearly all 200 men aboard; the other capsized, with the loss of half the crew. By 5.00 a.m. Dietl's troops were disembarking; the local Norwegian Army commander gave up the town without a fight, although some of his men were able to retreat into the hinterland.

The occupation of Trondheim also involved a risky voyage for the Germans, although it lay 400 miles south of Narvik. The strike force consisted of the heavy cruiser *Admiral Hipper* and five destroyers, with another regiment of mountain troops – 1,700 men – aboard. Two patrol boats stationed outside the entrance to

Trondheimfjord sounded the alarm, but the *Hipper* slipped through the narrows past the coastal forts; the dozy garrisons did not open fire. She dropped anchor at the town of Trondheim about an hour later, at 4.25 a.m. A thousand men were quickly put ashore to take control; Trondheim itself did not have a garrison. The inhabitants of Norway's third city awoke to find themselves under German occupation. Other detachments captured – from the rear – the coastal fortifications past which the battle group had just sailed.

Bergen lay 300 miles further to the south. The attack force here consisted of the light cruisers *Köln* and *Königsberg*, two torpedo boats, and some S-boats (*Schnellboote*, German motor torpedo boats or MTBs, which were later known by their British designation as 'E-boats'). On board were 1,900 infantry. Just after 1.00 a.m. the force was spotted by patrol boats but the Norwegians were caught by surprise, and in the exchange of fire half a dozen of them were killed – and a similar number of German sailors. After that the invaders quickly took control of the town.

Egersund, 135 miles down the coast from Bergen, was important as the starting point for the underwater telegraph cable to Scotland. Two minesweepers had been deployed there, and they arrived at 4.15 a.m. Stavanger, some 35 miles to the north of Egersund, and the location of an important airfield, was taken a few hours later, and by German airborne forces, rather than by the Navy. The airfield was quickly turned into an advance base for the Luftwaffe.

At Kristiansand, on the south coast – guarding the entrance to the Skagerrak – the invasion force consisted of the light cruiser *Karlsruhe*, two torpedo boats and some S-boats, with nearly 1,000 soldiers aboard. The landing was delayed six hours by fog and the relatively alert garrisons of the coastal batteries, but no shots were fired during the final advance. The port was in German hands by midday.

So far on 9 April fortune had favoured the bold. At Oslo the situation changed, as the laws of probability took effect. The force tasked to take the Norwegian capital was commanded by Admiral Oskar Kummetz; with two heavy cruisers it was the largest of six naval detachments. The *Blücher* – sister ship of the *Hipper* and the *Prinz Eugen* – was brand-new and had just completed working up; the *Lützow* (formerly the *Deutschland*) was a Panzerschiff of the same class as the *Admiral Graf Spee*. The force also included the light cruiser *Emden*, three torpedo boats and some patrol boats. Some 2,000 spearhead troops were being carried aboard the warships. At about midnight the leading German torpedo boat had been challenged by a small patrol boat, which provided some advance warning to the defenders. To reach Oslo itself the German force had to pass through a narrow channel protected by the Oscarborg Fortress. The *Blücher* now led the column, steaming about 600 yards ahead of the *Lützow*.

The German admiral believed the Norwegians could not, or would not, use their heavy coastal guns against his ships. Indeed, the coastal forts were only partly manned, and only two of the Krupp 280mm guns could be operated, along with some smaller batteries. The gunners inflicted heavy damage on the superstructure of the *Blücher*, but the fatal blow came from a shore-based torpedo battery firing at a range of 500 yards. The green crew of the cruiser were unable to save their ship, and the *Blücher* capsized and sank at 6.25 a.m. Casualty figures were shrouded by German secrecy, but a recent reliable source estimates that between 350 and 400 men were killed; over 1,000 survivors made their way ashore.[1] The *Lützow* was also hit by gunfire, but her officers were able to turn the column of ships around.

There was a second string to the German bow, a planned airborne seizure of Oslo's airport. This operation was like the one at Stavanger – although a combination of the naval failure and bad weather meant the Germans had to land their transport planes – loaded with infantry – under ground fire without a parachute drop. Meanwhile groups of Luftwaffe bombers had been flying over the town, hoping to use what would now be called 'shock and awe' tactics to cow the local authorities. At 2.00 p.m. the undefended capital surrendered; half an hour later the first German troops marched into the city from the nearby airfield.

Operation WESER EXERCISE included the simultaneous military occupation of Denmark. This was accomplished without resistance. At 7.30 p.m. on 9 April General Nikolaus von Falkenhorst, in overall charge of the Army formations taking part in the operation, reported his view of the situation to the Wehrmacht high command: 'The occupation of Norway and Denmark has been accomplished according to orders.'[2] Despite an element of oversimplification – Falkenhorst had himself not yet been able to set foot in Norway, and German power there hung by a thread – the report was essentially correct. From Narvik to Oslo the daring WESER EXERCISE *coup de main* had succeeded. The prize indeed was valuable; the losses, so far, were acceptable, even that of the *Blücher*. But within days the German hold on Norway would be severely tested.

Early on the morning of 9 April, a telephone call from the duty officer at the British War Cabinet Office in London woke General Hastings Ismay out of deep sleep. Ismay was the War Cabinet's secretary and a vital cog in the military machinery. He could hardly take in the report – that the Germans had seized Copenhagen, Oslo and all the main ports of Norway. Ismay arranged a meeting of the Chiefs of Staff for 6.30 a.m. (7.30 Norwegian time). 'As I hurried into my clothes I realised, for the first time in my life, the devastating and demoralising effect of surprise.'[3]

PLANNING FOR NORWAY

The naval battle for Norway had come about as a collision. Both the Allies and the Germans had been secretly planning action against the neutral Scandinavian country. Both sides were caught by surprise.

Allied grand strategy was confused and hesitant. Britain and France had gone to war with Germany counting on their economic strength and global position. There was, however, a growing body of opinion among their political and military leaders that time might not be on the Allied side, and that they could not win a long war – not least because Germany had blockade-proof access to raw materials via its Soviet quasi-ally. The British and French leaders were now eager to exert pressure by denying Germany access to the iron ore mines of northern Sweden. Superior Allied sea power meant an expeditionary force could be despatched to northern Norway; from there it might even move east (125 miles) by railway to occupy the Swedish mines. At the very least Allied warships could block the sea routes along which the iron ore was shipped during the winter months; when the Baltic Sea was frozen, the bulk ore was normally transported west by rail to Narvik and then by sea to Germany through the Norwegian 'Leads' (inshore waters).

Allied interest in northern Europe was heightened by the Soviet invasion of Finland in November 1939. The USSR was regarded as effectively an ally of Germany, but also a 'weak link'; moreover, the provision of aid to the Finns could serve as a pretext for Allied action in Scandinavia. (None of the planners can have imagined that Soviet Russia would become their ally, and that the main strategic importance of Norway in 1942–44 would be as a German base for attacking Allied supply convoys to Murmansk and Arkhangelsk.) A small expeditionary force was about to be despatched to northern Norway in mid-March 1940, when the Finnish surrender made the British and French pause. Then, at the meeting of the Allied Supreme War Council on 28 March it was finally agreed that in the next week or so two small minefields would be laid in Norwegian territorial waters; the operation was code-named WILFRED. More important, the Allies also revived a project (Plan R.4) to despatch, soon after the minelaying, a small detachment of ground forces to Scandinavia. The assumption was that the minelaying would incite German counter-measures against Norwegian territory, which could be used as a pretext. An initial wave of British and French troops would be followed by the build-up of a strong ground force in Narvik (promising access to the Swedish mines); a further military presence in central Norway would be made through the port of Trondheim. From hindsight, there was certainly an underestimation of with ability of with Hitler's armed forces to project power to the north.

The minelaying part of the Allied plan, scheduled for 5 April, was relatively simple, but a disagreement over strategy postponed it for three days – a fatal delay. Along with the minelaying were put back preparations for the troop landings at Bergen and Trondheim, and a naval raid to destroy the Stavanger airfield.

Churchill wrote to the Foreign Secretary, Lord Halifax, in March, bemoaning the surrender of Finland and expressing concern about German intentions: 'Whether they have some positive plan of their own wh[ich] will open upon us, I cannot tell. It w[oul]d seem to me astounding if they have not.'[4] The Germans were indeed making their own plans. Although the Army and the Luftwaffe were mainly interested in the Netherlands, Belgium and France, Admiral Raeder convinced Hitler that control of Norway was essential to prosecute the maritime war against Britain – this was a supposed lesson of World War I. In December the Führer did authorise contingency planning for an invasion. Although Norway lacked the military forces – and possibly the political will – to block a German takeover, the Royal Navy could be expected to intervene in strength. Raeder was prepared to accept heavy losses. Norway was important as a forward base for cruiser and U-boat anti-shipping operations in the Atlantic and because Swedish iron ore was needed for new warships. Battle there also guaranteed for the men and ships of the Kriegsmarine a prominent and active role in Hitler's war effort.

On 19 February, the German dictator accelerated the invasion planning, and appointed a senior German general, Nicolaus von Falkenhorst, to oversee it, with a tri-service staff. The end result was the directive for Operation WESER EXERCISE; preparations were to be completed by 20 March. Hitler decided to go ahead with WESER EXERCISE partly because he was receiving intelligence reports of imminent Allied action; he also knew that coming shorter nights would make conditions for a surprise attack less favourable. In addition, the U-boat force was standing by to support the invasion, and it could not be kept out of the general commerce war indefinitely. At the end of March Hitler ordered that WESER EXERCISE would begin between 8 and 10 April, and that the great offensive against France would begin very shortly after that. The Naval War Staff war diary detailed Hitler's attitude, two days before the first ships departed: 'He considered Operation WESER EXERCISE to be particularly daring – in fact one of the rashest undertakings in the history of modern warfare. Precisely that would ensure its success . . . He described the state of anxiety he would feel until the success of the operation as one of the strongest nervous tensions of his life.'[5]

As we have already seen, in the final plan combat ships would run in spearhead forces, with simultaneous strikes at six places, alongside airborne landings. Merchant ships surreptitiously stationed offshore would then bring in heavy equipment, supplies and support troops, before the British could prepare a naval response. Because these merchant ships were slower than the warships, and were supposed to be inconspicuous, they had to depart earlier and steam independently; the first seven ships left Hamburg on 3 April. One of three merchant ships supporting the occupation of Bergen, the 5,300-ton MV *Rio de Janeiro*, was torpedoed and sunk in the Skagerrak at midday on 8 April, by the Polish submarine *Orzel* (operating under British command). The submarine could not know what its target had been transporting, but local Norwegians realised the survivors were soldiers and part of an invasion force. The authorities in Oslo received this information by the early evening of the 8th. Preoccupied with reports of British minelaying that morning, they took no action.

The main elements of the German invasion fleet, intended for the simultaneous strikes against Narvik and Trondheim, had sallied forth from bases in northwestern Germany on Saturday night, 6/7 April. The plan was that elements attacking the Norwegian west coast ports would sail together across the North Sea. As the fleet progressed into the Norwegian Sea and up the coast of Norway, groups of ships would peel off. Each group would simultaneously enter Norwegian waters on the night of 8/9 April. Admiral Marschall, the officer originally assigned to lead the fleet, was replaced shortly before the start of the operation – evidently after a clash with Raeder. His substitute was Admiral Günther Lütjens.

The backbone of Lütjens's fleet comprised two new battleships, the *Scharnhorst* and the *Gneisenau*, perhaps the most famous warship twins in the 1939–45 conflict. They took their names from the two armoured cruisers lost at the Battle of the Falkland Islands in 1914; these ships in turn had been named after two Prussian military reformers of the Napoleonic Wars. They were among the most handsome vessels of their era, with raked *Atlantik* bows. Like all the ships of the expedition, they carried highly visible recognition markings to prevent attacks by friendly aircraft; huge swastika flags were painted on the deck fore and aft, and the tops of their turrets were now all yellow. They were not taking direct part in the landing but would provide long-range cover. In addition, their presence was intended to deceive the British into thinking – in the first hours – that what was going on was a commerce-raiding breakout into the Atlantic.

SEA/AIR OPERATIONS OFF NORWAY, APRIL–MAY 1940

The Home Fleet was the main battle fleet of the Royal Navy.[6] Its main wartime base was at Scapa Flow in the Orkney Islands. Admiral Charles Forbes had been C-in-C, Home Fleet, since April 1938. He was a capable officer, a gunnery specialist who had served on Admiral Jellicoe's staff at Jutland. In the first part of April 1940 Forbes thought that he had three tasks. The first was to prevent another breakout by German heavy ships into the Atlantic from northern Germany. The second was to cover the British minelaying operation in the Leads, scheduled for 8 April (Monday). The third was to prepare a response to any German counter-measures that might follow – possibly hurrying Allied support troops to Bergen, Stavanger, Narvik and Trondheim in accordance with Plan R.4.

On Friday, 5 April, Forbes had detached a task group north from Scapa Flow to cover the minelaying force. Admiral William Whitworth, commander of the Home Fleet Battle Cruiser Squadron, flew his flag in the newly modernised battle cruiser *Renown*; four destroyers including HMS *Glowworm* provided an escort. In truth Forbes and the Admiralty were more concerned with overawing the Norwegians than with fighting German warships; the new minefield would be 1,000 miles from the nearest enemy base.

However, the British detected signs of German naval activity off the North Sea ports on Saturday, 6 April. The following morning a squadron of RAF Blenheim light bombers sighted and attacked a large force of German warships in the North Sea. Faulty radio procedures meant that no sighting report was sent. Only after the planes returned to base late on Sunday afternoon could the news be relayed to the Admiralty, and more time passed before the Home Fleet was put on alert. Admiral Forbes departed from Scapa Flow with his main force – the battleships *Rodney* and *Valiant*, the battle cruiser *Repulse*, two cruisers and ten destroyers – at about 8.15 on Sunday evening.

Forbes and the Admiralty now had two handicaps. They were late; the German force – Lütjens's battle group – now had a head start of eighteen hours; it reached the 175-mile-wide choke point between the Shetland Islands and Bergen before the Home Fleet left port. And the British incorrectly assumed that this was another German fleet breakout – not the beginning of an invasion of central and northern Norway.

Just after midnight on Saturday the British government had received a warning from its Copenhagen embassy, obtained via local American diplomats, that a major German operation was planned; this would take in the arc from Jutland in Denmark to Narvik in northern Norway. This information – fundamentally correct – was forwarded by the Admiralty to the Home Fleet early on Sunday afternoon, but with a dismissive rider: 'all these reports are of doubtful value and may well be only a further move in the war of nerves'.[7] And shortly after dawn on Monday, some twenty-four hours before the Germans reached the target ports, came a more definite – but puzzling – warning. The destroyer *Glowworm*, which had left the *Renown*'s screen to search for a sailor who had fallen overboard, reported she was engaging a superior enemy force some 150 miles northwest of Trondheim and then – at 8.55 a.m. – ceased contact. In the afternoon, numerous reports arrived that German heavy ships – battleships or cruisers – actually bound for Oslo in southern Norway – had passed through the Great Belt and into the Kattegat (the exits from the Baltic Sea).

The *Glowworm* mystery was not cleared up until after the war. She had encountered and pursued enemy destroyers – part of Lütjens's screen – and this led her into an engagement with the heavy cruiser *Admiral Hipper*. The *Hipper* and the *Glowworm* fought an uneven and confused battle in poor visibility and at very close quarters. The destroyer was later credited with having rammed and crippled its enemy, and her captain, Lt Commander Gerard Roope, would be awarded a posthumous Victoria Cross in July 1945. The *Hipper* was actually not heavily damaged; she would be able to proceed with her invasion mission at Trondheim.

On Tuesday morning, after a stormy night at sea and an hour before the simultaneous attack on the Norwegian ports began, another event added to the general confusion. The battle cruiser *Renown* with its destroyer screen ran into the *Scharnhorst* and the *Gneisenau* out in the Norwegian Sea, about 200 miles WSW of Narvik. Lütjens dashed off a report: 'Am in battle with heavy forces grid square 3440 AF.'[8] It was the first battle between capital ships since Jutland in 1916, and the only such engagement during the Norwegian campaign. The big ships were not dissimilar. Displacements were nearly the same, although the *Renown* was longer. She had much more powerful guns, six 15-inch compared to nine 11-inch (but there were two German ships). The enemy ships were newer and better armoured, but the British ship had just been rebuilt. Steaming through intermittent snow squalls and exchanging many salvoes at long range, the *Renown*'s guns hit both German ships, causing some damage. The uncertainty of the situation – Lütjens believed he might be fighting the much superior *Nelson* as well as a 'Renown' class ship – and storm damage to the forward turrets of his two ships, prompted the German admiral to break off contact. The *Scharnhorst* and the *Gneisenau* hurried home to the safety of Wilhelmshaven, along with the *Admiral Hipper*, arriving on 13 April; for seven weeks they would take no further part in the campaign.

The inconclusive duel between the *Renown* and the enemy battleships was followed by the German occupation of the Norwegian ports, a development which ultimately determined the outcome of the campaign. But in the short term the success – marred only by the loss of the *Blücher* – could not last. The aim of an unopposed peaceful occupation of Denmark and Norway on German terms, with the installation of compliant governments, had not been achieved. Denmark had been taken without resistance, but the Third Reich would have to fight for Norway. The Allies had been caught by surprise, but elements of the British fleet had been at sea and ready for action.

The concentration of Allied submarines in the Skagerrak – the most well-timed part of Allied naval preparations – achieved early successes. The *Orzel* has already been mentioned. On Tuesday evening the British *Truant* encountered the light cruiser *Karlsruhe* on her way home from Kristiansand. The German vessel was hit by one torpedo (out of a salvo of ten) and was so badly damaged that she had to be finished off by her escort. The following evening the *Spearfish* caught the *Lützow* returning to Germany after her frightening trip up and down Oslofjord. The stern of the ship was badly damaged by the submarine torpedo, and she was lucky to make it back to Germany; she would be out of action for a year. (After the loss of the *Graf Spee*, the damage caused to the *Lützow* by one torpedo was more evidence of the limitations of the 'pocket battleship' design.)

British aircraft generally lacked the range and training to operate from home bases against German ships. The striking exception was the attack on Bergen by Royal Navy Skua fighter-dive bombers operating from a shore base on Orkney. The light cruiser *Königsberg* had been damaged by Norwegian shore batteries on the morning of Tuesday, 9 April. Although other ships pulled out during the day, the *Königsberg* was left behind to complete repairs. On Wednesday morning the Skuas caught her tied up against a jetty, and began dive-bomber attacks. Crippled by six hits or near misses, the *Königsberg* capsized – the first major warship to be sunk in combat by aircraft. (The dive bomber would prove to be a potent anti-shipping weapon in the hands of German, American and Japanese pilots; the *Königsberg* was to be the only major warship sunk by British aircraft using dive-bomber tactics.)

Admiral Raeder had originally insisted on all warships putting back to sea immediately after the initial landings. The *Admiral Hipper* sailed from Trondheim on Tuesday evening. But for the German Navy, mounting six simultaneous landings, Narvik turned out to be 'a port too far'. The destroyer flotilla at Narvik, led by Commodore Friedrich Bonte, could not begin the long voyage home until they had refuelled. Only one of two planned tankers reached Narvik (from the 'neutral' Soviet port of Murmansk), and on Wednesday morning the German flotilla was still in port. Bonte counted on four U-boats stationed at the mouth of the Ofotfjord to stop any British ships approaching Narvik, or at least to provide a warning. This did not happen. A flotilla of five British destroyers under Captain Bernard Warburton-Lee had arrived at the entrance to the fjord on Tuesday evening with orders to investigate the situation at Narvik. Despite having received a warning from the Norwegian shore station that a German flotilla was present, and that it was larger than his own force, Warburton-Lee pressed on up the fjord during the night.

In a sharp battle around Narvik on Wednesday morning, the British sank two German destroyers, including Bonte's flagship; the German commodore was among those killed. Three other destroyers were damaged. Germans vessels in other parts of the Ofotfjord counter-attacked, threatening to trap the British.

Although the British made good their withdrawal, the destroyers *Hardy* and *Hunter* were sunk, and Warburton-Lee was killed; on 7 June 1940 he would be posthumously awarded the first Victoria Cross of the war.

The survivors of the German flotilla were now themselves trapped. The second attack on Narvik came three days later, on Saturday, 13 April; it was among the most dramatic moments in the Royal Navy's wartime history. The battleship *Warspite* steamed up the fjord, flying the flag of Admiral Whitworth (who had transferred from the *Renown*); he was accompanied by nine destroyers and supported by aircraft from the carrier *Furious*. One by one the surviving German destroyers were picked off in the haze; all ten enemy destroyers which entered Narvik on 9 April had now been sunk or scuttled themselves.

Despite their Narvik victories, the British had missed other opportunities, up and down the coast and available for a day or two, to counter-attack. An immediate RAF air strike against the Luftwaffe transport aircraft which had landed at the strategically positioned Stavanger airfield was ruled out by existing limited-war prohibitions on attacking ground targets. Naval action against Bergen or Trondheim on 9 or 10 April might have destroyed some more German ships. Admiral Forbes did at midday on the 9th detach four cruisers and seven destroyers to attack Bergen, but this raiding party was recalled by the Admiralty.

The most critical decision, and one for which the Admiralty was responsible, had been made two days before the invasion, when the movement of enemy warships was first detected. On the evening of the 7th, Admiral Pound in London had ordered the standing down of the battalions tasked to implement Plan R.4. They had actually been aboard ships in the Firth of Forth and on the Clyde, ready to proceed at short notice to Stavanger, Bergen, Trondheim and Narvik. The assumption was that landing operations were not now the best use of the four cruisers at Rosyth in the Firth of Forth or of the escorts for the transports on the Clyde. The decision was implemented on the morning of the 8th. The soldiers on board the Rosyth cruisers were hurriedly sent ashore, without their equipment, and the ships were assigned to their 'proper' function of providing a scouting screen for the Home Fleet. On the other side of Scotland the transports on the Clyde were left immobile in port. The British had eliminated their own capability to mount immediate counter-landings.

A two-and-a-half-month campaign for Norway now began, which represented something new in military history, 'warfare in three dimensions'.[9] As far as the naval dimension was concerned, the Allies (mainly the British) were at this stage in the war – for a month or so – able to concentrate large forces in the Norwegian Sea. This was the only area where large enemy surface ships could be expected; after June 1940, when Italy entered the war and France was defeated, the situation would be very different. In early April 1940 five of

Britain's fourteen capital ships were operating in the Home Fleet: the *Rodney*, the *Valiant*, the *Warspite*, the *Renown* and the *Repulse*.[10] Admiral Forbes had enough big ships to deal with two German battle cruisers armed with 11-inch guns – if they put to sea again, and if he could catch them. Other ships available were the aircraft carrier *Furious*, fourteen cruisers, fifty-one destroyers and twenty submarines.[11]

And yet one unexpected feature of the fighting was the inability of the Allies to exploit their conventional naval superiority. This was largely caused by the emergence of the air dimension, exploited effectively by the Germans. They used airborne forces – parachutists or the surprise landing of troop-carrying transport planes – to seize forward airfields. Those airfields (in addition to bases in northern Germany and Denmark) were then used by Luftwaffe medium bombers to limit operations by the Royal Navy in the North Sea and the southern Norwegian Sea.

A highly significant encounter took place on the afternoon of the first day of the campaign (9 April). The main element of the Home Fleet – the *Rodney* and the *Valiant*, the cruiser *Sheffield* and escorting destroyers – was about 50 miles off the coast of Norway, and at a latitude between that of Bergen and Stavanger. They had been heading south since the previous evening, intent on dealing with a German force that had been reported emerging through the Danish straits (this was the task group that would attack Oslo). The weather had now cleared, and Admiral Forbes's ships came under sustained air attack from the machines of bomber wings KG 26 and KG 30 of Fliegerkorps X flying out of bases in northern Germany. The flagship, the battleship *Rodney*, was hit by a 500kg (1100lb) bomb dropped in a dive-bomber attack by a Junkers Ju 88. Fortunately the bomb did not fully detonate, and it was in any event too small to seriously damage the battleship. The smaller British ships were more vulnerable, however, and the *Gurkha*, a large new 'Tribal' class destroyer, was sunk after suffering a number of hits and near misses; she was the first British warship destroyed by enemy aircraft. A week later, on 16–17 April, the heavy cruiser *Suffolk* was detached to bombard the newly captured enemy air bases at Stavanger. She came under a seven-hour bomber attack and was only able to limp back to Scapa, her quarterdeck awash. After this Admiral Forbes became very cautious about operating his ships too far to the south, within range of major German air bases.

For most of the Norwegian campaign the German air attacks were made by unescorted twin-engined medium bombers, Heinkel He 111s and Junkers Ju 88s. The He 111 was the standard Luftwaffe bomber. The Ju 88, which had just entered service in 1939, was regarded as something of a 'wonder weapon', a Schnellbomber capable of high speed, and equipped with air brakes to permit dive bombing (in practice, given the size of the aircraft, this was a steep dive – 60 degrees – rather than a near-vertical one). Fortunately for the British, only a handful of Germany Navy torpedo carriers – Heinkel He 115 floatplanes – were available, and they were slow and achieved few results. The Luftwaffe also proved to be adept at co-ordinating long-range reconnaissance planes and air strikes, but without torpedoes or proper armour-piercing bombs it was very difficult to fatally damage capital ships or even cruisers.

The first weeks off Norway also made clear the limitations of the British sea/air power. At the critical point, despite knowing that Operation WILFRED was about to be carried out, Forbes left his only carrier, the *Furious*, behind in the Clyde, 450 miles from Scapa Flow. Even when the carrier did rejoin (on the morning of 10 April) she had no fighter planes embarked to defend the fleet, only eighteen Swordfish torpedo planes. The Admiralty had in previous months detached the two other Home Fleet carriers – the new *Ark Royal* and the *Glorious* – to the distant eastern Mediterranean for aircrew training.[12]

Meanwhile the shore-based bomber squadrons of the RAF lacked aircraft capable of successfully mounting long-range strikes against naval targets at sea. Like the Germans, the British had not yet fitted torpedoes to their modern medium bombers. Long-range British Wellingtons and Hampdens (twin-engined bombers) attempted some unescorted bomb attacks on the German fleet during the Norwegian campaign, but they had few successes and suffered heavy losses. RAF reconnaissance machines included a small number of the new four-engined Short Sunderland flying boats, but they had only limited success in supporting the fleet, partly due to the weather.

Above all, the Luftwaffe had the great advantage of being able to operate from newly captured bases in Norway and Denmark, which could be reinforced directly from home; RAF bombers based in Britain were unable to reach any target north of Bergen. It was only with great difficulty that a few British land-based fighter squadrons were flown into the Namsos and Narvik areas (from a carrier) towards the end of the campaign. One of the biggest causes of the Allied failure was the lack of ground-attack aircraft in Norway; carrier aircraft made some attempts to provide support, but they had limited impact.

Meanwhile at the beginning of the war British warships – like those of other navies – lacked sufficient anti-aircraft (AA) guns and fire-control systems to defend themselves independently, especially against faster aircraft and dive bombers. British destroyers effectively had no long- or medium-range AA defence at all. Even battleships and cruisers had only a few AA guns, although they did mount 'directors' for co-ordinating fire against high-level bombers.

While the Germans might seem to come out of the Norwegian campaign exhibiting a high degree of technical competence, there was one area where they were almost completely unsuccessful: submarine warfare. The U-boats were pulled out of the anti-shipping war at the beginning of March 1940, in preparation for Operation WESER EXERCISE. They were deployed in six groups up and down the Norwegian coast, and around Scapa Flow. It turned out, however, that German torpedoes suffered from grave technical problems. This was true both for those torpedoes designed to go off when they hit an enemy ship, and for those with magnetic 'pistols' (detonators) designed to explode the torpedo as it passed under the target. Had the U-boats' torpedoes functioned properly, the Royal Navy would have suffered much heavier losses off Norway.

Neither side had made preparations to fight a prolonged ground campaign in Norway. The German planners had hoped that the surprise simultaneous onslaught would sweep the Norwegians off their feet. The critical German military failure at Oslo – the sinking of the cruiser *Blücher* and the delayed arrival of the airborne troops – meant that the Norwegian royal family and government were able to escape the capital. The Norwegian Army had no time to mobilise, but within a couple of days it began to offer some resistance to the lightly equipped German spearheads which, out in the countryside, were hindered by steep terrain and deep snow.

The main thing, however, was that the invaders were able to channel troops through the short and safe crossing from the Baltic and through the Kattegat to the port of Oslo. From Oslo they had the advantage of rail transport to the north. A total of 108,000 men, 16,000 horses and 20,000 vehicles were ferried by sea to Norway across the narrow entrance to the Baltic in the two months before mid-June – in addition to some tens of thousands of men moved by air in the first weeks of the campaign.[13] British submarines had some success against this shipping, but no attempt was made to interfere with it using aircraft. On 23–25 April three French 'super-destroyers' carried out a 36-knot raid into the Skagerrak from Rosyth, but on the whole it was impractical to use surface ships. The Germans relied on small and relatively fast cargo and passenger ships, and their losses were not great.

As for the Allies, even when their expeditionary troops were re-assembled they were unable to mount an effective counter-blow. In the first weeks they should have been able to re-take either Trondheim or Narvik – both with isolated German bridgeheads – had they been able to make up their minds about which place to give priority to. When they finally decided to go for Trondheim the danger of enemy aircraft made them abandon plans for a direct attack on the town; instead they mounted a pincer movement of British and French troops from north and south. The first Allied 'amphibious' operation of World War II took place on 16–18 April and was directed against the small ports of Namsos and Åndalsnes, which were about 85 miles to the north and south (respectively) of Trondheim. The initial landings were unopposed by

German forces, but as a result of dividing their efforts the attackers could not ensure the security of either place, and this also put greater demands on their navies. The Luftwaffe was used effectively to attack advance ports and shipping (damaging the French light cruiser *Émile Bertin*). Meanwhile Allied movement inland from Namsos and Åndalsnes was slow. All the while two German infantry divisions were making their way up the two snow-covered central valleys from Oslo to the northwest. On 30 April they linked up with the bridge-head force at Trondheim.

By this time the Allies had decided to pull out of central Norway. The evacuation from Åndalsnes and Namsos – the first of a number of such dispiriting operations in 1940–42 – was completed with losses at the start of May. By this time the first Junkers Ju 87 Stuka wing had arrived at Trondheim, and the deadly single-engined dive bomber achieved its first successes against the British and French (one big destroyer from each navy) in the evacuation of Namsos.

This shambolic performance provoked prolonged sessions – later known as the Norway debate – in the British House of Commons on 7–8 May, a month after the invasion. Prime Minister Chamberlain's opponents, outside his Conservative Party and within it, lambasted the government's conduct of the war thus far. The government won the eventual vote, but such was the level of discontent in the House that on 9 May Chamberlain agreed to resign in favour of Winston Churchill. Historians argue over the contradiction between Churchill's advance to supreme power and his actual activities as First Lord of the Admiralty with direct responsibility for much that happened – or did not happen – in Norway. As Churchill himself noted in the draft version of his war memoirs, 'it was a marvel – I really do not know how – I survived and maintained my position in public esteem while all the blame was thrown on poor Mr Chamberlain'.[14]

Neither Churchill nor Chamberlain was directly to blame for the cack-handed response to Operation WESER EXERCISE. It is unfair to describe the Norwegian campaign as a 'Churchillian disaster'.[15] The Norway debate was really about Chamberlain's long-term weaknesses as a war leader. As well as his identification with Appeasement, he had famously declared on 5 April – four days before the German invasion – that Hitler had 'missed the bus' in terms of war strategy. Despite his involvement in the Norwegian affair, on 10 May Churchill took over, leading a coalition government. He was also Minister of Defence, so he would continue to have oversight over the conduct of the war at sea. On the same day the Wehrmacht finally began its main assault on the Netherlands, Belgium and France. Some ninety-three German divisions were in action; five days later the French government reported to London that an extreme military crisis had begun.

NARVIK AND OPERATION JUNO, MAY–JUNE 1940

The massive German invasion on 10 May reduced the Norwegian campaign – now essentially the siege of Narvik – to the status of a sideshow. General Dietl's mountain troops were still marooned in the town, although some supplies and reinforcements reached them by air, or even by rail via Sweden. An infantry relief column was advancing north from the Trondheim area to Narvik, a distance of some 350 miles as the crow flies, but longer in view of the tortuously winding motor roads. (There was then no railway north of Trondheim.)

Since 13 April the Allies had dithered about whether or not to attack Narvik directly. In mid-April they established a forward base at Harstad on the Vågsfjord, and a month later they had gradually assembled some 30,000 British and French troops. Harstad was only about 30 miles northwest of Narvik, but due to the convoluted geography of the islands and fjords the practical distances were much greater. The British eventually reactivated the small Norwegian airfield at Bardufoss, north of Narvik, and flew in some aircraft for Royal Navy carriers. Disagreements, however, were frequent between British Army and Navy leaders on the spot. The local British Army commander in the Narvik area, General P.J. Mackesy, refused to carry out an attack without what he regarded as sufficient preparations, and he was eventually relieved.

The Allied operations around Narvik in the last three weeks of May are in most respects irrelevant, especially in view of the catastrophic setbacks in Belgium and France. Indeed, on 24 May the British government secretly decided to evacuate all of Norway. Nevertheless, it was decided to save face by completing the attack on Narvik. This operation was tactically successful and was – if only in miniature – the first of a long series of Allied 'combined operations'. On the night of 12/13 May troops of the French Foreign Legion, using a handful of prototype British landing craft (of the MLC type), were able to establish an advance base at Bjerkvik on the north side of the Ofotfjord, opposite Narvik. 'We are used to travelling on camels across the desert', said one Legionnaire officer, 'and here you give us boats, and we have to cross the water.'[16] British warships provided gunfire support. On 28 May French and Polish troops mounted another assault over to the south side of the fjord and took Narvik itself. Dietl's men retreated down the railway line towards the Swedish frontier. The Allied troops put some of the ore loading facilities out of commission, but almost immediately their evacuation began. The main withdrawal convoy left Harstad on 7 June. On 10 June the remaining Norwegian troops surrendered to Dietl; three days later the German relief column yomped in from the south.

The final Allied naval evacuation was complex. There were a large number of transports to protect. Escort forces were limited, as cruisers and destroyers had been pulled back to the south to aid the Dunkirk evacuation, reinforce the Mediterranean Fleet, and even protect the British Isles from invasion.

Developments in Iceland caused complications. The island, larger than Scotland but with a population of only 120,000, had been a sovereign state under the Danish Crown. The British had taken over the Faroes a few days after the German invasion of Denmark on 9 April, and the Danish ambassador in Washington arranged for Greenland to come under American protection. The Icelandic government, however, insisted on neutrality, and in consequence a bloodless invasion took place. Two cruisers from the Royal Navy arrived in Reykjavik on 10 May, and a small force of Royal Marines came ashore; they were replaced a few weeks later by a British Army garrison (replaced in turn by Canadians and – in 1941 – US Marines). Allied naval and air bases set up in Iceland eventually played a vital part in the North Atlantic war. The Germans did develop a secret plan to seize the island, Operation ICARUS (IKARUS), and in the early days the British worried about another Norwegian-style *coup de main*. This was more of a threat once the Germans obtained full use of Trondheim, just 725 miles away, at the start of May. An incorrect British report on 5 June about German naval movements led to the hasty despatch of part of the Home Fleet to cover the east coast of Iceland. This force included the only two fast capital ships, the battle cruisers *Renown* and *Repulse*, and their deployment to Iceland left exposed Allied shipping movements now taking place off the Norwegian coast.

The Germans, whose surface navy had been inactive since its self-destructive spurt of activity in early April, now mounted another daring battleship raid, Operation JUNO. The origins of JUNO lay in mid-May, when the aim was to prevent the fall of Narvik. By June, Narvik having been temporarily abandoned, the aim was to prevent the destruction of the German troops who had fallen back along the railway to the Swedish border. Admiral Marschall, back in post as the Fleet Commander (Flottenchef), with the *Scharnhorst* and the *Gneisenau*, the heavy cruiser *Hipper*, and four destroyers, was assigned the primary task of raiding the Allied forward base at Harstad near Narvik, destroying shipping and installations there. There was another, underlying, reason why Admiral Raeder and the Naval War Staff put forward this risky operation. In the campaign in the Netherlands, Belgium and France, the German Army and Luftwaffe were clearly racing towards victory – the Dunkirk evacuation would begin on 26 May. Admiral Raeder was desperate to give the Navy a prominent role in the final victory of the European war, despite the risks involved.

What the Germans did not know was that the Allies were about to evacuate the Narvik region. After taking a couple of weeks to complete the training of the battleships, Admiral Marschall sailed from Kiel on 4 June with the *Scharnhorst*, the *Gneisenau*, the *Hipper* and four destroyers. Yet again, a daring German naval initiative caught the British Admiralty and the Home Fleet off guard. Marschall's battle group spent the day of 7 June and the morning of the 8th circling 250 miles west of Narvik. During this time they intercepted and sank the SS *Orama*, a 20,000-ton liner serving as a troopship (but fortunately with no troops aboard). Marschall detached the *Hipper* and the destroyers to German-held Trondheim to refuel and then, in the late afternoon of 8 June, the two battleships ran into the fleet carrier *Glorious*, which was steaming back to Scapa Flow with the escorting destroyers *Acasta* and *Ardent*.

The *Glorious* had, the day before, recovered the RAF Hurricane fighters temporarily based at Bardufoss. (This was no mean feat, as the RAF pilots were not trained for carrier landings, and their fighters were not fitted with tail hooks.) Now, proceeding at 17 knots, the carrier had no air patrol aloft, and she was unable to mount an air strike using her torpedo planes. Attempts at evasive manoeuvre were poorly executed. The visibility was good, and at a range of 28,000 yards (about 16 miles) the German battleships opened accurate fire on the lightly armoured carrier. About an hour later she capsized. Much the larger part of the crew, including the officers in charge, went down with the ship or perished in the life rafts. The sinking of the *Glorious* and her escort is one of the more controversial episodes of the whole sea war; the consensus of historians is that a major cause of the tragedy was the bad judgement of the carrier's captain, Guy D'Oyly-Hughes.[17]

Whatever the human error, however, the response to Operation JUNO involved broader communications and intelligence failures. The inter-service codebreaking and traffic monitoring centre at Bletchley Park had detected signs of a major German naval operation (JUNO), but this information had not been shared with the Operational Intelligence Centre (OIC) at the Admiralty. Indeed, so secret was the evacuation from the Narvik area that the OIC had not been informed that it was taking place. Neither the Home Fleet nor the Admiralty received any radio alarm signals from the *Glorious* and her escorts; they first learned the carrier had sunk when the Germans publicly announced it on the afternoon of the following day, 9 June. As a result, many of the surviving crewmen of the *Glorious* group died in their life rafts.

The escorting destroyers had also gone down with almost all hands, after heroic attempts to drive off the German battleships. Before she sank, the *Acasta* was able to hit the *Scharnhorst* with a torpedo. This caused severe damage; Marschall had to escort the badly damaged battleship to the shelter of Trondheim. The *Scharnhorst* would be out of action for six months, and – unknown to either side – the immediate extreme threat to the British evacuation convoys had come to an end.

Despite the loss of one of their three remaining Home Fleet carriers, the outcome could have been even worse. Three big convoys of Allied merchant ships leaving Norway had been within range of the JUNO battle group. One (six liners and 15,000 troops) passed through the danger zone west of Narvik on the 7th; two more passed through on the 9th, one with seven ships and 10,000 troops, the other with eight slow supply ships. At this latitude in early June there was no darkness to hide these shipping movements. The Home Fleet, meanwhile, was scattered all over the northeastern Atlantic; and the only big ships providing (distant) cover for the evacuation convoys were the battleship *Valiant* and carrier *Ark Royal*.

The German battle group had sunk the *Glorious* and her two destroyers, but Admiral Raeder judged that Marschall had mishandled his mission: he had not followed his orders to attack Harstad, and he had suffered unnecessary damage in the action with the carrier's escorts. This was surely unreasonable. Raeder did not take into account the fact that there would have been nothing left to attack at Harstad; meanwhile the carrier was a major British asset. Marschall was replaced as Flottenchef by Admiral Lütjens; he would not be given another command afloat. He was the second commander of the battle fleet to be sacked after a conflict with Raeder and the Naval War Staff, Admiral Böhm having been removed in the previous autumn. Meanwhile, Admiral Kummetz, who had led the *Blücher* to disaster at Oslo in the initial invasion, was eventually awarded the Knight's Cross. (Kummetz would go on to command a battle group in another major German setback off Norway, the Battle of the Barents Sea on 31 December 1942.)

Germany now controlled all of Norway, but two further events brought the campaign to a less satisfactory end. There was one final demonstration of the shortcomings of British naval aviation, in the form of a disastrous raid by the *Ark Royal*'s aircraft against the damaged *Scharnhorst* in Trondheim on 13 June. No hits were achieved and the strike force was savaged by modern Luftwaffe shore-based fighters; eight out of sixteen Skua aircraft were lost. A week later, however, came a compensating success. The big submarine *Clyde* put a torpedo into the *Gneisenau* when she and the *Hipper* – now both under Admiral Lütjens's command – attempted another sortie from Trondheim. A train could have been driven through the gaping holes on either side of the battleship's bow. The *Scharnhorst* and the *Gneisenau* now both limped back to Germany for long periods of repair. (Six Swordfish from the Orkneys mounted a torpedo attack on the *Scharnhorst* south of Bergen on the afternoon of 21 June – the first such attack on a capital ship at sea – but they achieved no hits.) In any event the two battleships, much the most powerful ships of the Kriegsmarine, would not be able to undertake operations again until the end of 1940.

CHAPTER 3

THE DEFENCE OF THE BRITISH ISLES

DUNKIRK, 1 JUNE 1940

The English Channel was the single most important body of water in the strategic geography of World War II. Stretching 340 miles, it is only 21 miles wide at the Dover Strait; it opens to a width of nearly 100 miles at its western end. The Channel saved Britain – and the future Allied cause – in the late summer of 1940. It would dominate Allied strategy from 1942 to 1944. In late May and early June 1940 it separated the men of the British Expeditionary Force (BEF) at Dunkirk from the safety of England.

Saturday, 1 June was the seventh day of the Dunkirk evacuation, code-named Operation DYNAMO. A junior artillery officer, Richard Austin, watched the coming dawn from Malo-les-Bains beach, just east of the port.

> Over there in front of us, German-wards, the horizon whitens. It is a pale steady dawn, breaking with a slight haze that presages another scorching day. Whatever is to be our fate, we are evidently going to have a fine day for it. Behind us the red fires of Dunkirk fade to orange in the gathering light, thinning till they are no longer visible, and Dunkirk resumes its daytime hue, unrelieved funereal black.[1]

Some 194,620 British and French troops from Dunkirk had already been disembarked in British ports. Only 39,000 British troops remained on the morning of the 1st.[2]

The popular conception of Dunkirk involves masses of civilian-manned 'little ships' crossing the Channel to pluck the BEF off the beaches piecemeal. This is an enduring myth. In reality, one official figure has 5,031 troops 'lifted' by private motorboats, out of a total of 338,226.[3] The evacuation was mainly carried out by British destroyers and by the civilian ships ('personnel vessels') which had been taken up from the merchant fleet since September 1939 for transporting the large BEF to France and supplying it there. These latter vessels were relatively small for merchant ships, but they were mostly in the 1,000–3,000-ton range and they were much bigger than pleasure boats. The retreating British troops did assemble on the beaches stretching 10 miles east of Dunkirk – at Malo-les-Bains, Bray and La Panne. Two-thirds, however, walked from those beaches to the port itself. There, they were picked up from the moles which protected the outer harbour. (The inner port of Dunkirk – a complex of half a dozen docks linked to the outer harbour by a narrow channel – had mostly been put out of service by a week of air raids.) The small craft did, however, play a vital role in the later days, shuttling soldiers from the beaches to larger vessels offshore.

Saturday's first movements were typical. The Southern Railway paddle steamer *Whippingham*, now a personnel vessel, cast off from the mole under cover of darkness at 1.30 a.m., headed across the Channel for Margate; she was heavily overladen with 2,700 troops. Shortly afterwards the fast coastal passenger ship *Lady of Mann* left for Dover with 1,500 casualties. The destroyers *Vanquisher*, *Icarus* and *Windsor* left the mole shortly after dawn, carrying a total of 2,807 troops; the personnel ship *Maid of Orleans* followed with another 1,856. On 1 June large British vessels made forty-eight trips to England from the port, and forty-seven from the beaches. Some eighty-one trips were carried out by smaller vessels (with loads of under 200 men).[4]

This Saturday was the costliest day of the Dunkirk evacuation because of the number of Allied ships taking part and the weight of the enemy air attack. The weather was clear and bright, better flying weather for the Luftwaffe than the low cloud of previous days. In the evening the SNO (senior naval officer) at Dunkirk, Captain W.G. Tennant, would report on the situation: 'Things are getting very hot for ships. Over 100 bombers on ships near here since 0530. Many casualties. Have directed that no ships sail during daylight.'[5] At 7.30 a.m. the first wave of attackers, mostly Junkers Ju 87 Stuka dive bombers, had arrived; within an hour they had inflicted heavy damage. A tugboat captain described the first attack on the destroyer HMS *Keith*, the flagship of the officer controlling offshore movements, Admiral Frederic Wake-Walker: 'A British destroyer outside of us began to fire on enemy planes and bombs began to fall near her as she steamed about. At full speed with the helm hard to port nine fell in a line in the water, along her starboard side, and they exploded underwater, heeling the destroyer over on her beam ends . . .'[6] The *Keith* then suffered a direct hit at 8.00 a.m., and sank at 9.40. Wake-Walker was forced to transfer to an MTB. Another destroyer, HMS *Basilisk*, was hit at 8.00 off La Panne, and finished off by a second attack at noon. More tragic still was the fate of the minesweeper HMS *Skipjack*, which had been picking troops off the beach at Malo-les-Bains. Hit by several bombs at about 8.45 a.m., she almost immediately capsized and sank – with 275 soldiers trapped below decks.

The Luftwaffe attacks continued to be effective through the early afternoon. The British destroyer *Ivanhoe*, which had picked up 1,000 troops from La Panne, was hit by a bomb. She stayed afloat, but at 8.00 a.m. the troops on board had to be transferred to the destroyer *Havant* and two other ships. The *Havant*, in turn, was hit an hour later; those aboard had – again – to be transferred to other ships, before the destroyer rolled over and sank at 10.15 a.m. Shortly after that, the transport *Prague* with 3,000 French troops aboard was damaged and had to be towed to the English coast and beached. A fourth destroyer, the French *Foudroyant*, was bombed and sunk at 10.30. Two British personnel vessels went down in these attacks, the paddle steamer *Brighton Queen* and the *Scotia*, the latter an LMS railway steamer used in peacetime in the Irish Sea. Both the transports carried French troops, many of whom would not survive; between 200 and 300 men out of some 2,000 aboard the *Scotia* were lost.

The Royal Air Force was blamed for not doing enough to protect the evacuation. In reality the British did put a number of fighter aircraft over the Dunkirk area and its approaches, but the short-range Spitfires and Hurricanes were operating at a considerable distance from their bases and could not provide constant cover. The effort to concentrate large formations meant there were deadly intervals between the arrival of each group of fighters. Altogether the RAF lost thirty-one aircraft on 1 June, and the Germans ten fighters and nineteen bombers.[7]

Despite the considerable losses, this Saturday saw the second largest total of troops evacuated, exceeded only by the number on 31 May. Some 64,429 were listed as landed in England on 1 June. Austin, the artillery officer, survived the day and recalled his rescue – after standing in a queue in deep water off Malo during the night of 1/2 June.

> The gunwale of the lifeboat stood three feet above the surface of the water. Reaching up, I could just grasp it with the tips of my fingers. When I tried to haul myself up I couldn't move an inch. The weight of my waterlogged clothes . . . beat me completely . . . Two powerful hands reached over the gunwale and fastened themselves into my arm-pits. Another pair of hands stretched down and hooked-on to the belt at the back of my great-coat. Before I had time to realise it I was pulled up and pitched head-first into the bottom of the boat.

The lifeboat took Austin out to the paddle steamer *Medway Queen*, aboard which he made his way to the safety of Ramsgate, with some 400 other survivors.[8]

THE BRITISH EVACUATION FROM FRANCE

Because the Allied May 1940 campaign was such a fiasco it is easy to forget that a great effort had been made to establish a large presence of the British Army and Royal Air Force in France and to prepare for the arrival of even bigger forces. Between September 1939 and May 1940 the British moved nearly 400,000 personnel, 69,000 vehicles and 724,000 tons of supplies, ammunition and petrol to France.[9] A range of ports from Boulogne to Saint-Nazaire was used; Cherbourg was especially important for personnel movements. The Germans were unable to interfere. The shipping resources assembled by the War Office and the Admiralty to support this expeditionary force would turn out to be crucial for the subsequent withdrawal from Dunkirk and the French western ports. Although most combat troops were in the eight British divisions near the Belgian border, they were supported by a large British supply organisation stretching back to the ports of northwestern France.

The German spring offensive into the Netherlands, Belgium and France began on 10 May 1940. Meanwhile the left flank of the British and French armies advanced, as planned, north into formerly neutral Belgium in order to create a forward defence line there. This turned out to be a strategic blunder, as the Wehrmacht also mounted a surprise and very rapid offensive with its armoured divisions from the Ardennes due west towards the Channel. Within ten days the BEF and the French First Army were cut off in Belgium and the tip of northeastern France. The lead German tanks reached the coast about 60 miles southwest of Dunkirk on 20 May. The nearby Channel ports of Calais and Boulogne quickly fell. Some 400,000 British and French troops had been cut off in the Lille–Dunkirk pocket; Britain was threatened with the loss of most of its field army.

On 23–24 May the enemy advance paused. Rather than sending their mobile troops up the coast to threaten Dunkirk, the last open French port in the north-east, the German generals on the spot decided to regroup, closing up their forces. At midday on the 24th Hitler issued his famous 'halt order' (*Haltbefehl*) confirming the short-lived pause. Historians still debate the reasons for this weighty decision, but the explanation is probably straightforward. In geographical terms the Germans had only cut off a small portion of the French north-eastern borderlands although hundreds of thousands of Allied troops were trapped there. The main strategic task for the Wehrmacht was to achieve a rapid, decisive victory over the French Army and occupy the great bulk of French territory, by advancing southwest across the Somme towards Paris. This had to be accomplished as soon as possible, before the French could regain their balance. Another element of Hitler's decision may have been the influence of Göring, who wanted his Luftwaffe (rather than the Army) to be given the credit for the entrapment of the Allied forces in the northeast. In any event, no one on the German side – or indeed the Allied side – thought a seaborne evacuation on a large scale from the Lille–Dunkirk pocket was a practical possibility.[10]

Whatever its cause, the 'halt order' did give the Allied ground forces in the pocket vital time. At first it had been hoped to mount counter-attacks north and south of the German thrust to the Channel, but the overall situation was very confused and the French high command had lost touch with reality. On the evening of Saturday, 25 May, General Gort, leading the BEF, began to pull back his forces. The French were hoping to maintain and defend the whole Lille–Dunkirk pocket, so that it could present a threat to the rear of the advancing Wehrmacht. On Sunday, however, London instructed Gort that the preservation of his troops was to be the predominant consideration. The general replied that even in the best circumstances the larger part of his expeditionary force would be lost. In the event the British were able to pull the three corps of the BEF back into the area around Dunkirk, lay out – together with the French Army – a reasonably stout defensive line there, and assemble shipping. The surrounding terrain was favourable to defence, with marshes, sand dunes and canals; it is not often recalled that a German garrison would hold an isolated position at Dunkirk for eight months, from September 1944 to the end of the war.

The post-war West German official history noted that the Dunkirk evacuation was 'mastered from the British Isles with astonishing skill and improvisation'.[11] Much of the credit for this impressive achievement must go to Admiral Bertram Ramsay. One of the two or three most outstanding British flag officers of the whole war, he would later be in charge of amphibious landings in North Africa (1942) and Sicily (1943), as well as D-Day in 1944; one reason Bert Ramsay is not better known is that his life was cut short when his Hudson aircraft crashed outside Paris in January 1945. On the outbreak of war he occupied a shore post as Flag Officer, Dover. With the breakthrough of the Panzer divisions he was, on 19 May, assigned the task of arranging new emergency supply routes to the BEF through Boulogne, Calais, Dunkirk and Belgian ports. Then, as the full extent of the crisis emerged, he began to put together the full-scale evacuation of the Allied forces. Based in Dover Castle, Ramsay was the right man in the right place, a highly effective organiser, with a detailed knowledge of the waters off Dunkirk. He worked with another admiral, James Somerville, soon to be prominent in the Mediterranean and the Indian

Ocean, and on his staff was Commander F.J. Walker (later the greatest of the Atlantic escort-group commanders).

The Admiralty began to prepare orders for an evacuation on 22 May, which was given the code name DYNAMO. The emergency operation began on the evening of the 26th, with the first troops arriving at Dover just before midnight.[12] The situation was badly complicated by the surrender of Belgian forces on the following night (27/28 May); this opened the eastern front of the pocket to the enemy and ended any thought of using Ostend for the evacuation.

Dunkirk was the third largest port in France, but much of it was rendered unusable by German bombing, which developed on 27 May. Unexpectedly, however, it was discovered by the SNO, Captain Tennant, on the night of 27/28 May that large vessels – destroyers and civilian-manned personnel ships – could be berthed alongside the two long breakwaters on either side of the outer harbour. This greatly improved the loading capacity of the port, and meant the soldiers did not have to be taken in small boats off the beaches.

The shortest distance from Dunkirk to Dover was about 40 miles, but sandbanks and the position of German artillery along the coast west of Dunkirk initially demanded a roundabout route over twice that length; on the 30th a shorter shipping lane (Route 'X') to the Kentish ports was established. Throughout the evacuation period the sea was calm, and on some days low cloud cover reduced the threat of air attack. The embarkation of Allied soldiers continued for seven days. It had been expected that the night of 1/2 June would be the last time of movement, but about 25,000 troops, most of them French, were taken off on each of the next three days. The final departure would be the old destroyer HMS *Shikari* with 383 French soldiers aboard; she left Dunkirk at 3.40 on the morning of the 4th.

The Luftwaffe caused considerable losses to the evacuation fleet, and the Germans even strafed the beaches, but the evacuation was possible only because of the near complete control of the surface of the sea by the Allied navies. The German Navy was incapable of intervening in the Dunkirk saga on a significant scale. The head of the Naval War Staff, Admiral Schniewind, reported on 26 May that transport by the enemy of large numbers of troops was not possible, but that smaller ships could evacuate troops without equipment, even off the beaches. Nevertheless, the Kriegsmarine did not currently have means available to interfere with this. A handful of small U-boats did attack the evacuation shipping, and the Allies had their first encounter with S-boats operating from Borkum and later Den Helder in the Netherlands. On the night of 23/24 May, *S 21* and *S 23* crippled the big French destroyer *Jaguar* off Boulogne, and over the next few nights S-boats sank or damaged a few British and French warships and transports involved in Operation DYNAMO. Three years of intense coastal warfare in the Channel and the North Sea between S-boats and British MTBs had begun.

Other misconceptions about Dunkirk are that it was the only British evacuation from France, and the last one. The campaign in France actually lasted another three weeks after Dunkirk. A second German offensive, across the Somme, began on 5 June.[13] Paris fell on the 14th and a new French government capitulated on the 22nd. The British evacuation from the Le Havre area (beyond the Somme) began on 9 June; code-named Operation CYCLE, it succeeded in taking off 15,000 British troops. There was one dramatic failure when most of the 51st (Highland) Division was captured at the little port of Saint-Valery-en-Caux near Dieppe on 12 June.

The final withdrawal, Operation AERIAL, involved a large number of British forces – many of them Army and RAF support personnel – in northwestern France, using ports from Cherbourg to La Pallice on the Biscay coast. This took place mainly over the period 17–20 June and was less fraught than DYNAMO at Dunkirk. Working ports were available, 133 ships were involved (many of them large ocean-going vessels), and some equipment was re-embarked. About 140,000 British personnel were evacuated as part of AERIAL, as well as 47,000 Allied troops, many of them Poles and Czechoslovaks, who had been fighting alongside the French Army.

The single worst British shipping disaster of the entire 1939–45 war occurred off Saint-Nazaire on the afternoon 17 June. The 16,000-ton Cunard liner *Lancastria* was bombed by a Ju 88 of KG 30, the Luftwaffe anti-shipping group (now operating from Amsterdam). The advancing German Army had been about 90 miles away from Saint-Nazaire. The *Lancastria* had been hastily loaded before the bombing with over 5,200 service personnel and some civilians for the expected short trip across the Channel; this was at least three times her normal load as a troopship. The big liner capsized and sank in twenty minutes, trapping many passengers below decks; she had been anchored out in the Loire estuary, several miles offshore, and continuing air attacks hampered rescue efforts. The total loss seems to have been about 2,000, considerably more than the number of deaths in the *Titanic* sinking of 1912. News of the disaster was not released for five weeks, but it is an exaggeration to label this as a cover-up.[14]

OPERATION SEA LION

This book is about the flow of real events on the seas during World War II. But what also needs to be considered is something that *never* happened: the German invasion of the British Isles. The inability or unwillingness of the Wehrmacht to knock Britain out of the war by *direct* military means – seaborne invasion – was one of the most important features of the war. This was true both in 1940 – when Britain was certainly at its most vulnerable – and perhaps also in the year that followed. A successful invasion would have given the Third Reich and Italy secure control at least of Western and Central Europe.

The origins of the German invasion plan can be found in a wide-ranging memorandum produced on 30 June 1940 by Hitler's chief military adviser in the Wehrmacht high command, General Alfred Jodl. This was a week after the French surrender, and three weeks after Italy entered the war on Germany's side. Jodl presented a landing operation (*Landung*) as one of several military options. The war could take the form of *direct* action against the 'English motherland' or of *indirect* actions against Britain's overseas possessions ('the periphery'). For direct action, the options included a siege by sea and air, 'terror' air attacks on the civilian population and/or a landing in Britain followed by occupation. For Jodl the purpose of a landing by the Army was not to defeat Britain militarily. Instead, the proposal was that in September 1940, thirty German divisions would deliver the *Todesstoss* (*coup de grâce*). It would strike a Britain whose economy had been paralysed by the Luftwaffe and the Kriegsmarine and which had been rendered defenceless; this result would be accomplished by an increasing tempo of air and sea attacks over the next two months, until the end of August or the beginning of September.[15] Tentative preparations for the invasion option were secretly ordered by the OKW on 2 July, and by Hitler's Directive No. 16 two weeks later. The second document used the code name SEA LION (SEELÖWE) and set an end-date for preparations of mid-August.[16]

Explaining in broad terms why SEA LION did not happen involves looking at a complex interplay of factors. Two of the fundamental ones were weather and time. Striking across the southern North Sea or the English Channel (and supplying a beachhead or 'lodgement') was not practical after about the middle of September. Autumn storms and rougher seas would make the crossing hazardous for the small transport vessels available to the invaders. In fact SEA LION was effectively cancelled on 17 September, six days before the autumnal equinox. Whatever else can be said, Hitler's armed forces really had a window of opportunity of only two months from the time of the 16 July directive, and this time was completely inadequate.

The ultimate decision about an invasion lay with Hitler. He was no military genius, but even a more able military leader would have been thrown off balance by the unexpected speed of the success in France, the range of grand-strategic choices now available and the complexities of a large and unprecedented amphibious operation involving competing branches of the Wehrmacht.

Hitler was also an inveterate opportunist, and as a result it is difficult for historians to reconstruct with any certainty a consistent military-political grand strategy. But he clearly had competing global objectives. He was aware that his Wehrmacht had for the moment a unique military advantage – the result of a mid-1930s head start in rearmament and the sudden – unexpected – collapse of France. The Führer was torn between fighting Britain or fighting Russia. He *did* want to secure an agreement with a new British government, bringing an end to the fighting and forcing acceptance of the new order in Europe in which the Third Reich would be dominant; this might require invasion, blockade or attacks on British colonies. But he also wanted to smash Soviet Russia, despite the August 1939 Non-Aggression Pact. This eastern mission had very deep ideological and political-economic roots for him; in addition a land war with Russia would allow full use of Germany's strongest asset, her army. The German dictator was probably realistic enough to know that he ought actively to fight only one of these enemies at a time.

Of the three Wehrmacht services, the Army and the Luftwaffe were confident that they could deal with their British opposite numbers. Göring's air-power enthusiasts even thought they could achieve victory on their own; the air campaign (which we now know as the Battle of Britain) would in fact begin on 8 August.[17] Admiral Raeder and the Naval War Staff, however, opposed an invasion attempt. This was partly because British superiority at sea was so great. Admiral Raeder began the 'premature war' with his September 1939 comment, already quoted (see p. 5), that the numerical inferiority of his surface forces meant that they could do no more than 'show that they know how to die gallantly'. The battles off Norway from April to June, when most German surface warships were sunk or crippled, had confirmed that fear. When the German Navy considered SEA LION in the high summer of 1940 it had, ready for war, only one heavy cruiser, two light cruisers and four destroyers. In home waters, the Royal Navy had five capital ships, an aircraft carrier, eleven cruisers and eighty destroyers; in the Mediterranean were another seven capital ships, two carriers, seven cruisers and thirty destroyers.[18] For Raeder and his admirals – like the leaders of most other major navies – amphibious operations were not a major part of their role. (The Kriegsmarine had taken part in the invasion of Norway, but that was essentially a *coup de main* against an unprepared neutral.) The naval leadership was far more interested in the deployment of submarines and surface raiders against British shipping and in building up a proper battleship fleet.

When reporting to Hitler on 11 July Admiral Raeder made plain the disparity of naval strength, as well as his professional opposition to SEA LION. In the words of his minute:

> The OBdM [C-in-C, Navy] regards a landing in England only as a last resort in efforts to force England to make peace. [He] is convinced that the cutting

> of her sea trades by U-boat warfare and air attacks on convoys, as well as heavy air attacks on the large English centres (Liverpool) will in any event force England to make peace. As a result the OBdM cannot for his part advocate a landing in Britain as he did in the case of the landing in Norway. Prerequisites are: complete air superiority and clearing a mine-free area for transports and disembarkation ... Further [prerequisites]: it would be necessary to seal off the transport area with flanking minefields. Lengthy preparation of transport shipping.

Hitler seems to have been convinced by these arguments. On Wednesday, 31 July, in a conference at the Berghof, his residence in the Bavarian Alps, the German dictator repeated the technical arguments against invasion which Raeder had emphasised, regarding preparations for the landing and the weather. 'Our small navy is 15% [the size] of the enemy, the number of destroyers is 8% that of the enemy, the number of motor torpedo boats equally is 10–12% that of the enemy.'[19] (Interestingly, Hitler did not, in these comments, stress the RAF as an impediment to invasion.)

An awareness of British naval superiority forced the Wehrmacht leaders to make planning choices, which in turn made their task more difficult and risky. General Jodl's preliminary operational outline of 12 July noted that '*England is in possession of command of the sea*' (his emphasis).[20] In reality the British, at this time, were expecting that if an attack came it would be on their east coast (East Anglia), with the invasion fleet departing from the enemy's North Sea ports. The German Army and Navy agreed, however, that the only possible landing area was the eastern part of the *Channel* coast (Kent, Sussex and Hampshire), west of the Dover Strait, where the sea approach route would be shortest and the Luftwaffe could provide air cover. But this choice meant that the British could concentrate their own defensive ground forces. Meanwhile, the closeness to Britain of the Channel embarkation ports, the need for mine clearing and mine-laying, and the size of the invasion force meant that there could be little element of surprise.

These military and naval realities were a large element in Hitler's decision not to go through with SEA LION. Instead he made the fatal decision to prepare for an invasion of the Soviet Union. He informed his senior commanders to this effect at the Berghof meeting. This was eight days before the beginning of the Battle of Britain; four and a half months before the issuing of the BARBAROSSA directive (15 December) setting out the basic invasion plan for the USSR; and nearly thirteen months before 22 June 1941 and the actual surprise attack.[21]

The decision to attack Russia was, of course, kept a deep secret. Meanwhile the Führer and OKW planners were prepared to see what pressure could be put on Britain. This took the form of a large-scale air campaign (directed in the first instance against RAF installations and aircraft factories) and the assembly of an improvised invasion fleet in the ports of the Netherlands, Belgium and northern France. In OKW Directive No. 17 of 1 August, Hitler ordered 'intensified air and sea warfare' against the UK, beginning with the attacks on RAF bases and the aircraft industry. After achieving local air superiority, the attacks would be directed against ports and food stores. Remarkably, nothing was said in this directive about how these operations would facilitate an invasion.[22]

In view of this decision to invade Russia rather than Britain, made at the highest level in the Third Reich, the details of the development of the SEA LION invasion plan after 31 July are largely irrelevant. Nevertheless, they do raise the question of what would have happened had Hitler changed his mind, and they give a sense of the strengths and weaknesses of the two sides.

The limited size of the German Navy, especially after Norway, has already been mentioned. Another fundamental weakness of the German military was that it was completely lacking in purpose-built amphibious craft or doctrine.[23] No serious thought had been given to an invasion of Britain before May 1940. Organisationally, it was difficult for the three Wehrmacht services to work together in what the British would call a 'combined operation'. Hitler never appointed an overall commander for Operation SEA LION, and there was limited co-ordinated planning between the Army and Kriegsmarine, let alone between the Luftwaffe and the other services.

In his initial 30 June paper, General Jodl had proposed a broad-front landing on the south coast, from Dover to as far west as Bournemouth; this would allow the German troops room to manoeuvre. The SEA LION directive (16 July) identified the same broad frontage. The leaders of the Kriegsmarine, however, insisted that British naval superiority compelled a much narrower frontage, a smaller initial force and a slower rate of build-up. The landing area needed to be as far away as possible from the enemy naval bases in the central and western Channel (Portsmouth and Plymouth) and in the Thames estuary (Harwich and Sheerness). It was only the short passage across the Dover Strait that – in theory – could be defended by German flanking minefields (and long-range coastal artillery at Cap Gris-Nez). From this maritime perspective the Navy wanted a front of only 50 miles from Folkestone (just west of Dover) west to Beachy Head, which was about a hundred miles east of Bournemouth. This was a third of the frontage originally proposed by the Army. This limitation, ultimately forced by British naval supremacy, made the invasion riskier from the point of view of ground fighting, and less attractive to the generals. General Halder, the Chief of the Army General Staff, feared the consequences of a narrow landing in the difficult country of east Sussex and southern Kent: 'I might as well put the troops which have just landed through a *Wurstmaschine* [sausage machine].'[24] On 7 August a compromise was reached: three main – eastern – landing areas, 'B', 'C' and 'D', were set out between Folkestone and Beachy Head: a fourth area, 'E', to the west near Brighton, was to be taken under Army responsibility, with only a limited re-supply element.[25]

In the final version of the plan nine divisions of the German 9th and 16th Armies (from Field Marshal von Rundstedt's Army Group A) were ear-marked for involvement in the first wave. A tenth, airborne, division would be dropped between Folkestone and Dover. Even though the first-day landings (on what was known as S-Day) were to involve only the spearhead of each division, this operation was very ambitious and had no precedent.

The initial Allied seaborne landing in Sicily in July 1943 would involve only seven divisions, and the D-Day seaborne landing in Normandy on the morning of 6 June 1944 involved only five.[26] The Allies spent a year and a half building landing craft and training troops before the invasion of Sicily. Even the abortive American-backed cross-Channel plans for 1942–43 (operations SLEDGEHAMMER and ROUNDUP) were planned on the basis of using purpose-built small landing craft (produced in very large numbers). By the time of the invasion of Sicily in 1943 a whole family of Allied landing vessels had been developed and deployed, including mother ships for landing craft, and tank and vehicle landing vessels of various sizes.[27]

The Germans in 1940, in contrast, were almost entirely dependent on a jumble of civilian coastal and river shipping in the form of tugboats, trawlers, barges and coastal vessels, hastily assembled in ports of the Netherlands, Belgium and France (often looted from recently occupied countries).[28] By the beginning of September the SEA LION invasion fleet had reached 168 transports (mostly small freighters, typically of about 4,000 tons), 1,910 barges (powered and unpowered) and 419 'tugs' (including trawlers).[29] Various contraptions were devised for the barges, especially to load and unload heavy vehicles and the large number of horses expected; even then, some of these were not ready until after the operation was officially cancelled in September 1940. All the same, by early September the build-up began to approach – on paper – the capacity needed to carry the assault forces across the Channel, and then (for areas B, C and D) to bring in reinforcements and supplies in repeat voyages.

Elaborate timetables were drawn up for numerous convoys of small ships. Some were to proceed down the coast from Rotterdam and Antwerp, to join forces from the main embarkation ports of Ostend, Dunkirk, Calais, Boulogne and Le Havre. The largest element for the three eastern landing areas (B, C and D), which was conceived as mainly a shore-to-shore operation, was a 'tow' (*Schleppzug*), consisting of a small tugboat or trawler (acting as a towing vessel) and two barges filled with infantry or supplies. Each of the three Transport Groups (*Transportflotte*) would cross the Channel in very long columns, formed mainly from lines of tows. For example, the longest column, Transport Group D, was supposed to proceed from Boulogne to landing area D (between Beachy Head and Hastings), carrying the assault elements of the German 26th and 38th Infantry Divisions. With a width of nearly a mile, the group would have stretched for 12.5 miles, including 165 tows; they were in four columns, each in line-astern formation. Maximum speed was about 4 knots. As the long column, running west parallel to the coastline, approached the objective each tow would turn to starboard through 90 degrees, and the whole formation, now in line abreast, would head for the shore. There the process of running the barges ashore (an awkward process because half of them would be unpowered) would be attempted. It was reckoned it would take nine days to land the first wave.

The Brighton landing (Transport Group E) would have involved a longer (100-mile) crossing from Le Havre, and in seas that were expected to be rougher. As a result it was to be an improvised ship-to-shore landing. The landing force, the assault elements of the 8th and 28th Infantry Divisions and the 6th Mountain Division, would have been carried on small coastal cargo ships ('transports') towing barges (rather than on tug-barge tows). The troops would transfer to the barges for the landing, although some would speed ashore in six-man Army assault boats (designed for river crossings).

These complicated manoeuvres, across the open waters of the Channel and under fire in the tricky coastal shallows, were to be performed by 15,000 rapidly drafted crewmen, some from the merchant marine. There was little time for basic training in small craft, let alone for testing the practicalities of the lumbering barge phalanxes. In his final report (dated 28 October) Captain Gustav Kleikamp, naval chief at Calais and designated commander of Transport Group C, made damning comments about the prospects of the plan's success:

> On account of starting too late [in the late summer] and of insufficient preparation and of the complete lack of training of the vessels and barges concerned in sailing formation, there would have been, in my opinion, the very greatest difficulty . . . to conduct a transport fleet in the desired order to the landing area requested by the troops on the opposite enemy coast at the end of September or at the beginning of October, especially not at night.[30]

The Royal Navy assembled a considerable force to deal with a German invasion, from the time, at the end of May, when it emerged as a serious prospect. The clear British superiority in conventional naval forces has already been noted. The heavy ships of the Home Fleet were not risked prematurely in sea areas exposed to enemy air attacks and mines. Admiral Forbes, C-in-C of the Home Fleet, was reluctant to move his battleships south from Scapa Flow until invasion actually seemed likely. He took the view that the role of his fleet was traditional command of the seas. He did not accept, even in September, that there was a serious invasion threat – and he was correct. (The admiral's independence of mind – and reluctance to take the advice of the First Sea Lord – seems to have been one of the reasons why Pound replaced him in December with Admiral John Tovey.)

Nevertheless, light cruisers and destroyers were moved to more southerly ports, although this left fewer escorts available to cover Atlantic convoys and a smaller pool of destroyers available to ensure the safe operation of the Home Fleet capital ships. In late September the naval forces in the Channel and the southern part of the North Sea included the old battleship *Revenge*, two cruisers and six destroyers at Plymouth, a new light cruiser and sixteen destroyers at Portsmouth, and three new light cruisers and two older ones in the Nore Command (the Thames estuary), along with twenty destroyers and four corvettes.[31] During the invasion scare of mid-September the *Hood* and the *Nelson* were moved from Scapa Flow to Rosyth (near Edinburgh) to join the *Rodney*.

Cruisers, destroyers and MTBs mounted sporadic raids against French and Belgian Channel ports. For a few weeks RAF attacks were carried out against barges in the embarkation ports. The British official history, based on German figures, maintained that by 21 September something like a tenth of the enemy vessels that had been assembled or were on their way to assembly posts had been lost or damaged as a result of British action. This included 21 of 170 transports (coastal steamships), 214 of 1,918 barges, and 5 out of 386 tugs.[32] Had the barge build-up continued, it would have been vulnerable to air attack, both in harbour and during the crossing.

There were, to be sure, weaknesses on the British side. Although the Royal Navy (along with the Italians) had pioneered motor torpedo boats (MTBs) in World War I, little further development had taken place until the late 1930s. Even then, there were only about a dozen MTBs (at Felixstowe and Portsmouth), and the vessels on hand were technically inferior to the German S-boats; Coastal Forces did not yet exist as a command. Likewise the ability of the aircraft of Coastal Command, and of the RAF in general, to attack ships at sea was still distinctly limited.[33] All the same, the forces of the unchallenged Royal Navy and the undefeated RAF did present a considerable threat to an invasion force.

The Germans had only limited means to defend their convoys and supply routes. The German plan envisaged ten days of minelaying on either flank of the main cross-Channel route before S-Day, to prevent a breakthrough of British light naval forces. This minelaying effort would surely have removed any element of surprise. In addition the mines would be hard to lay and relatively easy to sweep; they were also exposed to strong Channel currents. German supporting light forces were weak. Five of the surviving German destroyers were sent down the Channel from Wilhelmshaven to Cherbourg in early September. Two dozen U-boats would be brought in to help cover both flanks of the invasion route. It was hoped to keep the British heavy ships in the north by a feint against the British North Sea coast, Operation HERBSTREISE ('Autumn Journey'). This was a dummy ship-to-shore landing expedition, which was supposed to take place a week before S-Day. It involved fifteen ships, including the surviving big liners *Bremen* and *Europa*, escorted by the heavy cruiser *Admiral Hipper* and three light cruisers.

The combination of the extremely difficult task, the lack of time and training, and the strength of British resistance on and above the sea made the invasion a most dubious proposition. Walter Ansel, who was an amphibious planner in the US Navy in the Mediterranean, wrote one of the best-informed books on invasion preparations. His view was that 'execution of operation *Sea Lion* on 27 September as set up held the sole prospect of a major German disaster'.[34]

Front-line officers in the German Army and Kriegsmarine were assembling troops and shipping for SEA LION in late August and September. For them the operation was a real event, not a bluff. The British defenders also took the threat seriously. The assembly of invasion shipping in ports from Amsterdam and Antwerp west to Le Havre and Cherbourg was evident by the beginning of September, and it coincided with more heavy Luftwaffe attacks, especially on London. On the night of 10/11 September there was a major invasion scare in southern England, connected with the ongoing transfer of enemy invasion shipping to embarkation ports in the Channel. The Prime Minister, who in the middle of August had played down the cross-Channel invasion threat, now told a secret session of the House of Commons on 17 September that 1,700 barges and 200 sea-going ships had been observed. 'If this is all a pretence and a stratagem to pin us down here, it has been executed with surprising thoroughness and on a gigantic scale'.[35] Nevertheless, on that same day, in Berlin, the execution of SEA LION was secretly postponed; the invasion plan would never be taken up again.

The stillborn Operation SEA LION had implications. In early November 1940 Churchill could declare in the House of Common that 'the plain fact that an invasion . . . has not been mounted . . . and that all these anxious months . . . have passed safely away – that fact constitutes in itself one of the historical victories of the British Isles . . .'[36] That was true, and the confrontation had also made clearer the relative strength and strategic priorities of the two sides. Not only was the Third Reich weak at sea, but the German high command demonstrated an inability to co-ordinate the activities of the three armed services. None of the three Wehrmacht services supported amphibious *assault* (rather than a *Todesstoss*) as the primary means to defeat Britain. Churchill, meanwhile, had not been above exaggerating the invasion threat to bolster national unity, at least before and after the September 'scare'. It is remarkable that at a time of supposed existential danger the British War Cabinet was prepared to send an expedition with troops and ships to Dakar in West Africa and reinforcements of major warships, tanks and aircraft to Egypt.[37]

Finally, there is the question of why Hitler did not pursue SEA LION. Was this for essentially *political* reasons – a belief that Britain would be forced to make peace in any event, and/or a fundamental continental orientation against 'Bolshevik' Russia? Or was it because the Führer realised that in *military* terms the invasion was risky or impossible, in view of British strength? Both elements played a part – as well as the short time available to mount an attack – but there is no denying that British powers of military resistance *were* significant.

If British strength saved the country from invasion, which forces were most important? The government emphasised that the *home defence* forces of the British Army were numerically larger than they had been in 1914–18 or before the fall of France, but this was essentially just morale-boosting propaganda. The truth is that the pre-war Army had been weak, and it had then lost equipment and cohesion in the aftermath of Dunkirk. Meanwhile the entire fighting strength of the German Army, spectacularly successful in two campaigns, was now available to fight against Britain. The German generals were rightly confident that they could deal with the conquest of at least southern Britain *if* three dozen divisions could be put ashore and supplied.

The Royal Air Force was certainly more important as a defensive factor than the Army. The popular and historical consensus today is that the fighter pilots of the RAF saved Britain in 1940. That was also, it must be said, the line which Churchill took in his public speeches in August and September.[38] Of course Fighter Command did inflict heavy losses and it did compel the Luftwaffe to end the daytime bombing campaign at the end of September. For that, the courage of the RAF fighter pilots and the technical capabilities of the unique air defence system deserve the fullest credit.

On the other hand, the *deterrent* role of the much superior Royal Navy was surely an essential factor, even if its ships were not actually called upon to fight. Initially Churchill had made more of the Navy than the RAF. In his famous 'We shall fight them on the beaches' speech immediately after Dunkirk – and before the air battle began – Churchill spoke of the 'solid assurances of sea power'.[39] British naval strength made the Kriegsmarine very reluctant to attempt the invasion in the first place, and checked any lingering ambitions in August and early September. The realities of the island nation and British sea power were crucial. Admiral John Jervis, First Lord of the Admiralty from 1801 to 1804, had wittily dismissed an earlier invasion threat: 'I do not say the French can't come, I only say they can't come by sea.'[40] This was true, too, of the Germans a century and a half later.

A counterfactual SEA LION before October 1940 can perhaps be considered, but after that there is little point in the exercise. During the winter of 1940–41 the ground forces defending Britain recovered from Dunkirk and were re-equipped and reinforced. Coastal defences were strengthened. Air defences, already strong, were built up. Hitler's next major directive, No. 18 of 12 November 1940, was very much about *indirect* operations, against Gibraltar or the Atlantic islands (the Azores and the Cape Verde Islands). There was a reference here to reverting to SEA LION in the future (the spring of 1941), but at the insistence of General Jodl this had been moved to the very end of the text, making it an after-thought.[41] At a meeting with Mussolini in Salzburg in January 1941, Hitler made clear his antipathy to Soviet Russia, as well as his position on SEA LION:

> In any case, it is no longer a question of landing in England. Hitler said that the undertaking would be extremely difficult and that if it failed the first time it could not be attempted again. Added to this there is the fact that while England now fears the loaded pistol of an invasion, after a failure she would know that Germany holds only an empty pistol.[42]

In the spring of 1941 German heavy ships – battleships and a heavy cruiser – were based at the western end of the Channel, at Brest. An Operation HAIFISCH ('Shark') was drafted as a successor to SEA LION, but it was only a diversion plan for the June 1941 invasion of Russia. As late as the autumn of 1941 the British planners had to reckon with a possible *Blitzkrieg* defeat of the USSR and a rapid return of German ground and air forces to the Channel coast. During that winter, however, it became clear that the Wehrmacht was wholly entangled in the east, and at the same time the US entered the war on Britain's side. In February 1942 a final discussion about SEA LION took place between Hitler and Admiral Raeder. The admiral noted that the operation could certainly not be carried out in 1942 and was tying up valuable personnel and shipping. The conclusion was recorded: 'C-in-C, Navy, requests the lead-time be extended from eight to twelve months. *The Führer concurs*.'[43]

CHAPTER 4

THE BITTER FATE OF THE FRENCH NAVY

1940–44

MERS EL-KÉBIR, 3 JULY 1940

Mers el-Kébir was a partially finished naval base in Algeria, located just west of Oran and set under the heights of Djebel Santon. In early July 1940 what had been termed *le Toulon africain* was a refuge for the important warships of a defeated France.

Since the war began Admiral Marcel Gensoul had led the elite squadron of the French Navy. Originally based at Brest in Brittany, the *Force de Raid* was made up of some of the most powerful warships in Europe: the battleships *Dunkerque* and *Strasbourg* (completed in 1937 and 1938), three new light cruisers and a flotilla of super-destroyers (*contre-torpilleurs*). The two battleships were similar to the *Scharnhorst* and the *Gneisenau*, smaller but more heavily armed – with eight 13-inch guns. Able to make 30 knots, they were the fastest Allied capital ships afloat.[1] Increasing tension with Italy saw redeployment of Gensoul's ships in early April 1940 to ports in Algeria (Mers el-Kébir, Oran and Algiers); from there the task force could swing to either the central Mediterranean or the Atlantic.

The successful German assault in the west began on 10 May, and the danger of Italy entering the war grew. Responding to this, two more battleships, the *Bretagne* and the *Provence*, were moved to Mers el-Kébir. With massive tripod foremasts and two tall thin funnels, they had been completed in 1916. Their armament was ten 13.4-inch guns but they were much smaller and slower than the 'Dunkerque' class. Eight weeks later all four battleships were still tied up against the mole at Mers el-Kébir. Six super-destroyers of the Force de Raid were moored nearby. France's situation had worsened. The government fled Paris, and on 14 June the Germans entered the city. Marshal Pétain formed a new cabinet at Bordeaux on 16 June; a senior member was Admiral François Darlan, the French Navy C-in-C. Regarding the war situation as hopeless, the Pétain government signed the armistice with Nazi Germany at Compiègne on the 22nd. The terms provided for a rump French state in the south, but a German *zone occupée* in the north and west (including Paris). As for the French Navy, the armistice stipulated that it was to be demobilised under Axis supervision.

Eleven days later, on Wednesday morning, 3 July, the destroyer HMS *Foxhound* arrived off Mers el-Kébir; the time was an hour or so after sunrise. Half an hour later three British battleships and an aircraft carrier became visible far out to sea to the northwest. Aboard the *Foxhound* was Captain Cedric Holland, former British naval attaché in Paris. Holland requested an interview with Admiral Gensoul aboard the *Dunkerque*. Gensoul at first refused, on the basis of Holland's lack of seniority, but Holland sent him written terms for removing his ships from possible German control. At about 10.10 a.m. the French admiral sent his ships a signal: 'English fleet has proposed unacceptable armistice. Be prepared to answer force with force.'[2]

The terms of the 'unacceptable armistice' had been decided by the British War Cabinet a week earlier, when the possibility arose of important French ships falling into enemy hands. Four options would be offered to the French admiral: (1) continuation of the war against Germany and Italy; (2) internment in a British port; (3) internment in a French Caribbean port; or (4) self-destruction. If, within hours, none of these options was accepted the ships would be attacked and sunk. This action was code-named Operation CATAPULT.

Marcel Gensoul would have been an extraordinary officer had he chosen any of these four alternatives, and had he done so quickly. Having at first refused to parley he then, about midday, rejected concessions. After some difficulty Gensoul had contacted the French naval headquarters, temporarily located at Nérac in southwestern France. Gensoul dealt with Admiral Darlan's Chief of Staff, who agreed that he should respond with force, and who ordered French warships elsewhere to support Gensoul. Admiral Darlan was at Clermont-Ferrand, en route to the town of Vichy, where the government of the *zone libre* under Pétain was setting up its capital. An indirect participant in the discussion (via a civilian telephone), Darlan provided no further guidance and then, in the afternoon of this critical day, cut himself out of the communications loop. Gensoul may have been realistic when he reported to Nérac that the choice lay between sinking his ships and having them sunk, although he was later criticised for not sending the full British terms (which included internment). Had Gensoul agreed to scuttle his ships, lives would certainly have been saved (and the admiral could not have predicted that only one of his ships would suffer heavy losses). He later defended his refusal by saying that scuttling his fleet in the face of British threats would have been against the 'honour of the flag'.[3] But he and the French Admiralty did 'decide' – to do nothing.

The British, for their part, could not allow the French (or the Germans and Italians) time to take counter-measures, nor could they expose their own vessels to prolonged risk. The main ships involved were the battle cruiser *Hood*, the battleships *Valiant* and *Resolution*, and the carrier *Ark Royal*. Based at Gibraltar and commanded by Admiral James Somerville, they had just been designated as a new Force H. Somerville was a senior officer on the retired list, who had played a major role in the Dunkirk evacuation and had been despatched to Gibraltar from Britain only six days earlier. At 5.15 p.m., after several postponements, Somerville issued a final fifteen-minute ultimatum by signal lamp. Dusk was approaching, and the Admiralty had radioed demands for decisive measures. Receiving no reply from the French, Somerville finally took action. At 5.54 p.m. the British big-gun ships opened fire at a range of 17,500 yards (about 10 miles). For ten minutes they fired salvoes; nearly 150 15-inch shells plunged into the harbour area. To avoid provoking an incident Gensoul had delayed moving his ships or preparing them for action. They had poor fields of fire, and their counter-fire was ineffective. (This was the first of two occasions when the *Hood* would engage another capital ship; a year later the enemy would be more dangerous – the giant battle cruiser blew up after a hit from the *Bismarck* in the Denmark Strait.)

The *Bretagne* suffered a fatal hit almost immediately, which detonated her magazines; she capsized at 6.07 p.m. with heavy loss of life – over 977 officers and men. (She was a vessel similar in size and age to the US battleship *Arizona*, sunk at Pearl Harbor, whose losses – 1,177 men – were only slightly higher.) The *Provence* suffered a fire and flooding, but her captain was able to beach her. The new *Dunkerque* was damaged by four shells and lost power, but was successfully beached near the shore. The super-destroyers cast off; four made it out of the harbour, but the stern of the *Mogador* was blown off. The *Strasbourg*, straddled by shellfire at her moorings, had been struck by only splinters. She followed the flotilla through the net entrance, skirting magnetic mines laid by British Swordfish aircraft during the day, and then steamed east along the coast. Somerville had thought the mines would prevent a breakout. His battleships, far out to sea, were moving in the wrong direction. The *Hood* and the Force H cruisers attempted a pursuit, but the admiral recalled them as night fell. Attacks by *Ark Royal* planes also failed. The *Strasbourg* crossed the Mediterranean and arrived safely at Toulon the following evening.

THE *MARINE NATIONALE* AND THE FRENCH DEFEAT

On 3 July 1940, simultaneously with the confrontation at Mers el-Kébir, steps had been taken by the British to deal with other French ships. These included vessels that had taken shelter in Britain after the fall of northern France, as well as the task force which had been operating alongside the Royal Navy in the eastern Mediterranean. Armed boarding parties took over, undamaged, the ships at Portsmouth, Plymouth and other British ports. These included the *Courbet* and the *Paris* (two old dreadnoughts serving as training ships), as well as four destroyers, six torpedo boats, five submarines and numerous small craft. The potentially more dangerous situation at Alexandria in Egypt was resolved through the good sense of Admiral Andrew Cunningham and Admiral René-Émile Godfroy. The French commander agreed to disarm his considerable force; this comprised the 1916 battleship *Lorraine*, the heavy cruisers *Duquesne*, *Suffren* and *Tourville*, the light cruiser *Duguay-Trouin* and three destroyers. Godfroy refused, however, to serve alongside the British. Indeed, his ships and their crews would not join the Allies until May 1943, six months after the Allied TORCH landings in Morocco and Algeria.

The British continued to use brute force where necessary. The *Ark Royal* launched a second torpedo-plane attack against Mers el-Kébir on 6 July, after the French government publicly (and foolishly) announced that damage caused three days earlier had been limited. The new strike had a very serious effect on the beached *Dunkerque*; a torpedo hit a patrol boat tied up alongside, which led to the massive explosion of the boat's depth charges. Quick repairs to the *Dunkerque* were no longer possible, and she could not now follow the *Strasbourg* to safety. Dockyard facilities in North Africa were inadequate and the *Dunkerque* was only transferred to Toulon in February 1942; even there her repairs were never completed.

Meanwhile on 7 July a British force – the carrier *Hermes* and two heavy cruisers – was in action off the West African port of Dakar (Senegal), to which the incomplete new battleship *Richelieu* had been evacuated. The British put forward to the local French commander the same four options as at Mers el-Kébir; like Admiral Gensoul, he refused them all. During the night a British motorboat dropped depth charges under the battleship's stern, but these failed to explode. Six Swordfish biplanes from the *Hermes* attacked on the following morning. One torpedo struck home, badly damaging the hull and machinery of the *Richelieu* and effectively immobilised her. There was no loss of life.

To understand the decisions and actions of the British and French governments in June and July 1940 it is necessary to look back at the development of the French Navy and its leadership, and at its wartime operations up to June 1940. In September 1939 the second strongest navy in Europe had been not that of Germany or Italy, but the French *Marine Nationale*. This was true despite the fact that it was a junior service to the French Army and that under the 1922 Washington Treaty French diplomats had accepted a capital ship limit of 175,000 tons (compared to 525,000 tons for Britain). Quantitative limitations on smaller ships – cruisers, destroyers and submarines – were not accepted by the French, and a building race began with Italy. Seven 10,000-ton 'Washington Treaty' heavy cruisers were constructed in the 1920s, armed with 8-inch guns.[4] The last – the *Algérie* – entered service in 1934. In the 1930s, along with the other naval powers, the French turned to smaller cruisers with 6-inch guns. All told, nineteen cruisers were in commission in September 1939.

Since the late 1800s the French had taken a great interest in torpedo flotillas as an alternative to a battleship fleet; this was the basis of a naval doctrine known as the *Jeune École*. A prominent and unique element of the French naval construction in the inter-war years was the *contre-torpilleur*, often translated as 'super-destroyer' because of its large size (up to 2,400 tons), heavy armament and high speed. The French also built a smaller number of more conventionally sized (1,400-ton) destroyers (*torpilleurs d'escadre*, literally 'fleet torpedo boats'), twenty-six in the 1920s, and six in the late 1930s. There was a large force of eighty-one submarines. Most were small boats of 600–630 tons (smaller even than the German Type VII class); they were intended for coastal defence and the Mediterranean operations. A third of the undersea fleet – thirty-one units – were 1,500-ton, long-range types. Naval aviation was weak. Unlike the Italians, the French had an aircraft carrier, but the *Béarn*, although a converted battleship (like HMS *Eagle*), was slow and relatively small; she was used only as an aircraft ferry in 1939–40.

Battleship construction resumed in 1933, when the most likely enemy became Germany rather than Italy. The French, indeed, initiated the first round of a European battleship-building race by laying down the 26,500-ton *Dunkerque* (1932) and *Strasbourg* (1934). These were within France's Washington Treaty replacement tonnage allowance, and they were designed primarily to deal with the three German 'pocket battleships'. The Italians, however, responded by beginning the extensive modernisation of their four battleships, and the Germans laid down enlarged pocket battleships in the form of the *Scharnhorst* and the *Gneisenau*. When, in 1934, the Italians announced plans to construct two full-size (35,000-ton) battleships, the French began two of their own. The *Richelieu* and the *Jean Bart* would be scaled-up versions of the 'Dunkerque' class, with heavier, 15-inch guns.

The pre-eminent individual in the French naval command from the late 1930s until 1942 was the *Amiral de la Flotte* François Darlan. He had risen through the bureaucracy to become C-in-C of the Navy in January 1937. Darlan would be a major figure in Marshal Pétain's collaborationist government in 1940–42, but he was not originally a man of the right. His father had been a member of the Chamber of Deputies, and had briefly served as the Republic's Minister of Justice. Darlan *père* had belonged to the Radical-Socialists (although that party was not as far to the left as its name suggests). Political and family connections had given the ambitious young Darlan posts close to his godfather, the Radical-Socialist deputy Georges Leygues, who was Minister of the Navy on and off from 1917 to 1933.

Darlan was physically unimpressive; a (tall) American general who met him in 1942 described 'a little man with watery blue eyes and petulant lips', 'stubby [and] ingratiating'.[5] A gunnery officer by specialisation, Darlan had spent most of the 1914–18 war on the land front, with naval heavy batteries supporting the Army at Verdun and elsewhere. He had commanded the Brest-based Atlantic Squadron from 1934 to 1936, flying his flag in the *Provence*.

The French C-in-C was not especially hostile to the Royal Navy, although he maintained that his great-grandfather had been killed at Trafalgar. There was no doubt a degree of envy, mixed with respect, in his view of the much larger British fleet. Darlan also regarded the British as both imperial rivals and lukewarm allies. In the first nine months of the war, however, the French C-in-C played a major part in war planning, in co-operation with Churchill (then First Lord of the Admiralty) and Admiral Pound. Like Churchill, he urged offensive operations against the Germans in Scandinavia or the Balkans. He also welcomed the replacement of Neville Chamberlain as Prime Minister by the more bellicose Churchill in May 1940.

French ships, notably Admiral Gensoul's Force de Raid, worked together with the Royal Navy in the effort to hunt down German surface raiders. Warships and merchantmen were sent to support the Norwegian operation. The light cruiser *Émile Bertin*, as already mentioned, was damaged by a German bomber; three French super-destroyers, operating from Rosyth, mounted a deep raid into the Skagerrak. After the full-scale German offensive in the west began, French destroyers and torpedo boats suffered very heavily at the hands of the Luftwaffe and S-boats in the Channel; eight destroyers were lost, mainly during the Dunkirk evacuation.

Darlan had hoped from the outset of the war in September 1939 to be able to use his navy against Italy, but he had been thwarted by Mussolini's caution. When Italy did enter the war on 11 June 1940 the French Navy belatedly seized its opportunity. Toulon-based ships were committed to action on the night of 14/15 June, as harbour installations at Genoa were bombarded by cruisers and destroyers. By this time Admiral Darlan and the naval command had been forced to abandon their wartime headquarters outside Paris. In the first crisis days after the evacuation of the capital Darlan had been made Minister of the Navy – replacing a civilian – while keeping his post as C-in-C. The admiral was not among those early defeatists who called for an armistice with Germany. Nevertheless, Pétain regarded Darlan as an efficient, effective and loyal figure.

When *le Maréchal* formed his government on 16 June Darlan stayed on in his dual role.

The immediate challenge in these last days of the Third Republic, however, was evacuating the fleet from ports threatened by the German advance. In the south Toulon was still very distant from the fighting, but on the north and west coasts, especially at Brest in Brittany and at Saint-Nazaire in the Loire estuary, enemy ground formations were rolling forward towards major naval bases and shipyards.

The *Richelieu* and the *Jean Bart*, the two incomplete new battleships, had narrow escapes. The *Richelieu* had been launched at Brest in January 1939, and was structurally complete by June 1940; she was completing her sea trials. Early on the morning of 18 June the Brest naval commandant learned that the enemy were only hours away. He began a rapid evacuation of ships that could be moved, the most important of which was the *Richelieu*. In the evening she left Brest with the cadets of the *École Navale*, the French naval academy, embarked. The escape of the *Jean Bart* from Saint-Nazaire a few hours later was even more hair-raising. The ship's hull had been floated in a dry dock only in March 1940; three months later she was able to move under her own power, but only one of her two main turrets was in place. The short channel between her fitting-out basin and the navigable part of the Loire river was still in the process of being dredged. The great ship was, however, with great effort, eased through the channel. The original intention had been to send the two sister ships to the Clyde, but the impending armistice negotiations meant that the *Richelieu* was sent to Dakar and the *Jean Bart* to Casablanca. Just over two weeks later came the British actions at Mers el-Kébir and Dakar.

What can be said, in conclusion, about this tragic fighting between allied navies? Churchill was the prime mover behind Operation CATAPULT, although here he had the full support of the First Sea Lord, Admiral Pound. The British Prime Minister delivered a speech in the House of Commons on 4 July, the day after Mers el-Kébir. 'I leave the judgement of our action, with confidence, to Parliament', he declared. 'I leave it to the nation, and I leave it to the United States. I leave it to the world and to history'. The same day Admiral Somerville, who carried out CATAPULT, wrote privately that he was appalled by 'this absolutely bloody business' which he considered 'the biggest political blunder of modern times'.[6]

In terms of judgement about British actions in July 1940, historians often ignore one basic reality: in military terms little was achieved. The British certainly did not sink or eliminate the French Navy. The Royal Navy used serious force against only one base, Mers el-Kébir, and British forces succeeded in destroying – with heavy loss of French life – an old battleship of little combat value (the *Bretagne*). The *Strasbourg* and most of the destroyers at Mers el-Kébir escaped. The *Dunkerque* suffered only minor damage on the 3rd. She could have followed the *Strasbourg* back to France within a few days, had it not been for the fortunate – for the British – chain of events (the exploding patrol boat) on the 6th. The damaged battleship *Provence* would be evacuated to Toulon in early November 1940. Elsewhere, the British did not put out of commission the six modern French light cruisers based in Algiers, let alone the four heavy cruisers at Toulon. From the scattered and very large flotillas of destroyers and submarines just one vessel (the *Mogador)* was heavily damaged. Only a handful of vessels rallied to the Free French of General Charles de Gaulle.

The British did take control of or intern a number of French ships in home ports and at Alexandria, and the immobilisation of the *Richelieu* at Dakar removed, for the moment at least, a potential threat. But the action at Mers el-Kébir was counter-productive: ships were moved from North Africa to the French mainland, where the risk of German seizure was greater. Mers el-Kébir and Dakar, moreover, worsened British relations with the successor government at Vichy and outraged the tight-knit French naval officer corps.

However, even bearing in mind that the British actions were *intended* – as a worst case – to cause much more damage than they actually did (e.g. sinking all four battleships at Mers el-Kébir), it is hard to avoid the conclusion that the decisions of Churchill and Admiral Pound were correct. Britain was in the gravest danger; the Royal Navy was faced with multiple challenges. In July 1940 Britain was not yet *immediately* threatened by invasion, but the potential danger was there, and any strengthening of potential enemy fleets had to be prevented. The entry of Italy into the war presented heavy new tasks. Only six days after Mers el-Kébir, on 9 July 1940, the Mediterranean Fleet would fight a naval engagement with the main body of the Italian Navy off Calabria, at Punta Stilo.[7] Admiral Darlan had secretly set up procedures to scuttle his fleet should the German occupiers attempt to seize it, but there could be no guarantee in the medium or long term that he would remain at his post, that the ruthless leaders of Nazi Germany would not increase their control or that the collaborationist French government would not trade the fleet for other concessions. Finally, there is little point in comparing the violence at Mers el-Kébir and the peaceful outcome at Alexandria; the two situations were completely different. In Algeria the British had only a limited window of opportunity. This permitted very little time for negotiation before the French moved their ships or reinforced them. It is also true that firm British action had a political dimension, to signal – especially to the United States – British determination to continue the war, and to take the most ruthless measures. But that does not detract from the immediate military logic of the decision to attack the French fleet.

VICHY AND THE FREE FRENCH, JULY 1940–OCTOBER 1942

The Vichy government consolidated its position in the unoccupied part of mainland France. Marshal Pétain and his colleagues aspired to a policy of collaboration with the Third Reich. Meanwhile General de Gaulle in London created a government-in-exile, along with small Free French armed forces. There now ensued a two-and-a-half-year struggle for control of the extensive overseas French territories, all of which originally accepted the continuity of Vichy as the legitimate government of France. This global struggle inevitably had a large naval dimension, not least because a number of the colonial governors were admirals and because the French Navy provided much of what protection was available to them. On various occasions Admiral Raeder urged Hitler to secure the co-operation of Vichy for his (Raeder's) planned oceanic operations. Although the German dictator had to balance French interests against those of Italy and Spain, Vichy was granted considerable latitude in the maintenance and deployment of its armed forces – more than under the original 22 June 1940 armistice provisions – in order to allow them to defend the outlying territories against British attack. Many of these territories occupied positions of strategic importance, some on maritime supply lines; among these were Madagascar, Indochina, western North Africa, Syria and Lebanon, Nouvelle-Calédonie and French Polynesia.

French West Africa, with its port of Dakar, was especially important. It threatened the British route around Africa to the new fighting front on the border of Libya and Egypt. And for military leaders in Washington concerned with 'hemispheric defence', Dakar was the nearest point to the Americas. The British and the French supporters of the anti-Vichy General de Gaulle had, with the enthusiastic participation of the ever-belligerent Churchill, in early August developed a plan, Operation MENACE, to seize the port. It was hoped to persuade the local French authorities to change sides, but if necessary Free French or even British landing forces would impose the change. It turned out to be the first 'opposed' Allied amphibious operation of the war.

The expedition arrived on 23 September 1940. The British had – despite the continuing threat of invasion at home – committed a considerable naval force. This comprised the battleships *Barham* and *Resolution*, the carrier *Ark Royal*, four cruisers and ten destroyers. Nearly 8,000 troops and their equipment had been loaded aboard eleven transports. The tragic battle was confused. A dense fog on the first two days complicated the tactical situation, as did the defenders' smoke screens. The covering British fleet eventually exchanged fire with the defenders who, two and a half months after Mers el-Kébir, put up a stout resistance. On the first day the British sank a French submarine and forced the super-destroyer *L'Audacieux* to beach herself. On the 24th they sank a second submarine, but the *Barham* was damaged by gunfire. Urged on by London, the attack continued on the third day. Now the *Resolution* was hit amidships by a torpedo fired from the surviving French submarine, the *Bévéziers*. The battleship avoided the fate of her sister, the *Royal Oak*, but she would be under repair for a year. The attack on the *Resolution* would be the most 'successful' wartime action of the French submarine force. Operation MENACE was now abandoned.

It was thought at the time that MENACE had been spoiled by loose talk in London, especially among the Free French. Security was indeed poor, but evidently neither the authorities at Dakar nor the government in Vichy had received advance warning. The main problems were a poorly planned operation and the loyalty to Vichy of the local French units. There was considerable post-war controversy about the presence at Dakar of a powerful group of French warships, which had been sent from mainland France and allowed to pass through the Strait of Gibraltar on 9 September, under the noses of British naval and air forces. The main French naval force at Dakar had originally consisted only of two hastily evacuated ships, both new and incomplete – the battleship *Richelieu* and the destroyer *Le Hardi*. (There were also three submarines and some smaller vessels; the French coastal batteries, 240mm (9.4-inch) guns, were also significant.) The reinforcements from Toulon took the form of two modern light cruisers (the *Montcalm* and the *Georges Leygues*) and three super-destroyers (including *L'Audacieux*). The local naval commander in Gibraltar, the senior admiral Dudley North, was later relieved of his post, and after the war there were accusations that he had been made a scapegoat for the Dakar fiasco. A number of systemic failings did indeed facilitate the French passage of the strait, but the fact remains that North was aware that Operation MENACE was in the offing, and he should have shown more initiative. (It is irrelevant that the reinforcement task force had actually been sent from Toulon and past Gibraltar *not* to defend Dakar, but to restore Vichy authority in colonies further south, in French Equatorial Africa.)[8]

On a more positive note (for the British), some of the Free French troops intended for Dakar joined an incursion into Gabon, the last pro-Vichy part of French Equatorial Africa. The Battle of Libreville, the main port of Gabon, was the occasion for a tragic duel between two warships, on opposite sides of a French civil war: the *Savorgnan de Brazza*, a Free French sloop (*aviso colonial*), engaged and sank her sister ship, the pro-Vichy *Bougainville*. Securing all of French Equatorial Africa would prove important in Allied global strategy in 1941–42. It provided a route along which British and later American warplanes – starting from Takoradi in the Gold Coast (now Ghana) – could be ferried to the battles against Rommel in Libya and Egypt.

Meanwhile, the importance of Admiral Darlan grew within Pétain's government. After June 1940 the admiral believed Britain would follow France in coming to terms with the Axis, and from his point of view the sooner this happened the better. For him there was no likelihood of effective American intervention in the war, and 'Bolshevik' Russia was an existential threat to France, not a potential ally. Co-operation with Germany would lead to amelioration of the armistice terms. The Third Reich was going to control Europe; France would have to fall in with Berlin, while keeping its empire. In February 1941 Darlan became *Vice-président* (de facto premier) under Pétain, and the Marshal's legal successor. Shortly afterwards he became – simultaneously – Foreign Minister and Minister of the Interior, while keeping his naval position; in May 1941 he had meetings with Hitler and Ribbentrop at the Berghof. Other naval officers were installed in important posts both in the unoccupied zone and in the French overseas possessions. It was said, not wholly in jest, that two-thirds of France was controlled by the Germans, and the other third by the Navy.[9] In April 1942 Berlin put pressure on Pétain to replace Darlan with the civilian politician Pierre Laval, whom it regarded as politically more reliable. The admiral remained as C-in-C of the French armed forces, but he was now outside the cabinet.

The slow British process of rolling up Vichy's overseas possessions continued. Pétain and Darlan allowed the Luftwaffe to use airfields in Syria to support an anti-British uprising in Iraq. In response, in June and July 1941 British and Free French troops invaded Syria and Lebanon. There was bitter fighting on land, while the Vichy Navy attempted to bring in supplies. A year later, in May 1942, the British began the invasion of Madagascar, which had become a point where German and Japanese strategic thrusts might join up.[10] In the Pacific, Nouvelle-Calédonie and the New Hebrides had come over to the Free French in 1940. Nouméa and Espiritu Santo – featured in the film *South Pacific* – would be major American naval and air bases in the Guadalcanal campaign of late 1942. French Polynesia (*Océanie*) became an early American naval base in 1942, and a link in the transpacific supply chain to Australia. Meanwhile the pro-Vichy governor-general of French Indochina, another admiral, accepted the presence of Japanese forces in northern Indochina in September 1940, and in the southern part of the country in July 1941; these advances would prove fatal to the British defence of Singapore.

THE FRENCH NAVY FROM OPERATION TORCH TO THE LIBERATION, NOVEMBER 1942–SEPTEMBER 1944

The invasion of French North Africa in November 1942 – the famous Operation TORCH – was outlined in the introduction to this book. Its relationship to the

Battle of the Atlantic and to the development of Allied amphibious warfare will be described in greater detail in chapters 12 and 13, respectively. But here, we will look ahead to the fatal effects of the invasion for Admiral Darlan and for the French Navy.[11]

By the autumn of 1942 most of the ships of the French Navy were concentrated at Toulon in the – misleadingly named – *Forces de Haute Mer* ('High Seas Force'), under the command of Admiral Jean de Laborde. The Germans allowed only a small proportion of the ships to be kept at operational readiness. De Laborde flew his flag in the fast battleship *Strasbourg*. Under Admiral Marquis, commander of the Toulon Naval District, were training ships. In the remaining pro-Vichy overseas territories other warships were scattered in small detachments, rather in the manner of the Jeune École. Destroyers and submarines were based at Algiers and Oran, and at Bizerte in Tunisia. Casablanca in Morocco served as a forward base outside the Mediterranean, and the incomplete battleship *Jean Bart* was still located there. The battleship *Richelieu* was still at Dakar, with the three cruisers that had slipped past Gibraltar in September 1940 and some destroyers.

The Allied landings, carried out with complete surprise and on a very large scale, came on Sunday, 8 November 1942. On the previous night President Roosevelt had announced by radio that the Allies were arriving to defend French territory against impending German and Italian action. Pétain robustly rejected this in his own broadcast the following morning: 'We are attacked; we shall defend ourselves; this is the order I am giving.'[12]

In Morocco the American troops were successfully put ashore on the Atlantic coast north and south of Casablanca. The operations off Casablanca itself were supported by an American task force including the new battleship *Massachusetts*, the fleet carrier *Ranger*, an escort carrier, four cruisers and fourteen destroyers. One heavy turret aboard the incomplete *Jean Bart* was capable of being fired, and an exchange of artillery fire took place. The French battleship did not hit any of the American ships off Casablanca, and she suffered considerable damage from long-range shelling and American dive-bomber attacks.

Unusually for World War II, an amphibious landing was directly opposed by surface ships. During the Sunday morning the French cruisers and destroyers of the 2nd Light Squadron (*2e Escadre Légère*) charged up the coast towards the landing ships off Fedala. They made skilful use of smoke screens but took heavy losses. The light cruiser *Primauget* was damaged by naval gunfire, and then by American air attacks; she was burnt out after being beached; she would be the only French cruiser lost in action during the war. Also eliminated in the fighting were five destroyers. Some eleven French submarines had been based at Casablanca, but they had no success against the American warships despite four attempted attacks; eight of the boats were lost as a result of Allied action. Altogether 462 French naval personnel were killed in these needless battles.[13]

French destroyers were engaged off Oran twice by British cruisers, on the 8th and the 9th. Two were sunk on the morning of the 8th when they sortied to attack the landing, and a super-destroyer and a destroyer were sunk or scuttled on Monday morning, when they attempted to escape to Toulon. Three submarines put to sea, where two were destroyed by British escorts.

The local authorities in Algeria hesitated to change sides, partly because of the order from Pétain, partly because of the non-appearance of General Henri Giraud, a figurehead leader proposed by the Allies. In the end these bloody skirmishes were brought to a halt by the intervention of Darlan. The admiral had just flown to Algiers, apparently unaware of impending invasion, and was caught up in events. He discussed the situation with the local French military and with representatives of the Americans. On the Sunday evening (the 8th) he agreed in principle to an armistice in North Africa, although it was only on the Tuesday morning (the 10th) that his agreement was followed by a direct order. In the meantime Darlan's close friend, Admiral Jean-Pierre Esteva, who was governor-general of Tunisia, obeyed the 11 November directive of the government in Vichy (on the mainland) to continue resisting the Allied landings. At the crucial moment he had failed to block the arrival of German troop-carrying aircraft; his fatal inaction – and tactically brilliant improvisation by the Wehrmacht – condemned the Allies to six months of heavy fighting in Tunisia.

Back in metropolitan France, the German Army began its advance into the Vichy zone on Wednesday, 11 November 1942. There was no resistance. The French commanders might have saved much of their fleet had they acted decisively. Nothing, however, was done in the first three days after the Allied landings in North Africa. It was only on the Wednesday afternoon that, from Algiers, Darlan 'invited' Admiral de Laborde to move his ships from Toulon to Dakar. The Toulon admiral, senior to Darlan and a long-term career rival, remained loyal to Pétain; he replied with one word: '*Merde!*'[14] Advancing German forces took up position around Toulon, but did not occupy the naval fortress itself. Only on the early morning of 27 November, nearly three weeks after the beginning of TORCH, and two weeks after the German occupation of the rest of Vichy territory, did an advance into the naval base begin.

The main ships of the High Seas Force were tied up at Toulon in a long row of parallel berths. The French crews turned out, at least, to be efficient at demolishing their own fleet. The *sabordage* was an event unique in World War II. The ships were sunk at their berths, their guns spiked and turbines rendered useless. The fast battleships *Strasbourg* and *Dunkerque* (the latter in dry dock), the heavy cruisers *Algérie, Colbert*, *Dupleix* and *Foch*, three new light cruisers, twenty-five destroyers, sixteen submarines and many smaller vessels were scuttled. Only three submarines made their way out to sea. The old battleship *Provence*, another survivor of Mers el-Kébir and now a training ship, was also sunk. A handful of vessels that had been laid up could not be scuttled; they were taken over in turn by the Italians (and later the Germans.) Some 28,000 French naval personnel were imprisoned. The quixotic Admiral de Laborde refused to leave the sinking *Strasbourg* without a direct order from Marshal Pétain – which he received.

Admiral Darlan was now an embarrassment to the Allies. He had helped ensure that the Vichy forces in North Africa ceased fighting, but he had not – as initially hoped – delivered the French fleet in Toulon. He had no support in the French Army, and as a very prominent collaborator he was unacceptable to western public opinion. The situation was resolved six weeks later, on 24 December, when the admiral was shot and fatally injured in his office in Algiers by a young monarchist student. After the Liberation of France in 1944 a number of the senior Vichy naval officers would be tried and imprisoned, including admirals Auphan, de Laborde, Abrial, Marquis and Esteva; Admiral de Laborde was actually condemned to death, although his sentence was commuted to life imprisonment. Admiral Gensoul, the commander at Mers el-Kébir during the British Operation CATAPULT in July 1940, who had been sidelined after that event by Darlan, was not brought to trial.

The Free French Naval Forces (*Forces Navales Françaises Libres*, or FNFL) under General de Gaulle, formed in the summer of 1940, remained a small organisation. It had the use of a few of the vessels held in Britain in July 1940; the largest active ones were three destroyers and five submarines. Of more real military value, escorting Atlantic convoys, were nine 'Flower' class corvettes supplied by the British. The role of French naval forces operating alongside the British and Americans became much more substantial in the summer of 1943. A provisional government was created in Algiers in June 1943, effectively led by General de Gaulle. The availability of substantial manpower in Africa made the French ground forces an important military factor on the Allied side.

There was a similar position with naval forces. De Gaulle's FNFL were now overshadowed by ships and personnel from the interned ships at Alexandria and the former pro-Vichy squadrons at Casablanca, Dakar and Martinique. Of the 42,000 personnel serving in the reconstituted Marine Nationale (serving with the Allies) in August 1943, only 6,000 had come from the FNFL.[15] A naval headquarters was set up in Algiers in August 1943 under Rear Admiral André Lemonnier. The admiral had served in the Vichy Navy as captain of the cruiser *Georges Leygues*, fighting against the British and Free French at Dakar in September 1940.

The Vichy general governing French West Africa had decided in November 1942, thanks partly to the intervention of Admiral Darlan, that the time was now right to change sides. As a result the *Richelieu*, trapped in a damaged state at Dakar, could finally enter service. The big ship was rapidly refitted in the New York Navy Yard, partly using heavy guns and other equipment cannibalised from the damaged and incomplete *Jean Bart* at Casablanca. The *Richelieu* then served alongside the Royal Navy, off Norway in 1943, and in the (British) Eastern Fleet, based at Ceylon, in 1944–45. In addition, four of the most modern French cruisers (the *Émile Bertin*, the *Montcalm*, the *Georges Leygues* and the *Gloire*) and four super-destroyers were brought to the US for extensive modernisation.

Admiral Godfroy's Alexandria squadron – the old battleship *Lorraine* and four cruisers – had been disarmed in July 1940 and were also now returned to Allied service. These and other older French ships were refitted in North Africa rather than America and received only a limited amount of new equipment. The French also received new ships from their allies in 1943–44. The British provided a small destroyer, six 'River' class frigates and two submarines; the Americans supplied (in early 1944) six destroyer escorts, which operated in the Mediterranean.

The reformed French Navy took part in the liberation of Corsica in September and October 1943. The island had been occupied by Italy after the 1940 armistice. German troops only arrived in July 1943 and in small numbers; there was some fighting, but, hard-pressed elsewhere, the Wehrmacht decided not to defend the island. The participation of the French in the landings in northern France in 1944 was essentially of symbolic importance. At Normandy the cruisers *Georges Leygues* and *Montcalm* provided gunfire support off the OMAHA beaches, and a destroyer and nine frigates and corvettes took part as convoy escorts. In contrast, the French Navy played a major role in the invasion of southern France, Operation DRAGOON, in August 1944. In the support force were the surviving old battleship, the *Lorraine* (from the Alexandria squadron), five French cruisers, three super-destroyers, and fourteen smaller destroyers and other escorts.

The ships of the French Navy returned to Toulon – the port now wrecked by German sabotage and Allied bombing – on 13 September 1944. The ruins of the other main French naval base, Brest in Brittany, the home base of the Force de Raid in 1939–40, was surrendered by its German garrison six days later.

* * *

We now need to turn back three years to the summer and autumn of 1940, just after the fall of France, and consider the end of the first period of World War II at sea. In broad geopolitical terms, June 1940 broke up the first anti-German alliance. On the other hand, Hitler, due in large part to his enemy's naval supremacy, abandoned plans to invade Britain (effectively at the end of July 1940). This meant that no 'direct' resolution of the war in favour of Nazi Germany was possible. The conflict would now enter a second period, of stand-off between the British Empire and the Third Reich, in which a major element would be an 'indirect' attempt to weaken British power.

This second period would also see increasing pressure on the far-flung British Empire by two other revisionist powers, Italy and Japan. For nine months more, until June 1941 and the invasion of Russia, the Empire would be fighting on its own. Even after June 1941, the long-term survival of the new Russian ally would be in doubt, and Imperial Japan, with its powerful navy, would become a more dangerous threat. The only clearly positive development during this period – an extremely important one – would be a rapid increase of diplomatic and economic support from the neutral United States.

In more narrow terms of maritime war, the first period had been fought by peacetime forces. All the major powers had begun extensive naval rearmament in the late 1930s, but as far as capital ships – battleships and aircraft carriers – were concerned, most of the new generation were still not ready for service. The maritime war up to June 1940 had been a regional, northern European conflict, effectively between Britain and Germany. But this was not to be a repetition of the North Sea conflict of 1914–18. Even before the defeat of France, the invasion of Norway in April 1940 had shown that the fighting would be different. At least as far as the Kriegsmarine was concerned, this was not an accident: the German naval leadership had no desire to see history repeat itself. The unanticipated French calamity was also important for accelerating American rearmament – not least in President Roosevelt's 'Two-Ocean Navy' legislation of June 1940 and his calls for increased aircraft production.[16]

The maritime elements of the fighting had been significant. The Norwegian campaign would prove to be, geographically, one of the most widespread amphibious campaigns of the whole 1939–45 war. Neither side, however, had made special preparations for this type of fighting, and the target of the landings was a poorly defended neutral country. Six weeks later British control of the Channel made the Dunkirk evacuation possible. Although very far from a victory, Dunkirk was extremely important both militarily and politically. Even more crucial, lack of control of the Channel and the North Sea meant the Germans were unable to implement their ambitious SEA LION plan, even against a weakened and isolated Britain.

The balance of power at sea, previously heavily in the Allied favour, had been tilted but not transformed. German control both over the Norwegian ports and also over those of western France meant that the long-term potential for an oceanic anti-shipping war, by submarines and even by the surface ships of the Kriegsmarine, seemed to be much enhanced. At the same time the Third Reich had spread its control over western and northern Europe, and Stalin's Russia was continuing a policy of benevolent neutrality towards it. As a result, the naval blockade of the Third Reich was a much less viable strategy than had seemed the case in August 1939. French defeats had also encouraged Italy to enter the war; in the second period of the war the Royal Navy would have to contend on its own with a second sea war, in the Mediterranean.

The features of the sea war had not been what was expected, at least by the admirals. The fighting off Norway had shown that shore-based aviation could limit the movement of a big fleet, at least in coastal waters, even if attacking aircraft were available in only small numbers and even if they had only limited anti-ship capability. The suffering of Allied ships at Dunkirk had been a second demonstration of sea/air power as – less obviously – had been the British carrier strike against the French fleet in Algeria.

The events of the first period dashed expectations that submarine activity would be limited by international law or checked by technical developments in A/S warfare. The Germans had early success against major British warships, but as of June 1940, the U-boat force was much too small to mount a strategic threat to Britain's oceanic trade routes. Indeed, British available commercial tonnage had improved by taking over much of the merchant fleets of Norway, the Netherlands and other countries invaded by Germany.

France had been defeated. Germany dominated the Continent. Britain faced a perplexing new world, without a clear sense of the course to recovery and final victory, but at least without any fear of immediate defeat.

PART II

THE BRITISH EMPIRE AT BAY

JUNE 1940–APRIL 1942

. . . you may recall my remarks the evening we discussed War Plans for the Navy. I stated that if Britain wins decisively against Germany we could win everywhere; but that if she loses the problem confronting us would be very great; and, while we might not lose everywhere, we might, possibly, not win anywhere.

Admiral Harold Stark USN,
memorandum, 12 November 1940

It was the illusion that a Two-Hemisphere Empire can be defended by a One-Hemisphere Navy that sealed the fate of Singapore.

Admiral Herbert Richmond RN,
Statesmen and Sea Power (1946)

CHAPTER 5

THE BATTLE OF THE ATLANTIC, ROUND ONE

June 1940–December 1941

ATLANTIC CONVOY BATTLES, 16–19 OCTOBER 1940

With the fall of France in June 1940, the vital British shipping routes to the Empire and the United States were shifted to the north, funnelled in and out of the North Channel, the strait between Scotland and Northern Ireland. Liverpool became the main destination and departure point. In the third week of October convoys SC.7 and HX.79 converged in a sea area about 500 miles northwest of the United Kingdom. Both had left assembly ports in Nova Scotia some two weeks earlier.

Ocean convoys were organised throughout the war in line abreast, with short parallel columns. At night these columns were about 5 cable lengths (1,000 yards) apart; during the day 3 cable lengths (600 yards). Within the columns 2 cable lengths (400 yards) separated each merchant ship from the one behind it. The slow convoy SC.7 was made up of nine columns, each with five or six merchant ships. The command ship, carrying the convoy commodore, was usually positioned at the head of the central column; for SC.7 this ship was the SS *Assyrian*.

At this point in the war little protection was provided for the long middle reach of the transatlantic crossing. Enemy attacks there were thought unlikely, and escorts were still scarce. SC.7 was protected by the sloop HMS *Scarborough*, HX.79 by two armed merchant cruisers, intended to ward off surface raiders. The procedure at the time was that short-range escorts from Britain would join up to cover the final stage of the voyage at about longitude 20°W.

On the afternoon of Wednesday, 16 October 1940, SC.7 was sighted about 450 miles northwest of the British mainland by the *U 48*. The submarine radioed the convoy's position to its shore headquarters near Paris, headed by Admiral

Dönitz (now Commander, U-boats).[1] Shortly afterwards the escort of the convoy was reinforced, as planned, by two Liverpool-based vessels, the sloop *Fowey* and one of the new 'Flower' class corvettes, the *Bluebell*. The *U 48* was a medium-sized Type VII submarine; she carried fourteen torpedoes and had five launch tubes. Early on Thursday morning the U-boat sank a big tanker and damaged another ship, but at dawn she was forced to crash dive when a four-engined Sunderland flying boat arrived overhead from Northern Ireland. The *Scarborough* – the original transocean escort – set off in pursuit. Although the sloop dropped depth charges, she failed to sink the *U 48*; the *Scarborough* was also unable to rejoin the convoy, and so could not help provide protection on following nights. Early on Friday morning, however, SC.7 was joined by two more small warships from Britain, the sloop *Leith* and the corvette *Heartsease*. The captain of the *Leith* took over as escort commander.

The massacre of the convoy SC.7 began on Friday evening, when it ran into a patrol line of five submarines set up by U-boat HQ. Nine ships were torpedoed and sunk during the moonlit night, by submarines operating on the surface. Six were victims of the U-boat 'ace' Otto Kretschmer, who took his *U 99* into the middle of the convoy. One of the numerous attacks described in Kretschmer's log for that night was against the SS *Fiscus*:

> 23:55. Fire a bow torpedo at a large freighter of some 6,000 tons, at a range of 750 metres. Hit abreast foremast. Immediately after the torpedo explosion, there is another explosion with a high column of flame from the bow to the bridge. The smoke rises some 200 metres. Bow apparently shattered. Ship continues to burn with a green flame.[2]

The *Fiscus* was loaded with a cargo of steel, and she sank immediately with her entire crew of twenty-eight. Joachim Schepke in the *U 100* sank three more freighters.

The four remaining escorts failed to fend off any of the attackers, let alone sink them. The U-boats had low silhouettes; on the surface they were as fast as the sloops, faster than the corvettes, and twice as fast as the merchant ships. The ASDIC (sonar) of the escorts could not detect surfaced submarines, and they lacked radar and even effective 'star shells' (flares) to illuminate the area of the convoy. The British warships had not operated together beforehand, and their captains could only communicate by signal lamp; voice radio between escorts was not yet available.

The escorts in any event fell behind the convoy, as they picked up survivors from the sinking merchantmen. The *Bluebell* ended up with 200 men on board, four times her normal complement. Rescue operations were understandable, but they left the remaining merchant ships more vulnerable. In the end, even the convoy flagship was sunk, although the commodore was eventually rescued. The slaughter of SC.7 ended at dawn on Saturday; the Germans ran out of torpedoes and targets.

The October convoy disaster did not end there. On Saturday morning Günther Prien, the hero of the Scapa Flow attack and still in command of the *U 47*, sighted the 'fast' convoy HX.79. The reported position was about 50 miles behind SC.7 – and U-boat HQ vectored in four boats. The two British armed merchant cruisers had by now been detached from the convoy, but a reasonably strong UK-based escort arrived piecemeal in the course of the morning. It including two older destroyers, three corvettes and an armed trawler.

The poor co-ordination and technical problems evident in the defence of SC.7 were repeated. The 'pack' attack began on Saturday night and lasted through the early hours of Sunday. Some ten merchant ships were lost, as well as two stragglers, out of a total of forty-nine. The proportion of losses was lower than that for SC.7, but the attack was still a stunning German victory. Dönitz noted this in his war diary: 'The operations justify the principles on which U-boat tactics and training have been developed since 1935, i.e. that U-boats *in packs* should attack the convoys.'[3] Prien, his triumphs multiplying, was awarded the Knight's Cross with Oak Leaves, the latest version of the Wehrmacht medal.

The pack attacks did indeed demonstrate the potential of the U-boats, when they could operate from bases in France and when they worked in groups, even against convoys and even against ASDIC-equipped escorts. Indeed, these actions fit a common image of what the Atlantic convoy war was like.

However, the tragic fate of SC.7 and HX.79 needs to be contrasted with the great majority of inbound North Atlantic convoys, in late 1940 and up to the end of 1941. Of the next fifty-five slow convoys, SC.8 to SC.62 (the last SC convoy in 1941), forty-six suffered no losses at all, and the total number of merchant ships lost while in these convoys – over fifteen months – was fifty-three out of 2,007 ships – a loss rate of 2.6 per cent. Of the ninety-one faster HX convoys in the same period, HX.80 to HX.167, seventy-nine suffered no losses; for all of them, the number of merchant ships lost amounted to thirty-one out of 3,690 (0.8 per cent).[4] The two October 1940 attacks, terrible as they were for the merchant ship crews, were exceptions to the rule. For the Royal Navy they demonstrated a *future* strategic danger rather than a current one.

MERCHANT SHIPS UNDER ATTACK

Britain's unique global power came in part from a huge fleet of cargo and passenger ships. In 1939 the merchant ship tonnage of the British Empire was

17.9 million tons (GRT),[5] out of a world total of 68.6 million. The US possessed the second largest shipping fleet, but it amounted to only 11.4 million tons. The fleet of Britain's 1939 ally, France, consisted of just 2.9 million tons.[6] The shipbuilding industry was also a special strength. In the 1920s and 1930s over 40 per cent of world merchant ship tonnage was still built in British yards. Production in 1938 was 972,000 tons. By comparison, in the following year American shipyards delivered only 341,000 tons of merchant ships.[7]

In the nine months before the French collapse, abundant shipping was available. Considerable tonnage was needed to deploy and supply the British Expeditionary Force in France and – in April 1940 – to support a campaign in Norway. Nevertheless, movement was confined to relatively short routes in northwestern Europe. Meanwhile the German Navy was small; its North Sea bases were far from the shipping lanes. Even the fall of France did not at first seem threatening from a maritime point of view. Shipping was no longer needed to supply France. Britain gained direct control over many vessels from the merchant fleets of the states overrun by Germany, especially Norway, the Netherlands and – later – Greece. According to official statistics, the amount of merchant shipping under British control was about 18.5 million tons at the end of March 1940, and had reached 21.8 million a year later; at the end of 1941 the total was still 21.6 million. These figures included foreign-flag vessels under British control, which made up 4.6 million tons in March 1941 and 5.1 million tons in December 1941.[8]

In contrast to 1914–18, the British did not delay in introducing convoys in 1939, although a heavy escort was only provided in dangerous waters. A considerable proportion of shipping continued to sail independently. The first eastbound transatlantic convoy (HX.1) had departed on 16 September 1939 from Halifax, Nova Scotia. It comprised eighteen merchant vessels and arrived in Liverpool on 30 September. The last such convoy (HX.358) departed on 23 May 1945. SC convoys were 'slow' eastbound convoys with the same destination. The designation came from the assembly point at Sydney, Cape Breton, Nova Scotia. Convoy SC.1 departed in August 1940, and SC.177 on 26 May 1945; the speed of the ships in these slow convoys was 7–9 knots. Westbound ('outward') transatlantic convoys were mainly designated in the 'OB' series from Liverpool; these began with OB.1 in September 1939. In July 1941 northern outward convoys, to Halifax, were designated as the 'ON' series, which continued until ON.335 in May 1945.

Also important, however, was the north–south route via Gibraltar and Freetown (the large natural harbour in Sierra Leone). This led both to South America and around the Cape of Good Hope to what the British termed the 'Indian Ocean Area'. (The Mediterranean sea lane to the Indian Ocean via Suez was closed to nearly all British shipping from June 1940 to the middle of 1943.) After the fall of France these southbound convoys, like the transatlantic ones, were routed to and from Liverpool. Inbound convoys assembled at Freetown; they began in September 1939 as SL.1, and continued to the end of 1944 (SL.178). The outward-bound southern convoys (designated 'OS' from July 1941) made the outward trip to Freetown, where they dispersed.

As well as food and raw materials, British convoys also carried military personnel – brought as reinforcements to the United Kingdom from the distant Dominions, or sent from the UK to fight overseas campaigns. 'TC' convoys brought Canadian troops *to* the UK from December 1939. From the middle of 1940 to 1942 the movement of troops and supplies *from* Britain (and Australia) was mainly to North Africa. The large British 'WS' ('Winston Special') series began in August 1940 and continued to WS.33 in August 1943. Normally military personnel were moved in special convoys of fast converted passenger ships. In addition, throughout the war what were known as the 'monsters', a handful of huge ocean liners like the *Queen Mary* or the *Queen Elizabeth*, sailed independently, protected by their high speed.

As already indicated, this British oceanic trade network had been, on paper at least, an important target of overall German grand strategy. This had been true from the first months of the war, notably in Hitler's directive of November 1939. After the victory in France and the inconclusive air campaign of August–September 1940 these attacks were resumed. They continued in early 1941, even as German planners secretly deployed their forces for the invasion of Russia. Directive No. 23 of 6 February 1941 was entitled 'Directive for operations against the English war economy' and identified the attack on shipping as a key means of damaging the enemy war effort. Hitler openly announced this strategy three weeks later, on 24 February, in a speech which he made at the Hofbräuhaus in Munich. The *Kampf zur See* had been held up, he admitted, but the German Navy had not slept through the winter; it had been completing new U-boats and training their crews. 'Those gentlemen [the British] should prepare for a difference from March or April [1941] onwards'. 'One thing is clear', the Führer declared, 'wherever Britain touches the continent, we will immediately oppose it, and wherever British ships put to sea, our U-boats and aeroplanes will be deployed against them until the hour of decision comes.'[9]

The German Wehrmacht had several means for attacking British shipping. Surface ships, submarines, aircraft and mines could be deployed on the high seas or on the approaches to ports. In addition, the ports themselves and their facilities – warehouses, cranes, railway connections – could be destroyed by air raids.

The submarine force would turn out to be the most effective anti-shipping weapon, although in the spring and early summer of 1940 the available U-boats had been concentrated off Norway. Some months were needed to prepare the new, and much better-situated, bases in northwestern France and Norway.

An example of the most common class of German submarine (a Type VII) was the *U 99*, Otto Kretschmer's boat in the October 1940 attack on convoy SC.7. She was a brand-new vessel, having been commissioned in April 1940, and sailing on her first war patrol in mid-June. The Type VII class displaced only about 750 tons. The main armament consisted of five torpedo tubes, four forward and one aft. A total of fourteen torpedoes would be carried. The Type VIIs could be built quickly – a grand total of 703 would be completed by the time production halted in 1943. They were manoeuvrable, and could crash dive in thirty seconds. But they were originally intended for short-range – North Sea – operations. They could not operate effectively much beyond the middle of the Atlantic without vulnerable supply vessels, and in 1940–41 these were surface ships. The larger Type IX U-boats were originally designed for long-range operations (against France) in the western Mediterranean. The first version displaced 1,016 tons and was 30 feet longer than the Type VIIs. Only thirty to thirty-five were in service by the end of 1941, and only 194 would be completed during the whole war.

Compared to the submarines of the other naval powers, the Kriegsmarine boats were of uniformly recent construction; the first Type VII (the *U 27*) had been commissioned only in August 1936, the first Type IX (the *U 37*) in August 1938. The Type VII and Type IX U-boats were powered by two diesel engines which propelled them on the surface at a top speed of about 17 knots in a calm sea; in good conditions they could cover 400 nautical miles in a day. The diesels also charged the batteries powering two electric motors for use when submerged. Underwater speed was slow – 7 or 8 knots for a very short burst of an hour or so, and 3 or 4 knots for longer periods.

Karl Dönitz was a veteran U-boat man. In 1918 he had commanded submarines in the Mediterranean and was captured by the British. (He had not been very successful; indeed during his first attack the boat had broached.) After a decade of conventional service in surface ships in the 1920s he became one of the leaders of rebuilding the U-boat force. When the war began the future Commander, U-boats, was only forty-seven years old and did not yet hold flag rank. Dönitz led the submarine force from a headquarters in Wilhelmshaven, before moving briefly to Paris in the summer of 1940, and then in November of that year to Lorient on the southern coast of Brittany. He was an able commander who inspired loyalty.

Dönitz was certainly an innovator. He strongly supported the U-boat arm at the expense of other parts of the Navy, but that was only realistic given the late start of the Third Reich in construction of large surface ships and the 'premature' war. Two other things in particular stood out in his wartime leadership, one tactical-operational, the other grand-strategic. To overcome – or exploit –

the convoy system, Dönitz had long advocated co-ordinated U-boat attacks with central control from shore. He had not been able to put this into practice before the Norwegian campaign, but afterwards it became the core of his tactical doctrine. The boats operated as a 'pack' (*Rudel*), co-ordinating their movements by radio and swamping the defences. As part of the *Rudeltaktik* the U-boats attacked at night, manoeuvring on the surface while running on their diesels. This gave them higher relative speed and a better chance to see their target.

What might be called the grand-strategic element of Dönitz's policy was an emphasis on sinking as many merchant ships as possible. U-boat deployments were to be based not so much on specific tasks as on mathematical calculations, in which the object was to maximise the tonnage sunk per U-boat over a particular time period. From the point of view of the *Tonnagekrieg* – the 'tonnage war', as this approach became known – it did not matter *where* merchant ships were sunk; victory would come by the most efficient reduction of the enemy shipping pool as a whole.[10]

Both of the concepts of Admiral Dönitz had inherent weaknesses. The *Rudeltaktik* involved a highly sophisticated command-and-control system, but use of radio communications could give away the position of the U-boats by allowing British direction finding (DF) and message interception.[11] In addition, it depended on the continuing ability of U-boats to concentrate at speed while moving on the surface; this would become much more difficult as Allied radar and A/S aircraft developed. And the Tonnagekrieg concept was generally unrealistic, based on an underestimate of British and American potential to produce replacement merchant ships.

In the short term these inherent problems were not evident. The determining feature of this round of the submarine war in the Atlantic – in 1940–41 – was the lack of U-boats. In July 1940, after the Norwegian and French campaigns, and when the Battle of the Atlantic really commenced, the Kriegsmarine possessed three fewer U-boats than it had at the start of the war. There were only thirty *Frontboote* ('front-line boats'), and no more than a third of those could be engaged in Atlantic shipping attacks at any one time; they also needed to move to and from their bases and to refit between war patrols. The low point of Frontboot availability actually came in February 1941, when only twenty-one were available; it would not be until July 1941 that the number of boats on hand exceeded pre-war strength.

In the 1930s Admiral Raeder, the long-time C-in-C of the Kriegsmarine, had wanted to create a conventional 'balanced' fleet. Once the war began, however, he strongly supported submarine construction, urged on by Dönitz. The target was twenty boats a month, aiming for a fleet of 300 in 1943. With hindsight, this made sense. It was not, however, the kind of expensive long-term programme that the German masters of the 'lightning war' – the Blitzkrieg – found inherently attractive, at least not in 1940. At that time Hitler and the German high command expected the war with Britain to be over quickly, and they had limited resources and continental ambitions. In any event, some twelve to thirteen months were required to build even a medium-sized Type VII boat, and it was only in July 1941 that the monthly completion rate reached at least twenty. Even then, for each new boat the better part of a year of trials and training (mostly in the Baltic) was required before she and her crew were ready for operations.

The central importance of the submarine as an anti-shipping weapon was not evident to Hitler and his military advisers in the early stages of the war. Hitler's Directive No. 13 (6 February 1941) had been mainly about concentrating *air* attacks on Britain against major ports (ships in harbour and dock installations). This echoed his Directive No. 9 of 29 November 1939, which had stressed attacking the British economy by port attacks and minelaying, but made no reference at all to U-boats. The Luftwaffe did mount a campaign of large-scale night attacks in the spring of 1941 against western UK ports, attacking Glasgow (with Clydebank) in March, Belfast in April and May, and – especially – Liverpool in May. Because of the strength of the British air defences and the lack of escort fighters the Luftwaffe bombers could only operate at night, so precision attacks were impossible. In any event the bombers were already redeploying to the Mediterranean and Russia, and from June 1941 attacks on British ports virtually ceased.

Limited attempts were made to attack merchant ships at sea. The twin-engined medium bombers, mainly the Heinkel He 111 and the Junkers Ju 88, had an operational radius of only about 700 miles and could not fly far into the Atlantic. However, in August 1940 the four-engined aircraft Focke-Wulf Fw 200 Condor appeared, with an operational radius of 950 miles. In October 1940, a week after the U-boat massacre of convoys SC.7 and HX.79, an Fw 200 bombed and crippled the 42,000-ton liner *Empress of Britain* 70 miles northwest of Ireland; this enabled a U-boat to finish her off two days later.[12] In February 1941 six Fw 200s achieved another major success, against convoy OB.290, sinking seven ships. The secret 'Battle of the Atlantic' directive, which Churchill issued in early March 1941, presented the threat to shipping from the Focke-Wulf and other bombers as one comparable to that from U-boats. Fortunately for the British, only a handful of Fw 200s were available – about twenty-five aircraft. The aircraft itself was a hastily adapted Lufthansa airliner.

Tactical co-ordination was poor, and there was never an integrated sea/air threat in the Atlantic, where long-range aircraft located the convoys and directed U-boats against them. This reflected two fundamental German weaknesses, inter-service rivalry and a relative lack of interest in the sea/air war. James

Corum, one of the leading historians of the subject, argued that this was 'the Luftwaffe's single greatest failure in developing an air war doctrine'.[13] Göring certainly opposed any attempt by the Kriegsmarine to control its own aircraft. The senior leadership of the Navy, meanwhile, also had only limited understanding of or interest in sea/air warfare. The pre-war Navy had had a few aircraft – seaplanes and flying boats for reconnaissance – but they were slow and relatively short-ranged.

Meanwhile the British introduced counter-measures against the air threat. Merchant ships and escorts were provided with more AA guns. Catapults were fitted to some freighters for launching Hurricane fighter planes. Later, in 1941, the first small 'escort' aircraft carrier was despatched to cover the shipping route most threatened by air attacks (the UK–Gibraltar route). The conversion of HMS *Audacity* (from a captured German merchantman) had begun in January 1941. Although she could only carry a few fighters, these were able to break up German air attacks. In September 1941 an American-supplied Grumman fighter from the *Audacity* shot down an Fw 200, and more successes followed. The little carrier had a short career, being sunk by a U-boat in December 1941. But more escort carriers would become available in 1942, and many more in 1943.

CHURCHILL'S 'BATTLE OF THE ATLANTIC'

The Battle of the Atlantic is a story of repeated tactical encounters between submarines, escorts and merchant ships, taking place over a five-year period. It is a challenge to explain this concisely. The American naval historian Samuel Eliot Morison put the problem well: the history of the Battle of the Atlantic 'is exceedingly difficult to relate in an acceptable literary form'.[14]

Despite the drama and heroism of individual convoy battles and attacks on lone merchantmen, limited space means that a broad-brush approach is needed. Table 5.1 lays out the dynamics of the first period of the anti-shipping war in the Atlantic.

Figures for both tonnage and ships lost are listed, to make the physical destruction clearer.[15] The average size of an ocean-going merchant ship in this period of the war was about 4,000–5,000 tons; short-range coastal ships (in UK waters) were two-thirds this size. Losses also have to be compared to overall tonnage of shipping available at the start of the war and to new construction. British shipyards were turning out 1 million tons of merchant ships a year in 1940 and 1941, and the Empire began the war with 17.9 million tons.

In terms of where ships were sunk, Table 5.1 shows that until the summer of 1940 more were lost in UK waters than in the open Atlantic ('UK waters' includes the North Sea, the Channel and near approaches from the west). After

Table 5.1. The Battle of the Atlantic, 1939–41

Year/ quarter	N. Atlantic tonnage lost	N. Atlantic ships lost	UK waters tonnage lost	UK waters ships lost	U-boats oper.	U-boats t&t	U-boats lost
1939/iv	249,000	47	457,000	165	49	8	9
1940/i	122,000	28	426,000	153	32	24	10
1940/ii	370,000	66	573,000	221	46	6	6
1940/iii	586,000	119	486,000	151	28	23	4
1940/iv	727,000	136	307,000	125	27	37	4
1941/i	896,000	174	241,000	114	22	67	5
1941/ii	904,000	171	286,000	173	32	81	7
1941/iii	366,000	99	90,000	42	65	93	6
1941/iv	255,490	52	123,000	51	80	118	17
Sub-total	4,476,000	892	2,990,000	1,195			
Total (all theatres)	9,075,000	2,479					68

Source: Rosk/1, pp. 599–600, 614, 617–18.
Notes: Losses are for Allied and neutral countries' merchant ships due to enemy action *of all types*, not just due to U-boats. Tonnage is GRT. U-boat numbers are total for German Navy (all theatres) at the start of each quarter; 'oper.' is operational U-boats, 't&t' is units involved in training and trials. U-boat figures include losses from all causes and in all theatres.

this the proportion in the North Atlantic grew; this was mainly because U-boats began to use forward bases in western France and Norway. The majority (52 per cent) of the 9,075,000 tons of shipping lost in *all* theatres in 1939–41 was the result of submarine attack. Of the 7,466,000 tons of shipping lost in the North Atlantic and UK waters (4,476,000 + 2,990,000) the proportion sunk by U-boats was considerably higher; at this time Axis submarine operations in the Mediterranean, the South Atlantic, the Indian Ocean and the Pacific were on a very small scale.[16]

Finally, figures in Table 5.1 for U-boats available in 1939–41 show the very limited number of operational boats involved – at least until the fourth quarter of 1941. Also evident is the rapid growth of the potential undersea threat for the *next* period of the war (1942–43). The number of submarines 'on trials and in training' rose from eight in September 1939 to 118 two years later.

For the British, the commerce war began to assume greater prominence in the later months of 1940. In December the British Prime Minister wrote to President Roosevelt outlining what was probably his genuine view of the war: 'It is . . . in shipping and in the power to transport across the oceans, particularly the Atlantic Ocean, that in 1941 the crunch of the whole war will be found.' Churchill coined the term 'Battle of the Atlantic' in a secret directive of 6 March

1941. This directive ordered that priority be given to maintaining the flow of merchant shipping, and protecting it against submarine, air and surface ship attack. In late April he used the term publicly in a radio broadcast, citing Hitler's Munich speech: 'In February, as you may remember, that bad man, in one of his raving outbursts, threatened us with a terrifying increase in the numbers and activities of his U-boats and in his air attacks.' Britain was now fighting the German attack 'with might and main'. 'That', the Prime Minister declared, 'is what is called the Battle of the Atlantic which, in order to survive, we have got to win on salt water just as decisively as we had to win the Battle of Britain last August and September in the air.'[17]

Britain did indeed take important steps to deal with this challenge. At the grand-strategic level, policies were introduced to reduce imports to the UK, and it turned out that tonnage requirements were actually substantially less than pre-war expectations. At the same time, measures were taken to rationalise and increase the flow of goods coming through the western ports; the creation of a Ministry of War Transport, under the businessman Frederick Leathers, brought together the ministries of Transport and Shipping.

Another basic measure was the construction (and repair) of merchant ships. Shipyards in the UK were still busy with warships, but progress was made with the construction of standard merchant ship designs. Britain completed 810,000 tons of merchant vessels in 1940, and 1,156,000 tons in 1941. By the autumn of 1940 the British government turned increasingly to North America, especially the United States. Fewer merchant ships were available for purchase than had been expected, and new construction in existing shipyards had to compete with US Navy warship programmes. In November 1940 (the month of President Roosevelt's re-election), a British purchasing mission began to fund development of new shipyards for 'emergency' merchant ships on green-field sites in the US. Only 34,000 tons (five vessels) were completed for Britain in American shipyards in 1941, but the pre-Pearl Harbor investment would pay critical dividends in 1942 and afterwards, and for the US as well as Britain.[18]

The shortage of escort ships was also tackled. Construction of the classic escort, the destroyer, continued; some eleven were launched in 1940, and twenty-five in 1941. However, destroyers were expensive, multi-purpose vessels. They were built in specialist naval shipyards; they could operate at high speed with the main fleet and take part in mass torpedo attacks. Another British ocean-going warship type – the sloop – had been built in the 1930s and had a potential escort role (AA or A/S). Sloops were similar in size to destroyers (1,000 tons), but slower and not armed for fleet actions. Relatively few were as yet in commission. Some fifty-five fleet destroyers of the 'V' and 'W' classes, left over from the big World War I programmes, were available in 1939. As the war progressed, most were taken in hand and converted to specialised escorts against U-boats or aircraft, fitted with more effective guns, sensors and depth charges, and sometimes with new fuel tanks (and fewer boilers) for extended range. There were also fifty 'four-stacker' ex-American destroyers, which President Roosevelt agreed to supply to Britain in September 1940 – and promptly delivered – in exchange for base rights in the Western Hemisphere. They were renamed with town names which were used in both the US and the UK. The 'Towns' have been described as 'fifty ships that saved the world', but they were over-age vessels and not in good condition. Their military value as ocean-going escorts was limited, even after their modification in the UK; they sank only three U-boats.[19] They were very important diplomatically – as a symbol of American support to Britain – but that story will be told in Chapter 8.

Fortunately, belated steps had been taken shortly before the war to strengthen the escort force. In early 1939 the Admiralty ordered a class of small (1,000-ton) destroyers. These 'Hunt' class vessels were named after fox-hunting packs (in an era when such activity was smiled upon); the first, HMS *Atherstone* (named after the Atherstone Hunt in the Midlands), was completed in March 1940. There were twenty-three vessels in the first batch, mostly available by the end of 1941, with another sixty-one entering service in 1942 and 1943.

Work also began on a very large class of small escorts, the 'Flower' class. The first sixty were ordered in the summer of 1939, as the likelihood of war increased, and a further eighty-one by the middle of 1940. The classification 'corvette' was revived, and the first class was named after flowering plants. The lead ship was HMS *Gladiolus*, laid down in October 1939 and commissioned in April 1940; she would be lost with her entire crew of sixty-five men while escorting a convoy south of Iceland in October 1941. The 'Flowers' were immortalised by the writing of Nicholas Monsarrat about the fictional HMS *Compass Rose* in the novel *The Cruel Sea*; Monsarrat himself served in HMS *Campanula*.

The 'Flower' class, based on a 'whale-catcher' design, were rotund little ships with a single funnel. Their length was about 200 feet – two-thirds that of a destroyer; displacement was 950 tons. They could be constructed in the British (or Canadian) commercial shipyards which normally built small merchant vessels. Commercial steam engines (not special purpose steam turbines as in destroyers) drove a single screw (propeller); maximum speed was 16 knots, a little less than that of a surfaced U-boat. Main armament was originally one 4-inch gun and about forty depth charges; they were equipped with ASDIC and – later – with radar. The 'Flowers' (like the Type VII U-boats) were not originally intended for Atlantic operations; vessels in the first group built rolled excessively and had limited fuel capacity. Nevertheless, they could operate with some effectiveness in the open ocean, and later batches had improved range and habitability. As soon as it became clear in the summer of 1940 that an Atlantic escort was going to be required, the Admiralty ordered a larger twin-screw escort vessel (called a 'frigate'); the 'River' class began to enter service at the very end of 1941.

The 'Flowers', meanwhile, were also a major type used by the Royal Canadian Navy (RCN) throughout much of the war. Originally the Canadian shipyards were to build sixty corvettes, half to be supplied to the British. When the Royal Navy shifted its new construction to the more capable frigates, the Canadian-built 'Flower' class remained as the core of the so-called 'sheep dog navy' which was active off Canada's east coast. Operating in difficult weather conditions, with limited training and second-rate sonar, and tasked with escorting slower (more vulnerable) merchantmen, the Newfoundland Escort Force of the RCN had some major failures in the autumn of 1941, when U-boats extended their operations into Canadian waters. Eastbound convoy SC.42 lost sixteen ships southeast of Greenland to U-boats in September 1941, and SC.52 had to abort its transatlantic trip. The Canadians would have to persevere with corvettes into 1942 and 1943.

British destroyers and corvettes began to have more and more success against the U-boats. In a series of interconnected convoy battles in the western Atlantic in March 1941 British escorts accounted for three of the bemedalled captains involved in the attack on SC.7 and HX.79. Prien and Schepke went down with their boats, and Kretschmer was captured and spent the rest of the war in Canada. Schepke's *U 100* was rammed and sunk; this event was doubly significant, as the first 'kill' achieved with the help of radar, an early Type 286M set aboard the destroyer HMS *Vanoc*. In a common German chronology of the U-boat campaign, March 1941 was seen as the end of a first, short 'Happy Time' (*glückliche Zeit*).

Throughout the year the number and effectiveness of the British and Canadian surface escorts increased. In December 1941, at the end of the first round of the U-boat war, the 36th Escort Group (EG.36) under Captain F.J. 'Johnnie' Walker – two sloops and seven corvettes – led the outstanding defence of convoy HG.76, inbound from Gibraltar. For the first time the escorts inflicted a large number of 'kills' – four U-boats. Walker, a pre-war A/S specialist, was awarded the DSO for this operation; he would go on to become the most successful British escort commander of the war. Like the October 1940 wolf-pack attack on SC.7 and HX.79, the defence of HG.76 was not typical of that time. British 'success' in this period was still largely passive. Merchant ships avoided attack, but escorts did not destroy U-boats. The losses of German submarines in the Atlantic stayed about the same – eleven in the first half of the year, fourteen in the second. But the defence of HG.76 certainly showed the potential of well-led and well-equipped escorts.

That the Atlantic battle was also a sea/air war became evident even in this first period. The operations of British patrol planes were gradually extended out into the ocean. Coastal Command was a separate organisation within the Royal Air Force (alongside Fighter Command and Bomber Command), eventually with four operational groups. From the outbreak of war No. 15 Group was responsible for the Western Approaches, the area of the Atlantic lying directly to the west of Ireland and Great Britain; No. 19 Group was formed in early 1941 to take responsibility for the southwest.

Initially the planes of Coastal Command lacked range and a weapon able to sink a U-boat. Even surfaced submarines could be detected by them only in daytime and clear weather. The patrol planes still had some effect, as they forced the U-boats to submerge, in this way cutting their speed by three-quarters, and reducing their ability to locate targets. Aircraft could also direct better-armed surface ships into an attack.

During 1940–41 the aircraft and equipment of Coastal Command gradually improved in terms of quantity and quality.[20] More of the big four-engined Short Sunderland flying boats began to enter service, although production was initially slow. Further orders of twin-engined Lockheed Hudson shore-based patrol planes arrived from America in 1940, and at the start of 1941 the first Consolidated Catalina flying boats. Potentially even more important because of its size and range was the Consolidated Model 32 heavy bomber, which began to enter RAF Coastal Command service in small numbers in late 1941 as the 'Liberator'. As the U-boat threat increased, aircraft of other types were seconded from RAF Bomber Command, including twin-engined Bristol Blenheim and Beaufort light bombers and Armstrong Whitworth Whitley and Vickers Wellington medium bombers. Coastal Command aircraft operating from Northern Ireland and Scotland helped force the U-boats further and further out from the North Channel approaches, which meant that the area in which the convoys could hide from their attackers was greatly increased. Meanwhile invaluable air bases became available in Iceland (occupied in May 1940). Airborne radar (ASV) and more effective weapons (powerful depth charges) gradually entered service. Nevertheless, the ability actually to sink U-boats would not really develop until 1942. Only after two and a half years of war, in July 1942, did a Coastal Command aircraft destroy a U-boat in the Atlantic on its own, rather than in co-operation with a surface ship.[21]

As for the Germans, a challenge for the British with sea/air operations was organisational. As already mentioned, the shore-based aircraft of Coastal Command had been kept within the RAF when the ship-based Fleet Air Arm was transferred to the Royal Navy in 1937–39. Nevertheless, in December 1940, partly as a result of the autumn shipping losses, Coastal Command was put under the *operational* control of the Admiralty, although in other respects it remained within the RAF; it continued to be led by RAF air marshals, by Frederick Bowhill until June 1941, and then by Philip Joubert de la Ferté. Co-operation between the services was now certainly better than in Germany or in the US. The headquarters of RAF No. 15 Group was co-located in Liverpool with the Western Approaches command of the Navy.

Alongside surface ships and aircraft, the British were able to develop electronic warfare. ASDIC (sonar) has already been mentioned. Radar was steadily developed for use in aircraft and surface ships. The first generation of warship radars, Type 286, were based on the RAF airborne ASV Mk I radar; this Type 286 (with the relatively long wavelength of 1.5 metres) was not ideal, but it allowed escorting destroyers and corvettes to detect surfaced U-boats at night – something which ASDIC could not do.[22]

Intelligence, more generally, played an increasing role in the Battle of the Atlantic. Since Admiral Dönitz's pack tactics demanded frequent use of radios, it was possible for the British to get a reasonably good picture of their operations using shore-based direction finding (DF). When it became possible in 1942 to mount high-frequency DF (HF/DF, or 'huff-duff') on board escorts – something the Germans thought technically unlikely – this became a very important tactical tool.

Above and beyond that was the role of 'special intelligence', now generally referred to as 'Ultra'. Some decades after the end of World War II – in the late 1970s – it was revealed that British codebreaking had been very successful.[23] The achievements of the mathematician Alan Turing and the codebreakers at the signals intelligence centre at Bletchley Park, north of London (also known as the Government Code and Cypher School or GC&CS), have now become an essential part of the British narrative of the war. In the early summer of 1941 Bletchley Park developed the ability to decrypt important signals sent by the Germans using the Enigma code machine. This was the result of a combination of efforts to capture code materials from vulnerable German vessels in the northern seas and some good fortune, notably the taking of Lemp's *U 110* in May 1941, with an Enigma machine and code materials aboard. Naval intelligence-gathering of all kinds, especially about submarines, but also about Axis warships and auxiliary cruisers (raiders), was skilfully co-ordinated by the Operational Intelligence Centre (OIC), set up in the Admiralty building in London. A key role was played here by Paymaster-Commander Norman Denning. The decryption of U-boat sighting reports and of directives from U-boat HQ, coming on top of DF, gave the British the ability to route convoys around concentrations of U-boats. This was especially significant in the second half of 1941, when the number of U-boats available was still small compared to the expanse of the North Atlantic; British convoys had plenty of room for evasive manoeuvre.

In the summer of 1941 overall British shipping losses in the North Atlantic, mostly from U-boats, attacks, took a remarkable drop. The monthly total fell from 302,000 tons (GRT) in June (comparable to seventy-five ships of 4,000 tons) to 61,000 tons in July (comparable to fifteen ships; see also Table 5.1 above). Writing in 1993, and attempting to argue the overall importance of British codebreaking in shortening World War II as a whole, the British historian F.H. Hinsley maintained that in the second half of 1941, 'The first victory over the U-boats had already . . . been achieved *entirely on the basis of Ultra*' (my emphasis). This was, Hinsley claimed, 'At a time when the British anti-submarine defences were woefully weak and merchant shipping woefully scarce, and when the U-boat fleet was at last becoming a formidable force.'[24] Harry Hinsley was both an important participant in wartime intelligence (as a remarkably young man) and one of the great historians of World War II. But each of these points – the weak defences, the scarcity of merchant shipping, and the strength of the U-boat force – is debatable.

British A/S defences had been steadily improving in quantity and quality. The actual shipping problem was not acute, and as we have seen, it was being dealt with. The official historian of British wartime merchant shipping did state that the summer of 1941 was 'the most anxious moment of the war' because the volume of imports had been declining and the future flow of imports was unclear,[25] but anxiety regarding the future was not the same as current reality.

As for Hinsley's central point about Ultra, evasive routing of convoys was indeed made possible in part by the Ultra breakthrough (and in part by DF). But other factors were involved. An Admiralty instruction of June 1941 stipulated that merchant ships capable of a speed up to 15 knots should sail in convoy, rather than independently; the earlier limit had been 13 knots, and this change reduced the number of 'independents' lost in the Atlantic from thirty-five ships a month to only twelve.[26]

Another major non-Ultra explanation for the decline of Atlantic sinkings was the dispersal of the U-boat campaign. The Italian armed forces had suffered major setbacks at the hands of the British towards the end of 1941, and in response Hitler ordered twenty U-boats into the Mediterranean. Although these submarines had much success against British warships, they were not able to return to the Atlantic. Meanwhile six U-boats were sent to defend occupied Norway and to support the campaign against northern Russia.

The United States Navy became increasingly involved in the Atlantic in the late autumn of 1941 (see Chapter 8, pp. 165–9), but this had only a limited effect on the U-boat war. More important as a limiting factor was American neutrality – and the German desire that it should continue. U-boats were not yet operating in the western Atlantic. The attack on Pearl Harbor, and the German declaration of war on the US four days later (on 11 December 1941), would drastically change that situation, although initially to the advantage of the Third Reich.

GERMAN HEAVY SHIPS AT SEA

As well as U-boat operations, the year from the summer of 1940 to the summer of 1941 saw the greatest activity of German heavy ships in the Atlantic and also the depredations of disguised commerce raiders, operating in the spirit of Admiral Raeder's Kreuzerkrieg. The commerce raiders – sometimes described as 'auxiliary cruisers' (*Hilfskreuzer*) – could operate against shipping all across the world, and were intended to compel the British to spread their forces thinly over the oceans. The first batch of six disguised raiders, which had sailed in the spring and summer of 1940, were fast merchantmen armed with six 5.9-inch guns, torpedo tubes and a floatplane. With three later vessels, they achieved considerable success in the South Atlantic, the Indian Ocean and the Pacific. The force was small, however, and from the middle of 1941 it became more difficult to break out into the Atlantic or to return home to a European port. More and more Allied patrols made the seas more dangerous; the *Pinguin* and *Atlantis* were caught and sunk by British cruisers in 1941 (in the latter case as a result of Ultra decrypts). From 1942 the last two raiders were based in Japan (where the final survivor, the *Michel*, was sunk by an American submarine in October 1943). Altogether nine auxiliary cruisers accounted for 138 ships (858,000 tons) between April 1940 and October 1943.[27]

German heavy warships – battleships and heavy cruisers – sank fewer tons of British merchant shipping, but they had a more dramatic effect and unlike the U-boats caused the suspension of convoys. They were sent out into the Atlantic and beyond, once the damage from the 1940 Norwegian campaign had been repaired. The Naval War Staff took advantage of the long winter nights, and the new availability of transit bases in Norway, as part of the 'intensified' war on shipping ordered by Hitler in August 1940.

Work on the Z-Plan battleships had halted immediately on the outbreak of war. The shipyards continued to work only on three vessels that were near completion: the battleships *Bismarck* and *Tirpitz*, and the 'Austrian' heavy cruiser *Prinz Eugen*. At the end of 1940 the units actually available for Atlantic operations were the battleships *Scharnhorst* and *Gneisenau*, and the heavy cruisers *Admiral Scheer*, *Lützow* (ex-*Deutschland*) and *Admiral Hipper*.[28]

The renewed warship raiding campaign began with the breakout of the *Admiral Scheer*; she had missed the Norwegian fighting while completing a major refit. Under the command of Captain Theodor Krancke, the heavy cruiser (pocket battleship) sortied into the dark Atlantic through the Denmark Strait (between Iceland and Greenland) in October 1940. She intercepted convoy HX.84 in the mid-Atlantic and sank its sole escort, the armed merchant cruiser HMS *Jervis Bay*. The hopeless battle in failing light gave the convoy time to scatter, although six out of thirty-eight ships were sunk. The diesel-powered *Scheer* spent five months on the high seas, cruising as far as the Seychelles in the Indian Ocean; she was re-supplied by strategically pre-positioned German supply ships. She sank eleven more vessels before slipping home, again through the Denmark Strait, in March 1941. For his epic voyage of 46,000 miles Krancke was awarded the Reich's highest military award (the Knight's Cross with Oak Leaves) and promoted to the rank of rear admiral; he later became naval representative at the Führer's headquarters.

The second ship to sail, in December 1940, was the heavy cruiser *Admiral Hipper*. She had been repaired after minor damage in the Norwegian campaign – the collision with the *Glowworm* off Trondheim. Neither the *Hipper* nor her sister ship, the *Prinz Eugen*, would prove to be effective long-range commerce-raiders, due to their temperamental high-pressure boilers and relatively short range. The *Hipper* caused a stir on her arrival at Brest in northwestern France at the end of the month – the first big ship to use one of the western bases. She carried out one cruise into the Atlantic in February 1941 before returning for repairs to Germany via the Denmark Strait.

Operation BERLIN, the sortie of the battleships *Scharnhorst* and *Gneisenau* which began in late January 1941, was the high point of the heavy ship Kreuzerkrieg in the Atlantic. In command was Admiral Günther Lütjens. Born in 1889, he was two years older than Dönitz, and during the 1914–18 war had commanded a torpedo-boat flotilla off Flanders. In April 1940 Lütjens had been C-in-C, Scouting Force. After the temporary removal of the Fleet Commander (Flottenchef), Admiral Wilhelm Marschall, Lütjens took over the naval forces that covered the Norwegian invasion; in this capacity he commanded the *Scharnhorst* and the *Gneisenau* in the inconclusive duel with the *Renown* off Narvik. In June 1940 he permanently took over from Marschall as Flottenchef. Tight-lipped and humourless, Lütjens was an effective tactical commander.

The *Scharnhorst* and the *Gneisenau* departed from Kiel on 23 January 1941. Admiral John Tovey had replaced Admiral Forbes as C-in-C of the Home Fleet the previous month. Tovey had been in charge of Admiral Pound's destroyers in the Mediterranean Fleet in the late 1930s, and more recently commander of Admiral Cunningham's light forces – cruisers and destroyers – there. The

Admiralty were aware that a major German sortie was possible. Advance warning came from analysis of German radio traffic, and from reports that a battle group had passed through the Kattegat and Skagerrak. Tovey now posted Home Fleet cruisers north and south of Iceland and took the Home Fleet to sea. Lütjens first attempted to take his ships through the Faroes–Iceland gap, but a British cruiser was sighted and the German ships hastily pulled back. After killing some time in the Norwegian Sea, Lütjens dashed through the Denmark Strait a week later – without incident; by this time Tovey had had to return to Scapa Flow to refuel.

Taking on fuel from tankers, the *Scharnhorst* and the *Gneisenau* operated in the Atlantic for nearly two months. A number of convoys escorted by slow British battleships were encountered, but contact was avoided. In mid-March they sank sixteen ships sailing independently off Newfoundland. The two battleships reached Brest on 22 March after a two-month cruise of nearly 18,000 miles, which had taken them briefly to the west coast of Africa.

The long mission had been very successful, but it put a considerable strain on the machinery of the ships. The *Scharnhorst* had serious problems with her boilers and would be under repair until July 1941. Meanwhile, the strategically valuable surface ship bases in northwestern France were vulnerable to attack The two ships came under repeated air raids from the UK. Early in April the *Gneisenau* was hit by a Coastal Command torpedo bomber in Brest harbour (a daring attack for which the British pilot was posthumously awarded the Victoria Cross). The battleship was badly damaged; she was put in dry dock and three days later a British bomber hit her there. Neither the *Gneisenau* nor the *Scharnhorst* would be battle-ready for several – critical – months.

Admiral Lütjens's second Atlantic sortie, code-named RHINE EXERCISE (RHEINÜBUNG), would be one of the most dramatic naval actions of World War II. The intention of the Naval War Staff was now to mount repeated raids by surface ships into the Atlantic. When the *Scharnhorst* and the *Gneisenau* arrived in Brest, Raeder had immediately begun to plan a bigger operation for the new moon period of late April. This would introduce the Navy's newest ships, the battleship *Bismarck* and the cruiser *Prinz Eugen*. The two vessels would attack convoys as a unit, the battleship distracting or destroying the British escort – which might be a cruiser or one of the older battleships – while the *Prinz Eugen* attacked the merchant ships with torpedoes and heavy artillery.

A mine explosion near the *Prinz Eugen* off Kiel in April 1941 damaged that cruiser sufficiently to force postponement of RHINE EXERCISE to the next new moon period at the end of May. Lütjens and Admiral Raeder now disagreed about whether the operation should go ahead. Lütjens feared that if his battle group went out on its own the British would be able to concentrate their forces against it. He preferred to wait until at least one of the battleships at Brest was back in service; delay would also allow use of the *Bismarck*'s sister ship, the *Tirpitz*, which was currently working up in the Baltic. Lütjens was also concerned that the summer months were the time of long daylight in northern latitudes, making it difficult to break clear of any enemy ships that had made contact.

Admiral Raeder wanted immediate action, ostensibly to keep up the pressure on the British convoy system. He claimed in his memoirs that he was also concerned about growing American participation in the Atlantic war.[29] In addition, the Grossadmiral may have wanted to achieve another striking victory for the Kriegsmarine before the Army covered itself in glory again in the Russian campaign. He probably also expected that a repetition of Operation BERLIN could be staged without great difficulties at this time; the Royal Navy was under great pressure in the eastern Mediterranean, with the failure of the Greek campaign and the Axis threat to Crete. Hitler knew about plans for the new Atlantic raid; he visited the *Bismarck* and the *Tirpitz* at the port of Gotenhafen (now Gdynia, near Danzig) on 5 May 1941, and had a meeting with Captain Lindemann of the *Bismarck*, who put forward his concerns, especially over the danger from carrier aircraft. (An Italian battleship had been damaged by an aircraft torpedo at sea in late March.) Hitler accepted the risk. It is probable – although there is no direct evidence – that he believed the Atlantic actions would help distract attention from his preparations for a surprise attack on the USSR (which on 30 April was set to begin on 22 June).

The surface forces of the Royal Navy were still in a strong position in the Atlantic. Admiral Tovey's Home Fleet now operated from a better-protected permanent base at Scapa Flow. The first two new battleships, the *King George V* and the *Prince of Wales*, were now in service. Also with the Home Fleet were the powerful post-war *Rodney* with her nine 16-inch guns, and two battle cruisers: the *Hood* with eight 15-inch guns and the *Repulse*, with six 15-inch guns; unfortunately, the *Rodney* was only capable of 23 knots, and the *Hood* and the *Repulse* had not been fully modernised. The Gibraltar-based Force H, under Admiral Somerville, was positioned to operate in either the western Mediterranean or the Atlantic. This now included the third battle cruiser, the modernised *Renown*, as well as the carrier *Ark Royal*. Even newer British fleet carriers were now coming into service. Force H first two had gone to the Mediterranean (where they had much success against the Italians), but Admiral Tovey received the third, the *Victorious*, in May 1941. The four unmodernised 'Revenge' class battleships were slow, but two of them were in the western Atlantic defending important convoys, as was the 23-knot battleship *Nelson*.

The limitations of the Royal Navy in the Atlantic in May 1941 at the time of the *Bismarck* chase were the result of the commitment of much of the fleet to the Mediterranean. Leaving out cruisers and destroyers, the forces operating there under Admiral Cunningham included the relatively fast battleships of the 'Queen Elizabeth' class, including the recently modernised *Queen Elizabeth*, *Valiant* and *Warspite*. Also there was the new armoured carrier *Formidable*, while an older carrier, the *Furious*, was tied up in Mediterranean duties (ferrying aircraft to Malta); the *Eagle*, meanwhile, was returning from Alexandria via the Cape of Good Hope.[30] All these ships could have played a major active role against the *Bismarck* and the *Prinz Eugen* had Britain not been fighting a battle-fleet war on two fronts.

Unlike the earlier Atlantic breakouts, Lütjens and the *Bismarck* battle group failed to achieve surprise or to slip unseen into the open ocean through the passages north or south of Iceland. Having left Gotenhafen in the early hours of Monday, 19 May 1941, and passed through the Great Belt during the night, the *Bismarck* and the *Prinz Eugen* were sighted by a Swedish cruiser in the Kattegat on Tuesday. On Wednesday afternoon they were spotted in a fjord near Bergen by a long-range RAF reconnaissance Spitfire from Wick in northeastern Scotland. Tovey had sufficient warning to send his heavy ships out to reinforce the cruisers that were screening the access routes to the Atlantic. The *Hood* and the *Prince of Wales*, under Admiral Holland, new commander of the Home Fleet Battle Cruiser Squadron, sortied from Scapa Flow at 12.50 a.m. on Thursday morning. Their destination was the most likely interception point, the exit from the Denmark Strait, with its 100-mile-wide ice-free passage between Iceland and Greenland.

Some twenty-two hours later, at 10.45 p.m. on Thursday, Tovey himself departed from Scapa Flow aboard the *King George V*, along with the carrier *Victorious*, cruisers and destroyers. His aim was to cover Lütjens's southern route, between the Faroes and Iceland. The battle cruiser *Repulse* sortied from the Clyde and joined Tovey at sea. The battleship *Rodney* had departed independently from the Clyde at midday, en route for a refit in the United States.[31]

Admiral Lütjens made a number of fateful – and fatal – decisions. He refuelled the *Prinz Eugen* in Norway, but not the *Bismarck*. Even though he knew that his battle group had been sighted and that he had lost the element of overall surprise, he decided at midday on Thursday to proceed immediately into the Atlantic, and to take the route north of Iceland. This choice was probably based on mistaken Luftwaffe reports that all the Home Fleet's capital ships were still at Scapa Flow.

Early on Friday evening, 23 May, the two radar-equipped British cruisers which had been covering the eastern entrance to the Denmark Strait detected the approaching German battle group and fell in behind it as 'shadowers', one of them using her new Type 284 radar rangefinder. (In the January 1941 sortie Lütjens had been able to break contact with the ships following him; radar and long summer daylight now made this much more difficult.) The next day, worse was to come for the German admiral. In the early light of a brilliantly clear Saturday morning, as the German battle group exited from the strait, west of Iceland, Lütjens was stunned to run into two British capital ships. He had been ambushed.

On paper the British had a clear gunnery advantage, with eight 15-inch (*Hood*) and ten 14-inch guns (*Prince of Wales*) against eight 15-inch guns. The *Bismarck* and her sister ship the *Tirpitz* are often depicted as leviathans, but they were in some respects built to a conservative design. The gun battery of eight 15-inch guns (in four turrets) was identical to that of the *Hood* and the nine British battleships built for World War I; it was inferior to that of the 1927 'Nelson' class (nine 16-inch guns). Although capable of 29 knots the *Bismarck* was not especially fast. On the other hand, the ship's dimensions and heavy armour did make her less vulnerable to battle damage. And British intelligence had underestimated her size; the *Bismarck* was supposed to be a 35,000-ton ship, but she actually had a standard displacement of 41,700 tons and a deep load displacement of 52,600 tons.

The *Prince of Wales* was a new battleship of the 'King George V' class. Her guns were only 14-inch, but she had ten of them, in three turrets. She was very well armoured, and with a standard displacement of 36,700 tons she also now exceeded the old treaty limit. Capable of 28 knots, the vessel was considerably faster than earlier British battleships. Her radar suite was the most comprehensive of any ship in the world. On the negative side, she had been completed only two months earlier, so her crew were not fully trained, and some of her equipment had teething problems; she had had to put to sea with shipyard technicians still on board.

The *Hood*, the ultimate battle cruiser – the last and biggest ever built – displaced 42,300 tons. She had been designed before the Battle of Jutland, but altered while under construction to increase her protection. She had been due for a major modernisation in 1940, but this was interrupted by the beginning of the war. The limited horizontal armour of the *Hood* made her vulnerable to very long-range plunging shellfire.[32]

The *Hood* (flagship of Admiral Holland) and the *Prince of Wales* completed their interception of the German battle group and opened fire. The resulting engagement on the morning of 24 May was very short, and for the British catastrophic. Admiral Holland turned towards the enemy to close the range as rapidly as possible, but the angle of approach restricted the fire from the rear turrets of his ships and provided a better target for the German guns. The British could not at first tell the two German ships apart, and they wasted some of their salvoes on the *Prinz Eugen*. The fifth salvo from the *Bismarck*, fired at 6.00 a.m. at a range of 16,000 yards (about 9 miles), caused a very intense magazine fire aboard the

Hood, after which the giant vessel broke in half and sank, with almost her entire crew of 1,418 men (there were three survivors). One of the *Bismarck*'s junior gunnery officers (and the most senior crew member to survive), Lieutenant Müllenheim-Rechberg, observed what happened through the eyepiece of his gun director: 'At first the *Hood* was nowhere to be seen; in her place was a colossal pillar of black smoke reaching into the sky. Gradually, at the foot of the pillar, I made out the bow of the battle cruiser projecting upwards at an angle, a sure sign she had broken in two.'[33] Vice Admiral Holland, who went down with his flagship, was one of the most senior officers in the British armed forces to be killed in action in the 1939–45 war. A further exchange involving the *Bismarck* resulted in several hits on the *Prince of Wales* and was accompanied by a partial gunnery breakdown aboard the British battleship. In this situation her captain decided to lay a smoke screen and break off the action.

The sudden loss of the *Hood* is surely one of the most stunning events in the naval history of the 1939–45 war. A Board of Inquiry was held in the summer of 1941, its evidence based on observations from other British ships during the battle; after 1945 more information was obtained from the German side. The wreck lay at a depth of 2,800 metres, so considerable advances in oceanographic technology were required before the site could be reached. An expedition led by the oceanographer David Mearns located the remains of the *Hood* in July 2001, and the main pieces of the hull and the surrounding debris field were examined externally by a remotely operated vehicle (ROV). This unique opportunity did not fundamentally challenge the original judgement that the *Hood* had been destroyed by a 15-inch shell from the *Bismarck* which penetrated her relatively thin horizontal armour and caused an intense magazine fire involving some 120 tons of cordite in the after magazines.[34] (Three smaller British battle cruisers had been sunk after massive internal explosions at Jutland in 1916.)

Although the Battle of the Denmark Strait was a defeat for the Royal Navy, it also had fatal consequences for Operation RHINE EXERCISE. Unlike the *Hood*, the *Prince of Wales* had at least succeeded in damaging the *Bismarck*. The German battleship was hit by three 14-inch shells. She suffered only minor structural damage, but did develop a serious fuel leak. This – and the loss of the element of operational surprise – put paid to Admiral Lütjens's original full-scale commerce-raiding expedition. He now changed his plans and headed for Saint-Nazaire in western France to effect repairs. In the early evening of the Saturday battle the *Bismarck* briefly reversed course; this was to allow the undamaged *Prinz Eugen* to break loose from the shadowing British cruisers and set out on an independent – and unsuccessful – hunt for British shipping.

Around midnight on 24–25 May (Saturday to Sunday), a few hours after the *Prinz Eugen* had parted company, British torpedo planes mounted an attack on the *Bismarck*. This was the threat which had most worried Admiral Lütjens since the planning stage of RHINE EXERCISE. The Swordfish biplanes from the *Victorious* achieved a torpedo hit, but did no serious damage (although the *Bismarck*'s fuel leak may have been made worse). The fleet carrier had been commissioned only two months earlier (like the *Prince of Wales*) and had been rushed to sea when the German breakout began; she had been about to embark on a convoy escort mission as part of her working up. As a result, nine Swordfish of 825 Squadron made up her entire strike force, and they had not had recent torpedo-attack training.

After the Swordfish attack there followed – on Sunday the 25th – a chain of errors and bad judgements on both sides. The shadowing British cruisers lost contact in the early hours of the day. The Admiralty and Tovey – unaware of the extent of damage to the *Bismarck* – did not know whether the enemy battle group were headed west into the Atlantic for commerce raiding, south to a French base, or back home through the Faroes–Iceland gap. Admiral Lütjens, for his part, did not realise that the enemy cruisers had lost contact, as their radar emissions could still be detected. A few hours after dawn on Sunday, and evidently thinking his position was known, Lütjens made several long radio reports to Berlin. These transmissions could not be immediately decrypted, but they enabled British DF stations to ascertain the *Bismarck*'s general location. Then, however, the data was misplotted aboard the *King George V*, which charged off for seven hours in the wrong direction. Fortunately Lütjens had reduced his speed to conserve fuel – partly because he had neglected to top up his bunkers in Norway – and so the British error did not prove fatal.

By Sunday evening the Admiralty had a good sense of the *Bismarck*'s position and was convinced she was headed for France. On Monday (the 26th) British aircraft sighted the German battleship. In mid-morning she was spotted by a long-range Catalina flying boat from Northern Ireland. The Catalinas had been bought from America and reached operational status in the RAF in early 1941; this one had a US Navy co-pilot and was equipped with (British) ASV Mk II search radar. A second sighting was made by a Swordfish from the fleet carrier *Ark Royal*, which was steaming up from Gibraltar. However, Tovey's *King George V* and the *Rodney*, now operating together, were too far behind to intercept the *Bismarck* if she maintained her course and speed; they were also short of fuel. The German battleship was running through heavy seas, but the only thing that stood in the way of her arrival in a safe French port was the *Ark Royal* air group.

The battle doctrine of the Fleet Air Arm, developed in the 1930s, was often described as 'Find, fix and strike'. It was recognised that one or even two air-dropped torpedoes would have little chance of sinking a heavily armoured battleship, but the damage caused might 'fix' the target – slow it down or stop it – allowing British heavy ships to catch up and engage with their heavy artillery. The British Swordfish torpedo bombers had the configuration of World War I aircraft: biplanes with fixed (non-retractable) wheels, and with open cockpits. These characteristics give the attacks by the Swordfish from the *Victorious* (on Saturday) and the *Ark Royal* (on Monday) an aspect at once heroic and quixotic. The Swordfish has often been described as 'rickety' or 'ancient', but in reality it was neither: it was a large, robust aircraft that could operate in rough weather. The prototype first flew in April 1934 (only a year and a half before the first Spitfire); and Swordfish remained in production – as an A/S aircraft – until August 1944. Some of the machines which took part in the two *Bismarck* attacks were equipped with ASV Mk IIN radar. The aircraft was certainly vulnerable to modern enemy fighters, but there were none of those in the mid-Atlantic. Flying with well-trained and courageous crew members, the Swordfish was an effective weapon, and the *Ark Royal* had thirty of them on board.

The first attempt on Monday by the *Ark Royal* torpedo bombers was mounted late in the afternoon. As it happened, the object of their attack was the cruiser *Sheffield*, which had closed in to shadow the *Bismarck*. The torpedoes all exploded as they hit the water, due to their over-sensitive magnetic detonators. The *Ark Royal* was now, however, not far away, and her air group was able to land, rearm, and mount another strike on Monday evening – this time their torpedoes were fitted with more reliable contact detonators. The *Bismarck* had thick armour, but her air defences were weak. She mounted only four twin 4.1-inch and four twin 37mm on either beam.[35]

Despite flying through a heavy gale, the Swordfish achieved three torpedo hits. The critical one was near the *Bismarck*'s stern, and it jammed her rudder machinery. The battleship could now only move in circles, or very slowly, while manoeuvring with her outboard propellers. Lütjens sent a doom-laden message to Berlin explaining his situation. A few hours after dawn on Tuesday, 27 May, the *King George V* and the *Rodney*, a more lethal team than the *Hood* and the *Prince of Wales*, caught up with the staggering German battleship. They opened fire with accurate gunnery; this time no second enemy ship diverted the British gunlayers. The *Bismarck* was unable to achieve any hits before her gunfire-control equipment and guns were put out of action. About fifteen minutes into the action the first British hit, by the 16-inch guns of the *Rodney*, ravaged the *Bismarck*'s forward superstructure and bridge, probably killing Admiral Lütjens. The two British battleships then poured 300 to 400 heavy shells into the crippled vessel, while accompanying heavy cruisers fired guns and torpedoes.

All of the *Bismarck*'s guns were put out of action and her superstructure was wrecked. Nevertheless, the ship had been designed with a very broad beam, good compartmentalisation and thick armour. Because the *Bismarck* took hits both to port and to starboard, she avoided the immediate danger of capsizing. Admiral Tovey ordered the cruiser *Dorsetshire* to fire torpedoes to finish her. The *Bismarck* sank at 10.39 a.m. Over 2,000 German naval personnel went down with her; there were only 114 survivors. Who actually sank the *Bismarck* is an academic question. Some German survivors claimed that the ship had been scuttled, but in any event aircraft torpedoes, battleship and cruiser gunfire and the torpedoes of the *Dorsetshire* had caused fatal damage. Whatever happened, the hulk would certainly have gone to the bottom within a few hours. Like the *Hood*, the remains of the *Bismarck* became accessible only half a century after the battle. The wreck was located by Robert Ballard in June 1989 at a depth of 4,790 metres; it was lying on the bottom, upright and reasonably intact.

On 6 June, ten days after the loss of the *Bismarck*, Admiral Raeder was summoned to the Berghof to explain events to the Führer. The written report made available to Hitler was not critical of the late Admiral Lütjens or his decisions. An underestimation of British radar was noted. It had been wrongly believed that British warships were not equipped with *DeTe* (*Dezimeter-Telegraphie*) 'location equipment'; the assumption had been that there was still a good chance of an unobserved passage into the Atlantic. The mission (Raeder asserted) had been justified, and the taking of risks was inevitable, unless German surface ships were to give up all attempts to attack British trade.

Hitler asked the obvious question: why had Lütjens not returned home after sinking the *Hood*? Admiral Raeder replied that a return through the northern narrows would have presented 'far more dangers' than a sortie into the open Atlantic. Asked why Lütjens did not finish off the *Prince of Wales*, Raeder answered that the British battleship had taken evasive action, and that Lütjens had evidently not wanted to risk damage that would have prevented his commerce-raiding mission.

Lütjens had in fact made bad decisions; some of them have already been mentioned. He had persevered with RHINE EXERCISE even when he knew his battle group had been sighted in southern Norway; he had not topped up the *Bismarck*'s fuel bunkers there; he had risked an engagement with the *Prince of Wales* and the *Hood*, rather than turning away; he had not turned for home through the Denmark Strait after sinking the *Hood*; he broke radio silence on 25 May. Admiral Raeder and the Naval War Staff, however, bore an even greater responsibility; they had underestimated Navy. A balanced preview of the *Bismarck* operation should have taken into account the quantitative and qualitative superiority of the British forces in the Atlantic. They had become stronger during 1941, despite distractions and losses in the Mediterranean. The Royal

Navy in the Atlantic now had a greater number of modern ships – battleships, aircraft carriers and cruisers. More ships and aircraft were equipped with radar. RAF air coverage over the North Atlantic, based in the United Kingdom, Iceland and Newfoundland, was also much better. Signals intelligence had improved – at this stage due not so much to Enigma decrypts as to better radio direction finding (DF) and traffic analysis (TA). In addition, the growing RAF bomber force made the use of forward bases like Brest and Saint-Nazaire hazardous for big German surface ships. In effect they made co-ordinated German operations very difficult.

The Third Reich, meanwhile, was still much inferior at sea. Ocean surveillance by the Luftwaffe in the mid-Atlantic was almost non-existent. The U-boat force was still small, and little effort had been made to co-ordinate its actions with the *Bismarck* battle group. In any event, Lütjens's unexpected turn to the south, made after being damaged by the *Prince of Wales* in the Denmark Strait, meant that the small number of slow-moving U-boats that had been deployed in the western Atlantic (the WEST group) were completely out of position to cover his retreat to Saint-Nazaire. On 26–27 May Luftwaffe aircraft from France could not cover the retreating battleship or threaten the British warships closing in on her (although the severe weather was a factor limiting German air operations at this time).

The *Prinz Eugen* put into Brest on 1 June 1941. The heavy cruiser had not sunk any merchant ships, and she now had mechanical problems. Meanwhile the British, thanks to Enigma decrypts, were able to roll up much of the German supply-ship network in the open Atlantic. Information from special intelligence led to another significant – if little remembered – action on 13 June 1941, two weeks after the loss of the *Bismarck*. A squadron of land-based RAF Beaufort torpedo bombers from Leuchars and Wick in Scotland intercepted and put a torpedo into the heavy cruiser *Lützow*, which was en route to the Atlantic via Norway. The 'unlucky' *Deutschland/Lützow* – hit by Republican bombers during the Spanish Civil War, badly damaged by a torpedo during the 1940 Norwegian campaign – limped back to Germany and spent six more months under repair. The sortie was the last attempted breakout by a German heavy ship into the North Atlantic and the seas beyond. Meanwhile, in late July 1941 the *Scharnhorst*, which had arrived in northwestern France back in March 1941 after Operation BERLIN, was sent to conduct gunnery training at La Pallice. Despite being 240 miles south of Brest, the ship was caught in daylight by some of the RAF's new four-engined Halifax bombers. Hit while at anchor by five bombs, the *Scharnhorst* would be under repair for eight months.

Hitler had already decided against any repetition of operations BERLIN and RHINE EXERCISE. His resolve was strengthened in the autumn of 1941 when the nature of

World War II changed: the Third Reich became bogged down in a war of attrition with Russia. Interdicting the Allied supply line to northern Russia – rather than the convoy route across the Atlantic – became the highest priority.[36] In September 1941, to Admiral Raeder's surprise, the Führer made the crucial decision to position the operational base of the German heavy ships in Norway, rather than in France.

The story of German heavy ship operations in the Atlantic ended in February 1942, seven months after the loss of the *Bismarck*. This was the time of the 'Channel breakthrough' (*Kanaldurchbruch*), which the Germans code-named Operation CERBERUS (ZERBERUS) and the British called the 'Channel Dash'. The *Scharnhorst*, the *Gneisenau* and the *Prinz Eugen* had now been in northwestern France for the better part of a year, but had taken part in no operations. The bases in France were vulnerable to air attack, but with growing British and American naval and air power in the Atlantic, any attempt to return home through the northern straits had now become very risky. Hitler supported a daring solution, a surprise breakthrough up the Channel and through the Dover Strait into the North Sea. Admiral Raeder regarded this as too hazardous, and there was also some sentiment in the Kriegsmarine for keeping the Atlantic surface ship campaign in play. Britain had in December lost two of the Home Fleet capital ships – the *Prince of Wales* and the *Repulse* – to Japanese Navy torpedo bombers.[37] But Hitler insisted that the big ships be brought home via the Channel, or that they should be decommissioned.

Under the command of Admiral Otto Ciliax, the three big ships, with an escort of six destroyers, departed from Brest on the evening of Wednesday, 11 February 1942. Aside from the element of surprise and some bad luck by the British forces watching Brest, the *Kanaldurchbruch* exploited German technical strengths with the jamming of British coastal radar and the deployment of a dense screen of Luftwaffe fighters.

The *Gneisenau* struck a mine in the North Sea on the evening of the 12th, but she passed through the Kiel Canal on the following day and was put in dry dock in the Deutsche Werke shipyard in Kiel. The ship was not de-ammunitioned; two weeks later an RAF night raid on Kiel caused a magazine explosion which badly damaged her and killed 112 of her crew. She was towed east across the Baltic to Gotenhafen, where her guns were removed; two of her 11-inch triple turrets were emplaced on dry land in Norway, defending Bergen and Trondheim.

The Channel Dash was a clever and daring operation and an embarrassment to the British. But fundamentally it marked the end of an era and another German strategic failure. The heavy ships of the Kriegsmarine would never again operate in the North Atlantic.

CHAPTER 6

THE STRUGGLE FOR THE MEDITERRANEAN

July 1940–December 1941

THE BATTLE OFF CALABRIA, 9 JULY 1940

Calabria is the toe of the Italian 'boot'. Fifty miles south of the coast here, on the afternoon of Tuesday, 9 July, a full-scale fleet action took place, larger than any of the sea battles fought so far in World War II. It was the fourth week of the Anglo-Italian naval war, and the day before the beginning of the Battle of Britain.

Both sides were running small but important convoys across the central Mediterranean. On Saturday, 6 July, four fast merchantmen – a troopship and three cargo ships – had departed from Naples for the two-day voyage to Benghazi in eastern Libya. They carried vital reinforcements for the Army there. Meanwhile the British were preparing two convoys of their own, to evacuate stores from Malta.

The headquarters of the Italian Navy, the *Regia Marina*, was known as the *Supermarina*. It was located in Rome, on the Flaminio embankment of the Tiber and was headed by Admiral Domenico Cavagnari. On 2 July Marshal Pietro Badoglio, Chief of the Defence Staff, had ordered the larger part of the Regia Marina to prepare for sea. Cavagnari passed on the order to the fleet, and on Sunday (7 July) the various 'divisions' sortied into the central Mediterranean from the main southern naval base at Taranto, and from Augusta and Palermo in Sicily. If the convoy close escort is included, the total force committed comprised the battleships *Giulio Cesare* and *Conte di Cavour*, six heavy cruisers, eight light cruisers and sixteen destroyers. In overall operational command, aboard the *Cesare*, was Admiral Inigo Campioni.

Meanwhile, Admiral Andrew Cunningham, the C-in-C of the British Mediterranean Fleet, had set out from Alexandria in Egypt on Sunday night (7/8 July). Cunningham did not know about the enemy's Benghazi convoy; his immediate task was to protect his own planned convoys from Malta. Cunningham flew his flag in the *Warspite* and had two of the older battleships under his command, the *Malaya* and the *Royal Sovereign*; a fourth, the slower *Ramillies*, had been left behind. Cunningham also commanded the carrier *Eagle*, five light cruisers and sixteen destroyers. Steaming at 15 knots, his fleet would need more than twenty-four hours to reach the edge of the central Mediterranean; it arrived at that point early on Tuesday morning.

After the fall of France, Britain had established a second – smaller – fleet in the western Mediterranean. Force H, based in Gibraltar, was intended to operate either in the Atlantic or in the Mediterranean. As Flag Officer, Force H, Admiral James Somerville came under the direct control of the Admiralty. The two fleets covered the two exits out of the Mediterranean; Somerville described them as Gog and Magog, after the twin guardians of the City of London. On Monday morning, flying his flag in the battle cruiser *Hood*, Somerville put to sea with the carrier *Ark Royal*, the battleships *Valiant* and *Resolution*, and supporting ships. Only a week had passed since these ships had shelled the French at Mers el-Kébir. Somerville's task was now to support Cunningham by mounting a diversion against the Italians from the west; Force H was to bombard the port of Cagliari in Sardinia.

The British and the Italians each quickly realised that the other side had heavy ships at sea. An Italian submarine reported Cunningham's departure from Alexandria at about midnight on 7/8 July, and just after dawn on Monday a British submarine in the central Mediterranean sighted large Italian warships. The Supermarina was also aware of the Monday morning departure of Force H; Spain was a neutral country friendly to the Axis, and there were Italian observers in Algeciras, across the bay from Gibraltar. The Italian convoy arrived in Benghazi without incident on Monday afternoon and evening, but many warships of the Regia Marina were still in the southern part of the central Mediterranean.

British doctrine was clear. 'The Board of Admiralty cannot emphasise too strongly that in all cases, especially when dealing with an enemy who is reluctant to engage in close action, no opportunity must be allowed to pass of attaining what is in fact the ultimate object of the Royal Navy – the destruction of the main enemy force when and wherever encountered.'[1] Admiral Cunningham commanded his fleet in this spirit. As he passed the western end of Crete early on Tuesday he turned his ships to the northwest to cut the Italians off from their main base at Taranto.

Meanwhile Italian planes had tracked Cunningham's approach west across the Mediterranean on Monday, and mounted high-level bombing attacks from Aegean island air bases and from Libya. During the night, however, contact with the British fleet was lost, and not regained until early on Tuesday afternoon. The

Supermarina was also concerned about the advance of Force H. Late on Monday evening it instructed Admiral Campioni to concentrate all his forces off Calabria, where they could be supported by land-based aircraft.

Cunningham's fleet was stretched out over some 16 miles and divided into three parts. Five light cruisers commanded by Admiral John Tovey scouted ahead; a 'fast' group of ships comprising the *Warspite* and five destroyers made up the middle group; the two slower battleships, with the carrier and ten destroyers, brought up the rear. In the middle of Tuesday afternoon (9 July) Tovey's vanguard, now racing to the west, encountered the main part of the Italian fleet steaming NNE in three parallel columns. At about 3.00 p.m. the cruiser *Neptune* sent the message 'Enemy Battle Fleet in sight'; it was the first time this signal had been seen in the Mediterranean since Nelson's time. The nearest headland on the Calabrian mainland was Punta Stilo, a name often given to the battle.[2]

One of the junior officers aboard the *Neptune* recalled the events of that afternoon:

> Visibility was extreme and the first thing I saw was the masts of a great number of ships which were below the horizon . . . it soon became clear that we were approaching a large fleet of destroyers, cruisers and battleships.
>
> It took some time to get within range and I think that the enemy battleships must have opened fire some time before we could. Once battle was joined everything became very confusing and visibility was obscured by cordite smoke, smoke screens, and cascades of water from bursting shells. The approaching shells sounded like express trains and the confusion was added to by the need to keep shifting targets as cruisers and destroyers appeared through the smoke.[3]

Events were indeed confusing. There were many ships, and the two sides were different but not that unequal. All five battleships engaged dated from World War I. The three 33,000-ton British vessels mounted 15-inch guns. (For all Campioni knew there could be four such ships, if the *Ramillies* was included.) The two 29,000-ton Italian ships mounted only 12.6-inch guns. On the other hand, both had been modernised, and with a speed of 27 knots were faster than their British equivalents. At the moment of the battle Cunningham had only four fully operational cruisers. The Italians had six heavy cruisers and four light cruisers, with four more light cruisers approaching from the southwest.

The light cruisers screening each fleet exchanged fire at the very long range of 22,000 yards (12.5 miles) for about fifteen minutes. Then, at 3.26 p.m., the *Warspite* opened up with her big guns at 26,000 yards, engaging first the Italian light cruisers and then (from 3.53 p.m.) the two Italian battleships. In this second phase the *Malaya* also opened fire at maximum range, but her shells fell well short; the *Royal Sovereign* was too slow to get into range at all. The six Italian heavy (8-inch-gun) cruisers slid into position ahead of their battleships and exchanged fire at long range with Tovey's four light (6-inch-gun) cruisers. Cunningham reported later that Tovey handled his ships 'superbly'; four months later he would be transferred to command the Home Fleet at Scapa Flow.

For about ten minutes the *Cesare* and the *Cavour* returned fire. Then, at 3.59 p.m., the *Cesare* was hit amidships by a 15-inch shell from the *Warspite*, causing a temporary reduction in her speed. Cunningham remembered the event: 'I had been watching the great splashes of our 15-inch salvoes straddling the target when . . . I saw the great orange-colour flash of a heavy explosion at the base of the enemy flagship's funnels. It was followed by an upheaval of smoke, and I knew she had been heavily hit.'[4] The Italian admiral ordered a turn to the west under cover of a smoke screen, and his destroyers mounted a long-range torpedo attack to ensure the British kept their distance. Cut off from Taranto, Campioni's ships made their way in some disorder towards the ports in Sicily. Cunningham feared a trap by enemy light forces and did not, as he put it, 'plunge straight into the smoke screen'. He attempted to work around the smoke to the north and reached a point only 25 miles from the mainland, but was unable to pursue. With dusk approaching, the enemy below the horizon and his destroyers short of fuel, Cunningham turned away to the south at 6.30.

The gunnery duel was only one aspect. Calabria was arguably the first ever sea/air fleet battle; it involved a British aircraft carrier and many land-based bombers of the Italian Air Force, the *Regia Aeronautica*. Cunningham's *Eagle* had been commissioned as a carrier in 1924, after a six-year conversion; she had been laid down (in 1913) on the Tyne as a battleship for Chile. The maximum speed of the *Eagle* was only 24 knots, and despite her large size (24,000 tons) her air group in July 1940 numbered only seventeen Swordfish torpedo planes and two obsolete biplane fighters. Steaming astern of the battleships, the *Eagle* launched two torpedo-plane strikes during the main battle, as well as scouting and A/S patrols. Malta did not yet have any land-based offensive air strike capability, but RAF flying boats from there proved invaluable as scouts. The Italian ships were steaming at high speed; the British carrier aircraft were few and flown by inexperienced crews. All the same, there were many targets, and it is surprising that nothing at all was achieved. Any Italian ship that had been 'fixed' (slowed down or stopped) by air attack would surely have been finished off by British guns or torpedoes. (There was one successful air attack: a Swordfish sank a destroyer during an attack on Augusta in Sicily on the night of 10/11 July.)

The other element of this sea/air battle consisted of the Italian bombers, mostly Savoia-Marchetti SM.79 and SM.81 trimotors; each could carry four or five 250kg (550lb) bombs. Large numbers of bombers and trained crews were available in the first weeks of Italy's war; the Italian Air Force did not have the commitments in North Africa and the Balkans which would so burden it later on. Formation attacks from a high level (10,000 feet) began on Monday and Tuesday, 8 and 9 July, as the two British fleets approached. These attacks were generally ineffective, because the rapidly moving targets could manoeuvre away from the falling bombs. The few hits and near misses with relatively small bombs caused little damage. The Italian Air Force as yet had no operational dive-bomber or torpedo-bomber squadrons.

The British were clearly concerned about the bomber threat. Admiral Somerville was well aware of the danger after his experience in the Dunkirk evacuation only six weeks earlier. He abandoned the attack on Cagliari and returned to Gibraltar, because he did not think his diversionary mission was worth the air risk to his ships. Cunningham, too, came under heavy air attack on Thursday and Friday (11–12 July). As he put it in a letter to Admiral Pound in London, 'Literally we have had to fight our way back to Alexandria against air attack'. Somerville thought his old friend now took the air threat more seriously: 'Andrew B. has quite changed his tune as a result of his recent experiences'.[5]

The Battle off Calabria was indecisive. No ships were lost in the main fleet engagement. (A submarine sank one of the Force H destroyers during the return to Gibraltar and, as mentioned, an Italian destroyer was torpedoed at Augusta.) The convoys, Italian and British, arrived safely at their destinations; the British convoys sailed from Malta bound for Alexandria, the first late on Tuesday evening (the 9th) – with Cunningham's wife and nieces among the passengers – and the second on Wednesday. Still, 9 July 1940 saw the first classic fleet action in World War II, the first gunnery battle which involved at least two capital ships on either side. Cunningham described the Battle off Calabria as 'irritating and disappointing', but in driving off the enemy fleet and demonstrating the current impotence of the vaunted Italian Air Force he had won a significant moral victory.[6]

SEA/AIR BATTLES IN THE MEDITERRANEAN

Italy declared war on Britain and France on 10 June 1940. When Hitler had suddenly triggered a European conflict nine months earlier Mussolini had stood back, on grounds of unreadiness. Now it seemed that French defeat was certain, and that Britain would be forced, at the least, to negotiate a peace. The Italian government wanted to be able to make claims in this re-ordered world, where it had interests in the Balkans, Tunisia, Egypt and East Africa. Sea power was a significant factor; Mussolini was concerned not just with local control over *Mare Nostrum* (Latin for 'Our Sea', the Roman name for the Mediterranean), but also with exit routes into the wider oceans. The armed forces, however had undertaken little concrete planning. Once the war became a real and a protracted one, Mussolini and Fascist Italy were in deep trouble.

Mussolini's main naval adviser was Admiral Domenico Cavagnari. Like Admiral Raeder he was in his mid sixties, and he had been in post long enough to put his stamp on the naval service. Cavagnari had been de facto Minister of the Italian Navy (under Mussolini) since 1933, and Chief of Staff (*Capo di Stato Maggiore*) since 1934. He had overseen a build-up of the fleet – with France as the most likely enemy – and he had loyally supported Mussolini's foreign policy ventures.

The Regia Marina of 1940 was larger than the German Kriegsmarine and a considerably better-balanced force. As a naval power, however, Italy had certainly not been in the same league as Britain, the US or Japan. The pre-Fascist government in Rome accepted a capital ship limit of 175,000 tons under the 1922 Washington Naval Treaty, which was the same as that of France, but much less than the 525,000 tons allowed for Britain. Naval competition with France in the 1920s led to the production of vessels suited to a future war in the central and western Mediterranean, with sizeable cruiser, destroyer and submarine programmes. Italian shipyards produced handsome and innovative modern ships, distinguished by high speed. There were seven heavy cruisers, all named after cities in Dalmatia or the Tyrol, the *Italia irredenta* gained from Austria-Hungary after World War I – Pola, Fiume, Gorizia, Zara, Trieste, Trento and Bolzano. In June 1940 the Italians also possessed twelve modern light cruisers. Escort vessels included forty-four destroyers, also very fast, and thirty new 620-ton torpedo boats. A very large submarine force numbered over a hundred boats.

Italy was caught up in the early 1930s in a European naval building race (mainly German–French and French–Italian). France began two fast battleships (the *Strasbourg* and the *Dunkerque*) as a reply to the German pocket battleships. Italy responded first by beginning the comprehensive reconstruction of two of its (four) existing battleships (the *Conte di Cavour* and the *Giulio Cesare*), which dated from World War I. As converted, they displaced 29,000 tons and mounted ten 12.6-inch guns in four turrets; they were now capable of 27 knots. Then, in October 1934, two full-sized battleships with 15-inch guns (in three turrets), the *Littorio* and the *Vittorio Veneto*, were laid down at Genoa and Trieste. This was consistent with international naval rearmament agreements, as Italy had replacement tonnage available.[7] Under the terms of the Washington Treaty Britain could only start battleship construction in January 1937. The new Italian battleships were supposed to displace 35,000 tons but were completed at 40,700. They were capable of speeds of 30 knots and would be 4 or 5 knots faster than the older British battleships operating in the

Mediterranean. Comprehensive reconstruction of the two remaining unmodernised battleships originally built during World War I, the *Caio Duilio* and the *Andrea Doria*, was also begun. (These last two rebuilt vessels were not fully operational until after July 1940, and so missed the Battle off Calabria.)[8]

A serious shortcoming was the lack of aircraft carriers, despite the fact that Italy had an allowance of 60,000 tons under the Washington Treaty, and France had an aircraft-carrier programme. Admiral Cavagnari had not supported carrier construction, and the Italian military leadership argued that such a vessel would be unnecessary in view of the large number of land-based aircraft available (operated by the Air Force). An independent Italian Air Force had been created in 1923. Italy was the homeland of prominent air-war theorist Giulio Douhet (1868–1930), who had argued that wars would be won by air power alone, and that aircraft deployed for support of armies and navies were a wasted asset. In 1930–31 and 1933 the Fascist leader Italo Balbo led mass formations of Regia Aeronautica flying boats across the Atlantic, first to South America and then to the United States. The early events of the war, however, showed a serious lack of inter-service co-ordination. After the Battle off Calabria, Foreign Minister Ciano (himself the son of an admiral) wrote that the 'real controversy in naval conflicts is not between us and the British, but between our air force and our navy'.[9]

Other telling shortcomings of the Regia Marina included limited fuel oil supplies, limited training in night fighting and lack of radar and sonar.

For the British Royal Navy, the Mediterranean had been a centre of activity for over a century and a half. This had developed over decades of rivalry with France and Spain and had then become even more important with the establishment of strategic bases in Gibraltar and at Malta and the opening of the Suez Canal in 1869. Major fleet units had been based in the Mediterranean, and the Navy was very familiar with the theatre of operations.

Nevertheless, a continued British role in the Mediterranean raised several questions in the high summer of 1940, especially with the abandonment of the Continent and the threat of invasion. Allied naval dominance of the western basin of the Mediterranean had ended with the fall of France. There were serious discussions in Whitehall about whether the position in the eastern basin should or could be maintained. More recently the British historian Correlli Barnett, in his major history of the wartime Royal Navy, went so far as to question the wisdom of a 'blue water strategy', which he described as 'using maritime power to sustain land campaigns in far-off peripheral theatres'. Barnett was thinking in particular of the war in the Mediterranean in 1940–44.[10]

The question could be narrowed down to whether the British government was correct in summer 1940 to commit naval and other resources to the Mediterranean. In terms of what was known at the time and what we know now, the decision was a sound one. The petroleum resources of the Middle East were an important asset, and it would be highly undesirable for them to fall into the hands of an oil-starved Italy and Germany. In military terms, Britain on its own was certainly not going to be able to fight the German Army on land in north-western Europe. Italy was the weaker Axis partner; southern Europe and the Middle East offered the only viable theatre for British action. At the strategic level, loss of territories controlled by Britain in the eastern Mediterranean would have greatly damaged the prestige of the Empire. Attempts on other exposed territories by Japan and Spain would have been encouraged. British influence in the Balkans and Turkey would have declined. Unrest would have been provoked among subject peoples in India and elsewhere. And a setback of this magnitude, following failure in Norway and France, would have made intervention on Britain's side by either the US or the USSR less likely.

Admiral Raeder and the German Naval War Staff made the same case to Hitler in September 1940:

> Decisive strategic significance for the German-Italian war effort in the Mediterranean area: Gibraltar and the Suez Canal.
>
> Exclusion of England from the Mediterranean – Vital importance of the domination of the Mediterranean area for the position of the central powers [*sic*] in southeastern Europe, Asia Minor, Arabia, Egypt and the African area – Guarantee of unlimited sources of raw materials – Establishment of new and strategically favourable bases for further operations against the British Empire – Crucial difficulties for British import traffic from the South Atlantic as a result of the loss of Gibraltar – Preparations for this undertaking [*Aktion*], which should not be considered a secondary undertaking, but rather a main undertaking [*Hauptaktion*] against England, must be begun at once so that it can be carried out before the entry of US [into the war].[11]

Hitler informally approved this concept but, as we will see later, it was hard to bring it to life and sustain it.

Britain's Mediterranean strategy seemed even sounder *after* the pivotal summer of 1940. By the autumn and winter the British Isles were more secure. Local defence forces were built up in Britain, and the Americans began to provide greater support. In addition, by this time operations in North and East Africa and the Mediterranean had confirmed the suspected military weakness of Fascist Italy. And the strategy made more sense still when the German Wehrmacht was thrown into the Russian campaign in the summer of 1941.

The Admiralty had kept a large naval force at Alexandria to deter the Italians, even during the campaigns in Norway and France. This comprised four battleships, an aircraft carrier and about nine cruisers, twenty-six destroyers and twelve submarines. The most important units over the next eighteen months would be the five 'Queen Elizabeth' class battleships, although they would not all be in the theatre at the same time. They were the best battleships built during World War I, and had formed the famous 5th Battle Squadron at Jutland. Capable of relatively high speed, they were each armed with eight 15-inch guns. Three of them, the *Queen Elizabeth*, the *Valiant* and the *Warspite*, had been rebuilt in the late 1930s with new machinery, radar, enhanced main-gun range finders and better AA systems. Even the less extensively modified *Barham* and *Malaya* were capable of successfully engaging any of the Italian battleships.[12]

Andrew Cunningham was the aggressive C-in-C of the Mediterranean Fleet, an officer in the Nelson mould, and now generally regarded as the outstanding British flag officer of the 1939–45 war. A Scot, he did not come from a naval family. Much of his career had been spent in destroyers and in the Mediterranean. In the summer of 1937 he became second in command of the Mediterranean Fleet under Admiral Pound, before being made Deputy Chief of Naval Staff (DCNS) at the Admiralty in 1938. He returned to the Mediterranean as C-in-C in June 1939, after the unexpected promotion of Pound to the position of First Sea Lord. (He himself would replace Pound as First Sea Lord in 1943.)

On the morning of 19 July, ten days after the Battle off Calabria, a smaller naval action was fought west of Crete, off Cape Spada. A cruiser-destroyer force ran into two Italian light cruisers. The Australian cruiser *Sydney* stopped one of the Italian ships with gunfire, and the destroyers finished her off with torpedoes; the *Bartolomeo Colleoni* was the first major loss of the Italian Navy.

Meanwhile, Admiral Cunningham had requested reinforcements. These were despatched by the Admiralty in August 1940, at the height of the Battle of Britain and of the invasion threat. In Operation HATS, a carrier, a battleship and two AA cruisers were rushed across the Mediterranean.[13] The 23,400-ton HMS *Illustrious* was a great improvement over the *Eagle*. Commissioned only in May 1940, she was the first of the new armoured aircraft carriers, with a Type 79 air search radar and the latest British naval fighter planes. The modernised battleship *Valiant* was also fitted with radar. Escorted by Force H while on their way to the central Mediterranean, the new ships joined up with Cunningham near Malta on 2 September. During the transfer Admiral Campioni took the Italian battle fleet to sea from Taranto. It now included four battleships, among them the two new 15-inch-gun 'Littorio' class. He was kept on a tight leash by the Supermarina, however, and was unable to prevent the strengthening of the enemy fleet at Alexandria.

By November 1940 all six of the Italian battleships were operational and had been concentrated with many smaller vessels at Taranto (in Apulia, the heel of the Italian 'boot'). The British had for some time – since the Munich Crisis of 1938 – been considering an attack on this southern base, and now a plan was put into effect. The Mediterranean Fleet departed Alexandria on 6 November. An air attack was mounted by Swordfish torpedo planes on the night of 9/10 November, launched from the *Illustrious* at a range of 170 miles. The attacking force was small, with twenty-one aircraft, only half of which carried torpedoes. The six battleships were moored in a shallow anchorage enclosed by a torpedo net, but numerous torpedo hits were achieved. The *Littorio* was damaged, and the *Conte di Cavour* and the newly modernised *Caio Duilio* were sunk in shallow water. The attack halved – for a time – the strength of the Italian battle fleet. The *Littorio* would be under repair until March 1941, the *Duilio* until May; repair work on the *Cavour* was never completed. The other heavy ships were pulled back for a time to Naples and other ports further north, which limited their operations in the central Mediterranean.

The Battle of Cape Spartivento took place in late November, and ran along similar lines to the July action off Calabria. The British were sending small but important convoys from Gibraltar to Malta and Alexandria and from Alexandria to Malta, and at the same time the battleship *Ramillies* and two cruisers were being transferred from Alexandria, via Malta, to the Atlantic. Meanwhile Cunningham mounted strikes with his two carriers against Leros in the Aegean, and against Tripoli.

Somerville set out on 25 November 1940, with Force H; his ships now consisted of the modernised battle cruiser *Renown*, the *Ark Royal*, four cruisers and eight destroyers. Axis observers again provided details of his departure from Gibraltar, and contrary to the expectations in London the Supermarina ordered Admiral Campioni to sortie from Naples into the western Mediterranean with the undamaged *Vittorio Veneto* and the *Cesare*. The Italian battleships were supported by a strong force of six cruisers and several destroyers. Campioni's mission was to trap the weaker Force H.

The Admiralty did not know where the undamaged Italian heavy ships were based, after Taranto. The Supermarina, for its part, did not know that Somerville had joined up at sea east of Gibraltar with the three fast cargo ships of the east-bound COLLAR convoy, which had sailed directly from the UK. On Wednesday morning (27 November), elements of the opposing fleets converged off Cape Spartivento, the southern tip of Sardinia. Just before noon, Force H and the detachment from Alexandria (the *Ramillies* and the cruisers *Berwick* and *Newcastle*) came together. After this, neither the British nor the Italians had a clear advantage in terms of naval forces. As for air strength, Somerville had the *Ark Royal*, with fourteen Swordfish and, for the first time, strong fighter cover in the form of twenty-four Fairey Fulmars; the Fulmar was an eight-gun fighter with a Merlin engine (but unfortunately it was a big two-seater that was rather slow for a fighter). The Italian fleet was operating close to Regia Aeronautica bases on Sardinia.

As soon as Admiral Campioni realised he was up against a combined British force with an aircraft carrier, he turned to the east and ran for home behind a smoke screen. The stern chase to the northeast involved a long-range artillery duel off Cape Spartivento, lasting for about fifty minutes. Somerville's cruiser vanguard was commanded by Admiral Holland, who would die six months later aboard the *Hood*. As in the Battle off Calabria, two big-gun capital ships took part on either side: the *Vittorio Veneto* and the *Cesare* were opposed by the *Renown* and the *Ramillies*, although the latter was too slow to actually get into range. It would be the last surface action on this scale until the naval Battle of Guadalcanal on 14–15 November 1942.[14] Artillery fire at very long range had little effect; one ship on each side suffered minor damage.

By early afternoon, with his lead ships only 30 miles from the Sardinian coast and even his cruisers evidently having no chance of catching up with the fleeing Italians, Somerville broke off and turned south to protect the COLLAR convoy, which he saw as his main task. This decision provoked an angry reaction from London, where there was dissatisfaction that the enemy had again not been engaged decisively. A senior admiral was hastily despatched to Gibraltar to conduct a Board of Inquiry. This body concluded that Somerville had acted correctly, but the British admiral regarded such heavy-handed intervention from London as a 'bloody outrage'; Cunningham shared his anger.[15]

The British convoys passed safely to their destinations with no damage. The Regia Marina was once again swept from the sea. The Italian Air Force intervened late, in small numbers, and without effect. But the carrier planes from the *Ark Royal*, on a clear summer day and in the absence of an enemy fighter defence, were not able to pick off any of the Italian warships. Campioni's sortie into the western Mediterranean had not been anticipated, and the British had been caught with their fleets divided. Cunningham, with the main body of his Alexandria-based fleet (the *Warspite*, the *Valiant* and the carrier *Illustrious*), was well away from the action, 160 miles to the east of Malta.

Cape Spartivento had a major impact on the Italian side, on top of other setbacks on land and sea. The Italian Army's advance towards Cairo had stalled in western Egypt. A foolhardy invasion of Greece, launched from Albania at the end of October 1940, had been stopped by the Greek Army. On 5 December Mussolini replaced his cautious Chief of the Defence Staff, Marshal Badoglio; three days later Admiral Cavagnari was also dismissed. Mussolini saw the Battle of Cape Spartivento as another naval failure, for which the Supermarina were responsible. The Italian Navy's new Chief of Staff, Admiral Arturo Riccardi, would remain in post in Rome until 1943. Admiral Campioni, unsuccessful off Calabria and Cape Spartivento, was replaced as battle fleet commander by Admiral Angelo Iachino, who had previously commanded the cruiser force.[16]

Berlin had meanwhile been watching developments in the Mediterranean. As already mentioned, Admiral Raeder in early September 1940 had suggested to Hitler that German grand strategy be directed towards attacking British overseas interests. The impracticality of a landing in the British Isles had already become clear, and at the same time the admiral opposed the invasion of Russia (already in its planning stages). In early November an OKW directive proposed Operation FELIX, an advance across Spain to Gibraltar and the (Spanish) Canary Islands. In December, however, General Franco said he would not take part, at least at the current time; his refusal was based on a lack of Spanish preparation. This is not the place to look in depth at grand-strategic counterfactuals, but with hindsight it certainly would have been hugely advantageous, in both offensive and defensive terms, for Axis forces to have occupied Gibraltar and blocked the western entry into the Mediterranean.[17] What is clear with hindsight is the fragility of German power in the south. The Third Reich ultimately relied here on ineffectual and squabbling partners in the form of Italy, Vichy France and Spain.

Even though a large-scale strategic commitment was ruled out by Hitler – above all due to preparations for the Russian campaign – the need to prop up Germany's Italian allies had become evident. Stalemate in Africa turned into Italian military defeat. Hardly had Marshal Badoglio been sacked than British Empire ground forces mounted a counter-attack in Egypt and pursued the Italian forces back into Cyrenaica (eastern Libya). Tobruk, the forward supply port, was captured in January 1941 and Benghazi in early February. Altogether some 130,000 prisoners were taken. A small German Army support force was despatched, General Erwin Rommel's famous Afrika Korps. The elements of a motorised division arrived in March 1941 and a Panzer division followed in April and May.

More important for the war at sea was the arrival of the Luftwaffe. An Anglo-Italian naval war was transformed into an Anglo-German sea/air war, which would last until 1944. Hitler approved the movement of some air formations to the Mediterranean in late November 1940, and in January 1941 X. Fliegerkorps began to arrive from northern Europe. German planes were initially based at Regia Aeronautica airfields in Sicily, from which they quickly asserted control over the narrows and the approaches to Malta.

In previous months, off Calabria and elsewhere, Italian bombers attacking in formation from high altitude had had little effect. The Junkers Ju 87 Stuka dive bomber proved to be a much more deadly weapon.[18] Even without special naval training or weapons, the Stuka crews were able to deliver a much more accurate attack, albeit one only effective when directed against lightly armoured ships, at a short range, and in the absence of defending fighters. The availability of radar and better defensive carrier fighters in the Mediterranean towards the end of 1940 had made the British over-confident. In addition, there had been an important failure of intelligence: Cunningham was not informed about the arrival of numerous German aircraft in Sicily until 9 January 1941, the day before they inflicted heavy damage.[19]

Before 1939 the Admiralty was aware of the dangers of operating within range of airfield-based aircraft. As already mentioned, the latest British carriers – after the *Ark Royal* – had been designed with substantial (3-inch) armoured decks and an enclosed hangar. On the other hand, there were still not sufficient fighter planes to provide an active defence in the form of what would later be called a CAP or 'combat air patrol'. The rapidly developed Fairey Fulmar had folding wings; it was similar to the Hurricane and Spitfire fighters in that it had a powerful Merlin engine and was armed with eight machine guns. But it was a big two-seater that could only attain a speed of 265 mph. As a result, the Fulmar was considerably slower than the Junkers Ju 88 bomber (although faster than a Stuka). Moreover, that January the *Illustrious* carried only fifteen of these fighters.

The changed sea/air balance became evident in Operation EXCESS, another complex British convoy operation, which began on 6 January 1941. Four days later, on the afternoon of 10 January, the Royal Navy's armoured carrier concept was tested in battle. The *Illustrious*, in company with the battleships *Warspite* and *Valiant*, was caught by German aircraft 60 miles west of Malta; these ships of the Mediterranean Fleet were on their way to rendezvous with an east-bound convoy. The *Illustrious* was subjected to an attack by Stukas of II./StG 2 'Immelmann' (*Gruppe* II of *Stukageschwader* 2). Dropping 500kg (1,100lb) bombs, the dive bombers achieved six hits and killed 126 crew members. Saved by her armoured deck, the damaged carrier was towed to Malta, but she then suffered further bomb damage during two weeks under repair. Only with much difficulty was the ship patched up enough to steam back to Alexandria. From there she later passed through the Suez Canal, and around the Cape to the neutral US for repair. The *Illustrious* would not be back in service until November 1941.[20] As shocking to the Royal Navy was the complete loss on 11 January of the *Southampton*, which had come from the west with Cunningham's Mediterranean Fleet. The 11,700-ton light cruiser was a modern ship – commissioned in 1937 – with what was believed to be a good AA armament. Stukas attacking at long range caught her crew off-guard. The bombs caused a serious fire which could not be contained; the ship had to be abandoned, and the burning hulk scuttled. The *Southampton* was the first major British warship sunk as a result of air attack.

For the moment Cunningham was able to maintain his strength in the eastern Mediterranean. The *Illustrious* was replaced in early March by her sister ship, the *Formidable* (commissioned in November 1940). The new carrier was sent to Alexandria, not directly across the Mediterranean, but via the safer and much longer Cape route.

The British government had meanwhile decided to commit troops to support the Greek Army against the Italians. In early March 1941 a series of convoys (Operation LUSTRE) sailed from Alexandria to Piraeus (the port of Athens); this eventually brought in four British Empire divisions. Although this expedition to Greece turned out to be a strategic blunder, it led to the greatest success of the Royal Navy in the Mediterranean in 1941, the Battle of Cape Matapan.

The Supermarina was under pressure from the Germans to use the Italian battle fleet more actively. At the suggestion of Admiral Iachino, the new fleet C-in-C, an ambush was prepared against the British troop convoys to Greece. This was a daring operation, with the battleship *Vittorio Veneto* and eight cruisers operating south of Crete (the island then being controlled by the British). Admiral Cunningham was warned by Enigma intercepts (decrypted at Bletchley Park) from the Luftwaffe and the Italian Navy that a major operation was under way. He was able secretly to concentrate his own ships. They made contact with the Italians on the morning of 28 March. This turned into another stern chase as the faster Italian fleet raced away to the northwest. The Fleet Air Arm technique of 'Find, fix and strike' was again effective. In the afternoon Swordfish and Albacore torpedo bombers from the *Formidable* succeeded in hitting and immobilising the *Vittorio Veneto*.[21] The battleship was able to get under way, but in the evening British planes immobilised the heavy cruiser *Pola*. These air strikes took place off Cape Matapan, the southern tip of mainland Greece. The damaged *Vittorio Veneto* limped north to safety, but Iachino sent a heavy cruiser division back to support the *Pola*. This force was destroyed in a night engagement fought at point-blank range with Cunningham's battleships, the *Warspite*, the *Valiant* and the *Barham*, making effective use of their radar. The *Fiume*, the *Pola* and the *Zara* were sunk, as well as two destroyers. Some 2,300 Italian sailors were lost, including Admiral Cattaneo, commanding the cruiser division. The British suffered no casualties, except for a torpedo bomber crew.

This demonstration of sea power did not strengthen the British position on land in the Balkans. The German Blitzkrieg in Greece and Yugoslavia came on 6 April 1941 – a week after Cape Matapan. Mainland Greece was overrun in a matter of weeks; the British forces sent there were successfully evacuated in another Dunkirk-style operation. The prospects for holding the big island of Crete, which occupied a strategic position north of the convoy route from Alexandria to Malta, seemed good. The German Air Force, however, quickly organised an airborne invasion. In Operation MERCURY (MERKUR), which began on Tuesday, 20 May, parachute troops seized airfields, and transport planes flew in reinforcements.

The Battle of Crete was especially damaging for the Royal Navy, which had positioned its ships to deal with a seaborne landing. Cunningham remained ashore at his headquarters in Alexandria to co-ordinate the movement of four task groups. Two British cruiser-destroyer forces succeeded in blocking invasion shipping coming from the north, improvised convoys made up of local fishing vessels (*caiques*). No large Italian fleet units were deployed to support the invasion. But the Germans had powerful air strength available after their operations of Yugoslavia and Greece; other Luftwaffe aircraft were now based in Libya.

As the British screening naval forces were withdrawn from northwest of Crete on Thursday, 22 May they came under heavy air attack. Two cruisers sent to rescue the crew of a British destroyer that had been sunk came under mass air attack themselves. The new *Gloucester* went down after four bomb hits, and the men in the water could not be rescued; 800 were lost. The even newer *Fiji* was so severely damaged that she had to be abandoned. The *Warspite* was also badly hit and could not be repaired at Alexandria. Sent to a shipyard in the United States, the historic battleship would not return to service until March 1942; when she did it would be in the Indian Ocean, not the Mediterranean.

German medium bombers damaged the *Warspite*'s sister ship, the *Barham*, on the 27th; four days later the old AA cruiser *Calcutta* was sunk off Alexandria. The most serious single setback was the damage to the carrier *Formidable*, which was attacked on the 26th by a formation of Stukas operating from Libya. This came after an ineffectual strike by the carrier against Axis air bases in the Aegean; the Stuka attack came two days after the loss of the *Hood* in the Denmark Strait. Two bomb hits meant the *Formidable* had to be withdrawn from the Mediterranean, eventually joining the *Warspite* and the *Illustrious* in American shipyards. After this the Royal Navy in the eastern Mediterranean would have no carrier until the end of 1943.

Three cruisers and six destroyers had been sunk at sea in the battle for Crete. A fourth vessel, the heavy cruiser *York*, had to be scuttled in Crete's Suda Bay. She had been damaged by an Italian explosive speedboat in March and run aground; she was wrecked by German bombers on 18 May. In addition to the *Formidable* and the two crippled battleships, five cruisers and five destroyers were badly damaged. Admiral Cunningham famously stated that it had been essential to give the British Army all possible support, and the honour of his service was at stake: 'It takes the Navy three years to build a ship: but 300 to build a tradition'. Demanding the immediate despatch of RAF reinforcements, the admiral stressed the gravity of the situation. 'We are on the verge of disaster here for we stand to lose fleet and thus Malta, Cyprus and Egypt unless we act at once . . .'[22] The sea/air battle off Crete in May 1941 was to prove the single most costly action fought by the Royal Navy in World War II.

AXIS SEA ROUTES TO NORTH AFRICA

The Mediterranean war, especially in 1940–41, was a prolonged and singularly interlocked affair. This was true in terms of both geography and the different forms of warfare involved.[23] There was a land war in North Africa, with the strategic goal of the Suez Canal. There was a sea/air war in which British convoys ran between east and west, and Axis ones between north and south. The convoys came under attack from the surface ships, submarines and aircraft. It was an asymmetrical struggle, but the two sides were quite evenly matched in 1940–41.

When they entered the war the Italians had a large garrison in Libya, heavily dependent on supplies and reinforcements brought across the Mediterranean; the civilian population also required some imports. Libya was served by one medium-sized port, Tripoli, but from there the coastal road, the *Via Balbo*, stretched 1,000 miles to the fighting front on the border of Cyrenaica and Egypt. Benghazi, 620 miles to the east of Tripoli, was a considerably smaller port; Tobruk, 290 miles further east and exposed to British attack, was smaller still. There were better ports to the west of Libya at Tunis and Bizerte, with only a short crossing from Sicily. They, however, were located in Tunisia, which was a territory of Vichy France and also much further away from the fighting front.

Axis ground forces did play an active role. The Italian Army for a time posed a direct threat to Egypt and the Suez Canal in late 1940. Then, in the wake of Wavell's winter offensive came a German-led counter-attack. Rommel drove the British back past Benghazi to the Egyptian border in April 1941; by the middle of the month Tobruk had been bypassed and besieged by German and Italian forces. There the front stabilised until December 1941.

Italian supply convoys to Libya, at first mostly from Naples, began as soon as the war broke out. Overall, the main activity of the Italian Navy was providing escort, mainly in 1940–42. (There were also numerous convoys to Albania in 1940–41 in support of the Italian campaign against the Greeks.) At first, in 1940, the British could do little to stop this shipping. The Naples–Tripoli route was too far from Alexandria, not to mention Gibraltar, for it to be at serious risk from big British surface ships. Suda Bay in western Crete was a nearer base, but it had few facilities and was lost to the British in May 1941. After that the German-held airfields on Crete and in eastern Libya threatened the passage of British warships into the central Mediterranean from the east, through what the Royal Navy came to know as 'Bomb Alley'. Even submarines had to travel a considerable distance from Alexandria to reach potential targets. The distances also ruled out long-range air attack from Egypt using the machines available to the RAF in 1940–41.

All this made Malta critically important. Located south of Sicily, it lay directly across the Axis convoy route to North Africa. Malta had been the main base in the Mediterranean for the Royal Navy since the island was seized by Admiral Nelson in 1800. By the time the war with Italy began, however, Malta seemed more a liability than an asset. In the late 1930s the headquarters of the Mediterranean Fleet had been moved to Alexandria because of the danger of Italian air attack. The position of the island was all the more exposed after the unexpected surrender of the French in July 1940. The Regia Aeronautica launched a bombing campaign as soon as the war began. These raids were limited in scale compared to what would come later, but it took considerable time to build up a defensive fighter force (mainly RAF Hurricane fighters flown in from aircraft carriers). And then, in January 1941, the German bombers (X. Fliegerkorps) moved to Sicily and through the spring pounded Malta with heavy air raids.[24]

In the first part of 1941 most of the Italian supply ship losses – in total not large – were caused by submarines, but in the summer RAF air attacks from Malta became more important. In November and December 1941 surface ships based on the island had great success. All these activities were facilitated by air reconnaissance (from Malta) and by signals intelligence. The codebreakers at Bletchley Park were frequently able to decrypt Italian naval signals, and when the Germans recommended (as an increased security measure) adoption of the Swedish Hagelin C-38m cypher machine from the summer of 1941 the British task became even easier. The growing ability to read Luftwaffe Enigma messages in 1941 also provided detailed information on routes and individual convoy movements.

The Royal Navy had possessed a considerable submarine force in 1939, overall some sixty boats. There were a dozen boats in the Mediterranean in June 1940, but many of them were large and not suited to the shallow and relatively clear local waters. Until February 1941 the Admiralty rules of engagement limited attacks on merchant ships. In addition Italian A/S escorts proved to be unexpectedly effective, and a number of British boats were lost. In the six wartime months of 1940 British submarines sank only ten Italian merchant ships, totalling 44,500 tons.

As months passed more of the new 640-ton 'U' class submarines began to arrive, based from February 1941 in Malta itself. In May 1941 the recently commissioned HMS *Upholder*, commanded by Lt Commander Malcolm Wanklyn, sank the 22,000-ton liner *Conte Rosso* in a convoy off the coast of Sicily; Wanklyn was awarded the Victoria Cross. Bound for Tripoli, and employed as a troopship, the *Conte Rosso* had 2,700 men on board, of whom nearly half drowned. In mid-September 1941, forewarned by Bletchley Park decrypts of German signals, the *Upholder* intercepted another southbound convoy 60 miles off Tripoli and sank the former liners *Neptunia* and *Oceania*, sister ships of 19,500 tons with a total of 6,500 troops on board.[25] Wanklyn was the most successful British submarine commander of the war; he and his crew would be lost with the *Upholder* in March 1942. Overall British submarines did much more in 1941 than in 1940, accounting for ninety-one enemy merchant ships, totalling 288,000 tons.[26]

As far as air strength on Malta was concerned, the emphasis was on short-range defensive fighters, but there were also some reconnaissance planes, and a handful of FAA Swordfish torpedo planes and RAF light and medium bombers. In the summer of 1941 Malta began to provide a base for more strike aircraft, some of them radar-equipped. In the late summer and autumn they sank twenty-four Axis merchant ships, totalling 102,000 tons.[27]

From mid-April 1941 British destroyers were based in Malta. On the night of 15/16 April, in heavy weather off Cape Bon in Tunisia, four of them ambushed an Italian convoy which was taking a roundabout route from Tripoli. All five transports and all three escorting destroyers were sunk, for the loss of one British destroyer. Despite the heavy losses suffered off Crete in May, the Royal Navy became an increasing threat to Axis shipping in the central Mediterranean. A group of cruisers and destroyers, Force K, was moved to Malta in October 1941. On the night of 8/9 November it achieved one of the Royal Navy's most spectacular wartime victories when the light cruisers *Aurora* and *Penelope*, with two destroyers, ambushed and completely destroyed a convoy of seven merchant ships. The BETA (or *Duisburg*) convoy had been carrying 35,000 tons of stores, including nearly 400 vehicles and 17,000 tons of fuel. Seven Italian destroyers were escorting the convoy, with distant cover provided by the heavy cruisers *Trieste* and *Trento*; one of the destroyers was sunk. Mussolini, according to Foreign Minister Ciano, considered this the most humiliating day for Italy since the beginning of the war.[28] Pressed by the Germans, the Italians now began to transfer supplies to North Africa aboard fast cruisers and destroyers. A month after sinking the BETA convoy a British destroyer flotilla, forewarned by Ultra, intercepted and sank the light cruisers *Da Barbiano* and *Da Giussano* in a night attack off Tunisia.

Unfortunately, from the British point of view, November and December 1941 marked the peak of success for attacks against Italian supply shipping. At the very end of the year heavy losses to Force K reduced the threat from Malta. Three cruisers ran onto an Italian minefield north of Tripoli on 19 December; the *Neptune* and a destroyer were sunk, and the *Penelope* and the *Aurora* were damaged. Meanwhile the German decision to transfer Luftwaffe forces from the

Russian front would lead in January 1942 to heavy air strikes to suppress Malta's offensive capability.[29]

In some respects the British naval position in the Mediterranean looked very favourable, especially after the victories at Taranto and Cape Matapan. The post-war 'staff history' prepared by the British Admiralty later asserted that the Royal Navy had established 'command of the sea' in the Mediterranean by October 1940, but this is too strong a claim. With only distant operating bases at Gibraltar and Alexandria and with the availability on Malta of only small offensive striking forces, there was little to stop the flow of Axis supplies to North Africa (even with the aid of Ultra). According to Italian figures, 354,600 tons of cargo were sent between June 1940 and January 1941 (an average of 47,000 tons a month), of which only 8,000 tons failed to arrive across the whole six and a half months. In the same period 41,500 personnel were transported, and under 800 men were lost.[30]

For most of 1941, as well, a high proportion of the Axis shipments (based on cargo tonnage) continued to arrive safely. The weight of cargo despatched averaged over 90,000 tons a month for the period February to November 1941; it dropped to 47,700 tons in December, mainly as a result of the arrival of Force K. The proportion of this cargo which arrived was over 90 per cent for the first six months of 1941, but between 70 and 80 per cent for five of the last months; the bad month was November 1941, when 79,200 tons were despatched and only 29,800 tons arrived (38 per cent). Some ninety-three supply ships bound for Libya in 1941 were sunk, a total of 378,000 tons. Only 30,800 tons were sunk in the first quarter of 1941, but 131,300 in the fourth.[31]

BRITISH SEA ROUTES TO NORTH AFRICA AND MALTA

Although a few special British convoys were run across the Mediterranean from Gibraltar to Alexandria, they were very much the exceptions (until the summer of 1943). The risks were too high, and each attempt required a full fleet escort. The most important was Operation TIGER in April–May 1941, when five fast merchant ships with Army supplies were rushed through the Mediterranean, along with the modernised battleship *Queen Elizabeth*. On the whole the defence of Egypt and the Suez Canal was dependent on very long maritime supply lines, and in the case of forces from Britain they came around Africa. Convoys of troopships and supplies sailed down the African west coast and around the Cape of Good Hope, then via the Indian Ocean and the Red Sea. The first WS convoy (a heavy cruiser and the Cunard liners *Queen Elizabeth* and *Mauretania*) had departed at the end of June 1940 with 10,000 troops; subsequent convoys sailed monthly. Altogether some fourteen WS convoys were sent in 1940–41; only one ship was lost en route.

Once London decided to reinforce the Middle East, growing numbers of troops and equipment were sent. In the period from the end of August to December 1940 some 76,000 personnel were sent from the UK, and 49,400 from Australia, New Zealand and India. In the first seven months of 1941, the number sent rose to 239,000 British Empire personnel: 144,000 from the UK, 60,000 from Australia and New Zealand, and 35,000 from India and South Africa. Shipping of 'military cargo' to the Indian Ocean Area, which was made up of the Middle East, the Persian Gulf and India, came to 854,700 tons in the seven months from June to December 1941, an average of 122,100 tons a month.[32] This leads to a feature of the 'Desert War' that is often overlooked: the British prevailed because they could reinforce Egypt using oceanic links faster than the Axis could reinforce Libya using the much shorter convoy route across the central Mediterranean.

British supply operations *within* the Mediterranean were also important. A considerable amount of shipping was involved in moving troops to Greece and supplying them there during the first months of 1941. Short-range supply operations along the coast of Egypt and Cyrenaica also contributed to British success. The most important were those taking supplies into the isolated fortress at Tobruk from April to December 1941. British warships also provided gunfire support, but it was notable that there was no attempt to turn the Axis flank by a significant amphibious operation.

The best-known British convoys within the Mediterranean in 1940–41 were involved with supporting besieged Malta. A number of these were special operations to ferry aircraft into the island to defend it from Axis bombers. The distance from British-held airfields to Malta was, for most of the period 1940–42, too far for British single-engined fighter aircraft of the time to fly, from either end of the Mediterranean. In a method pioneered off Norway, RAF fighters were flown to Malta from carriers. Altogether there were thirteen of these operations in 1940–41, the first in August 1940.

Weapons, equipment and fuel were also brought to Malta by individual fast warships, 38-knot cruiser-minelayers like HMS *Manxman*, and by submarines. The quantities these ships could carry was relatively small, and merchant ships in the 'Malta convoys' were of greater importance. These Malta convoys, as already described, were often very complex operations, involving movements from both Gibraltar and Alexandria and very heavy warship escort. The prototype was the July 1940 operation that led to the Battle off Calabria. The first proper convoy was MF.2, a fast convoy of three cargo ships, escorted by three cruisers and four destroyers, which left Alexandria on 29 August 1940 and arrived in Malta four days later. This was part of Operation HATS, already mentioned (see above, p. 119). A similar operation in late November involved small convoys from either end of the Mediterranean, including the COLLAR convoy, linked to the Battle of Cape Spartivento.

The threat to the convoys and the air bombing of Malta itself increased in January 1941 with the arrival in Sicily of the German X. Fliegerkorps. As already mentioned, in Operation EXCESS the *Southampton* was lost and the *Illustrious* damaged. Nevertheless, three small convoys (MC.4, MW.5 and ME.6) did arrive safely in Piraeus, Malta and Alexandria. Fortunately for the British, the bulk of X. Fliegerkorps was moved away from Sicily to North Africa and the Balkans, and by the summer of 1941 many German fighters and bombers were sent to the Russian front. Air attacks on Malta and the convoys were now mostly left to the Italians, who were less effective. In July 1941 the British Operation SUBSTANCE resulted in the safe passage of six cargo ships to Malta, including troop reinforcements.

The Malta convoys were also threatened in the summer of 1941 by the heavy ships of the Italian fleet, which had now completed repairs after Taranto and Cape Matapan. Admiral Iachino took a major force to sea at the end of August 1941, intending to intercept a British convoy that was believed to be bound for Malta from Gibraltar. There was, however, no convoy, and the main outcome was to waste dwindling Italian supplies of fuel oil. A real British convoy (GM.2) was sent from Gibraltar in September, as part of Operation HALBERD. The Admiralty had reinforced Admiral Somerville's Force H with a powerful heavy escort. It consisted of three of the most powerful British battleships, the 16-inch-gun *Nelson* and *Rodney*, and the new *Prince of Wales*. The *Ark Royal* provided air support. Air attacks were mounted only by the Regia Aeronautica, without Luftwaffe help. A number of hastily organised torpedo-bomber squadrons had been organised; the *Aerosiluranti* squadrons were mostly equipped with Savoia-Marchetti SM.79 trimotor bombers, each carrying an external torpedo. Only one merchant ship out of nine in GM.2 was sunk, by an SM.79. The *Nelson* was, however, also damaged by another SM.79 torpedo hit; she would not complete her repairs and return to the fleet until April 1942. A number of Italian scout planes and bombers were shot down or driven off by the Fulmar fighters of the *Ark Royal* CAP and by AA fire. Admiral Iachino took the *Littorio* and the *Vittorio Veneto* to sea from Naples, but he withdrew the battleships when, once again, his air support failed to arrive.

While Somerville's Force H was operating successfully in the western basin, Cunningham's Mediterranean Fleet at Alexandria had made good some of its losses around Crete, even without an aircraft carrier. It now included the modernised battleships *Queen Elizabeth* and *Valiant*, and the *Barham* returned to the fleet in September 1941 after repairs in South Africa. The ships from Alexandria were in the last months of 1941 having considerable success in supporting the coastal flank of British Army fighting in the Western Desert. Unfortunately for both Somerville and Cunningham, a new factor was now introduced into the Mediterranean campaign in the form of German U-boats.

One of the surprising features of the Mediterranean campaign since June 1940 had been the poor showing of the Italian submarine force. When Italy entered the war in June 1940 the Regia Marina possessed 115 submarines – the largest underwater fleet in the world, except for that of the USSR (and the Soviet Navy included a large number of very small coastal submarines). Preparing in the 1920s and 1930s for a Mediterranean naval war with France, the Italians put a major effort into submarine construction, with Mussolini offering enthusiastic support. In wartime there was an early success: a submarine sank the old light cruiser HMS *Calypso* south of Crete on the second day of the fighting, but after that the Italian boats had only occasional success: in 1940–41 they sank the new cruiser *Bonaventure*, a destroyer and a submarine. The Italians seldom succeeded in co-ordinating submarine operations with their surface fleet, and the boats tended to be deployed in static patrol areas. Heavy losses were suffered; the British sank ten boats in the first month of the war, partly thanks to code-breaking.[33] Meanwhile, some of the best Italian submarines were sent to operate in the Atlantic.

The first U-boats arrived in September 1941, fifteen months after the Mediterranean war began. Hitler had first raised the possibility of deploying submarines in late August, when the objective was to provide some naval support to Rommel's Panzergruppe Afrika (the successor to the Afrika Korps). Six boats sailed in the first wave, part of a total of thirty-five that were despatched during the autumn and winter of 1941–42; of these, two were sunk en route, and six had to turn back. All were medium-sized Type VII boats, judged best suited for Mediterranean operations. Admirals Raeder and Dönitz both opposed diversion of U-boats from the Atlantic 'tonnage war', in which the objective was to sink as much merchant tonnage as possible; there were indeed relatively few cargo ships to attack within the Mediterranean. On the other hand, the submarines had great successes against warships. On 13 November 1941 the *U 81* successfully attacked the carrier *Ark Royal* east of Gibraltar, when she was returning from flying off RAF Hurricanes to Malta. The '*Ark*' was at the time perhaps the most famous ship in the Royal Navy, not least because German propaganda had repeatedly reported her as sunk. This time the luck of the big ship had run out. She was only hit by one torpedo, and stayed afloat for fifteen hours. She could have been saved except for poor damage control; only one crew member was lost. She was the first modern fleet carrier to be sunk in the 1939–45 war.

More tragic was the fate of the *Barham*, sunk a week and a half later at the other end of the Mediterranean. On 25 November 1941 the battleship was supporting the British Army's CRUSADER offensive in Libya, along with her sister ships *Valiant* and *Queen Elizabeth*. The *Barham* was hit by three torpedoes fired at point-blank range by the *U 331*. Surely the most dramatic naval newsreel footage of World War II was taken by a Gaumont-British News cameraman (John Turner) aboard the nearby *Valiant*, who later recalled the scene:

> As she turned on her side and the funnel touched the water, terrifying in its suddenness, there was a terrible, unforgettable explosion and . . . she died and blew up – her whole inside, turrets, machinery, pieces of ship flung high in the air. A huge pall of smoke, red glow in the centre, rose above the water, billowing out and mercifully covering the dreadful scene that must have been enacted in those dark oily seas.[34]

Loss of life was very heavy. The following month another U-boat sank the light cruiser *Galatea* with most of her crew, in a night attack off Alexandria.

On 19 December 1941 a direct attack was made on the British Mediterranean Fleet in Alexandria. This would be the greatest success of the Regia Marina. The Italians had a long interest in unconventional naval operations, dating back to their daring coastal operations against the Austro-Hungarian Navy in 1917–18. A special attack unit was formed, which in March 1941 took the name of *Decima MAS* (*X^a Flottiglia Mezzi d'Assalto*). The unit had success with explosive speedboats crippling the heavy cruiser *York* in harbour at Suda Bay in Crete in March 1941 (but also suffering a disastrous failure in an attack on Valletta, Malta, in July 1941, in which Vittorio Moccagatta, the commander of the unit, was killed). Also developed was a submersible attack craft or manned torpedo, officially designated as an SLC (*Siluro a lenta corsa*, low-speed torpedo). These midget submarines had a detachable limpet-mine warhead and could be transported on the deck of a submarine; two 'assault divers' (*nuotatori d'assalto*) rode astride the SLC.[35] At Alexandria on the night of 18/19 December 1941 the two surviving Mediterranean Fleet battleships, the *Queen Elizabeth* and the *Valiant* (both extensively modernised in the 1930s), were badly damaged by assault divers riding three SLCs from the submarine *Scirè*. The *Queen Elizabeth* would be under repair in Egypt until June 1942; she was then sent around the Cape to the US, and returned to service only in June 1943. The *Valiant* was repaired in Alexandria and Durban (South Africa), and by August 1942 was operational in the Kenya-based Eastern Fleet. After the loss of the *Barham* and the December 1941 attack no battleships were available to the Mediterranean Fleet. In his report on the effect of two dozen torpedo planes at Taranto in November 1940

Cunningham had remarked that 'as an example of "economy of force" it is probably unsurpassed';[36] the attack on Alexandria by six assault divers was even more exemplary.

The British had launched a long-prepared and successful land offensive, Operation CRUSADER, in November and December 1941. In his summary of December events Admiral Cunningham noted the irony: 'The striking power of the fleet was thus seriously reduced just at the time when we had at last reached a position to operate offensively in the Central Mediterranean.'[37] Even worse was to follow for much of 1942, with the outbreak of war in the Far East. The Mediterranean Fleet based in Alexandria never regained its former strength, and in 1942 British sea power was concentrated in the western basin.

CHAPTER 7

DEFENDING THE MOTHERLAND

The Embattled Soviet Navy, June 1941–December 1944

THE TALLINN CATASTROPHE, 28–29 AUGUST 1941

Ten weeks had passed since Hitler's surprise attack on the USSR on 22 June 1941. Now, in late August 1941, a large part of the Soviet Navy was based in Tallinn, the capital of Estonia, and these ships were in grave danger. Estonia had been annexed by the Soviet Union in the summer of 1940, and soon afterwards the main base of the Red-Banner Baltic Fleet had moved forward to Tallinn.[1] The Estonian port took the place of Kronshtadt, a port on Kotlin Island, at the eastern end of the Gulf of Finland, near Leningrad. A network of Soviet defensive minefields and coastal batteries had been constructed at the western entrance to the Gulf of Finland on territory seized from Estonia and Finland; these defences prevented the Kriegsmarine from moving its big ships forward. The situation on the land front, however, was perilous. The retreating Red Army formations in Estonia had fallen back on Tallinn; German ground troops had now encircled the city and cut the rail line to Leningrad.

Admiral V.F. Tributs, C-in-C of the Baltic Fleet since April 1939, had requested permission to pull his fleet units back to Kronshtadt. The C-in-C of the Northwestern Theatre, Marshal Voroshilov (in Leningrad), had at first refused this, as had the People's Commissar of the Navy, Admiral Nikolai Kuznetsov (in Moscow), and – apparently – Stalin himself. By Tuesday, 26 August, however, advancing German troops were close enough to shell Tallinn harbour, and the high command was forced to relent.

Now, Tributs had quickly to arrange the evacuation of a very large number of warships, transports and naval auxiliaries. They were carrying the remnants of Tallinn's defenders (many of them wounded), as well as Soviet civilians. He organised this mass of ships into three covering groups and four convoys.

On the outbreak of the war the major surface combat ships in the Baltic Fleet comprised two battleships, two cruisers, nineteen destroyers and nine corvettes. Of the larger ships, only the cruiser *Kirov* had to be moved to safety that August. A sister ship, the *Maksim Gorkii*, was under repair in Leningrad; her bow had been blown off by a mine in June.[2] The battleships *Marat* and *Oktiabrskaia Revoliutsiia*, built during World War I, had been moved from Tallinn back to Kronshtadt in the first week of the war. But the destroyers and smaller warships remained, and were now organised in three detachments to escort the merchant ships.

The Main Body included the *Kirov*, three modern destroyers, the old destroyer *Iakov Sverdlov*, twenty-four smaller ships and an icebreaker; Tributs and part of his staff were aboard the *Kirov*. In the Covering Force, under Admiral Iurii Panteleev, the most important warships were the destroyer leader *Minsk* and two other new destroyers. Three old destroyers and three corvettes made up the Rear Guard.

The largest merchant ships, including nineteen transports, were grouped in four convoys, each with a number of small escorts. Altogether there were 200 vessels of all kinds, including minesweepers, motor torpedo boats, submarines, tugboats and harbour craft. The transports were all relatively small, 1,500–4,000 tons. Two-thirds came from the merchant fleets of the annexed Baltic states. Most of the ships were overloaded.

Embarkation began on Wednesday afternoon (the 27th). Rough seas delayed departure, and as a result the minesweepers were not able to clear a safe channel to the east during daylight. The first ships began to move only on Thursday afternoon.

The obstacle preventing a safe withdrawal was a maze of minefields north of Cape Juminda, which is a headland on the Estonian coast about 30 miles north-east of Tallinn. The mines had been laid by Finnish and German ships from Helsinki, and the danger zone stretched about 35 miles from east to west, and about 20 miles from north to south. Evacuation had been left far too late. Route planning had been done at the last moment and there were too few minesweepers.

The Soviet ships approached the Juminda barrage in the last hour of daylight on Thursday. Luftwaffe attacks began, carried out by Ju 88 bombers from Finland. Four ships were lost, including the transport SS *Alev* with 1,280 people aboard, among them 800 wounded soldiers; she was damaged by the air attack and then drifted onto one of the minefields; only six of those aboard were rescued. A similar ghastly fate awaited the overloaded headquarters ship SS *Vironia*; she sank in five minutes during the night, taking 1,500 passengers with her. The short hours of darkness gave some protection from air attack. Many other ships, not damaged by bombs, ran onto the Juminda minefield during

Thursday night. From the Main Body the destroyer *Iakov Sverdlov* sank with heavy loss of life; among those killed aboard her was Johannes Lauristin, the Communist Prime Minister the Soviets had installed in Estonia in 1940.

After the minesweepers of the Main Detachment were damaged, Admiral Panteleev was ordered to provide replacements from his Covering Force. This left his force vulnerable to mines; Panteleev's flagship, the *Minsk*, struck one at 9.40 p.m. The *Skoryi*, the destroyer astern, was ordered to go ahead and take the *Minsk* in tow. The admiral later recalled the events:

> Having received all instructions for towing, and wishing us luck, the *Skoryi* steamed ahead. Her stern slowly went past our bow, the towline began to tighten. The destroyer's stern light glistened like a little star . . .
>
> To all of us the explosion seemed far away and deep. I remember only the shout of the signalman in the darkness: 'It's the *Skoryi*.'
>
> The sailor's voice was cut short. I saw how the destroyer drifted to port, her stem rose out of the water, and at the same time the stern, with the propellers and rudder, came up . . . The ship's hull bent like a jack-knife and swiftly sank below the waves. A striking sound like dozens of cupboards full of dishes falling over could be heard, and the scraping of metal, and the hissing of steam, literally molten steel sank in the water . . . All this seemed like a nightmare. Dozens of heads bobbed up in the sea, and indistinct shouting could be heard.

The boats of the *Minsk* picked up about 100 men. At 10.45 p.m. Panteleev ordered his ships to drop anchor.[3]

The Rear Guard proceeded without minesweepers and suffered the loss of all three outdated destroyers and two of three corvettes. Of the civilian convoys, Convoy No. 1 lost the transport SS *Ella* with 850 passengers; Convoy No. 3 lost the SS *Everita* with nearly 1,500 troops. From the flagship, Admiral Tributs finally ordered all ships to drop anchor and await daylight. Some fifteen smaller vessels had gone down from the convoys by this time.

Even worse was to come at sunrise on Friday morning (the 29th), when the ships were exposed again to air attacks, and in greater strength. The *Kirov* and the other surviving ships from the three fleet groups which had passed through the minefield now made off east to Kronshtadt, with damaged vessels – including the *Minsk* – in tow. The surviving merchant ships and the slower escorts were left behind. Several more were mined before they could get clear of Cape Juminda. These included the last corvette and the transport SS *Balkhash* from Convoy No. 3; some 3,815 people seem to have been lost with the *Balkhash*, evidently the most lethal sinking in the evacuation. Very few of these vessels carried AA guns, and the handful of short-range Soviet fighter planes available were sent up to cover the retreating warships rather than the transport ships. Several more ships went down with heavy loss of life during the day, others beached themselves on nearby islands. Some damaged vessels were finished off by the Luftwaffe on Saturday. Large numbers of survivors were rescued, others made their way to islands like Suursaari (Hogland), where they were eventually picked up by rescue ships from Kronshtadt. Altogether 28,600 Army and Navy personnel and 13,400 civilians had begun the desperate evacuation. In the end 26,000 made it to Leningrad and Kronshtadt – many after having been picked up from sunken ships. Lost were nineteen warships, including five destroyers, three corvettes and two submarines. Some forty-three other ships went down, including eighteen transports. Altogether about 15,000 people perished. In human terms this would be the worst convoy disaster of the whole war.[4]

REBUILDING THE SOVIET NAVY IN THE 1930S

Russia's naval tradition dated from the early eighteenth century, further back than that of the US, Germany or Japan. For much of the nineteenth century it had operated the world's third-largest navy, after Britain and France. In the Cold War the Soviet fleet would be second only to that of the US. Unfortunately, in 1941 the Soviet Navy was the weakest of those of any of the great powers.

Geographically, Russia was, like France and Germany, a continental power; indeed, it was almost a continent in its own right. But this meant that the four Russian fleets – Baltic, Black Sea, Pacific and Northern – were cut off from one another. And long land frontiers meant that the first priority for military expenditure was the ground forces that guarded them. Meanwhile, the early twentieth century had been disastrous for the Russian Navy. A war was fought with Japan in 1904–05, to which nearly all ships of the Baltic Fleet – the main naval force – were sent; after an epic global cruise most were sunk or captured. Reconstruction began slowly. In World War I naval losses of the small Baltic and Black Sea fleets were low, but then the 1917 revolution and civil war ravaged trained personnel and equipment. Red Army ground forces finally prevailed in 1920, but only after a period when foreign powers and counter-revolutionaries had occupied nearly all Russia's ports; very little naval strength remained in the Black Sea, the Arctic north or the Pacific. Part of the Baltic Fleet survived at Petrograd/Leningrad and at Kronshtadt, but in bad repair. Worse still, the forward defences in the Baltic Sea were lost when Finland and the Baltic states gained their independence.

The 1920s was a decade of gradual recovery for the country as a whole, and also for the remains of the Navy. Military forces were a luxury for Russia in that decade, and most funds available were devoted to the ground forces. Of the surviving ships, the older ones were scrapped, and the newer ones repaired – notably three Baltic dreadnoughts, commissioned during World War I, which were given new revolutionary names – *Marat* (a radical leader of the French Revolution), *Oktiabrskaia Revoliutsiia* ('October Revolution') and *Parizhskaia Kommuna* ('Paris Commune'). A few vessels half-built in 1914–17 were completed. The Black Sea Fleet was reinforced in 1929 by a battleship and a cruiser sent from the Baltic. The infamous White Sea–Baltic Canal (*Belomorkanal*), dug by forced labourers of the Gulag, made it possible to transfer destroyers and submarines from the Baltic to the White Sea. Meanwhile the opening of the Northern Sea Route around the Arctic coast of Russia allowed icebreakers to escort small groups of ships between the White Sea and the Pacific. Small fleets were created in the Pacific (1932) and the Arctic north (1933), which were provided with a few of the older destroyers from the Baltic.

In the late 1920s Stalin secured his political power, an industrialisation drive began and foreign threats seemed to multiply. Although the new mechanised ground forces still had first call on resources, the future of the fleet began to be discussed. The few survivors of the tsarist naval officer corps envisaged a traditional 'balanced fleet' with battleships and cruisers. Others, however, advocated doctrines not that different from those of the French Jeune École, with a 'mosquito fleet' of MTBs. The effectiveness of the German U-boat fleet had been demonstrated in 1914–18, and some naval leaders favoured a fleet organised around the submarine. These relatively inexpensive alternatives were also favoured by the Army-dominated General Staff. In addition, the biggest immediate threat seemed to come from Japan (which annexed Manchuria in 1931), so forces were needed that could be transferred by rail from European Russia to eastern Siberia. Through the first half of the 1930s there was a concentration on MTBs and small submarines, as well as aviation and coastal artillery.

The USSR built more MTBs and submarines than any of the other naval powers, but this strength was misleading. The MTBs were mostly small, unseaworthy and short-ranged. Some of the early Soviet-designed submarines were failures. Others were small. The 95 'M' type boats (the 'M' stood for *malyi* or 'small'), which joined the fleet from 1934 onwards, were coastal-defence boats. The pre-war versions displaced about 160–200 tons and were only 120 feet long, armed with two torpedoes and manned by a crew of twenty; their main virtue was that they could be moved from base to base by railway. There were some good conventional boats. The 840-ton 'S' type began to join the fleet in 1936 but only sixteen were in service in June 1941. Although these were known as the 'Stalinets' ('Stalinist') type, they were designed by a German firm in Bremen.

More numerous but smaller and slower were the 600-ton 'Shch' type ('shch' being the transliteration of a single letter of the Cyrillic alphabet). The first was commissioned in the Baltic in 1933; some eighty-one were with the fleets in June 1941. Finally, there were in the Baltic eleven ocean-going submarines (or submarine-cruisers) of the 1,490-ton 'K' (*Kreiser*) type, the first of which entered service in the Baltic in December 1939.

New surface ship construction had begun in 1927 with a class of 450-ton corvettes,[5] followed by a few big (2,200-ton) destroyers ('leaders'), built – very slowly – in Russia with French assistance. Then came a large class of 1,600-ton conventional destroyers, their design influenced by consultants from Fascist Italy. The first of the 1,600 tonners, the *Gnevnyi* ('Tempestuous'), was laid down in Leningrad in November 1935, and through 1942 nearly fifty units were built, but spread across all four fleets. At the same time construction began in Leningrad and Nikolaev (on the Black Sea) of the first four of a class of six 7,900-ton light cruisers, armed with nine 7.1-inch guns. These were designed, like the destroyers, with Italian technical help; the turbines for the first unit completed, the *Kirov*, were supplied by a firm in Italy. The four built in the Baltic (the *Kirov* and the *Maksim Gorkii*) and the Black Sea (the *Voroshilov* and the *Molotov*) would be the only large modern warships the Soviet Navy would operate during the war.

The decision to create an ocean-going fleet of conventional surface ships dated from the end of 1935. It was linked to the new round of international naval competition. Japan had announced it would no longer be subject to naval arms limitation treaties, and the Anglo-German Naval Agreement allowed the expansion of the Kriegsmarine. A Soviet shipbuilding programme was developed in 1937–39 as part of the Third and Fourth Five-Year Plans for the national economy (covering the period 1938–47). The version of August 1939 envisaged fifteen new battleships and sixteen battle cruisers, two aircraft carriers and twenty-two new light cruisers, as well as numerous destroyer leaders, destroyers, corvettes, submarines and smaller vessels. Submarines were still highly rated, and 247 new boats were included in the plans.[6]

The programme developed in 1937–39 was highly unrealistic to start with; it was delayed by extreme political events, shipyard limitations, lack of steel and armour plate, and the beginning of the European war. The first new battleship, the *Sovetskii Soiuz* ('Soviet Union'), was laid down in Leningrad in July 1938. Some 880 feet long and displacing 59,000 tons, she would have been inferior in size only to the Japanese 'Yamato' class (840 feet, 68,000 tons); armament was nine 16-inch guns. Three more of the 'Sovetskii Soiuz' class were begun later, one at Nikolaev, and the other two in a huge indoor double slipway built at Molotovsk (now Severodvinsk), near Arkhangelsk. Work also commenced on two battle cruisers, armed with nine 12-inch guns, at Leningrad and Nikolaev in

November 1939. Some 790 feet long and displacing 40,000 tons, they would have been larger than the 'Scharnhorst' class (741 feet, 32,000 tons). When 22 June 1941 came, none of the battleships or battle cruisers had reached even the launching stage. A few of the improved 'Chapaev' class of 11,100-ton light cruisers were launched, but they would not be completed until well after 1945. In October 1940 as tension with Germany increased, it was decreed that measures needed to be taken to prioritise construction of cruisers, destroyers, corvettes and submarines; no more battleships or battle cruisers were to be begun, and construction of one of the two Molotovsk battleships would be abandoned. In July 1941, a desperate month after the invasion, another decree halted all work on capital ships and cruisers.

Neither of the aircraft carriers included in the Ten-Year Plan was actually laid down. Nevertheless, aviation was an important component of the Soviet Navy. In June 1941 there were 2,700 naval aircraft, with 1,200 in the Pacific Fleet, 710 in the Baltic Fleet, and 640 in the Black Sea Fleet. Each of the three major fleets contained a torpedo-bomber regiment (comparable to an RAF wing) with twin-engined Iliushin DB-3T and DB-3F aircraft, as well as many smaller MBR-2 flying boats. The fighters and light bombers, however, were the same types as those of the Red Army Air Force (VVS), and they were inferior to most Luftwaffe types.

The command structure of this growing navy in 1941 was unlike any other. The larger part of the tsarist-era officer corps left after the 1917 revolution; some who remained in Soviet service retired or were removed in the early 1930s. Ranks and officer status were restored in both the Army and Navy in 1935. (The rank of admiral – and of general in the Army – was restored only in May 1940.) With the big shipbuilding programme came major reorganisation. In December 1937 a separate People's Commissariat (Ministry) of the Navy was created – separate from that of the Army – along with a Main Naval Staff (*GMSh*). Unfortunately this was also the time of Stalin's Purges. *Five* heads of the Navy in succession were dismissed, tried and shot between June 1937 and January 1939. Other victims were the commanders of all four fleets and a considerable number of other 'command staff' and commissars.

The intensity of the terror slowed at the end of 1938. In the Navy Nikolai Kuznetsov was appointed to the post of People's Commissar in April 1939, at the age of only thirty-four – half the age of Admiral Raeder. A peasant boy from northern Russia, Kuznetsov had joined the new Soviet Navy in 1919 aged fifteen. His studies and shipboard experience were good. He served for a year as chief naval adviser to the Republican Navy in the Spanish Civil War, and in 1938 he replaced the purged commander of the Pacific Fleet, before moving to Moscow. Kuznetsov kept his team of fleet commanders together from 1939 and throughout the war: four admirals, Tributs in the Baltic, Oktiabrskii in the Black Sea, Golovko in the Northern Fleet and Iumashev in the Pacific.

The final pre-war development was co-operation with Nazi Germany under the infamous Non-Aggression Pact of August 1939. Although mainly remembered for the partition of Poland, the pact's important features also included maritime factors. For Germany, increased trade with the USSR provided a route around the British–French naval blockade. For the USSR, the free hand Germany conceded in the Baltic allowed a strengthening of the military position there, as the line of defence was pushed 250 miles to the west, back to where it had been before 1917. As already mentioned, a complex defensive system of Soviet coastal artillery and minefields was laid out to block access to the Gulf of Riga and the Gulf of Finland. Forward naval bases were re-established in Estonia, Latvia and Finland, partly by forced treaties with these small states, partly by military attack (against Finland in 1939), and partly by outright annexation (of Estonia and Latvia in July 1940).

The Soviets obtained technical assistance from Germany, and in exchange provided the Kriegsmarine with secret help. The Germans sold them the incomplete *Lützow*, the fourth 'Admiral Hipper' class heavy cruiser; she was towed to Leningrad in April 1940 (but never completed). As for the Germans, they were provided with a secret naval anchorage (which the Germans called *Basis Nord*) at Zapadnaia Litsa Bay, 35 miles west of Murmansk. After the fall of France in June 1940 the small German raider *Komet* was allowed to transit the Northern Sea Route to attack British shipping in the Pacific.

THE GREAT RETREAT, 1941–42

Admiral Kuznetsov had put the Soviet Navy on an alert status on 19 June 1941. The main warship bases were distant from the frontier, and the initial surprise attacks by the Luftwaffe on the 22nd concentrated on forward Army airfields. German planes dropped some mines off Kronshtadt and Sevastopol, but they were quickly swept. Many of the air squadrons that were part of the Navy suffered heavy losses in the first desperate weeks, including bombers sent out on unescorted strikes against enemy ground targets.

In June 1941 the largest of the Soviet Navy's four fleets was in the Baltic. Admiral Tributs commanded a force with two old battleships, two modern cruisers, fourteen new and seven older destroyers, and eight corvettes. There were forty-two MTBs in two brigades, but only thirty-two minesweepers. The three brigades of submarines contained seventy boats, twenty-three of them of the coastal defence 'M' type. Naval air strength was 709 machines.[7]

The two fleets skirmished at sea, as the Germans, Finns and Soviets all laid minefields at the entrances to the Gulf of Finland and the Gulf of Riga (the Irben Strait). A Soviet covering force ran onto a minefield; the destroyer *Gnevnyi* was sunk on 23 June, and the bow of the cruiser *Maksim Gorkii* was blown off. The cruiser *Kirov* and a flotilla of new destroyers laid mines covering the Gulf of Riga and then withdrew north to Tallinn. The first Soviet success occurred in the sixth week of the war, on 28 July, when the submarine *Shch-307* torpedoed and sank the *U 144* off the entrance to the Gulf of Finland.

In both the Baltic and the Black Sea the real crisis of the fleets was caused by the deep retreat of the Red Army. The Wehrmacht quickly overran western Latvia, taking the new Soviet forward naval base at Liepāja (Libau) from the land side on the fifth day of the war. A submarine flotilla (*divizion*) had been based there; most of the boats managed to escape. Soviet ground forces on the Estonian mainland fell back on Tallinn, with the resulting catastrophe already described.

The Baltic islands of Saaremaa (Ösel) and Hiiumaa (Dagö) in northwestern Estonia were strategically valuable to the Soviets as they anchored from the south the defences covering the entrance to the Gulf of Finland. The island also provided a base for long-range air attacks on Berlin – the first of which was mounted on 7/8 August by a squadron of naval DB-3T torpedo bombers flying from Saaremaa.[8] These forward outposts, however, could not be held. The larger of the two main islands, Saaremaa, was taken by small German landings at the start of October, and Hiiumaa two weeks later. On the northern side the entrance to the Gulf of Finland was Hanko, a forward position on a peninsula seized from Finland in 1940. The Red Army garrison held out here until December 1941, under siege by the Finns. The rear guard at Hanko was picked up by a convoy which had left Kronshtadt on 29 November; it comprised the new 7,500-ton Dutch-built liner *Iosif Stalin*, two modern destroyers and some minesweepers.[9] Having embarked some 5,600 Red Army troops, the liner was crippled by three mines as she threaded her way through a German minefield northwest of Tallinn. About a third of the passengers were transferred to other vessels, but the hulk drifted ashore, where 3,000 survivors fell into German hands.

By September 1941 the main forces of the Baltic Fleet had been squeezed into the eastern end of the Gulf of Finland. Leningrad seemed in imminent danger of capture. Detailed plans were made to scuttle the ships of the fleet if the city fell. In late September 1941 the Germans assembled warships west of the entrance to the Gulf of Finland under Admiral Ciliax, tasked to prevent a possible breakout to Sweden. This was surely an unlikely possibility, but the force included the new battleship *Tirpitz*, the pocket battleship *Admiral Scheer*, four light cruisers, three destroyers and five torpedo boats.

In any event the Soviet warships at Kronshtadt and Leningrad were vulnerable to attacks by German bombers, now operating from nearby airfields. A number were hit or damaged, including, on 21 September, the battleship *Marat*. Heavily armoured battleships (unlike aircraft carriers or cruisers) were normally hard to sink with bombs, but the *Marat* was a small, first-generation dreadnought, and she was hit by a special 1,000kg (2,200lb) heavy bomb dropped by a Stuka. The magazine of her forward triple turret exploded and the entire forward part of the ship was destroyed; the captain and over 300 crew members died. The ship sank in very shallow water at Kronshtadt, but she would never be seaworthy again. Her surviving three turrets, with nine 12-inch guns, were operational, and she served as a static battery for the rest of the siege of Leningrad. The sister ship of the *Marat*, the *Oktiabrskaia Revoliutsiia*, survived hits by six smaller bombs. Six days later, off Oranienbaum, the historic cruiser *Avrora*, still a training ship, was sunk in shallow water by German artillery.[10]

After the air attacks and the Tallinn catastrophe, the Baltic Fleet was left with three damaged heavy ships, the *Oktiabrskaia Revoliutsiia*, the *Kirov* and the patched-up *Maksim Gorkii*, as well as eleven new destroyers. None of these large surface ships would play any further part in the war as sea-going units. But one of the unique features of the Soviet Navy, in the Baltic and elsewhere, was the transfer of personnel from the warships of the fleet to the land front, mostly in special naval infantry units. Some 69,000 Baltic Fleet sailors were transferred to the land front to fight alongside the Red Army in 1941, and 35,000 in 1942.[11] Meanwhile, the incomplete hulls of large fleet units laid down before 22 June 1941 rusted on their slipways – the battleship *Sovetskii Soiuz*, the battle cruiser *Kronshtadt*, four 'Chapaev' class cruisers.

The situation for the Soviet Navy in the Black Sea after June 1941 was more favourable. Admiral Filipp Oktiabrskii commanded much the largest operational force of the Soviet Navy, with the old battleship *Parizhskaia Kommuna*, six cruisers, eight new destroyers and five old ones. There were also forty-four submarines (nineteen small), forty-two MTBs and 640 aircraft.[12] On the Axis side, the Germans had at first no ships at all in the Black Sea, and limited air strength. Romania, allied with Germany, had a navy with only two destroyers and a submarine.

The war began with a flurry of naval action. A German attempt to block Sevastopol with air-dropped magnetic mines failed. Soviet ships bombarded the Romanian port of Constanţa, but the destroyer leader *Moskva* ran onto a minefield on 25 June, and was lost. Long-range naval aircraft were expended in raids against ground targets in Romania, including the Ploieşti oil centre.

The advance of the German and Romanian armies in the south was not as rapid as in the Baltic, but Soviet ground forces were steadily forced back. The main Black Sea shipyard, at Nikolaev, near the mouth of the Dnepr river, fell on 17 August, in the eighth week of the war. Captured on building ways, still at an early stage of construction, were the two giants, the battleship *Sovetskaia Ukraina* and the battle cruiser *Sevastopol*. The Russians managed to evacuate across the Black Sea the hulls of the uncompleted 11,100-ton cruisers *Frunze* and *Kuibyshev* and some destroyers. These were sent to the small Georgian port of Poti, but there were no facilities for completing ships there; the cruisers would not enter service until 1950.

Odessa, the second largest port in the USSR, was bypassed by the advancing Wehrmacht. The Soviets conducted what was in some respects their best naval operation of the war, using their superior fleet to ferry reinforcements into the besieged city. The battle for Odessa lasted from early August until the middle of October – a month after the fall of Kiev. The final evacuation, when it came, was orderly, and the Russians benefited from lessons learned at such high cost at Tallinn.

At the end of September, before Odessa fell, the Germans broke through demoralised Soviet troops guarding the northern entrance to the Crimea peninsula at Perekop. Perhaps the greatest siege of the whole war now began, for the naval base of Sevastopol.

The Germans – despite having few tanks – overran all the rest of the Crimea, a peninsula about the size of Sicily. Warships – notably the destroyer leader *Tashkent* – and submarines of the Black Sea Fleet kept up a flow of reinforcements and supplies from the small ports in the Kuban (the region southeast of the Sea of Azov). The big ships of the fleet, including the battleship *Parizhskaia Kommuna*, provided artillery support. Sevastopol had strong coastal defence guns, but only improvised defences on the land side. Sailors drafted ashore defended the base, and they were reinforced by soldiers evacuated from Odessa.

There were still no Axis naval forces in the region, but the Luftwaffe dominated the skies. On the morning of 7 November 1941 the 4,800-ton cargo liner MV *Armenia*, overloaded with about 5,000 civilians and wounded soldiers, was torpedoed by a lone Heinkel He 111 off Yalta, although she was apparently marked as a hospital ship. The *Armenia* sank in less than five minutes, and only eight survivors were picked up. Four days later Stukas sank the old cruiser *Chervona Ukraïna* ('Red Ukraine' in Ukrainian) at Sevastopol; she had been Admiral Kuznetsov's own command in the 1920s and the 1930s.

At the end of December 1941 the Soviets carried out landings at Kerch and Feodosiia on the eastern side of the Crimea. This was, notably, the first major amphibious operation carried out by any of the Allies. (The first *major* British 'combined operation' came in May 1942, the invasion of Madagascar.) The crossing of the Kerch Strait, beginning on 26 December, was short-range and conducted by small craft. It was notable for the role of Sergei Gorshkov, then a rear admiral commanding the Azov Flotilla (later he would be C-in-C of the Soviet Navy for three decades during the Cold War). More striking was the Soviet attack on the port of Feodosiia, 60 miles to the west, on the neck of the Kerch Peninsula. The first wave arrived in the middle of a winter storm aboard the cruisers *Krasnyi Kavkaz* ('Red Caucasus') and *Krasnyi Krym* ('Red Crimea'), and three destroyers. On three consecutive nights the Soviets landed a total of 29,000 troops at Feodosiia aboard fourteen transports. Altogether, at Kerch and Feodosiia the force put ashore comprised 42,000 men in six infantry divisions. The operation delayed the German attack on Sevastopol, but Feodosiia itself had to be given up at the end of January.

In the end the Germans were able to wear down the garrison of Sevastopol. The large number of Soviet troops that had been ferried into the Crimea during the winter were unable to hold out against the concentrated strength of the German Army and the ground-attack elements of the Luftwaffe. In early July 1942 the defenders of the fortress were overwhelmed. With this ended the first phase of the operations of the Black Sea Fleet.

The Northern Fleet, created in 1933, was the smallest of the four. In June 1941, Admiral Golovko commanded five new destroyers, three outdated ones and seven corvettes. Initial submarine strength was only twenty-two boats, six of the small 'M' type.[13] After the war began eight submarines were despatched to the Northern Fleet through the Belomor Canal from the Baltic, including four of the large (1,500-ton) 'K' type.

Unlike Soviet warships in the Baltic and the Black Sea, those in the Northern Fleet had ready access to the world's oceans, from ice-free Murmansk on the Barents Sea. Murmansk was some 600 miles north, by sea, from the much older White Sea port of Arkhangelsk, which had better port facilities and good connections to the main railway system. Unfortunately frozen seas closed Arkhangelsk from October/November to May/June, which was why Murmansk had been created as an emergency supply port (then called Romanov) during World War I; a railway spur had been hastily laid out to the south in 1915–17. Murmansk lies 35 miles down a long fjord, best known as the Kola Inlet. Near the mouth of the fjord, at Poliarnyi, was established the main base of the Northern Fleet.

Murmansk seemed very vulnerable in the first days of the war, being situated only 60 miles east along the coast from the Finnish port of Petsamo. The Germans had deployed two mountain divisions to northern Norway, and at the end of June 1941 they began to march across the trackless tundra towards Murmansk; the operation was assigned the exotic code name PLATINUM FOX (PLATINFUCHS). The attack stalled at the Litsa river, only halfway to Murmansk.

The terrain was extremely difficult, and the invaders had only limited ground forces and very long supply lines; they faced determined Soviet resistance and suffered heavy losses. As a result, the Litsa would remain the line of the front until the late summer of 1944.

Enemy air and naval forces in the north were also initially limited. Admiral Raeder and the German Naval War Staff believed Murmansk to be of great strategic importance, but they mistakenly assumed the Army would quickly take the port. A handful of German destroyers were eventually brought up north and based in the small Norwegian port of Kirkenes, about 100 miles west of Murmansk on the Varangerfjord.

As for the Soviet Northern Fleet, it did not at first attempt any active operations with surface ships. Submarine successes in 1941 were limited to three enemy ships, totalling 6,400 tons, and a small A/S trawler. Some 11,000 sailors from the Northern Fleet were transferred to fight alongside the Red Army on the main land fronts; others secured the coast west of Murmansk. The British provided some help. Aircraft from the Home Fleet carriers *Furious* and *Victorious* raided Petsamo and Kirkenes on 30 July but suffered heavy losses. In early September the *Argus* flew off two dozen RAF Hurricane fighters to bolster the air defence of Murmansk and Poliarnyi, and a few British submarines operated from Poliarnyi. More important, in early September two British cruisers intercepted a German convoy carrying reinforcements to the Murmansk front. Although the two troopships escaped, the German Army decided to use the safer but slower overland route through Finland. The first British supply convoy from Iceland to Arkhangelsk sailed in August 1941 and arrived without loss. In the first nine months after June 1941 Germans could do little to intercept the convoys, but by the summer of the following year their ships, U-boats and aircraft had become a mortal threat.[14]

THE NAVAL WAR ON THE EASTERN FRONT, 1942–44

The Soviet Navy recovered and developed in the later part of the war, but it remained a junior service. Hundreds of thousands of Soviet sailors continued to serve on the land front. Aircraft of naval aviation units were often diverted for missions in direct support of the Red Army. Many resources were devoted to naval flotillas on inland waters, in Europe on the Volga, Dnepr and Danube rivers, and on lakes Ladoga and Onega.

Admiral Kuznetsov and the Main Naval Staff, based in Moscow, had little role in overall war planning and often learned of operations only as they were taking place; Kuznetsov was not formally a member of Stalin's high command, the *Stavka VGK*, until February 1945. A Stavka decree of March 1944 did raise the Navy's status. All fleets and lake/river flotillas were now (in principle) subordinated directly to Admiral Kuznetsov. In practice the Northern Fleet and the Black Sea Fleet were under Kuznetsov, while the Baltic Fleet was operationally subordinate to the (Army) C-in-C of the Leningrad Army Group (*Front*). The March 1944 decree also specified that air units were to be used essentially for naval missions, although in exceptional cases they could be deployed to support the land front.[15]

The personnel strength of the active fleets (and river flotillas) peaked at about 280,000 in the spring of 1942, dropped to a low of about 230,000 in the autumn of 1943, and then gradually rose to about 310,000 in 1945.[16] Unlike the other major Allied powers, there was very little new construction of large warships during the war, just the completion of a handful of the vessels that had been on the stocks on 22 June 1941. Any 'new' surface ship construction was concentrated on coastal forces – MTBs, minesweepers and small diesel patrol boats of the 'sub-chaser' (*okhotnik*) type.

The most positive development – as elsewhere – was in sea/air warfare. Naval aviation, which had been under General S.F. Zhavoronkov since 1939, began to be rebuilt in 1942. The process accelerated in 1942–44, with the arrival of Lend-Lease equipment. Aircraft operated were still mainly the same Russian-built and Lend-Lease types used by the Red Army Air Force – land-based fighters, attack planes (*shturmoviki*) and light and medium bombers. They gained a numerical superiority, and aircraft quality approached that of the Luftwaffe. No purpose-built 'naval' aircraft were in service except small Soviet-built flying boats and, late in the war, the American-supplied PBY Catalina. Prominent in *minno-torpednaia aviatsiia* (torpedo bomber aviation) were regiments of the American-built Douglas A-20s, used for attacks with torpedoes and 'skip-bombing'.[17] According to Russian data, air attacks accounted for 57 per cent of enemy warships sunk by Soviet forces and 47 per cent of transport ships; in contrast, surface ships were responsible for only 7 per cent of warships sunk and 3 per cent of transport ships.[18]

The situation of Admiral Golovko's Northern Fleet after the winter of 1941–42 was better than that in the other fleets. There had been no desperate retreats or punishing losses of warships. The Belomor Canal was now blocked by the Finns, but reinforcements were available. From the Pacific Fleet three new destroyers arrived via the Northern Sea Route, and six submarines were despatched for transit through the Panama Canal.[19] In 1943 five small 'M' type submarines were transferred north by rail and two 'S' class by a circuitous inland water route.

Britain and the US provided other equipment. In 1943 MTBs, large minesweepers and other coastal craft arrived by sea. In the late summer of 1944 nine ex-American four-stacker destroyers were transferred, along with four new (small) British-built submarines. The destroyers were originally among the fifty vessels provided to Britain in the 1940 'destroyers for bases' deal. The biggest additions were a British battleship and an American light cruiser. They were interim compensation for the Soviet share of the Italian fleet captured in 1943, and were transferred to northern Russia in April 1944. HMS *Royal Sovereign* became the *Arkhangelsk*, and USS *Milwaukee* became the *Murmansk*. Both vessels were outdated, but they were fitted with modern electronics. The *Arkhangelsk*, with a destroyer screen, did apparently mount one sortie in support of convoy JW.59 in August 1944.[20]

Aside from supporting the arrival and departure of the Allied convoys, the Northern Fleet also escorted shipping between Murmansk and Arkhangelsk. Offensive missions included attacking German supply ships in the Varangerfjord. Soviet attacks grew in intensity in 1943 and 1944, combined-arms operations involving aircraft, submarines and MTBs, but they were never able to completely isolate German ground forces. The Northern Fleet submarine brigade accounted for eighteen small supply vessels in 1942, totalling 19,000 tons, and eight in 1943, totalling 26,700 tons.[21] The German forces, for their part, sank only two Northern Fleet ships in 1941, a destroyer and a corvette, but losses mounted. In 1942 another Soviet destroyer was lost in a storm and two corvettes sunk by the enemy, as well as nine submarines. In 1943 Soviet losses were ten submarines, and in 1944 a destroyer, a corvette and four submarines.[22]

The last phase of the war came after September 1944, when Finland signed an armistice. The German forces had to pull back from the approaches to Murmansk, and in October the Red Army launched the 'Petsamo–Kirkenes Operation'. Soviet coastal forces and aircraft took part on a large scale, but the enemy were able to retreat 350 miles to a more defendable position at Lyngenfjord, north of Narvik.

For Admiral Oktiabrskii's Black Sea Fleet the situation became more difficult after the fall of Sevastopol in July 1942. The Germans also captured Rostov that month and then most of the North Caucasus, effectively detaching the Transcaucasus – and the whole Black Sea – from the 'mainland' of the USSR. Having lost the use of Sevastopol in the autumn of 1941, the fleet had had to fall back on Batumi and Poti, small Georgian ports; now even these bases were cut off from most of the USSR. Preparations were made to scuttle the fleet in case the Wehrmacht took all of the Transcaucasus.

On paper the Black Sea Fleet consisted in the late summer of 1942 of the battleship *Parizhskaia Kommuna* (restored to its tsarist name, *Sevastopol*, in 1943), the cruisers *Molotov*, *Voroshilov*, *Krasnyi Kavkaz* and *Krasnyi Krym*, six modern destroyers and two older ones. There were also thirty-four submarines, of which twenty were operational.[23] The Axis attempted to build up their naval forces in the Black Sea with small ships transported by river and railway, including a number of S-boats, which arrived in the spring of 1942, and six small Type IIB U-boats, which entered service in the autumn.

The main naval fighting in late 1942 and 1943 was along the northeastern coast of the Black Sea. The southern German armies were now in retreat, and the Soviet high command planned an ambitious landing near Novorossiisk to block the escape route over the Kerch Strait to the Crimea. Several rifle brigades, with light tanks, were to land at Iuzhnaia Ozereika, a few miles west of Novorossiisk. The cruiser *Voroshilov* and three destroyers provided a preliminary bombardment. On the morning of 4 February 1943 Soviet small craft brought the troops ashore, as artillery support was provided by the cruisers *Krasnyi Kavkaz* and *Krasnyi Krym* and three other destroyers. The Iuzhnaia Ozereika landing force was wiped out; a secondary landing nearer Novorossiisk held on and was reinforced, but there was no Soviet breakout. Admiral Oktiabrskii was dismissed as C-in-C after the Iuzhnaia Ozereika debacle; his replacement was Admiral Vladimirskii, the commander of the Battle Force (*Eskadra*) of the Black Sea Fleet. The Germans were able to keep control of their bridgehead on the Kuban coast from February to September 1943, when they evacuated it by sea.

The Russians now began to prepare for a return to the Crimea. As part of this they suffered their most serious surface ship loss since 1941. On the morning of 6 October 1943, three destroyers were caught south of the Kerch Peninsula, after carrying out a night bombardment of Crimean ports. Stukas damaged the large destroyer *Kharkov*; the *Sposobnyi* tried to take the damaged vessel in tow but was herself hit and sunk by a second dive-bomber sortie, as was the third destroyer, the *Besposhchadnyi*. These vessels made up nearly half the surviving modern destroyer force in the Black Sea. Only 170 of the combined crews of some 900 men were rescued. Stalin himself was highly critical, and on 11 October he issued a directive condemning the 'unnecessary' loss of three major warships. The Black Sea Fleet was to carry out no operations without the authority of the local army group commander, and 'Long-range operations of the fleet's major surface ships are to take place only with permission of the Stavka VGK.'[24] With this ended major surface ship operations, not only in the Black Sea, but also in the Baltic.

The Soviet jump into the eastern Crimea was attempted three weeks later, on 31 October 1943, with landings by an armada of Soviet small craft, one near the town of Kerch, the other at the village of Eltigen. The Germans were able to blockade the Eltigen landing zone, and eventually – in December – to crush it.[25] The northern Soviet beachhead at Kerch held out, although not until early April

1944 could a further advance west into the centre of the Crimea be mounted. In March 1944, a year after sacking Admiral Oktiabrskii, the State Defence Committee (*GKO*) removed Admiral Vladimirskii, and also demoted Admiral G.A. Stepanov, the acting head of the Main Naval Staff in Moscow. This was formally because of the loss of the three destroyers (in October 1943), but probably also because of the stalemate at Kerch; Oktiabrskii meanwhile was brought back as Black Sea C-in-C.

Hitler's 'strategy' at this late stage in the war (1943–45) involved obstinate defence of all territory held. German and Romanian forces were kept in the Crimea and actually reinforced by sea. The Soviet ground offensive into the Crimea began in early April 1944, and within two weeks the enemy had been bottled up in Sevastopol. The final withdrawal, by sea, was carried out under heavy Soviet attacks, mostly by aircraft. Nevertheless, in the last month, from mid-April to mid-May 1944, some 130,000 Axis troops were evacuated by sea to Romania. Soviet submarines remained active, operating from Poti, although they had only a limited impact on Axis shipping both from the Crimea and from the Kuban bridgehead further east. In 1943 five steamers totalling 28,000 tons were sunk, as well as four German landing craft.[26]

The Red Army advance moved rapidly to the northwestern coast of the Black Sea, but Soviet warships played only a minor part. Odessa and Nikolaev were liberated in April 1944. A flotilla (*divizion*) of MTBs – many of them American-built Vosper PT boats – was sent around the Crimea to a base near the mouth of the Dnepr river. In late August 1944 Romania changed sides, and the remaining U-boats were scuttled. Three outdated Italian-built destroyers of the Romanian Navy were handed over and incorporated into the Black Sea Fleet.

The symbolic end of the naval war in the Black Sea was the return of the battle force to Sevastopol. On the morning of 5 November 1944 a column of ships entered the North Harbour, led by the 'Guards cruiser' *Krasnyi Krym* and including the battleship *Sevastopol*, the cruisers *Voroshilov* and *Molotov*, the five surviving Soviet destroyers and three ex-Romanian destroyers. The *Krasnyi Krym* flew the signal 'Greetings from the victors to an undefeated Sevastopol'.[27]

The Baltic Fleet did little in the winter of 1941–42. The Gulf of Finland froze during the winter, and sea-going operations were only possible from April to December. However, that was now only a secondary factor compared to the terrible situation of the *Blokada*, the Siege of Leningrad. It lasted for 900 days, and was accompanied by a famine in the winter of 1941–42 in which 1 million people died. The situation stabilised in the summer of 1942, after many of the survivors were evacuated. But Leningrad and Kronshtadt were cut off from the Russian 'mainland' until January 1943 when a small railway corridor was opened; until then they were supplied by small boats crossing Lake Ladoga (and by an ice road in winter). It was not until the Red Army offensive of January 1944 that the Germans were pushed fully away from the embattled city.

In 1942 the Germans were still worried about possible Baltic operations by Soviet surface ships. In April 1942, at the beginning of the 'campaigning' (ice-free) season, they mounted co-ordinated air strikes codenamed Operation ICE JAM (EISSTOSS) against the warships in the port of Leningrad, but with little success. The Russian surface ships, from battleship to corvettes, were used for the next two years as floating artillery batteries. Their gunfire was especially important in the breakout from the Oranienbaum bridgehead in January 1944; small craft had ferried large numbers of Soviet troops into the bridgehead.

Coastal forces and submarines skirmished in the eastern Gulf of Finland. Fierce battles were fought for small islands; the Soviets held Moshchnyi (Lavansaari), the Germans held Bolshoi and Malyi Tiuters, and the Finns held Suursaari (Hogland). Extensive minefields were laid to contain the Soviet fleet. In 1942 heroic efforts by Soviet submariners did break through at high cost. In total twenty-three merchant ships totalling 52,000 tons were sunk in the Gulf of Finland and the Baltic, for the loss of ten submarines (out of twenty-eight taking part).[28] Before the beginning of the 1943 ice-free season the Germans and Finns laid a double submarine net from west of Tallinn to west of Helsinki. This ended, for sixteen months, any further Soviet submarine breakouts.

In the northern sector of the Soviet–German front, the enemy position remained stable, despite the Soviet victory at Stalingrad at the beginning of 1943. Even after the Germans were pushed back from Leningrad in January 1944, they still held the Baltic region (Estonia and Latvia). The enemy position began to crumble after the Red Army offensive in Belorussia in June 1944. Two follow-on drives were mounted, one along the coast of Estonia towards Tallinn, and a second, south of Latvia, which reached the Gulf of Riga. Another offensive, also in June, forced the Finns to conclude a peace treaty (signed in early September). With Tallinn and Helsinki now both free of German control, access through the Gulf of Finland to the Baltic was finally open again, albeit with a very large mine danger.

Despite these setbacks, Hitler and the C-in-C of the German Navy, now Admiral Dönitz, wanted to preserve a bridgehead in Latvia. This was intended partly to provide a starting point for a hoped-for strategic counter-attack and partly to protect the central Baltic as a training area for a re-equipped U-boat fleet.[29] A number of the surviving cruisers, destroyers and torpedo boats of the Kriegsmarine were committed as gunfire support vessels.[30] The cruiser *Prinz Eugen* shelled a Red Army toehold on the Gulf of Riga and made possible the withdrawal of troops from Estonia west into Courland (Kurland), the northern part of Latvia. The Russians mounted a sizeable amphibious operation to recapture the Baltic islands of Muhu, Hiiumaa and Saaremaa, starting at the end of September 1944. The pocket battleships *Lützow* and *Admiral Scheer*, with accompanying destroyers, provided gunfire artillery support in November 1944 to the ground troops holding the Sõrve (Sworbe) Peninsula on the southern tip of Saaremaa Island; this position commanded the entrance into the Gulf of Riga. Soviet air squadrons attached to the Navy became a more important element in the Baltic, as elsewhere. The most striking single success was the sinking of the *Niobe*, a small German anti-aircraft cruiser (*flakschiff*) in Kotka harbour in eastern Finland in July 1944. The attack was carried out by a large formation of aircraft, including Pe-2 dive bombers and A-20 medium bombers. The 4,000-ton *Niobe* was an old Dutch cruiser, then the *Gelderland*, which had been seized by the Germans in 1940; the intended target was apparently the largest ship in the Finnish Navy, the coast-defence ship *Väinämöinen*. A Soviet bomber also sank the 850-ton German torpedo boat *T 18* off Tallinn in September 1944. No successful attacks, either by aircraft or by submarines, were achieved against larger German warships operating in the Baltic in late 1944, despite an air attack on the *Admiral Scheer* in November off the Sõrve Peninsula.[31]

The paper strength of the Soviet Baltic Fleet towards the end of the war comprised a battleship, two cruisers, ten destroyers and six corvettes. In March 1944 the Stavka ordered the Baltic Fleet to prepare both submarines and major (*krupnye*) warships for operations, but such action did not prove feasible.[32] None of these vessels were committed to battle, either in 1944 or 1945. The main surface ship strength available took the form of MTBs (some now supplied by the US).

In the autumn of 1944 fifteen Soviet submarines were able to operate in the open Baltic for the first time since 1942, after they were transferred (under 'friendly' Finnish escort) with their tenders to Turku and Hanko, ports in western Finland. Operating as far south as Pomerania, their total success over three months of operations at the end of 1944 came to thirteen small merchant ships, totalling 36,000 tons. They would go on to have a more striking impact in the spring of 1945.[33]

CHAPTER 8

AN UNDECLARED NAVAL WAR

The Neutral US and the Axis Threat

THE SINKING OF USS *REUBEN JAMES*, 31 OCTOBER 1941

Have you heard of a ship called the good *Reuben James*
Manned by hard-fighting men both of honour and fame?
She flew the Stars and Stripes of this land of the free
But tonight she's in her grave on the bottom of the sea.

These lines come from a patriotic folk song by Woody Guthrie, written in 1942 and honouring a tragic and now little-remembered incident of the year before. USS *Reuben James* was a four-stacker destroyer, commissioned in 1920. Like most American destroyers she was named after a prominent officer or enlisted man of the US Navy; Boatswain's Mate Reuben James had fought the Barbary pirates alongside Captain Stephen Decatur at the beginning of the 1800s. In the spring of 1941, while America was still neutral, the ship was assigned to patrol duties off the East Coast.

In September 1941 President Roosevelt ordered American warships to escort British convoys across the western part of the Atlantic, and to defend them against German U-boats and surface raiders. As part of this effort the *Reuben James* joined four other US destroyers in Task Unit 4.1.3.[1] The first mission of 'Taffy 3', at the start of October, was to escort the big British westbound convoy ON.20 on the second part of its North Atlantic voyage from Liverpool to Halifax, Nova Scotia. Taffy 3 took over from three British destroyers at what was now called the 'Mid-Ocean Meeting Point' or MOMP.

The second and final convoy mission for the *Reuben James* came at the end of October. Task Unit 4.1.3 escorted the eastbound British convoy HX.156, with fifty-eight merchant ships. On 31 October, with one more day to go before the rendezvous with the British escorts at the MOMP, the *Reuben James* was stationed on the convoy's port quarter. HX.156 was now about 625 miles due west of the Irish coast. Unfortunately, the convoy was sighted before dawn by one of the U-boats of wolfpack STOSSTRUPP ('Shock Troop'). The *U 552* was a Type VIIC submarine on her sixth patrol. Her commander was the very able Lieutenant Erich Topp, who would survive the war as the third most successful U-boat skipper and become an admiral in the West German Navy.

The first contact was reported in the U-boat's log: 'Convoy sighted in broad moonlight, lying roughly 5 nm to the east. Large ships.' After nearly three and a half hours, with dawn approaching, Topp had been unable to work his way through the destroyer screen. He decided to attack one of the escorts: 'From a range of 1,000 m we attack destroyer silhouette with a spread of two torpedoes and sink her. Both torpedoes hit. A huge tongue of flame. The wreck is blown to smithereens by the detonation of its own depth charges.'[2]

At the last moment the escorts had learned from local radio intercepts that a U-boat was shadowing the convoy. This did not save the *Reuben James*, which was hit forward on her port side. She was probably struck by only one torpedo (not two), but it set off an ammunition magazine. Shipfitter 1st Class Fred Zapasnik had the good fortune to be in the after part of the ship. He fought his way up a ladder to the top deck, as water flooded in from above: 'since it was still dark, I could not see what had happened. After my eyes adjusted to the darkness, I was horrified to see that there wasn't anything left of the ship forward of the fourth [rear] stack, which was lying across the deck right in front of me.'[3]

The front portion of the *Reuben James* had sunk in seconds after the explosion. The stern section stayed afloat for about five minutes. Some of the men there were able to get into life rafts; others just jumped into the oily water. Then two of the ship's own depth charges detonated in the water, as they plummeted to their pre-set depth. The explosion killed many of those in the water. Only a third of the crew were picked up by the other American destroyers. Some 115 men out of a crew of 159 'hard-fighting men both of honour and fame' perished, including Lt Commander Heywood Edwards and all his officers; only two men were saved from the forward part of the ship. The following day, at the MOMP, British escorts took over. Convoy HX.156 reached Liverpool without further loss on 5 November.

Lieutenant Topp learned quickly from radio broadcasts that he had sunk an American ship. He realised 'how politically explosive' his action had been; it recalled the events of 1917 when U-boat warfare brought America into the war. He was alone with his thoughts until he returned to base: 'The tension a man endures when he thinks he is making history, however unintentionaly, is indeed enormous.'[4]

Tell me what was their names, tell me what was their names,
Did you have a friend on the good *Reuben James*?
What was their names, tell me, what was their names?
Did you have a friend on the good *Reuben James*?

THE EUROPEAN WAR AND THE TWO-OCEAN NAVY

The *Reuben James* had been part of a very powerful navy. The United States is sometimes portrayed as a nation quite unprepared for war in 1939–41, with an army weaker than that of Belgium. In reality America possessed one of the two biggest navies in the world and maintained a large shipbuilding programme throughout the 1920s and 1930s. Since the late 1930s the country had been actively engaged in an accelerating naval arms race. The US Navy was larger than the Japanese Navy, and roughly comparable in size to the early-war Royal Navy. While the US Navy had fewer cruisers and escort ships than the British, it was ahead in some critical areas, especially naval aviation.

The US had not possessed a full-scale ocean-going fleet, along the lines of the great European navies, until the 1890s. In 1898 a victorious naval war was fought with Spain, and in the first decade of the twentieth century the country began to see the results of a major shipbuilding programme. America had a large population, abundant resources and rapidly growing industry, but it did not have extensive overseas colonies, and its merchant fleet was much smaller than that of Britain. America did produce the best-known advocate of 'sea power', in the form of Captain Alfred Thayer Mahan USN. Mahan's core argument, a highly influential one, was that navies were essential to a world power; he based his case on the rise of Britain in preceding centuries. Mahan also believed that sea power required battleships and the ability to win decisive battles. Mahan's views were taken as gospel by the leaders of the US Navy, and they influenced statesmen and naval officers at home and in other countries.

When World War I began, however, the US was still not among the very largest naval powers. The US Navy included only ten dreadnought battleships, compared to twenty-nine dreadnought battleships and nine battle cruisers in the British Royal Navy, and seventeen dreadnought battleships and seven battle cruisers in the German Navy. In the summer of 1916, immediately after the Battle of Jutland, Congress authorised by an overwhelming vote a five-year, $500-million rolling programme of naval construction. This included ten battleships and six battle cruisers (all armed with 16-inch guns), as well as numerous cruisers, destroyers and smaller ships. The aim was a navy at least comparable to that of any other power, one which would allow the United States (still a neutral state) to assert its influence on a global scale in the post-war period.

To the dismay of the Mahanists, the construction of the battle fleet was delayed when the US actually entered the war in April 1917. This came as a result of the unexpected need to build destroyers and other escorts to deal with the threat of German U-boats. As with much of the American war effort, a late start and long distances meant that World War I ended before a full operational contribution by the US Navy could be made. Nevertheless, 279 new destroyers were ordered; a total of 273 were completed, an unprecedented amount; few were finished in time for active war service. They were known as 'flush-deckers' (because, unlike the previous class, they did not have a raised forecastle) or as 'four stackers' (because they had four thin funnels). They displaced just over 1,000 tons and each was armed with four 4-inch guns and twelve torpedo tubes. The first was the *Caldwell* (DD-69),[5] laid down in December 1916 and commissioned a year later; the last was the *Pruitt* (DD-347), commissioned in September 1922. The *Reuben James* was DD-245. About a hundred of these ships were scrapped or lost between the wars. By 1940 there were only 169 remaining – many in 'mothballs' (long-term storage) – but this still made up a very considerable reserve.

The period from 1919 to 1922 was a strange one. The main wartime threat to Britain and the US, the Navy of Imperial Germany, had disappeared, but a serious naval building race was taking place between the victors. One of them had been a central participant in the sea war (Britain), and the other two had effectively been onlookers but were rivals with one another (the US and Japan). The Washington Naval Conference of 1921–22, mentioned in previous chapters sensibly slowed down this competition. Under the terms of the 1922 Washington Naval Treaty the United States and Britain agreed to parity in battleship numbers and tonnage; the Japanese accepted 60 per cent of the other two. A building 'holiday', initially of ten years, began.

Most of the capital ships of the American 1916 'Big Navy' programme were cancelled or broken up for scrap before completion. In the end only the first three American 16-inch-gun battleships entered service (three of the four planned 'Colorado' class). The six bigger battleships of the (first) 'South Dakota' class (41,400 tons) were not even launched.[6] Two of the six 40,000-ton (890 feet long) battle cruisers (laid down in September 1920 and January 1921) were completed – in 1927 – as the aircraft carriers *Saratoga* and *Lexington*; the other four were cancelled. Under the terms of the supplementary 1930 London Naval Treaty the powers scrapped some of their older dreadnoughts and the US Navy was left with fifteen capital ships – balanced against fifteen British and nine Japanese in a 5:5:3 ratio. The building 'holiday' was extended for five years.

Despite the agreement on capital ships, naval competition continued; this especially involved cruisers. As we have seen, the Washington Naval Treaty did not cap the numbers of these ships, but it did limit their specifications; cruisers could not exceed 10,000 tons, and their guns could be no bigger than 8-inch. The Japanese began a major 'treaty' cruiser programme, followed by Britain and the US. The first American heavy cruiser was the *Pensacola*, laid down in 1925 and completed in 1928. The London Naval Treaty of April 1930 modified the rules, making a distinction between 'heavy' and 'light' cruisers (the latter with 6-inch guns). For Britain, the US and Japan it set numerical and tonnage limitations for cruisers, destroyers and submarines; the US Navy was permitted eighteen heavy cruisers (totalling 180,000 tons), as well as light cruisers (CL) totalling 143,500 tons.[7] Some fifteen American heavy cruisers had been laid down by 1931; three more would be laid down in 1933–35. With their high speed and size they would play a big part in the Pacific war, and seven of the eighteen would be sunk.

Later, during the Great Depression, warship building was an element of President Franklin D. Roosevelt's New Deal public works programme. Roosevelt, who entered office in 1933 and was re-elected by a landslide in 1936, certainly took an interest in the outside world and in the American armed forces, especially the Navy. Before being incapacitated by polio at the age of thirty-nine, the wealthy New Yorker had been a keen amateur yachtsman, and he always had a strong interest in the details of maritime power. He had been Assistant Secretary of the Navy from 1913 to 1920, a time when the fleet was greatly expanded and sent into a shooting war. Serving under Woodrow Wilson, he fully supported the President's advocacy of a leading and active role for America in world affairs, for which sea power was an essential component.

Warship construction acted as 'pump priming' for an economy in depression. It also now seemed an appropriate precaution. The international scene had become more troubling, with Japanese aggression in Manchuria in 1931–32 and the success of the Nazis in Germany in 1933. As part of the New Deal emergency funding programme of March 1933 the US Navy was able to order construction of the – later to be famous – carriers *Yorktown* and *Enterprise*, four large light cruisers, twenty destroyers and other ships. More radical was the Vinson–Trammell Act of March 1934. With this, Congress provided blanket authorisation for building up and maintaining the US Navy at full (Washington/London) treaty strength of 'under-age' warships over the course of the next eight fiscal years.[8] Influential in steering the programme through the legislature was a long-serving Democratic Congressman from Georgia, Carl Vinson, who was the chair of the House Naval Affairs Committee. The Second Vinson Act of May 1938 extended the principle of the 1934 law into a period when the international naval arms limitations were no longer in effect (after 31 December 1936). It authorised the enlargement of warship tonnage by 20 per cent. In addition, the President was authorised to raise tonnage of individual battleships to over

35,000 tons, if he judged that other states were now prepared to exceed the Washington Treaty limit. This latter provision allowed the laying down of the 48,110-ton 'Iowa' class, the first two vessels being ordered on 1 July 1939 (and laid down in June 1940).

There was a huge acceleration of American shipbuilding in June–July 1940. However, it is important to bear in mind that *before* this, from 1934 until the beginning of 1940, the US had actually begun construction of a very large number of new warships. This development, in itself, had big implications in terms of international rivalry (especially with Japan) and the eventual conduct of World War II. The warships involved included six 35,000-ton fast battleships (the 'North Carolina' and – new – 'South Dakota' class), two more carriers (the *Wasp* and the *Hornet*), six more cruisers, sixty-nine destroyers and thirty submarines. In terms of the coming Atlantic war it was significant that American shipyards had also begun construction of the 'Benson/Gleaves' class, a standard 1,620-ton destroyer with five 5-inch guns and ten torpedo tubes; this would eventually be built in large numbers, with repeat orders. The lead ship, USS *Benson*, was laid down in May 1938 and commissioned in July 1940.[9] All these ships, combined with the construction of the 1920s, would provide the force of vessels with which the US Navy, in 1942, turned the tide in the Pacific and contributed significantly to the war in Europe.

In the spring of 1940 the international situation had worsened, with the outbreak of the 'European war'. The French capitulation in June and the possibility of British defeat made the international danger to the US seem even greater. On 14 June, two weeks after Dunkirk, the President signed into law the Naval Expansion Act of 1940 (also known as the Third Vinson Act) which allowed for a further 11 per cent increase of authorised under-age tonnage, beyond that of 1938; the increase amounted to 167,000 tons, giving a total of 586,857 tons. That in itself would have been remarkable, but a month later, after the fall of France, Congress passed the Vinson–Walsh Act, better known as the Two-Ocean Navy Act. Authorised tonnage was increased by 70 per cent, to a total 1,892,857 tons. The giant programme involved long-term plans to construct seven battleships (two more of the 'Iowa' class and five of the 60,500-ton 'Montana' class), six 'Alaska' class battle cruisers, eleven 'Essex' class aircraft carriers, eight 'Baltimore' class heavy cruisers, thirty-six 'Cleveland' and 'Atlanta' class light cruisers, 204 destroyers and seventy-three submarines.[10] The programme was intended to be completed by 1946–47. It would take a long time to roll out, and wartime challenges would bring major alterations. However, one of the battleships in the Fiscal Year 1941 programme, USS *Missouri*, would have an historic role. Launched at the New York Navy Yard in January 1944 and entering active Pacific service a year later, she would be the setting for the Japanese surrender ceremony.

American naval aviation will be discussed more fully in a later chapter.[11] It should be stressed here, however, that it was an extremely important aspect of the US Navy's strength. The structure of military aviation was quite different from that in Britain. There the Royal Air Force played a central role and one, from the point of view of the Royal Navy, that had not been positive. In the US – as in Japan – the Army and Navy each had its own air arm. This was of great advantage to the US Navy, as it was able to develop its own very effective carrier aircraft. The top levels of the naval command, while still committed to the battleship as the core weapon of the fleet, were more receptive to aviation than were their opposite numbers in Britain (and Germany), and there were a significant number of flag officers prepared to champion aviation. Seven large aircraft carriers were operational by December 1941 (and unlike the Royal Navy the neutral Americans had so far suffered no war losses).

On the negative side, the US Navy (unlike the Japanese Navy) was not allowed airfield-based long-range combat aircraft, while the US Army Air Corps had no organisation comparable to RAF Coastal Command nor any central interest in operating over the sea. (The Air Corps did in May 1938 stage an interception by new B-17 bombers of the Italian liner *Rex* over 600 miles out in the Atlantic, but this was more a public relations stunt than a thought-through policy.) The US Navy was, however, allowed flying boats, and it developed and procured in the late 1930s large numbers of the effective Consolidated PBY.[12] The type was intended to be a 'patrol bomber' to support the battle fleet, but this was in reality a role to which it was ill-suited. As a 'platform', however, the PBY would prove to have valuable reconnaissance and anti-submarine capabilities. Some US naval aircraft, as we have seen, would be sold to France, Britain, Russia and other countries in 1939–41, including the PBY.

The number of combat aircraft in the US Navy rose from about 1,000 during the 1930s to nearly 2,000 in 1938. The 1938 Naval Expansion Act raised the total to 3,000, and in May 1940 the President made a speech to a joint session of Congress, proposing production of 50,000 aircraft a year, and an establishment of 50,000 aircraft for the US armed services. In June 1940 the target for all naval aircraft was raised to 4,500, then 10,000, and, under the July 1940 Two-Ocean Navy Act, to 15,000. This level of production took a long time to realise (although less time than was required for heavy warships); actual combat strength in July 1941 was 1,774 (3,191 a year later). But, indicative of rapid expansion to come, the number of US Navy training planes rose from 363 in July 1940, to 1,444 in July 1941.[13]

Another way to look at the growth of the US Navy in these years is through its changing budget. From about \$300–350 million a year in most of the 1920s and the first half of the 1930s, it quadrupled to \$1,138 million in 1940 and \$4,466 million in 1941.[14]

ONE-SIDED NEUTRALITY

American entry into World War I in 1917 was formally a response to German submarine attacks on merchant ships, involving in some cases the death or injury of US citizens. The best-known cases involved the liners *Lusitania* and *Arabic*, and the Channel ferry *Sussex*. In February 1917 the German government, going back on earlier agreements, began a policy of 'unrestricted' U-boat warfare. On 2 April President Woodrow Wilson requested a declaration of war against Germany: 'I advise that the Congress declare the recent course of the Imperial German Government to be in fact nothing less than war against the government and people of the United States; that it formally accept the status of belligerent which has thus been thrust upon it'.[15]

There was a period of frenzied patriotic enthusiasm in 1917–18, and Allied victory in November 1918 was followed by the prominent role of President Wilson at the 1919 Paris Peace Conference. Thereafter, much of public opinion turned against the war, and with it involvement in the outside world. Intervention in 1917 had cost the lives of tens of thousands of American soldiers, seemed to have been of no benefit to the US, and was followed by a confused peace process and continued global instability. Many people in the US came to the view that the country had been tricked into taking up arms by the Allies and by American arms manufacturers hoping to profit from the bloodshed. Their view was that in future the US should isolate itself from external conflicts. When another period of international fighting developed in the 1930s (in Ethiopia, Spain and China) it was difficult to kindle support for American action to head off aggression and conflict.

President Roosevelt, who came to power at the same time as Hitler, was a liberal internationalist, but he realised that effective action would be hard to bring about, given the power of Congress and the attitudes of the public at large. The response of Congress to external turmoil was to pass a series of Neutrality Acts intended to avoid a repetition of the events of 1915–17, mainly by limiting arms sales to foreign countries, the use of American merchant ships and the activities of American citizens abroad.

In September 1939 international tension and local conflicts escalated to large-scale war in Europe involving three great powers. The United States was a neutral. The government and public opinion favoured, both in the European and the East Asian wars, one side over the other (Britain and France over Germany and Italy; China over Japan). But there was still little public taste for direct intervention, and in any event the armed forces, especially the US Army, were largely unready to play a role abroad. Only Congress could declare war, and it would be foolish to take the country into a conflict without overwhelming support there.

President Roosevelt could only follow public opinion. In November 1939, however, he was able to have the Neutrality Acts modified to allow the shipment of American-produced arms, provided they were carried by foreign vessels (the 'cash and carry' policy). The situation turned for the worse with the unexpected crisis of the Allied forces. France surrendered in June 1940; Nazi Germany emerged as the dominant state in continental Europe; Italy joined forces with Germany; Britain seemed in danger of negotiated surrender or invasion. And then there was Japan, a country long regarded by both American armed services as a potential enemy, not least because of the exposed American colony in the Philippines. Japan continued the war of aggression with China that had begun in 1937. It now threatened to take advantage of the collapse or weakness of the European imperial powers – the Netherlands, France and even Britain – to take effective control of their Asian possessions.

The American government and many American citizens were alarmed, but the only politically realistic policy seemed – as already described – to be to build up the capability of the nation (or the American hemisphere) for self-defence. The President attempted to implement this on a bipartisan basis, appointing in July 1940 prominent non-isolationist Republicans as the cabinet members in charge of the US Army (Henry L. Stimson) and US Navy (Frank Knox). In September 1940, at the President's urging, Congress also approved the Selective Service Act, introducing peacetime conscription, essentially for the expanding US Army.[16]

It happened that 1940 was an election year in the United States. President Roosevelt would seek in November an unprecedented third four-year term in office. He campaigned on a platform of keeping the United States out of *direct* involvement in the war. Nevertheless, relations with the British developed at a remarkable pace. Roosevelt began a long-term private correspondence in September 1939 with Churchill, who was then First Lord of the Admiralty (the two men had scarcely met previously). In August 1940 the US sent special observers to London including, on the naval side, Admiral Robert L. Ghormley. After several months of discussion Washington agreed, at the start of September 1940 – the height of the invasion scare – to supply Britain with fifty of the outdated 'flush-decker' US Navy destroyers, in exchange for long-term base rights in Newfoundland, Bermuda and the West Indies. As mentioned earlier, transfer of the ships began in Newfoundland in October 1940, and the first of them reached British home waters in November.

Germany, Italy and Japan, meanwhile, were aware of the potential importance of the US in the current international situation – although they certainly underestimated the country's military potential. In September 1940 their representatives met in Berlin and signed the Tripartite Pact. As well as improving mutual relations between the signatories (essentially creating the 'Axis'), the pact focused on the US. The objective was to deter American entry into the war, either in Europe or in the Far East, along the lines of the declaration of war by Congress in April 1917. The three partners stated that if America went to war against any one of them, the other signatories would come to the aid of the state involved.

Franklin Roosevelt won a decisive victory on 5 November 1940, and the Democrats kept control of both the Senate and the House. The re-elected President gained greater freedom of action and could become more outspoken. And at the same time wartime events in the winter of 1940–41 provided assurances that Britain was not a lost cause; aid to that country would not be wasted. One of Roosevelt's first acts after the election was the announcement of Lend-Lease, proposed in a mid-December speech. Signed into law in March 1941, this programme was of the greatest importance because the British were running out of foreign exchange to purchase munitions. After introducing Lend-Lease the President, in December 1940, put forward the notion of America as an 'Arsenal of Democracy'. Under this policy the country would provide weapons to countries fighting aggression, while not itself becoming involved in the fighting.

Britain (and, from late summer 1941, Russia) began to receive military equipment and other resources from the US. Production for future allies also accelerated the mobilisation of *American* arms production (although, in the short term, some weapons were shipped to Britain and Russia at the expense of the American forces). This is not the place to go into the details of Lend-Lease. Naval supplies would certainly not be the largest part of the programme, but it supplied – by 1943–45 – much of the air strength of the British Fleet Air Arm, many of the long-range aircraft used for sea/air warfare by the RAF, and dozens of escort carriers and destroyer escorts and hundreds of landing craft and merchant ships.

In another remarkably un-neutral step the American government agreed, in April 1941, to repair damaged British warships in American shipyards. The first was the battleship *Malaya*, which entered the New York Navy Yard that month after having been torpedoed by a U-boat in the Atlantic; work continued for four months. More extensive repairs were required to the carrier *Illustrious*, damaged by Stukas off Malta in January 1941; she arrived at the Norfolk Navy Yard in Virginia in May. Other British warships followed.

Merchant shipping was also provided by the US. As already mentioned, this had been called 'the crunch of the whole war' in a letter from Churchill to President Roosevelt of December 1940 (see p. 92). The Prime Minister estimated that 3 million tons would be required, which only the US could provide, by new construction or by transferring vessels surplus to current American needs. One of the most important developments here began before the advent of Lend-Lease.

This was British investment in December 1940 in two new shipyards in the United States, which would build very large numbers of standard-type merchant vessels – the future 'Liberty ships'. The programme would later be much expanded. American shipyards produced only about 500,000 tons of merchant ships in 1940; they would produce 19 million tons in 1943. In the eighteen months before Pearl Harbor the British ordered or purchased sixty new large merchant ships (600,000 tons) and 900,000 tons of second-hand ships. The United States also helped Britain acquire 1 million tons of shipping from Axis or occupied countries that had ended up in American ports. In addition, a large number of merchant ships were repaired in American shipyards.[17]

In the summer of 1941 Roosevelt abandoned any restraint in his condemnation of Germany. The President made a remarkable radio speech on 27 May 1941 – by coincidence the day on which the *Bismarck* was sunk. Announcing a state of 'Unlimited National Emergency', the President began by declaring that 'a European war has developed, as the Nazis always intended it should develop, into a world war for world domination'. For the first time he attacked the Nazi leader personally: 'Adolf Hitler never considered the domination of Europe as an end in itself'. Hitler's 'plan of world domination' was being blocked only by the 'epic resistance' of the British Empire and the 'magnificent defence of China'. The maritime aspect was stressed: 'Control of the seas' was crucial to a German victory and failure to achieve it would lead to Germany's 'certain defeat'. 'All freedom . . . depends on freedom of the seas.' America would ensure this freedom by shipbuilding and by protecting merchant ships at sea. It would also defend itself not only by passive defence but by securing forward points, such as the Cape Verde Islands and Iceland.[18]

Alongside these open developments, remarkable in themselves, covert discussions about war had begun in Washington. Admiral Harold R. Stark was Chief of Naval Operations – comparable to the British First Sea Lord – from August 1939 to March 1942. Stark was generally known by his Academy nickname as 'Betty'. Unlike his counterpart, General George Marshall, who led the US Army throughout World War II and later served as Secretary of State, Stark is little remembered today. He was sidetracked into secondary posts in early 1942 (for reasons that will become clear in chapters 9 and 10). But before that Stark made a deep impact on American grand strategy. He was on good personal terms with the President, whom he had met as a young destroyer commander in 1914, when Roosevelt was Assistant Secretary of the Navy. By 1939 Stark had a range of service experience, but he held the relatively junior post of commander of cruisers in the Pacific-based 'Battle Force'. That August he was appointed by President Roosevelt to the post of Chief of Naval Operations, over the heads of some fifty more senior officers, including Admiral Ernest King.[19]

In late November 1940, in the aftermath of the signing of the Tripartite Pact and of Roosevelt's election victory, Stark submitted a long memorandum on US global strategy to the Secretary of the Navy – and indirectly to the President. Four alternative approaches were set out: (a) 'hemispheric defence' of the Americas; (b) an offensive strategy in the Pacific, while staying on the defensive against Germany and Italy; (c) an equal division of effort the between Pacific and the Atlantic; (d) an offensive in the Atlantic, while remaining on the defensive in the Pacific. After a thoughtful discussion the admiral came down for option 'd', or 'Dog' in the American phonetic alphabet of the time. In opting for 'Dog', Stark stressed the danger that the defeat of Britain would present to the United States. His strategic emphasis was unexpected, as the admirals had normally concentrated on the Pacific, and on the Japanese Navy as their most likely opponent.

The leadership of the American military informally accepted the 'Germany First' concept – the US Army had always favoured this. The President, however, did not formally commit himself.[20] In early 1941 secret staff talks began in Washington, the 'American–British Conversations' or ABC-1. The planners were mainly concerned about a potential future war in which Britain and the United States were allied against Germany and Italy, but they did also consider possible involvement by Japan. ABC-1 went so far as to draft out a general war plan, which on the American side would develop into RAINBOW 5 (so called because the US was envisaged fighting a spectrum of enemies). There was also highly important technical co-operation between Britain and the United States in issues like cryptography, electronics and nuclear weapons.

Co-operation between the British Empire and the neutral United States was emphasised by the summit meeting in Newfoundland at Argentia (or Placentia Bay) in August 1941; it is often known as the Atlantic Conference. The President arrived aboard the heavy cruiser *Augusta*, the Prime Minister in the new battleship *Prince of Wales*. A few weeks before, the two powers had already jointly responded to Japanese actions in the Far East (the military occupation of southern French Indochina) by imposing heavy economic sanctions.[21] The most widely publicised feature of the conference was a joint political programme, the Atlantic Charter, which spoke directly about 'the destruction of Nazi tyranny'. The conference made a secret agreement about joint action, including arrangements for American warships to escort convoys across the Atlantic.

RATTLESNAKES OF THE ATLANTIC

As already described in Chapter 5, the government of the Third Reich did follow a policy of naval restraint in the early months of the war – despite the sinking of the British liner *Athenia* in September 1939. Germany also confined U-boat operations to an area from which Washington had already prohibited the passage of American ships. As a result, the chances of an 'incident' were at first much reduced. Although the leaders of the German Navy wanted to extend the U-boat war, the number of submarines available was limited. Moreover, after the invasion of Russia in 1941, Hitler was anxious to avoid a confrontation with the United States, at least until Russia was defeated.

The United States organised a Neutrality Patrol on the outbreak of the European war, nominally cooperating with some of the Latin American countries. The patrol zone extended some 300 miles out into the Atlantic, but this so-called 'chastity belt' had little real impact. More serious steps were taken in the autumn of 1940, as additional American ships were made ready for service. In November, the Patrol Force, US Fleet, was set up in the Atlantic. Admiral Stark selected Ernest J. King to command the Patrol Force, an appointment with great long-term implications. Seemingly at the end of his career in 1939 (he was already sixty-three in 1940), Admiral King was an energetic officer with a wide range of experience, and no lack of ambition. In February 1941 a more fundamental reorganisation took place when the post of C-in-C, US Fleet, was ended, with the removal of its incumbent by President Roosevelt; Admiral Richardson had run afoul of the President, in part because of his opposition to forward-basing the major part of his ships in Hawaii in the summer of 1940. The operational ships of the US Navy were now essentially divided into the Pacific Fleet, under Admiral Husband Kimmel (Richardson's replacement), and the Atlantic Fleet under King. (There was also a small Asiatic Fleet in the Philippines.)

Most of the large combat ships of the US Navy – battleships, carriers and cruisers – remained in the Pacific. The core of Admiral King's command was originally three old battleships which had mainly a training role. In March 1941, however, the decision was made to transfer significant reinforcements from the Pacific, with an eye to confronting the German surface raiders. These included three somewhat newer battleships, the 'Idaho' class (armed with 14-inch guns and completed in 1917), a carrier (the *Yorktown*) and four new light cruisers. This transfer was completed by the end of May 1941.

The fourth Neutrality Act of November 1939 allowed arms shipments in foreign vessels but barred American ships from a demarcated zone around the coast of northern Europe and (after June 1940) the Mediterranean. This included a zone around the British Isles. At the end of March 1941, as part of extended U-boat operations, Hitler had announced that the Kriegsmarine operational area (originally set out in August 1940) was being extended into the North Atlantic. It would now include the seas around Iceland and about half the transatlantic convoy route. The northern part of the operational area was extended as far west as 38°W. (This was a meridian – a line of longitude – just to the east of the southern tip of Greenland.) The US government protested this action, and in response seized German, Italian and Danish ships in American ports.[22] Meanwhile in April 1941 the Americans extended their own security zone far out into the Atlantic to the line 26°'W (just west of Iceland). At the end of May, Roosevelt also decided to take over the occupation of Iceland – where the British had landed a small number of troops twelve months before, shortly after the invasion of Norway. Task Force 19, an expeditionary convoy with eight transports carrying a brigade of US Marines, arrived in July 1941. Hvalfjörður (near Reykjavik) was established as an advance base for the Atlantic Fleet, 2,000 miles east of the American mainland. Congress was only informed of this action after it had taken place. The supply line to Iceland now became a potential flashpoint between German and 'neutral' American forces.

Despite these developments there were relatively few incidents between German and American vessels. On 21 May 1941, however, the *U 69* sank the American merchant ship *Robin Moor* off West Africa. The submarine's captain had ascertained the nationality of the vessel, but decided that she was carrying contraband. He observed prize rules to the extent of letting the crew and passengers (forty-six people) take to the lifeboats before the ship was torpedoed and shelled. The attack provoked a major diplomatic incident. When details of the sinking became known, the American government punished Germany by freezing its assets and closing all consulates, leaving only the Washington embassy.

The now overlapping American and German zones inevitably led to conflict. Churchill secretly reported to his Cabinet colleagues that the President had told him at the Atlantic Conference that 'he would wage war, but not declare it, and that he would become more and more provocative. If the Germans did not like it, they could attack American forces!'[23] At the start of September 1941 the four-stacker destroyer *Greer* was attacked (but not hit) south of Iceland by the *U 652*, which the *Greer* had been tracking in co-operation with a British aircraft. A week later the President delivered a strong condemnation of the attack in a radio address. The *Greer*, he declared, had been sailing 'in waters which the Government of the United States had declared to be waters of self-defence – surrounding outposts of American protection in the Atlantic [i.e. Iceland]'. Decisive action would now be taken against these 'Nazi submarines and raiders' which were 'the rattlesnakes of the Atlantic':

> in the waters which we deem necessary for our defence, American naval vessels and American planes will no longer wait until Axis submarines lurking under the water, or Axis raiders on the surface of the sea, strike their deadly blow . . . From now on, if German or Italian vessels of war enter the waters, the protection of which is necessary for American defence, they do so at their own peril.[24]

In mid-September 'escort groups' of American destroyers began to accompany convoys between Newfoundland and the mid-Atlantic (to the MOMP). The first (eastbound) convoy was HX.150; the first westbound convoy (from the MOMP) was ON.18, at the end of the month. On 17 October the *U 568* hit and damaged with a torpedo the new destroyer *Kearny*, one of an escort group of five American destroyers called in to support eastbound convoy SC.48.

The third incident, two weeks later, involved the *Reuben James*, which sank at longitude 27°5′W, well within the US security zone (bounded by 26°W). There was one surprising thing about this incident on 31 October: the loss of the destroyer and the death of over a hundred American sailors did *not* lead to American entry into the war against Germany, or even cause a major protest by Washington. Congress did in the middle of the following month amend the Neutrality Acts to arm American merchant ships, and to allow them to call at a port of one of the 'belligerents' (i.e. the British); this important change, however, had been initiated before the *Reuben James* incident.

In the last two or three months before Pearl Harbor the US Navy stretched neutrality to breaking point, with activities well beyond the escort of convoys. On 6 November the light cruiser USS *Omaha*, patrolling in the South Atlantic, ran into a German blockade-runner northwest of Brazil. Disguised as an American merchantman, the MV *Odenwald* had sailed from Japan with a cargo of rubber. The crew tried to scuttle her, but the Americans were able to save the vessel, and claimed her as a prize, along with her cargo.

Potentially more dangerous were preparations further north, where it was only by chance and a period of German naval inactivity that nothing dramatic came of them. From September Task Group 1.3, including battleships and cruisers, was based in Iceland, ready to intercept any German surface raider which attempted to break out through the Denmark Strait, as the *Bismarck* had done in May. In early November 1941 radio intercepts revealed that another German heavy ship was preparing to sally forth into the Atlantic. The old battleships *Idaho* and *Mississippi*, the heavy cruisers *Wichita* and *Tuscaloosa*, and three destroyers were despatched to cover the Denmark Strait. This was to have been the heavy cruiser *Admiral Scheer*, but in the end her sortie was cancelled due to machinery problems. No confrontation with the US Navy took place.

At about the same time, on 9 November, a special convoy, WS.124, departed from Halifax. It was carrying 22,000 men who had just been ferried across the Atlantic from Britain. This was the British 18th Division and other troops intended for Egypt and the battlefields of North Africa. The soldiers had transferred to six large American transports, including the three biggest and fastest liners that had been taken up from civilian service, the SS *Washington*,

Manhattan and *America*, now renamed USS *Mount Vernon*, *Wakefield* and *West Point*. The large escort of WS.124 was also exclusively American. The fleet carrier *Ranger* went part of the way with the convoy, and the rest of the escort comprised the heavy cruisers *Quincy* and *Vincennes*, six destroyers and a fast oiler. At the time of the Pearl Harbor attack WS.124 was still en route across the South Atlantic to Durban, South Africa, where the changeover to a British escort was to take place.

American activities in the Atlantic in the autumn of 1941 have sometimes been called an 'undeclared naval war'. Although American crews had to endure the wintry seas of the North Atlantic the *Reuben James* was the only loss, and no German U-boats or surface raiders were sunk by American ships or aircraft. Nevertheless, these events were important. The US Navy gained valuable operational experience. Admiral King enhanced his reputation to the extent that he would shortly be made C-in-C of the entire US Navy. Hitler, meanwhile, decided in late November 1941 that there was little more that the United States could do to help Britain than it was currently doing, even if it were at war with Germany. For this reason he did not discourage Japan from an aggressive foreign policy, and had little hesitation about declaring war on the United States after the news – unexpected by him – of the Japanese Pearl Harbor attack. On 11 December the German declaration of war, and Hitler's speech to the Reichstag announcing it, made much of American naval activities in the Atlantic. Unwarranted attacks on U-boats and blockade runners were cited as a justification for Germany's decision.

CHAPTER 9

JAPAN ATTACKS BRITAIN AND AMERICA

December 1941–April 1942

PEARL HARBOR, 7 DECEMBER 1941

Commander Genda Minoru saw the flag signal 'Take Off' hoisted aboard the aircraft carrier *Akagi*, the flagship of Japan's Mobile Force.

> All vessels of the force simultaneously turned their heads against the wind direction and increased their speed. First fighters, then dive bombers and other bombers in that order revved up engines and took off one after another. Each carrier sent in a report of 'Take Off complete' successively . . . It was at 0130 on 8 December Tokyo Time [6.00 a.m., 7 December, local time], and the point was 230 miles due north of Pearl Harbor. The dawn had already come on the sea. Planes which took off in the air circled over the fleet once and then twice, and then disappeared into clouds far away to the south . . . I who watched them take off at the bridge was filled with deep emotion and couldn't help feeling my blood boil up.[1]

Genda's excitement was understandable; he was the chief planner of the Pearl Harbor air raid.

The gaggle of Japanese planes reached the north shore of Oahu in broad daylight, at about 7.40 on that Sunday morning. One of the Hawaiian Islands, Oahu has the area of Greater London. Pearl Harbor, capacious but shallow, is an indentation on the south coast – a lagoon separated from the Pacific by a dredged channel. Honolulu lay to the east.

Ford Island took up much of the space in the centre of the harbour, and ship moorings of the American naval base were positioned all around it. The main targets of the Japanese attack were tied up on the east side of the island, along what was known as 'Battleship Row'. Nearest the exit channel to the south was the *California*, the flagship of the Battle Force, then two pairs of battleships side by side, the *Maryland* and the *Oklahoma*, and the *Tennessee* and the *West Virginia*. The *Arizona* and the *Nevada*, moored behind one another, brought up the rear. Smaller vessels – cruisers, destroyers, submarines – were tied up alongside piers on the southeastern side of the harbour. Opposite Ford Island an eighth battleship, the *Pennsylvania*, lay in dry dock.

The first wave of the raid was made up of Nakajima B5N/KATE 'attack planes' (carrying either torpedoes or very heavy bombs), Aichi D3A/VAL dive bombers and escorting Mitsubishi A6M fighters.[2] As he reached the north coast of Oahu the strike leader, Commander Fuchida Mitsuo, fired flares to signal the start of the attack. The big formation broke into half a dozen elements, each assigned to one target area.

Chief Petty Officer Mori Jūzō from the carrier *Sōryū* flew across Oahu in a B5N torpedo bomber. Realising that his assigned zone contained no important targets, Mori spent ten harrowing minutes assessing the situation and putting himself in a new attack position. He turned around to attack an undamaged target – the *California*. His intense training took over and, 'moving like an automaton', he brought the big plane from 3,000 feet to near the level of the water. 'Suddenly the battleship appeared to have leaped forward directly in front of my speeding plane', Mori recalled, 'it towered ahead of the bomber like a great mountain peak. Prepared for release . . . Stand by! *Release torpedo*!'[3] Hit by two torpedoes during the course of the raid, the *California* settled to the harbour bottom, her superstructure still jutting out of the water. The other battleships moored outboard, the *Oklahoma* and the *West Virginia*, suffered multiple torpedo hits. The *Nevada*, on her own at the end of the line, took only one torpedo.

A few minutes later Fuchida's B5N level bombers arrived.[4] Aboard the *Tennessee* the battle station of Signalman Richard Burge, a young Texan, was in the powder magazine deep below No. 2 turret. After a bomb hit damaged the turret, Burge was sent topside to help with firefighting: 'I watched the fleet destroyed right before my eyes', he later recalled:

> The USS *Arizona* was anchored fifty feet to the stern of our ship. She took several bombs and torpedoes and raised up and quickly sank to the bottom of the harbour. The USS *West Virginia* and the USS *Oklahoma* took several torpedoes. The *West Virginia* sank alongside us. The USS *Oklahoma* which was anchored forward of the *West Virginia* capsized completely. The USS *Maryland* anchored forward of us took a bomb and its bow sank.[5]

Russell McCurdy was a young Marine stationed in the massive fighting top of the *Arizona*, on the battleship mainmast, high above the main deck: 'there was a really violent explosion in the front part of the ship, which caused the old *Arizona* to toss and shake . . . Our entire magazine and forward oil storage had exploded; tons of TNT and thousands of gallons of fuel oil poured into the water. Black smoke billowed into the sky as the oil caught fire'. An observer closer to the site of the explosion, Lt Commander Harley F. Smart later recounted the horror of what happened. Smart 'could see men on *Arizona* walking on deck and burning alive. They had their helmets on, their clothes were all seared off. Actually they were only recognizable because of their helmets. They were a ghostly crew as they walked out of those flames. And then they just dropped dead'.[6]

A second wave of Japanese attackers arrived about thirty minutes later, made up of dive bombers and a few fighters. By this time the harbour was obscured by oil smoke, and AA fire was more intense. The *Nevada* made a dramatic attempt to move through the channel and out to sea, but the battleship was so badly damaged that she had to be beached. Other Japanese planes attacked the airfields on Oahu to make sure that they could not be used for counter-strikes against the Japanese fleet as it withdrew. The last of the attackers left to return to their carriers by 12.30 p.m.

THE IMPERIAL JAPANESE NAVY

Why did Japan go to war in December 1941, not just against the US at Pearl Harbor (and the Philippines), but also against the British Empire?

Japan had been fortunate not to become another Asian victim of European imperialism. Instead, however, it became an active participant, alongside European powers, in the exploitation of a weak China. Japan annexed Formosa in 1895, and Korea in 1910. In 1931 all of Manchuria was seized and in the summer of 1937 full-scale war with China began. Historians of the 'Pacific' conflict often neglect Japanese involvement in this war with China for over four years before Pearl Harbor.[7] This increased the influence of the military in Tokyo and mobilised the Japanese economy for war, years ahead of the conflict with Britain and the US. Meanwhile, the leaders and personnel of the Emperor's armed forces took part in extensive military operations.

Sea power, in the sense of 'using the sea for one's own purpose and depriving the enemy of its use' (Admiral Richmond), was actually extremely important for the conduct and strategy of the Sino-Japanese War. Japanese operations in China were possible only because the Imperial Navy had near-complete control of Chinese coastal waters. Most of the Japanese troops fighting in China were moved there by sea, as were their supplies. And an important strategic aim of the invading forces throughout the war was to deprive the defenders of the use of Chinese and other ports to bring in military supplies from outside the country.[8]

The Nationalist Party (*Kuomintang*) of China under Chiang Kai-shek had begun to unify and strengthen China in the late 1920s, after decades of conflict between rival warlords. It had taken the first tentative steps to rebuild a navy, constructing two 2,500-ton Japanese-designed light 'cruisers' (launched in 1931) and even ordering two Type II U-boats from Germany (the order was cancelled under Japanese pressure). But in the summer of 1937, when China went to war, its coastline was still largely undefended by ships or coastal defences, while Japan had the third largest navy in the world and a string of nearby bases.

The Japanese Navy did not actually have to fight Chinese forces at sea, but it gained extensive operational experience, carrying out large-scale amphibious operations and engaging in air warfare. The China Area Fleet (China *Hōmen Kantai*) was organised within the Japanese Navy in October 1937. The capture of Shanghai coincided with a landing by two divisions of the Japanese Army at Hangzhou Bay south of the city in November 1937. Although the main fighting by the Japanese Army moved inland by the start of 1938, naval landings were carried out to seize Canton (Guangzhou) on the south coast in October 1938, as well as a number of other ports on the South China Sea and the strategic island of Hainan (in February 1939). Altogether the Japanese carried out sixteen amphibious landings in China between August 1937 and March 1941.[9]

The experience gained in China does much to explain the stunning success achieved by the Japanese armed forces – not just the Army but also the Navy – in the Pacific and Southeast Asia in December 1941 and the first months that followed. The air element of the Navy was especially prominent. Three aircraft carriers (the *Kaga*, the *Ryūjō* and the *Hōshō*) supported the initial battles around Shanghai in the autumn of 1937, along with long-range G3M/NELL medium bombers flying from Formosa (then part of Japan). It was Japanese Navy bombers that sank the American gunboat *Panay* near Nanjing in December 1937. In May 1939, after the Nationalist government had withdrawn to west-central China, Navy medium bombers took part in a series of long-range strategic raids against the new capital at Chungking (now Chongqing). Between 1937 and 1941 the Imperial Japanese Navy lost 680 aircrew and 554 naval aircraft, which gives a sense of the effort involved.[10]

Meanwhile, the early victories of Nazi Germany provided extraordinary opportunities for the expansion of Japan's empire. France and the Netherlands were occupied. Their resource-rich colonies in Southeast Asia, notably French Indochina and the Netherlands Indies (*Nederlands-Indië*), lay undefended, and open to Japanese action. Britain had been thrown out of Europe at Dunkirk, and the Royal Navy was fully tied up in the Atlantic and the Mediterranean.

Another potential threat to Japan seemed to have ended with the military catastrophe suffered by the Red Army during the German invasion of June 1941.

In September 1940 Japanese troops entered northern Indochina, leaving the pro-Vichy colonial government in place. Ten months later, in late July 1941, bases were seized in southern Indochina. In response, Washington froze all Japanese assets in the US and embargoed oil exports; the British and the Dutch government-in-exile followed suit. Attempts were made to resolve the confrontation, including the despatch of special ambassadors from Tokyo to Washington. These attempts foundered on demands that Japan renounce the Tripartite Pact (signed in September 1940 with Germany and Italy) and withdraw its forces not only from the French colony, but also from China. In October 1941 General Tōjō Hideki and a cabinet of uncompromising nationalists came to power, and an Imperial Conference finalised the decision to take the resources of Southeast Asia by force.

The Imperial Japanese Navy was crucial for this expansionist policy. The Japanese state had only been transformed under a modernising government at the end of the 1860s. The new navy, inspired and trained by the British, fought first in the China war of 1894–95. Then, after rapid expansion and with a battle fleet built in foreign (mostly British) shipyards, it took part in a major and triumphant naval war against Russia in 1904–05. The Japanese fleet developed into one of the most important in the world during the second decade of the twentieth century, in parallel with that of the United States. This was partly due to the advent of new naval technology and new construction, and partly due to the disappearance of German and Russian rivals in 1917–18.

The first two dreadnoughts (armed with 12-inch guns and built in Japanese shipyards) were commissioned in 1912. Four super-dreadnoughts with 14-inch guns were commissioned in 1915–18, and four similarly armed battle cruisers in 1913–15. Finally, two battleships with 16-inch guns (the *Nagato* and the *Mutsu*), comparable to the British 'Queen Elizabeth' class, were completed in 1919 and 1921.[11] After 1918 a naval construction race began, as mentioned in Chapter 8. The US Naval Act of 1916 envisaged the construction of ten battleships and six battle cruisers over a five-year period. The programme was designed primarily with Germany and the British Empire in mind, but it also affected Japan. The government in Tokyo responded by ordering the second battleship with 16-inch guns (the *Mutsu*), and two enlarged versions; these were followed by orders for two 41,000-ton battle cruisers.

This shipbuilding arms race (in which Britain also took part) was very expensive, especially in the immediate aftermath of the 1914–18 war. As already mentioned, at the Washington Conference in 1921–22 the five naval powers agreed to limit construction. The signatories agreed to the ten-year building 'holiday' for capital ships (later extended for a further five years). The Japanese accepted that their fleet of capital ships would be 60 per cent of that of each of the US and Britain – the 5:5:3 ratio – which corresponded roughly to the existing balance of the most recent vessels. By the early 1930s Japan had nine capital ships,[12] and Britain and the US each had fifteen. Japan also carried out an extensive modernisation programme for the existing battleships, increasing the range of their guns, their speed and their armour protection. The Washington Treaty to some extent compensated for Japan's capital ship inferiority by providing that no new fortifications and naval bases would be established in the Pacific; this reduced a potential threat by denying the British and Americans advance naval bases from which to attack or blockade Japan.[13]

Partly to make up for the capital ship inferiority, Japan began a major programme for the construction of big cruisers, the number of which was not limited by the treaty. Construction of 10,000-ton 'treaty' cruisers was followed less enthusiastically by Britain and the US, in a smaller version of the post-war naval arms race.[14] To contain this new competition the London Naval Treaty of 1930 limited Japanese heavy cruiser numbers to twelve (totalling 108,000 tons), while the US Navy was permitted eighteen (totalling 192,000 tons).[15] This was the time of an upsurge of nationalism in Japan, which coincided with the seizure of Manchuria by local Japanese Army units. There was much disquiet in the Navy and among ultra-nationalists about accepting a 'demeaning' balance of forces with the US and Britain.

The leaders of the Imperial Navy were certainly innovative in a technical sense, and their destroyers were another example. Like the cruisers, they were powerful ships, also built with with a mid-Pacific battle in mind. Twenty 'Special Type' ('Fubuki' class) destroyers were laid down from 1926 and completed by 1932. Some 388 feet long, they displaced 1,750 tons and were each armed with six 5-inch guns and nine torpedo tubes able to launch 24-inch torpedoes. The US Navy had just produced a numerically huge destroyer class of nearly 200 four-stackers. The Japanese vessels at least were *qualitatively* superior; the American ships were 314 feet long, displaced 1,215 tons, and were each armed with four 4-inch guns and twelve 21-inch torpedo tubes. Four more classes of similar big Japanese destroyers, over forty vessels, were completed for the Japanese Navy before December 1941. Based on lessons learned in the Russo-Japanese War and at Jutland, much time was spent in realistic training for night-battle, using destroyers. The Japanese also developed their submarine fleet, with an emphasis on large, fast boats that could support the battle fleet.[16]

Japan withdrew from the second London Naval Treaty in January 1935. Legally, after 31 December 1936 there were no limits for Japan on the size or number of her warships. The Japanese Navy began construction of extremely large capital ships, beginning with two super-battleships of 62,000 tons (the treaty limit had been 35,000 tons). Each would be armed with nine 18.1-inch guns and capable of 27 knots. The *Yamato* and the *Musashi* were laid down in November 1937 and March 1938, and no details of their specifications were publicly announced.

In the 1930s Japanese naval aviation also developed rapidly; this would be most important for the future Pacific war. As already mentioned, there was no independent Japanese Air Force, so the Navy did not suffer the crippling loss of leading personnel and control of aircraft which the Royal Navy suffered in 1918. Permitted carrier tonnage was set under the Washington Treaty at 81,000 tons, which was 60 per cent of the American and British totals. The Americans converted two 'cancelled' battle cruisers into very large carriers. The Japanese did the same: the hulls of the battle cruiser *Akagi* and the battleship *Kaga* became carriers, displacing, respectively, 36,500 tons and 38,200 tons. Two medium-sized (17,000-ton) carriers, the *Sōryū* and the *Hiryū*, were laid down in 1934 and 1936.[17] After the naval disarmament treaty expired two excellent ships of 25,675 tons, the *Shōkaku* and the *Zuikaku*, were built. Completed in August and September 1941 respectively, they reached service just in time to join the four earlier carriers in the Pearl Harbor raid. Two smaller carriers were in operation by the early 1930s, and provision was made to quickly convert some fast auxiliaries and passenger ships into carriers; one was ready by December 1941, and four more would enter service by the middle of 1942.

The quality and quantity of Japanese carrier aircraft were high. They were much superior to their British equivalents by the end of the 1930s, and in some respects even better than those of the US Navy. The Japanese Navy also developed powerful shore-based medium bombers (torpedo carriers) – something which the organisational arrangements in Britain and America did not permit. These successful designs resulted partly from the planning and development work carried out under Admiral Yamamoto Isoroku when he was working in the Naval Aviation Department from 1930 to 1935. The Japanese were also fortunate that a Mitsubishi design team led by Horikoshi Jirō created a new naval fighter plane, the A6M Zero, which performed very well in combat and had extraordinary range, operating from both carriers and land bases. The crews of naval aircraft were thoroughly trained and, as mentioned already, many of them gained vital operational experience in the air war over China.

Japanese naval ambitions were fired by strong ultra-nationalist feelings. This was, however, only part of the story; there was also a rational element of insecurity. Japan was far from the economic super-power that would emerge in the 1950s and 1960s. It had a large population but was, on the eve of 1941, still a poor agricultural country whose main export was textiles. The Japanese gross domestic product (GDP) at that time has been calculated as $232 billion, compared to $800 billion for the US and $683 billion for the British Empire. Steel production was only 7 million tons a year in 1938, a quarter that of the US, and three-quarters that of Britain. The US produced over 3 million motor cars in 1940; in that year Japanese construction of all motor vehicles (including trucks and buses) was only 43,000.[18] So the Japanese were labouring under a very considerable handicap.

Furthermore, the shipbuilding programme of Britain, and even more that of the United States, now threatened to overwhelm Japan. This involved not so much the huge American Two-Ocean Navy Act of July 1940 – which would take some time to actually produce ships and aircraft – but also legislation passed in the mid-1930s. The Vinson–Trammell Act of 1934 authorised building up the US Navy to full treaty status over the next eight years, and the Second Vinson Act of May 1938 envisaged exceeding the previous treaty limit by 20 per cent. The Chief of the Naval General Staff, Admiral Nagano Osami, laid out the position at a secret civilian–military Liaison Conference in July 1941: 'As for war with the United States, although there is now a chance of achieving victory, the chances will diminish as time goes by. By the latter half of next year [1942] it will be difficult for us to cope with the United States; after that the situation will become increasingly worse.'[19]

The Japanese Navy drafted detailed plans for operations in the event of war. The writings of the American navalist Alfred Thayer Mahan, the traditions of the British Royal Navy and the experience of the 1904–05 war with Russia were all important influences. The destruction of the Russian fleet in 1905 at Tsushima (between Korea and Japan) became a model for an 'attrition/decisive battle' strategy: an enemy fleet advancing on Japan would be worn down by attrition and then destroyed in a decisive battle. The US Navy was the most likely opponent. In the inter-war years the potential theatre of operations extended across the Central Pacific. The Marshalls, the Carolines, and the islands of Saipan and Tinian in the Marianas, formerly colonies of Imperial Germany, had come under Japanese control, as a result of the country's participation in the 1914–18 war on the Allied side.[20] By the mid-1930s Japanese strategists thought the decisive battle might be fought between the Bonin Islands and the Marianas (about 1,000 miles southeast of Japan), and by the end of the decade the position of the battle had shifted as far east as the Marshall Islands (2,500 miles away).

For the admirals of the Japanese Navy, as for those of the other big naval powers, the central element of sea power was still composed of battleships. Aircraft carriers, cruisers and destroyers, however, would observe and wear down the oncoming US battle fleet. Submarines were given a bigger role from the mid-1920s. In the 1930s the aviation element (carrier-based and land-based) grew in importance, as the range and size of aircraft increased.

The Japanese armed forces re-examined their strategic plans during the summer of 1940, in light of the changing international situation. The Army up to this point had concentrated its planning and modernisation programmes not so much on war with China as on war with Soviet Russia. In mid-1940 the generals became more interested in an operation directed towards the forsaken European colonies in Southeast Asia. In late July 1940 civilian and military leaders agreed to the extension of Japanese influence into Southeast Asia, with the establishment of bases in Indochina, a territory which was formally controlled by French colonial authorities who had accepted the Vichy government. For the first time a hugely ambitious campaign to take control of this whole region was looked at seriously.

The Naval General Staff (NGS) developed, with the Army, a complex series of joint thrusts directed toward Southeast Asia; this would become known as the Southern Operation. The Navy did assume, for planning purposes, that occupation of the Netherlands Indies or operations against British possessions in Asia (Hong Kong, Borneo, Malaya) would probably lead to war with the United States. The strategy adopted by the admirals involved stripping out from the Combined Fleet,[21] at least for a short time, a considerable element of the Navy's 'attrition' forces, mainly the Second Fleet heavy cruisers and the air flotillas of land-based bombers. The assumption was that other forces left in home waters – battleships, carriers, destroyers, submarines – could deal with any rash American movement directly across the Pacific. Such an initiative by the US Navy was less likely now that a quarter of its strength had been moved to the Atlantic.

The clearest available presentation of the NGS's view of Japanese strategic intentions was Nagano's speech to the Imperial Conference of 6 September 1941.[22] Nagano, it must be said, was neither ignorant of technical matters nor a short-sighted nationalist. He had studied English at Harvard, served for five years in the US, and had held the posts of Navy Minister (1936–37) and C-in-C of the Combined Fleet (1937). (And at sixty-one he was younger than admirals Pound or King.) The probability of a prolonged war was very high, Nagano argued. The best prospect for Japan – but one that could not readily be expected – was an early American or British lunge into waters controlled by Japan. The better-prepared Imperial Navy could turn this into a decisive naval victory. But Nagano maintained that more than even a decisive naval victory would be required to bring the war to an end, because in his view the American position was 'impregnable'. As he put it: 'our Empire does not have the means to take the offensive, overcome the enemy, and make them give up the will to fight'.[23] In

Nagano's view the most important thing was, at the outset of the war, to take the enemy bases (Singapore, Manila) and resource areas (Malaya, Netherlands Indies), 'making our operational position tenable and at the same time obtaining vital raw materials ... our Empire will have secured strategic areas in the Southwest Pacific, established an impregnable position, and laid the basis for a prolonged war'.[24] Although not explicitly stated, Nagano's expectation probably was that the position of Britain, the natural ally of the US was *not* 'impregnable'. Britain could be defeated by losing her empire or even by a German cross-Channel invasion. With this British defeat, the US would lose the will to fight.

Alongside this grand-strategic plan for the Southern Operation and its consequences, there was an alternative. Admiral Yamamoto, since 1939 C-in-C of the Combined Fleet, had devised the Hawaiian Operation. This was a very long-range strike against Hawaii by six of his aircraft carriers.

Shortly before the September 1940 signing of the Tripartite Pact with Germany and Italy, which involved a steep worsening of relations with the United States and Britain, Yamamoto had a private meeting with the then Prime Minister, Prince Konoe Fumimaro. 'If I am told to fight regardless of the consequences,' the admiral reportedly said, 'I shall run wild for the first six months or a year, but I have utterly no confidence for the second or third year.'[25] This comment is often quoted, partly because it was so prescient – the Combined Fleet did indeed overrun the western and Central Pacific, only to be smashed at Midway in June 1942. The quote is also sometimes used – incorrectly – to establish Yamamoto's credentials as a realist.

In fact, Yamamoto was not opposing war with the US, he was opposing the Imperial Navy's conventional strategy. The fleet, he believed, would be able to make spectacular gains in the first six months against the small peacetime enemy forces committed to the western Pacific. It would not, however, be able to deal with the American counter-attack, when it came, by relying on the 'attrition/decisive battle' strategy of the 1920s and 1930s. Yamamoto was more explicit in a letter to Navy Minister Oikawa in January 1941. The Combined Fleet, he said, was training for its set-piece battle, with each type of ship having a pre-determined role. Such a battle, however, might well never occur in a war with the United States and Britain. Yamamoto had a radical alternative proposal: 'The most important thing we have to do ... is to fiercely attack and destroy the US main fleet at the outset of the war, so that the morale of the US Navy and her people [*sic*] goes down to such an extent that it cannot be recovered.' Specifically, Yamamoto proposed to attack and physically block the fleet base at Pearl Harbor.[26] What the C-in-C of the Combined Fleet was actually proposing was a *decisive battle*, staged further east even than the Marshall Islands. It brought together the attrition and ambush phases of the classic strategy, and moved the site of the decisive battle to Hawaii. To achieve complete victory, Admiral Yamamoto planned to concentrate a powerful submarine force, but above all he needed all of the Navy's big aircraft carriers.

The Hawaiian Operation – the Pearl Harbor raid – finally took shape as a kind of 'private venture', distinct from the strategy of the Naval General Staff. As C-in-C of the Combined Fleet, Yamamoto regarded himself – especially in wartime – as directly subordinate to the Emperor and not to the NGS. In the summer and early autumn of 1941 Admiral Nagano and the planners in Tokyo were concentrating on the Southern Operation and co-ordination with the Army. For them, the the Hawaiian Operation was merely a 'raid', an auxiliary strike intended to impede – for a short period of time – the movement west of the US Pacific Fleet.

From the point of view of the NGS this did not justify risking all the carrier forces, and in any event some of the carriers and their planes were required to support, from the outset, the Southern Operation. This was also the view of Admiral Kondō Nobutake, appointed in September 1941 to be C-in-C of the Second Fleet (the core of the future 'Southern Force'). Kondō was a powerful figure in his own right; he had served as Vice Chief of the NGS, under Nagano. The NGS wanted to assign him at least three of the best-trained large aircraft carriers, and half the tankers which Yamamoto had earmarked for the Hawaiian Operation. Such a disposition would have left Admiral Nagumo Chūichi's Hawaii attack fleet, the Mobile Force, with only two new and untrained big carriers (the *Shōkaku* and the *Zuikaku*), and perhaps one more experienced ship.

In mid-October 1941 Yamamoto threatened resignation if there was no agreement to keep his mass striking force of six carriers together. In Tokyo, Admiral Nagano and the NGS were forced to give way and accept the plan of the Combined Fleet. Delivered on the very eve of war, Yamamoto's threat had carried great weight. The NGS also now made a judgement that British, Dutch and American forces in the western Pacific and Southeast Asia had still not been reinforced. It reckoned that *land-based* Navy attack planes, with long-range fighter escort, would provide sufficient support in the first weeks of the Southern Operation in the Philippines and Malaya.

THE HAWAIIAN OPERATION AND AFTERWARDS: THE US NAVY DEFEATED

The Americans would hold half a dozen inquests into the surprise attack. The 1946 congressional inquiry framed the question most clearly: 'Why, with some of the finest intelligence available in our history, with the almost certain knowledge that war was at hand, with plans that contemplated the precise type of attack . . . why was it possible for a Pearl Harbor to occur?'[27]

The first explanation must be that Pearl Harbor was – in a technical sense – an exceptionally well-planned and executed attack. Admiral Yamamoto created a planning staff in January 1941 and began training in the following summer. In April 1941 he approved the proposal of Admiral Ozawa Jisaburō to concentrate the existing carrier force into a new First Air Fleet. The commander of the First Air Fleet was Admiral Nagumo Chūichi. An able and well-connected officer, Nagumo lacked experience with carrier operations, but his Chief of Staff, Admiral Kusaka Ryūnosuke, was a long-time aviation specialist. In early November 1941 the famous tactical designation *Kidō Butai* ('Mobile Force') was assigned to the carrier fleet, with its supporting ships.

The ships of the Mobile Force began to leave the Inland Sea, one by one, on the night of 17/18 November, bound for a remote anchorage in the Kurile Islands to the north of Japan. Having assembled, the force departed from Hitokappu Bay (now Kasatka Bay in the Russian Federation) on 26 November – the carriers *Akagi, Kaga, Hiryū, Shōkaku, Sōryū* and *Zuikaku*, the fast battleships *Hiei* and *Kirishima*, three cruisers, eight destroyers and three submarines, with a crucial refuelling group of eight tankers. The North Pacific was normally empty of civilian shipping, but the 3,700-mile passage was extremely risky. Refuelling at sea was still in its infancy, and it was not unreasonable to think – as the Americans did – that a large, long-range raid was not a practical proposition.

The problems of the unthinkable voyage were overcome thanks to detailed preparatory staff work in the Combined Fleet and thorough implementation by Admiral Nagumo and his captains. Complete surprise was achieved. The lead air crews had been very well trained. Admiral Nagumo is sometimes criticised for not carrying out a third wave of attacks on Pearl Harbor, targeting oil tanks and repair facilities. But he was surely right not to risk his irreplaceable ships. Operating so far from base, any damaged Japanese ships had a good chance of being sunk.

What the congressional inquiry called the 'finest' intelligence was indeed very fine. The Americans and British could read Japanese diplomatic codes (based on the so-called PURPLE machine). Their codebreakers had made little progress reading naval messages encrypted in what was then called the 'AN-Code' (later known as JN-25). Intercept stations at Pearl Harbor, Manila and Singapore were able to obtain considerable information about naval organisation and movements by radio direction finding (DF) and traffic analysis (TA), but the Mobile Force and other Japanese operational fleet units generally maintained radio silence in the final approach to war. Air reconnaissance revealed Japanese fleet movements in Southeast Asia in the last days before the war – but it was not of any help in the North Pacific.

Some weeks before Pearl Harbor PURPLE decrypts revealed that, despite continuing negotiations in Washington, the Japanese government had given up attempting to normalise relations with the US, Britain and the Dutch government-in-exile. Tokyo was no longer trying to resolve the issues of its military presence in French Indochina, frozen assets and the oil embargo. On 6 December another intercept made clear that 1.00 p.m. on the following day in Washington (7.30 a.m. in Hawaii) would be an important time. From the same source the Americans knew about Japanese communications preparations, including destruction of embassy code machines. From DF and TA they knew on 26 November about the creation of a new naval headquarters oriented towards Southeast Asia, actually Admiral Kondo's Second Fleet. On 6 December British patrol planes spotted a large Japanese troop convoy in the Gulf of Siam, probably headed to land forces in neutral Thailand.

Both in Washington and in London the top leaders expected, in these last days, the outbreak of war in the Far East. They assumed, however, that the key events would be played out in Southeast Asia and take the form of an invasion of Thailand or the Netherlands Indies. The possibility also existed of a strike against British territory in the Far East, something which became very evident in the final days from codebreaking. What was not thought probable was a strike against Hawaii. As the 1946 congressional inquiry put it: 'So completely did everything point to the south that it appears everyone was blinded to significant, albeit somewhat disguised, handwriting on the wall suggesting an attack on us elsewhere.'[28]

Admiral Stark in Washington learned on the morning of 7 December (Washington time) that the Japanese were about to break off relations and had specified delivery of a diplomatic note at 1.00 p.m. He decided this information did not merit being passed on immediately to Admiral Husband Kimmel at Pearl Harbor. In 1944 a Naval Court of Inquiry could note that Stark 'had failed to display the sound judgement expected of him.'[29]

Admiral Kimmel and General Walter Short, the head of the US Army's Hawaiian Department, were rightly held responsible for the unreadiness of the local defences, although there were no doubt also institutional failings beyond their control. There was no overall commander in Hawaii (or the Philippines); authority was divided between the two services. Some attention had been paid to the risk of a possible air attack on Hawaii, in both pre-war US Navy manoeuvres and 1941 contingency planning, but few concrete steps were taken to deal with such an event. The US Army was responsible for the main air defence of the Hawaiian Islands, but Short, an infantryman, was more concerned with 'fifth columnists' among the large ethnic Japanese population. Meanwhile the US Army high command had ordered long-range B-17 bombers to the Philippines, rather than using them to patrol the airspace around Hawaii. Admiral Kimmel's priorities were training his fleet and preparing to implement pre-war plans set out in Washington. These envisaged distracting the Japanese from a naval drive

1. **British Ocean Liner: SS *Athenia***

The *Athenia* was the first ship to be sunk by a U-boat in World War II. The 13,500-ton passenger vessel of the Donaldson Atlantic Line left Glasgow for Montreal on 1 September 1939. She was torpedoed two days later by the *U 30*, commanded by Lt Fritz-Julius Lemp. The liner took fourteen hours to sink but over a hundred passengers and crew were drowned. Officially the prize rules of the German Navy forbade attacks on merchant ships without warning. The government in Berlin denied responsibility; Lemp later reported he had thought the *Athenia* was a Royal Navy auxiliary cruiser.

2. **German Type VII U-boat**

The commissioning ceremony for the *U 203* in the icy waters of Kiel in February 1941. She was a Type VII, which made up much of the largest class of U-boat – a total of 703 units would be completed. The *U 30*, which sank the *Athenia*, was also a Type VII. Designed for operations in the eastern Atlantic, the Type VIIs were relatively small; the *U 30* displaced 616 tons and was 211 feet long. The *U 30* served as a training boat for most of the war and was scuttled at Flensburg on 4 May 1945; the *U 203* was sunk by British ships and aircraft off Greenland in April 1943.

3. **The Invasion of Norway, 9 April 1940**

Troops board the heavy cruiser *Admiral Hipper* at the North Sea port of Cuxhaven on 6 April 1940, in preparation for the invasion of Norway, Operation WESER EXERCISE. These forces took part in the attack on Trondheim on 9 April; it was the most successful of five operations carried out by the Wehrmacht. The sister ship of the *Hipper*, the newly built *Blücher*, was sunk by shore batteries during the approach to Oslo.

4. **Admiral Erich Raeder in Norway, 1940**

The C-in-C of the German Navy arrives in Norway after the invasion. An ardent nationalist and backer of a powerful ocean-going navy, Raeder did not disagree with Hitler's foreign policy. He was, however, surprised by the outbreak of war with the major powers. Still, once fighting began, Raeder pushed for active use of his fleet in Norway and for commerce raiding. Hitler dismissed him in January 1943, critical of the performance of the Navy's surface ships.

5. **Battleship: HMS *Warspite***

In April 1940, the battleship *Warspite* sailed up a Norwegian fjord to wipe out the German destroyer flotilla which had landed troops at Narvik. Armed with eight 15-inch guns, she had been extensively modernised in the late 1930s. Her combat career would later be the most active of any Allied capital ship.

6. **Bomber: German Junkers Ju 88**

The Ju 88 medium bomber was one of the key weapons of the sea/air war. More than any other Luftwaffe aircraft it extended German power over the seas around continental Europe during 1939–44 – in the North Sea, off Norway, in the Baltic, in the Bay of Biscay and in the Mediterranean. This photograph shows an aircraft of *Kampfgeschwader* (KG) 30, a specialist anti-shipping wing based at Comiso in Sicily.

7. **British Troops Arriving from Dunkirk, 31 May 1940**

Soldiers arrive at Dover aboard two of the many destroyers which took part in the evacuation. Despite the enduring myth that the troops of the British Expeditionary Force (BEF) were rescued off the beaches by 'the little ships' (motor boats, yachts and tugboats), the great majority travelled home aboard warships and BEF transport ships. In any event, the successful evacuation by sea was crucial for Britain's ability to continue the war.

8. **Mers el-Kébir, 3 July 1940**

The French battleship *Dunkerque* lies damaged and run aground at a base in Algeria. Two weeks after France surrendered to Germany, she and other ships had been bombarded by the Royal Navy. The British demanded that the French vessels be immediately removed from possible German control; they were to be disarmed or moved to a safe port but Admiral Gensoul refused to comply. The British opened fire, sinking the battleship *Bretagne* with heavy loss of life and damaging the *Dunkerque*.

9. **Battle off Calabria, 9 July 1940**

The battleship *Giulio Cesare* was Admiral Campioni's flagship in the first fleet battle of World War II. With another battleship and fourteen cruisers she engaged the British Mediterranean fleet off Calabria, the southern 'toe' of Italy. HMS *Warspite* succeeded in hitting the *Cesare* with one 15-inch shell; Campioni withdrew behind a smokescreen with his faster fleet and returned to base.

10. **Torpedo Bombers: Fairey Swordfish of the Fleet Air Arm**

A biplane capable of only 140 mph, the Fairey Swordfish had non-retractable wheels and the crew of three sat in an open cockpit. Nevertheless, Swordfish could carry a 1,670 lb (760 kg) torpedo, and they achieved hits on the *Dunkerque* at Mers el-Kébir, the Italian fleet at Taranto, and the *Bismarck*. This photograph shows Swordfish aboard the *Illustrious* in October 1942, toward the end of the type's torpedo-bomber career.

11. **Lofoten Commando Raid, 4 March 1941**

A raiding party of British Army special forces (Commandos) aboard an LCM(1) landing craft leave the small port of Stamsund in Norway after destroying valuable fish-oil storage tanks. Codenamed Operation CLAYMORE, this raid on the Lofoten Islands, west of Narvik, was the first of a long series of amphibious or 'combined' operations which culminated in the 1944 D-Day landings.

12. **Soviet Retreat, August 1941**

A Soviet attempt to evacuate the encircled Estonian port of Tallinn ended in catastrophe: air attacks and mines sank over 40 ships and killed 15,000 soldiers and civilians. For a time, the Red Army held the entry to the Gulf of Finland with the Hanko fortress (in southwest Finland). In December two destroyers and the 7,500-ton Dutch-built liner, the *Iosif Stalin*, arrived from Kronshtadt to pull out the rear guard. On the return voyage the liner hit mines; the wreck drifted ashore in Estonia and 3,000 survivors fell into German hands.

13. **Soviet Reinforcements Embarking for Besieged Sevastopol, 1942**

The Soviet naval base at Sevastopol in the Crimea was encircled by the Germans in October 1941. This photograph shows troops embarking on the 2,900-ton destroyer leader the *Tashkent* in the port of Novorossiisk, on the mainland east of the Crimea. The *Tashkent* made a number of wartime trips to the Crimea and sank at Novorossiisk on 2 July 1942, two days before the fall of Sevastopol.

14. **Admirals Stark, Pound and King, August 1941**

In August 1941, at the Atlantic Conference, British Admiral Dudley Pound (centre) confers with two senior officers from the neutral US. Pound had unexpectedly become First Sea Lord and Chief of Naval Staff (CNS) in July 1939, after the illness of the incumbent. To the left is Admiral Stark, the Chief of Naval Operations; to the right stands Admiral King, who would replace Stark and take overall charge of the US Navy from March 1942 to 1945.

15. **'Flower' Class Corvette: HMS *Azalea***

The dazzle-painted HMS *Azalea*, pictured here, was a member of a very large 'Flower' class of 925-ton class escorts. Built in Britain and Canada, the 'Flowers' were commissioned from 1940 onwards; the designation 'corvette' was revived for them. The 'Flowers' were celebrated by Nicholas Monsarrat in his novel *The Cruel Sea*.

16. **Liberty Ship: SS *Samuel Chase***

The SS *Samuel Chase* steams off the Maine coast in 1944. These 'emergency cargo' ships, built mostly in the US, were the backbone of the Allied global war effort. The first 'Liberty' ship was completed in September 1941 and a total of 2,755 went to sea in 1941–45.

17. **The Sinking of the USS *Reuben James*, 31 October 1941**

The American destroyer was sunk by the *U 552* while escorting a British convoy; 115 of her crew were lost. This was five weeks before Pearl Harbor. In September, President Roosevelt had ordered US Navy ships to escort British Atlantic convoys. Two other US Navy destroyers had been attacked, in an undeclared naval war with Germany. The photograph depicts the *Reuben James* in 1932.

18. **Admiral Isoroku Yamamoto**

Undoubtedly the most famous Japanese admiral of World War II, Yamamoto was an intelligent and forward-looking officer. He oversaw the creation of a powerful Japanese naval air arm in the 1930s and took command of the Combined Fleet in 1939. The surprise attack on Pearl Harbor was conceived and organised by him.

19. **Japanese Super-Battleship: the *Yamato***

The *Yamato* on her sea trials in October 1941. She and her sister ship, the *Musashi*, were constructed in great secrecy. The Japanese hoped that the unprecedented qualities of the two vessels would compensate for the potential of the Americans and British to construct more big-gun ships.

!0. **Pacific Disaster: Pearl Harbor, 7 December 1941**

Che main target of the Hawaiian Operation was 'Battleship Row'. The *Oklahoma* was hit by five orpedoes and capsized. This photograph shows her upturned hull (right); 429 members of ıer crew would be lost. The powerful *Maryland* (left) was moored inboard and protected from orpedoes.

1. **Pacific Disaster: The Loss of HMS *Prince of Wales* and *Repulse*, 10 December 1941**

he new battleship *Prince of Wales* arrives at the naval base at Singapore on 6 December. A new ,astern Fleet had been created, literally on the eve of the Japanese Southern Operation. Forming orce Z with the battle cruiser *Repulse* and four destroyers, the *Prince of Wales* left the base on 8)ecember; their mission was to break up Japanese landings in southern Thailand. Force Z was aught in a mass attack of Japanese shore-based bombers from Indochina and both big ships were ınk.

22. ***Kreuzerkrieg*: The Battleship *Scharnhorst* and *U 124*, March 1941**

This photograph was taken from the *U 124*, when German vessels were operating against British shipping near the Cape Verde Islands. Operation BERLIN, the Atlantic raid of the *Scharnhorst* and her sister ship, the *Gneisenau*, was the most successful episode of the *Kreuzerkrieg* (cruiser war), which was then a central part of the German Navy's strategy. The daring voyage began in Kiel in January 1941 and ended in late March with the arrival of the ships in the port of Brest in occupied France.

23. **The RAF Attacks German battleships, 18 December 1941**

Two new RAF Halifax bombers fly over the port of Brest in occupied France. In dry dock, directly in front of the lead bomber, are the camouflaged *Scharnhorst* and *Gneisenau*. This raid did not damage the battleships, but hits made earlier in the year had shown it was too dangerous to base large German warships in France. In February 1942, Hitler ordered the battleships and the cruiser *Prinz Eugen* back to Germany via the Channel.

24. **Malta Convoys: The Battle of Sirte, 22 March 1942**

Four cargo ships bringing supplies to Malta from the east were escorted by the Mediterranean Fleet's surviving warships – five light cruisers and fifteen destroyers. In a five-hour battle the escort succeeded in driving off a superior Italian force including a battleship, two heavy cruisers and a light cruiser. This photograph, taken from the HMS *Euryalus*, shows the HMS *Cleopatra* laying a smokescreen.

25. **Butch O'Hare, 20 February 1942**

Lt Edward 'Butch' O'Hare (right) poses for a publicity photograph with Lt Commander John S. Thach, leader of O'Hare's fighter squadron (VF-3), on 20 February 1942. O'Hare became a national hero by shooting down several Japanese bombers attacking the carrier *Lexington* on 20 February. In the background is a Grumman F4F-3 Wildcat fighter of the type flown by VF-3.

26. **The Battle of Midway: The Carrier *Hiryū*, 4 June 1942**

The *Hiryū* manoeuvres to avoid bombs dropped by US Army Air Force B-17s. These early attacks by shore-based bombers from Midway Atoll caused no losses to the enemy fleet. Later in the morning, however, a ship-based dive-bomber attack from a US Navy task force inflicted fatal damage on three of the four Japanese carriers. The undamaged *Hiryū* managed a counter-strike, but she was put out of action in the afternoon and sank on the morning of 5 June.

7. **The Battle of Midway: Aboard the *Yorktown*, 4 June 1942**

he flagship of Admiral Fletcher, she was heavily damaged by planes from the carrier *Hiryū* on June. Attempts were made to tow the damaged vessel to safety, but she was torpedoed by a ıbmarine on 7 June.

. **Fighter Plane: Japanese A6M/ZEKE Fighter**

ıe Mitsubishi A6M (or 'Zero') fighter, codenamed ZEKE by the Allies, played a major role in pan's early conquests. This example was the first to fall intact into American hands; flying from e carrier *Ryūjō*, it had crash landed on a remote Aleutian island in July 1942. Test-flights in the S enabled the development of effective tactics to deal with it.

29. **Malta Convoys: Operation PEDESTAL, 10–15 August 1942**

Taken from the HMS *Victorious*, this photograph shows the *Indomitable* and the *Eagle*. A fourth carrier was present, as well as two battleships, three cruisers and thirteen destroyers. Radar and better aircraft, including Sea Hurricane fighters, gave the convoy protection from air attack. Nevertheless, a U-boat sank the *Eagle*, and the *Indomitable* was damaged by a bomb; attacked by aircraft and MTBs, only five out of fifteen merchant ships got through.

30. **Beachhead: Dieppe, 19 August 1942**

A Churchill IV heavy tank lies knocked out on the beach. Operation JUBILEE was the most unsuccessful Allied amphibious operation of World War II. It demonstrated the difficulties of overcoming the German defences and especially the problems of taking a defended port; a full-scale invasion would have to find some other route for putting troops, vehicles and supplies ashore against British and Dutch territories in Southeast Asia by a US naval demonstration against the Marshall Islands. Kimmel's flying boat squadrons were training for this, rather than patrolling around the Hawaiian Islands.

Short and Kimmel had been given 'war warnings' from Washington on 24 and 27 November, and intelligence was shared with them regarding Japanese communications preparations and force movements. Even if their commands were apparently not directly threatened, simple precautions were not taken. Kimmel and Short were dismissed from their posts almost immediately after the attack, and in February 1942, after a high-level inquiry, they were retired from military service. The attack on the naval base and airfields on Oahu was the greatest defeat in American military history. The two men were certainly not solely responsible for the debacle, but they were the officers in charge.

Despite the drama and humiliation of Pearl Harbor, American losses were shocking rather than devastating. Panic reigned for a few days in Washington. Admiral Stark and others feared the imminent invasion of the Hawaiian Islands. American leaders had turned from underestimating the Japanese to seeing them as all-powerful. But the effect was short term.

Nearly 200 American planes (mostly from the Army) had been destroyed, most of them on the ground, but many of them were obsolescent and they were easily replaced. Two thousand naval personnel were killed – more than half of them aboard the *Arizona*, including Admiral Isaac Kidd, the commander of Battleship Division 1.[30] Five battleships had been sunk or put out of action – a very large loss – and the US Navy leadership was still dominated by the 'gun club', the advocates of the traditional capital ship. But the vessels sunk or seriously damaged were all 21-knot battleships which were too slow to take part in modern fleet actions. Only the *Arizona* and the *Oklahoma*, two of the oldest battleships, and comparable to the British 'R' class, had been total losses. Three more, which sank upright in shallow water, would take two or more years in shipyards to repair (although time spent there included extensive modernisation work). Damage to other fleet units was strictly limited. Most important, none of the three Pacific Fleet aircraft carriers was in Pearl Harbor on 7 December, but there was also little damage to the cruiser or destroyer force.

Above all, the raid represented a complete misunderstanding on the part of the Japanese of politics and popular opinion in the United States. The attack had been made on American territory, on a Sunday morning, without a declaration of war. As the British ambassador, Lord Halifax, put it on the evening after the attack: 'I can't imagine any way in which they could have acted so completely to rally, unite and infuriate American opinion'.[31] The decision of Hitler and Mussolini to throw their lot in with Japanese three days later, with declarations of war on 11 December, tarred Germany and Italy with the same brush.

Nevertheless, whatever the long-term implications of Pearl Harbor, the Pacific Fleet had been damaged and the naval command stunned. From this point of view Japanese calculations paid off. There was no likelihood that the US Navy could now defend American territories in the western and central Pacific, let alone contribute, directly or indirectly, to the defence of the 'Malay Barrier' (Singapore, Sumatra and Java).

The Japanese capture of Guam, between Wake Atoll and the Philippines, was carried out quickly. Ceded by Spain to the US in 1898, it had never been fortified. Guam was one of the Mariana Islands, and was easily attacked from Japanese-held Saipan. The invasion came on 10 December; the small garrison of a few hundred sailors and Marines had no chance against a Japanese brigade and a number of warships.

Wake Atoll was much smaller and more remote, but events there were more dramatic. The atoll consisted of three low-lying coral islands measuring less than 3 square miles. It lay some 2,300 miles to the west of Hawaii and was valuable as an airstrip for ferrying long-range planes across the Pacific and (potentially) as a seaplane base. In the autumn a battalion of Marines was landed to defend the island and a carrier flew in twelve Marine F4F Wildcat fighter planes. The Japanese attacked the atoll as part of their simultaneous first strike. A long-range bomber strike from the Marshall Islands (to the south) destroyed most of the Marine fighter planes on the ground. However, an attempt by a small enemy force to effect a landing on 11 December was driven off by Marine artillery and four surviving fighter planes. Two elderly destroyers, the *Hayate* and the *Kisaragi*, were sunk, the first Japanese surface ships to be lost in the whole war. The Americans considered a major fleet operation to support Wake. However, the top leadership of the US Pacific Fleet was in flux, and it took time to assemble a task force from the carriers that had been at sea on 7 December. In the end it was not possible even to evacuate the Marine garrison or the civilians who had been working on the Wake facilities. The Japanese called in two of the Pearl Harbor carriers, the *Hiryū* and the *Sōryū*, to support a second, successful landing. This took place on 22 December and resulted in an American surrender.

The United States did not fight a naval campaign in defence of the Philippines. The surface ships of the US Asiatic Fleet – two cruisers and thirteen destroyers – had been moved south from Manila to safer waters before the fighting began. Nevertheless, the islands were strategically important. The threat of future intervention from the Philippines against Japanese shipping routes from Southeast Asia was one of the main reasons for the whole pre-emptive attack on the United States. American operations in the Philippines also demonstrated a fatal lack of joint war planning. The US Army and the US Navy took different views on whether the islands were defensible or not. The US Navy believed that a concentration of two dozen submarines could block Japanese attempts to invade the islands. Equally naïve was the attempt by the US Army Air Force (AAF) to use air power to block invasion (and indeed to control the whole Pacific) by deploying B-17 bombers.

The Americans did not believe that the Japanese could reach their airfield complex in central Luzon with escorted bombers, but on the first day of the war the long-range flight of A6M Zero fighters demonstrated that this was incorrect. Meanwhile the inadequate and badly defended bases were attacked with devastating results; a third of the B-17 force was destroyed on the ground and the rest flew south, out of range. The main Japanese invasion of the Philippines came at Lingayen Gulf in northwestern Luzon on 22 December, with over fifty transport ships from Formosa and the Pescadores[32] carrying the 18th Infantry Division; it was attacked at sea neither by aircraft nor by submarines. A couple of US submarines did enter the gulf but had no effect. Other American boats achieved almost nothing in the course of several months.

Once ashore, the Japanese met no effective ground troops. The attempt by General Douglas MacArthur to set up an all-round defence of Luzon was a failure. He had to fall back on an earlier plan of creating an enclave in the rugged Bataan Peninsula northwest of Manila, as well as keeping control of the island fortress of Corregidor at the entrance to Manila Bay. Bataan did hold out for four months – until 9 April – and Corregidor surrendered even later, on 6 May. This was a more impressive performance than that of the British and Dutch 'imperial' armies, and the Japanese Army general concerned was censured by his own side for a failure to achieve a quick victory. The most remarkable feature of these events was the survival of General MacArthur's reputation.

THE SOUTHERN OPERATION: THE ROYAL NAVY DEFEATED

From the naval point of view, the opening of the Pacific war can be divided into two distinct events. Japan's Hawaiian Operation – Pearl Harbor – has burned into the American collective memory. But for the Japanese government, and for the British, the Southern Operation meant more.

The British, for their part, had long worried about how they could defend their colonial empire and economic interests in the Far East. Indeed in the 1920s Japan became the main global threat as far as Royal Navy planning was concerned; this did not change until the resurgence of Germany in the mid-1930s. The solution devised in the 1920s was to develop a base at Singapore, at the southern tip of Malaya. To this base the 'main fleet' in Europe could be sent, in the event of increased tension or even war with Japan.

By 1939–40 Britain's global position had changed for the worse. It was now fighting a full-scale war in Europe, and from June 1940 a desperate one. No warships were available to send to the Far East. Moreover, the hypothetical threat had become more definite in 1937–40, as the Japanese moved towards Singapore. They took control of China's southwestern coast in 1938, bypassing the British colony at Hong Kong, and in the summer of 1940 they sent forces into northern Indochina.

The situation seemed to improve in early 1941, as the Americans took on a bigger role. The secret military staff 'conversations' (known as ABC-1, see p. 165 above) between the American and British military, held in Washington, touched on Japan. The broad plan – strange as it might seem from a post-Pearl Harbor perspective – was to commit some (neutral) American heavy ships to the Atlantic; this would allow the Royal Navy to reinforce Singapore and prepare a defence of the Malay Barrier. The American Pacific Fleet (stationed from the summer of 1940 in Hawaii rather than on the West Coast) would tie down the Japanese fleet. By May 1941 the British Admiralty was considering a new Eastern Fleet with three to six of the older big-gun ships, a carrier and supporting vessels. Admiral Tom Phillips, Admiral Sir Dudley Pound's deputy as Vice Chief of Naval Staff (VCNS), was assigned as provisional C-in-C. Phillips had no recent combat experience, but he was expected to function well as a naval diplomat, co-operating with the other two British services and negotiating with the Dominions and potential American and Dutch allies.

The planned gradual build-up was jerked forward by events – with tragic consequences. In August the Prime Minister travelled to Argentia, Newfoundland, aboard the new battleship *Prince of Wales* to confer with President Roosevelt. Shortly afterwards he proposed that such a ship be sent to the Far East, where its technical quality and speed would impress and deter the Japanese. The Admiralty resisted, but two important developments in October led the British government to renew the plan. One was the appointment of General Tōjō's bellicose government, the other was the crisis of the Red Army and the threatened fall of Moscow, which might tempt the Japanese to make war on the USSR and invade Siberia. Sending a British battleship could provide an immediate deterrent to rash Japanese action.

On 25 October the *Prince of Wales* departed from Scotland, with Admiral Phillips aboard. She would join forces in the Indian Ocean with the battle cruiser *Repulse*. Churchill made a major public speech on 10 November declaring that 'a powerful naval force of heavy ships' was being deployed. He also summed up the basic strategy: 'this movement of our naval forces, in conjunction with the United States Main fleet, may give a practical proof to all who have eyes to see [i.e. the Japanese government] that the forces of freedom and democracy have by no means reached the limits of their power'. On 3 December *The Times* announced the arrival in Singapore of the two big ships and the creation of the Eastern Fleet under Phillips.[33]

The deterrent strategy did not work. The forces which would carry out the Japanese Southern Operation were already at sea. A detachment of Japanese infantry landed from three transports at Kota Bharu in northern Malaya an hour or so before the Pearl Harbor attack. Its task was to capture the nearby RAF aerodrome and to prevent air strikes against Japanese ships to the north, in the Gulf of Siam. A much larger force was put ashore there from sixteen transports, at Singora on the Kra Isthmus in neutral Thailand. The British had counted on sea/air power to shatter an invading force even before it came ashore. A network of RAF air bases had been laid out, but the second-rate fighter and bomber squadrons available were not up to the task.

Phillips decided to use his surface ships for a 'high-speed descent' to disrupt the enemy landings on the Kra Isthmus. The *Prince of Wales* and the *Repulse*, with four escorting destroyers, sailed north from Singapore on the evening of 8 December.[34] They were now designated as Force Z. Neither Phillips nor the Admiralty had an accurate idea of the threat to be faced. The Joint Intelligence Committee (JIC) in London in November had concluded that any Japanese operations in the South China Sea would require aircraft carriers, and that land-based aircraft would not be a factor.[35]

As part of its oceanic attrition strategy the Japanese Navy – stemming partly from the initiative of Admiral Yamamoto in the early 1930s – had developed the concept of a long-range torpedo-carrying 'land-based attack aircraft', known by the abbreviation *rikkō*. The advanced Mitsubishi G3M began development in 1933 and first flew in 1935. It was a twin-engined medium bomber with an exceptional operating radius of 1,300 miles. A successor design, the G4M, first flew in October 1939. The G3M had been used in the China war since 1937, and a civilian version had made record-breaking long-distance flights outside Japan. Nevertheless, the availability of six large operational attack plane formations (naval air groups or NAGs) was evidently not known to the British.[36] The base units were very mobile; three naval air groups were rapidly moved to southern Indochina from the home islands and from Formosa on the eve of the war.

Force Z had no effective air cover. Admiral Phillips, realising on the afternoon of the 9th that his ships had been spotted by enemy scout planes, turned back before he reached the Kra Isthmus. At midday on the 10th, however, on the way home to Singapore and off the coast of central Malaya, the British fleet came under a mass attack. The enemy strike force comprised about ninety (unescorted) attack planes flying from Indochina. The torpedo attacks were lethal; first the *Prince of Wales* and then the *Repulse* were hit. The battle cruiser sank first, and half an hour later the *Prince of Wales*; Admiral Phillips went down with his flagship. Only three Japanese planes were lost. The destruction of Force Z was the worst moment of the whole war for the Royal Navy, and in a number of respects worse for the Allies than Pearl Harbor. It was also a turning point in sea/air warfare: modern, manoeuvring capital ships had been found and sunk at sea by bombers.

Churchill is sometimes blamed for risking the big ships. In reality the disaster had two causes. The first was the underestimation by the Admiralty of the capability of the Japanese Navy (including its shore-based bombers). The second cause was the tactical decisions made by an admiral with no modern combat experience. As one air-minded flag officer put it, 'Phillips like a lot of Admirals never believed in the air & now poor devil he knows.'[37] The 'high-speed descent', with only four escorting destroyers, may have been in the Nelsonian tradition, but it was highly risky, even without the Japanese air threat. Force Z had been shadowed by Japanese submarines, and Phillips narrowly missed a night action with Admiral Kondō's Second Fleet main units, which could well have destroyed Force Z; these were the fast battleships *Haruna* and *Kongō*, seven heavy cruisers, a light cruiser and fourteen destroyers.

There could be no further British attempt to challenge the bridgehead of the Japanese Army in Thailand and northern Malaya. Seasonal bad weather and the impenetrability of the terrain had been counted upon; neither slowed the enemy. In an eight-week 'dash advance' land campaign, the Japanese drove towards Singapore, outmanoeuvring and outfighting the more numerous British and Indian troops. Singapore fell on 15 February 1942. Some 70,000 British, Australian and Indian troops were captured. The largest surrender in the military history of the United Kingdom, it was the beginning of the end of the British Empire.

Meanwhile the Japanese had made rapid progress into the Netherlands Indies. The meticulously planned conquest of the Malay Barrier was a demonstration of brilliant staff work and well-conducted amphibious warfare. Simultaneous attacks were mounted over a wide area, with military units 'leap-frogging' over one another. The ground forces committed were not very large; the Japanese Army was mainly deployed in the Asian mainland, fighting in China or confronting the USSR. Most of the air support was provided by the Navy – the naval air groups of the land-based Eleventh Air Fleet and – after a delay of over a month – the carriers of the Mobile Force (by now back from Hawaii).

In mid-December the Japanese took without difficulty the small ports on the west coast of Borneo, situated on the far side of the South China Sea. After gaining control of most of the Philippines and establishing a firm bridgehead in Malaya, they began to consolidate their position. The port and airfield at Rabaul in the Bismarck Archipelago, north of New Guinea, were seized on 23 January. Such was the importance of Rabaul that the invasion was supported by air attacks from four of the Mobile Force carriers. Little resistance was put up by the small Australian garrison.[38] At the same time the Japanese began an advance south through the Netherlands Indies, past the islands of Borneo and Celebes (now Sulawesi), with little resistance from the Dutch or their allies. The climax of the campaign was the capture of Java, the central element of the Malay Barrier and the Dutch administrative centre in the Netherlands Indies, which was very densely populated, with some 50 million of the 70 million inhabitants of the Netherlands Indies living here; Java was also a centre for oil production.

By mid-February the Japanese had prepared two big invasion convoys, one aimed for the eastern part of Java, near Surabaya, and the other for the western part, near Batavia (now Jakarta), the colonial capital. The Surabaya convoy assembled in the southwestern Philippines. Its forty-one ships transported the 48th Division which had fought on Luzon, and the 56th Regiment. The convoy bound for western Java, some fifty-six ships, assembled at Cam Ranh Bay in Indochina. On board was the headquarters of the Sixteenth Army,[39] the soldiers of the 2nd Division (later destroyed on Guadalcanal), and a regiment of the 38th Division. The convoys put to sea on 18 and 19 February.

Admiral Nagumo's Mobile Force supported the invasion by raiding Port Darwin in northern Australia, the main Allied support base for Java. The *Akagi*, the *Kaga*, the *Hiryū* and the *Sōryū* sailed from the Palau island group in the western Carolines, then through the eastern part of the Malay Barrier, and into the Indian Ocean. On the morning of 19 February nearly 200 carrier planes raided Port Darwin, joined by very long-range rikkō strikes from captured bases in the Netherlands Indies. The Australian port was effectively put out of action.

The Battle of the Java Sea began on 27 February. It was the first major surface battle of the Pacific war, and the prototype of a long series of cruiser-destroyer actions fought in 1942 and 1943. Despite the activities of the Imperial Navy off China from 1937 onwards, and in the Hawaiian and Southern operations, the Battle of the Java Sea was the first major conventional naval battle which Japanese warships had fought for thirty-six years – since Tsushima in 1905.

It was an event for which the fleet had planned and trained for decades. As already mentioned, the Japanese had developed powerful cruiser and destroyer forces as part of the inter-war plan to 'wear down and ambush' the US Navy in the Central Pacific. A 24-inch, 3-ton torpedo had been developed. The Type 93 used oxygen rather than compressed air as its oxidiser; this was a complex and volatile technology which the Royal Navy had invented and then abandoned as impractical. The torpedo had a theoretical range of 40,000 metres (25 miles) at 36 knots. Its explosive charge was 1,080 pounds. The Allies knew nothing of this weapon in February 1942, or for some months afterwards. (After the war, the naval historian Samuel Eliot Morison would assign the name 'Long Lance' to the Type 93, but this designation was used neither by the Japanese nor by the wartime US Navy.)

The heavy cruisers that played a central part in the Java Sea and later battles were equipped to fire barrages of these heavy torpedoes; they mounted twelve torpedo tubes (4×3), as well as their artillery of ten 8-inch guns (in five turrets). The two ships that fought at the Java Sea were the *Nachi* and the *Haguro*. Admiral Takagi Takeo, who flew his flag in the *Nachi*, also had under his command two destroyer squadrons, each with six to eight destroyers and led by a light cruiser.[40]

The Allied commander in the Battle of the Java Sea, the Dutch Admiral Karel Doorman, was aboard the modern light cruiser *De Ruyter*. He led a very mixed 'Combined Striking Force' with four other ships – the heavy cruisers *Houston* and *Exeter*, and the light cruisers *Perth* and *Java*. Some of these ships had been damaged by Japanese bombers earlier in the campaign, and all were in need of overhaul. The Dutch *Java* dated from 1922, but the *Houston* was the former flagship of the US Asiatic Fleet. HMS *Exeter* had played a gallant part in the *Graf Spee* battle, and the Australian *Perth* was a sister ship of the *Ajax* and the *Achilles*. Light forces comprised four American, three British and two Dutch destroyers.

Doorman took the Striking Force north into the Java Sea from near Surabaya on 27 February. Over a seven-hour period, beginning in the late afternoon, he attempted to break through the Japanese escort force to get at the eastern convoy. An indecisive gunnery action was fought at very long range; the machinery of the *Exeter* was crippled by an 8-inch shell, and she had to withdraw to Surabaya. In a second stage, under a full moon, a torpedo salvo from the *Nachi* and the *Haguro*, fired at a range of 10,900 yards (over 6 miles), sank the two Dutch cruisers. Doorman went down with his flagship, after ordering the *Houston* and the *Perth* to make their way to Batavia. It was the last sea fight in a gallant Dutch naval tradition stretching back to the seventeenth century.[41]

On the following evening (28 February) the *Houston* and the *Perth* attempted but failed to reach the safety of the Indian Ocean through the Sunda Strait between Java and Sumatra. They sailed by chance towards the anchorage at Bantam (Banten) Bay, where twenty-seven transports had just begun to land part of the Japanese western convoy. At first only one Japanese destroyer was involved, but powerful reinforcements, including the heavy cruisers *Mogami* and *Mikuma* (under Admiral Kurita Takeo – a commander later famous in the 1944 Battle of Leyte Gulf), quickly arrived from the north. In a confused gun and torpedo mêlée the *Houston* and the *Perth* were sunk by destroyer torpedoes. Four large Japanese transports and a minesweeper also went down in the barrage of torpedoes fired from the *Mogami*. One victim of this friendly fire was the commander of the Sixteenth Army, General Imamura – he was able to swim to safety.

The *Exeter*, damaged on the afternoon of the 27th, made a desperate daytime dash out of Surabaya with two destroyers on the morning of 1 March, hoping to break through the Sunda Strait. The three ships were intercepted and boxed in south of Borneo by two Japanese heavy cruiser groups. Admiral Takahashi with the *Ashigara* and the *Myōkō* now supported Admiral Takagi's *Nachi* and *Haguro*. All three Allied ships were sunk in a one-sided gunnery and torpedo action fought at midday; no Japanese ships were lost or damaged. With this ended the naval defence of the Malay Barrier.

The two big convoys had brought the Japanese Army to Java with very little loss. On 25 February the Allied headquarters on Java was wound up; it had been created in early January as the ABDA (American-British-Dutch-Australian) Command under the British general Archibald Wavell. It was the first (and least successful) inter-Allied headquarters at theatre level. Now, with Malaya, Singapore and the Dutch East Indies lost, General Wavell departed for India. The rest of the land fighting was quickly over; the Dutch forces on Java capitulated on 9 March. The first campaign of the Pacific war was over.

The Japanese Navy now struck out into the Indian Ocean. They seized the Andaman Islands in March, and at the beginning of April a Japanese squadron under Admiral Ozawa Jisaburō sortied from Mergui (now Myeik) on the west coast of Burma and raided the Bay of Bengal. His force included the small carrier *Ryūjō* and six cruisers. Operating south of Calcutta and in the rear area of the British Burma front, they sank twenty-three merchant ships, totalling over 100,000 tons; no opposition was met from British ships or aircraft.

An even bolder Japanese thrust was directed at the same time against Ceylon, Operation C. This expedition is often ignored in histories of the sea war; in reality it had similarities to both the Pearl Harbor raid and the Battle of Midway. On 26 March, Admiral Nagumo departed from Starling Bay in Celebes with one of the most powerful fleets the Imperial Navy would ever assemble. The Mobile Force now consisted of the *Akagi*, the *Hiryū*, the *Sōryū*, the *Shōkaku* and the *Zuikaku*, five of the Pearl Harbor carriers; they carried some 400 aircraft.[42] Four fast battleships, three cruisers and eleven destroyers accompanied the carriers. Steaming south through the Ombai Strait (north of Timor) into the Indian Ocean, the Mobile Force proceeded at high speed to the west, refuelling at sea south of Java.

Operation 'C' had both operational and strategic goals. The former was to prevent interference by the British Eastern Fleet with convoys supporting the Japanese troops in Burma (the overland supply route was poor).[43] The strategic goal was to bring about a decisive battle with the British Eastern Fleet and to destroy it before it could be reinforced.

Neither side had an accurate knowledge of the other's strength. Japanese intelligence estimated in early March that two battleships, two carriers, two heavy cruisers and four to seven light cruisers were available at Ceylon and Bombay, and 350 planes based on Ceylon. They expected that this force would shortly be reinforced by six additional battleships, two carriers and another 250 aircraft. The British, for their part, had advance warning of the raid, but they expected a *smaller* enemy force consisting of a couple of carriers escorted by cruisers.[44]

On 5 April the ship strength of the Eastern Fleet was on paper stronger than the Japanese assessment, but the assembly of the fleet had only been completed in the very last few weeks before Operation 'c'. Admiral James Somerville had been told he was to take over the Eastern Fleet on 2 January. It was only on 17 February that he departed from the Clyde aboard the newly repaired carrier *Formidable*; having travelled around the Cape, he reached Colombo on the west coast of Ceylon only on 26 March. The Eastern Fleet included the *Indomitable* (the newest of the 'Illustrious' class) which had been ferrying RAF fighters around the Indian Ocean. His third carrier, the *Hermes*, 10,000 tons and commissioned in 1924, had been in the Far East for some years but was of little operational value. Although the *Formidable* and the *Indomitable* were very impressive vessels, the total air strength of the three carriers was made up of only thirty-nine fighters and fifty-seven strike aircraft. The latter were all outmoded Swordfish and Albacore biplanes; for their crews, daytime operations in the face of A6M Zero fighters would be suicidal. Never had the long-term weakness of British carrier air power been more evident.

The only effective British battleship, the ubiquitous *Warspite*, had arrived on 22 March; like the *Formidable*, she was Mediterranean veteran, and had sailed halfway around the world (via Sydney) from a Puget Sound repair yard. Four more battleships with 15-inch guns, the *Ramillies*, the *Resolution*, the *Revenge* and the *Royal Sovereign*, had been concentrated in Ceylon in the past few weeks, having previously been engaged in long-range convoy escort. They were slightly newer than the *Warspite*, but slower and unmodernised. They were suitable only for convoy work and coastal bombardment. The two heavy cruisers in the Eastern Fleet, the *Dorsetshire* (which had torpedoed the *Bismarck* the year before) and the *Cornwall*, had been hunting for surface raiders in the southern oceans. There was also a mixed batch of five light cruisers and sixteen destroyers, mostly old, and seven submarines.

Somerville was one of the most able and experienced admirals, having commanded Force H at Gibraltar from July 1940. He had two major advantages, although in the end they permitted his survival rather than enabled a British victory. First, there was his main operating base. The new fleet was using an emergency anchorage 400 miles south of Ceylon in the Maldive Islands at Addu Atoll (code-named Port 'T'). Addu had very few facilities or defences, and an awful equatorial climate, but the Japanese did not know of its existence. The other British advantage was codebreaking. Almost at the moment of his arrival in Ceylon Somerville received information about Japanese intentions from both his Colombo-based intercept unit (the Far East Combined Bureau, or FECB) and the Americans.[45] A signal, decrypted from the JN-25B naval code by the FECB on 28 March, gave information about a planned raid by a carrier force originating from Celebes; this would strike a location, probably Colombo, on 1 or 2 April. On the negative side, Ceylon lacked long-range reconnaissance aircraft; only six Catalinas were available.

The decrypt did not give the strength of the attacking force, but Somerville informed the Admiralty that the enemy had just two carriers and four cruisers – a very dangerous underestimate.[46] He had only just assumed command, and he was aware of the lack of training of his ships and air crews. Nevertheless, he thought that there was a chance of hitting the approaching Japanese with a surprise flanking attack, especially with radar-equipped torpedo bombers mounting night attacks from his carriers. This was a scenario not totally different from the one that Admiral Nimitz would envisage at Midway two months later.

On Tuesday, 31 March, warships at Colombo, Trincomalee (Ceylon) and Addu put to sea and assembled south of Ceylon. Critically, the date given in the decrypted message was inaccurate, because the initial departure of the Mobile Force from Celebes had been delayed. On the morning of Friday (the 3rd), with no further sign of enemy movement and the short-legged 'R' class battleships needing to return to base shortly to refuel, Somerville detached the *Cornwall* and the *Dorsetshire* to Colombo and the *Hermes* to Trincomalee. He continued exercising the rest of his ships until the evening, when he turned south to Addu. He arrived there at midday on Saturday; then, at 4.00 p.m. a Catalina sighted enemy ships SSE of Ceylon, evidently bound for Colombo. Somerville was too far away to intercept, but he thought he might be able to hit the Japanese on their return trip after the raid, and he took his fast ships to sea very early on Sunday.

On Easter Sunday, 5 April, the Mobile Force launched a massive strike against the port, naval base and airfields at Colombo. The strike leader was Commander Fuchida Mitsuo, who had been commander of the attacks on Pearl Harbor and Port Darwin. It was not a repetition of 7 December. Thanks to the intelligence warnings most of the Allied merchant ships had cleared the port. The RAF did put several squadrons of Hurricane fighters up, although these suffered badly at the hands of the escorting Zeros. In the early afternoon a second wave caught the *Dorsetshire* and the *Cornwall* at sea, hurriedly sailing back from Colombo to rejoin the main fleet. They were sunk in a mass attack by Aichi D3A/VAL dive bombers.

Admiral Somerville had in many respects been very lucky. His premature sortie and return to base kept his main forces completely clear of the Japanese attack force. Nagumo did not attempt a 360° air search, nor did he loiter off

Colombo. By the evening of the 5th – repeating his cautious behaviour at Pearl Harbor – he was heading rapidly away to the southeast. In the course of the day Somerville had suddenly realised that he was not the hunter but the fox, and that he was facing a much superior enemy force; his main concern now was to avoid contact. By Tuesday the 7th he had decided that most of the fleet would have to be withdrawn from Ceylon to safer bases in East Africa and at Bombay.

On Thursday the 9th, Admiral Nagumo returned to attack Trincomalee, the other major naval port on Ceylon, on the east coast. Although his approach was detected, the air defence of the port was even less effective than at Colombo. In addition, the *Hermes* was caught at sea and sunk by a swarm of dive bombers, along with the destroyer *Vampire*, which had survived the December attack on Force Z.

Overall, one explanation for this humiliating defeat was the weakness of British carrier aircraft, in terms of both number and quality. Less obvious, but still telling, was the almost complete lack of shore-based air power on Ceylon; two dozen RAF Blenheim light bombers could achieve nothing against Japanese warships and half a dozen Catalinas could not provide adequate ocean surveillance. The rival demands of the Atlantic U-boat war and the Mediterranean war must of course be taken into account, as well as previous losses on the Malay Barrier. Nevertheless, there was a profound mismatch of resource allocation at the strategic level, especially because of the British strategic bombing obsession. A month after a few dozen British planes tried to defend Ceylon, the RAF would send 1,000 heavy and medium bombers against Cologne.

The British government and military planners now took the threat extremely seriously. Ceylon and southern India were virtually defenceless in the spring of 1942. The Axis powers did not actually have a global strategy, but from the Allied perspective the ultimate peril involved co-ordination of enemy operations in the Suez–Caucasus–western Indian Ocean region. Winston Churchill apparently once declared that the Japanese raid on Ceylon had been 'the most dangerous moment of the war and the one that caused [him] most alarm'.[47] However, the strategic threat should not be exaggerated. The Japanese Army high command, overburdened on other fronts and realistic about the long-range supply problem, refused to provide troops for a landing in Ceylon (or India).[48]

Nothing of strategic value was achieved by the Japanese. As the historian John Lundstrom put it, the Ceylon operation turned out to be 'almost meaningless'.[49] It is true that the British were forced to withdraw their warships from Ceylon to the East African coast. Although they contemplated a number of amphibious counter-attacks against Burma, Malaya or Sumatra in 1943 and 1944 these would come to nothing. But that was largely because of the higher priority given to other theatres and a lack of assault shipping.

We know with hindsight that the rapid revival of the US Navy would rule out any further Japanese adventures. Two American carriers mounted a raid against Tokyo on 18 April (nine days after the Trincomalee raid), and then the loss of four Mobile Force carriers at the Battle of Midway on 4 June profoundly shifted the strategic balance. Operation 'C' was, for the Japanese, a symptom of confused grand strategy and a waste of valuable assets and time, which would have been better used consolidating the position in the South Pacific. The implications of this Japanese inattention will be discussed in the following two chapters.

* * *

These dramatic events of April 1942 brought to a close the second period of the 1939–45 war, one which had begun with the fall of France in June 1940. In broad geopolitical terms, the British Empire had – between June 1940 and June 1941 – survived a single-handed confrontation with Germany and Italy, despite their dominant position in continental Europe. The Mediterranean and North Africa emerged as the most important overseas theatre for the British, but not for the Germans. Hitler's decision to invade the Soviet Union was a most important one, diverting Wehrmacht forces from the war against Britain.

Meanwhile the position of the neutral US had become more important for both sides. This contributed to some restraint in Hitler's war on shipping (to avoid a full-scale American entry into the war on the lines of 1917). Meanwhile, President Roosevelt had to deal with a Congress (and a population) that opposed involvement in the war, but he steered the country into an increasingly one-sided, pro-British form of neutrality.

But in December 1941 the war became a global one, in a way that most of the war leaders had not expected. The Japanese onslaught called an American bluff and brutally laid bare the limitations of British power. The final months (December 1941 to March 1942) saw the catastrophic collapse of the British position in the Far East and Southeast Asia. In the words of Admiral Richmond, the great naval historian, 'It was the illusion that a Two-Hemisphere Empire can be defended by a One-Hemisphere Navy that sealed the fate of Singapore.'[50]

This collapse, however, would surely – in time – be compensated for by the participation in the war of Russian and American allies, each in its own way at least as powerful as Britain. The full-scale involvement of the US, with all its forces and resources, and the Russian survival after the initial Blitzkrieg assault, meant Hitler's hopes for a rapid and decisive victory were now dashed. The shrewder leaders of Germany and Japan now thought in terms of slowing the expected Allied counter-offensive which was bound to develop, and pondering whether the resource base they had so rapidly acquired could allow a stalemate outcome.

In more narrowly maritime terms, the main fighting had been, until the last months of this second period, confined largely to the European side of the North Atlantic and to the Mediterranean. In both these areas, and in scattered engagements in the more remote areas of the 'world ocean', the Royal Navy was able to deny use of the sea to Britain's enemies. Germany could not invade the British Isles, and indeed Axis forces made no real headway against even the extended British-controlled overseas territories – despite the urgings of Admiral Raeder.

A fundamental achievement of the British of this period was that they continued to make use of a global shipping network, both on the transatlantic routes and, to a smaller extent, in supplying the Middle East (around the Cape of Good Hope). Construction of merchant ships was still on a relatively small scale, but so were losses, and the British Empire had begun the war with a huge pool of shipping.

The technology of sea power had begun to change in this period. Both Britain and her enemies had now been able to put some of their new capital ships into service. The British kept their advantage, with their inter-war head start, and a monopoly on carrier aviation. There were more British battleships and carriers under construction; in contrast, for the Germans the completion of the *Bismarck* and the *Tirpitz* would be the end of the road, and activity in Italian shipyards had also petered out. Despite some successes, it became clear that German surface ships could have little long-term value as commerce raiders. The Italian Navy was on paper much superior to the German one – and to the British forces in the Mediterranean – but its large surface ships made few successful sorties. Nevertheless, German (and to lesser extent Italian) aviation made British control of the sea far from complete. The British Empire's arterial route through the Mediterranean to the Indian subcontinent and the Far East remained closed to normal British shipping; meanwhile Axis convoys, supported by Axis air patrols, were able to sustain ground forces in North Africa, and to enable them to mount successful offensives towards the Suez Canal.

Too few U-boats were available from 1940 until early 1942 to seriously endanger the main Atlantic route, especially when some of the limited number were diverted to the Mediterranean or Norway. The U-boat building programme had been accelerated in the summer of 1940, but many months were required to deploy an effective force. Meanwhile the British were putting more escort ships to sea, improving tactics, and developing effective A/S aircraft and electronics. The year 1941 also saw vital breakthroughs in British codebreaking.

British maritime aviation had gradually improved in this second period of the war, especially with the arrival of the first three new armoured fleet carriers and the development of RAF Coastal Command. British carrier aircraft were still too few in number, and too poor in quality. Nevertheless, a significant number of major ships of Britain's opponents had been crippled by air attack in port: the *Dunkerque* and the *Richelieu* in July 1940, and the *Littorio*, the *Conte di Cavour* and the *Caio Duilio* at Taranto in November. At sea in the same period Fleet Air Arm planes damaged the *Vittorio Veneto* off Cape Matapan in March 1941, and the *Bismarck* in May. Land-based RAF aircraft caused serious damage to the *Lützow* in the Atlantic in June 1941, the *Scharnhorst* off La Rochelle in July 1941 and the *Gneisenau* in Kiel in February 1942.

German aviation also had an increased impact (especially in the Mediterranean and from February 1941). On the other hand, the Junkers Ju 87 and Ju 88 dive bombers were most effective against more lightly armoured warships and merchantmen; no British battleship or aircraft carrier was sunk by the Luftwaffe in 1940–41. The Germans also failed to develop long-range anti-shipping aircraft or deploy significant numbers of medium-range types over the ports and crucial convoy routes in the eastern Atlantic. This was due partly to inter-service rivalry, and partly to the demands of the fighting in the Mediterranean land front and in Russia.

Despite some successes, British, Italian and German sea/air operations were less impressive than those carried out by the Imperial Japanese Navy; this was true in terms of both carrier aviation and land-based bombers. The six-carrier strike against Oahu on 7 December 1941, and the mass torpedo-plane attack on the British Eastern Fleet off Malaya three days later were something entirely new in the history of naval warfare.

In European waters, neither side had the capability to carry out major amphibious operations. The Germans could not mount a cross-Channel landing. The Italians could not take Malta. The British raiding strategy remained at pinprick level.[51] Reinforcing and supporting the ground campaign in North Africa required a considerable amount of British shipping but the lack, so far, of large-scale amphibious expeditions meant that the demands on Allied shipping were manageable; this would become a greater challenge in late 1942 and 1943. In contrast to developments in Europe, the Japanese amphibious campaign mounted from December 1941 to March 1942 against Malaya, the Philippines and the Netherlands Indies was stunningly successful. Air power was a major factor. The Japanese demonstrated exceptional skill, but the weakness of the defending forces was also a major contributing factor.

In the spring of 1942 two questions remained. Could the Axis powers consolidate their gains? And how quickly could the Allies recover from their winter of defeats?

PART III

GLOBAL WAR AT SEA

APRIL–DECEMBER 1942

Through the skill and devotion to duty of our armed forces of all branches in the Midway area, our citizens can now rejoice that a momentous victory is in the making. It was on a Sunday just six months ago that the Japanese made their peacetime attack on our fleet and army activities on Oahu. Pearl Harbor has now been partially avenged. Vengeance will not be complete until Japanese sea power has been reduced to impotence. We have made substantial progress in that direction. Perhaps we will be forgiven if we claim we are about midway to our objective.

Admiral Chester Nimitz USN, press communiqué,
6 June 1942

CHAPTER 10

THE PACIFIC IN THE BALANCE

From Carrier Raids to Midway

USS *LEXINGTON* OFF RABAUL, 20 FEBRUARY 1942

The last week of February 1942 was a low point for the Allies. Singapore had fallen, and now the Malay Barrier was being overrun. The US Navy was still reeling from Pearl Harbor. The surviving ships, however, began to raid exposed Japanese-held positions. Task Force 11 (TF 11), built around the carrier *Lexington*, left Pearl Harbor on 31 January; in command was Admiral Wilson Brown. The *Lexington* (CV-2) was a very large ship. Converted from an uncompleted battle cruiser, she displaced 37,000 tons and was nearly 900 feet from bow to stern – considerably longer than even the giant HMS *Hood* (860 feet). After reaching the South Pacific and liaising at sea with the Australian naval command, Brown decided to attack shipping in the harbour at Rabaul in the Bismarck Archipelago, which had been seized by the enemy on the 23rd. The raid might also distract the Japanese from their impending invasion of Java. TF 11 now included the carrier, four heavy cruisers and ten destroyers. Brown proposed a carrier strike, and then a cruiser bombardment; this was accepted by his superiors in Hawaii and Washington.

Admiral Brown left the Nouméa–Fiji area on 16 February and intended to hit Rabaul at dawn on the 21st. The morning before, on 20 February, his task force was spotted NNE of Bougainville in the Solomon Islands by a four-engined Kawanishi H6K/MAVIS flying boat from Rabaul, which lay some 450 miles to the west.

The *Lexington* provided TF 11 with what was for its time a formidable air defence system. The CXAM-1 radar, its big mattress antenna mounted above the carrier's huge funnel, could locate high-flying aircraft at a range of 75–80 miles. The equipment had limits: CXAM-1 could not provide direct information about the altitude of an approaching aircraft ('bogie'), nor could operators readily tell the 'echoes' of friendly planes from enemy ones.[1] Manual plotting was required, as the equipment could not yet provide an electronic plan view. But the carrier's fighter director officer (FDO) was able to play a key role in interpreting the mass of information and directing fighters towards single or multiple 'bogies'.

The *Lexington* air group contained about seventy-five aircraft in four squadrons: fighters (squadron VF-3), torpedo planes (VT-2), scouts (VS-2) and bombers (VB-2). Especially important were the eighteen Grumman F4F-3 Wildcat fighters of the VF-3, known to the Navy as 'Fighting Three'.[2] The Wildcat was much the best Allied naval fighter available up until the spring of 1943. This was true even for the *Lexington*'s F4F-3s, which carried only four .50-calibre machine guns. (The later 'standard' F4F-4 carried six guns; it was also fitted with folding wings, which allowed stowage of more aircraft on a carrier.)

The slow Japanese 'snooper' radioed a report home to Rabaul and then tried to hide in the clouds. After about forty minutes it was attacked and shot down in flames by two Wildcats from the combat air patrol (CAP) vectored in by the FDO. One of the F4F-3s was flown by the CO of VF-3, Lt Commander John Thach, who had been developing fighter tactics against the A6M Zero fighter. A second flying boat suffered the same fate as the first some two hours later, at noon, shot down by another pair of Wildcats.

The newly formed Japanese 4th Naval Air Group at Rabaul responded very quickly to the sighting reports. It was equipped with the twin-engined Mitsubishi G4M/BETTY, the main aircraft type in the force that destroyed Force Z off Malaya in December. Only two of the three bomber squadrons (*chūtai*) had arrived. Moreover the rapid advance meant that aerial torpedoes had not yet been delivered; the attackers would have to resort to high-level-formation bombing, and they each carried only two 250kg (550lb) bombs. The 4th NAG included fighters, but these lacked the range to escort the long strike.

The air-defence function of TF 11 now became critical. The Japanese had split their squadrons to hunt the intruding task force; at 3.42 p.m. *Lexington*'s radar picked up Chūtai 2 about 80 miles to the west. At 4.15 a fresh 'division' of six Wildcats was launched, which jumped the tight V-formation of enemy bombers. The range capability of the G4M bomber had been gained by using a light structure and leaving off armour and self-sealing fuel tanks. American AA fire was poor, but fighters shot down eight of the nine bombers over the task force in a ten-minute air battle, and the ninth was destroyed while running for home. 'I even had to remind some members of my staff that this was not a football game', Admiral Brown later recalled.[3] Four of the Japanese aircraft were able to drop their bombs, but the CO of the *Lexington*, Frederick Sherman – a future task force commander – manoeuvred his big ship to dodge the bombs falling from 10,000 feet. A war correspondent aboard the *Lexington* watched the pilot of a crippled bomber try to crash into the carrier, dropping lower and lower:

> Finally, when he was down to a height of no more than 300 feet, the 1.1-in and 20-mm fire . . . seemed to really take effect . . . While still 200 yards behind the *Lexington*'s zigzagging stern the bomber finally stalled in the air. Its wings ceased to carry its weight, and the nose dropped in a precipitate dive into the sea. An instant later only a huge pillar of black smoke marked the grave of the bomber and its crew.[4]

The attack by the nine bombers of Chūtai 1, some fifteen minutes later, was even more dramatic. Most of the *Lexington*'s CAP had engaged in the first attack. When the second wave arrived – unexpectedly from the east – there were only two F4F-3s on station, and the guns of one of them had jammed. The lead plane, however, was flown by Lieutenant Edward O'Hare, an Annapolis graduate who had won his wings in 1940. He was an outstanding shot, and in a series of attacks was able to destroy three of the bombers, including that of 4th NAG strike leader, Lt Commander Itō Takuzo; two more were damaged. Lt Commander Thach was amazed that O'Hare survived the bombers' defensive fire: 'Imagine this little gnat absolutely alone tearing into that formation.'[5] The four surviving G4Ms turned for home, but two of them had to ditch in the sea. In all only two bombers made it back to Rabaul, survivors of seventeen planes sent out; eighty-eight Japanese naval airmen had been lost. Two US Navy fighters were lost, with one pilot. No ship in TF 11 was hit.

With his task force sighted and surprise lost, Admiral Brown abandoned the Rabaul raid; this caution did not go down well with Admiral King, the US Navy C-in-C, and Brown would soon be recalled to a post in Washington, an important one but ashore. More defeats lay ahead – including the loss of the *Lexington* at the Battle of the Coral Sea in May. But 'Butch' O'Hare became a badly needed national hero. The President personally presented him with the Medal of Honor on 21 April. The citation described the air battle as 'one of the most daring, if not the most daring, single action in the history of combat aviation'.[6] Post-war sources showed that O'Hare had only destroyed three bombers (not the five claimed), but he had indeed broken up a dangerous attack. He died flying an early night-fighter in late 1943; Chicago's O'Hare Airport was named after him. The complete destruction of Chūtai 2, the first air-to-air combat of American carrier planes, was perhaps even more significant than O'Hare's single-handed defence against Chūtai 1. The air battles of 20 February 1942 marked a milestone in sea/air warfare; they demonstrated, for the first time in this war, the combat potential of the United States Navy.

THE FIRST MONTHS OF THE PACIFIC WAR

During the late winter of 1941–42 both sides made some fundamental decisions about strategy, decisions that would determine the course of the entire Pacific war. What the leaders of the Japanese armed forces termed the 'first phase' of the war had been completed in April 1942. The overthrow of British and Dutch power in Southeast Asia had gone ahead more rapidly and at lower cost than expected, although the final conquest of the American garrison of the Philippines was delayed – Corregidor held out until 6 May. Opinions in Tokyo were divided about what to do next. The Army was not interested in expansion into the islands of the Pacific Ocean or Australia, and made no plans for operations there. It was fully employed in China and Southeast Asia, and among the generals there was also support for an offensive in Siberia against the embattled Soviets. The Navy, in contrast, did favour advances to the south and east, although disagreements developed within the service about where in this vast ocean the attacks should be made. Admiral Nagano's Naval General Staff (NGS) took a broader view of the war as a whole, and had to interact with the Army high command. Admiral Yamamoto and the Combined Fleet pursued above all a decisive naval victory. In 1941 pre-war planning there had been a conflict between the Southern (against Southeast Asia) and Hawaiian operations. Now there were disagreements about the relative priority of the Central Pacific and the South Pacific, rival theatres of operations some 3,500 miles apart.[7]

As early as the beginning of January, senior staff officers in the Combined Fleet began to develop plans for the 'second phase', which would involve capture of US outposts in the Central Pacific (including the Hawaiian Islands), while forcing a decisive naval battle with the weakened US Navy. But until March 1942 most of the Japanese ships were tied up in the first-phase campaign. In particular, the six big carriers concentrated in the Mobile Force undertook operational tasks. They supported the second attack on Wake in December, covered the attack on Rabaul in late January, and then assisted the invasion of Java in mid-February (with the Port Darwin air strike). The Indian Ocean raid followed, and kept them busy until the middle of April.

After the capture of Rabaul, senior officers of the NGS proposed cutting Allied supply lines to Australia with operations in the South Pacific. Combined Fleet planners, however, continued to emphasise the Central Pacific, and completed detailed planning in late March for a full-scale fleet attack on the American-held Midway Atoll, which it was hoped would bring the US Pacific Fleet out for a crushing defeat. This operation was accepted by the NGS at a meeting on 2–5 April, although Admiral Yamamoto had (for a second time) to threaten resignation to get his way.[8] The code name was Operation MI. Yamamoto did accept short-term diversions of some forces for the invasion of Port Moresby in the South Pacific and of the Aleutian Islands in the north.

The Allies also had decisions to make. There were concrete inter-Allied issues to be resolved, unlike the situation with the Axis powers.[9] The global organisational structure was in flux after the chaotic defeats and the retreats of the first four months of the war, including the collapse of the ABDA command in Southeast Asia and continuing pressure in the Pacific. The British were hard pressed in the Mediterranean and Middle East, faced with an invasion of India (from Burma), still fearful of a threat to Britain itself (should the Soviet Union be defeated), and heavily engaged in the Battle of the Atlantic. The forces and resources they could deploy against Japan were still limited.

In response, in March and early April 1942 the western Allies accepted a proposal by President Roosevelt to divide the world into three command areas. The US now became responsible for the entire Pacific region, including the defence of Australia and New Zealand; and 'supreme command' for the whole area was now to be American. The zone for which the British were responsible was the Indian Ocean area (and the Mediterranean). Roosevelt's third zone, the North and South Atlantic and 'plans for a new front on the European continent', would be a joint British–American responsibility.[10]

There was another decision to be made, about which of these areas would have priority, and whether the 'Germany First' strategy still obtained. This will be discussed later; in the short term it was not an issue, as basic defensive measures clearly had to be put into effect first. The US Army did agree to send troops equivalent to three or four divisions, and significant air strength, to the South Pacific. This would help to defend Australia, and the approaches to it from the north (from eastern New Guinea) as well as the strategic supply line from the east (the New Hebrides and Samoa).

Likewise the issue of the American command structure in this vast global region was not relevant to the desperate naval battles of May and June 1942. At the end of March the Joint Chiefs of Staff in Washington set up two commands, the South West Pacific Area (SWPA) and the Pacific Ocean Area (POA), but this only became a vital distinction later in the summer.[11] Of more immediate importance, soon after Pearl Harbor a secure line of communications and a base system began to be laid out from the Panama Canal and the West Coast of the US to Australia. In mid-February an American convoy arrived at Bora Bora, northwest of Tahiti in French Polynesia. A fortified base and refuelling station, code-named BOBCAT, was set up. From there the supply line ran west past Samoa and Fiji to the forward port at Nouméa in French Nouvelle-Calédonie.

Meanwhile the command structure in the US Navy was taking shape. Between the wars the Navy had been administered by the Chief of Naval Operations

(CNO) in Washington, who was subordinate to the civilian Secretary of the Navy. The battle force was normally concentrated on the West Coast, and was led by the Commander-in-Chief, US Fleet (CINCUS). After Pearl Harbor Admiral Harold Stark remained as CNO, but in mid-December Admiral Ernest King was appointed as overall commander-in-chief of the 'US Fleet'. King asked to use the title 'COMINCH', taking the view that the losses at Pearl Harbor had made the old title of CINCUS (pronounced 'Sink-us') an embarrassment. The 'fleet' headquarters of CINCUS/COMINCH was moved from Hawaii to Washington; the senior American admiral was no longer serving afloat, ready to lead his battle line into a new Pacific Jutland. Stark as CNO was now – for a time – in charge of logistics and long-term planning, under the Secretary of the Navy. King was in charge of operations, under the President – who was the commander-in-chief of all US armed forces. Subordinate to King were the leaders of the Pacific Fleet (Admiral Chester Nimitz) and the Atlantic Fleet (Admiral Royal E. Ingersoll).

This arrangement at the top level was simplified when, in early March 1942, Admiral Stark asked to be relieved of his post as CNO. Partly this was because he was concerned about the confusion of his authority with that of King, and partly it was because he was aware of his damaged professional position after Pearl Harbor and later defeats. The President sent Stark to London as Commander, US Naval Forces Europe (COMNAVEUR), but this was at the time a post of only limited practical importance. Admiral King became CNO and COMINCH, and had nominal authority over nearly all aspects of the US Navy.

King was to be one of the most important wartime leaders. He would control the largest navy in the world, and had a powerful influence on Allied global strategy. A working class boy from an industrial town in Ohio – the son of two immigrants from Britain – he had achieved steady advance in the Navy on the basis of intellect, energy, ambition and personality. He excelled at Annapolis and attended the Naval War College. He undertook a broad range of service, including submarines in the 1920s and aircraft in the 1930s. Qualifying as a pilot at the age of forty-eight, he was the second captain of the carrier *Lexington*. He also served for a number of years in the Bureau of Aeronautics (BuAer), from 1933 to 1936 as its head. An ambitious officer, King had hoped to become CNO, but in the spring of 1939 Stark had been appointed instead. Having turned sixty in November 1939, King's naval career seemed effectively over; he was posted to the General Board of the US Navy, an advisory committee which was normally an honourable duty before final retirement.

King was then saved by developments in the European war and by Admiral Stark – one of his few personal friends in the upper ranks of the Navy. France fell and Britain was besieged. As we have seen, the Atlantic, with its German U-boats and surface raiders, suddenly assumed great potential importance.[12]

Stark selected King in December 1940 to head a revitalised Atlantic force, a group of ships hitherto largely devoted to training. The new Secretary of the Navy, Frank Knox, had also been impressed by King's administrative work on the General Board. King dealt effectively with his tasks, especially in the second half of 1941 when escort of British convoys began and US Marines garrisoned Iceland.

The decision to appoint King, now sixty-three, as COMINCH in the week after Pearl Harbor was understandable. His intelligence, will power and broad expertise were known to the President, Secretary Knox and Admiral Stark. King had now commanded a fleet in combat conditions. His aviation expertise was an additional strength. Above all he was a tough officer of ruthless energy; as King himself famously later put it, 'When they get into trouble, they call on us sons of bitches.'[13]

The appointment of King as COMINCH was one of two key appointments that had been decided by Roosevelt and Secretary Knox by 15 December 1941. The other was the selection of Admiral Chester Nimitz to replace Husband Kimmel as C-in-C, Pacific Fleet, or CINCPAC. The choice was less obvious than that of King. Unlike King, Nimitz had no background in aviation, although he had served in submarines, and they were expected to play a major role in the Pacific. He had extensive experience in the Navy's personnel department, the improbably named Bureau of Navigation; he was deputy head from 1935 to 1938, and head from August 1939 to December 1941, at a time when the Navy was rapidly expanding. He had evidently made an impression as an efficient administrator on the President, Knox and Admiral William D. Leahy (CNO, 1937–39, and an influential adviser to Roosevelt). His recent service with the fleet was confined to nine months from September 1938 to June 1939, when he commanded, in quick succession, a cruiser division and a battleship division. But he certainly bore no responsibility for what had happened in Pearl Harbor on the morning of 7 December or the weeks before. In any event, Nimitz arrived in embattled Oahu by flying boat on the morning of Christmas Day; he formally assumed command, standing on the deck of the submarine *Grayling*, on the 31st. He made the important decision to break with tradition and commanded his fleet from a shore headquarters, rather than the flag bridge of a major warship.

Nimitz's father had been a small-town hotel-keeper from the frontier of Texas, who died before Chester was born. Both his parents were of German descent; his mother, although born in the US, was more comfortable speaking German than English. Nimitz was an affable man, with a store of folksy anecdotes – quite the opposite of King. He made the shrewd decision to keep most of Kimmel's headquarters staff. But in the first months of his role Nimitz had few obvious achievements. In February 1942 he was not among those selected when Secretary Knox, at the President's request, polled nine senior admirals (including King and Stark) to identify the forty most competent flag officers in the Navy. The historian Richard Frank has speculated that Nimitz 'appeared primarily as a paper-pushing personnel specialist who enjoyed the particular favour of President Roosevelt'.[14] This image would change in the months to come.

A crucial factor behind the Pacific battles of the first half of 1942 was the inter-war development of carrier aviation in the US Navy, especially in the 1930s. This contrasted with what had happened in the Royal Navy. The Americans possessed the advantage that their naval aviation was directly under the control of the Navy rather than under an independent air force. More important than just the superior design and larger numbers of US Navy aircraft was the organisational element, the presence of a significant number of senior officers in the American fleet who championed aviation. There was a degree of tension between a majority of 'gun club' traditionalists ('black shoe' officers) and a minority of aviation ('brown shoe') advocates, but the minority was vocal and influential. Also, unlike the British, the US Navy could focus almost entirely on a possible war with another country that had a carrier fleet – Japan.

The Americans were by the late 1930s substantially ahead of Britain in the quantity and quality of naval aircraft. In 1938–41 the US Navy was able to introduce a generation of all-metal monoplane carrier aircraft, with enclosed cockpits and retractable undercarriages. The quality of American aircraft, even in 1941–42, was as good as that of their Japanese counterparts.[15] The Grumman F4F Wildcat has already been mentioned. The Douglas TBD Devastator torpedo bomber, although it entered fleet service in late 1937, was technically much superior to the British Swordfish biplane and comparable to the Nakajima B5N/KATE. Another Douglas type, the SBD Dauntless 'scout bomber', entered fleet service in early 1941 and was comparable to the Aichi D3Y/VAL. The SBD Dauntless was intended to be a multi-role aircraft, a dive bomber, a 'scout' and an auxiliary interceptor. It would have a sensational impact as a dive bomber in the battles of 1942.[16]

Equally as important was the *number* of aircraft available on each carrier. US Navy ships deployed much larger air groups than the British, partly because they made more use of flight-deck parking.[17] The air group of USS *Enterprise* at Midway in June 1942 was typical of the American fleet carriers: seventy-eight planes, including twenty-seven F4F fighters, thirty-seven SBD dive bombers, and fourteen TBD torpedo planes. In contrast, the similar fleet carrier HMS *Victorious* in the August 1942 PEDESTAL convoy in the Mediterranean carried only forty-seven planes: twenty-four fighters and twenty-three biplane torpedo bombers. Japanese fleet carrier procedure was somewhat different from that of the Americans, but they operated air groups that were only slightly smaller (and considerably larger than those aboard the British carriers). The air group of the fleet carrier *Zuikaku* at the Battle of the Coral Sea, for example, consisted of sixty-seven planes – twenty-five fighters, twenty-two dive bombers and twenty torpedo bombers.[18]

The activities of the US Pacific Fleet, operating from Pearl Harbor in the first months of 1942, were relatively limited. It was detached from the struggle of the ill-fated ABDA command in the Netherlands Indies (not to mention the British Eastern Fleet at Ceylon). Urged on by Admiral King in Washington, Nimitz sent his surviving ships out on hit-and-run raids against widely spread out (and as yet weakly defended) Japanese-held territories. The carrier–cruiser task forces had extraordinary mobility, and the raids gave their aircrew invaluable experience.

Despite the Pearl Harbor catastrophe the relative *effective* strength of the American and Japanese sides was not all that different. The Japanese now had a considerable advantage in terms of the number of operational battleships in the Pacific, but for both navies most of the big vessels in service were too slow to keep up with the carriers. The Japanese had six fleet carriers and three light carriers. Five American fleet carriers were available for the Pacific by the spring: the *Lexington*, the *Saratoga*, the *Yorktown*, the *Enterprise* and the *Hornet*, as well as the escort carrier *Long Island.* The *Saratoga* was torpedoed by a Japanese submarine southwest of Oahu on 11 January, and she was then under repair for five months; the Japanese believed she had been sunk and this led them to underestimate American strength. In theory two more fleet carriers could have been deployed from the Atlantic (following the *Hornet*) in these months, the *Ranger* and the *Wasp*. The two sides were about roughly equal in terms of the number and quality of heavy cruisers, destroyers and submarines.

After the abortive sortie to relieve Wake in mid-December the first US Navy operation followed Admiral Kimmel's pre-war plans, with air strikes on the Marshall Islands in the Central Pacific. These took place on 1 February and were launched by Admiral Bill Halsey with the *Enterprise* (in TF 8) and Admiral Frank Jack Fletcher with the *Yorktown* (in TF 17). More daring was Admiral Brown's attempt to raid Rabaul with the *Lexington* (in TF 11) in late February. The objective was in the South Pacific, nearly 1,500 miles from Pearl Harbor. Three weeks later, in mid-March, the *Yorktown* and the *Lexington*, operating together in the Coral Sea, launched a raid over a mountain range in New Guinea and attacked the Japanese force which had landed at Salamaua and Lae on the northeastern coast of that huge island. More adventurous still had been the raid at the end of February by Halsey and the *Enterprise* on Wake Atoll in the Central Pacific, followed by a second raid on 4 March 1942 against tiny Marcus Island (Minami-Torishima). Marcus was a remote pre-war Japanese possession; it was 'only' 1,100 miles southeast of Tokyo, and nearly 3,000 miles from Pearl Harbor.

Best known was the 'Doolittle raid', a bomber attack on Japan itself, launched from one of Halsey's carriers on 18 April. The *Enterprise*, now part of TF 16, had sortied from Pearl Harbor and made a rendezvous in the empty ocean north of the Hawaiian Islands with the *Hornet*, a half-sister of the *Yorktown* and *Enterprise* and commissioned only in October 1941. (The *Hornet*'s CO was Marc Mitscher who in 1944–45 would command the whole 'fast carrier force'.) The carrier had arrived from the US West Coast carrying sixteen new twin-engined US Army B-25 Mitchell bombers commanded by Lt Colonel James Doolittle. After a two-week dash to the west, Halsey launched the bombers towards the Japanese mainland, mostly against Tokyo. They were supposed to reach landing strips in unoccupied north China after dropping their bombs. However, because TF 16 was sighted by a picket boat they had to be launched prematurely, and after raiding Japan the crews were forced to crash-land in China or bail out there. At a press conference a few days later Roosevelt joked that the bombers had come from 'our new secret base at Shangri-La' (after the fictional Tibetan setting of the 1937 movie *Lost Horizon*). The Japanese, however, knew full well that the bombers had come from a carrier (as a result of the sinking of one of their picket ships and the interrogation of captured fliers).

Little physical damage was caused by the raid. It has been argued by at least one historian that although Admiral King supported the Doolittle raid it was a 'publicity stunt' which endangered valuable ships. The raid also made it impossible for the Navy to mass four carriers which might have enabled it to win a decisive early victory at the Coral Sea battle in early May.[19] News of the 'Tokyo' raid did, however, buck up American public opinion, serving as delayed revenge for Pearl Harbor; the attack also forced the enemy to devote resources to home defence.

The Doolittle raid is sometimes linked to the Midway victory, supposedly provoking the Japanese into mounting their ill-fated June expedition into the Central Pacific. In fact the Combined Fleet had been planning such an operation since January, and it was given the go-ahead on 2–5 April, two weeks before Doolittle and his B-25s arrived for their 'thirty seconds over Tokyo'.[20]

THE BATTLE OF THE CORAL SEA

The Coral Sea is a 'marginal' sea of the Pacific, bordered on the west by the Queensland coast of Australia (with the Great Barrier Reef), on the north by New Guinea and the Solomon Islands, and on the east by New Hebrides and Nouvelle-Calédonie. To the south lies another large marginal sea, the Tasman, which stretches between Australia and New Zealand.

Port Moresby is situated in the northwestern corner of the Coral Sea, a small trading port on the south coast of Papua (the eastern end of New Guinea). In 1942 it was a place of strategic importance for both sides. The Japanese could use it to raid northeastern Australia; the Allies could use it as a forward base to counter-attack towards Rabaul. For the Japanese the invasion route to Moresby involved a long circuitous voyage from Rabaul, around the eastern tip of Papua – a distance of some 1,000 miles. The Australians and Americans had hurriedly created air bases around Moresby, and it was garrisoned by the Australian 30th Brigade.

Operation MO, as planned, was not very different from expeditions the tireless Japanese had undertaken since December 1941 in Malaya, the Netherlands Indies and New Guinea. Convoys of Japanese Army troops in transport ships were supported by warships, including aircraft carriers, and long-range Japanese Navy bombers. There had been some Allied naval and air resistance to earlier operations, but as the weeks passed this had become weaker and weaker. On three occasions – at Rabaul, Wake and Lae–Salamaua (in Papua) – individual raiding American carriers had attempted counter-strikes. These, however, occurred weeks or even months after the original invasion and had little effect. The difference this time was that the Japanese were further from their main bases, and that the Allies were closer to Australia. And Allied strength had finally begun to rise.

As with the earlier invasions, the Japanese forces were numerically small. The main unit in Operation MO comprised 5,000 soldiers from the South Seas Detachment (*Nankai Shitai*, essentially an Army infantry regiment). This unit had carried out the (second) attack on Wake in December 1941, and also the January 1942 attack on Rabaul. Also involved were 500 men of the naval infantry.[21] The invasion force would be embarked at Rabaul on eleven slow transports.

Throughout the war the Japanese naval planners favoured complex operations, involving multiple forces and phased movements. Operation MO was no exception, and it included the occupation of Tulagi, 850 miles to the east. This was the (undefended) administrative centre of the British Solomon Islands; it was located just north of the (later) more famous island of Guadalcanal. A seaplane tender based here would support long-range reconnaissance flights by four-engined H6K/MAVIS flying boats.

Several forces of warships covered the two landings. Near the Moresby transports was the 11,600-ton *Shōhō*. Originally built as a fast submarine tender, she had been converted into a light carrier in 1941. At this time she only carried twelve fighters and eight torpedo planes. But Admiral Yamamoto had also committed his two newest fleet carriers, the *Shōkaku* and the *Zuikaku*, to support Operation MO. Veterans of Pearl Harbor, Port Darwin and Ceylon, they had been detached from the Mobile Force in mid-April as it passed north through the Formosa Strait, homeward bound from the Indian Ocean operation. They stopped briefly at Truk, and then approached the battle zone escorted by two heavy cruisers and six destroyers. The carrier strike force was now commanded by Admiral Takagi Takeo, who had been the senior Japanese commander in the Battle of the Java Sea. In overall command of Operation MO (under the general direction of Admiral Yamamoto and the Combined Fleet) was Admiral Inouye Shigeyoshi. He was C-in-C of the Fourth Fleet, with his headquarters at Truk in the Caroline Islands.

The most important advantage for the Allies in the lead-up to the battle was that they knew the Japanese were coming, thanks to radio intelligence. A great amount has been written regarding codebreaking in the Pacific war (and the basic story came out three decades before the revelations about Bletchley Park and Ultra).[22] As already mentioned, the Americans had developed a sophisticated system of signals intelligence, which included the ability to fix the general location of radio transmissions (DF), understand enemy radio networks (traffic analysis), and even to begin to decrypt the contents of the messages. The Americans had two major codebreaking centres by the spring of 1942, one at Pearl Harbor (Station HYPO) and the other at the Navy Department in Washington (Op-20-G). There were also smaller but important Allied codebreaking groups in Melbourne (later known as FRUMEL) and Colombo (FECB). Since February 1942 good progress had been made in reading Japanese naval signals. A particularly important figure was Commander Joseph Rochefort and his team of cryptanalysts in Hawaii. Admiral Nimitz had accepted the advice of his intelligence chief, Commander Edwin T. Layton, that radio intelligence was of singular importance. As a result Nimitz was confident by the second week of April that the Japanese were planning an expedition against Port Moresby, and that it would be supported by aircraft carriers; Admiral King in Washington assented.

The Americans were able to deploy two of their carriers to the South Pacific as TF 17, under the overall command of Admiral Frank Jack Fletcher; these were the *Yorktown* and the *Lexington*. The *Yorktown* left Pearl Harbor for the South Pacific in mid-February, and the *Lexington* left in mid-April. Fletcher had commanded a cruiser division in the Pacific at the time of Pearl Harbor. Although he grew up in Iowa his family had naval connections; his uncle had been an admiral. Both men had won the Medal of Honor at Vera Cruz during a confrontation with Mexico in 1914.

A considerable number of land-based aircraft from the USAAF and the Royal Australian Air Force (RAAF) had been assembled in Queensland (north-eastern Australia) and at Port Moresby. The other two available carriers available to Nimitz were the *Hornet* and the *Enterprise*. Nimitz intended to send them south after they returned to Pearl Harbor from the Doolittle raid (which struck Tokyo on 18 April). They departed Pearl Harbor on 30 April, but Operation MO began before they could reach the South Pacific. Having missed the battle, they then had to hurry back north.

On Sunday, 3 May the Japanese landed a small detachment at the island of Tulagi. Admiral Fletcher, whose ships were operating to the south, in the Coral Sea, responded quickly. On the Monday morning the *Yorktown* launched a strike force of sixty aircraft. The American planes sank the destroyer *Kikuzuki* and several smaller vessels. The *Kikuzuki* was the first significant warship ever sunk by a US Navy carrier,[23] but this raid on 4 May was most important because it made the Japanese aware that at least one American carrier was operating in the area. Nevertheless, on Monday afternoon the main part of Japanese Operation MO began, when the transports of the Southern Detachment set out from Rabaul.

Admiral Takagi, flying his flag in the heavy cruiser *Myōkō*, had been steaming north of the Solomons with the carriers *Shōkaku* and *Zuikaku* and their escort. He now brought his battle group past the east end of the island chain, rounding the island of San Cristobal (now Makira) at midday on Tuesday, and then heading west into the Coral Sea. During several days of confusion the fleets moved towards one another. Then, on 7 May, the Japanese and Allied navies finally came into contact.

The invasion force was approaching the Jomard Passage to the east of Papua (after which it would have passed into the Coral Sea and turned west towards Port Moresby). In nearby support were the light carrier *Shōhō* and the four cruisers of *Sentai* 6 (the 6th Division), a force commanded by Admiral Gotō Aritomo in the heavy cruiser *Aoba*.[24] On Wednesday, 6 May, they had been sighted and attacked by long-range USAAF bombers from Australia, staged through Port Moresby, but no damage was suffered.

At about 7.30 a.m. on Thursday, 7 May, a scout plane from the *Shōkaku* reported a carrier some 200 miles to the south, well out in the Coral Sea. About forty-five minutes later a plane from the *Yorktown* reported two carriers to the northwest, approaching the tip of New Guinea. Both sightings were quite inaccurate, due to misidentification and miscommunication; such events demonstrated the uncertainty of these early carrier operations.

Both sides launched full-scale air attacks. The American strike from the *Yorktown* and the *Enterprise* did not find the false sighting, but did stumble on the light carrier *Shōhō*. Attacked by waves of dive bombers and torpedo bombers over a period of twenty minutes, the *Shōhō* sank quickly, not unlike the unfortunate HMS *Hermes* off Trincomalee a month before. 'Scratch one flat top!' was the famous report of one of the air commanders.[25] Half an hour later the squadrons from the *Shōkaku* and the *Zuikaku* reached their reported objective. The 'carrier' turned out to be a naval oiler, which was crippled by a dive-bomber attack; an escorting destroyer was sunk. Fletcher's carrier force was actually well to the west, not to the south.

Fletcher and TF 17 had got the better of the first day. On the second day, Friday (the 8th), the situation was clearer and the fighting more deadly – for both sides. The two groups of ships were about 240 miles apart when they sighted one another; Takagi's two carriers were now NNE of the Americans. All four carriers launched their planes between 9.00 and 10.00 a.m.; the strike forces also arrived over their targets at about the same time (11.00–12.00). The *Shōkaku* was hit by three bombs, badly damaged, and was unable to operate her aircraft.

Meanwhile, mortal damage was inflicted on the *Lexington*. The converted battle cruiser was a very large ship, but she was hit nearly simultaneously by torpedo bombers and dive bombers. Two torpedo hits on the port side were followed by two bomb hits. She was able to maintain her speed and resume air operations, and by 1.00 p.m. the fires seemed to have been brought under control. Then there was a large explosion caused by a leak of petrol vapour from damaged storage tanks. The resulting blaze could not be contained. At 5.07 p.m., after a series of explosions in the afternoon, Captain Sherman had to order the burning ship abandoned; some 216 men were killed from a very large crew of about 2,800. The burning hulk was sunk two hours later, finished off by the torpedoes of an American destroyer. She would be the largest American warship lost to enemy action in World War II.

The *Yorktown* had avoided a number of torpedoes but was hit by one bomb, which caused significant damage. It was important that the Japanese believed she, too, had been sunk, meaning both American carriers had been accounted for. This would contribute to their underestimation of their opponents' strength at Midway a month later.

The invasion convoy had turned around on Thursday morning once it became clear enemy carriers were present. On Friday afternoon, with all his carrier air power out of action, Admiral Inoue ordered a postponement of the Port Moresby operation.

The Coral Sea is famous as the first naval battle in which the surface ships of the two sides did not sight one another. It was also the first in which both sides had aircraft carriers, and in which they were the principal weapon.[26] It was a fleet action, but neither side deployed battleships.

At one level it can be seen as a Japanese victory – and the leaders of the Imperial Navy regarded it that way. The Japanese had exchanged a light carrier for a fleet carrier. Admiral King vetoed the proposal that Fletcher be awarded the

Distinguished Service Medal (DSM) for his conduct of the operation. (This may have had a personal element; King had been the captain of the *Lexington* in the early 1930s).[27] On the other hand the action of Fletcher's task force had stopped the planned invasion of Port Moresby and brought an end to Operation MO.

With hindsight the battle was even more important. The Mobile Force had been seriously weakened, with a light carrier sunk and the two most modern fleet carriers unable to take part in the Battle of Midway because of damage to the *Shōkaku* and the loss of air crew. The seaborne expedition against Port Moresby was not just delayed, but never attempted again. In the second half of 1942 the Japanese would devote considerable futile effort to taking Port Moresby overland across Papua, and their forces had to divide their efforts in the South Pacific between Papua and Guadalcanal. In terms of military theory, Operation MO was the 'culminating point' of the great Japanese Pacific advance.

THE BATTLE OF MIDWAY

Meanwhile, the Japanese Combined Fleet command were following through their plan to take the American-held Midway Atoll. This had been approved by the Naval General Staff in early April and formally set in train with an order from Imperial General Headquarters (IGHQ) on 5 May. Admiral Yamamoto hoped this operation would bring the American fleet out to suffer the decisive defeat which had not occurred at Pearl Harbor. Midway Atoll itself lay 1,300 miles northwest of Hawaii, and was made up of three tiny islands, one of which had an airfield.

Admiral Yamamoto intended a complex operation mounted on the largest possible scale. The ships directed against Midway Atoll itself were deployed in five major groups. First of all, there was the invasion force of fifteen transports, which was to sail from Saipan in the Marianas. A large support force was created from the fast battleships and cruisers of Admiral Kondō's Second Fleet. Advancing ahead was the Mobile Force (the Kidō Butai), the famous carrier task force commanded by Admiral Nagumo. Several hundred miles behind the carriers steamed the Main Body of the Combined Fleet; this included the three best battleships, with Admiral Yamamoto himself flying his flag in the huge *Yamato*.[28] Potentially important, but less often taken into account by historians, was a fifth force, a concentration of fleet submarines tasked to ambush the American battle fleet. Some 1,400 miles to the north of Midway Atoll, in Alaskan waters, a simultaneous operation was being carried out to invade two islands at the western end of the Aleutians – Attu and Kiska.

Dispersal was evident at both the strategic and operational level. In April three Japanese carriers (the *Shōhō*, the *Shōkaku* and the *Zuikaku*) had been sent to support the Port Moresby operation, and because of the Coral Sea action none of these ships were now available in the Central Pacific.[29] Two smaller carriers (the *Ryūjō* and the *Junyō*) were being sent to support the landing in the Aleutian Islands by attacking the US base at Dutch Harbor, 1,700 miles northeast of Midway.[30] Yamamoto's plan divided the surface ships into three groups, too far apart to support one another; two small carriers (the *Zuihō* and the *Hōshō*) were tied up supporting the Main Body and the Second Fleet, respectively.

Admiral Yamamoto expected to achieve surprise. Little concrete intelligence was available to the Japanese about the ships currently available to the US, but they assumed that since the start of the war the enemy had lost three fleet carriers to submarine attack and in the Coral Sea battle. A significant number of US aircraft based on Midway itself would have to be dealt with. But the Combined Fleet would have the initiative, and the Americans would not be able to position their fleet until the Japanese approach to Midway had been detected; by that time the exposed airfield on the atoll would have been neutralised. Indeed it was hoped that Midway would rapidly be converted into a Japanese forward air base for the later stages of the decisive sea/air battle.

Japanese operational intelligence was inadequate. Unlike the Americans, the Combined Fleet was advancing through the empty North Pacific, well beyond the normal bases from which even long-range bombers and flying boats could support it. Yamamoto had hoped to arrange a reconnaissance flight over Pearl Harbor on 31 May to check for the presence of the American fleet; the intention was to deploy very long-range Kawanishi H8K/EMILY flying boats, refuelling from a submarine, but this daring enterprise had to be cancelled. The whole Japanese submarine force, which might have detected American movement, was, for technical reasons, deployed too late between Hawaii and Midway. Above all the vanguard element, the Mobile Force, did not devote sufficient effort to scouting its flanks using carrier scouts or catapult floatplanes.

The Allied codebreaking advantage, which had already played such an important role in the pre-positioning of naval units in the Coral Sea, was even more critical in May for Midway. The role of Joseph Rochefort and his team at Station HYPO is well known. American codebreakers were able to discover Japanese intentions to advance into the Central Pacific (early May); they later learned what Japanese naval forces would be involved, and they obtained a good idea of the direction of approach. Radio intelligence would not be so important during the battle itself, partly because the Japanese observed radio silence and changed their code system at the end of May. At the operational intelligence level the Americans also had the great advantage that radar-equipped PBY flying boats were making long-range ocean surveillance patrols from Midway.

Admiral King in Washington was uncertain about how to proceed. He was concerned to keep some of his carriers in the South Pacific, and he had become more risk-averse after the Coral Sea battle and the loss of the *Lexington*. Even when he permitted Nimitz to follow his intelligence advice and bring his carriers north to defend Midway and Hawaii in the Central Pacific, he urged Nimitz to be cautious, 'to employ strong attrition tactics and not – repeat – not allow our forces to accept such decisive action as would be likely to incur heavy losses in our carrier and cruisers'.[31]

Admiral Nimitz took the initiative in concentrating his forces in the Central Pacific, and he did not ignore the opportunity for decisive action. He built up US Army and Marine air strength on Midway, and moved two carrier task forces into a position northeast of the atoll. TF 16 was built around the *Enterprise* and *Hornet* (the Tokyo raiders), with two heavy cruisers and six destroyers. It was now commanded by Admiral Raymond A. Spruance, as Bill Halsey had developed a debilitating skin disease while returning from the South Pacific with his carriers; this was after their fruitless race south to support Fletcher in the Coral Sea. Spruance had been commander of Halsey's cruiser escort (CruDiv 5), flying his flag aboard USS *Northampton*. An exceptionally able officer, Spruance had already been chosen by Admiral Nimitz to take over as his chief of staff (replacing Admiral Milo F. Draemel). Spruance's replacement, commanding the TF 16 cruisers (Task Group 16.2), was Admiral Thomas Kinkaid, who would himself have an important career in the later part of the war.

The other task force was TF 17, still commanded by Frank Jack Fletcher. This force was built around the *Yorktown*, the carrier damaged at the Coral Sea battle and very quickly repaired at Pearl Harbor,[32] with six cruisers and nine destroyers. Spruance's task force departed Pearl Harbor on 28 May; Fletcher followed on the 30th.

Even if he had not obtained outstanding signals intelligence Nimitz would have had some advance warning. The carrier force under Admiral Kakuta Kakuji mounted an ineffective air raid against the American base at Dutch Harbor in the eastern Aleutians in the early morning of 3 June, and then a second raid on the following day.[33] And on the morning of the 3rd the Occupation Force, which had left Saipan on 27 May, was sighted at long range to the southwest of Midway by a PBY based on the atoll.[34]

Admiral Nagumo's Mobile Force began the main battle, as planned, before sunrise on Thursday, 4 June. The Mobile Force launched a big carrier strike against Midway to neutralise the air base. This included a large part of the available aircraft of the Mobile Force, seventy-two strike planes, escorted by thirty-six fighters; a second wave was held in reserve. The raid force arrived over Midway at 6.20 a.m. Many of the fighters that the Americans put up to defend the atoll were shot down in fierce air battles, but the attackers did not put the airfield out of action. The strike leader radioed that a second strike would be needed. Japanese losses – mainly to AA fire – were considerable; eleven planes shot down and fourteen heavily damaged.

Meanwhile a PBY from Midway had at 5.34 on that same morning made another and much more important discovery to the northwest, sighting some of the Mobile Force carriers. Before the Japanese strike force arrived over Midway an assortment of USAAF and Marine aircraft had taken off from the island to attack these carriers; the first arrived over the Mobile Force at 7.00 a.m. Their attacks lasted for some time and caused a great deal of excitement aboard the Japanese fleet, but no hits were achieved and the planes from Midway suffered heavy losses.

At 7.15 a.m., in the midst of these attacks, and while the first Japanese strike was beginning its return from Midway, Admiral Nagumo ordered that the second wave of planes (D3A/VAL dive bombers and B5N/KATE torpedo planes) be prepared for a repeat strike on the atoll. This involved rearming the B5Ns with general purpose bombs for airfield attack, rather than anti-ship torpedoes. Then between 7.40 and 8.20, the admiral received reports from his scout planes that American ships, including at least one carrier, had been sighted within range to the east. Nagumo had sent out a small – inadequate – long-range float-plane search from two of his cruisers. One scout was launched late; another flew near the American task forces but failed to spot them. The first report of enemy ships was transmitted at 7.28. Had the search been conducted differently the American carriers might well have been located in time for Nagumo to launch a strike with his reserve aircraft.[35] For want of a nail . . . The Japanese admiral now made the critical decision not to launch his second wave immediately, and to begin rearming his attack planes with torpedoes in place of bombs.

Meanwhile, between 7.00 and 8.30 a.m., air strikes were launched by the two American task forces, operating semi-independently, but with Fletcher in local command as the senior officer. Fletcher's TF 17 (*Yorktown*) was somewhat to the north of Spruance's TF 16 (*Enterprise* and *Hornet*). The first – decisive – American carrier strike on the morning of the 4th turned out to be very well timed in terms of Japanese vulnerability, but was not well organised. Admiral Spruance decided to launch aircraft and send them off to strike the Japanese fleet as soon as possible, without waiting to form the squadrons into fully co-ordinated groups.

The opposing carrier forces were about 150 miles apart. Not all the first elements sent off by Spruance's TF 16 could find the Japanese, but the *Hornet*'s torpedo bomber squadron (VT-8, known as 'Torpedo 8') approached on its own from about 9.40. It lacked a fighter escort. Every one of the fifteen TBD

Devastators were shot down by the Zero CAP (combat air patrol) and all but one of the VT-8 crew members were killed. Only a few of the planes had even got close enough to drop their torpedoes against the enemy carriers, and no effective hits were achieved. The only positive result of the sacrifice of VT-8 was that it expended the fuel and ammunition of the enemy CAP, and put it out of position. The Japanese air defence was further dislocated by the arrival from another direction of another torpedo squadron (VT-3), this one from the *Yorktown* in Fletcher's TF 17. In addition, the rapid evasive manoeuvres demanded of the Japanese carriers had prevented the launch of any reinforcement for the original CAP. Nagumo's fleet did not have the advantage of radar or fighter-direction systems.

Fortunately for the Americans, the *Yorktown* (TF 17) and the *Enterprise* (TF 16) SBD Dauntless dive bombers arrived together – to some extent by chance – at the critical moment, about 10.20 a.m. They were flying at 13,000 feet and were not intercepted by the Japanese CAP. Japanese dive bombers and torpedo planes, belatedly readying for a strike on the American carriers, were being rearmed and refuelled in the hangar decks of their carriers (the deck below the flight deck). By this time the Mobile Fleet carriers were spread out in a line stretching some 17 miles (southwest to northeast), but in sea/air battle terms they were close together. As Admiral Ugaki Matome, Yamamoto's chief of staff, put it later, they 'were concentrated in one group, offering many eggs in one basket'.[36] Three of the carriers were attacked by dive bombers pretty much simultaneously, from about 10.20 to 10.30. The *Kaga* and the *Akagi* (Admiral Nagumo's flagship), to the southwest, were engaged by two squadrons from the *Enterprise*, and the *Sōryū*, furthest to the northeast, by a squadron from the *Yorktown*. Because aircraft in the hangar decks were fuelled and were in the middle of a hasty process of rearmament, hits by a relatively small number of American 500lb bombs caused fires and devastation. This was true even on the *Akagi*, which received only one direct bomb hit. (No effective American torpedo hits were achieved at any point in the battle.) Within ten minutes the battle had been lost. Three Japanese carriers were no longer capable of operating aircraft, and in fact had been irreparably damaged, although they took a number of hours to sink. It is not the case, as described by Commander Fuchida Mitsuo, the leader of the *Akagi* air group and author of an influential account of the battle, that his ship was within five minutes of launching a decisive counter-strike when the dive bombers pounced.[37] By 10.50 a.m. Admiral Nagumo, apparently against his will, was transferred to a light cruiser.

The fourth carrier, the *Hiryū*, although situated between the *Sōryū* and the *Akagi*, had by chance not come under dive-bomber attack. She was the flagship of the 2nd Carrier Division, with the able Admiral Yamaguchi Tamon aboard. Just before 11.00 a.m. the *Hiryū* mounted the *only* attack against the American carriers, comprising two escorted waves, the first by eighteen D3A/VAL dive bombers and the second by ten B5N/KATE torpedo bombers, following the returning Americans. The dive bombers attacked the *Yorktown* in TF 17 about an hour later and achieved three hits. The target was badly damaged, and Admiral Fletcher was forced to transfer to the cruiser *Astoria*. At 2.30 the B5Ns attacked the same carrier, which had resumed steaming. She was hit by two torpedoes. The ship lost power and developed a heavy list. At 3.00 p.m. she had to be abandoned.

The two American task forces were now operating some tens of miles apart, and the *Enterprise* and *Hornet* were not attacked by the *Hiryū* planes, or indeed by any other Japanese planes at any point in the battle. At 5.00 p.m. a second strike by two dozen *Enterprise* SBDs found the *Hiryū* and inflicted fatal damage, forcing most of the crew to be taken off. The hulk did not actually sink until the following morning. Admiral Yamaguchi apparently chose to die aboard his ship.

With this ended the Pearl Harbor task force, known to posterity as the Kidō Butai (Mobile Force). As one of the codebreakers at Hawaii later recalled: 'Even for me, it was sobering to realize that in one afternoon Nagumo's Kidō Butai had passed into history with Napoleon's Old Guard, Nelson's Band of Brothers, and Stonewall Jackson's Foot Cavalry'.[38]

Yamamoto, far away to the west with the Main Body, attempted to turn the disastrous situation around. Shortly after the *Hiryū* suffered its fatal damage, he ordered a 'charge' to the east with his surface ships, to bring about a night battle with the American fleet; in line with this – and the loss of the carriers – he replaced Nagumo with Admiral Kondō as tactical commander. A division of heavy cruisers, Sentai 7 under Admiral Kurita Takeo, was ordered to bombard the airfield on Midway to prevent it being used by the enemy on the 5th. But early on Friday morning Yamamoto cancelled Operation MI, and prepared to return with his surviving ships to Japan. Sentai 7 had been ordered to reverse course, but while retreating two of the ships collided. On Saturday morning as they withdrew at very slow speed to the west they were caught by a large dive-bomber attack. The *Mikuma* was sunk and the *Mogami* badly damaged. Sensational close-up aerial photographs were published in the American press showing the *Mikuma* before she sank, adrift and on fire, and with her superstructure and guns devastated.

Scattered fighting continued, both off Midway and in the Aleutian Islands – where the Japanese continued their operations. The Japanese submarine *I-168* succeeded in torpedoing the badly damaged *Yorktown* on Saturday afternoon, as the largely abandoned carrier was being towed slowly home. She sank the following day. The wreck, remarkably intact, was found and filmed in 1998, at an extreme depth of 16,650 feet, by an expedition led by Robert Ballard.[39]

Churchill once wrote about the responsibilities borne by Admiral Jellicoe, the C-in-C of the British Grand Fleet, in World War I: 'Jellicoe was the only man on either side who could lose the war in an afternoon.'[40] In some respects this would actually happen to another admiral a quarter of a century after Jutland; the Pacific war was lost by Admiral Yamamoto Isoroku in ten minutes on 4 June. The Imperial Navy lost four of its six fleet carriers in the course of that day.[41] Even after the loss of the *Yorktown* the US Navy now had three fleet carriers in the Pacific, and a fourth, the *Wasp*, was in the process of being transferred from the Atlantic.[42] Midway had not been captured, and neither that atoll nor Hawaii would ever be threatened again. Admiral Ugaki Matome, Yamamoto's chief of staff, recorded a gloomy conclusion in his diary on 7 June 1942: 'we are now forced to do our utmost to cope with the worst case. This should be kept in mind as a lesson showing that war is not predictable.'[43]

Tempting as it is, this is not the place for extensive counterfactuals.[44] Of course, the battle on 4 June could have gone a different way. The outcome might have been a comparable American defeat after a mass strike by the air groups of the Mobile Force. It might have been a draw if, following Admiral King's orders from Washington, Nimitz, Fletcher and Spruance had kept their distance to preserve their fleets intact. In either case it is hard to see how Midway Atoll could have been held by the Americans.[45] However, as Admiral Nagano had observed back in September 1941, even a decisive naval victory would not end the war against an 'impregnable' United States. Admiral Yamamoto exaggerated how demoralising even a great defeat would be for the Americans. And in any event massive US naval reinforcements, including numerous new fleet carriers, would have begun to reach the Pacific Fleet in the autumn of 1943.

The US Navy certainly won the battle. There is, however, another issue about how 'miraculous' or 'incredible' the American victory at Midway actually was. The historian Samuel Eliot Morison later described the American Pacific Fleet as 'a David to Yamamoto's Goliath'.[46] In reality the *effective* forces – aircraft – available to the two sides in the area northwest of Midway on 4 June were similar in quantity and quality. The American combat aircraft on Midway Atoll were less capable than those aboard the TF 16 and TF 17 carriers, but there were ninety-nine of them (including twenty-eight Marine fighters). The small number (twenty-one) of US Army heavy and medium bombers received much credit at the time in the American press, but they caused no damage at all. All the same, by their very presence the Midway-based planes did preoccupy and distract the Japanese. In addition the atoll was the forward base for thirty PBY flying boats, which provided a great advantage in terms of reconnaissance on 3–5 June.

Granted that the comparative number of the carrier aircraft involved was the most important combat ratio, the four Japanese carriers in the Mobile Force were only slightly superior to the three American carriers (which had larger air groups); Admiral Nagumo had 246 carrier planes, compared to 233 aboard TF 16 and TF 17. The Americans had a potential battle advantage in the availability of radar (and fighter-direction systems) as a 'force multiplier', but this had little actual effect on 4 June. Given the distances involved, ship-mounted surface-search radar could not be used to detect Japanese ships, although search radar was valuable in the PBY patrol planes from Midway (but was not then available on any US Navy carrier aircraft). As for air-defence radar and fighter-direction systems, TF 16 was never actually attacked, so they were never tested there. In the event, small formations from the *Hiryū* were able to break through to TF 17 and cripple the *Yorktown*.

Neither side used submarines effectively, although quite a number of fleet boats were at sea. Twelve American submarines were deployed in a patrol line west of Midway, but only the Mobile Force penetrated far enough to reach them. The huge (2,370-ton) American submarine *Nautilus* did make contact, and at about 2.00 p.m. on 4 June fired four torpedoes at the burning wreck of the *Kaga*; only one torpedo hit and it was a dud. The thirteen Japanese submarines assigned to the main battle area west of Midway failed in both their reconnaissance and attack missions; the exception was the *I-168* which caught up with the *Yorktown* when she was under tow two days after the battle.[47]

The historian John Prados perhaps went too far in the opposite direction, arguing that for both Coral Sea and Midway 'there is a good case to be made that these Allied victories were not incredible but inevitable' in view of systemic weaknesses of the Japanese Navy.[48] However, there is some weight in this argument, and the odds for the US Navy were certainly improved by mistakes in the Japanese overall plan.

Admirals King, Nimitz, Fletcher and Spruance were all awarded the US Navy's Distinguished Service Medal after the Midway victory. Nimitz, for his part, made the crucial call that intelligence gathered from intercepts was plausible (and not a ruse). He accepted that Midway Atoll would be the focus of the Japanese attack, and he also entrusted the battle to the aircraft carriers. Probably wisely, he did not interfere at a distance with his task force commanders in the actual running of the battle of 4 June.[49]

Tactical command afloat was left vague. TF 16 and TF 17 operated very close to one another, but Admiral Fletcher was in overall tactical command at the outset. On the American side historical credit for the victory was influenced by events later in the war; Spruance would become (with Admiral Bill Halsey) *the* sea-going commander of the Pacific Fleet and won great victories in 1944–45, while Fletcher's career was sidetracked in the autumn of 1942. In fairness it should be stressed that Fletcher was in overall charge on Thursday morning during the decisive air strike against the Mobile Force. Only in the early afternoon, as a result of the damage to his flagship, the *Yorktown*, by the *Hiryū* dive bombers, did Fletcher delegate command to Spruance. The historian Samuel Eliot Morison's verdict that 'Fletcher did well, but Spruance's performance was superb' does seem to be based on something other than the actual events.[50] Another officer who did not receive credit at the time for an undoubted contribution to the victory was Commander Joseph Rochefort; this was partly because of a bureaucratic conflict between Station HYPO in Hawaii and the naval intelligence centre in Washington. The DSM was posthumously awarded to Rochefort only in 1985, a decade after his death.

CHAPTER 11

THE SOUTH PACIFIC

The American Offensives at Guadalcanal, the Solomons and New Guinea, August 1942–May 1944

GUADALCANAL AND SAVO ISLAND, 7–9 AUGUST 1942

Guadalcanal Diary, written by the American journalist Richard Tregaskis, is a classic of war reporting and became well known as a wartime film. The book begins with a description of life on board an unnamed troopship:

> On the deck, Marines lined the starboard rail, and strained their eyes and pointed their field glasses toward the high, irregular dark mass that lay beyond the sheen of the water, beyond the silently moving shapes that were our accompanying ships. The land mass was Guadalcanal Island. The sky was still dark: there was yet no pre-dawn glow, but the rugged black mountains were quite distinct against the lighter sky.[1]

It was the early morning of Friday, 7 August 1942: American Marines were about to launch Operation WATCHTOWER, a landing on the islands of Tulagi and Guadalcanal in the British Solomon Islands.

For that period of the war, WATCHTOWER was a big invasion, including the whole 1st Marine Division, with 19,000 men, carried by a convoy of nineteen large transport ships. The Japanese – the small local garrisons and those higher up the chain of command at Rabaul, Truk and Tokyo – were caught by surprise. They had occupied Tulagi in early May; it lay on the outermost edge of their Pacific conquests. In August there were still no beach defences, and few defending troops. The Japanese Navy was completing an airstrip on the plain of northern Guadalcanal near Lunga Point, but no aircraft had yet been flown in.

Tulagi, nestled below the Florida (now Nggela) Islands, had a fine anchorage and a comparatively healthy climate. It had been the tiny administrative centre of the British Solomon Islands Protectorate. Most of the small Japanese garrison –

naval infantry of a Special Naval Landing Force (SNLF) battalion and some aviation personnel – were now located here, and in a bloody skirmish they fought to the last man. The much larger island of Guadalcanal lay 25 miles to the south, across a body of water that would soon be known by the Allies as Ironbottom Sound. The Japanese there were engineers laying out the airstrip, and they fled into the jungle when the Marines came ashore.

The covering force, under Admiral Fletcher, was Task Force 61. It included the carriers *Saratoga*, *Enterprise* and *Wasp* and was on station 120 miles to the southeast. The carriers provided air cover over the anchored invasion convoy on Friday and Saturday as it began to unload. On Friday afternoon the Japanese Navy were able to mount small long-range raids from Rabaul, 550 miles to the northwest, starting with two dozen bomb-laden G4M/BETTY medium bombers. These caused no damage to the invasion fleet; during a second strike on Saturday, however, a G4M crashed into the transport *George F. Elliot*, causing a fire which sank her. The low-flying attackers suffered heavy losses from American fighters and AA guns.

The sombre volcanic stump of Savo Island lay to the west of the sound, between Guadalcanal and Tulagi, where the invasion fleet lay anchored. By Saturday evening (8 August) the routes into the sound, north and south of Savo, were covered by Allied warships. There were two cruisers in the southern channel, and three in the northern one; to the west of each group patrolled a radar-equipped picket destroyer.

Unusually for a Pacific war operation, the naval forces included a significant non-American element. The cruiser screen was commanded by Admiral Victor Crutchley RN, who had commanded the battleship *Warspite* in the Battle of Narvik in 1940.

Unfortunately, Admiral Richmond Kelly Turner, the American commander of the Amphibious Force, had summoned Crutchley to a conference aboard his flagship off Lunga Point. To save time Crutchley travelled in his own flagship, the *Australia*; this weakened the cruiser screen; it also meant that the guard force off Savo now lacked a competent tactical commander.

During Saturday (the 8th) a force of Japanese cruisers and destroyers under Admiral Mikawa Gunichi had raced southeast from Rabaul down the New Georgia Sound; this was the central channel of the Solomon Islands – later better known as 'the Slot'. Sighting reports by a submarine and Allied land-based aircraft were delayed or misunderstood, and the approaching Japanese did not come under air attack. After midnight on Sunday the column of ships led by Mikawa's flagship, the heavy cruiser *Chōkai*, reached the approaches to Savo. The radar of the American picket destroyers did not detect the Japanese column, which Mikawa skilfully led through the southern passage between Guadalcanal and Savo. Surprise was complete. At 1.43 a.m. on the 9th, the destroyer USS *Patterson* radioed the alarm: 'Warning! Warning! Strange ships entering the harbor!'[2] It was too late. At 1.40 a.m. Mikawa's ships opened up on the southern Allied cruiser force covering the passage south of Savo, first with a salvo of torpedoes, and then with all their guns. The Australian heavy cruiser HMAS *Canberra* and, behind her, the USS *Chicago* were the first victims. The *Canberra* was struck by a torpedo and a rain of shells; within minutes she lost all power and began to list. The *Chicago* took a less lethal torpedo hit well forward, but she moved to the west out of the battle zone. Her CO, who in Crutchley's absence was in command of the cruiser screen, neglected to radio a warning to the ships covering the north passage.

Proceeding further to the north, Mikawa, his force now breaking into two disorderly columns, opened fire on three American heavy cruisers, the *Vincennes*, the *Quincy* and the *Astoria*. Captain Ōmae Toshikazu, Mikawa's Chief of Staff, witnessed the battle from the bridge of the *Chōkai*:

> we sighted another group of enemy ships 30 degrees to port. *Chōkai* searchlights illuminated these targets, and fire was opened on an enemy cruiser at 0153. *Chōkai* searchlights were used for the double purpose of spotting enemy targets and informing our own ships of the flagship's location. They were effective in both roles, fairly screaming to their colleagues, 'Here is *Chōkai*! Fire on *that* target! . . . Now that target! This is *Chōkai*! Hit *that* target!'
>
> The initial firing range of 7,000 metres closed with amazing swiftness. Every other salvo caused another enemy ship to break into flames.[3]

The Japanese shells were igniting the fuel tanks of the floatplanes sitting on the catapults of the American heavy cruisers; the resulting fires made the whole ship highly visible. The *Astoria* was irreparably damaged by heavy shells. The same thing happened to the next ship forward in the American line, the *Quincy*, which was also hit by two torpedoes; she capsized little more than half an hour after the action began. The lead ship, the *Vincennes*, was hit by torpedoes as well as gunfire, but she lasted fifteen minutes longer, sinking at about 2.50 a.m.

The *Canberra* was abandoned near dawn on the 9th, and finished off by an American destroyer. The *Astoria* finally went down at noon. Four major Allied warships had been lost; the Japanese suffered only minor damage. The Battle of Savo Island – the Japanese called it the Battle of the Solomons Sea – was one of the worst defeats ever suffered by the US Navy; news of the scale of losses would not be released until October. About 1,270 Allied sailors were killed in the attack or would later die from their wounds.[4]

During the morning after the battle Admiral Turner hurriedly unloaded what food and ammunition he could. In the early afternoon of 9 August he departed for the safety of distant Nouméa with his transports and surviving warships. The Marine landing force were left to fend for themselves.

STRATEGY FOR THE SOUTH PACIFIC

The victory in the Battle of Midway on 4 June 1942 had allowed the Allies to take the initiative earlier than they had expected.[5] In theory there were a number of directions this advance could have followed, but some were ruled out by geography, the forces available and the range of existing aircraft. Midway had been the site of the defensive victory but to the west, between that atoll and mainland Japan, there was nothing but empty ocean for 2,500 miles. Further south, the pre-war planned track of the US Navy west across the Central Pacific through the Marshalls, the Carolines and the Marianas – the so-called war plan ORANGE – was also impractical; the distances between objectives were currently too great (that advance would only begin in late 1943).

In contrast, the South Pacific, beyond the equator, had many advantages as an area of concentration and a line of advance. In the first half of 1942 considerable Allied forces had been assembled here, to protect Australia and its supply lines to the US. Unlike in the Central Pacific, the Japanese were still taking initiatives here, even after Midway. Allied forces deployed in the South Pacific would protect Australia and Allied bases like Nouvelle-Calédonie and Espiritu Santo, while also being available to begin a step-by-step advance to the north towards the Philippines and the Japanese-controlled island mandates, each stage covered by land-based aircraft.

Of the Allies, it was American forces and decision-makers who were crucial. The US, it will be recalled, had taken overall responsibility for all wartime operations in the Pacific region in April 1942. Admiral King in Washington had actually begun consideration of an advance into the southern Solomons in the dark days of February 1942. Nevertheless, it was only on 2 July – a month after Midway – that a general offensive towards Rabaul (in the Bismarck Archipelago, north of New Guinea) was approved by King and by General George Marshall, the Army Chief of Staff. Guadalcanal was only specified as one of the early objectives after 5 July, when signals intelligence picked up the first information about Japanese intentions to construct an airstrip in there. This threat to Espiritu Santo and Nouvelle-Calédonie lent a sense of greater urgency to the planning.[6]

This was 'Task 1' of the three-part offensive plan of 2 July 1942, a plan which was based partly on geography and partly on inter-service diplomacy. Task 1 was given the code name Operation WATCHTOWER, and was originally scheduled to commence on 1 August, with Admiral Nimitz in Hawaii in overall control. The second task agreed on 2 July involved the seizure of the remaining Solomons and of Papua (eastern New Guinea); the third and final task was the capture of Rabaul and nearby positions in the Bismarck Archipelago; both these latter tasks would be commanded by General Douglas MacArthur from his headquarters in Brisbane, Australia.

As far as Guadalcanal and the later Solomons campaign was concerned, there was competition for warships, planes, troops and transport ships with General MacArthur's South West Pacific Area (SWPA). MacArthur agreed about the importance of Rabaul as an objective. All the same, the continuing threat to Port Moresby and northern Australia prompted him to concentrate the meagre troops and aircraft available on the New Guinea side of the approaches to Rabaul. In the short term, however, Task 1 would be conducted by a force under the control of the US Navy; this was the new 1st Marine Division, which was in the process of deploying to the Pacific. In July 1942 there were seven US Army infantry divisions scattered across the Pacific (outside the continental US and Alaska). Nearly all of them, however, were inexperienced, and none had training in amphibious warfare.

More important, there was rivalry with the 'European' theatre. The larger issue concerned global grand strategy. 'Germany First' was for the Allied supreme leadership the fundamental concept of the war. An amphibious operation across the English Channel and the (later) alternative of a landing in North Africa preoccupied civilian leaders and top-level military planners in Washington and London. The North African variant, leading to Operation TORCH in November 1942, was confirmed at the highest level only in late July 1942, a few weeks after the WATCHTOWER plan for the South Pacific was agreed.

Territories of the British Empire (Australia, New Zealand, the British Solomons, eastern New Guinea and later the Gilbert Islands) were central to this Pacific campaign. Nevertheless, pressures in Europe and Burma made London reluctant to see Allied forces committed to more than a defensive holding operation in the Pacific (even after Midway). The British certainly had few men and little equipment of their own to make available.

The Japanese also had to consider their long-term strategy. As with the Allies there was a debate on service lines about grand strategy, with the Japanese Army being more concerned with China and even a possible campaign against the Soviet Union. Of western enemies, the Army section of the Imperial General Headquarters (IGHQ) in Tokyo was at first more concerned with Britain than with the United States.

As a result, strategy for the vast Pacific region was dominated by the Imperial Navy, for some months after Midway. Priority was given to the consolidation of an eastern perimeter. A toehold now existed in the Aleutians, but after the losses suffered on 4 June there was no prospect of further advance there. The same was true of another Central Pacific offensive against Midway, let alone one against Hawaii. In the South Pacific the Naval General Staff also abandoned rash plans for expeditions to Nouvelle-Calédonie, Fiji or Samoa.

The Japanese were determined, however, to protect Rabaul by consolidating its eastern approaches, in the Solomons. Much of the early air fighting in New Guinea was also controlled by the still powerful shore-based aviation elements of the Imperial Navy. The Imperial Army also took part, providing the ground troops needed to defend the main base at Rabaul – where a newly organised 17th 'Army' (essentially a weak corps) was centred. A small number of Army ground troops took part in offensive moves against Port Moresby. The first had been the seaborne MO operation, abandoned in May 1942 after meeting American resistance in the Battle of the Coral Sea. The second was an overland drive which began in mid-July 1942, a few weeks before the American invasion of Guadalcanal. There was very little Japanese Army ground or air presence in the South Pacific. Excluding occupation forces equivalent to three divisions in the Philippines and the former Netherlands Indies, Army strength initially comprised part of one division deployed in Papua. As the extent of the campaign on Guadalcanal became clear, however, the Japanese Army would commit the main ground formations required.

The most important American forward naval base in the South Pacific, developed after the Coral Sea battle, was at Nouméa. This was a fine harbour in the French colony of Nouvelle-Calédonie (originally named New Caledonia by Captain Cook, and usually known to English-speakers by this name). Unlike the situation in most of the French overseas colonies, the settler-leaders here had followed de Gaulle in 1940, eventually ejecting the pro-Vichy governor. The island lay nearly 1,200 miles to the southeast of Guadalcanal. In the summer of 1942 the Americans also built early air bases for the US Army Air Force (AAF) on Espiritu Santo; this was about 600 miles from Guadalcanal, also to the southeast. Espiritu Santo was part of the unique British–French condominium of the New Hebrides (now Vanuatu). Air bases on Espiritu Santo were used by four-engined B-17s, and they would also enable shorter-range planes to be ferried into Guadalcanal.

The first Commander, South Pacific Area (COMSOPAC), was Admiral Robert L. Ghormley. He had arrived in Nouméa in mid-May and established his headquarters on a transport ship tied up in the harbour. Ghormley was in charge of all Allied forces in the theatre, and also responsible for the chain of islands leading east towards the US. He was directly subordinate to Admiral Nimitz, far away to the north in Hawaii. Admiral Fletcher commanded Ghormley's sea-going forces. The head of Ghormley's Amphibious Force was Admiral Turner, who was directly in charge of the landings at Guadalcanal and Tulagi.

The Japanese mid-Pacific base was at the atoll of Truk (now Chuuk) in the Caroline Islands. It lay at about the same distance (some 1,200 miles) from Guadalcanal as Nouméa, although in the opposite direction, to the northwest. The Japanese had the advantage that Rabaul, their forward air and naval base, was only 550 miles away from Guadalcanal. They also had use of an intermediate naval anchorage in the Shortland Islands, at the southern tip of Bougainville, the biggest island in the Solomons. The Shortlands were only 375 miles from Guadalcanal, less than a day's steaming at 20 knots. On the negative side, because of the speed of their advance the Japanese lacked, in the autumn of 1942, adequate forward air bases in the Solomons – although they belatedly began to construct them.

THE LONG BATTLE FOR GUADALCANAL

Probably more than any other prolonged campaign in World War II – except perhaps the battle for Malta – the battle for Guadalcanal saw the close integration of naval, air and land fighting.[7] Guadalcanal was needed by the Americans as an air base; the air base was threatened and defended by ground troops, but also attacked by bombers and naval artillery; all the ground troops and their supplies had to be brought in by sea; the air base in turn threatened the supply lines of the counter-attacking Japanese troops. Another similarity between the fighting at Malta and Guadalcanal was that the two sides were different but evenly matched.

For the sake of clarity the Battle of Guadalcanal can be broken down into different kinds of fighting. First of all there were the initial landings on Tulagi and Guadalcanal and the main ground fighting until January 1943. Guadalcanal itself is a large island, about two-thirds the size of Crete, but was then – as now – very thinly populated. The fighting on the island, once it began, was confined to a small enclave on the northwestern coast near Lunga Point, around the airstrip begun by the Japanese. The rugged terrain, broken by small rivers and swamps, was covered by jungle and meadows of tall kunai grass.

On the American side the initial landing, and the fighting on the ground for the epic first two months of the battle, was carried out by the men of the US Marine Corps (USMC). Three infantry regiments of Marines (in addition to smaller units) had come ashore at Guadalcanal and Tulagi, the larger part of General Alexander Vandegrift's 1st Marine Division. The USMC traced its origins back to 1775, providing a landing role for the US Navy; their tasks were originally similar to those of the (British) Royal Marines.[8] As time went by the

USMC developed a unique spearhead role for an 'isolated' state with a small standing army and a distrust of military elitism. The 5th Marine Regiment was among the first units to be sent to France in 1917, and as part of the 4th Marine Brigade it fought in major land battles.[9] The 6th Regiment was the core of the intervention force when the neutral US occupied Iceland in 1941. The Marines had continued a more traditional role in the 1920s as a 'police' force protecting US interests in the Caribbean and Central America; the 4th Regiment had served as the American military presence in China in the 1930s.

By the 1920s and 1930s the planned role of the corps in a possible full-scale conventional war (most likely with Japan) had become the seizure and defence of 'advance bases'. A Fleet Marine Force was established in 1933 as a centre for training and development. A considerable number of exercises were carried out with the Navy and a body of written doctrine developed. A small land-based air support element was created. As US participation in World War II approached, Marine brigades and then Marine divisions (each made up of two or three infantry regiments) began to be formed in the Atlantic and Pacific. (By 1945 there would be six USMC divisions, with eighteen infantry regiments.)

Operation WATCHTOWER in August 1942 was essentially about the seizure and defence of an advance base. This was exactly the role laid out for the USMC in the 1930s, but the fighting did not begin as a full-scale amphibious assault against entrenched troops. As already described, the Marines achieved surprise. Although the lightly equipped Japanese naval infantry battalion on Tulagi resisted fanatically, alongside aviation ground crew and aviators, they were eliminated in two days.

Bitter fighting took place as the Japanese Army gradually landed reinforcements on Guadalcanal to the east and west of the American-held airfield perimeter, but the number of men was initially small. The Japanese command had seriously underestimated the size of the original enemy landing and its early reinforcement. The first Japanese Army reinforcements (the Ichiki Detachment, a battalion of 900 men, originally part of a force tasked to occupy Midway) were brought in by six destroyers from Truk on 18 August (D+11).[10] The detachment (led by Colonel Ichiki Kiyonao) was wiped out when they attempted a direct assault on the American defences. The Marines won an important morale-boosting victory, and demonstrated that Americans were able to take on the Japanese Army in jungle conditions.

The essence of the Guadalcanal campaign was the ability of either side to bring in reinforcements and supplies. Japanese reinforcements included an Army brigade group (the Kawaguchi Detachment) which landed from destroyers, after having been transferred to Rabaul from the Philippines. At the end of August and the beginning of September this group mounted a fanatical attack on the defensive position at 'Bloody Ridge' and again failed to break through the Marine positions.

The Japanese, for their part, were unable to interrupt the build-up of the American garrison, especially once Washington gave the highest priority to Guadalcanal. In mid-September another Marine regiment arrived, and on 13 October a US Army regiment. Ten days later came another major ground offensive, the Battle of Henderson Field (known to the Japanese as the Battle of Lunga Point). It was launched by the Japanese 2nd Division with a regiment of the 38th Division, under the direct leadership of General Hyakutake Harukichi, commander of the Seventeenth Army. The attack was again repelled with heavy losses. In the first week of November the rest of the Japanese 38th Division, transferred from Java, was brought in by sea, raising Japanese strength on the island to 30,000 men. It was not possible, however, to mount a full-scale attack, after the failure of a reinforcement transport convoy in mid-November.

Despite its decisive role and historical fame, the long land battle for Guadalcanal was not particularly bloody – compared to later operations – at least for the Americans. The total of US personnel killed over six months was 1,207 Marines and 562 men from the US Army. Japanese losses were much higher, nearly 21,000; many died from disease or malnutrition.[11]

The second dimension of the Guadalcanal fighting was in the air; the sole object of all the ground fighting was the captured airstrip. On 20 August (D+13) the first USMC aircraft – F4F Wildcat fighters and SBD Dauntless dive bombers – flew in from the escort carrier *Long Island*. The airfield was now known by the US code name for Guadalcanal, CACTUS. It also bore the name 'Henderson Field', after a Marine major who had been killed leading a bomber strike from Midway on 4 June. In that June battle the Marine fliers, untested and equipped with second-line aircraft, had suffered heavy losses and achieved little. On Guadalcanal, with better aircraft and more experience, and flying alongside US Navy and AAF planes, things were different. The Marine flyers played a central role in keeping the airfield open, supporting the ground troops, and attacking Japanese ships near the island.

The air squadrons of the Japanese Navy, flying from their airfields near Rabaul, responded very quickly to the first landings on Guadalcanal. The Zero fighter plane was still technically superior to the US Navy and AAF fighters they encountered; it was heavily armed, highly manoeuvrable, and could operate at very long range. The Navy's G4M/BETTY twin-engined bomber also had long range and could reach Guadalcanal from Rabaul without difficulty. Nevertheless, the Japanese bombers had poor protection and were proving highly vulnerable. The Americans, for their part, could in 1942 mount nothing more than nuisance raids against distant Rabaul, mostly by a handful of AAF B-17s staging through Port Moresby.

The Americans were still very wary of Japanese long-range torpedo bombers, and this was the main reason Admiral Fletcher pulled back his carriers from near Guadalcanal in the first days of the battle. Nevertheless, the Japanese were able to use their shore-based naval aviation only to a limited extent to prevent the American build-up. The last sea/air battle came at the very end of the campaign, on the night of 29/30 January 1943. An inept American admiral had exposed his squadron to attack southeast of Guadalcanal near Rennell Island. The cruiser *Chicago*, which had survived both a midget submarine attack in Sydney harbour and the Battle of Savo Island, was sunk by long-range G4M/BETTY torpedo bombers from Rabaul. This would prove to be the last major success of the Japanese rikkō (land-based attack aircraft) concept which had proved so effective against the *Prince of Wales* and the *Repulse* off Malaya in December 1941.

American strike aircraft based on the Guadalcanal airfields, mostly SBDs and the new Grumman TBF Avengers, were able to gain control over the waters north of Guadalcanal. The Japanese were unable to bring in reinforcements during the hours of daylight; they had to rely on their destroyers making trips between the Shortland Islands and Guadalcanal under cover of darkness.

The third – naval – dimension of the Guadalcanal naval campaign is perhaps best known for a series of night surface battles. The Battle of Savo Island, as we have seen, was a Japanese triumph, although Admiral Mikawa missed an extraordinary chance to destroy the American transport fleet. This, as Richard Frank observed, 'would have ended the campaign shortly in ignominious defeat for the Allies'. Mikawa's Chief of Staff, Captain Ōmae Toshikazu, argued that his chief was influenced by a doctrine which stressed the destruction of enemy warships and furthermore that he was worried about an air attack from the American carriers.[12] In any event, after Savo Island four further night battles were fought (two in November separated by only one night). The Japanese force of fast battleships, cruisers and destroyers, so successful in the Netherlands Indies, had been only been slightly weakened at Midway. The Japanese were better trained for night fighting – part of their general battle doctrine – with better optical equipment. Most American cruisers did not even carry torpedoes; the Japanese, in contrast, could fire barrages of long-range, wakeless torpedoes from their cruisers and destroyers. On the other hand, the tactics of the US Navy gradually improved, and the Americans had the advantage of radar.

None of the later night engagements was as bad for the US Navy as Savo Island. Cape Esperance is situated at the northwestern coast of Guadalcanal; in mid-October the very able Admiral Norman Scott intercepted a Japanese airfield bombardment force there, made up of three heavy cruisers. In the battle the enemy admiral was mortally wounded, and the heavy cruiser *Furutaka* sunk by gunfire and torpedoes. The two battles fought in mid-November, and part of the naval Battle of Guadalcanal were the most important and will be dealt with below. The final night engagement, the Battle of Tassafaronga, took place on the night of 30/31 November just after the critical period of the Guadalcanal campaign. An inexperienced American admiral with a cruiser force took on a Japanese destroyer flotilla bringing reinforcements and commanded by the veteran admiral Tanaka Raizō. One Japanese destroyer was sunk, but torpedoes sank the *Northampton*, and badly damaged three other heavy cruisers.

The first eight American MTBs arrived in the middle of October, carried aboard transport ships. Based at Tulagi, the PT boats operated in the waters around Guadalcanal, and their brave crews received a good deal of publicity, but despite some exaggerated claims they had little success in 1942.

Submarines played a role in the Guadalcanal campaign. The Americans had the first success near Rabaul, when the old *S-44* sank the heavy cruiser *Kako* as she returned from the Savo Island battle. The US Navy submarine force was only reinforced in November, when the main naval fighting had passed the critical point and there were fewer targets. For the Japanese, Guadalcanal would be the single most successful period of submarine operations, especially in the waters between Nouvelle-Calédonie and Guadalcanal, which the Americans called 'Torpedo Junction' (after the 1940 Glenn Miller song 'Tuxedo Junction'). The *I-26* damaged the *Saratoga* in August, and for the second time in the year the giant carrier had to return to the West Coast for lengthy repairs (on this occasion for three months). With one extraordinary torpedo salvo on 14 September, the *I-19* mortally damaged the carrier *Wasp* and a destroyer, and caused damage to the new battleship *North Carolina*. The battleship had to be sent to Pearl Harbor for repairs and was unavailable until late November. The removal of the *Saratoga*, the *Wasp* and the *North Carolina* seriously changed the balance of forces, but on top of that in October the *I-176* seriously damaged the heavy cruiser *Chester*, and in November the *I-26* (again) finished off the damaged light cruiser *Juneau*.

Guadalcanal led to two major battles between aircraft-carrier fleets. Midway is often seen as the decisive battle of the war; four Japanese carriers went down, and after that the US Navy was certainly in an advantageous position. As already mentioned, on 7 August the Guadalcanal landing was directly supported by three American fleet carriers: the *Enterprise*, the *Saratoga* and the *Wasp*. (A fourth, the *Hornet*, was held back by Admiral Nimitz for a few weeks as a reserve at Pearl Harbor.) On 7 August the Japanese had fully available – and based in home waters, not the South Pacific – only two fleet carriers and a small light carrier. The *Shōkaku* and the *Zuikaku* had fought at Coral Sea but missed Midway. The 8,000-ton *Ryūjō*, commissioned in 1933, had supported the Philippines invasion.

The light carrier *Zuihō* was in dry dock, so not available. Two medium-sized carriers were working up; the *Junyō* and the *Hiyō* had been converted from NYK Line luxury ocean liners while under construction and were capable of a respectable speed of 26 knots. At 24,000 tons, they were about the same size as the *Hiryū* and the *Sōryū* (lost at Midway), and each was designed to carry an air group of fifty planes. The *Junyō* had actually operated in the Aleutians at the time of Midway, but afterwards had to complete her fitting out and undergo a refit. The *Hiyō* was only commissioned on 31 July, and then required intensive training in home waters with her sister ship; the two vessels only departed for Truk and then the South Pacific on 4 October.

The first carrier action was the Battle of the Eastern Solomons (known to the Japanese as the Second Battle of the Solomon Sea). It took place on 24 August, two and a half weeks after the Guadalcanal landing. In overall command of the American fleet, Task Force 61, was Admiral Fletcher. He was an obvious choice; Admiral Halsey was still on medical leave in Washington, and Admiral Spruance – paired with Fletcher at Midway – had become Nimitz's Chief of Staff. In command of the Japanese carriers, now designated as the Third Fleet, was still Admiral Nagumo.

The *Shōkaku*, the *Zuikaku* and the *Ryūjō* had come down from Japan and were now cruising to the north of the eastern Solomon Islands; the American fleet was positioned to the east. The Americans still had an advantage, at least in aircraft carriers; their three fleet carriers were up against the two fleet carriers and the light carrier. At the beginning of the actual battle, however, only the *Saratoga* and the *Enterprise* were engaged, as Fletcher had sent the *Wasp* task force south to refuel its destroyer screen. There was a heavy exchange of air attacks. The *Ryūjō*, sent forward, was sunk by *Saratoga* dive bombers. However, the *Enterprise* was badly damaged and forced to steam to Pearl Harbor for repairs, not returning to the South Pacific until mid-September. The American fleet did block the Japanese attempt to directly reinforce Guadalcanal from Truk using transport ships; a convoy was crippled and forced to turn back by Marine dive bombers from Guadalcanal.

The Battle of the Eastern Solomons was also Admiral Fletcher's last sea-going combat command. On 30 August, six days after the battle, the *Saratoga* was torpedoed by the *I-26*. When Fletcher returned to Pearl Harbor on 21 September aboard his damaged flagship he was sent to Washington on leave. A month later, on 23 October, Nimitz was informed that Fletcher would not be returning and had been assigned to a senior shore post, Naval District 13, with headquarters in Seattle. The reasons for Fletcher's removal are complex, and include the ambitions of the 'aviators' among the senior officers of the US Navy and a command crisis in the South Pacific. Above all, Admiral King did not have confidence in him and thought him over-cautious. Fletcher was treated shabbily by King and by historians; S.E. Morison commented in 1963 that 'during the rest of the war [he] received commands more commensurate with his abilities'. Only recently has there been an attempt to give Fletcher the credit he deserves.[13]

Two carriers, the *Enterprise* and the *Saratoga*, had been removed from the theatre. Even worse, in the middle of September the *Wasp* was sunk after being hit by three torpedoes fired by the *I-19*. This left Admiral Ghormley – and indeed the whole Pacific Fleet – with only the *Hornet*, which had come down from Pearl Harbor to join TF 61 at the end of August; this weak situation continued for two months. To add to the catalogue of woes, the *South Dakota* struck a rock at Tonga on 6 September and the *North Carolina* was torpedoed by a submarine on the 14th;[14] both new fast battleships had to join the queue of vessels undergoing lengthy repairs at Pearl Harbor.

The second carrier duel, the Battle of the Santa Cruz, was fought two months later, on 26 October, and this time the Japanese were the victors. The background to the battle involved a crisis in the American command in the South Pacific. American naval strength, especially in carriers, had been drastically weakened. Admiral Fletcher had been sent on leave. Two new Japanese divisions had been landed on Guadalcanal, and the enemy looked set to overrun Henderson Field and the rest of the airfield complex at Lunga Point. The Marine ground force on Guadalcanal was exhausted and riddled with disease. Admiral Ghormley, Commander, South Pacific Area (COMSOPAC), based ashore in Nouméa in Nouvelle-Calédonie, swamped himself in detail, failed to visit the battle zone on Guadalcanal and became increasingly pessimistic. A very senior officer, he had been a confidant of President Roosevelt, and was sent to besieged Britain in 1940 as a special observer. However, he had not held a sea command since 1938 and was unfamiliar with carrier operations. Nimitz and King now lost confidence in him. Halsey, his health now recovered, and Spruance (currently Nimitz's Chief of Staff) flew down from Pearl Harbor to Nouméa with sealed instructions to remove Ghormley. On 18 October Halsey took over as COMSOPAC; as Halsey famously put it, when he opened his orders: 'Jesus Christ and General Jackson! This is the hottest potato they've ever handed me!'[15]

A much more aggressive commander than Ghormley, Halsey was also faced with the possible loss of Henderson Field and with complaints by the other services about the lack of support being given by the fleet. A week after taking command as COMSOPAC and once the carrier *Enterprise* had returned from repairs, Halsey ordered that ship and the *Hornet* to carry out a daring sweep to the north; Admiral Thomas Kinkaid, flying his flag in the *Enterprise*, was put in charge of the whole force, TF 61. The sea/air battle took place on 25–26 October about 350 miles east of Guadalcanal near the Santa Cruz Islands, which the

Americans used as the name of the battle. (The Japanese would call this the Battle of the South Pacific.) On the Japanese side Admiral Yamamoto was in overall charge, aboard the *Yamato*, which was anchored at Truk. The sea-going overall commander was Admiral Kondō, aboard the heavy cruiser *Atago*. Admiral Nagumo commanded the main carrier force.

The two sides operated in roughly the same area as in late August, but this time the Japanese had the numerical advantage. The *Hiyō* and *Junyō* air groups had finally completed their training in the Home Islands. The two carriers departed on 11 October, with the *Zuihō*, to join the *Shōkaku* and the *Zuikaku* in the South Pacific. Fortunately for the Americans the *Hiyō* suffered accidental damage and had to be withdrawn to Truk, but the Japanese force remained twice the size of the American one. The Battle of Santa Cruz would be the last time in which the Japanese carrier air groups would ever engage the American ones on equal or better terms, either quantitative or qualitative.

The hard-fought sea/air battle resulted in the loss of the *Hornet*, the target of furious attacks by dive bombers and torpedo planes from the Japanese carriers. The *Enterprise* escaped both the air attacks and (on the night after the battle, 26/27 October) two hunting packs of surface ships, each containing a pair of fast battleships. No ships were lost by the Imperial Navy, although the *Shōkaku* and the *Zuihō* were damaged. The Japanese did lose more planes and aircrew, thanks partly to the presence of the *Enterprise* and the escorting battleship *South Dakota*, with their powerful AA batteries. Both had been recently equipped with several of the new quad mounts of the Swedish-designed Bofors 40mm AA gun, a great improvement on the earlier 1.1-inch (28mm). All the same, half the American carrier force had been sunk, while the Japanese had lost no ships. The outcome was masked by American successes two weeks later, but the Battle of Santa Cruz had still been a defeat for the US Navy.

The decisive action was fought on 12–15 November, in what the Americans call the Battle of Guadalcanal and the Japanese the Third Battle of the Solomon Sea. It was very different from Santa Cruz; it was fought at night between surface ships, and the aircraft carriers had only a limited role. The solitary carriers still available to each side, the *Junyō* and the *Enterprise*, were kept well back, out of danger. The Japanese planned a decisive reinforcement of the Army troops fighting on Guadalcanal, bringing up more men and supplies. Rather than a piecemeal run down the Slot with troops carried aboard destroyers, they used eleven cargo ships, new and fast vessels of about 7,000 tons each.

The complex Japanese plan set in motion multiple naval forces to smother and suppress Henderson Field with battleship and cruiser gunfire. Serious local American naval opposition was not expected, but if enemy ships were met they would be overwhelmed. The core of the Japanese force was two 'Kongō' class fast battleships. Big, handsome vessels with two funnels and eight 14-inch guns each, they were British-designed and based on the battle cruiser HMS *Lion* (commissioned in 1912). The *Kongō* was actually Vickers-built, the last Japanese capital ship ordered in Britain; the *Haruna*, *Hiei* and *Kirishima* were constructed in Japan.

Although the four ships – laid down as far back as 1911–12 – were the oldest Japanese capital ships, they were the most active of these vessels in the Pacific war. Modernised twice in the 1920s and 1930s and capable of 30 knots, they were the only Japanese big-gun ships operational in 1941 that could keep up with the aircraft carriers. While the other six pre-war battleships remained in home waters, two of the 'Kongō' class escorted the Pearl Harbor strike force, and the other two covered the invasion of Malaya and stalked the *Prince of Wales* and the *Repulse*. All four took part in the invasion of the Netherlands Indies, escorted the April raid into the Indian Ocean, and were present at Midway. In mid-October, Admiral Kurita Takeo had been detached with the *Kongō* and the *Haruna* to carry out a saturation bombardment of Henderson Field. On the night of 13/14 October the two battleships fired nearly 1,000 heavy shells; many aircraft and stores had been destroyed or damaged. Now, in mid-November, the *Hiei* and the *Kirishima* were ordered to repeat that success.

The first attack force, under the overall command of Admiral Abe Hiroaki, departed from the Shortland Islands on Thursday, 12 November. In addition to the *Hiei* and the *Kirishima*, Abe's 'Volunteer Attack Force' comprised the small cruiser *Nagara* and fourteen destroyers. To contest control of the approaches to Guadalcanal, Admiral Halsey had thrown together a task group of cruisers and destroyers under Admiral Daniel Callaghan. These included ships from the smaller force of Admiral Norman Scott, the experienced commander who had fought and won the Battle of Cape Esperance a month before. Dan Callaghan had been President Roosevelt's naval aide for three years, and then Admiral Ghormley's chief of staff at Nouméa. He had been put by Ghormley in charge of the cruiser-destroyer force, despite the fact that he lacked Scott's experience and indeed had held a sea-going command for only two weeks. Callaghan's flagship, the heavy cruiser *San Francisco*, was not equipped with the latest SG search radar. His eight destroyers were of different classes and had not operated together before. (The force included the *Fletcher* and the *O'Bannon*, the first combat use of the US Navy's new class of large destroyers.)[16]

The two fleets collided head-on southeast of Savo Island in the early hours of Friday (the night of 12/13 November). The confused mêlée lasted only half an hour, illuminated by flares, searchlights and burning ships. The *Atlanta*, a new light (AA) cruiser, was damaged by Japanese shells and torpedoes, and then hit by gunfire from the flagship *San Francisco*, which had been positioned astern of her in the American column. Admiral Scott, aboard the *Atlanta*, was killed, probably as a result of this friendly fire. The *San Francisco* then duelled at very short range (2,500 yards) with Admiral Abe's flagship, the battleship *Hiei*. This unbalanced exchange led to the death of Callaghan on the cruiser's bridge. (Callaghan and Scott were the first US flag officers to be killed in action since Admiral Kidd at Pearl Harbor; both were posthumously awarded the Medal of Honor.) Nevertheless, a shell hit from the *San Francisco* put the steering gear of the Japanese battleship out of commission. The guns of the *San Francisco* and other American ships – nothing bigger than 8-inch – could not penetrate the armoured decks of the *Hiei*, but they caused great damage to her topside structures and equipment.

On the American side, the cruisers now following the *San Francisco* – the *Portland*, the *Helena* and the *Juneau* – were shot up or torpedoed but not mortally damaged. Two of the American destroyers were sunk immediately, and two more went down a few hours later; on the Japanese side one destroyer was sunk and another fatally damaged. The second Japanese battleship, the *Kirishima*, 1,000 yards astern of the *Hiei*, suffered only a glancing blow from a 6-inch shell. In any event Abe decided to call off the battleship bombardment.

During the day of Friday (13 November), damaged ships were finished off. The battleship *Hiei* limped north of Savo. After dawn Admiral Abe was taken off his flagship by a destroyer; he would play no further part in the three-day battle. (Admiral Yamamoto subsequently sacked him for his failure to carry through the airfield attack.) After repeated air strikes, mostly by US Navy dive bombers and torpedo planes, the abandoned hulk sank during Friday night. As three of the damaged American cruisers were limping back to Nouméa on Friday the *Juneau* was torpedoed by a submarine. She exploded and sank within moments. The crew numbered over 700 men; most were killed instantly, but about 100 died more slowly in the water. The *Juneau* went down in the open sea southeast of Guadalcanal and attempts to rescue survivors came too late; only ten men were picked up.[17]

On Friday night (13/14 November) another Japanese force of three heavy cruisers arrived to bombard Henderson Field. In command was Admiral Mikawa, the victor of Savo Island. A number of American planes were destroyed on the ground, but the airstrip was not put out of action; the events of the following day were to show that this had been a critical failure. Much more damage would have been inflicted by the 14-inch guns of the battleships had Admiral Abe completed his mission the previous night.

During Saturday planes from Henderson Field, reinforced by fighters and dive bombers flown in from the *Enterprise*, pounced on Mikawa's retreating bombardment force and sank the heavy cruiser *Kinugasa*. But the most important development involved the passage down the Slot in the other direction of the eleven troop transports from the Shortlands, escorted by Admiral Tanaka.

They were subjected to repeated air attacks from Henderson Field. As Saturday afternoon progressed the Japanese transports were one by one sunk, damaged or forced to turn back; some of the troops on board were safely transferred to the escorting destroyers, but with the loss of much of their equipment.

The fourth night surface action of the Guadalcanal campaign took place on Saturday night (14/15 November), forty-eight hours after the deaths of admirals Callaghan and Scott. The battleship *Kirishima* and the small cruiser *Nagara*, with several destroyers, had steamed towards Truk on Friday. They joined forces with another group of warships, the most important of which were the heavy cruisers *Atago* and *Takao*. Admiral Kondō himself, aboard the *Atago*, took personal charge. The warships headed south together on Saturday, with the *Kirishima*, the *Atago* and the *Takao* forming the bombardment group.

The battle was again fought around Savo, although this time mainly to the west of the island, at the end of the Slot. Admiral Halsey had taken the daring – and probably foolhardy – decision to commit two battleships in these confined waters. Construction of 'fast' battleships, two of the 'North Carolina' class and four of the 'South Dakota' class, had begun in 1938. The two classes were similar, 37,500-ton ships each with nine 16-inch guns, and twenty dual-purpose 5-inch guns. They were capable of 28 knots. The *North Carolina* and *Washington* were commissioned in the summer before Pearl Harbor, and the *South Dakota* and her three sisters joined the fleet in 1942.[18]

Admiral Willis Augustus 'Ching' Lee, commanding the battleship task group, was an able commander and a radar expert. The battle opened badly when the *South Dakota* suffered an electrical power failure, and problems developed with the ship's radar. She took numerous gunfire hits at a range of 5,000 yards, but no serious damage was caused. The enemy concentrated his fire on the *South Dakota*. The *Washington*, with Admiral Lee on board, was able to use her gunnery radar effectively; she remained undetected and undamaged.[19] The *Kirishima* was apparently hit by twenty 16-inch shells, a deadly onslaught. The *Atago* suffered only minor damage, and the *Takao* was not hit at all, but Kondō still cancelled the planned bombardment of Henderson Field.

Meanwhile, Admiral Tanaka arrived with his destroyers and the four surviving transports. It was much later in the night than in the original plan, so he decided to run the transports aground. About 2,000 men of the 38th Division were landed on the island, as well as some ammunition and food. After that Guadalcanal would only be reinforced by destroyers dropping oil drums offshore, and the troops on the island went hungry.

For the Americans the crisis on Guadalcanal was over. The Japanese IGHQ decided to fall back on the central Solomons. More American ground-force reinforcements – soldiers and Marines – arrived. The saga of Guadalcanal ended two months later in early February, when the Japanese pulled out. They did succeed in evacuating nearly 10,000 men from the island aboard a number of destroyers, without interference.

American warship losses in the six months of the Guadalcanal campaign were higher than those of the Japanese; the US Navy did not lose any battleships (and the Japanese lost two), but the Allies lost two fleet carriers (against a small light carrier), eight cruisers (against three) and fifteen destroyers (against eleven). American aircraft losses were marginally lower (although the Japanese, flying long-range offensive missions, lost many more aircrew).[20] The Imperial Navy started the war with fewer warships, and certainly had less capacity for building replacements; it could not afford just to trade losses. The main thing about this Verdun of the Pacific war, however, was that the Americans held Guadalcanal, the starting point of their drive towards Japan.

THE ADVANCE UP THE SOLOMONS, FEBRUARY–NOVEMBER 1943

Task 2 of the campaign plan sketched out in Washington in July 1942 involved an offensive up the chain of the Solomons to capture Rabaul.[21]

From the new American bases at Guadalcanal and Tulagi it was about 470 miles in a northwesterly direction to the final objective in the Solomons: Buka, a tiny island off the northern tip of Bougainville. The Solomons are two parallel lines of islands, and nearly all the fighting was on the western line.[22] Northwest of Guadalcanal were the Russell Islands, which were occupied by the Americans without serious Japanese resistance in February 1943. Then came New Georgia, with the newly built Japanese airstrip at Munda; its capture was slowly completed in the course of a poorly conducted American campaign which lasted from the end of June until mid-September. Beyond New Georgia lay Kolombangara with another Japanese air base at Vila; further north still was the island of Vella Lavella, which was invaded by the Americans in August 1943. Finally, there was the biggest island in the Solomons, Bougainville, which was only 270 miles from Rabaul; it was close enough to serve as a base from which Allied bombers, with fighter escort, could attack the port and airfield complex of the Japanese fortress.

For the first eight months of 1943 only a limited number of major warships from either navy operated in the South Pacific, due mainly to the losses suffered in 1942. There were none of the big fleet actions which had featured in the previous year, neither side deploying carriers or battleships in the central or western Solomons (or around New Guinea). All the same, there was a large amount of sea/air fighting, with both sides basing their aircraft on land.

The American forces began to be equipped with a new generation of fighter aircraft, for the first time markedly superior to those of the Japanese. The US

Navy F4F Wildcat and the AAF P-39 Airacobra and P-40 Warhawk remained in service, but they were supplemented with new types. The first of the Army's twin-engined long-range Lockheed P-38 Lightning fighters arrived on Guadalcanal in November 1942, and the Vought F4U Corsairs of the US Marines followed in February 1943. VMF-214, the so-called 'Black Sheep' squadron – later one of the best-known Marine units, thanks to a 1970s US television series – was commanded by Major Gregory 'Pappy' Boyington. Formed in September 1943, the squadron flew Corsairs from Guadalcanal, the Russell Islands and New Georgia.

The air-minded Admiral Yamamoto, in the last of his fateful – and fatal – command decisions, decided to forestall a further American advance against Rabaul from Guadalcanal and New Guinea by means of a major air campaign, code-named I-GO. This high level of activity was surely ordered partly in response to the humiliating destruction of an eight-ship convoy carrying Imperial Army troops from Rabaul to New Guinea in March 1943 (the Battle of the Bismarck Sea).[23] In any event I-GO involved attacking Allied air and naval bases near Guadalcanal (the Tulagi anchorage), as well as those at Port Moresby and Milne Bay in eastern New Guinea. The admiral decided to strip aircraft from his carrier air groups and fly them from Rabaul and new forward land bases in the Solomons.

The I-GO blitz, carried out in a series of air raids from 7 to 16 April, was a failure. It did not cause serious losses to the enemy. Allied air forces held their own, and the Imperial Navy's carrier-trained air groups were badly depleted. The Japanese carriers, in the end, would not see any action for twenty months after the Battle of Santa Cruz in October 1942.

The operation also led to the death of Yamamoto. The little admiral came to Rabaul to personally oversee the air strikes. On 18 April, having concluded – incorrectly – that I-GO had been successfully completed, and at the urging of his chief of staff, Admiral Ugaki, Yamamoto flew from Rabaul to visit one of the advance air bases off the southern end of Bougainville. Orders timetabling the visit had been radioed four days earlier and decrypted by the Americans. The decision to carry out an attack on Yamamoto was apparently approved by admirals Nimitz and Halsey, despite the danger of revealing the extent of the Allied codebreaking success. (It is sometimes asserted that President Roosevelt was directly involved in the decision; there is no evidence that this was the case.)[24] There was an irony in the killing of the Japanese Navy C-in-C by aircraft from the US Army; at the time only the twin-engined P-38 Lightning had sufficient range for the flight from Guadalcanal. Some sixteen P-38s intercepted the two G4M/BETTY bombers which were carrying Yamamoto and his party. Both planes were shot down. The admiral's body was recovered from the jungle crash site, and later carried from Truk to Tokyo aboard the super-battleship *Yamato*. A state funeral would be held in Tokyo a month and a half later on 5 June.

Yamamoto's replacement as C-in-C of the Combined Fleet was Admiral Koga Mineichi. A year younger than his predecessor, Koga had been the C-in-C of the China Area Fleet. He lacked Yamamoto's experience in naval aviation, but continued the 'decisive battle' mentality of his predecessor.[25] In Tokyo, Admiral Nagano remained as Chief of the Naval General Staff (on 15 February 1943 his portrait had appeared on the cover of *Time* magazine).

In late June 1943 the Americans really began their advance up the Solomons towards Rabaul, with Marine and Army landings on New Georgia. From the naval point of view the Combined Fleet had little strength to deploy, especially in the first weeks, as Admiral Koga had just sent major forces north from Rabaul to Truk and Tokyo, in a forsaken attempt to deal with the American counter-attack in the Aleutians.[26]

There were three significant battles between Japanese and American cruiser-destroyer forces in the central Solomons, mostly to intercept 'Tokyo Express' supply convoys to island garrisons. The most important was the base and airfield at Vila on the island of Kolombangara, north of New Georgia. The Americans had radar-controlled guns in their new light cruisers, the Japanese had excellent torpedoes. In early July, at Kula Gulf (north of New Georgia) an American cruiser-destroyer force under Admiral Walden Ainsworth engaged ten Japanese destroyers and lost the light cruiser *Helena* to a long-range Type 93 torpedo.

A little more than a week later the Battle of Kolombangara was fought in the same waters. This time Ainsworth's force came out ahead, sinking the light cruiser *Jintsu* and killing the Japanese admiral aboard. With hindsight this engagement was also a remarkable event because the two greatest naval historians of World War II were present. Commander Stephen Roskill RN was executive officer of the New Zealand cruiser *Leander* (sister ship of the light cruisers that fought the *Admiral Graf Spee*). The *Leander* had replaced the *Helena*, and in fact took a torpedo hit herself, which she survived. Roskill was injured and nearly swept overboard. Meanwhile Samuel Eliot Morison was an observer aboard the *America* flagship. The Harvard University maritime historian had been invited by President Roosevelt to write a multi-volume history of the naval war, and had been given a reserve commission as a lieutenant commander. Morison's cruiser was also hit by a torpedo, but fortunately this one was a dud.[27]

The Battle of Vella Gulf (between Kolombangara and Vella Lavella) fought on 6–7 August was even more successful for the Americans, as their destroyers were allowed to fight independently. The force sank three enemy destroyers with no loss to themselves. Five nights earlier, and not far away, had taken place the incident – later to become famous – in which an American MTB, *PT-109*, commanded by Lieutenant John F. Kennedy, was rammed and sunk by the destroyer *Amagiri* west of Kolombangara; the Japanese ship was en route to

Rabaul after a supply trip to Kolombangara. The future President succeeded in saving injured members of his crew.

A week after the Battle of Vella Gulf, on 15 August, the Americans landed on Vella Lavella. This was an extremely significant event, because the attack bypassed the now large Japanese garrison on Kolombangara and marked the beginning of 'leap-frogging' in the Solomons campaign. (The Japanese were later able to evacuate 9,000 men, most of the garrison, from Kolombangara, by sea.)

Both sides were now re-considering the importance of Rabaul. In July 1943 General Marshall had proposed bypassing the big enemy base, and this was accepted by Admiral King. The radical adjustment of strategy was secretly approved in August by the Combined Chiefs of Staff at the QUADRANT inter-Allied conference, held in Quebec. This was one of the most important examples of Pacific leap-frogging. Rather than a direct assault on the fortress, General MacArthur was to seal it off by seizing islands in the Bismarck Archipelago to the west of Rabaul and advancing along the north coast of New Guinea. (The Admiralty Islands were invaded in February 1944; see the following section, p. 249.) During these same autumn months, on 30 September 1943, an Imperial Conference in Tokyo secretly re-cast national strategy, setting up an 'absolute national defence zone' (*zettai kokubō ken*). In the South Pacific, this zone included western New Guinea, but not Rabaul. This 'third phase' of Japanese grand strategy was essentially defensive.[28] On the other hand, regions to the east of the zone – including Rabaul and Bougainville, as well as the Gilbert Islands and the Marshall Islands – would not be abandoned. And when the Americans directly threatened Rabaul by attacking Bougainville, Admiral Koga and the Imperial Navy responded in force.

Bougainville lies at the northwestern end of the Solomons. The island was about the size of Cyprus, and twice as big as Guadalcanal. The garrison was the largest encountered so far, some 40,000 men, including a considerable number of front-line personnel of the Seventeenth Army, some of whom had fought on Guadalcanal. The terrain was very rough, with two central mountain ranges covered by a dense rain forest, unbroken by roads. Movement across the island in any strength was difficult. As elsewhere, the flexibility which came from sea control allowed the Americans to avoid the main centres of resistance. The new 3rd Marine Division landed on the undefended western coast at Torokina in Empress Augusta Bay on 1 November 1943 (Operation CHERRYBLOSSOM).

The landing provoked major Japanese air and warship movements. The biggest surface ship battle since November 1942 took place in Empress Augusta Bay, as a Japanese battle group under Admiral Ōmori Sentarō raced to land an infantry force and counter-attack the beachhead.[29] In the force were the heavy cruisers *Myōkō* and *Haguro*, as well as two light cruisers, the *Sendai* and the new *Agano*. The attempt to repeat Admiral Mikawa's success at Savo Island was frustrated. The defending American force comprised the *Montpelier*, the *Cleveland*, the *Columbia* and the *Denver*, four new 'Cleveland' class light cruisers, each armed with twelve 6-inch guns (but no torpedo tubes). The enemy squadron was driven off in a night battle on 1/2 November with the sinking of the *Sendai* and a destroyer; the Americans lost no ships.[30]

Once again, Rabaul was reinforced by planes from the carrier fleet, this time on the orders of Admiral Koga, rather than (as in April 1943) by Yamamoto. In Operation RO some 173 aircraft were flown into Rabaul from Truk, having been detached from their carriers. Accepting over-optimistic reports of American losses at the Battle of Empress Augusta Bay, Admiral Koga ordered the heavy cruisers of his Second Fleet (now under Admiral Kurita, who had replaced Admiral Kondō in September 1943) to move south from Truk to Rabaul. The Americans responded violently with ground- and carrier-based strikes on Rabaul, which broke up the counter-attack. This important episode will be described at greater length at the beginning of Chapter 18.

Meanwhile, on Bougainville the Americans did not need to conquer the whole island. They were confident enough just to set up a defensive perimeter around the landing zone. This time the Japanese were neither able to break through nor to execute a successful evacuation. The garrison on Bougainville – General Hyakutake and the remnants of the Seventeenth Army from Guadalcanal – remained in limbo until the end of the war. Some 25,000 Japanese troops would surrender on the island in September 1945.

In 1943 airfields were rapidly laid out within the American perimeter on Bougainville. The first major strike against Rabaul organised by 'AirSols', the joint Army–Navy headquarters controlling air activities in the Solomon Islands, took place in mid-December. After one final air battle in February 1944 the surviving Japanese naval air force on Rabaul was pulled back north to Truk in the Central Pacific.

The tidal wave of the Allied advance now left Rabaul and its garrison in the distant rear. On 4 September 1945 General Imamura and Admiral Kusaka surrendered all remaining forces on New Britain to an Australian general; the ceremony took place on the deck of the new light carrier HMS *Glory*. (New Britain, of course, was part of the British Empire.) The Japanese garrison of Rabaul had included 57,000 soldiers and 32,000 naval personnel.

NEW GUINEA, JANUARY 1942–MAY 1944

The long battle for New Guinea was a less obvious part of the war at sea than the Solomons campaign. It was largely fought between the Japanese Army and American and Australian ground and air forces. Neither side committed major naval forces to the area on a long-term basis. No naval combat on the scale of the Guadalcanal campaign took place, not even the smaller cruiser-destroyer battles that featured in the central and northern Solomons in 1943. All the same, sea power played a crucial role in the Allied success.

The second largest island in the world (after Greenland), New Guinea stretches over 1,000 miles from east to west. Before December 1941 the western half of the island was part of the Netherlands Indies, the eastern half under British control. New Guinea and neighbouring islands were sparsely settled, with an equatorial climate and endemic malaria, an environment difficult for outsiders to adapt to. Because the terrain was rugged and there were few roads and no railways, a conventional land campaign was impossible; even overland *movement* was difficult. Land-based aviation was singularly important as a supporting force, but the two sides depended heavily on use of the sea to transport and supply their troops.

For the Australians, Japanese control of New Guinea would present a mortal danger, threatening their home territory; this was true at least until the middle of 1942. For General Douglas MacArthur, on the other hand, the big island could serve as the route for the return to the Philippines, where he hoped that it would be his forces rather than those of Admiral Nimitz which would play the main role. For the Japanese, New Guinea became in January 1942 the south-eastern corner post of their Pacific empire; it covered the eastern approaches to their resource region in the occupied Netherlands Indies and Borneo, as well as the southern approaches to the Philippines.

First of all there was Rabaul. As we have seen, this was the overall focus of Japanese and Allied strategy in the South Pacific for two years, from January 1942 to the summer of 1943. Although set on the island of New Britain in the Bismarck Archipelago, Rabaul was part of the New Guinea region. The small town had been the capital of Papua until it was heavily damaged by a catastrophic volcanic eruption in 1937 and the administrative centre was moved to Lae on the mainland of Papua–New Guinea.[31]

As already described, the first stage of the campaign on New Guinea proper involved the eastern tip of the huge island, Papua, and especially Port Moresby. Japan had seized bases, in January 1942, at Rabaul, and in March on the north coast of Papua–New Guinea itself, at Lae and nearby Salamaua (25 miles south of Lae). The Japanese seaborne expedition of May 1942 against Port Moresby (on the southern coast of Papua) failed with the Coral Sea battle. A new approach was attempted after this setback, as Japanese forces in July 1942 were trans-shipped 170 miles east along the coast from Lae–Salamaua to Buna, directly north of Port Moresby. From Buna an Imperial Army detachment was to trek some 100 miles south over the Owen Stanley mountains along the so-called Kokoda Trail to take the Australian-held strongpoint.

In support of this advance, the Japanese Navy landed a small force at Milne Bay in late August 1942, using naval infantry (SNLF), supported by a small force of light cruisers and destroyers. Milne Bay was at the eastern tip of Papua, and an RAAF forward airfield was being been laid out there. Forewarned by radio decrypts, the Australians had been able to reinforce their land garrison, and after two weeks the Japanese landing party had to withdraw, suffering heavy losses. Although small in scale, the Battle of Milne Bay was the first time in the war that the Japanese had to permanently abandon one of their amphibious operations; it was also their last such attack. Meanwhile their overland Kokoda Trail expedition was stopped north of Moresby at the end of September. The Army column was gradually pushed back by the Australians, with American help, to the starting point at Buna; this place then had to be evacuated by sea in January 1943. The scale of the fighting in Papua was considerably larger than the more famous American campaign on Guadalcanal, and the number of casualties higher.

The Japanese Army had previously not been greatly interested in the Japanese Navy's adventures in the South Pacific; its leaders were more concerned with China, Russia and Burma. Now the defeat at Midway and the heavy fighting on Guadalcanal focused the attention of the Army section of the IGHQ on the southern ocean. Striving to regain the initiative in eastern New Guinea, the Army headquarters sent ground troops and air units as reinforcements, forming a new Eighteenth Army (essentially a corps) under General Adachi Hatazō in November 1942. The east-central part of the north coast was reinforced by two infantry divisions and by air squadrons.

However, attempts to transport a third division from Rabaul to Lae by sea ended in disaster in early March 1943. In one of the most dramatic episodes of the sea/air war, land-based Allied aircraft – mostly twin-engined AAF A-20s and B-25s – intercepted a Japanese convoy en route from Rabaul to Lae. The sea/air action is inaccurately known as the Battle of the Bismarck Sea; it was essentially a convoy attack, the most lethal part of which occurred in the Solomon Sea on the approaches to Lae, rather than in the Bismarck Sea (north of New Britain).

In any event the result was highly significant. There were eight transports in the convoy, three of them above 6,000 tons. All were sunk, as well as four of the eight escorting destroyers. Of the 6,900 troops who embarked, only 1,200 arrived. General Adachi and the commander of the 51st Division were themselves caught up in the attack (they survived). After this heavy – and, for the Japanese Navy, humiliating – defeat, the use of large ships on the New Guinea supply run had to be abandoned, and reliance placed on less efficient coastal barges. In Rabaul the catastrophe led to the removal of Admiral Mikawa as commander of the Eighth Fleet; in better days for Japan Mikawa had been the victor at Savo Island.

High-level American debates about offensive strategy in the Pacific had now ended in compromise. General MacArthur wanted sole command, with emphasis on New Guinea, but Admiral King and the leaders of the US Navy had other ideas. Nevertheless, it was agreed at the end of 1942 that one element of the advance would be the continuation of MacArthur's offensive in eastern New Guinea, initially with a view to taking Rabaul.

Naval support was essential for MacArthur's advance. The ships of the Southwest Pacific Force were renamed the Seventh Fleet in March 1943.[32] Admiral Arthur Carpender, the first commander of the fleet, did not work effectively with MacArthur, the Australians or the US Army; in November 1943 Admiral Thomas Kinkaid replaced him as head of 'MacArthur's Navy'. Kinkaid was an ambitious officer from a naval family; he was the brother-in-law of Admiral Kimmel, who had been in command at Pearl Harbor on 7 December 1941. He served as naval attaché in Rome from 1938 to 1941. After Pearl Harbor he took command of a Pacific cruiser division. Although he had no pre-war aviation experience, Kinkaid had led the American carrier task force (TF 61) that fought the Battle of Santa Cruz in October 1942. That engagement did not go well, and the admiral was shifted sideways to become commander of the North Pacific Force in January 1943. There he proved himself as an effective 'joint' leader during the operations in the Aleutians to re-take Attu (May 1943) and Kiska (August 1943), working smoothly with the US Army and the Canadians.[33] With this experience he was selected to return to the South Pacific in November and take up the challenge of working with Douglas MacArthur at his headquarters in Brisbane. Meanwhile Admiral Daniel E. Barbey, one of the US Navy's leading specialists in amphibious warfare, had become commander of local amphibious forces in January 1943; in March 1943 these were re-labelled as VII Amphibious Force ('VII 'Phib').

The Seventh Fleet was small. It had only a few large warships, the only combat role of which, in the New Guinea area in 1943–44, would be to provide gunfire support for amphibious landings. At the turn of 1943 these vessels included the Australian cruisers *Australia* and *Shropshire*, one or two of the new 'Brooklyn' class light cruisers and less than a dozen destroyers.[34] Even amphibious 'lift' (capability) was at first limited to shore-to-shore operations; these used various small ships and 'fast transports', converted from old four-stacker destroyers, as well as the new landing vessels (LSTs, LCTs and LCIs) as they became available. Only in late 1943 would VII 'Phib obtain assault ships for longer-range operations. The Japanese, for their part, had few warships in the New Guinea fighting, although they did deploy some of their medium-size, *Ro*-type submarines – with little effect.

Allied amphibious operations in New Guinea began in May and June 1943 on a small scale, and were intended to open supply lines to troops advancing overland. In September Barbey and VII 'Phib supported a more ambitious shore-to-shore operation from Milne Bay and Buna; this was launched against Lae, with Australian troops attacking from the land side. The Japanese were soon pressed back beyond the Huon Peninsula

A strategic position was now the Vitiaz Strait, a 30-mile narrows separating New Guinea's Huon Peninsula from the western end of New Britain and blocking the way, beyond the 'Bismarcks Barrier', to the long northern coastline of New Guinea.[35] Cape Gloucester (New Britain), on the north side of the strait, was captured at the end of December 1943 with a big landing involving the whole of the 1st Marine Division (the veterans of Guadalcanal).

New Ireland is a long island situated beyond the other (northern) tip of New Britain. About 200 miles west of New Ireland, and 200 miles north of New Guinea, on the northwest edge of the Bismarck Sea, lie the Admiralty Islands. Here in late February the US Army's 1st Cavalry Division carried out a landing on Los Negros and succeeding in overcoming unexpected but ineffective Japanese opposition. Within a few weeks another island in the Admiralties, Manus, had been occupied; largely undefended by the Japanese, it would provide an important Allied naval base 1944–45.[36]

Meanwhile, the Japanese assembled the main combat ground and air forces of the Eighteenth Army on the north coast of New Guinea, to the west of the Vitiaz Strait, at Madang, Hansa Bay and Wewak; many of the troops here had retreated overland from the Huon Peninsula. The campaign continued to go badly for General Adachi and his forces. Japanese air strength was worn down by AAF attacks. Initially General MacArthur planned for a landing in Hansa Bay, but his codebreakers provided evidence that the Japanese rear area was weakly defended. Making use of the growing capabilities of Admiral Barbey's VII 'Phib, MacArthur jumped 200–300 miles further west, to the rear area of Aitape and Hollandia (now Jayapura) on 22 April 1944. The code name for the Hollandia attack was Operation RECKLESS, but the landing encountered little serious resistance. The remnants of the Japanese Eighteenth Army, some 50,000 men, were now trapped far to the east. By the end of July 1944 the Americans had reached the western tip of New Guinea, the Vogelkop (named after its resemblance on the map to a bird's head).

The American landing at Biak, an island lying to the east of the Vogelkop, on 27 May 1944 brought to an end the main part of New Guinea campaign – and the fighting in the South Pacific. Biak was near the western end of New Guinea, and the commander of the Japanese Southwest Area Fleet (then based in Surabaya, Java) was concerned about the threat to the prize territory of the

Netherlands Indies; Surabaya had just been attacked by a British-led carrier task force.[37] The high command in Tokyo incorrectly believed this was the main Allied line of advance – rather than through the Mariana Islands. Operation KON was set up in June 1944 to reinforce Biak. A task group under the command of Admiral Ugaki was formed with the super-battleships *Yamato* and *Musashi*, the heavy cruisers *Myōkō* and *Haguro* and the new light cruiser *Noshiro*, with destroyers. They departed from their forward base in the southwestern Philippines on 10 June, supporting a group of transports. Operation KON was cancelled two days later, when alarming news arrived of major American air strikes against the Marianas, 1,450 miles to the north, in the Central Pacific.[38] From this a different decisive battle was to ensue, fought on American terms in the Philippine Sea.

CHAPTER 12

THE BATTLE OF THE ATLANTIC, ROUND TWO

January–December 1942

LIBERTY FLEET DAY, 27 SEPTEMBER 1941

On Saturday, 27 September 1941, slipway No. 1 of Bethlehem-Fairfield, a huge new emergency shipyard in Baltimore, was the central site of 'Liberty Fleet Day': here took place the launching of the first Liberty ship, the SS *Patrick Henry*. The namesake of this vessel was famous to all Americans for his words on the eve of the Revolution: 'Give me liberty, or give me death.'[1]

The aim of Liberty Fleet Day was to showcase the shipbuilding capability of the United States, and across the country fourteen facilities were involved. The *Patrick Henry* was launched in Baltimore by the wife of Vice President Wallace. Admiral Emory S. Land, the head of the US Maritime Commission, was also present. President Roosevelt was spending the weekend at his Hyde Park estate in upstate New York, but a 'radio-recording' of his speech was played at Bethlehem-Fairfield and at the other shipyards.

In his address the President declared that between dawn and dusk fourteen ships were being launched, on the Atlantic, Pacific and Gulf coasts. Roosevelt was trying to mobilise public opinion. American warships were now escorting Atlantic convoys; two weeks earlier, after the destroyer *Greer* was attacked, he had condemned the U-boats as 'rattlesnakes of the Atlantic'. Now he said that 'Our shipbuilding program . . . is one of our answers to the aggressors who would strike at our liberty'. The President spoke out, too, against the isolationists and against restrictive neutrality legislation; he urged his fellow countrymen not to 'listen to those few Americans who preach the gospel of fear – who say in effect that they are still in favour of freedom of the seas but who would have the United States tie up our vessels in our ports'. 'We propose', he declared, 'that these ships sail the seas as they are supposed to'.[2]

The Liberty ships were hugely significant in the conduct of World War II. They, more than any other merchant vessels, would make possible the movement – essential for victory – of Allied supplies, food and raw materials between continents. Built to a very basic British tramp-steamer design, the 'ugly ducklings' had been optimised in the US for mass production (and fitted for oil fuel rather than coal). Their official designation was EC2-S-C1; the 'EC' stood for 'Emergency Cargo'. With a simple reciprocating steam engine (rather than a steam turbine or diesel) and one propeller, they were capable of only 11 knots. Their welded hulls were prone to structural failure; they were not intended to last very long. But they were large – 440 feet long – and could carry about 10,000 tons of cargo.[3]

They became available in astonishing numbers. A total of 2,755 of them would be completed in 1941–45, far more than any other large cargo ship. Three other Liberty ships were launched that same day, the *Adabelle Lykes* at Wilmington, Delaware, and the *Star of Oregon* and the *John C. Fremont* on the West Coast. Two 'Ocean' class vessels launched on 27 September at Henry Kaiser's Todd-California yard in San Francisco Bay were essentially Liberty ships; the *Ocean Venture* and the *Ocean Voice* were being built in a shipyard organised by the British in the winter of 1940–41 to build thirty 'emergency' merchant ships.[4] Liberty ships could be built very rapidly. The keel of the *Patrick Henry* had been laid down on 30 April 1941; she would be delivered on 30 December and so took only 244 days to construct. By the summer of 1942 the building time for a Liberty ship at Bethlehem-Fairfield had been reduced to just fifty days.

Liberty ships were only the best-known products of Allied (mainly American) wartime shipbuilding. The Maritime Commission had been set up under President Roosevelt's New Deal in the late 1930s to revitalise and co-ordinate American shipbuilding. A number of standard cargo ship designs were developed, which were faster and better built than the later Liberty ships. The so-called 'C-boats' were all ocean-going and came in three basic sizes. Two of the ships launched on 27 September were of the 397-foot C1 type, two more were of the 459-foot C2 type. Also launched were three 492-foot C3 type vessels. Two of these later became 'attack transports' (APAs) for amphibious landings, the SS *African Planet* (as USS *George Clymer*) and the SS *Fredrick Funston* (commissioned into the US Navy without a name change); the SS *Steel Artisan*, a C3 launched at Western Pipe and Steel in San Francisco, would eventually be fitted with a flight deck to become the British escort carrier HMS *Attacker*. The final merchant ship launched on 27 September was the tanker *Sinclair Superflame*, built at Quincy, Massachusetts. Also launched on that day, in addition to the fourteen cargo ships, were two 'Gleaves' class destroyers.

Two of the Liberty ships launched on 27 September would be sunk, as well as both the 'Ocean' class. Two of the C-boats (the *James MacKay* and the *Louise Lykes*) were lost with all hands – eighty-five men each – to U-boat attacks in 1942.

THE U-BOAT WAR

The Atlantic sea war of 1942 was in many ways different from that of the previous year. On 11 December 1941, when Hitler declared war on the US, the Kriegsmarine suddenly found itself in an altered, but not wholly unexpected, conflict. The Royal Navy, for its part, had a powerful new active ally across the Atlantic. On the other hand, the war for control of the seas continued much as it had in 1941, especially on the vital North Atlantic route. Organising shipping and the struggle between escorts and attackers went on with only incremental changes. This was true even for the US Navy, which had been fighting an 'undeclared war' in the Atlantic from September 1941.

Table 12.1 shows the unprecedented scale of shipping losses in the North Atlantic theatre in 1942, and also the rapid growth of the U-boat force. Towards the end of the year, in his annual November 1942 speech in Munich, Hitler boasted that 24 million tons of Allied shipping had been sunk in the war so far, twice that of World War I.[5] That was an exaggeration, but there had certainly been a high and growing cost to Britain and the United States. In *each* quarter of 1942 the tonnage lost in the Atlantic was at about the same level as the *worst* three months of 1941 (the spring quarter). The highest monthly loss in 1942 – June – was the worst monthly loss for whole war; it came to 624,000 tons,

Table 12.1. The Battle of the Atlantic, 1942

Year/ quarter	N. Atlantic tonnage lost	N. Atlantic ships lost	U-boats oper.	U-boats t&t	U-boats lost
1942/i	1,241,000	216	91	158	11
1942/ii	1,591,000	310	121	164	10
1942/iii	1,469,000	289	140	191	32
1942/iv	1,171,000	191	196	169	34
Total (N. Atlantic)	5,471,000	1,006			
Total (All theatres)	7,791,000	1,664			87

Source: Rosk/2, pp. 467–9, 475, 486.
Notes: Losses are for Allied and neutral countries' merchant ships due to enemy action *of all types*, not just due to U-boats. Tonnage is GRT. U-boat numbers are total for German Navy (all theatres) at the start of each quarter; 'oper.' is operational U-boats, 't&t' is units involved in training and trials. U-boat figures include losses from all causes and in all theatres.

or 124 ships. November 1942 was almost as bad, at 509,000 tons (eighty-three ships). These figures need to be compared to the 365,000 tons (sixty-three ships) lost in the Atlantic in March 1941, the worst month in that year.

The U-boats were now the only serious anti-shipping force on the transatlantic route. Admiral Raeder's Kreuzerkrieg had been abandoned – indeed the last gasp had effectively come seven months before the end of 1941, with the fatal *Bismarck* sortie. In any event, the battleships and cruisers finally departed up the Channel in February 1942. Likewise German maritime aviation was no longer a serious threat to ships, even on the UK–Gibraltar route.[6] At the same time the Luftwaffe's air attacks on British west-coast ports virtually ceased, due to the demands of the Russian and Mediterranean fronts; those terminals of the Atlantic shipping routes had been the targets of a major air campaign in the spring of 1941.

Most of the new U-boats were of the medium-sized Type VII, along with a small number of longer-range Type IXs. An expanding network of German shipyards had built about fifteen submarines a month in 1941, compared to less than five a month in 1940 – but this was still lower than Admiral Raeder's target of twenty a month. The number entering front-line service at the start of 1942 should have been higher, but a hard winter in 1941–42 meant ice covered much of the Baltic, and disrupted training there. All the same, as Table 12.1 shows, by the *end* of 1942 the Kriegsmarine had gone well beyond the 1939 target of 300 U-boats, although many of these were newly completed boats undergoing trials or training. Technically the boats had changed little; they were still armed with standard torpedoes with reliable contact detonators. The only innovations were more secure communications equipment and French-designed Metox radar detectors (from October 1942). Significant technical changes would not come until late 1943. A dozen supply U-boats to refuel and provision submarines in distant waters did enter service. They would be especially valuable in 1942 for extending the range of the smaller Type VIIs, which had been designed for operations no further from base than the North Sea and the eastern Atlantic. The Type XIV U-tanker, nicknamed the *Milchkuh* ('Milk cow'), could carry 430 tons of fuel.

The deadly attacks which these U-boats conducted in the North Atlantic (excluding for the moment the Arctic Sea) can be split into two parts, according to geography and time period. The first part consisted of the waters off the eastern seaboard of the United States and into the Caribbean Sea; protection of these waters was the responsibility of the US armed forces. The second part was the rest of the North Atlantic, mainly the central sector of the great ocean but also the waters off Canada; these areas were guarded by British and Canadian forces.[7]

The submarine attacks on the US seaboard were something new. In 1941 Hitler had wanted to avoid war with the US; now American shipping was fair game – a situation the leaders of the Kriegsmarine had argued for earlier. The US Navy was directly involved, as an enemy. The waters off the eastern seaboard were in fact the *only* place Germans and Americans would fight one another for the first six months of the war. It was the main location until December 1942 – when American soldiers finally collided with the Wehrmacht in Tunisia.

The US had entered the war after a Japanese surprise attack, and neither Berlin nor Washington had fully anticipated this remarkable U-boat campaign. At first the German naval command had few U-boats to spare, given deployments in the Mediterranean and off Norway, and training delays in the frozen Baltic. Admiral Dönitz was allowed to despatch a handful of his larger, Type IX, boats to the western Atlantic. The initial operation was assigned the code name DRUMBEAT (paukenschlag), and the five-month eastern seaboard offensive as a whole is often – inaccurately – known by this name. The *U 123* claimed the first victim, the British SS *Cyclops* (9,000 tons), off Nova Scotia on 12 January 1942. As the level of success became evident, the submarine assault was reinforced. Shorter-range Type VIIs were thrown in, now supported by supply ships and new U-tankers. Unprecedented success was achieved. The US Navy termed the main coastal zone between Maine and northern Florida the 'Eastern Sea Frontier'. Here 588,000 tons of shipping (100 vessels) were sunk by U-boats between January and June 1942. In March 1942 the main concentration of U-boat attacks began to move south. More than 960,000 tons of shipping (over 180 ships) were sunk in the Gulf Sea Frontier and the Caribbean Sea Frontier between February and September 1942. This region was of vital importance, as it was the centre of Allied petroleum production. The U-boat crews recalled these months as a (second) 'Happy Time'. For the Allies it was the opposite; one historian described it as 'the greatest maritime massacre in US history'.[8]

This devastation of Allied shipping was inflicted at very little cost to the U-boat fleet. The American press headlined in late January 1942 the memorable report 'Sighted sub, sank same', made by the crew of a US Navy Hudson bomber operating from Newfoundland. In reality, the first successful US air attack on the eastern seaboard would not occur until over five months later. This came on 7 July, when an AAF Hudson sank the *U 701* off Cape Hatteras, North Carolina. American surface ships also achieved very little; the first successful U-boat 'kill' did not come until mid-April, three months into the battle, when the four-stacker USS *Roper* sank the *U 85* off Norfolk, Virginia. Altogether American naval forces accounted for only eight U-boats in the period until mid-July 1942.[9]

This was to be one of the most controversial naval campaigns of World War II. Samuel Eliot Morison, the historian of the wartime US Navy, and an individual not normally given to blanket criticism of the service, was brutally frank in his account: 'the United States Navy was woefully unprepared, materially, and mentally, for the U-boat blitz on the Atlantic Coast that began in January 1942 . . . this unpreparedness was largely the Navy's own fault . . . it had no plans ready for a reasonable protection of shipping . . . and was unable to improvise them for several months'.[10]

Written in 1947, Morison's assessment is basically correct; some later historians have been at least equally critical. These months of heavy shipping losses were not the result of an overwhelming flood of U-boats; there were seldom more than a dozen on station off the US coast at any one time. The losses also did not stem from short-term difficulties in decrypting U-boat communications (which were changed in February 1942); unlike the earlier and later battles in the Central Atlantic, the Germans did not use wolfpack tactics or extensive radio communication in their long-range attacks off the American coast.

The main problem was the unwillingness of the US Navy to set up a coastal convoy system immediately, or at least to do so once a direct U-boat threat emerged in the second half of January. While Admiral King and his subordinates accepted the need for coastal convoys, they believed it impossible to assemble sufficient escort ships. Meanwhile neither the US Navy nor the AAF provided effective air cover in coastal waters, which were not far from their bases. In contrast, the British by this time were able to keep the U-boats 500–600 miles off their coasts – even though enemy submarines were operating from nearby bases in France and Norway.

The Americans had been given much detailed information about the U-boat danger and methods of combating it – at least since Admiral Ghormley arrived in London with his naval mission, fifteen months before Pearl Harbor.[11] The British had come to the conclusion that priority should be given to preserving shipping rather than sinking U-boats. They accepted that even weakly defended convoys were better than individual sailings. This was not something the American naval command readily accepted. Not even a partial convoy system was set up in American waters until the start of April 1942, and it was not functioning up and down the coast until May and June. Gradually surface escorts were provided, partly by reducing somewhat the number of transatlantic convoys; the British also provided a number of corvettes and A/S trawlers.

There were, to be sure, mitigating factors. The US had been suddenly thrown into two wars – against Japan and against Germany and Italy. Naturally, the American forces, and especially the US Navy, were preoccupied with a full-scale naval conflict in the Pacific. Moreover, there had been no reason to expect such a weight of transoceanic attack from an enemy fleet made up of short-range U-boats. In the Atlantic, green peacetime staffs and crews had to confront the expert U-boat command of Admiral Dönitz and his experienced (or at least well-trained) U-boat commanders. The British A/S system was indeed much superior to the American one in January 1942, but the Royal Navy and Coastal Command had had two years to develop it.

The lack of escorts might seem strange for a large navy, one of the two largest in the world, which had suffered virtually no war losses and was in the middle of a huge shipbuilding programme. It is worth recalling that the US had provided fifty destroyers to Britain at the end of 1940. The shortage of escorts was not caused by a wholesale movement of destroyers to the Pacific. The number of American destroyers in the Atlantic theatre was ninety-two in December 1941 and ninety-five in September 1942.[12] But even in the Atlantic the Eastern Sea Frontier had to compete with demands for US destroyers elsewhere. They were needed to serve in escort groups in the mid-Atlantic, for very heavily escorted US Army troopship convoys to Iceland and Northern Ireland, and to support American heavy ships. What is at least as important is the lack of adequate smaller sea-going escorts – sloops, frigates and corvettes. The closest approximation was a handful of (sloop-sized) US Coast Guard cutters.

Some historians lay the blame on Admiral King, whom President Roosevelt had made Commander-in-Chief, US Fleet (COMINCH), after Pearl Harbor. American command arrangements were inadequate, with argumentative Army–Navy relations – a weakness especially relevant for sea/air warfare. Even within the US Navy the organisational structure was awkward. The powers of King and Admiral Stark (Chief of Naval Operations) were confused until Stark's resignation in March 1942. At an operational level the superannuated Admiral Adolphus Andrews in New York commanded the Eastern Sea Frontier and Admiral Royal E. Ingersoll commanded the pool of ships and naval aircraft operating in the Atlantic. Neither admiral dealt effectively with the 1942 shipping crisis, but neither was openly criticised; Andrews remained in post until November 1943 and Ingersoll until November 1944. The professional leaders of the US Navy were (like the British) also traditionally more interested in battle fleets than in trade protection, more comfortable with an active offensive strategy than a passive, defensive one. These attitudes matched the actual American strategic profile, where overseas trade (and overseas supply) had not been central factors.

Ernest King cannot be blamed for the pre-war policies of the US Navy, but he did indeed (after Stark's departure in March 1942) have responsibility for the Navy's operations and organisation. On the face of it his fumbling of this shipping war was surprising; he had been C-in-C, Atlantic Fleet, throughout 1941, taking part in the 'undeclared naval war' of that autumn. He is often accused of Anglophobia, but perceptive judgement by a British contemporary who dealt with the admiral was more subtle: rather than being very anti-British 'he was rather excessively pro-American'. Ernest King has been described as 'the greatest naval leader of his century', but if so this was not his finest hour.[13]

Nor should the air element be ignored; King was certainly air-minded, but the US Army Air Force was outside his remit. Aviation was now recognised by the British as a key element in the Atlantic war, both as a 'killer' of U-boats and as a means of reducing their mobility (by forcing them to spend more time submerged). The USAAF set up the I Bomber Command, but over-sea training and routine convoy support was not a priority. Inter-service rivalry over this function, especially on the eastern seaboard, would not be resolved until the middle of 1943.

The second major area of Atlantic U-boat activity in 1942, moving away from the American eastern seaboard and the Caribbean, was in the central North Atlantic crossing and Canadian waters. Unlike the American coast, this was much more of a continuation of the 1941 submarine war between British naval forces and the Kriegsmarine, and many of the same factors were involved as in the previous year. Although American destroyers operated here in the early part of 1942, they had largely been removed from the Mid-Ocean Escort Force by the middle of the year. After that the crucial transatlantic supply route to the UK was again nearly wholly protected by British and Canadian vessels.

The course of the submarine war in 1942 – especially on the transatlantic route – is often explained by the availability (or unavailability) of signals intelligence. The reading of German signals by the codebreakers at Bletchley Park had certainly been an important factor in the second half of 1941, allowing convoys to be routed around observed U-boat concentrations. On 1 February 1942 the German Navy improved the security of their communications network supporting the Atlantic (and Mediterranean) U-boats (known as TRITON to the Germans and SHARK to the codebreakers). The submarines were now re-equipped with the M4 version of the Enigma machine, and for ten months the British codebreakers were unable to break into signals sent and received by it. The historian David Kahn would describe this as 'the most significant event in German cryptography during World War II'.[14] At about the same time (February 1942) the *B-Dienst* (*Beobachtungsdienst*), the radio intercept/decrypt section of naval intelligence, achieved a good ability to read the Allied Naval Cypher No. 3. This was extremely important, because it became their main tool for locating and attacking transatlantic convoys throughout the year. Because the Allies could not read TRITON signals they did not become aware of how much their own communications security had been compromised.

On the other hand, technical developments gradually introduced by the British in 1942 played a positive role in their A/S efforts in the central North

Atlantic. Although Bletchley Park could not decrypt TRITON its codebreakers continued to read messages sent by the main naval network (HEIMISCH/DOLPHIN), which covered surface ships and U-boat operations in the Baltic and Norway. Meanwhile high-frequency direction finding (HF/DF) from distant shore stations had provided an approximate location of U-boat transmissions. This mean that the British Operational Intelligence Centre still had information about the overall strength of the U-boat force and the timing of its war patrols.

From February 1942 this was supplemented by a compact shipboard version of HF/DF, a development that the Germans had not believed technically feasible. It was extremely valuable for accurately locating U-boats in the close vicinity of convoys, and could be used to locate – and then drive off – shadowers. Meanwhile radar carried by escorts rapidly improved, from the early 268M of 1941 to the centimetric Type 271, which was widely available in destroyers and corvettes by the spring of 1942.[15] These new technologies made night surface attacks by U-boats much more difficult and dangerous for the Germans.

In a speech in November 1942 Hitler mocked Allied claims for escort construction, declaring that Germany, too, could mass produce warships and that Allied escorts were nothing more than herring boats with guns on top. This was dangerous hyperbole, even if made in ignorance of the rapid development of Allied sensors. More British and Canadian 'herring boats' were now available. Most of the new convoy escorts entering service were still the 'Flower' class corvettes, but they were an improved version with longer range and better habitability. In January 1942, 110 British and sixty-seven Canadian 'Flowers' were in service in the North Atlantic, compared to only forty-seven British and twelve Canadian vessels a year earlier. British escorts were now equipped with heavier and more effective depth charges. The Royal Navy had also begun construction of a twin-screw escort, superseding the corvettes. These came on stream slowly; the first twelve of the 'River' class 'frigates' were commissioned between April 1942 and the end of the year.[16]

The long pause in the Central Atlantic in the first half of 1942 gave the Royal Navy time both to re-equip and to train their surface escorts. The Canadians were in a more difficult situation, with inexperienced and less well-trained crews, inferior equipment, and with the task of escorting slow and relatively vulnerable convoys in difficult weather conditions.

Aviation played a much larger part in the A/S war in the Central Atlantic in 1942 than in 1941. In 1941 only three submarines had been credited to shore-based Allied aircraft, out of thirty-five lost in action. In 1942 the number of U-boat losses caused by aircraft increased to thirty-five; five more were sunk by aircraft and ships operating together. These made up nearly half the eighty-seven U-boats lost that year.[17] Many of the British maritime patrol bombers were equipped with ASV Mk II radar and, at the beginning of 1942, with the much superior 10cm ASV Mk III sets. New types of air-dropped depth charges had more lethal potential. The radius of air operations over the Atlantic, from bases in Canada, Iceland and the UK, was progressively widening. Nevertheless, the 'Air Gap' – what the German called the 'Black Pit' – would remain in the mid-Atlantic until May 1943.

Considerable controversy surrounds the delay in closing the 'Air Gap'. The British could have been more single-minded. The RAF's Air Staff continued to concentrate the new British-built long-range four-engined bombers in the night attacks against German cities. (The first 'thousand-bomber raid' was mounted on Cologne in late May 1942.) The Prime Minister also preferred giving first priority to these offensive strikes against the Reich, rather than to defensive 'auxiliary' operations in the Battle of the Atlantic. In 1942 Coastal Command had to make do with shorter-range medium bombers and a handful of American-built long-range Liberator bombers provided under Lend-Lease and modified for very long-range (VLR) patrols. The RAF command also hoped to use airborne centimetric radar sets mainly as 'bombing aids' (to permit more accurate night bombing of German cities), rather than to release the equipment for A/S warfare. On the other hand, the best recent study of this question suggests that the most important factors included an underestimation of the potential U-boat danger in the eastern Atlantic, as well as the decision of Coastal Command to use the four-engined aircraft available in the Bay of Biscay, rather than preparing them for longer-range missions in the Central Atlantic.[18]

In any event, this was the technical balance when, in the summer of 1942, Admiral Dönitz and the U-boat staff moved the focus of the U-boat campaign back to the central North Atlantic. Operations on the American eastern seaboard had become less profitable and even riskier, and more U-boats were now available. The first major attack here since December 1941 came in mid-May 1942. It was mounted by wolfpack HECHT ('Pike') against convoy ONS.92, and seven ships were sunk without loss. In another attack in August, SC.94 lost eleven out of thirty-five merchant ships, as a result of an attack by nineteen U-boats (two of which were lost). The German submarines achieved several other significant convoy successes, especially when escorts were thinned out to cover the convoys involved in Operation TORCH (leading up to 8 November 1942) and its aftermath. This culminated with an attack on westbound convoy ON.154 in the mid-Atlantic in December 1942, when thirteen ships out of fifty were sunk, for the loss of one U-boat. But the overall threat to convoys in this area was still far from crisis level. Of fifty-four (eastbound) HX convoys in 1942 (HX.168 to HX.221), comprising 1,806 merchant ships, only *one* merchant ship was lost in the first half of 1942, and eight in the second half. For the fifty-three slower eastbound SC convoys (1,962 merchant ships), only one ship was lost in the first half of the year, and only thirty-nine in the second half.[19]

The long-range Type IX U-boats were also active in more distant waters, where British patrols were weaker, especially off the West African coast. One striking incident was the sinking of the RMS *Laconia* by the *U 156* in September 1942. After his attack the submarine's captain discovered that the big liner had been carrying many Italian prisoners-of-war, as well as civilians. He took life boats in tow and summoned help, but his submarine was then attacked and driven away by an American patrol plane. Following this Admiral Dönitz issued an order stating that 'No attempt of any kind may be made to rescue members of ships sunk . . . Rescue runs counter to the rudimentary demands of warfare for the destruction of enemy ships and crews.'[20] This order would be one of the main items raised against the admiral during the 1946 Nuremberg trial.

This section has treated A/S operations off the US East Coast and those in the mid-Atlantic separately, but of course the U-boats operating in both those sectors came from the same bases (mainly in France). The growing Allied air forces could also be used to attack the shipyards that built the submarines, their bases, and transit routes from the bases to the open oceans. In reality this had only limited effect. RAF Bomber Command directed many of its night raids against submarine-building shipyards. Raids targeted against Bremen, Hamburg, Kiel, Augsburg and elsewhere achieved only minimal success, and although the number of RAF raids increased, there was still an inability to hit such precision targets.[21] Attacks on the forward U-boat bases in France – located at Brest, Lorient, La Rochelle and Bordeaux – were also largely unsuccessful, thanks to the construction of huge bunkers there. Built by the Todt Organisation, these were some of the largest concrete structures of all time, and they protected the submarines and servicing facilities even from direct hits by heavy bombs.[22]

More successful – for a time – was an Allied campaign against U-boats as they crossed the Bay of Biscay, to and from their French west-coast bases. They could be attacked using Coastal Command aircraft based in southern England. The RAF now had experienced crews, and A/S aircraft equipped with effective weapons. Using ASV Mk II radar, and a searchlight ('Leigh Light') for the final approach, they could find and attack the U-boats at night or in overcast conditions. Even if the U-boats were not sunk, the patrolling aircraft slowed their pace transiting the bay, and this reduced their operational range once they reached the open sea. In August 1942, however, the Germans began to equip their U-boats with Metox, a (French-designed) radar detector. Meanwhile during the day British patrol planes were driven off by long-range fighters (the heavy-fighter version of the Ju 88 medium bomber), and by October 1942 the RAF had temporarily abandoned its operations.

A more basic tool for Allied victory in the Atlantic war was the construction of new merchant ships; shipbuilding was introduced in the first section of this chapter. The autumn of 1942 was a wartime turning point not only on the battlefront (El Alamein, Operation TORCH, Stalingrad, Guadalcanal), but also in the shipyards. Britain and her Allies had begun the war with large merchant shipping tonnage, but this had begun to decline. Now there was a distinct change, and in a favourable direction. Production of 'dry' (non-tanker) cargo ships in Allied shipyards on either side of the Atlantic exceeded losses for every month from August 1942 onwards (except for November 1942). By the second half of 1942 the shipyards were turning out about 1 million tons a month. Meanwhile, construction of tankers – vessels crucial for supplying a war of movement – consistently exceeded losses from November 1942 onwards (except for January 1943); production came to about 100,000 tons of tankers a month in the latter half of 1942, rising to 200,000 tons a month in first half of 1943.[23] This was largely due to the American output, the construction pump having been primed in the winter of 1940–41 by British initiatives. Output of merchant ships in the United Kingdom was limited by other shipbuilding programmes, including those for escorts and landing craft. Overall, between 1939 and 1945 production of merchant ships in the UK would be 8.3 million tons (deadweight), an average of 1.5 million tons a year; Canadian wartime production added 3.6 million tons. In contrast, the US produced 50 million tons, four-fifths of the total.[24] Whatever the source, the year 1942 saw such a rapid growth of Allied merchant ship construction that the success of Admiral Dönitz's 'tonnage war' was completely impossible.

There was, however, a problem of the distribution of these newly built ships among the Allies. Merchant shipping under British control decreased from 16.1 million tons (GRT) at the start of 1942 to 14.3 million tons twelve months later. The spring of 1943 would actually mark the low point, after which overall tonnage under British control gradually increased.[25] Before Pearl Harbor the British had been counting on 7 million (deadweight) tons of shipping to be provided by shipyards in the US. However, the unexpected American entry into the war meant that most of this was kept back for American use, especially on the long Pacific supply lines. The civilian War Shipping Administration (WSA), set up in Washington in February 1942, had only limited control of shipping allocation, especially in relation to the large demands of the American armed forces. Because of this, and because of shipping losses and the assignment of vessels to distant theatres and new Allied offensives, London was greatly worried by the end of 1942 about the decline of imports to the UK. Oliver Lyttelton, the British Minister of Production, representing Churchill, met with President Roosevelt in November and secured an informal promise that American shipping would be provided. Fortunately British import requirements turned out to have been overstated.

In global strategic terms the Battle of the Atlantic in 1942 was more than the 'tonnage war' and the safeguarding of supplies to Britain (or Russia). It was also about the use of control of the ocean for decisive Allied military initiatives. The US successfully began the movement of ground and air forces to Britain in the spring and summer of 1942, the main part of which was known as Operation BOLERO. This was accomplished by troopship convoys from New York and Halifax, mostly to the Clyde; the first was AT.10, which left New York on 15 January 1942. These convoys were sometimes very heavily escorted by American destroyers (which might have been better employed protecting shipping on the eastern seaboard). From August 1942 the convoys were supplemented by huge ocean liners like the *Queen Mary*, sailing independently at high speed. The first divisions and air groups were shipped over to support the defence of the United Kingdom and to prepare for Operation ROUNDUP, a cross-Channel landing proposed for early 1943. This early invasion plan was overtaken by other events, but in any case the Germans were not able to interfere with these transatlantic troop movements. No losses were suffered from enemy action.

The most important military initiative was Operation TORCH, the invasion of North Africa on 8 November 1942; the execution of this was outlined in the Introduction to this book. Hundreds of transports, merchant ships and warships were involved. Three American convoys carried invasion troops to Morocco directly from the US; nine British convoys transported American and British troops from the UK to Algeria. 'Follow-on' convoys were at sea as the first landings were taking place.

Although the Atlantic crossing and the landings in North Africa were a great success, they put demands on the overall carrying capacity of the Allied shipping system. These were as high as the depredations of the U-boats, although, of course, the effect was relatively short term; few ships were sunk and few lives lost. In all, the Royal Navy had to provide 125 escort ships, and fifty-two minesweepers for the British convoys. Many of the 'regular' convoys to Russia, Gibraltar and Sierra Leone (en route to the Indian Ocean) were postponed for months; escorts also had to be taken from the Home Fleet and coastal convoys. Complex re-routing of other merchant shipping took place; this was efficiently organised from London, but it meant that shipping followed indirect – and longer – routes. Operation TORCH and follow-on land operations in Algeria and Tunisia coincided with what Allied leaders and many historians have seen as a global shipping 'crisis'. The American historian Kevin Smith in an incisive study of 'convoy diplomacy' argued that TORCH was a 'premature' offensive, but that is true only in a technical logistical sense.[26] An early invasion of North Africa was essential for diplomatic, political and strategic reasons, and it was implemented successfully.

Operation TORCH demonstrated Allied control of the seas, as surface ships, submarines and aircraft of the German and Italian fleets were unable to locate the invading force at sea or to mount effective attacks before they came ashore. Part of the reason for this was that even as late as October 1942 the German Navy did not think that the Allies were strong enough to mount an invasion of North Africa, either in Algeria or Morocco. As for the Allies, although their codebreakers were still shut out of Atlantic U-boat communications at this time, radio direction finding (DF) and access to other German signals provided valuable information for the routing of the convoys.[27] U-boats did spot some of the British ships involved, but they did not connect these sightings to a major expedition. The only submarines in the area west of Morocco and Gibraltar at the end of October and early November were the ten U-boats of wolfpack STREITAXT ('Battle-axe'). These boats, however, were shifted north in pursuit of the last pre-TORCH convoy from Sierra Leone, SL.125. Some twelve merchant ships in the convoy were sunk, but the heavily escorted invasion convoys now passed safely through the danger zone the wolfpack had left. Only one ship was successfully attacked on the approach voyage, the C3 attack transport USS *Thomas Stone*, which was torpedoed in the Mediterranean en route to Algiers on the morning of 7 November. The troops on board were forced to take to their landing craft, but fortunately the loss of life was low.

Alerted by the initial landings, the Germans rallied their submarines to deal with the follow-on and supply convoys for TORCH. But even then they could achieve only limited success and this did not affect the outcome of the operation as a whole. On 11–12 November four American troopships at anchor near Casablanca were sunk by U-boats, but they had already unloaded the forces on board; two big British troopships were torpedoed and sunk on the voyage home. A few days later the escort carrier HMS *Avenger* was sent to the bottom by a U-boat west of Gibraltar. But only one TORCH supply convoy was really badly mauled, and even that occurred in the new year, two months after the initial landings. This was TMF.1 from Trinidad in the Caribbean, sailing with a British escort; seven out of nine oil tankers were lost to wolfpack DELFIN ('Dolphin') south of the Azores in early January 1943. Aside from these incidents the Allies had demonstrated their substantial control of the Atlantic, and the seizure of French North Africa now made that control all the greater.

THE RUSSIAN CONVOYS

Another way the year 1942 differed from most of 1941 was the importance of the Eastern Front. Shipping of war supplies to the USSR had become a major part of British–American global strategy, as the Red Army was for the moment taking the brunt of the Wehrmacht's assaults. The shortest route was from transit ports in Britain or Iceland, around the northern tip of Norway, to Murmansk and Arkhangelsk. The polar route was relatively short, at 1,500 miles (at 12 knots, a voyage of about five days), less than the distance from Alexandria to Malta. But it ran through the Norwegian Sea and the Barents Sea, and could be as much as 300 miles north of the Arctic Circle. The storms of winter were severe, and there was great seasonal variation. The successful defence of convoy JW.51B – the Battle of the Barents Sea – would be carried out in the near total darkness of December. The destruction of convoy PQ.17 took place in the endless daylight of early July, with no darkness to provide cover from patrol planes or bombers.

Norway was now important for another reason. Hitler feared a major British landing operation in this exposed region, an apprehension increased by British Commando raids in May and December 1941,[28] and by Allied disinformation. The outbreak of war with Russia in June 1941 gave Norway a new significance. Even in the autumn of 1941 U-boats and surface ships were sent north to protect the long exposed coastline. In December of 1941, with the Battle of Moscow, it became clear that Germany's war with the USSR – despite original expectations – might be a prolonged and demanding one. As a result the continued control of Norway and the interdiction of Allied supply lines to Russia became high-priority objectives for the German armed forces.

Convoys to northern Russia were within range of mass attacks by Luftwaffe twin-engined bombers, even if the ships were routed as far north as possible, near the pack ice. In those seas, too, the Germans could deploy their largest surface warships – battleships, cruisers and most of their destroyers. These surface warships, and a sizeable U-boat force, could operate from secure bases in northern Norway, beyond the effective range of Allied bombers.

The battleship *Tirpitz* was the most famous unit of Hitler's Norwegian fleet; after working up she left German waters in February 1942, never to return. She was the sister ship of the *Bismarck*; the two vessels were the only full-size battleships built for the Kriegsmarine. The *Tirpitz* had a reputation as a 'super-battleship' or 'floating fortress', and the British would devote an extraordinary effort over three years to trying to sink her, including the use of midget submarines, carrier air strikes and RAF heavy bombers.

The big ship's power can be exaggerated. The 'Bismarck' classships displaced considerably more than their declared 35,000 tons, and they were well armoured. However, the main battery of eight 15-inch guns was weaker than that of most of the other battleships designed in the 1930s. In addition, the Kriegsmarine faced a serious risk in moving their big ships up and down the Norwegian coast, and even in the far north there was the danger of attacks from carrier aircraft and submarines. The transit route along the coast of southwestern Norway was within range of British air bases in Scotland, and Allied submarines were stationed off the major Norwegian bases. The *Lützow* had been ambushed by RAF torpedo bombers in July 1941, and the *Prinz Eugen* was torpedoed by a submarine off Trondheim in February 1942; both heavy cruisers had to return home for long repairs. In March 1942 Albacore torpedo bombers from the carrier *Victorious* caught the *Tirpitz* off Narvik, after she had sortied from Trondheim to attack a convoy; the big ship was lucky to escape without damage.

The Royal Navy began to run 'PQ' convoys to northern Russia three months after the original invasion of the country, when local German sea/air forces were still weak. During the autumn and winter the long Arctic night provided cover.[29] Until the end of March 1942 only one merchant ship had been sunk, out of 110 despatched. PQ.13, 14 and 15 in March and April 1942 sailed with the loss of only a few merchant ships. The cost to the Royal Navy was greater. The new cruiser *Trinidad* was damaged in a skirmish with German destroyers in March 1942 while covering PQ.13; she was lost in May, on her way home from Murmansk. The *Edinburgh* (sister of the *Belfast*) was mortally damaged in April by two U-boat torpedoes and then scuttled; she had been escorting the homeward-bound QP.11 convoy.[30] PQ.16 in late May 1942 was subjected to heavy Luftwaffe attacks, losing six out of thirty-six merchant ships; a seventh vessel was sunk by a U-boat.

The next attack would be made on PQ.17, in July 1942. Morison would describe this as the 'grimmest convoy battle of the entire war' [31]; it would also arouse bitter controversy. The German naval plan was code-named Operation RÖSSELSPRUNG (KNIGHT'S MOVE). Heavy ships were to move to forward bases as soon as the convoy had been located by a U-boat patrol line northeast of Iceland. The *Tirpitz*, the heavy cruiser *Hipper*, and six destroyers would sail north from Trondheim to the Altafjord at the northern tip of Norway. The heavy cruisers ('pocket battleships') *Lützow* and *Scheer*, with six destroyers, already stationed at Narvik, would join them. The *Tirpitz* and the *Hipper* would fight any escort force, while the *Lützow* and *Scheer* would 'roll up' the convoy. On 15 June 1942 Admiral Raeder put the plan to Hitler, who approved it as long as all enemy carriers had been neutralised. He did not want another surprise like the sinking of the *Bismarck* or the March 1942 air attacks on the *Tirpitz*; this was also a week after the Battle of Midway. The move up to the Altafjord was approved, but the ships were not to move from beyond there without Hitler's permission. Meanwhile the Luftwaffe prepared mass attacks, mainly by the anti-shipping specialists of KG 26 and KG 30.

PQ.17 included thirty-six cargo-carrying merchant ships. Of these, twenty-one were American, ten British and two Soviet. The Russian Northern Fleet was weak,[32] and with other global commitments – notably convoys to Malta and operations in the Indian Ocean – the British had only limited naval strength to spare. The Royal Navy took the main responsibility for the Arctic convoys, but in the summer of 1942 the new American battleship *Washington* and the heavy cruisers *Wichita* and *Tuscaloosa* operated with Admiral Tovey's Home Fleet. (This part of 1942, along with the invasion of North Africa, was the only time during the entire war that modern US capital ships would operate in European waters.) Admiral Tovey had at his disposal, as well as the *Washington*, the fast battleship *Duke of York* – the Home Fleet flagship – and the aircraft carrier *Victorious*.[33] The heavy ships, however, all stood off well to the west of Bear Island at the entrance to the Barents Sea. A squadron of four heavy cruisers – the *Wichita* and the *Tuscaloosa* and the British *Norfolk* and *London* – shepherded the convoy from a distance. Even they were not intended to proceed east of Bear Island. The all-British close escort consisted of six destroyers, four corvettes and some smaller ships, under Commander John Broome.

The merchant ships departed Reykjavik on 27 June 1942.They suffered their first air attack on the sixth day out, but without loss. Two days after that, on Saturday, 4 July, strong air attacks began, co-ordinated with submarines. Two merchant ships were sunk, and one was mortally damaged.

As the convoy entered the zone of greatest danger, codebreaking played an important part in events. Although from February 1942 the Atlantic U-boat Enigma could not be read, there was still good access to the German messages to and from Norway regarding naval and air strengths, movements and intentions. Swedish intelligence also provided intercepted and (independently) decrypted German teleprinter messages transmitted on landlines passing through their territory.

Implementing RÖSSELSPRUNG, the German Naval War Staff had indeed ordered its big ships north from Trondheim (the *Tirpitz* and the *Hipper*) and Narvik (the *Lützow* and the *Scheer*). Admiral Otto Schniewind, the Flottenchef, now commanded the biggest surface force the Third Reich would ever assemble. The ships left Trondheim and Narvik on 2 and 3 July and reached the Altafjord by the morning of 4 July.[34] They would be unleashed against the convoy – once the reconnaissance situation was clear and Hitler was satisfied that the risk level was acceptable.

On Saturday evening (4 July) the Admiralty learned from decrypts that the battle group had been assembled at the Altafjord earlier in the day. There seemed a strong possibility that, its escort destroyers having refuelled (this could have been as early as midday), this force had already set out to intercept PQ.17.

Admiral Pound calculated that this attack could come at any time after the early hours of 5 July (Sunday). What the British did now know about were the operational limitations imposed from above on Admiral Schniewind; having reached the Altafjord his ships then did nothing for twenty-four hours. In the middle of the Saturday evening the Admiralty transmitted signals, which suggested an immediate threat by surface ships to the convoy. At about 9.00 p.m. Admiral Pound ordered the cruiser escort to withdraw to the west, and about half an hour later, at 9.23, came the fatal orders: 'Immediate. Owing to threat from surface ships, convoy is to disperse and proceed to Russian ports.' Thirteen minutes later came a second bald signal, referring to the first: 'Most immediate. [With reference] My 2123/4 [4 July] Convoy is to scatter.'[35] The ships were still 600 miles – two days' steaming – away from the safety of Russian ports.

Disaster followed the false alarm. Broome's six destroyers followed the cruisers, assuming that they would be required to support them in an imminent surface engagement with German heavy ships. Only the corvettes and smaller escorts remained. The merchant ships fanned out at about 10.15 p.m., still daylight at this northern latitude. On Sunday and Monday (5–6 July), sailing independently or in small groups, they were picked off, first of all by the U-boats and then by the bombers. In the end only eleven merchant vessels made it into Russian ports. Altogether PQ.17 suffered extremely heavy damage, losing twenty-four out of thirty-six merchant ships. Eight were sunk by U-boats, eight by the Luftwaffe, and eight were damaged by aircraft and finished off by submarines. Only five German bombers were lost. Matériel lost to the Soviets was great, including 3,350 motor vehicles and 430 tanks. The human cost to the Allies of the 'convoy to hell' was actually surprisingly low – some 153 merchant seamen.[36] Hitler finally gave permission for the heavy-ship sortie to proceed on Sunday morning (5 July). Admiral Schniewind's battle group headed east from the exit to the Altafjord to intercept the convoy, still some 400 miles away. Operation RÖSSELSPRUNG was, however, called off that evening, when it became clear that the Allied merchantmen could be destroyed without risking the precious heavy ships. (The Russians claimed that their submarine *K-21* damaged the *Tirpitz* with a torpedo that Sunday, but this was not the case.)

There was considerable controversy about who was responsible for the destruction of PQ.17. Admiral Tovey, in his despatch (published in October 1950), was sharply critical of the directions he received from the Admiralty. This was a judgement which Roskill supported in his official history of the sea war, published in 1956, thirteen years after Admiral Pound's death (in 1943). On Saturday evening Pound had decided to ignore the (correct) judgement of his intelligence staff – and of apparently most of his senior colleagues – that the *Tirpitz* battle group was probably still in port at the Altafjord. Pound's decision certainly proved, with hindsight, to be incorrect, but he had to make it based on the actual information which he possessed. He could not have left the decision to Tovey in the Home Fleet, as London had access to better intelligence and analysis. The controversial young historian David Irving suggested in his 1968 book *The Destruction of PQ.17* that the cause of the disaster was the decision by 'Jacky' Broome to withdraw his close escort destroyers. In a much-publicised lawsuit, refuting the claim, Broome won £40,000 – then a very considerable sum – from Irving and his publishers. Two important historians of the battle, Harry Hinsley and Werner Rahn, later argued that PQ.17 would have had to scatter in any event, once it was learned on 5 July that the German heavy ships had sortied.[37]

In early September 1942 PQ.18 departed for Loch Ewe. Autumn had come, and the convoy had at least eight hours of darkness out of every twenty-four. Admiral Tovey did not go to sea with the Home Fleet covering force, but kept his direct landline communications with the Admiralty. The big gun support – battleships *Duke of York* and the new *Anson* – was still kept west of Bear Island. The convoy, however, had an even larger close escort of fleet destroyers, whose torpedoes would hopefully deter the German heavy ships. More important, an (American-built) escort carrier, the aptly named HMS *Avenger*, stayed with the convoy. RAF strength had been built up at Murmansk; two dozen RAF Handley Page Hampden torpedo bombers had been sent there, and RAF Catalina flying boats helped keep the U-boats submerged. Hitler did not release the heavy ships to attack the convoy. The attacking bombers suffered considerable losses from Sea Hurricane carrier fighters and AA fire, and forty-one German aircraft failed to return to base. The convoy proceeded together all the way to Arkhangelsk.

Still, from the British point of view, PQ.18 indicated that the Arctic convoys were unsustainable. Of its forty-four merchant ships, eight were sunk by aircraft and three by U-boats. Churchill wrote to President Roosevelt concerning his opposition to further convoys (after January 1943), run 'under the present conditions of danger, waste and effort'. He observed that 'we used 77 warships for PQ.18 and think ourselves fortunate to have lost no more than one-third of the merchant ships'.[38] The original Allied intention had been to run monthly convoys to northern Russia. German counter-measures – and the demands of other theatres – had effectively shut down the Arctic convoy route.[39] The German Navy and the Luftwaffe had won a strategic victory which justified Hitler's decision to move his surface fleet to Norway from the eastern Atlantic. The most direct supply route to Russia would be greatly restricted, not only in the second half of 1942, but also for most of 1943.

The Arctic convoys were just one sea route to Russia. Total Lend-Lease deliveries from North America to Russia in 1942 were nearly 2.5 million tons. Of these only 950,000 tons went through northern Russia. There were two other routes, and now they became increasingly important.[40]

In August 1941 British and Soviet forces had jointly occupied neutral Persia (Iran) to eliminate German influence, and to establish a supply link. The problems with this route were the long voyage around Africa (until the opening of the Mediterranean in the autumn of 1943), inadequate port and transit facilities in Iran, and the distance from the Iranian border to the Soviet battle front. Major steps would be made to improve the transport infrastructure in 1943.

Sporadic use of the Siberian port of Vladivostok had begun after the June 1941 invasion, with ships sailing from the US West Coast. The outbreak of the Pacific war did not close this supply route, as the Japanese military were loath to open another war front. For these sailings the Americans initially transferred about thirty older merchant ships on the West Coast to the Soviet flag in the winter of 1942–43. The Pacific supply route took unescorted merchant ships through the Aleutian Islands, and across the Bering Sea to the Kamchatka Peninsula, where Petropavlovsk provided a fine ice-free harbour. For the final jump to Vladivostok, some cargoes went south on either side of Sakhalin, through the Strait of Tartary or the La Pérouse Strait (between southern Sakhalin and Hokkaidō.) By 1943 this little-known Pacific route would make up about half the Lend-Lease shipments to Russia (by tonnage).[41]

CHAPTER 13

BRITAIN AND THE BEGINNINGS OF AMPHIBIOUS OPERATIONS IN EUROPE

March 1941–December 1942

THE LOFOTEN RAID, 4 MARCH 1941

The Lofotens are an archipelago of ruggedly beautiful islands jutting out into the Atlantic from northern Norway. They run along the north side of the long Vestfjord. Narvik, at the far end of the Vestfjord, lies some 100 miles to the east.

Operation CLAYMORE (named after the Scottish broadsword) had been conceived in January 1941, and hastily planned. Before dawn on 4 March a British raiding force made its way into the Vestfjord. It had set out three days earlier from Scapa Flow and refuelled in the Faroes. The most important element were two sleek single-funnelled vessels. HMS *Queen Emma* and HMS *Princess Beatrix* were the very first Allied 'landing ships, infantry' (LSIs) or 'attack transports'. Now sailing under the white ensign, they had been built in the Netherlands just before the war as North Sea ferries. Sister ships some 380 feet long, with a tonnage of 4,136 tons (GRT) and a top speed of nearly 25 knots, they were now a long way from the Flushing–Harwich passenger route for which they had been designed, having made their way to Britain after the German invasion in May 1940. Each vessel was now modified with large sets of davits to lower eight landing craft, and could carry a 'Commando' of 250 British Army special forces, as well as demolition teams and Norwegian volunteers. A flotilla of six destroyers, mostly of the heavily gunned 'Tribal' class, formed the escort. Two cruisers provided distant support, and two of Admiral Tovey's Home Fleet battleships steamed 200 miles to the west, far beyond the horizon.

Weather conditions were unexpectedly good for early March. Low clouds protected the ships from any German scout planes as they sailed towards the Norwegian coast. On the morning of the 4th the temperature was well below freezing, but the day was fine and clear with brilliant sunshine. The sea was calm.

The *Queen Emma* landed No. 4 Commando in two fishing villages in the eastern part of the Lofotens, the more important of which was Svolvær. Some twenty miles further to the west, the *Princess Beatrix* landed No. 3 Commando in two other fishing villages. The supposed object of Operation CLAYMORE was to destroy the fish oil production facilities of which the Lofotens were a centre. The naval despatch described the situation in the middle of the morning: 'dense columns of heavy black smoke could be seen at Ports "X" [Svolvær] and "A" [Stamsund] rising to the tops of the surrounding mountains, a height of several thousand feet, sure evidence of the thoroughness with which the landing parties were carrying out their tasks of destruction'.[1] The Commandos also sank the large (6,132-ton) German factory ship SS *Hamburg* and a number of small enemy merchant ships.

The raid was unopposed. There were only a handful of military personnel in the port (twenty-five men were captured) but nearly 200 German merchant seamen. A Luftwaffe plane would shadow the force as it withdrew, but no air attack took place. The Commandos were ashore for only six hours, and they had all departed by 12.30 p.m., with no losses. The local population filled the snow-covered streets, and several hundred Norwegians elected to leave with the raiders.

Much was made of the Lofoten raid, both in contemporary British propaganda and by later historians. 'Henceforth,' Stephen Roskill concluded, 'no enemy coastal garrison could feel secure from surprise'.[2] It was no more than a pinprick but it certainly boosted British morale in a war against Germany that was not going well. Civilian cameramen had been taken along, and their newsreels would depict blindfolded prisoners and 'quislings', and the crowd of Norwegians who elected to depart with the raiders. As the Prime Minister put it to Admiral Tovey: 'this has given an immense amount of innocent pleasure at home'.[3] Substantial economic damage was indeed caused, and with no collateral physical harm to the Norwegian population. A quite different result, which only became known much later, was that the raid provided important intelligence. The armed whaler *Krebs*, one of the Kriegsmarine vessels stationed at the approaches to Narvik, had the misfortune to run into the destroyer *Somali* as the raid began. The little ship's captain and most of his crew were killed in the exchange of fire. The Germans had thrown their Enigma code machine over the side, but a boarding party captured vital documents that enabled the code-breakers at Bletchley Park to decrypt enemy naval signals in April and May, and guided their further breakthroughs.[4]

The Lofoten raid stoked Hitler's fear of an attack on Norway and warped his strategy, although this was not the intention of the CLAYMORE planners. In any event Hitler's fears would be stoked by another Commando raid on Vågsøy

(Vaagso) – not far from the Lofotens – in late December 1941. Most important, the Lofoten raid was the real beginning of 'combined operations'. The efficiency of close co-operation between the British Army and the Royal Navy had been demonstrated, along with some core elements of the Allied amphibious technology.

BRITISH RAIDING STRATEGY

Mighty oaks from little acorns grow. The victory of Britain and America in World War II, in both Europe and the Pacific, was achieved through mastery of amphibious or 'combined' operations, which grew to huge dimensions in the years after the Lofoten raid. The most important was the Normandy invasion of 6 June 1944. The American term 'amphibious' is generally used in this book rather than the British term 'combined',[5] as the subject is specifically about landings from the sea. Nevertheless, a key feature of these operations was that they did involve 'combined' naval, army and – usually – air force elements; these elements were physically and organisationally (and culturally) quite different from one another.

Amphibious operations did not seem a very likely form of future war in 1939. The Gallipoli invasion of 1915 had shown the many practical difficulties even of a medium-sized operation of this kind. Furthermore, at least in northern Europe, there seemed no scenario in which any of the powers would carry out a large-scale landing from the sea. And yet, in reality, Allied amphibious warfare did develop in the World War II period, and it did so along a number of paths: British compared to American, small-scale compared to mass-scale, navy-based compared to army-based. It is fair to say, however, that its most important point of origin was the British raids of 1940–41 against the coast of enemy-occupied Europe.

In the aftermath of Dunkirk and the surrender of France the British faced a strategic crisis. Churchill, the new Prime Minister, still favoured offensive action, not least to convince the Americans that Britain was alliance-worthy and not defeatist. Much of Europe had been subjected to occupation by the Wehrmacht, and this was believed to present fertile ground for rebellion, or at least development of an active underground. Meanwhile the Third Reich now had a very large coast to protect. To take advantage of this, new organisations were set up in London, outside the normal armed forces structure. Their task was to foment insurrection and sabotage in German-occupied territory and to carry out raiding operations on the coastline of occupied Europe. The first task was delegated to the – later famous – Special Operations Executive (SOE), formally set up on 22 July 1940. Meanwhile, a centre to develop landing operations was created in June; this became known as the Combined Operations Headquarters

(COHQ).[6] On 17 July, Admiral of the Fleet Roger Keyes, a very senior (retired) naval officer, was appointed as Director of Combined Operations. The sixty-seven-year-old admiral enjoyed Churchill's personal support and was evidently felt to have sufficient rank and prestige (and ambition) to deal with the three existing service chiefs of the Army, the Navy and the RAF.

Keyes had been chief of staff to the naval commander of the Dardanelles operation in 1915 and leader of the Zeebrugge raid in April 1918.[7] In 1940–41, he and his team formed elite assault units, developed a combined operations training establishment in Scotland, and promoted the development of specialised equipment. In operational terms, however, little was achieved. In particular, a plan to seize the strategic island of Pantelleria, south of Sicily, fell through. There was friction between Keyes and the conventional service chiefs – notably Admiral Pound. In October 1941 Keyes resigned over whether he held a command role or an advisory one. He was replaced by Lord Louis Mountbatten, another favourite of Churchill, but quite a different individual. 'Dickie' Mountbatten was a forty-year-old naval captain, who had previously commanded only a destroyer. A tall, imposing figure, Mountbatten was ambitious and extremely well connected; he was also a war hero as a result of his exploits as a destroyer captain in 1940–41.[8]

Whatever the shortcomings of Roger Keyes, COHQ under his tenure did develop 'special' forces capable of carrying out daring, small-scale attacks; Mountbatten was able to build on this. Originally elements of a Special Service Brigade set up within the British Army in June 1940, these battalions were informally known as Commandos (after Boer guerrilla bands), and the term became official in early 1941.

As important as the creation of doctrine and special units was the development and deployment by the British of naval vessels for amphibious landings. German preparation for an invasion in the opposite direction (Operation SEA LION) had been on a much tighter schedule – as a result of Hitler's continental objectives – and with little attempt at a genuine 'combined operation'. Preparations had been, of necessity, highly improvised, involving long columns of barges and tugboats, manned by mobilised civilians (see pp. 57–9). The British, in contrast, had more time and more patience.

Because, before 1940, amphibious operations were not expected to be a major type of operation in future war, there had been little material preparation. In Britain activity had been confined to building a handful of prototype landing-craft, and drafting some doctrinal statements. The Inter-Service Training and Development Centre (ISTDC) was set up in the late 1930s, partly inspired by Japanese developments in the war with China. The British did design a prototype assault landing craft just before the European war began. This was a wooden barge about 40 feet long and intended to be lowered and raised from the davits of a larger sea-going mother ship. Flat-bottomed and with a shallow draught, the craft was designed to be landed on an enemy-held beach, where the troops could rapidly disembark through a bow door. These craft were invaluable for the British raiding strategy of 1940–42, but no one can have imagined in 1939 that nearly 2,000 of these British 'landing craft, assault', or LCAs, would eventually be built.

In the US the Marine Corps had their own tradition of amphibious war. They developed a plywood craft similar to the LCA, partly on the initiative of the New Orleans industrialist Andrew Higgins. One version, the 'landing craft, personnel (large)' or LCP(L), was supplied to the British before Pearl Harbor, again with the raiding strategy in mind. In 1941 Higgins developed an improved type, which could carry more personnel and cargo than a British LCA, and in addition was fitted with a large bow door to discharge attacking troops and even a small vehicle such as a jeep. By early 1942 this vessel was designated as the dual-purpose 'landing craft, vehicle, personnel' or LCVP. (In the end some 20,000 LCVPs would enter service; they were by far the most numerous landing craft used in the war.)

The British, actually fighting a war and preparing for coastal raids, were inevitably moving faster than the armed forces of the neutral United States. Basic landing craft were developed and procured in quantity. The Royal Navy was also well ahead in the development of carrier ships for landing craft; the first were the *Princess Beatrix* and the *Queen Emma*, which carried the Lofoten raiders. This type of vessel was originally called an 'assault ship', but it was eventually re-designated as the 'landing ship, infantry', or LSI. In the course of 1940–41 much larger versions of the LSIs in the 10,000-ton range appeared, notably some converted cargo liners of the peacetime Glen Line. HMS *Glengyle*, for example, was converted to carry a battalion of troops and twelve LCAs, as well as some LCMs (landing craft, mechanised) capable of carrying vehicles.

The US Navy, after a belated start, eventually built a very large number of comparable vessels, which they called attack transports (APAs). These were usually large vessels, initially converted from large fast freighters or liners and later purpose-built. They could carry over twenty LCVPs in their davits. In the course of the war the availability of these 'combat loaders' would be a crucial means of projecting Allied power and a key determinant of Allied strategy.

Another important vessel for landing infantry was developed by the British and Americans in early 1942, at the urging of Mountbatten, now an admiral. This was originally specified as a small beachable 'raiding' ship, but became the 'landing craft, infantry' (LCI). It was a steel-hulled sea-going vessel but was capable of carrying about 180 troops – a company – and unloading them directly onto the beach. The first example, *LCI(L)-1*, was laid down in Camden, New Jersey, in July 1942 and commissioned three months later. The LCI was, at 158 feet, about half the length of that other mainstay of the Allied amphibious fleet (from mid war) – the tank-carrying LST ('landing ship, tank'). The LCI had a quarter of the crew and a fifth of the displacement of the LST. The LCIs were all built in the US; too big to be piggybacked on another ship, they made the daring crossing of the Atlantic in small groups, under their own power; the first group sailed in November 1942.[9]

Vessels intended to land personnel were essential. After the Blitzkrieg of May 1940, however, it became clear that modern large-scale warfare – even large raids – required the extensive use of tanks, trucks and other large vehicles. The British had developed the prototype of a landing craft capable of carrying a motor vehicle in the 1920s, and this was available in very small numbers in the 1930s. By 1940 a new steel version was on hand, as the 'landing craft, mechanised' Mk I or LCM(1). This was bigger than the (infantry-carrying) LCA, but it would still fit on the davits of a carrier ship, or could be placed on deck. The LCM had room for one small (16-ton) tank, which was lowered into it from the mother ship by a crane.[10]

The size of tanks and other vehicles increased, and more ambitious raids and other amphibious operations were planned. Accordingly, a larger 'landing craft, tank' (LCT) was developed in 1940 at Churchill's insistence. This vessel could carry three heavier (36-ton) tanks (or six smaller ones) or other vehicles, and land them onto an open beach through its bow door. With a length of 152 feet, the original LCT was a steel vessel much larger than an LCM or an LCA, and far too big to be carried in the davits of a mother ship or lowered from the deck by a crane. The LCT was to some extent 'sea-going'; it could operate in the Channel or the Mediterranean, but it could not safely cross the Atlantic.

The LCT could be used to land tanks, vehicles, stores and personnel which had been lowered into it by crane from a deep-draught transport ship; it was first used in the Mediterranean in the summer of 1941. The British and Americans also worked together in the winter of 1941–42 on an improved version. The resulting 117-foot Mk 5, or LCT(5), was smaller than the British original but was built in American factories in much larger numbers; the first was delivered in June 1942. As the Allies moved from raids to full-scale invasions – from 1943 – the LCT in its various versions would turn out to be an excellent vessel for transporting supplies and vehicles of all kinds onto any captured beach, in the absence of well-equipped or undamaged ports. It was an essential component of the shore-to-shore operations campaigns both in the Mediterranean and (by the US Navy and the US Army) in the South Pacific.

During the second half of 1941 the British devised a new type of ship which became the all-important LST. The vessel was conceived as an 'Atlantic' version of the LCT, able to transport a large number of tanks and vehicles long distances and land them onto a shallow beach. The first three examples were rebuilt from 380-foot tankers designed to operate in the shallow waters of Lake Maracaibo in Venezuela; they were commissioned in August 1941. HMS *Baquachero* took part in the invasion of Madagascar in May 1942 and all three demonstrated their worth in Algeria during Operation TORCH in November; they could each be loaded with twenty tanks. The British began construction of purpose-built vessels designated as LST(1)s. These could carry eighteen tanks, and sail at 18 knots, but the design was expensive and over-complicated. Only three were built, and construction progressed very slowly; the first, HMS *Boxer*, was ordered in March 1941 and commissioned only two years later.

When the British proposed construction of the LSTs in the United States, the American designers came back with a simpler, smaller and slower (12-knot) vessel. The Mk 2, or LST(2), was born, and despite an initial lack of interest by the US Navy it would become the single most important amphibious vessel of the war.[11] It could be built by inland metal-fabricating firms not experienced in shipbuilding. The *LST-1* was built well inland, at Pittsburgh; construction began in July 1942 and she was commissioned into the US Navy five months later. A slab-sided vessel, the LST was 328 feet long – about the length of a destroyer – and displaced 1,625 tons empty (4,800 GRT). The crew numbered about 100 officers and men. For propulsion it had two locomotive type General Motors (GM) diesels. Over 1,000 LSTs would be built. As well as their tank-landing role, the LSTs were exceptionally important as general-purpose vessels capable of bringing in supplies to newly occupied areas before working ports were available; this would be vital at Normandy in June and July 1944. LSTs were also used to piggyback LCTs across the Atlantic, from American shipyards and factories to Allied bases in the Mediterranean or the UK.

The final general element to be mentioned – developed before and during 1942 but in large-scale active service only later – were small amphibious vehicles. Unlike most of the inventory of equipment used for landing operations, they were inspired by the Americans rather than the British. The DUKW amphibious truck, intended for the US Army, was based on the standard GM six-wheel truck, but given an unarmoured boat hull and an auxiliary propeller drive.[12] The 'landing vehicle, tracked', or LVT, was a tracked personnel carrier originally intended for the US Marine Corps and first used on Guadalcanal for bringing in supplies; later versions were armoured for use as assault vehicles, and some were fitted with a tank turret.

This inventory of amphibious equipment is not simply a technical matter. Vessels for amphibious warfare made up a large proportion of the total Allied naval construction effort during the war years. For the UK, vessels for amphibious operations amounted to 26 per cent of naval construction; for the US the figure was 36 per cent.[13] These vessels – the deep-draught attack transports, the sea-going LSTs, LCIs and LCTs, and the ship-to-shore craft – were critical for successful landing operations. The first contested landings, in 1942, up to and including Guadalcanal–Tulagi in August, and Morocco–Algeria (TORCH) in November, mainly used the basic landing craft, and neither involved overcoming heavy beach defences. The whole range of vessels began to enter service in the summer and autumn of 1943 and they would be a decisive element for Allied victory in both Europe and the Pacific.[14]

This wealth of matériel was, to be sure, not available when the raiding strategy began to unfold at the Lofoten Islands in 1941. Another raid, in company strength, was mounted across the Channel by parachute troops rather than Commandos; this was against Bruneval, north of Le Havre, in late February 1942, and a new German radar set was captured. The raiding party was dropped on the objective from the air, but extracted from shore by Royal Navy LCA landing craft.

In late March 1942 a much more dramatic Commando raid (Operation CHARIOT) was directed against the port of Saint-Nazaire at the mouth of the Loire. Mountbatten was by now in charge of COHQ. The objective was the big dry dock designed for the liner *Normandie*; this dock, it was feared, might be used by the new battleship *Tirpitz*. The approach of the Commandos involved a 400-mile crossing from Falmouth in Cornwall by a force of three destroyers and numerous motor launches; it achieved surprise. One of the destroyers, HMS *Campbeltown*, a four-stacker transferred from the US Navy in 1940, was loaded with explosives and rammed into the gates of the dock. Landing parties destroyed port installations. More than 600 Commandos (from No. 2 Commando) and seamen took part; some 170 were killed and 215 captured, including most of the Commandos.[15] Five participants won the Victoria Cross. With hindsight the raid was unnecessary, as the *Tirpitz* was to spend its war in Norway, but that was not known at the time. The raiders did succeed in damaging an important objective heavily defended by the Germans; one result was the transfer of Admiral Dönitz and his U-boat command centre from Kernével in the exposed port of Lorient (65 miles north of Saint-Nazaire) to the safety of inland Paris.

Operation IRONCLAD, the little-remembered British amphibious operation against Vichy French Madagascar, now suddenly a place of strategic importance with the Japanese advance into the Indian Ocean, came in May 1942. An invasion rather than a raid, it was an important testing ground for amphibious techniques. In early March 1942 the British government approved a plan to take the excellent natural harbour at Diego Suarez (now Antsiranana), at the very northern end of the big island.

31. **The Cruiser *Mauritius* Escorts the Liner *Queen Mary*, August 1942**

The British Empire had many ocean-going passenger vessels available for troop movement. The most important were a dozen high-speed liners which the shipping planners called the 'monsters'. RMS *Queen Mary* visible on the horizon here, was one of the two largest. Some 965 feet long, she displaced 81,000 tons, and could carry as many as 15,000 troops. With a speed of 28 knots she was almost impossible for U-boats to intercept.

32. **Russian Convoy: PQ.18, 13–18 September 1942**

HMS *Eskimo* steams past in the foreground, and an underwater explosion raises spray near another destroyer, HMS *Ashanti*. This convoy was better protected from attack by German aircraft and U-boats than PQ.17 in July, but 11 merchant ships out 44 were lost, and a large escort was required. Frequent convoys to North Russia were abandoned until 1944, except in the winter months, when the arctic darkness provided protection.

33. **Guadalcanal: The Loss of USS *Wasp*, 15 September 1942**

American warships escorting a troop convoy to Guadalcanal were attacked by the submarine *I-19*. The fleet carrier *Wasp* burns in the background, while another torpedo hits one of her escorts, the destroyer *O'Brien*. The *Wasp* sank the same day, and the *O'Brien* went down while under tow to the US a month later.

34. **The Battle of Santa Cruz, 26 October 1942**

The carrier *Enterprise* under air attack, beneath dark clouds of exploding A/A shells. Visible on the horizon (right) are a destroyer and the new battleship *South Dakota*. The Japanese had lost four carriers at Midway but five months later they had assembled another force. The October battle would be the last time the Japanese fleet engaged the US Navy on equal or better terms. They lost more aircraft, but the Americans lost the carrier *Hornet*.

35. **Beachhead: French North Africa, 8 November 1942**

Allied forces on one of the three beaches near Algiers. Transport ships of the British-led Eastern Task Force stand offshore. Although Operation TORCH marked a vital turning point and was carried out on a very large scale, there was still little specialised amphibious shipping available. The troops who came ashore were mostly American, but naval forces in the Mediterranean were still mainly British.

36. **Admiral Darlan with Allied leaders in Algiers, 13 December 1942**

Darlan (far left) headed the French Navy in 1939. After the 1940 surrender he took a prominent role in the Vichy government. When the Allies invaded, Darlan was in Algiers; he agreed to cooperate with them. This photograph shows him at an Allied ceremony; to his left are Eisenhower Cunningham and General Henri Giraud. The 'Darlan deal' ensured a rapid Allied victory, but the admiral was a political embarrassment. He was assassinated two weeks later.

37. **Russian Convoy: The Battle of the Barents Sea, 31 December 1942**

Captain Robert Sherbrooke, aboard the HMS *Onslow*, led a flotilla of six destroyers which defended convoy JW.15B in a four-hour battle with two enemy heavy cruisers and six destroyers. JW.15B reached Murmansk without loss. This photograph shows the Onslow returning to Scapa Flow. The action coincided with the Stalingrad crisis; Hitler, in a rage at his navy's failure, ordered the big ships to be withdrawn from service and the removal of Admiral Raeder.

38. **Admiral Karl Dönitz and Albert Speer**

Dönitz (right) replaced Erich Raeder as C-in-C of the German Navy in January 1943. He is shown here with Albert Speer, Reichsminister for Armaments, who supported the programme to mass produce high-speed Type XXII submarines. Dönitz was fifteen years younger than Raeder; after Hitler's suicide he briefly replaced him as head of state.

39. **Escort Carrier: HMS *Biter***

Commissioned in May 1942, the HMS *Biter* operated off Oran during Operation TORCH. Here a lend-lease Grumman Martlet fighter and a Swordfish are 'spotted' forward on the flight deck. Most escort carriers were built in the US on new cargo ship hulls; the *Biter* had been converted from a C3 merchant ship. Capable of only 16–18 knots and vulnerable to enemy attack, the small carriers nevertheless had a vital role escorting convoys and supporting landings.

40. **Escort Carrier Aircraft Attack a U-boat, 12 June 1943**

The *U 118* under attack west of the Canaries by Grumman TBF planes from the new escort carrier, the USS *Bogue*; the boat was sunk with most of her crew. American escort carriers mostly operated in the southern part of the North Atlantic. They destroyed many U-boats, partly thanks to Ultra decrypts. Most of these sinkings took place after the Germans withdrew their boats from the northern parts of the Atlantic in May 1943.

41. **Patrol Bombers: Liberators of RAF Coastal Command**

In 1942–43, more and more long-range bombers became available to close the mid-Atlantic 'air gap'. U-boats were sunk or forced to sail at slow speed submerged, unable to concentrate for wolf-pack attacks on convoys. The most important Allied aircraft was the American-built Liberator. The antenna of a British ASV Mk II radar is visible under the wing of the Liberator III in the foreground; the third plane in line is equipped with more lethal centimetric radar.

42. **Home Fleet Commanders: Admirals Tovey and Fraser, May 1943**

Admiral Bruce Fraser is piped aboard the fleet flagship, the battleship *Duke of York*, in May 1943 to take over command from Admiral John Tovey. He is being greeted by Tovey, who had led the hunt for the *Bismarck* in May 1941. Fraser would be aboard the *Duke of York* in January 1944 when she sank the German battleship *Scharnhorst* off North Cape. He would later command the British Pacific fleet in 1944–45.

43. **Combat Loader: USS *Custer***

'Combat loaders' were central to Allied global military planning, acting as carrier-ships for landing craft. The British first developed these as Landing Ships Infantry (LSI); the Americans commissioned them in large numbers as Attack Transports (APA). The *Custer* was converted from a C3 cargo ship and commissioned as APA-38 in July 1943; she could carry twenty-four LCVPs, two LCM(3)s and a battalion of troops.

44. **Beachhead: Sicily, July 1943**

Operation HUSKY began on 10 July. Although smaller in scale than the invasion of North Africa, it was here that Allied amphibious warfare came of age. The most important single new type was the Landing Ship Tank; here big US Army trucks drive ashore across a floating pontoon from *LST-336* off Gela.

45. **Cruiser USS *Savannah* Hit by a Bomb off Salerno, 11 September 1943**

The Allied landing on mainland Italy at Salerno on 9 September met stiffer resistance. A dangerous new weapon was introduced in the form of a radio-controlled bomb, the 1.5-ton Fritz X. Nearly 200 crew members were killed when the large light cruiser *Savannah* was hit by a Fritz X, but the ship survived. The Fritz X was available in only small quantities and was vulnerable to electronic counter-measures; also, the Luftwaffe Do 217 medium bombers that carried and controlled it could be shot down by Allied fighter planes.

46. **The Italian Fleet Led into Captivity, 16 September 1943**

Italy surrendered in confused circumstance in early September. The fleet was concentrated at Malta and then transferred to Egypt. This photograph was taken from the bridge of the Italian battleship *Vittoria Veneto* as she steamed from Malta to Alexandria. Directly ahead is the battleship *Italia* (formerly *Littorio*), and leading the column is a British battleship.

47. **Leaders of the US Navy: Admirals Spruance, King and Nimitz**

Three of the most important admirals flew into Saipan on 17 July 1944. From left to right: Raymond Spruance was sea-going commander of the Pacific battle force, the Fifth Fleet. Ernest King, based in Washington, was US Navy C-in-C (COMINCH) and Chief of Naval Operation (CNO) and a major planner of Allied global strategy. Chester Nimitz, based in Hawaii, was C-in-C of the Pacific Fleet (CINCPAC) and of the Pacific Ocean Areas (POA). To the right is General Jarman, head of US Army forces in the POA.

48. **Fleet Submarine: USS *Trigger***

The *Trigger* was a standard American 'fleet' submarine. Displacing 1,526 tons and 311 feet long, she was much larger than the standard Type VII and Type IX U-boats, and was equipped with radar. Named after the Triggerfish, the submarine was commissioned in January 1942 and sailed on her first regular war patrol in June; she was sunk in the East China Sea on her twelfth patrol in March 1945.

9. **Fighter Plane, the Grumman F6F-3 Hellcat**

he Hellcat won air superiority over the Pacific. Grumman achieved the remarkable feat of rogressing from the Hellcat's first flight test in June 1942, to delivery to fighter squadrons six ionths later, and to combat action eight months after that. Powered by a huge 2,000hp Pratt & Vhitney radial engine, the Hellcat could easily out-perform its main opponent, the Japanese A6M ero.

. **Fleet Carrier: USS *Essex***

ie 'Essex' class aircraft carriers were the most powerful warships of World War II, and no fewer ian fourteen of them took part in combat operations. This photograph shows the USS *Essex* in Iay 1943 completing her work-up in the Atlantic. A large part of her air group is parked on the ght deck, 11 of the new F6F Hellcat fighters, 18 TBF torpedo planes and 24 SBD dive bombers; tal capacity was 80-90 aircraft.

51. **Air Raids on Rabaul, November 1943**

Rabaul, north of New Guinea, was the key Japanese base in the South Pacific. This extraordinary photograph of the *Haguro* in Simpson Harbour at Rabaul was taken during a raid by US Army B-25 bombers on 2 November; the heavy cruiser had just taken part in the Battle of Empress Augusta Bay. More damage was done to warships at Rabaul by two US Navy carrier raids a week later.

52. **Beachhead: Tarawa, 20–23 November 1943**

Operation GALVANIC, the invasion of the Gilberts, was the first of the US Marine Corps assaults on small but heavily defended islands in the Central Pacific. The main fighting was on Betio in Tarawa Atoll; the islet had an area of less than 300 acres. Poor intelligence and an inadequate naval bombardment led to high American losses. The obstacles could not be overcome even by the extensive use of LVT amphibious tractors – one of which is shown in this photograph, hung up on the devastated shoreline.

3. D-Day Commanders: General Eisenhower and Admiral Ramsay

)peration NEPTUNE, the 1944 Normandy invasion, was World War II's most important naval
peration. Two of the senior Allied officers involved are pictured here on D-Day, 6 June. General
)wight D. Eisenhower was commander of the Supreme Headquarters of the Allied Expeditionary
'orce (SHAEF) and the British Admiral Bertram Ramsay was 'Allied Naval Commander,
xpeditionary Force' (ANCXF).

1. Beachhead: Normandy, 6 June 1944

peration NEPTUNE was divided into five assault areas, two American, one Canadian, and two
ritish. The American OMAHA assault area proved the most difficult, partly due to the terrain and
e strength of the German defenders. The beach obstructions (*Hemmbalken*) are clearly visible in
is photograph, taken at the end of the day. The immobilised tank is an amphibious Sherman DD;
ost of the tanks that tried to 'swim' ashore foundered.

55. The Battle of the Philippine Sea, 18–19 June 1944

When the US invaded Saipan in the Marianas the Japanese responded with the entire Combined Fleet. On 19 June 1944 Task Force 58 fighters intercepted Japanese carrier planes, shooting down hundreds; the enemy carrier fleet never recovered. Shore-based aircraft were also destroyed in large numbers. This photo shows an action on 18 June over TF 52, which was covering the invasion fleet; a twin-engined bomber falls from the sky. The photograph was taken from the escort carrier (CVE) *Kitkun Bay*.

56. **Fleet Train: Tanker USS *Cahaba***

The tanker US *Cahaba* (AO-82) refuels the battleship *Iowa* and the fleet carrier *Shangri-La* underway at sea in 1945. The creation of the 'fleet train' was a key element of the US Navy's victory in the vast Pacific Ocean. By 1943–44 American task forces could remain at sea for long periods, fuelled by tankers like the *Cahaba*. Mobile forward bases were set up at Eniwetok, Majuro, Manus, Ulithi, Leyte and elsewhere, using a system of Service Squadrons (Servons).

. Leyte Gulf: The Battle off Samar, 25 October 1944

ıis dramatic photograph was taken from an American warship: the doomed escort carrier *ımbier Bay* is straddled by splashes from the shells fired by pursuing Japanese cruisers. An ıack group commanded by Admiral Kurita had surprised the task group covering the northern proaches to Leyte Gulf.

Kamikaze: Lingayen Gulf, 6 January 1945

ganised suicide air attacks began during the Leyte Gulf battle. They continued on a larger scale 1945, when the Americans moved north in the Philippines to invade the main island of Luzon. e largest landing was in Lingayen Gulf. The Japanese Navy, using land bases, responded with nerous kamikaze strikes on the fleet standing offshore. This dramatic photograph shows an M/ZEKE diving on the cruiser USS *Columbia*, one of several attacks on 6 January.

59. **Surrender and Sea Power: USS *Missouri*, 2 September 1945**

The Japanese delegation signed the surrender document on the veranda deck of the battleship *Missouri*, as she lay anchored in Tokyo Bay. Their backs can be seen in this photograph. One of th last fast battleships to be completed, the *Missouri* joined the fleet in January 1945.

The operation, commanded by the South African-born Admiral E.N. Syfret, was much bigger than the Lofoten raid. The initial landing involved a considerable number of troops – three British Army brigades (ten infantry battalions) and No. 5 Commando. The landing force included five ocean-going attack transports (LSIs), three troopships and six 'store ships' with vehicles and supplies, along with an LST. They operated from an advance base at Durban, South Africa. Naval covering forces included two big carriers (the *Illustrious* and the *Indomitable*), the old battleship *Ramillies*, two cruisers, eighteen destroyers and eight corvettes.

The local French garrison was small (1,500–3,000 men) and composed of colonial infantry – local recruits as well as some men from Senegal. There were a few French aircraft and warships (including three submarines, two of which would be sunk). The fighting in Diego Suarez itself only lasted one day. As the Royal Marine general who commanded the ground forces put it in his report, dated 15 June: 'there is much of interest in this, the first of many probable amphibious assaults which remained [*sic*] to be carried out during the war'.[16] The Vichy governor was 480 miles to the south, inland at Tananarive (Antananarivo). The takeover of the whole of Madagascar was a much more drawn-out affair, a land campaign involving colonial troops on either side. It ended with the local French surrender in November 1942.

CROSS-CHANNEL OPERATIONS

The entry of the United States into the war in December 1941 (and the Russian victory at the Battle of Moscow) transformed the medium- and long-term strategic prospects of Great Britain. Both the British and the Americans thought the programme of raids should continue, to keep the Germans off balance and provide Allied troops with combat experience. In addition, however, a full-scale invasion across the Channel could now be considered, to drive the enemy out of France and the Low Countries and destroy German power. After agreeing in principle at the start of April 1942 to an invasion of the Continent, a top-level discussion about the timing and location of the first major counter-offensive continued until the middle of the year. It was one of the best-known episodes of inter-Allied military diplomacy; competing strategic views were involved, and also the competing views of the various military services. As with the Germans in 1940, decision-making was constrained by the seasons; all parties agreed that from October through March sea/air conditions in the Channel ruled out a landing attempt in France or the Low Countries.

For their part, Churchill and his military chiefs were dubious about an amphibious operation in the immediate future, especially a full-scale cross-Channel one.

Any landing before October 1942 would have to be mounted mainly by British forces and in the face of a strong German garrison. It threatened to cause heavy (British) casualties on the scale of World War I and might well fail. Already fighting a major land campaign in Libya and Egypt, the British were more interested in a landing operation against the Vichy French territories in northwest Africa; they had assigned to this the preliminary code name GYMNAST. (The Prime Minister was also interested in a campaign in Norway – although his own generals were not enthusiastic.)

The US Army under General George Marshall and his planners favoured a methodical movement of ground and air forces from America to the UK in a build-up code-named BOLERO. This movement would be followed by a joint British–American invasion across the Channel into France (Operation ROUNDUP) in the spring of 1943. This preference also made the American military leaders (especially the US Army) look positively on raids and on an 'emergency' landing in northwestern France in the autumn of 1942, which was given the code name SLEDGEHAMMER. They also tended to oppose any other major operation that would interfere with a spring 1943 landing in France.

In the end practical difficulties and higher politics proved decisive. Roosevelt and Churchill were eager for a major operation in the West before the end of 1942, partly to do *something*, partly to keep Russia in the war and partly to focus public opinion on the war against Germany. Political factors were not irrelevant: in the US, congressional elections were scheduled to take place in early November, and some progress needed to be made before then in the war against the main enemy. In the end, after trips by political and military leaders back and forth across the Atlantic, it was agreed, on 25 July, at the highest level, that Allied forces would stage a major landing in northwest Africa (Morocco and Algeria). Operation GYMNAST was given the more inspiring designation, Operation TORCH. Formally, the emergency cross-Channel landing in 1942 (SLEDGEHAMMER) was still on the table, but no one now thought it would happen. There was continuing approval for the 1943 ROUNDUP landing in France, but a lack of clarity about what form it would take.

This was the context for the Dieppe raid (Operation JUBILEE). The amphibious attack took place in mid-August 1942, but it was first proposed in early April and was originally scheduled – as Operation RUTTER – for early July. In April the British Chiefs of Staff (COS) had approved a policy of raids to be undertaken in the coming summer. These were to be on the largest scale that the available equipment (i.e. landing craft) would allow. A 'super-raid' was to be launched against one of the ports on the German-held Channel coast.[17] Dieppe, a medium-sized French port between Le Havre and Dunkirk, which lay just over 60 miles from the British coastline, was chosen in April. The crossing could be made overnight, preserving the vital element of surprise, and Dieppe was within range of supporting RAF aircraft operating from southern England. Intelligence suggested that the port's defences were relatively weak.

Operation RUTTER/ JUBILEE was intended to be short and intense; Churchill described it to the Cabinet as a 'butcher and bolt' raid.[18] Serious damage was to be inflicted by the raiders on port installations and on nearby airfields. German invasion craft in the harbour were to be 'cut out' and brought back to Britain. Tactical surprise was a crucial factor, as there would be no heavy air or naval bombardment. This was a raid, not an invasion. The window of time available was small; an indirect tactical attack, coming ashore up or down the coast from the port and approaching it from the land side, was ruled out. The attackers had to get in and out before the strong German counter-attack began.

The scale of RUTTER/JUBILEE was substantially bigger than any British amphibious operation except Madagascar (which was not a raid); it dwarfed the Lofoten landing. Dieppe is often inaccurately described as a 'Commando raid'. Three British Commando battalions did take part in a supporting role, but the main force was two brigades – six battalions – of the 2nd Canadian Division, a regular infantry formation. Moreover, a Canadian tank regiment (sixty vehicles) with the new 39-ton Churchill heavy tank took part. RAF air power was committed in strength to protect and support the invasion, and it was hoped that heavy losses could be inflicted on the Luftwaffe. But for fear of killing French civilians an air bombardment of the town was deleted from the plan.

On the naval side thirteen attack flotillas, with several hundred vessels, set out from Southampton, Portsmouth and two smaller ports. Nine attack transports (LSIs) took part, including the *Queen Emma* and the *Princess Beatrix*; most were medium-size converted Channel ferries. They carried five Canadian battalions and No. 4 Commando, who were transferred to landing craft for the final leg through the darkness to shore. Three other battalions were transported all the way across the Channel (shore to shore) by small LCP(L) landing craft. The armoured force was transported in the same way, by twenty-four LCTs, most of them carrying three tanks. Support firepower was limited to nine small 'Hunt' class destroyers; the Admiralty did not oppose the raid, but because of the air danger it was not prepared to commit a battleship or a cruiser to provide gunfire support.

Operation JUBILEE was the single wholly unsuccessful major British or American amphibious operation of the entire war. The main force came ashore just before dawn, at 5.20 a.m., but was unable to fight its way off the beaches. Only half the tanks were landed, and they were unable to break into the town itself. The Canadian ground-force commander threw in his reserve infantry in a blind attempt to save the situation, and they too were trapped and destroyed. At 9.50

a.m. the withdrawal of the survivors was ordered, but it was already too late. Of nearly 5,000 Canadian troops involved, only 2,200 returned to England, and 3,400 were casualties; about 900 were killed in action, many others were taken prisoner. A quarter of 1,100 British Commandos were casualties.[19] Even the air battle went badly; the RAF suffered higher losses than the Luftwaffe. The Royal Navy probably came out the best of the three services, although the Royal Marine Commando thrown into the attack on the port suffered very heavy casualties. The Navy had successfully transported the invasion force. None of the attack transports was damaged, although one of the 'Hunts' was sunk after an air attack.

So much about the raid was badly planned. It was assumed that the Germans were weak and could be caught by surprise. Inexperienced Canadian troops were thrown into a violent battle demanding close adherence to timetables. Admiral Mountbatten was no land warfare expert, and he surely deserves some blame. He raised objections to changes to the original plan (imposed from above), but ended up accepting them. In the view of a critical Canadian historian, Mountbatten 'was the wrong man at the wrong time, in the wrong place, taking the easy route of least resistance just when he should have been most alert to the dangers'.[20]

The Allied troops at Dieppe fought bravely, and efforts have been made by historians to defend the value of the operation. Hitler did personally order the transfer of troops to defend the Atlantic coast defences during 1942, but steps had begun *before* the August raid. Dieppe did demonstrate the folly of both British super-raids and the American pressure to mount the 'emergency' Operation SLEDGEHAMMER in 1942. But by the time JUBILEE was carried out the Allies had already decided to land in North Africa instead. Some important lessons were indeed learned. German coastal defences could not be minimised. Better intelligence and planning were essential. Surprise was not enough; gunfire support was needed, both heavy naval guns offshore and direct support by specialised vessels operating closer inshore. Ports were too well protected to be taken in the initial assault; and some other means would have to be found to bring in massive reinforcements and supplies. Most of this should have been obvious without the catastrophe of JUBILEE. In any event Dieppe would be the last major amphibious operation against the Channel coast until June 1944.

OPERATION TORCH

Various aspects of the execution of Operation TORCH, the giant landing operation in North Africa, have already been discussed.[21] The object here is to put TORCH in context as the end-point of the first series of Allied amphibious operations, which began with the Lofoten raid. Some of same ships and forces took part, including the *Princess Beatrix* and the *Queen Emma* (they landed American troops west of Oran). These vessels from the Lofotens, however, were now crowded out by an armada of other transports.

The British and American decision to strike in North Africa was made at the highest level in late July 1942. It came after the postponement of the projected cross-Channel operations, and it marked the success of British strategy over the version preferred by the American military leaders. Operation TORCH was another example of 'hitting 'em where they ain't' – to use the much-quoted tactic from American baseball – although this time on a strategic scale. On the day of the landings there were no German combat forces in Morocco, Algeria or Tunisia. At the same time, as outlined earlier in this book, TORCH was a very ambitious operation, much larger in scale than Madagascar or Dieppe (or Guadalcanal). Allied forces converged from Scotland and the East Coast of the United States. Command of the Atlantic gave the Allies the oceanic flexibility required to accomplish this, and to achieve complete surprise.

The plans for the TORCH amphibious operation were worked out very rapidly, in August and September 1942. For six weeks, high-level arguments went on about which points in northwest Africa to attack. The Americans wanted to be sure of a secure port on the Atlantic coast of Africa in the event that the Germans – perhaps with Spanish help – closed the Strait of Gibraltar; this worst-case scenario would have trapped an Allied force landed on the Mediterranean coast of Algeria. Other Allied planners, mainly on the British side, discounted the Spanish danger and wanted the naval landings extended east towards Tunisia, or at least to eastern Algeria. From there Allied forces would be poised to cut *all* the supply lines to Axis forces in Libya and Egypt, and to prevent enemy troops and aircraft arriving in North Africa from across the Mediterranean.[22] However, only a limited number of Allied troops and landing craft were available, and the objectives could not be too close to enemy air bases in Sicily and Sardinia. At the time that the Allied staffs were working out their plans, the dangers of air and naval attack in the Mediterranean still appeared extreme. In the hard-fought Malta convoy of August 1942 (Operation PEDESTAL) two-thirds of a convoy of fourteen merchant ships had been lost.[23] In the end it was decided to make three major landings, at Casablanca in Morocco, and at Oran and Algiers in Algeria.

The command arrangements for TORCH were complex. The landing operation was not only much larger than its predecessors but, unlike them, it was inter-Allied. A joint headquarters was set up for the 'expeditionary force', bringing together not only army, navy and air force commands, but also British and American forces. Dwight Eisenhower was appointed C-in-C of the Allied Expeditionary Force. This was partly because most of the troops involved were from the US Army, but also because it was felt that an operation led by an

American general – rather than a British one – would be less likely to meet armed resistance from the Vichy-led forces in North Africa. A British admiral, Bert Ramsay, was the officer mainly responsible for the detailed naval planning. Admiral Andrew Cunningham had, however, secretly been assigned to be overall Allied Naval Commander, Expeditionary Force (ANCXF), while still stationed in Washington as head of the British naval mission; Ramsay served as his deputy. Admiral King in Washington had never been enthusiastic about TORCH, but in the end he willingly committed naval forces. He accepted, too, that Cunningham, at that time the most successful Allied flag officer of the war and a man with whom he had become acquainted in Washington, would have overall command of the entire TORCH naval element; this included the US Navy task force of Admiral Kent Hewitt, which operated off Morocco.

Operation TORCH also needs to be put into the context of Allied strategy. The active formations of the British Army were heavily involved in Egypt; eleven divisions from the British Empire fought at El Alamein in November. As a result the larger part of the Allied forces which invaded northwest Africa were from the US Army. The expeditionary force in Morocco comprised elements of an armoured division and two infantry divisions, all American. In Algeria were elements of another US armoured division, elements of three US infantry divisions, a British infantry division and British Commando battalions. The US Marine Corps might have been expected to play a part in the largest amphibious operation in American history, but Marine combat units were all in the Pacific, and both the US Army and US Navy favoured this situation. Some of the US Army divisions involved in TORCH had amphibious training, but this preparation had been rudimentary. The opinion of one of the most senior American staff officers, General Thomas Handy, was that 'we never put on an operation during the war where the risk was higher than in TORCH'.[24]

The invasion of North Africa (like that of Guadalcanal) was set in train before much of the amphibious war technology which was under development became available. The LST tank landing ship had not yet entered service with the US forces; tanks had to be moved from the US to Morocco aboard a converted rail ferry, and then unloaded at the small port of Safi in the south. For infantry, the LCI infantry landing ship and the DUKW amphibious truck were also not yet available. There was little preparation for offshore bombardment in direct support of the troops (although coastal batteries were engaged). Fortunately the invasion beaches were not fortified or defended.

The British had deployed for the Mediterranean landings the first specially modified headquarters ships, HMS *Bulolo* and HMS *Largs*, converted merchant vessels with greatly enhanced radio equipment. The necessity of such vessels had been learned at Dakar in 1940 and during later expeditions. Off Morocco the Americans had to use a conventional warship, the heavy cruiser *Augusta*, as a headquarters. This led to problems when she was required to steam away to support the naval action against the French – with General George Patton (the local land forces commander) still aboard.

Tactically the Allies had secured their initial objectives with light losses. And at the grand-strategic and diplomatic level American ground and air forces were now committed to a 'second front' against Germany. And yet at the tactical level the TORCH amphibious operation revealed significant shortcomings. These would have become important had French resistance not evaporated within two or three days – or if the enemy had been the Wehrmacht. There was a large non-combat wastage of poorly constructed landing craft. The US Army official history observed that from the point of view of logistics the November landings were 'an object lesson in disorderly planning and brilliant improvisation'.[25] At a higher, operational, level the Germans were able to rush troops by air to Tunisia. There they mounted a campaign which lasted until early May 1943, made high demands on the Allied supply system and greatly destabilised global shipping availability. Arguably, this forced a delay of ROUNDUP, the cross-Channel landing, from 1943 to 1944.[26]

In the longer term, however, while Hitler gained a few months, the Axis forces were doomed in North Africa from the time of Operation TORCH. The Allies, despite their untutored battlefield forces, had achieved complete surprise. They had been able to put ashore (perhaps not in all the right places) an unprecedentedly large landing force. The potential was now there to re-open the globally important Mediterranean shipping route and make a direct approach to Sicily and mainland Italy.[27] At a strategic and operational level Operation TORCH compared remarkably well with the German invasion of Norway in April 1940 (which also involved inexperienced ground forces on the attacking side). The difference was that in November 1942 the invaders, who depended entirely on sea transport, suffered only insignificant naval losses. Operation TORCH was a demonstration of the potential of large-scale amphibious warfare, even before the appropriate technology and organisational structure had been fully developed.

CHAPTER 14

THE MEDITERRANEAN

The British Regain the Initiative, January 1942–November 1942

THE BATTLE OF SIRTE, 22 MARCH 1942

The previous chapter was about the evolution of Allied amphibious capabilities and operations in Europe in 1941 and up to November 1942. This chapter moves back to early 1942 to follow a different strand: the fierce sea/air battles fought during that year around the Mediterranean convoys of both sides.

MW.10, a British Malta supply convoy, sailed from Alexandria on the morning of Friday, 20 March 1942.[1] Its main escort, Force B, left port in the evening. It would consist of three light cruisers, all that remained of the once powerful Mediterranean Fleet. The task force was led by Admiral Philip Vian, commander of the 15th Cruiser Squadron, aboard the brand-new *Cleopatra*. Vian's former flagship, the cruiser *Naiad*, had been sunk by a U-boat a week before, off the Egyptian coast. The admiral himself had been pulled 'wet and oily' from the sea. In company on 20 March were the *Euryalus* and the *Dido*. All three were new AA cruisers, with ten 5.25-inch guns and six torpedo tubes; they were vessels of only 5,600 tons, and the *Cleopatra* was far from fully worked up. A considerable force of ten modern fleet destroyers also set out with Vian from Alexandria. The convoy itself was made up of four cargo ships, large, fast and modern; close escort was provided by the old AA cruiser *Carlisle* and five small 'Hunt' class destroyers. From Malta the survivors of Force K, the light cruiser *Penelope* and a destroyer, sailed east to reinforce Vian; they would join up at 8.00 a.m. on Sunday, 22 March, the day of the surface battle.

Convoy MW.10 was sighted between Crete and Libya by Italian submarines and German aircraft on Saturday afternoon (21 March). At this time the British Army still held the Libyan coast as far as Gazala (west of Tobruk), and new long-range RAF Beaufighters of No. 201 Group provided some fighter cover.[2]

Diversionary operations had been mounted by the Army and the RAF to tie up Axis aircraft.

The Supermarina, the Italian naval high command in Rome, committed powerful surface forces. At about midnight on Saturday Admiral Angelo Iachino departed from Taranto with the battleship *Littorio* and four destroyers; Iachino had commanded the battle force of the Regia Marina since December 1940. A scouting force consisting of the heavy cruisers *Gorizia* and *Trento*, the light cruiser *Bande Nere* and five destroyers sortied from Messina in Sicily at about the same time. The two groups sailed converging courses across the central Mediterranean towards the expected position of the enemy convoy. During Sunday morning Admiral Vian was alerted to the movement of ships from Taranto as a result of a submarine sighting and decrypted Italian signals, and he detoured his ships onto a more southerly course.[3]

The action took place on the edge of the Gulf of Sirte, about 150 miles north of the Libyan town of Sirte (now Sidra).[4] The British ships came under repeated air attacks by Italian and German aircraft from mid-morning, but these had no effect, thanks to evasive manoeuvres and heavy expenditure of AA ammunition. Vian kept most of his warships between the convoy and the Italian warships threatening it from the north. Iachino sent his cruisers ahead, and the first distant sighting between surface ships took place at 2.00 p.m. At about 2.30 the British escort turned to the east and began to lay a smoke screen, and the two sides exchanged long-range gunfire. A daylight gunnery and torpedo engagement ensued and continued intermittently for about five hours. In this first phase the balance of firepower between the two cruiser forces was in favour of the Italians; sixteen 8-inch guns and eight 6-inch guns were ranged against six 6-inch and thirty 5.25-inch guns.

The Italian cruisers withdrew to the north at about 3.00 p.m., evidently to lure the British towards the approaching *Littorio*. At 3.30 the two Italian forces formed into a united battle group, and at 4.40 the gunnery duel north of the convoy resumed, this time with the addition of the nine 15-inch guns of the battleship. Captain Eric Bush of the *Euryalus* remembered the final stage:

> at 6.41 p.m., the battleship *Littorio* spotted *Euryalus* through a gap in the smoke screen. I saw flashes from her 15-in guns rippling down her side as she fired a salvo at us – an unarmoured ship. An age seemed to pass before her shells arrived with a deafening crash, as they plunged into the water all around us, engulfing the ship in columns of water masthead high. We'd been straddled . . . *Euryalus* shuddered and shook and then rocked so violently that I thought the topmast would come down, while fragments of shell scrammed through the air to bury themselves in our ship's sides.[5]

Bush's cruiser jigged sharply to starboard, and the next Italian salvo passed harmlessly overhead. Then the safety of the smoke again enveloped the British ship. Iachino did not attempt to skirt around the escorts to the east (into the clear waters upwind of the smoke screen).

At long range and with rapidly manoeuvring ships, there were few direct hits by either side. The British destroyers mounted three attacks out of the smoke screen, forcing the enemy to turn away. The Italian ships were certainly unwilling to enter the smoke, and they had been ordered to avoid a night engagement; both events would have neutralised their gunnery advantage. Just before dusk Iachino finally turned away. At about this time Vian ordered the merchant ships to proceed on to Malta, with individual escorts, while Force B itself turned east for a night-time dash back towards its base. The despatch reported the return: 'The Force arrived at Alexandria at 1230 [24 March] where they were honoured to receive the great demonstration which then ensued.'[6]

Sirte was a small engagement in which neither side lost any ships or suffered much damage. MW.10 comprised only four cargo ships. And yet the battle is rightly seen as an important British victory. The Prime Minister sent his personal congratulations to Vian via Admiral Cunningham:

> That one of the most powerful modern battleships afloat attended by two heavy and four light cruisers and a flotilla should have been routed and put to flight with severe torpedo and gunfire injury in broad daylight by a force of five British light cruisers and destroyers constitutes a naval episode of the highest distinction and entitles all ranks and ratings concerned, and above all their commander, to the compliments of the British Nation.[7]

C.S. Forester, a writer popular in both Britain and the United States, published *The Ship* in May 1943, a novel depicting the heroic action of a fictional cruiser, HMS *Artemis*, and her crew, based loosely on the *Penelope*. In the novel there are *two* enemy battleships, and hits on one of them by British cruiser gunfire and a destroyer torpedo finally lead to the Italian withdrawal (after a tense discussion between the fictional Italian admiral and his fictional German adviser). Admiral Cunningham's assessment, given when more accurate information about the forces involved had become available, was that Sirte had been a 'thoroughly deserved victory from a situation in which, had the roles been reversed, it is unthinkable that the convoy or much of the escort would not have been destroyed.'[8]

Although the British conduct of the sea fight on that Sunday afternoon battle was indeed exemplary, the larger picture was less positive. The delay caused by the Italian sortie meant that the four cargo ships could not approach port at Malta until some hours after dawn on Monday (23 March), and they then came under heavy air attack. One was sunk 20 miles south of the island. Another, the *Breconshire*, a veteran of half a dozen daring runs into Malta, was crippled eight miles from safety. Although towed through air attacks and rough seas into one of the Maltese ports, she was sunk there by bombing on the 27th. Her fate had been shared by the two other merchant ships from the convoy that did reach Valletta's Grand Harbour, on Monday; they were sunk there three days later. Of 26,000 tons of supplies aboard the four ships, only 4,000 tons were unloaded. A damaged fleet destroyer and two 'Hunts' were lost, before and after the Sunday afternoon battle. And MW.10 would be the last even partly successful convoy to reach Malta from the east until November 1942.

THE MALTA CONVOYS

The year 1941 had ended quite successfully for the British ground forces in North Africa. Operation CRUSADER, the first major British Army offensive against German troops, had apparently been a victory. The siege of Tobruk had been lifted, and General Rommel and his Italian allies had been thrown back from the Egyptian border deep into Cyrenaica. Benghazi itself was taken, and for a time the RAF was able to fly from bases in eastern Libya. The British command looked forward to the planned Operation ACROBAT, which would drive west towards Tripoli and throw the enemy out of Libya altogether.

The Axis forces were able to recover. At the end of January 1942 Rommel began a surprise counter-attack, quickly forcing the abandonment of Benghazi and a 200-mile British retreat to Gazala, just west of Tobruk. After a prolonged battle in late May and June 1942 the Germans and Italians suddenly reached and captured Tobruk (which had survived a six-month siege in 1941). The Axis leaders discussed the situation at the highest level; Rommel with his Panzer Army Afrika was allowed to pursue the enemy deep into Egypt, the British front collapsing in front of him. At the end of June the British established a new defensive line at El Alamein, 240 miles into Egypt, and only 70 miles from Alexandria.

Whether advancing or retreating, the British operations in Egypt and Libya in 1942 were dependent on the long maritime supply line around the Cape of Good Hope, mainly from the United Kingdom or the United States. The WS ('Winston Special') convoys continued to come through without loss. There were eleven of these convoys departing from the UK in 1942 (WS.15 to WS.25). The attack on Madagascar was mounted partly to secure the supply route from the Cape to the Red Sea and Suez. In 1942 total shipments of 'military cargo' to the Indian Ocean Area (the Middle East, the Persian Gulf and India) from the UK and North America came to 3,250,700 tons (270,900 tons a month).[9] More than anything else these ocean convoys were indispensable for eventual British success in Egypt and Libya in late 1942.

The Allied convoys *within* the Mediterranean were actually less important in strategic terms than the WS and other oceanic convoys, but they would be more famous and much more hard-fought. The Battle of Sirte was one of the first convoy battles of 1942, and it demonstrated the difficult position the Royal Navy faced in the Mediterranean in the first ten months of that year. Although the global strength of the Royal Navy continued to grow, the British naval forces at either end of the Mediterranean – Gog and Magog – were greatly weakened, even compared to their situation in 1940–41. Four battleships and three fleet carriers had been disabled as a result of enemy action, including devastating German air attacks off Crete in May 1941 and the midget submarine attack on Alexandria in December; one battleship and one carrier were total losses. Replacements could not be sent from Britain or America because of the successes of the Japanese Navy.

In the eastern basin no battleships or carriers were available and only a small number of cruisers and some destroyers and submarines. Indeed, in the second half of 1942, under threat from Rommel, the Mediterranean Fleet was withdrawn from Alexandria, and merchant shipping was concentrated at Haifa in Palestine and Port Said at the north end of the Suez Canal. At the start of April, Admiral Andrew Cunningham was secretly recalled from what had now become a naval backwater. His new post was head of the British Admiralty Delegation (BAD) in Washington, where it was hoped his prestige and toughness would serve as a counterweight to the American admiral Ernest King. His replacement in the rump Mediterranean Fleet would be Admiral Henry Harwood, the hero of the Battle of the River Plate in 1939 against the *Graf Spee*.

In the battles of 1940–41, Cunningham's Alexandria fleet had been the larger of the two British Mediterranean naval forces and had done most of the fighting. In 1942 the emphasis of the war at sea shifted to the western basin and to the British naval forces operating from Gibraltar. Force H could at least be reinforced from the Atlantic, where the danger had been reduced by the withdrawal of the *Scharnhorst* and the *Gneisenau* from northwestern France to Germany in February 1942. The pool of warships available to the British was still limited, as a number of them were required to cover the Indian Ocean and then to support the invasion of Madagascar in May 1942. For much of early 1942 no modern British fleet carrier was available even in the western basin. There were changes in personnel here too. In February 1942 Admiral Somerville was transferred away from Force H. As we have seen, he took over the Eastern Fleet in the Indian Ocean – shortly after the fall of Singapore.[10] His replacement at Gibraltar was

Admiral Neville Syfret, who had commanded a cruiser squadron in the Home Fleet.

Hitler had not adopted a 'Mediterranean' strategy in 1940–41, and with the full-scale demands of the Russian front it was now an even lower priority. But he still wanted to take advantage of any opportunities that might arise for weakening his vulnerable British enemy. The options were limited, however, by the weakness of German naval forces; there were still virtually no surface units in the Mediterranean.[11] Two more U-boats reached the Mediterranean in January 1942, joining the twenty-one survivors of the twenty-six boats that had arrived in 1941. Fourteen more submarines would arrive in the autumn and early winter of 1942. They did not have a major anti-shipping role, as there were relatively few Allied merchant ships to attack. Losses in 1942 amounted to fourteen boats, about a third of the force on hand. The loss of the *U 559* was especially important. The crew abandoned ship after she was damaged by British forces off Haifa in October 1942. Code materials were captured which enabled Bletchley Park to break into the TRITON/SHARK U-boat communications in December; this was a coup as important as the capture of the *U 110* in 1941. Two of the three British seamen who boarded the sinking submarine to retrieve code materials were drowned when she went down.

The most important German force in the sea/air battles of 1942 was the Luftwaffe, but with the war now being fought on a Europ-wide scale Göring's fighters and bombers were ever more thinly spread. In November 1941 Hitler had agreed to despatch an Air Fleet headquarters (*Luftflotte 4*) under Field Marshal Kesselring from Russia to the Mediterranean. These aircraft had much success in reducing Malta's effectiveness in a Blitz of April and May 1942, but they were soon withdrawn to Libya and Russia. The final brief attacks against the embattled island came in October 1942, but they were halted after heavy losses.

As for the Italians, the negative consequences of the decision made in 1937 to concentrate limited resources on a second battleship-building programme now became clear. The *Roma*, the sister ship of the *Littorio* and the *Veneto*, was commissioned in June 1942. The fourth 'Littorio' class, the *Impero*, was launched in the Ansaldo shipyard at Genoa in November 1939 but never completed.[12] A little noted fact, however, is that Italy did actually complete more new full-size battleships (three) than either Germany or Japan. Slow work continued on the carrier *Aquila*, but only one major combat vessel larger than a destroyer was completed in 1942. This was the lead ship of a class of small (3,800-ton) but very fast scout cruisers designed for an earlier era, when the aim was to fight the French super-destroyers. These vessels, the 'Capitani Romani' class, were named after famous military leaders of the Roman Empire. The first, *Attilio Regolo*, was commissioned in May 1942, and two more 'Capitani' followed in 1943. Otherwise the Italian Navy was very much a wasting asset, having as total losses in 1940–41 a battleship, eight cruisers, twenty-one destroyers, twenty escorts *(torpediniera)* and thirty-eight submarines. In 1942 losses were three cruisers, eight destroyers, four escorts and twenty-two submarines. Italy's remaining operational strength in the Mediterranean in September 1942 came to six battleships, two heavy cruisers, seven light cruisers, twenty-eight destroyers and thirty-five submarines.[13]

The Italian Navy faced an increasingly serious problem with its fuel supply. This mostly came from Romania and was received through German supply channels. Fuel was expended lavishly in the first months of a war that was expected to be short and victorious. After this the Navy became more cautious and fewer days were spent at sea. Even so, fuel reserves of 1,667,000 tons in June 1940 had fallen to 141,000 in January 1942. The Germans promised to deliver 50,000 tons of fuel a month, but managed less than half that. About 50,000–70,000 tons a month were required, mainly for convoy escorts.[14]

British naval operations from the west were at first confined to attempts to build up Malta's (defensive) air strength. The carrier *Eagle* made three trips into the Mediterranean in March 1942, and flew off thirty-one fighters to Malta. Earlier ferry missions had involved Hurricanes; the planes flown in during 1942 were now Spitfires, which could hold their own against the latest German and Italian fighters. The American fleet carrier *Wasp* took part in two ferry operations, in April and May 1942, the sole example in the whole war of a modern American capital ship operating in the Mediterranean.[15] Daring missions in dangerous waters, the voyages of the *Wasp* also served as tangible demonstrations of British–American co-operation and solidarity. Most of the forty-seven Spitfires despatched in the first cruise of the *Wasp* were destroyed on the ground on Malta shortly after arrival, but better preparations were made for the second batch of sixty-four Spitfires, launched from the *Wasp* and HMS *Eagle* in May.

The first full-scale British convoy operation of 1942 was much larger than MW.10, which Admiral Vian had defended in March (as described in the first part of this chapter). It took place in the (dark) new moon period of June 1942; the Italians knew these battles as the *Mezzo Giugno*. The British plan was complex, involving Operation HARPOON from Gibraltar, and Operation VIGOROUS from the east. As a result of earlier losses and other global demands, the escorting forces were weaker than for the Malta convoys in late 1941, or for the more famous PEDESTAL convoy that would follow in August 1942. The operation overlapped with preparations for convoy PQ.17 in the Arctic, which left Iceland on 27 June.

The HARPOON convoy (WS.19Z) started on the Clyde and passed Gibraltar on the night of 11/12 June; it was made up of five fast cargo ships and the big new tanker *Kentucky*. Air cover was provided only by the *Eagle* and the small *Argus*. Compared to the new fleet carriers these vessels were slow and could keep only half a dozen fighters aloft above the convoy as a CAP. The first air attacks were mounted from Sardinia on Sunday, 14 June, by the Italian Air Force. Its torpedo bombers, mostly Savoia-Marchetti SM.79 trimotors, presented a more dangerous threat than the high-level bombers had done in 1940–41. The torpedoes of the Aerosiluranti sank a cargo ship and damaged the cruiser *Liverpool* so badly that she had to be towed back to Gibraltar; the veteran cruiser would not complete repairs until the war's end. The departure of the *Liverpool* reduced an already small covering force. The unmodernised battleship *Malaya* accompanied the two small aircraft carriers, but they could not risk approaching the Sicilian narrows. Two light cruisers – one of them the task force flagship – had to be kept with the carriers rather than the convoy.

When WS.19Z, now down to five merchant ships, emerged from the Sicilian narrows heading east at dawn on Monday, 15 June, it was pounced on by an Italian cruiser squadron. The largest ship directly supporting the convoy was the small AA cruiser HMS *Cairo*; she was an elderly vessel armed with only eight 4-inch guns. There were also five British fleet destroyers and four destroyer escorts (of the 'Hunt' class). The escort was engaged by the Italian admiral Alberto Da Zara. His force, which had come down from Palermo during the night, comprised the light cruisers *Raimondo Montecuccoli* and *Eugenio di Savoia*, along with three destroyers. The Italians call the engagement which resulted the Battle of Pantelleria, after the nearby island to the north. Like Admiral Iachino at Sirte, Da Zara was not able to get in range of the convoy; British destroyer attacks and a smoke screen made him keep his distance. But Italian destroyers severely damaged two of their British counterparts, the *Bedouin* and the new *Partridge*. Meanwhile the convoy was still too far from Malta for effective RAF cover against German and Italian air strikes. The crippled *Bedouin* and one merchant ship were sunk by the attacking planes; and two merchant ships – including the vital *Kentucky* – were damaged so badly that they had to be scuttled. The convoy then ran onto a minefield laid off the entrance to Valletta's Grand Harbour, and the Polish-manned 'Hunt', *Kujawiak*, was sunk. In the end only two cargo vessels reached Malta from the west on Monday night.

No merchantmen at all would reach Malta from the east in the simultaneous Operation VIGOROUS, which set out with eleven merchant ships (Convoy MW.11). The convoy ships sailed on Friday, 12 June, from Haifa and Port Said (Rommel's advance had made Alexandria too vulnerable). The naval commander was Admiral Vian, the victor of the Battle of Sirte. He had neither carriers nor battleships, but there were now eight cruisers. Ashore in Egypt Admiral

Harwood, the new Mediterranean Fleet C-in-C, hoped that long-range land-based strike aircraft of RAF 201 Group and submarines might provide some protection against the Italian Navy. Passing through 'Bomb Alley' between Crete and Libya on Sunday, the convoy came under heavy air raids from either direction. There was also a new threat in the form of six German S-boats based in Libya; these craft had recently been moved to the Mediterranean via the French river system. Three merchant ships were lost to the air attacks; a destroyer was sunk by the S-boats on Sunday night, and the cruiser *Newcastle* was badly damaged by them.

Meanwhile the Supermarina had decided that of the two convoys the eastern one was the more important target. Admiral Iachino was despatched on what was to prove the last significant hunting expedition of the Italian battle fleet. He commanded the modern *Littorio* and *Veneto*, two heavy cruisers, two light cruisers and twelve destroyers. During the night of 14/15 June the admiral raced SSE across the central Mediterranean to intercept the VIGOROUS convoy. Long-range Allied attacks had some effect, but not enough. The heavy cruiser *Trento* was stopped by a Beaufort torpedo bomber from Malta, and then sunk by a submarine. The *Littorio* was hit from high altitude by an American B-24 Liberator from Egypt. But lacking clear intelligence on the Italian position and after several indecisive changes of course ordered by Admiral Harwood (still ashore in Egypt), Vian was given freedom of action. He decided to give up the attempt to reach Malta.[16] As the two sides returned to base the *Littorio* was torpedoed in a night attack off Cape Matapan by a Wellington medium bomber from Malta, and the British cruiser *Hermione* was torpedoed by a U-boat. The Italian battleship was under repair until the end of August, and a British cruiser was sunk.

The *Mezzo Giugno* was the closest thing to a major Italian naval victory in the whole war. Both British convoys failed. Two merchant ships reached Malta out of seventeen despatched. The Italians lost the heavy cruiser *Trento* as well as a considerable number of bomber aircraft; much fuel was expended. But a British cruiser was sunk and two more were badly damaged; five British destroyers were lost. After the battle Mussolini rushed in person to Taranto and Naples to award medals to the Italian naval commanders. The battle coincided with the Battle of Gazala, the fall of Tobruk to the Germans (21 June) and the retreat of the British Eighth Army deep into Egypt.

The best known of all the Malta convoys was Operation PEDESTAL, in August 1942; the Italians called it the *Mezzo Agosto* battle. It was one of the most hard-fought sea/air actions of World War II. The PEDESTAL convoy left the Clyde on 3 August 1942, with fourteen merchant ships, all large, modern and capable of high speed. To preserve secrecy it was given a bogus designation in the WS series, usually assigned to convoys routed around the Cape of Good Hope. In fact WS.21S was going to Malta. After it passed the Strait of Gibraltar on Monday, 10 August, the close escort was made up of four cruisers and eleven destroyers. In contrast to the HARPOON convoy, the Admiralty had been able to assemble a powerful covering force, supplementing Force H with ships from the Home Fleet and elsewhere.[17] This task group included the battleships *Nelson* and *Rodney*, armed with 16-inch guns, the fleet carriers *Indomitable* and *Victorious*, the older carriers *Furious* and *Eagle*, three cruisers and thirteen destroyers. This unprecedented concentration of naval might had been made possible as a result of global developments: the reduced threat from the Japanese Navy after the Battle of Midway (4 June) and the cancellation of the Russian convoys after PQ.17 (10 July). In overall command of the armada, flying his flag in the *Nelson*, was Admiral Syfret, who had led the attack on Madagascar in May. Syfret had been able to exercise the fleet with the convoys out in the Atlantic before passing Gibraltar, practising air defence and co-ordinated manoeuvres.

Like its predecessor, the PEDESTAL convoy had to batter its way through multiple threats and operate in narrow seas close to enemy air and naval bases. There was little element of surprise – both sides knew the darkness of the monthly new-moon period was the least dangerous time to run a convoy – and there was little chance to divert the enemy. A dummy British convoy sent as a diversion from Alexandria had little effect. Meanwhile, on the Axis side several hundred Axis planes were ready on Sardinia and Sicily. A strong Italian cruiser force was on alert, and a large number of Italian submarines and motor torpedo boats (MTBs) were deployed, reinforced by some German units.

The concentration of four British carriers was unprecedented. The total air group consisted of seventy-two fighters – Sea Hurricanes, Grumman Martlets and Fulmars – and twenty-eight Albacore torpedo planes. This was a small number compared to what four American Pacific carriers would have carried in the Pacific – perhaps 300 aircraft – but the *Furious* was operating as a ferry carrier and flew off thirty-six RAF Spitfires to Malta. The carriers had to turn back short of the Sicilian narrows, but as the convoy came close to Malta on the other side of the narrows it came under the protection of RAF planes from there, including 100 Spitfires, thirty-six long-range Beaufighters and thirty Beaufort torpedo bombers.

The carrier planes were able to fend off many of the Italian and German air attacks mounted from Sardinia and Sicily on Tuesday and Wednesday (11–12 August), thanks to radar-controlled fighter direction. At this time the Royal Navy's systems were more effective than those of the Americans in the Pacific. Admiral Syfret praised the naval interceptors in his despatch: 'Flying at great heights, constantly chasing the faster JU.88s, warning the fleet of approaching formations, breaking up the latter, and in the later stages doing their work in the face of superior enemy fighter forces, they were grand.'[18] However, a Stuka attack on Wednesday evening succeeded in damaging the *Indomitable* (just as the carrier task group reversed course to return to Gibraltar). Her flight deck was put out of service. She had to be sent to the US for repairs and would only return to the Mediterranean in February 1943.

Axis submarines posed a greater danger than to any previous Malta convoy. The Italians deployed five boats on the distant approaches to the island and the Germans deployed two U-boats. The *U 73* sank the *Eagle* with four torpedoes on Tuesday afternoon (the 11th), the first major success for the Mediterranean U-boats since the previous December. The old carrier went down in eight minutes and 131 officers and men perished – the heaviest loss of life of the whole PEDESTAL battle. The Italian submarine *Axum* mounted one of the most successful torpedo attacks of the war, certainly for the Regia Marina. A spread of four torpedoes achieved three important hits. The cruiser *Nigeria*, flagship of the close escort, was forced to return to Gibraltar. The small AA cruiser *Cairo*, veteran of the HARPOON battle, was sunk. The tanker *Ohio* was damaged; she was the sister ship of the ill-fated *Kentucky* in the HARPOON convoy and the most important merchantman in the convoy. During the night other Italian submarines picked off two damaged merchant ships.

The formation of the surviving ships and their escort became confused as the convoy entered the Sicilian narrows on Wednesday night (12/13 August). The Axis attack on the PEDESTAL convoy included one of the most successful actions by motor torpedo boats in the whole of World War II. The Italians had built about 50 *MAS* boats (*Motoscafo anti sommergibili*) before the war, but although very fast these pre-war MTBs were small (30 tons) and not very seaworthy. In 1941–42 a superior 60-ton MTB, the *Ms* (*Motosilurante*), was built, based on the German S-boat. The Kriegsmarine had also sent a small number of their own 81-ton S-boats to the Mediterranean. In the small hours of Thursday the convoy and its close escort, strung out after the air raids of the previous day, came under MTB attack east of Cape Bon on the Tunisian coast. The *Ms 16* and *Ms 22* succeeded in hitting the *Manchester* with two torpedoes, and she had to be scuttled. The light cruiser was the largest warship lost as a result of an MTB attack during the 1939–45 war. In the next few hours of darkness a mixed force of a dozen Italian and German MTBs achieved hits on five large merchant ships, which were sunk outright, abandoned or scuttled.

In protecting the final approach of the survivors on Thursday (the 13th), the RAF Spitfires and Beaufighters from Malta were less effective than the carrier fighters had been on the previous two days. The *Nigeria* and the *Cairo* had been the only ships capable of (radio) 'fighter direction' of defending aircraft from Malta. The convoy was now spread out, which reduced the effect of AA fire.

Two more cargo ships were sunk by German aircraft – the MV *Waimarama* in a spectacular explosion.

Unlike the June convoy, the PEDESTAL ships were not threatened by Italian surface ships, despite passing only a short distance from enemy bases. The Supermarina had decided that in view of the fuel shortage it would be unwise to send the battleships to sea. A striking force of four light cruisers and eight destroyers moving into position north of Sicily was recalled during Wednesday night when it was decided at the highest level that any fighters available would be used to escort bombers rather than cover the fleet. The Italian cruisers might have been in a position to annihilate the final ships of the convoy south of Pantelleria on Thursday morning, but in the event there would be no repetition of the successful action in the June battle. The British submarine *P42* was able to torpedo the *Bolzano* and the *Muzio Attendolo* as they made their way back to Messina; the two cruisers were damaged so seriously that they would never again be operational.

Three cargo ships reached Malta on Thursday afternoon (13 August). Another, damaged, ship arrived on Friday. On Saturday morning the big Texaco tanker *Ohio* reached Valletta. A famous photograph shows her passing the harbour entrance, low in the water and physically supported on either beam by a destroyer. Although the *Ohio* sank in the harbour, about 90 per cent of her cargo of fuel was recovered.

Operation PEDESTAL had been costly for the British. Two-thirds of the fourteen large cargo ships were lost; only five made it to Malta. The Royal Navy lost the *Eagle*, the cruisers *Manchester* and *Cairo*, and a destroyer. On the other hand, 47,000 tons of cargo were unloaded on the island, by far the largest total since Operation HALBERD in September 1941. The population and the garrison now had sufficient food and supplies to last it through the late autumn. By that time the Battle of El Alamein and Operation TORCH had made the Allied situation in the Mediterranean much more favourable.

After PEDESTAL there would be no attempt for three months to run a full-scale convoy into Malta, partly because escorts and merchant ships were required for Operation TORCH. Then on 17–20 November the STONEAGE convoy (MW.13) arrived in Malta from Alexandria, the first such convoy for six months. MW.13 consisted of four merchant ships escorted by a squadron of cruisers, and the journey was made with no losses. Malta was secure; it would now be possible not just to hold onto the island but to develop it for a powerful offensive role in 1943.

AXIS SEA ROUTES TO NORTH AFRICA

The other aspect of the Mediterranean shipping war in 1942, as in the preceding eighteen months, was the Axis supply routes from southern Europe to North

Africa. Over the previous two and a half years the Royal Navy had consistently outfought its Italian opponent, but it had not gained sea/air 'command' of the central Mediterranean even with the advantage of the Malta base. The Italians and Germans had been able to deploy, reinforce and supply their land forces in North Africa, and they had also gained control of the Aegean and Crete.

The Axis powers scrambled to regain the initiative in the Mediterranean in the winter of 1941–42 after the temporary success of Operation CRUSADER and after the successes of Malta-based surface ships, submarines and aircraft against their shipping. It would be essential to neutralise Malta by bombing attacks and even to consider the possibility of capturing the exposed island. Heavy attacks were mounted by the Luftwaffe in April and May 1942, but then largely ceased. By this time the German Air Force was being pulled in a number of directions, especially towards the fighting in Russia and northern Norway.

The Axis could have improved their position had they been able to capture Malta. This possibility had been raised in 1940 and 1941, but there was little development of the amphibious forces available in 1942, and the defensive ground and air forces on the British-held island were growing stronger. In January 1942, when the Axis armies were retreating back towards Tripoli (after Operation CRUSADER), Field Marshal Kesselring, who had just been appointed German C-in-C South, did approve in principle an invasion of Malta. Some planning was carried out for an operation which the Italians called 'c3' and the Germans called HERCULES (HERKULES). When they met near Salzburg in April 1942 Hitler and Mussolini discussed an attack on the island in July. It is sometimes argued that preparations were undone by Rommel's unexpected capture of Tobruk in June 1942 and his breakthrough into Egypt, which led to resources being channelled not to Malta but to a final push to Alexandria and the Suez Canal. More likely, the Axis did not have the capability to mount an amphibious landing. The argument of Reinhard Stumpf in the German official history seems convincing: 'what matters is whether, under prevailing circumstances, Malta could or could not have been taken in the summer of 1942, and the answer, in my opinion, is no'.[19]

The British were less successful at blocking the Axis supply route to North Africa over most of 1942 than they had been in the latter part of 1941. The Blitz on Malta and continuing pressure on the island's supply lines were sufficient to limit the activity of anti-shipping forces based there. There were some early British successes in the sea/air war, notably in January 1942 when RAF Beaufort torpedo bombers from Malta sank the Italian troopship *Victoria* (13,100 tons) en route to Tripoli. This proved, however, to be an isolated event. With the weakening of the British Mediterranean Fleet at Alexandria at the end of 1941 the Italians could risk sending out more warships to cover the convoys to North

Africa. Four 'battleship convoys' were sent (the first in December 1941). Operation M 43 at the start of January involved a nine-ship convoy bound for Tripoli, with an escort including four battleships. The *Duilio* remained with the merchant ships, and the *Littorio*, the *Cesare* and the *Doria* provided distant cover to the east. Once Rommel recaptured Cyrenaica (eastern Libya) in January and February 1942 there was little the diminished British Mediterranean Fleet could do, at least to block the convoys to Tripoli. Axis air bases were now positioned on both sides of the route from Alexandria to Malta ('Bomb Alley'), with Crete on one side and Libya and western Egypt on the other. In May 1942 an attempted raid by a destroyer force from Alexandria against a convoy to Benghazi ended in disaster. The flotilla was caught by Ju 88s flying from Crete, and three of the four destroyers were sunk. As for submarines, the 10th Flotilla had to pull out of Malta until July/August 1942. The low point was reached at the end of June when even the base facilities at Alexandria had to be abandoned, and the big submarine tender HMS *Medway* was torpedoed and sunk en route to Haifa in Palestine.

The capacity of the Axis-held North African ports was limited, and, as in 1940–41, only small convoys were despatched. Between January and October 1942, Axis losses in shipping tonnage on the Libyan route were typically about 10,000–20,000 tons a month, equivalent to two to four medium-sized vessels. This was certainly lower than in December 1941, when the total loss had been 37,800 tons, although the loss figure would rise again in August and October 1942. The weight of cargo despatched came to about 80,000 tons a month for January to November 1942, which was somewhat lower than the monthly figure for 1941. Cargoes landed in Libya were usually a reasonably high proportion (about 80 per cent) of what had been loaded on ships in Italy and Greece. A typical month saw 50,000–100,000 tons of cargo despatched (of which from a third to a half was for German – rather than the Italian – forces in North Africa). April 1942 was the most successful month of the war for the Axis Libyan convoys, with 151,600 tons of cargo despatched and 150,400 tons received. Shipping losses that April were only 5,500 tons – equivalent to one medium-sized ship. For most of the first seven months of 1942 the proportion of cargo which arrived was normally over 90 per cent (although in June 1942 it fell to 78 per cent). The situation became considerably more difficult in August and October, but even then successful arrivals (by cargo weight) still amounted to 67 per cent and 55 per cent respectively.[20]

The causes of loss were different from 1941. Sinkings were negligible for the first five months of 1942. From June to November, however, according to British figures, Axis losses in the Mediterranean came to seventy-one vessels. Of these, thirty were victims of Allied submarines and thirty-one of Allied aircraft; surface warships accounted for only two small merchantmen.[21] Special intelligence played a part in whatever British successes were achieved. One estimate suggests that a third of the vessels sunk on the Libyan route (not just in 1942) were the result of this.[22]

There have been debates about the effect of Allied attacks on shipping. The historian Martin van Creveld argued that '[t]he importance attributed to the "battle of the convoys" is grossly exaggerated'; '[a]t no time, except perhaps November–December 1941 did the aero-naval struggle in the central Mediterranean play a decisive part in events in North Africa'.[23]. Another way of looking at the 'Desert War', however, was that both armies – and the outcome of the campaign – depended on supplies brought in from overseas. Here the Allies were incomparably more successful, especially in view of their much longer supply routes.

The last two months of 1942 saw Operation TORCH and Rommel's defeat at El Alamein. The British Army began a long pursuit, during which the Axis Libyan supply ports were rolled up; Tobruk was captured on 13 November, Benghazi on 20 November and Tripoli on 23 January 1943. Meanwhile the advance from the west, inland from the TORCH landings, was slower than it might have been. However, it still eventually gave the Allies control of Oran, Algiers and Bône (now Annaba), in effect nearly the whole African shore of the western Mediterranean. This secured Malta and enabled a tightening of the blockade of Tunisia. British and American land-based air power in North Africa could finally eliminate the threat of the Axis air forces. The Mediterranean region, with the Allied navies and air forces in near complete control of its waters, would have an even more important role in 1943 and 1944. The western Allies were ready to move north to the European shore.

The situation had changed drastically since the Battle of Sirte eight months earlier. There was virtually no attempt by the Axis to use surface ships in the weeks after the TORCH landing in November 1942. Admiral Cunningham noted the dominance of the Royal Navy in these weeks in his final report: 'The complaisant [*sic*] attitude of the Italian Fleet, and the inactivity of the French main Fleet, unfortunately gave Force H no scope for action.'[24]

* * *

In the third period of the war, the year 1942, the European conflict had become an interconnected global one.[25] This was partly because of the entry of the US, completing the involvement of all the major powers. It was partly, too, the result of the territorial spread of Axis dominance. Germany now gained control of much of southern Russia and North Africa and, even more dramatically, Japan now controlled the western Pacific and Southeast Asia. In this third period, however, at least after the early spring of 1942, the offensive momentum of

Germany, Japan and Italy showed itself to have been spent. The Axis powers were neither able to extend their conquests, nor to consolidate their hold on what they had already taken.

One of the features of 1942 was the very limited use of American ground and air forces against the European Axis powers – at least until November. This was understandable, in view of the time required to mobilise from peacetime and move forces across an ocean. The same thing had happened after the American declaration of war in April 1917, but in addition the US was in 1941–42 fighting a parallel war in the Pacific. What *was* massively important was the mobilisation of industrial and human potential within the US, which would have such an impact in 1943–45.

The British naval historian Stephen Roskill called this third phase of the sea war 'the period of balance'.[26] Inevitably the maritime war in 1942 had also become truly global rather than 'European'. It now extended to the Pacific, the Indian Ocean and the Arctic north, in addition to the Atlantic, the Mediterranean, the Baltic and the Black Sea. Compared to later months, this phase saw a higher proportion of the American naval effort being devoted to Europe, with the *Wasp* ferrying aircraft to Malta and new American battleships, carriers and cruisers operating with the British Home Fleet. However, the main German–American action, if it can be called that, in 1942 was the devastatingly successful operation of U-boats off the US East Coast. Meanwhile, the Royal Navy and the US Navy had to retreat rapidly in the Indian Ocean and the Pacific Ocean in the first months of 1942. By the middle of the year, however, they were offering a degree of resistance (at Midway *decisive* resistance), and Japanese naval forces had clearly reached the limits of their powers. The end result was critical. 'The last months of 1942', Admiral Richmond later noted, 'marked the opening of a new phase of the war, in the beginning of the transition from the struggle for the command of the sea to the reaping of the benefits of that command.'[27]

The leadership of the fleets in 1942 was generally the same as in 1941. The exception was the United States, where Pearl Harbor was followed by the sacking of Admiral Kimmel and the departure of the CNO, Admiral Stark. The position of their successors, admirals Nimitz and King, was at first tenuous, but consolidation and then successful counter-attack would allow these men to dominate naval decision-making until 1945. Perhaps surprisingly there was little change in the Royal Navy, despite a naval catastrophe off Malaya and in the East Indies which was, in many respects, worse than Pearl Harbor. The leadership of the German and Japanese navies stayed the same, which was understandable given many victories.

The level of naval activity had greatly increased in 1942 with the deployment of peacetime American and Japanese navies. The character of the 'battle fleet' had changed. The aircraft carrier replaced the battleship as the capital ship, a development which all the major powers (and their non-expert civilian leaders) had recognised from the beginning of the year, and certainly from the time of the Battle of Midway. Germany and Italy now made belated preparations to deploy carriers, although it was for them already far too late. Meanwhile the role of land-based aircraft in the sea/air war had been emphasised by the sinking of the *Prince of Wales* and the *Repulse*, the continued success of the Luftwaffe in the Mediterranean and the growing role of RAF anti-shipping aircraft there, and the role of shore-based American aircraft in the Solomons and New Guinea. At the very heart of the fighting in 1942 were the island air bases at Guadalcanal and Malta.

The trade war developed globally in 1942. The era of the surface raider – cruisers and disguised raiders – was essentially over. The European Arctic was in some respects an exception, but even there heavy surface ships sank only a handful of Allied merchant ships; the damage was done by U-boats and aircraft. A distinction has to be made between economic/strategic (trade) convoys and front-line/operational convoys which carried personnel and supplies into dangerous combat zones. (The Russian convoys – most notably PQ.17 – fall between the two categories.) The Japanese front-line/operational convoys in the South Pacific (e.g. the 'Tokyo Express') and the British ones to Malta were central features of 1942; in 1943 they would not be so prominent.

As for the strategic submarine campaigns, neither the Japanese nor the Americans achieved much success in 1942, due to their naval doctrine, the distances to enemy shipping lanes, technical problems and the limited number of boats available. The Germans, in contrast, were now able to deploy the U-boat fleet in unprecedented strength. They were, however, forced to divert many boats away from the strategic anti-shipping campaign (the 'tonnage war') to operational campaigns in the Arctic and the Mediterranean. And the British and Canadians were able to put a larger number of well-equipped escort ships into commission and, above all, to use aircraft as a deadly, effective A/S weapon. Allied strategic convoy routes were relatively secure by the end of 1942, including the one from the US to Australia.

Amphibious operations had been much more important in 1942 than in the first three years of the war. The Axis had carried out such operations earlier in the conflict, notably in Norway and in the Pacific and Southeast Asia, but these had been mounted in a vacuum against unwary and undefended targets. In 1942 two combined operations, at Guadalcanal and in North Africa, proved to be pivotal. The Germans and the Italians, meanwhile, lacked the capability to mount any large operations of this kind in 1942; the continued inability to take Malta (or threaten the British Isles) was highly significant. And the run of Japanese successes came to an end. Allied sea/air defences in the Coral Sea blocked the amphibious attack against strategic Port Moresby in May 1942, and American resistance in the following month forced the Japanese to abandon the assault on Midway Atoll. The Allies had only one failure, at Dieppe, and that had been a raid rather than an attempt to take and hold an objective; German sea/air forces played little part in its defeat.

Still, 1942 had been a year of contested seas, rather than of wholesale Allied victory. But during that time the pre-conditions were established for war-winning developments in 1943–44.

PART IV

VICTORY AT SEA

JANUARY 1943–JUNE 1944

If there is anyone who thinks that combating convoys is no longer possible, he is a weakling and no true U-boat commander. The battle in the Atlantic is getting harder but it is the determining element in the waging of the war. Be aware of your high responsibility and understand that you must answer for your conduct. Do your best over this convoy. We must destroy it. If the conditions permit, do not dive to evade aircraft, but fire and fend them off. Move away from destroyers on the surface where possible. Be hard, push forward and attack. I believe in you. Commander-in-Chief.

Admiral Dönitz, signal to wolfpack
MOSEL, 21 May 1943

CHAPTER 15

THE BATTLE OF THE ATLANTIC, ROUND THREE

January 1943–May 1944

THE BATTLE OF THE BARENTS SEA, 31 DECEMBER 1942

When, on Wednesday, 30 December 1942, the British convoy JW.51B, bound for northern Russia, was sighted by a patrolling U-boat, Naval Command North (*Marineoberkommando Nord*) put into effect a pre-arranged plan, Operation REGENBOGEN (RAINBOW). This involved an attack by heavy cruisers and destroyers based at the Altafjord in northern Norway, 175 miles north of Narvik. Admiral Oskar Kummetz would be in command; his main units were the *Admiral Hipper* and the *Lützow*; the latter was the sister of the *Admiral Graf Spee* and had reached the far north only two weeks earlier. Supporting the heavy cruisers were six big destroyers. Battleships were not available; the *Tirpitz* was refitting at Trondheim and the *Scharnhorst* was still in dockyard hands in Germany.

Kummetz sortied on Wednesday evening and some hours later split his force into two divisions, each consisting of a cruiser and three destroyers. The *Hipper* group was to draw the British escort off to the north, while the *Lützow* group attacked the convoy from the south. The engagement was expected to take place some 200 miles from the German base, in the few hours of twilight on the forenoon of the following day, New Year's Eve.

The battle group operated under instructions which later proved controversial: 'exercise restraint even when the enemy is of the same strength, as taking major risks with the cruisers is not desired by the Führer.'[1] Hitler feared another loss of German prestige; the senior naval command, including Admiral Raeder, feared the final destruction of the 'core fleet' of heavy ships. Kummetz himself was no stranger to 'major risks'; he had commanded the thrust of the heavy cruisers *Blücher* and *Lützow* up the Oslofjord in April 1940. This ended with the loss of his flagship, the brand-new *Blücher* (sister ship of the *Hipper*), sunk by the Norwegian shore defences.

For the Allies this was the second large Allied Arctic convoy since PQ.17 in July 1942. With the memory of that disaster in mind, the Admiralty had changed the convoy series designation from 'PQ' to 'JW', and began with convoy JW.51. The first JW convoy was divided to make it easier to handle. Convoy JW.51A (sixteen merchant ships) slipped through the polar darkness and arrived off the Kola Inlet without incident on Christmas Day. The second element, JW.51B, was made up of twelve merchant ships and departed from Loch Ewe in Scotland on 22 December. HMS *Onslow* and five other fleet destroyers, commanded by Captain Robert Sherbrooke, provided close escort. Local support took the form of the light cruisers *Jamaica* and *Sheffield*, under Admiral R.L. Burnett.

The battle, spread over an area extending 25 miles from north to south, and 35 miles from east to west, lasted for about four hours of the late morning. The sea was relatively calm, but there were snow squalls. The cautious probing of the German cruisers and destroyers met smoke screens and aggressive counter-attacks by the British escorts. Alan Ross, a radio operator, watched events from the deck of the *Onslow*: 'As I walked aft to peer out in the half-light we slewed violently, repeated flashes of gunfire stabbing the horizon on our port beam. *Hipper* had altered her range and bearing, and now shell after shell was pitching just ahead of us.' Ross had only returned to the 'W/T office' when disaster struck: 'Within seconds flames and smoke had engulfed most of the forward part of the ship. We had been hit twice between the wheelhouse and the two for'ard guns, the second salvo killing the two gun crews, wiping out the fire and repair parties, and the ammunition supply party next to "B" gun.'[2] Captain Sherbrooke was partly blinded by shell splinters, and had to transfer command of the escorts to another officer.

The *Hipper* sank a corvette and mortally damaged the destroyer *Achates*, but at 11.35 the *Jamaica* and the *Sheffield* under Admiral Burnett emerged from the murk and hit the German flagship three times, taking advantage of their superior radar. At about this time Kummetz's instructions not to take risks were repeated, and in the next few minutes both German forces began a withdrawal. One of their destroyers, the *Friedrich Eckoldt*, blundered into the midst of Burnett's cruisers and was quickly sunk with all hands.

The main body of the convoy and its cargo of supplies reached Murmansk untouched on 3 January 1943. Admiral Tovey – the Home Fleet commander – expressed his satisfaction in a despatch: 'That an enemy force of at least one pocket battleship, one heavy cruiser and six destroyers, with all the advantages of surprise and concentration, should be held off for four hours by five destroyers and driven from the area by two 6-inch cruisers, without any loss to the convoy, is most creditable and satisfactory.'[3] The badly wounded Sherbrooke was awarded the Victoria Cross.

Hitler, attempting to follow events from his headquarters, 1,500 miles to the south in East Prussia, grew increasingly angry. Kummetz kept radio silence as his reunited battle group returned to base through the last night of the year. Even after he returned to the Altafjord early on 1 January, technical factors slowed the relaying of a report. On the afternoon of the 31st Admiral Krancke, the naval representative at Führer Headquarters, had made too much of a U-boat report suggesting heavy damage to the Allied convoy. Then, in the evening, the British had announced the successful defence.

Hitler felt misled, but there were deeper reasons for his frustration on this first day of the new year. In the past two months his war effort had clearly turned for the worse. The British and Americans had taken the initiative in North Africa; Rommel was now retreating headlong in Libya, and the Allies had landed in Morocco and Algeria. In Russia the German sixth Army had since mid-November been trapped at Stalingrad; with this, any chances of achieving the aim of the 1942 Russian campaign – reaching the oil regions of the Caucasus – had vanished. By the afternoon of the 1st, still with no report about REGENBOGEN, the Führer was in a rage. His comments were minuted by the now silent Admiral Krancke: '[Surface] ships were completely useless, and served only as a bulwark of revolution because the crews spent time lying around and were lacking in zeal; it [had] meant the death of the [1914–18 era] High Seas Fleet, it was now his [Hitler's] unalterable decision to get rid of these useless ships at last, to make more productive use of the good personnel, the good weapons, the armoured material [the armour plate]'.[4]

Five days later Admiral Raeder flew from Berlin to East Prussia for a meeting with Hitler. He was subjected to a monologue on the shortcomings of the German Navy and the worthlessness of the big ships. The Naval War Staff were allowed to make a final case for retaining the vessels, but this was rejected. To save face, Raeder's departure was delayed until 30 January 1943, the tenth anniversary of the Nazi seizure of power. Erich Raeder was almost sixty-seven years old and had commanded the German Navy for the last fifteen years. His replacement would be the fifty-one-year-old Admiral Karl Dönitz.

THE BRITISH VICTORY IN THE ATLANTIC

The traditional Kriegsmarine had failed – as Admiral Raeder had predicted it would in the first days of the 'premature' war. Raeder was a traditional nationalist who had been willing to work with Hitler, and he won the support of the Nazi leader while the Kriegsmarine had its early successes with surface warships and U-boats. During the war he had a different strategic conception from Hitler, oceanic rather than continental, but his outlook was still oriented towards

Weltmacht ('World Power'). Like many European naval officers of his generation, Raeder underestimated naval aviation and the potential of sea/air war, but probably no admiral could have won the bureaucratic dogfight with Göring's Luftwaffe. At Nuremberg the Grossadmiral was rightly convicted of planning and fighting a war of aggression; he was fortunate to avoid the death sentence imposed on his opposite numbers in the German Army and Luftwaffe. In the end he would serve a decade in Spandau Prison, before being released on grounds of ill health in 1955; he lived to see his memoirs published.

Hitler's appointment of Admiral Dönitz as C-in-C, Navy (*Oberbefehlshaber der Marine* or OBdM), began a new stage in the history of the Kriegsmarine. Rolf Carls, head of Naval Command North, and seven years Dönitz's senior, had been Raeder's preferred replacement, but Carls was passed over and was soon retired from active service, along with other older admirals. The head of the Naval War Staff, Kurt Fricke, also senior to Dönitz, was transferred from Berlin to head Naval Command South in the Balkans. Fricke's successor at the Naval War Staff, Wilhelm Meisel, was two years junior to the new OBdM. He was competent – he had commanded the *Admiral Hipper* until November 1942 – but he had little to do.

Dönitz was a more single-minded adherent of Hitler than Raeder. He was somewhat more effective than his predecessor – in wartime – in getting resources for the Kriegsmarine in competition with the other services, and he formed an effective working relationship with some leaders of the war economy, including Albert Speer. His participation in the operational side of the U-boat war was inevitably reduced when he took over the whole Kriegsmarine (although the submarine was now fully the main weapon of that service). His headquarters and that of the U-boat command moved from Paris to Charlottenburg in Berlin. Eberhard Godt, formerly head of operations in the U-boat staff, remained as head of the U-boat arm until the end of the war.

The new OBdM did not follow Hitler's wishes regarding the big ships, or continue with his own initial response to them. The proposal had been to withdraw the battleships and cruisers from operational duties, decommissioning some of them and retaining others only as training vessels. The *Scharnhorst* would have been kept in the Baltic and withdrawn from service in July 1943, the *Tirpitz* would have stayed in Norwegian waters until August 1943, and then been paid off. In February 1943, however, Dönitz put it to Hitler that the Russian convoys were still a vulnerable target, and won the decision that the *Tirpitz* and the *Lützow* would remain in northern Norway, to be joined by the *Scharnhorst*.

This chapter deals with the first eighteen months of the Dönitz era. The period falls into two quite different phases. The first was from January to May 1943, when the largest-ever concentration of U-boats was thrown against the

North Atlantic supply convoys; it ended with massive losses for the German submarine force and the decision by Admiral Dönitz to abandon attacks on the main northern Atlantic convoy route. The second phase ran from June 1943 to the end of May 1944, the eve of the Normandy landings; in these months the Allies consolidated their control over the North Atlantic, and crushed German attempts to regain the initiative. Overall developments, increasingly favourable to the Allies, are shown in Table 15.1.

In January 1943 the U-boat threat was indeed a powerful and increasing one. Twelve months earlier, at the start of what turned out to be a devastatingly successful campaign off the American coast, there had been ninety-one 'front-line boats' (*Frontboote*), sixty-five of them operating in the Atlantic. Now there were 213 front-line boats, 166 of them in the Atlantic. Ominously for the Allies, at the start of 1943 a further 187 U-boats were involved in running trials or training.[5] More than twenty new units were being completed each month. The simple number of Frontboote was not the only German strength. The Battle of the Atlantic is now popularly seen as a campaign in which 'special intelligence' gave the Allies a great advantage. However, at the start of 1943, it was the Germans who were ahead. From February the *B-Dienst* was again able to decrypt rapidly the Allied convoy codes, and only in June 1943 did the Allies become fully aware of their vulnerability and take effective counter-measures.

The Allies confronted a number of shipping 'crises' during the course of the war. Probably the most important one took place in the spring of 1943. This is often misunderstood and, in some respects, historians have made too much of

Table 15.1. The Battle of the Atlantic, January 1943–May 1944

Year/ quarter	N. Atlantic tonnage lost	N. Atlantic ships lost	U-boats oper.	U-boats t&t	U-boats lost
1943/i	938,000	155	212	181	40
1943/ii	417,000	77	240	185	75
1943/iii	177,000	28	207	208	73
1943/iv	127,000	25	175	237	53
1944/i	86,000	14	168	268	60
1944/ii	39,000	5	166	278	68
Total (N. Atlantic)	1,784,000	304			
Total (World)	3,839,000	716			369

Source: Rosk/2, pp. 475, 486; ibid./3,1, p. 364; ibid./3.2, pp. 478–9.
Notes: Losses are for Allied and neutral countries' merchant ships due to enemy action *of all types*, not just due to U-boats. Tonnage is GRT. U-boat numbers are total for German Navy (all theatres) at the start of each quarter; 'oper.' is operational U-boats, 't&t' is units involved in training and trials. U-boat figures include losses from all causes and in all theatres.

it. The rate of merchant ship sinkings at the hands of the U-boats was still very high in the first quarter of 1943, and at the Casablanca Conference (code-named SYMBOL) and elsewhere, the western Allies had taken on new and demanding shipping commitments with their planned offensives. On the positive side, however, in the winter of 1942–43 Allied global construction of merchant ships had cancelled out losses, and the output of shipyards – above all American shipyards – raced ahead.

In reality the 'crisis' was a symptom of the *success* of the British and American war effort rather than of its weakness. The American forces were now attacking in the South Pacific, where the very long shipping supply lines and the lack of port facilities tied up many ships. Major victories had been won in North Africa, although the shipping demands of that theatre – after Operation TORCH in November 1942 – also turned out to be larger and longer-lasting than expected. Moreover, the Allied powers had also agreed to carry out the invasion of Sicily (Operation HUSKY) in mid-1943. Supplies increasingly had to be sent to Russia via a long shipping route through Persia. There were plans at the Casablanca/SYMBOL Conference for a major amphibious operation in Burma, Operation ANAKIM; if carried out, ANAKIM would demand merchant ships in the distant Indian Ocean.

The British were concerned, at the highest level. As the Minister of War Transport, Lord Leathers, put it in March1943, 'We must cut the coat of our strategy according to the cloth of our shipping . . .'[6] To some extent the problem was sorted out. In the end ANAKIM was abandoned, and the costly northern Russian convoys were cut back. The British found that their import requirements for the UK were not as high as they had expected. A direct appeal by Prime Minister Churchill to President Roosevelt led to a decision in May 1943 which gave the British wartime control of 200 merchant ships.

Most obviously, the Allies were able to reduce the shipping losses from U-boat attacks that they had been suffering in 1942 and the first quarter of 1943. So, in overall terms, the feared shipping crisis was avoided, at least from the point of view of Britain and the war effort of the western Allies. Britain was kept supplied, and the ambitious major counter-attack plans of the British and American forces – short and long term – could be put in place without logistics being a bottle-neck. Nevertheless, the mismanagement of shipping was a contributing factor to a major famine in India in 1943.

As far as the battle with the U-boats in the Atlantic is concerned, it would be a mistake to exaggerate either top-level command or special intelligence as the key elements of the May 1943 turning point. The British admiral Max Horton did take over as C-in-C, Western Approaches, in November 1942, replacing Percy Noble – who was made head of the British Admiralty Delegation (BAD) in Washington (in place of Andrew Cunningham). Meanwhile Air Marshal John Slessor took over Coastal Command from Philip Joubert de la Ferté in February 1943. Both the new men were very able (Slessor would be awarded a knighthood in May), but the underlying structure was largely the work of their predecessors.

Allied intelligence – especially signals intelligence – was not *the* central causal factor, any more than in 1942. As already mentioned, the success of Bletchley Park against the U-boat communication system greatly improved from December 1942, and this allowed more evasive routing of convoys and concentration of escorts. There were weeks, however, where decryption lagged behind, notably in March 1943.[7] As far as the work of other 'backroom' civilians is concerned, more attention needs to be paid to the development of Operational Research. This was the analysis of the course of the battles and of convoy policy by non-naval advisers like the physicist Patrick Blackett; most important, this advice was taken seriously at the highest levels. (The failure – or inability – of Nazi Germany to exploit the talent of civilian 'outsiders' was a significant weakness in its war effort.)

In reality the heart of the spring 1943 victory were the British and Canadian sea/air forces, and their highly trained crews and first-rate electronic equipment. By January 1943 the Allied surface escort forces were steadily growing. On the northern convoy route the 'Flower' class were supplemented by new corvettes of the larger 'River' class, as well as a number of destroyer-size sloops. The accumulation of strength allowed the deployment of more and better-equipped escort groups, as well as new 'support groups'. The latter consisted of faster ships, including some new destroyers seconded from the main fleets; they could be rapidly deployed to reinforce the escort of the most threatened convoys. Most of these escort vessels had centimetric radar, and they all benefited from improved inter-ship communication. Moreover shipborne HF/DF (high-frequency direction finding) was now common. Much effort had been devoted to training and the development of tactics in the Royal Navy in the relatively quiet period of late 1942.

The aviation component of the sea/air war was now vital, above all the ability of aircraft to actually 'kill' U-boats rather than simply drive them underwater. Arguments continued at the highest levels of the Allied leadership about this, especially about giving the A/S forces a share of the new four-engined bombers, and the latest centimetric radar equipment. Involvement of long-range aircraft of the US Navy and the AAF in the northern convoy route was limited at this time, but the American supply of aircraft to the British was crucial. RAF Coastal Command had 118 land-based long-range patrol aircraft in January 1943 (compared to twenty-eight in July 1942). By July 1943 the number had risen to 150. Especially important for closing the 'Air Gap' was the VLR ('very long range') American-built Liberator.[8] The numbers of patrol planes alone made it difficult for the enemy to continue to use wolfpack tactics outside the 'Black Pit' in the Central Atlantic; the patrol planes stymied their rapid movement – on the surface – to concentrate for convoy attacks. A/S aircraft were still mainly land-based. The escort carrier would be a more important element later, but in the spring of 1943 there were still not many of them, and they were only beginning to be used in the North Atlantic; the American-built sister ships USS *Bogue* and HMS *Biter* arrived in March and April 1943.

Other long-range aircraft, medium and heavy bombers, supported by long-range RAF fighters, operated over the Bay of Biscay from bases in southwestern England. Indirect attacks on the U-boats, away from the convoys, had limited effect in the first five months of 1943. Air raids against German U-boat ship-yards achieved little, despite now being given priority by Allied leaders. Forward U-boat bases now incorporated heavily protected concrete bunkers. Transit routes across the Bay of Biscay, however, were becoming vulnerable again to British and American patrol aircraft. Coastal Command No. 19 Group began in March 1943 to operate RAF Wellington bombers and AAF B-24 Liberators, both equipped with accurate centimetric radar which could not be picked up by the U-boat Metox detectors.

Between 1 January and 31 May 1943, forty-five U-boats were sunk by shore-based aircraft, two by carrier aircraft, and eight by ships and aircraft operating together. Only twenty-nine enemy submarines were credited to surface ships operating on their own. The total number of U-boats sunk in these first five months of 1943 was ninety-six, compared to eighty-seven in all twelve months of 1942. The number sunk by shore-based aircraft, either on their own or shared with surface ships, rose to fifty-one from forty.[9]

The 1943 battles on the northern Atlantic supply route were fought mainly by the well-equipped and well-trained ships of the Royal Navy and the Royal Canadian Navy and, increasingly, the aircraft of RAF Coastal Command. Indeed, at a conference held in Washington in early March 1943 it was agreed that the Americans would withdraw completely from the northern route; this took effect at the end of April. The British and Canadians would now divide this route between them, with longitude 47°W (the line of the southern tip of Greenland, Cape Farewell) marking the dividing line. The failure to develop smooth co-operation between the western Allies at 'theatre' level was a feature of the Battle of the Atlantic in 1943 (and 1944), which might have become more dangerous in different circumstances. The US Navy command, and Admiral King in particular, were unwilling to submit the Battle of the Atlantic to an inter-Allied staff; especially problematic for them was the question of an overall command co-ordinating all aspects of the sea/air in the Atlantic. The commander-in-chief would probably have been British, and King was opposed to American warships fighting under foreign command. Even worse for King, of course, was the prospect of command by a fellow countryman in the form of a USAAF general.

The spring of 1943 is often seen as the climax of the Battle of the Atlantic, with the largest U-boat fleet ever deployed. Nevertheless, the overall level of losses in the – enlarged – eastbound convoys from North America to Britain remained low. Of twenty-five (fast) HX convoys in the first half of 1943 (HX.222 to HX.246), only eight suffered any losses to ships in convoy; the total in these six months was twenty-seven merchant ships out of 1,349 (2 per cent). Of the nineteen slower SC convoys (SC.116 to SC.135), only four took losses in convoy; the total losses were twenty-five merchant ships out of 901 (3 per cent).[10]

In the first months of 1943, U-boat operations were curtailed by the North Atlantic winter and the Ultra-based success in re-routing convoys. The pivotal and largest battles on the northern route took place in March 1943. The eastbound convoys HX.229 and SC.122 were attacked in the mid-Atlantic on 16–20 March, while beyond the range of patrol aircraft. Three wolfpacks were directly involved, totalling forty-one submarines. Some twenty-two merchant ships out of 110 were sunk, and only one U-boat was 'killed' in exchange.

After this the Allies began to gain the upper hand. The slow westbound convoy ONS.5 did lose twelve merchant ships, but in a wild battle on the foggy night of 5/6 May, the ships of the escort sank five U-boats; two more were 'killed' by aircraft as the convoy crossed the Atlantic, and two went down after a collision.

Despite the continuing shipping losses the British had decided that the best policy was to fight their way through on the shortest great-circle route from North America to the UK. The density of U-boats was high but a growing force of British and Canadian escort and support groups at sea was available; in addition, more VLR aircraft were in service to operate in what had been the 'Black Pit'. Westbound convoys HX.237 and SC.129 fought off thirty-six U-boats (7–14 May) with the loss of five merchant ships; four of the attackers were destroyed.

Faced with increased Allied strength, Admiral Dönitz and the U-boat command resorted to desperate measures. (Dönitz now had a simultaneous and acute shipping crisis of his own on the Italy–Tunisia route.)[11] On 1 May boats transiting the Bay of Biscay were ordered to stay on the surface to fight back against enemy patrol planes when time to dive was limited; they were to use their newly fitted 20mm AA guns. The order was in place for three months; while a number of patrol planes were shot down, U-boat losses were heavy. Meanwhile the U-boat packs that had actually reached the northern Atlantic convoy route – many of them with inexperienced crews – had to be urged on against increasingly lethal opposition from the escorts. On 21 May Dönitz despatched a frantic signal to wolfpack MOSEL ('Moselle') which was attacking HX.239: 'If there is anyone who thinks that combating convoys is no longer possible, he is a weakling and no true U-boat captain . . . *Hart sein, nach vorne kommen und angreifen* [Be hard, push forward and attack]'.[12] Despite this exhortation the convoy suffered no casualties. Dönitz had meanwhile suffered a personal tragedy when he learned that the *U 954* had gone missing during the attack on convoy SC.130 on 18–19 May. On board had been his twenty-one-year-old son; Sub-Lieutenant Peter Dönitz was lost with forty-five comrades when his boat was sunk by two escort ships.

Four days after Dönitz's appeal of 21 May the U-boats were stood down from the northern route, in view of the strength of the defences. The German command assumed the Allied advantage was temporary, based on advances in radar – they were unaware of shipborne HF/DF, let alone the comprehensive decryption of their communications. But with hindsight these events would actually mark the decisive defeat of the North Atlantic U-boat campaign. The month would later be remembered by the Kriegsmarine as 'Black May'; in this period some forty-one U-boats were sunk, mainly on the northern Atlantic convoy route but also in the Bay of Biscay.

THE RUSSIAN CONVOYS AND THE END OF THE GERMAN HEAVY SHIPS

After the Battle of the Barents Sea in late December 1942 two more convoys (JW.52 and JW.53) were run to Murmansk in January and February 1943, taking advantage of the long polar night. These had to endure the wild winter weather, but neither suffered losses from German action. Then, paradoxically, just at the time Hitler had given up on the surface navy and sacked Admiral Raeder, the Allies decided the Barents Sea was too dangerous an area. They drastically scaled back their Arctic convoys, and in the end this pause continued through most of the year, until the long nights reduced the danger. The next eastbound convoy (JW.54A) departed from Loch Ewe only eight months later, in mid-November 1943.

The British and American decision may or may not have been correct, but it was understandable. Operation TORCH and the fighting in Tunisia reduced the number of merchant ships and escorts available, as did the onslaught of an unprecedented number of U-boats in the North Atlantic; this was the height of Allied shipping difficulties. Meanwhile for the British Admiralty the German sea/air threat in the northern Atlantic route still seemed acute. At the end of March 1943, Churchill broke the news to Stalin about cancelled convoys, stressing the danger from the German fleet and the need for shipping for the planned invasion of Sicily.

Stalin was angry, not least because the postponement of the convoys coincided with the delay of the cross-Channel invasion. All the same, he was more restrained in his response than he had been in the autumn of 1942. The Red

Army's victory at Stalingrad meant Russia's military situation was no longer so desperate. The British and Americans were now engaged with a serious number of German troops in Tunisia, and the next planned move, into Sicily, was certainly most important. Meanwhile significant supplies were beginning to reach the USSR through the Persian corridor, Vladivostok and the Alaska–Siberia (ALSIB) air ferry route. In August and September 1943, however, the Soviets pressed for resumption of northern convoys, in view of the improving naval situation in the North Atlantic and the Mediterranean. Stalin wrote to Churchill in October, stressing that 'the northern route is the shortest, ensuring quickest delivery to the Soviet–German front . . . and that unless that route is properly used the USSR cannot get supplies on the required scale'.[13]

In September 1943 the *Tirpitz*, the *Scharnhorst* and ten destroyers carried out a brief raid against small Allied installations on Spitzbergen, the remote island 450 miles northwest of North Cape, in the Svalbard Archipelago. The expedition had no military importance, but it marked the swansong of the heavy ships. The *Tirpitz* lobbed 15-inch shells against small targets on the bleak Arctic shore – the only time her big guns would be fired in anger.

At the end of the month, after the battle group had returned to the Altafjord, British midget submarines mounted a daring attack. This was not the first attempt. In Operation TITLE in October 1942, a trawler had towed two converted torpedoes, intended to be ridden by two pairs of divers, into the Trondheimsfjord, where the *Tirpitz* was then anchored. Each 'chariot' was to carry its 'crew' slowly up to the target, where they would dismount and attach limpet mines. The chariots were towed to within 10 miles of the *Tirpitz*, but then broke adrift and the raid had to be abandoned.

For the Altafjord attack in September 1943 (code-named Operation SOURCE), the British used small submarines rather than manned torpedoes. The 'X-craft' were about 50 feet long and displaced 27 tons. The crew of four, including a diver, were accommodated within the small hull. The crew were to drop big explosive charges on the seabed, underneath their target. There were originally six X-craft in Operation SOURCE, with simultaneous attacks planned against the *Tirpitz*, the *Scharnhorst* and the *Lützow*. The mission was exceptionally dangerous, starting with the 1,300-mile voyage under submarine tow to the north of Norway; two X-craft were sunk en route. The four surviving X-craft cast off from their mother submarines at the entrance to the Altafjord, and the final approach – a voyage of 50 miles – took thirty-six hours, with crews having to cut through torpedo nets to reach their final target. The *X5*, with the mission commander, disappeared. Nevertheless, the *X6* and *X7* succeeded in planting several 2-ton demolition charges under the *Tirpitz*. Serious damage was caused. Code decrypts revealed that even temporary repairs would not be completed until March 1944. The

Scharnhorst was undamaged; she had left her mooring for gunnery practice. *X10*, assigned to attack her, was able in the end to return to the open sea. Her crew spent six days trapped in their floating coffin before one of the mother submarines rescued them.

By the end of 1943 the *Scharnhorst* remained the last active heavy ship in the Far North. The *Tirpitz* had been immobilised, and the *Lützow* sent home for a refit, along with half the destroyers. In November Admiral Kummetz, the battle group commander, departed on extended sick leave. Admiral Erich Bey was left in charge of the *Scharnhorst* and five destroyers.

In November 1943 the British began to run supply convoys to northern Russia again. JW.54A, JW.54B and JW.55A made the eastbound trip unhindered. With the German Army now pulling back before the Soviet onslaught, the renewed flow of supplies to northern Russia was an embarrassment for the Kriegsmarine. At his meeting with Hitler on 19–20 December Admiral Dönitz reported his intention to strike the next convoy. The attack was hastily prepared, and assigned a significant code name: Operation OSTFRONT (EASTERN FRONT).

Convoy JW.55B was sighted by German aircraft north of the Faroes on 22 December. Dönitz claimed in his memoirs that the naval staff shared his opinion that 'here was a splendid chance for the *Scharnhorst*'. In reality both Bey and the C-in-C, Navy Group North, Admiral Schniewind, at Kiel were opposed to the operation, in view of the weather, the short hours of twilight and the weakness of the Altafjord battle group.[14] Dönitz decided to press ahead, and in the afternoon of the Saturday the 25th, Bey received the 'execute' order: 'OSTFRONT 1700/25/12'.

Convoy JW.55B was made up of nineteen merchant ships. It was covered in the Barents Sea by Force 1, three Home Fleet cruisers. Meanwhile a separate Force 2 sailed from Iceland, with the battleship *Duke of York*, the cruiser *Jamaica* and four destroyers. Flying his flag in the *Duke of York* was Admiral Bruce Fraser, who had replaced Tovey as C-in-C, Home Fleet, in May 1943. Bletchley Park promptly decrypted the OSTFRONT 'execute' order, and at 2.17 a.m. on Sunday, the Admiralty despatched a warning to the *Duke of York*: 'Emergency: *Scharnhorst* probably sailed 1800 25 December'.[15] With this information and the expected position of the convoy, Admiral Fraser could make an educated guess about the course of the enemy ships. Admiral Bey, for his part, proceeded north at high speed from the Altafjord toward the estimated position of the convoy; he aimed to attack it at about 10.00 a.m. on the 26th, but he still lacked a clear idea of the strength or location of the British covering forces.

The Battle of North Cape was fought in a storm and semi-darkness on Sunday, 26 December. In the first of three phases Force 1 – the cruisers *Norfolk*,

Belfast and *Sheffield* – intercepted the German battle group, after making radar contact at 8.40 a.m. An hour later the two sides fought a running engagement until Bey broke off. A second phase, in the middle of the short Arctic 'day', took place as the *Scharnhorst*, now without her destroyer screen, approached the convoy from the north. Bey ran into the Force 1 cruisers again, failed to break through and decided to give up the whole operation. The *Scharnhorst* raced south back towards home, trailed by the British cruisers. In the last phase, in the complete darkness of late afternoon, the cruisers and the *Duke of York* force (coming up from the southwest) boxed her in.

Bey was a destroyer specialist with little experience handling heavy ships. (His most notable earlier service had been as commander of the German destroyers trapped at Narvik in April–May 1940.) In addition the battleship's Seetakt search radar had been disabled in the duel with the *Norfolk*. Fraser, in contrast, co-ordinated effectively the movements of his ships. The final duel began at 4.17 p.m, when the radar of the *Duke of York* picked up the enemy battleship. Half an hour later she fired star shells; the blaze of light caught the *Scharnhorst* with her guns still trained fore and aft. She was pounded by the radar-controlled 14-inch guns of the *Duke of York*, and was unable to achieve any hits with her own armament. Heavy shell damage slowed her enough for a British destroyer flotilla to catch up and fire torpedoes (initially achieving four hits). No British ship saw the *Scharnhorst* go down, but an underwater explosion was heard at 7.45 p.m. Only thirty-six survivors were picked up; neither Admiral Bey nor any of his officers were among them.

Admiral Fraser was promoted to full admiral in February 1944, and given command of the new Pacific Fleet later in the year. (In 1946 he would be raised to the peerage in 1946 as Baron Fraser of North Cape.) His battle appeared to be an old-fashioned surface action, but codebreaking and radar played a vital part. Dönitz, meanwhile, deserves much of the blame for the loss of the *Scharnhorst*. Early in the new year he and Hitler held what must have been a dispiriting post-mortem at Führer Headquarters in East Prussia. Dönitz told his Führer that the battle had shown that 'without the necessary radio location equipment [radar] it is no longer possible for surface ships . . . to fight'. Hitler believed the *Scharnhorst* should have taken on the British cruiser force more aggressively in the midday phase of the battle. Despite the nature of the orders he himself had actually given on previous occasions, Hitler claimed that since the loss of the *Graf Spee* in 1939 the German Navy had played it too safe.[16]

The *Tirpitz* was now the sole remaining surface threat to the Russian convoys. On 3 April 1944 the Home Fleet mounted Operation TUNGSTEN, an air strike on her anchorage in the Altafjord. The Admiralty knew from special intelligence that the repairs to the *Tirpitz* were nearing completion. Little remembered now, the air strike was probably the most elaborate carried out by the Fleet Air Arm (FAA) during the course of the war, and after Taranto the most successful. Admiral Fraser now commanded a powerful sea/air striking force, including the fleet carrier *Victorious*, the older *Furious* and four American-built escort carriers, HMS *Emperor*, *Fencer*, *Pursuer* and *Searcher*.[17]

Four and a half years into the war, the FAA was finally equipped with large numbers of modern aircraft. The carriers of Fraser's attack force had embarked 141 planes, including thirty-nine new Fairey Barracuda strike aircraft, twenty-eight Vought Corsairs and twenty Grumman Hellcats. The contrast with the ineffective operations off Norway in 1940 (when the carrier *Glorious* was lost) was sharp. Even in 1941 and 1942 British carriers had been equipped with Swordfish or Albacore biplane torpedo bombers; also not first-rate had been FAA fighters, the two-seat Fulmar and the navalised Sea Hurricane and Seafire, both improvisations with limited range. American-built fighters had begun to arrive in late 1940 in the form of the Grumman Martlet/Wildcat (F4F). This was the mix of aircraft that was still used by the British in the Mediterranean in late 1942 and the spring of 1943.

New American-built fighters with 2,000hp engines became available to the FAA under Lend-Lease in the summer of 1943. Eventually about 2,000 Corsairs and 1,000 Hellcats were received. The new squadrons were formed in the US, many at a naval air station at Quonset Point, Rhode Island. Also joining the fleet was the British-built Fairey Barracuda, which carried a torpedo externally, and could also be used as a dive bomber. First flown in December 1940, over 2,000 were eventually delivered during the war; the Barracuda began operational service at the time of the Salerno landing in September 1943.

In April 1944, the swarm of modern aircraft involved in Operation TUNGSTEN achieved near complete surprise in the early morning attack on the Altafjord. Protective nets around the *Tirpitz* and the narrowness of the anchorage ruled out the use of torpedoes. Dive-bombing by the Barracudas could not readily pierce the battleship's armoured deck, even with special 1,600lb armour-piercing (AP) bombs. Nevertheless, significant damage was achieved by strafing attacks and bombs; sixteen hits or near misses were achieved. Some 132 German crew members were killed (compared to only one man in the September 1943 X-craft attack). The *Tirpitz* would only be available for full service three months later, in July 1944. (The air strike coincided with another operation using the new aircraft, which took place on 19 April 1944 on the other side of the planet; the target was Sabang on Sumatra, and the Ceylon-based *Illustrious* had forty-two Corsairs and fifteen Barracudas embarked.)[18]

Repeat attacks on the *Tirpitz* were attempted in July and August 1944, operations MASCOT and GOODWOOD, with the strike forces being launched by the

Furious, the *Formidable* and the new fleet carrier *Indefatigable*. These were largely thwarted by German smoke screens.

Meanwhile, Allied supply from North America to northern Russia decreased from 950,000 tons in 1942 to 680,000 in 1943, the result of cancelled convoys. This made up only 14 per cent of supplies sent to Russia by tonnage; the figure increased slightly in the first half of 1944, but was still less than 20 per cent. Maritime supply of the USSR changed greatly in 1943, with the expansion of the routes via the Persian Gulf and the Pacific. In the late summer of 1942 American engineers had taken over the ports and routes of the 'Persian corridor'. Some 1.6 million tons of supplies were despatched from North America through Iran in 1943, and this flow was greatly aided by the re-opening of the Mediterranean.[19]

To the surprise of the Allies, the Japanese did not seriously interfere with individual sailings along the Pacific Lend-Lease route via the Aleutian Islands, with Petropavlovsk on the Kamchatka Peninsula as the main destination. The Americans now transferred some thirty Liberty ships to the USSR; the first, in January 1943, was the SS *Krasnogvardeets* ('Red Guard'). The Pacific route was far from ideal. Ice conditions limited transits; ships spent months tied up in port; American submarines mistakenly attacked several Soviet merchant ships in the final stages of the passage. There was an incident in 1943 at the opening of navigation in the La Pérouse Strait (between Sakhalin and Hokkaidō), when a Japanese icebreaker stopped and held two US-built merchant ships recently transferred to the Soviet flag (the two vessels were released that summer). All the same, in 1943 the Pacific became the route by which half the supplies – in terms of tonnage – from the US and Canada were sent. In 1943 this came to nearly 2.4 million tons.[20]

The British and Americans did not achieve the hoped for (and promised) totals of Lend-Lease aid to Russia under the so-called Second Protocol (July 1942 to June 1943). They did do so during Third Protocol period (July 1943 to June 1944), when the commitment of 5.1 millions tons was exceeded by 25 per cent.[21]

THE U-BOAT WAR, JUNE 1943–MAY 1944

Admiral Dönitz developed a good working relationship with Hitler despite the Atlantic setback. The German Navy, after all, was in many respects doing less badly than the Army and the Luftwaffe. Dönitz paid close attention to the attempted revival of the U-boat campaign, but as C-in-C, Navy, his time was now also taken up by more general problems, including Mediterranean supply and developments in Italy. He spoke at a meeting of Nazi regional leaders in Posen in October 1943, and it seems very likely that he was present there when

SS leader Heinrich Himmler made a speech describing explicitly the mass murder of the Jews.[22] Shell-Haus in central Berlin was burned out in a British air raid in November 1943; the naval headquarters was moved to a bunker complex in the northern suburbs of Berlin code-named KORALLE ('Coral'), the construction of which had begun during the summer.

The summer of 1943 was also the time that the Kriegsmarine decided to embark on a radical technical change of submarine construction. As recently as April 1943 the expanded programme involved more and more conventional (Type VII) U-boats. Now it was decided that no further Type VII and Type IX boats would be laid down. In their place an ambitious programme for constructing two new types began.

German engineers had considered leaping beyond a two-engine (diesel/electric) propulsion system to 'closed-cycle' technology; this would allow the boat to remain submerged at all times. The motor designed by Hellmuth Walter, which used hydrogen peroxide as a fuel, seemed to present the possibility of a true submarine, and a new streamlined hull was designed for it (the Type XVIII).[23] In the end the Walter motor presented unexpected technical problems, but it was proposed to Admiral Dönitz that the new hull could be adapted to conventional diesel/electric propulsion by installing much larger battery capacity. The so-called 'electro-boat' would be able to run underwater at higher speeds and for longer distances.

This improvisation became the 1,600-ton Type XXI U-boat, a replacement for the Type IX. At the same time, a small electro-boat, for use in the Mediterranean and elsewhere, was developed as the 230-ton Type XXIII. Equally innovative and ambitious was the programme to mass-produce these two types using prefabrication of hull sections at inland sites; this would increase production flow and reduce time exposed in vulnerable shipyards. Even with the best technical and industrial luck, however, it would take well over a year to bring significant numbers of the new boats into commission.[24]

In the meantime, in the autumn and winter of 1943, new equipment enhanced the existing U-boat fleet. More powerful AA armament has already been mentioned. The Naxos U detector would provide warning of aircraft using centimetric radar. A more important fundamental means of avoiding attack was the snorkel (German *Schnorchel*). This was a combined air-intake and exhaust system which allowed submarines to run their diesels and re-charge their batteries while 'snorting' (as the British put it) at periscope depth. Only the tip of the snorkel projected above the water, so it was difficult for enemy ships and aircraft to detect, even by radar. The first snorkel-equipped German boat was the *U 539*, which departed Lorient in January 1944. The effectiveness of the snorkel was limited. It took a long time to fit and accustom crews to its use;

meanwhile it forced the U-boats to move at a slow submerged speed while snorting, which was incompatible with wolfpack tactics.[25]

More active equipment included new torpedoes. The T5 (which the British called the GNAT) was mainly intended to destroy Allied escort ships by homing in on their machinery noise. This weapon was first used during an attack on a mid-Atlantic convoy (ON.202) in September 1943. A considerable number of escorts were sunk or seriously damaged by T5s, but the Allied navies were able to introduce effective counter-measures such as the 'Foxer', a noise-making decoy towed behind the escorts.

Significant, in a negative sense, was the continuing German weakness in sea/air warfare, especially at oceanic range. The Luftwaffe, which now controlled all German maritime aviation, could neither locate distant merchant convoys for the U-boats nor themselves effectively attack these targets with bombs, torpedoes or guided missiles. Only a handful of aircraft were made available to succeed the lumbering Focke-Wulf Fw 200 as a long-range patrol aircraft for ocean surveillance. More success was achieved at shorter ranges. The limited conventional German air-to-sea weaponry on hand – notably He 111 and Ju 88 torpedo bombers – was mostly in action in the Mediterranean or the Norwegian Sea.[26] The first use of the Henschel Hs 293 radio-controlled glider bomb carried by a Dornier Do 217 medium bomber occurred in August 1943 in a strike against British escorts. Later, in November 1943, a mass attack was mounted against homeward-bound Allied convoy SL.139/MKS.30, some 850 miles out to sea beyond the Bay of Biscay. Some twenty Heinkel He 177 bombers from II./KG 40 launched forty glider bombs, but only one small merchant ship was sunk. The Luftwaffe had some success in the Mediterranean against warships with the Hs 293 and the Fritz X radio-guided bomb, but the Allies enjoyed general air superiority and the number of German missiles and launch aircraft was limited. As with the T5 torpedo, the Allies developed effective technical counter-measures.

The Americans, for their part, developed their definitive A/S system only after the U-boats had been defeated. In May 1943 the US Navy did finally establish a headquarters to oversee intelligence and operations for its A/S effort in the Atlantic. This was designated the Tenth Fleet.[27] Admiral King himself was nominally in command, but Rear Admiral Francis Low – a long-time King subordinate – was Chief of Staff and effective head. The Tenth was a peculiar 'fleet', with a tiny core of about fifty people, and most of the 'enlisted' personnel being from the women's branch of the US Naval Reserve, the WAVES (Women Accepted for Volunteer Emergency Service). No ships or air squadrons were permanently attached to the Tenth Fleet, but it could call on resources from Admiral Ingersoll's Atlantic Fleet and the three 'sea frontiers'.

The sea/air war to maintain control of the North Atlantic now owed even more to American production. Lend-Lease in the summer of 1943 finally began to provide large numbers of 1,200-ton American-built vessels of the 'destroyer escort' (DE) type. Two-thirds the size of conventional destroyers, they had been inspired by the Royal Navy 'Hunt' class. The type had first been ordered in quantity by the British from the US in the middle of 1941, but production had been sidetracked by the need for landing craft. The British categorised these vessels as 'frigates' – following their earlier revival of the term 'corvette'. They were named after Royal Navy ship captains of the French wars; the first was HMS *Bayntun*, which entered active service in British waters in May–June 1943. (Another vessel was named after Captain Bligh of mutiny-on-the-*Bounty* fame.) Six entered service in the first half of 1943, fifty-nine in the second half, and thirteen in the first months of 1944. (Many more DEs served under the US flag, mainly in the Pacific.) Smaller numbers of frigates designed and built in Britain, the prefabricated 1,435-ton 'Loch' class, joined the fleet from the middle of 1943. By June 1944, there were 131 new British or Canadian frigates or sloops. For corvettes, the numbers were 102 'River' class (forty-five of them Canadian) and 205 'Flower' class (eighty-eight Canadian).[28]

Allied maritime patrol aircraft were still vital after the closing of the Atlantic ' Air Gap', although their numbers did not increase dramatically in the year after May 1943; Coastal Command had about the same number of land-based long-range aircraft involved in anti-U-boat operations in June 1944 as in September 1943 – some 480 planes. There were significant extensions to the Atlantic patrol-plane network. In October 1943 the Portuguese government – after the fall of Mussolini – finally allowed the British to base A/S aircraft in the Azores, 1,100 miles west of Gibraltar, which greatly improved coverage of the southern convoy route.

The Allies benefited for some time from Admiral Dönitz's ill-judged decision to have his boats fight it out if necessary with Allied aircraft on the surface, rather than submerge. There were fierce battles in the Bay of Biscay in July 1943. Some eighty-six U-boats tried to cross the bay; seventeen were sunk – nearly all by aircraft – and six others were forced to return to base.

A particular feature of the post-May 1943 consolidation phase in the Atlantic was the escort carrier or CVE ('CV' being the normal US Navy abbreviation for a carrier, 'E' for escort). The British in 1940 had developed the concept of a cheap 'auxiliary' carrier built on a merchant ship hull – an aviation parallel with the armed merchant cruiser. The first conversion was HMS *Audacity* – already mentioned in Chapter 5 – which operated briefly on the UK–Gibraltar route in late 1941. Although British shipyards would build a handful of escort carriers after the *Audacity*, the great majority of vessels operated by the Royal Navy would come from America.[29] The first batches were built on the C3 fast passenger-cargo ship hull. They had a flight deck nearly 500 feet long and a speed of 16–17 knots. Of the first six C3 conversions, four went to the Royal Navy in 1942 (as HMS *Archer*, *Avenger*, *Biter* and *Dasher*). An improved C3-based version entered service with both navies as the 'Bogue' class;[30] of these, three (*Attacker*, *Battler* and *Stalker*) were received by the Royal Navy in late 1942, eight more in the first half of 1943, eighteen in the second half, and five in early 1944.

It was the US Navy which made most effective use of the CVE, and indeed, its greatest operational contribution to the Atlantic campaign were 'hunter-killer' operations in the southern Atlantic shipping route (from the US East Coast to the Mediterranean). Offensive sweeps by carriers against U-boats had gone out of favour in the first months of the war, after the loss of HMS *Courageous*, and the Americans had found them to be of little use during the 1942 East Coast U-boat Blitz. Now A/S aircraft and sensors were much more capable and the number of U-boats available to hunt (on the southern route) was reasonably high; in addition, Ultra decrypts and HF/DF provided invaluable background information.

The first American hunter-killer group, consisting of the CVE *Bogue* and three old four-stacker destroyers, began operations south of the Azores in June 1943. The carrier's aircraft consisted of about twenty Wildcat fighters and Avenger torpedo bombers, both types being Grumman aircraft now built in massive quantities by General Motors. Even strengthened U-boat AA defences could not cope with a small swarm of torpedo planes and strafing fighters. This force was followed by similar task groups built around the escort carriers *Card*, *Core* and *Santee*.[31] In just over three months (June to August 1943) this handful of CVE task groups accounted for sixteen U-boats; eight were U-tankers, essential for effective long-range operations. The successful sweeps continued into 1944. A later American CVE, USS *Block Island*, was sunk off the Canaries by the *U 549* in late May 1944; the submarine was then destroyed by the carrier's surface escorts. The *Block Island* was the only American aircraft carrier – indeed the only large American warship of any type – lost in the war against the European Axis powers. A week later another US Navy hunter-killer group comprising the CVE *Guadalcanal* and five DEs succeeded in capturing the *U 505* north of the Cape Verde Islands.[32] (The boat survives in Chicago's Museum of Science and Industry.)

The Royal Navy did not achieve such dramatic results with the half-dozen escort carriers it operated on the Atlantic convoy routes; they accounted for only two U-boats in 1943. Rocket-armed Swordfish biplanes proved effective A/S weapons (remaining in service until the end of the war), but the big American-built Avengers were superior. British escort carriers operating with the Arctic convoys in the first half of 1944 sank six U-boats (two more together with surface escorts) and shot down seven German aircraft; the bomber danger was still significant here. Five other British escort carriers protected merchant ships in the Indian Ocean, beginning in October 1943.

The Kriegsmarine attempted one last major attack on the North Atlantic in September 1943, four months after 'Black May'. Nineteen U-boats were deployed in the North Atlantic as wolfpack LEUTHEN (named after a 1759 battle of the Seven Years' War). This time the U-boats carried T5 anti-escort torpedoes and were equipped with a superior Hohentwiel U radar search receiver, and beefed-up AA guns for self-defence. Westbound convoys ON.202 and ONS.18 were attacked together in the middle of September. Six merchant ships were torpedoed, and three escorts sunk by T5s, but three U-boats were destroyed. Special intelligence allowed the British to route later convoys around (smaller) U-boat concentrations and to reinforce the escort groups.

The Germans after May 1943 dispersed their U-boats to less well-protected ocean regions. This led to a changing pattern of Allied shipping losses, smaller in scale and far removed from the vital northern Atlantic main artery. In the period from January to May 1943, 1,355,000 tons of shipping had been lost in the North Atlantic and 771,000 tons (36 per cent of the global total) in other sea areas. In contrast, in the twelve months from June 1943 through May 1944, only 443,000 tons were lost in the decisive North Atlantic, compared to 1,290,654 tons (74 per cent of the global total) elsewhere. Breakdown by area is given in Table 15.2.[33]

Admiral King summed up the situation in a speech on Navy Day in October 1943: 'Submarines have not been driven from the seas, but they have changed status from a menace to a problem'. The de facto head of the Tenth Fleet, Admiral Low, accurately described the strategy of dispersed U-boat operations as a 'guerrilla war'.[34] The Allies kept nearly full control of the Atlantic Ocean from

Table 15.2. Allied Shipping Losses, June 1943–May 1944

Theatre	Tonnage lost	Ships lost
North Atlantic	443,000	76
UK home waters	30,825	23
Mediterranean	550,000	105
South Atlantic	147,000	27
Indian Ocean	533,000	87
Pacific	30,000	6
Total	1,733,000	294

Source: Rosk/3.1, p. 389.
Notes: Losses are for Allied and neutral countries' merchant ships due to enemy action *of all types*, not just due to U-boats. Tonnage is GRT.; in this period 70% of global losses (by tonnage) were caused by submarines, and 22% by aircraft (Rosk/3.1, p. 388).

Table 15.3. Troop Movements across the Atlantic (Eastbound), January 1943–June 1944

Quarter	Convoys	Personnel
1943/i	12	56,600
1943/ii	16	127,200
1943/iii	17	196,900
1943/iv	24	326,000
1944/i	40	403,300
1944/ii	40	433,400
Total	149	1,543,400

Source: Rosk/2, p. 452, ibid./3.2, p. 431.
Notes: 'Personnel' includes all services. In 1943 nearly all troop movements were by large liners sailing unescorted or in small UT convoys. Equipment had to be carried in slower and smaller ships. In 1944 troopships also sailed in normal convoys.

mid-1943 to mid-1944, enabling Britain, as well as the Allied forces in Sicily and mainland Italy, to be kept fully supplied. Meanwhile, BOLERO, the build-up of American troops for the full-scale invasion of northern Europe, was speeded up. The scale of movement is shown in Table 15.3. The first of a new series of UT troopship convoys arrived in Liverpool from America on 5 September 1943. Preparations would also involve the transfer back to the UK of British, American and Canadian troops from the Mediterranean.

By the end of May 1944 over 1.5 million American servicemen had been brought across the Atlantic, nearly 60 per cent in escorted convoys and over 30 per cent in unescorted liners (425,000 personnel in the *Queen Elizabeth* and the *Queen Mary* alone). There were no losses due to enemy action.[35]

CHAPTER 16

THE MEDITERRANEAN

The Allies Gain Control, November 1942–August 1944

THE SICILIAN CHANNEL AND NAPLES, 2–4 DECEMBER 1942

The naval situation in the Mediterranean began to change dramatically in the four weeks after Rommel was thrown back at El Alamein in Egypt and the American and British armies came ashore in Morocco and Algeria. On 20 November the STONEAGE convoy arrived in Malta from Port Said, ending the siege of the island; the dangers from 'Bomb Alley' between Crete and Libya were now much reduced. A week later a reconstituted Force K, the cruisers *Cleopatra*, *Euryalus* and *Dido*, supported by four destroyers, returned to Malta from Alexandria.

Two further events at the beginning of December 1942 showed just how much stronger the Allied sea/air presence had become. The first was a convoy battle in the Sicilian narrows. The British were now able to base large surface warships on the African shore of the western Mediterranean, something not possible since June 1940. A forward naval base was set up at Bône in eastern Algeria, and a newly established Force Q arrived on Monday, 30 November. Admiral Cecil Harcourt had under his command three light cruisers – the veteran *Aurora* and the new 'Dido' class *Argonaut* and *Sirius* – and two destroyers. The mission of Force Q was to cut off Tunisia; Harcourt's ships departed on their first mission on Tuesday evening, alerted to Axis convoy activity by Ultra decrypts.[1]

Several Italian convoys were at sea on that Tuesday night (1/2 December). Convoy 'H' sailed from Palermo in western Sicily in the morning, bound for Bizerta (now Bizerte) in Tunisia, a distance of some 220 miles. Convoy 'H', its ships taking part in the race to build up Axis forces in Tunisia, was made up of three medium-sized Italian cargo ships and the German *KT 1*.[2] The escort, large considering the number of cargo ships, comprised the destroyers *Da Recco*,

Folgore and *Camicia Nera* ('Blackshirt'), as well as two torpedo boats. Captain Aldo Cocchia, in command of the convoy and aboard *Da Recco*, had a year's experience on the Naples–Tripoli run.

Shortly after midnight on Wednesday, Force Q intercepted the convoy at the Skerki Bank, which lies at the western end of the Sicilian narrows. Harcourt's force was much stronger than the Italian escort, and it had the great advantage of radar. Convoy 'H' was already in some disorder as a result of missed signals; the British quickly sank the *KT 1*, and laid down accurate fire on the other cargo ships.

As Force Q looped around the convoy, the escorts attempted to counter-attack, with the *Folgore* ('Thunderbolt') arriving first. Cocchia, on the bridge of the *Da Rocco*, watched events unfold as the fire of the British ships lit up the horizon with multi-coloured tracer shells:

> They were of all colours: green, yellow, blue, red. Each British ship had been given projectiles with a tracer of its own colour . . . To the various bright lights were very soon added the white-blue beams of the searchlights and the incandescent globes of the 20mm machine guns. The *Folgore*, a small old destroyer, veteran of so many escort missions, tested in a thousand episodes, bore all alone the whole weight of battle . . .

The *Folgore* fired torpedoes, but no hits were achieved. Shattered by the fire of HMS *Argonaut*, she went down with most of her crew, including her captain, Lt Commander Ener Bettica. About fifteen minutes later the *Da Recco* in turn was hit forward; ammunition ignited and most of those on the bridge were killed or injured. Captain Cocchia was himself gravely injured but would be later awarded the Gold Medal for Military Valour (MOVM), as would the gallant Bettica (posthumously) and the captain of the *Camicia Nera*.[3] The *Da Recco* limped home, but the three cargo ships, in addition to the *KT 1*, were sunk; the total loss of Axis personnel, aboard the transports and the escort, numbered 2,200 men. Towards midnight of the following night (2/3 December) four destroyers from Malta's Force K sank the torpedo boat *Lupo* in Tunisian waters.

The ships of Force Q were undamaged during the Tuesday night battle. They were, however, caught at sea after dawn by a German Ju 88, and the destroyer *Quentin* was bombed and sunk.

The second event, the American air raid on Naples, took place two days later, on the afternoon of 4 December (the feast day of St Barbara, the patron saint of the Regia Marina). As Rommel's armies rolled back, the Allies captured an advance Italian airfield at Gambut, just west of Tobruk in Libya. Gambut had long runways and could be quickly exploited as a forward base for B-24 Liberator bombers of the IX Bomber Command, US Army Air Force; the big four-engined machines had begun to arrive in the Levant in small numbers in the late summer. The distance from Gambut to Naples was only 730 miles, so the B-24s were now well within range of what by November 1942 had become the main Italian operating base. The raid, the first by the Americans against Italian territory, was mounted by twenty B-24s from the 98th and 376th Bomb Groups (Heavy).

Although the RAF had mounted occasional night attacks on Naples, the AAF proved more effective. American bombers flew in daylight and could hit targets with a degree of precision. They arrived in the late afternoon from the direction of Mount Vesuvius. The B-24s had no fighter escorts, but they attacked at high altitude and achieved surprise; they did not meet opposition from defending fighters or AA guns. Indeed, the bombs were falling before the air raid alarm was even sounded. They were dropped from 20,000 feet, but the ships in the harbour were stationary and crowded together. Aboard the Italian warships the watertight doors were open, and many men were on deck. The cruisers of Admiral Da Zara's 7th Division, which had won the battle against the HARPOON convoy back in June, suffered most damage. Two of the three cruisers took direct hits by 1,000lb bombs. The *Muzio Attendolo* capsized four hours after the attack; she had just had her bow replaced after an attack by a British submarine during the PEDESTAL battle. The *Montecuccoli* would now be under repair until July 1943. The third cruiser, the *Eugenio di Savoia*, was damaged by a near miss, and put out of action for a month. There was heavy loss of life, both aboard the warships and among civilians in the port area.

The St Barbara's Day raid led to the abandonment of Naples as the major fleet base of the Italian Navy. On the evening of 6 December the three modern battleships – the *Littorio*, the *Vittorio Veneto* and the new *Roma* – departed under heavy destroyer escort for the pre-war main base at La Spezia, 370 miles to the north, near Genoa. The big ships would remain there until the end of Fascist Italy's war. They would be unable to operate in the central or eastern Mediterranean, or even to take part in the defence of Sicily or the southern mainland.

TUNISIA BLOCKADED

In midwinter of 1942–43 the struggle for the Mediterranean Sea became very different from the previous two years. Then, the maritime war had been a sea/air struggle largely between the Royal Navy and the German Luftwaffe, dominated by attacks on convoys. The land war had been one of rapid movement back and forth along the coastal strip of Libya and Egypt, as one side and then the other gained the initiative.

Now the Axis armies were no longer poised to take the Suez Canal, but in irretrievable retreat. Benghazi fell on 20 November 1942, Tripoli on 23 January 1943, and the British reached eastern Tunisia in early March. The Allies were now converging on a region 1,000 miles to the west of El Alamein. The Germans and Italians, however, had been able to establish a presence in Tunisia and construct a defensive line in the western mountains; they were even able in mid-February to mount a counter-attack at Kasserine against US troops advancing from Algeria.

Rather than evacuating what forces they could from Benghazi and Tripoli, or from newly occupied ports in Tunisia, Hitler and the German high command actually decided to *reinforce* North Africa. The assumption was that a sizeable bridgehead in Africa could be created and held, at least in Tunisia. The strategic rationale, not a wholly incorrect one, was that this would tie down considerable numbers of British and American troops, shipping and supplies in the Mediterranean and lessen the likelihood of a cross-Channel invasion in 1943. Meanwhile control of Tunisia and Sicily would keep a lock on the vital west–east Mediterranean shipping route. In addition, the Germans believed that the abandonment of North Africa might have a lethal effect on Italian morale, even leading their southern ally to leave the war. Not least important, they believed that the supply problems which had dogged the Axis armies in 1940–42 would be overcome with better ports in Tunisia and much shorter supply routes, readily covered by air from either side of the Mediterranean. It would now be the besieging Allies who would have long supply lines.

Admiral Raeder had produced a report ten days after the TORCH landings which stressed both the importance of Tunisia and the feasibility of supplying Axis forces there; he discussed this with Hitler at the Berghof on 19 November 1942:

> The decisive key position in the Mediterranean has been and still is Tunisia. The deployment of Axis forces in Tunisia compels the enemy to deploy considerable forces, which must be supplied over long and vulnerable routes. It simplifies the task of supplying our Panzer Army, which we have placed on interior lines [of communication], and it prevents enemy success by blocking the sea route through the Mediterranean.[4]

Details of the land fighting in Tunisia need not concern us here, but terrain, weather and Allied supply problems helped the Axis defence at least through March 1943.

From the point of view of the sea/air war the battle of the north–south convoys was renewed, but the Allies for the first time were able to decisively block the Axis supply route. In his November 1942 report Raeder had played down the danger presented by new Allied air bases. This was undoubtedly a misjudgement, as the central features of the present sea/air war were the powerful squadrons of the RAF and the US Army Air Force which could now operate over the Mediterranean. Allied aviation now repeated from the south shore of the Mediterranean the deadly role the Luftwaffe had previously played from the north.

As the Allied armies converged towards Tunisia, they began to establish a large number of forward air bases in western Libya and Algeria, supplementing their established – and now secure – air bases on Malta. Aircraft from the North African bases supported the Allied troops fighting on the approaches to Tunisia, and they also contested control of the waters of the central and western Mediterranean. By mid-April overall Allied air strength in the theatre was some 3,250 aircraft, versus 900 German and 900 Italian machines.[5]

The attack on Naples by the USAAF on 4 December 1942 was just the beginning of an important but largely unremembered air campaign. By January and February 1943 American B-17 and B-24 heavy bombers based in North Africa continued to attack ports and convoys, as well as airfields on the Italian mainland, Sicily and Sardinia. Medium bombers and long-range Allied fighters helped cut the Axis sea–air supply line from southern Italy and Sicily to Tunisia. At the same time air attacks on Axis airfields in Sardinia and Sicily wore down the ability of the Luftwaffe and the Regia Aeronautica to escort shipping and defend the approaches to Italy itself.

The Tunisian problem became more acute for the Germans in March 1943 after Rommel's counter-offensive ended. The reinforced Allied forces compressed the two armies of Army Group Africa (*Heeresgruppe Afrika*) into northeastern Tunisia. Rommel and others now urged the evacuation of Axis forces. Some form of Tunisian 'Dunkirk', into Sicily, would probably have been possible in March, without prohibitive cost, although it would have represented a considerable loss of prestige. However, Hitler still persisted in fighting for Tunisia – a parallel to his insistence on holding Stalingrad from November 1942 to February 1943. To achieve this end he stressed the importance of a full-scale effort to develop Axis sea transport to Tunisia, putting pressure on the Italians to make a maximum effort. Admiral Dönitz, now C-in-C of the German Navy, was sent to Rome to discuss procedures and organisation with Mussolini and Italian Navy Chief of Staff Admiral Arturo Riccardi.

The Axis shipping situation was precarious, despite better ports and shorter shipping routes. According to published post-war figures, in the period from November 1942 to May 1943 39,000 personnel (35,000 of them German) arrived in Tunisia; 3,100 were lost en route. Most of these were rushed across in a Mediterranean version of the Tokyo Express, aboard Italian destroyers rather than troopships. Losses of matériel were considerably higher. Some 314,000 tons were sent, of which 102,000 tons (more than 32 per cent) were lost. In addition to losses, considerably less was despatched than in 1942. The average monthly figure for matériel was only about 50,000 tons, compared to 80,000 tons a month in 1942. The monthly requirement of Axis forces in Tunisia was some 150,000–200,000 tons.[6]

Defensive minefields were laid on either side of the Axis shipping route to Tunisia, which prevented a repeat of the devastating 4 December attack by British surface ships. Nevertheless, the Royal Navy was able to lay mines in the channel, and there were increasing attacks by submarine and aircraft, as well as successful raids against ships in port at either end of the crossing. To the Axis commanders it was clear that this convoy channel, even so near Sicily, was extremely dangerous; it became known to them as the *rotta della morte*, the 'route of death'.

There was no flow in the other direction, bringing out German troops. Operation RETRIBUTION – so called by the British because of their experience of earlier evacuations from Dunkirk in 1940, and from mainland Greece and Crete in 1941 – was an all-out attempt by Admiral Cunningham to prevent any last-minute evacuation of Tunisia, but in the end almost nothing was attempted by the enemy. The Axis forces in the African bridgehead ceased fighting on 12 May 1943. The Allies captured about 265,000 prisoners, half German and half Italian; in addition the Axis armies suffered 40,000 men dead and wounded.[7] It was a huge victory.

The Allies had not only succeeded in blocking Axis sea and air supply; they had also established their own largely unchallenged line of communications to the Tunisian battlefields. Large numbers of reinforcements and masses of supplies poured in from either side, from the United States across the Atlantic via new captured forward ports at Oran and Algiers, or from the United Kingdom through the Suez Canal and via Tripoli in Libya. Neither route saw significant losses due to Axis submarines or aircraft. This confounded the German assumption that very long Allied supply lines (vulnerable to U-boat attack) would make success impossible.

From the middle of May 1943 – before the invasion of Sicily – the Mediterranean was again opened to convoyed shipping from Gibraltar to Suez. After an intense effort over two weeks in May 1943 British minesweepers cleared a safe passage in the central Mediterranean, the 'Tunisian War Channel'. Shipping could now proceed directly to Suez, saving a month and a half compared to the voyage around the Cape of Good Hope. In the summer over 400 ships a month made the passage, and in 1944 the monthly number had risen to 1,200.[8] This was most important for reinforcing the Indian Ocean and increasing Lend-Lease supplies to Russia via the Persian Gulf.

THE INVASION OF SICILY

At the Casablanca/SYMBOL Conference in January 1943 the Americans gave in to British pressure and agreed that the next full-scale operation would be directed against Sicily. The initial hope for a cross-Channel landing in late 1943 (Operation ROUNDUP) had been rejected by the British, who judged that a direct attack across the Channel into northern France was still impractical; German ground and air strength was too strong, and assault shipping was insufficient. The British also argued that strong Allied forces had been built up in North Africa and a jump into southern Europe, using sea power, would be the most efficient step. This strategy also had the potential to knock a weakened Italy out of the war, and it would re-open the globally important shipping route from Gibraltar to Suez and the Indian Ocean.

Planning for the invasion of Sicily, Operation HUSKY, began in February 1943, again under the overall command of General Eisenhower. On the face of it Sicily was a substantially more difficult task than the invasion of French North Africa. Operation TORCH in Morocco and Algeria had had the benefit of surprise. It had been directed against a peripheral area where there were no Axis troops or air units. And once ashore the Allies had encountered – as they largely expected – only a thin crust of Vichy hostility. Southern Europe seemed more difficult. The last British involvement here, in Greece in the spring of 1941, had been a spectacular failure. In 1943 the Italians had about 200,000 troops on Sicily, in four regular divisions but including many local reservists. The Germans had recently deployed an understrength Panzer division and an infantry (*Panzergrenadier*) division.

There was little the Italians or Germans could do to block the approach of the invasion fleet. In the end, *after* the actual landings, the Supermarina would make two attempts to despatch a small fast cruiser force to bombard Palermo (which had fallen on 23 July); both were called off before the ships neared their objective. On paper the Italian Navy was still a large force; the surface ships ready for sea consisted of five battleships, nine cruisers and about fifty destroyers and fleet torpedo boats. The old problems remained: inadequate supplies of fuel oil and the inability to provide air cover for the fleet at sea. In addition even the Italian ports were dangerous for heavy ships, thanks to Allied long-range bombers, especially those of the AAF. The St Barbara's Day raid on Naples in December 1942, with the sinking of the cruiser *Muzio Attendolo*, had been just the beginning. Another raid, by AAF B-17s in April 1943, caught Italy's last two operational heavy cruisers at their moorings near La Maddalena in Sardinia. The *Trieste* capsized and sank, and the *Gorizia* was badly damaged. The main naval base at La Spezia was now vulnerable; in early June 1943, B-17s damaged the battleships *Veneto* and *Roma* there. Even the Italian naval headquarters, the Supermarina, was in danger; in February 1943, it was moved out of central Rome to the Navy's communication centre at the village of Santa Rosa on the via Cassia, 11 miles north of the capital.

The enemy now had effective sea/air control over the central Mediterranean. On the Allied side, nearly all of the major warships involved in HUSKY were British. The Royal Navy had made good the ships damaged in 1941 and 1942 (in many cases thanks to American shipyards). Admiral Andrew Cunningham resumed the title of C-in-C, Mediterranean Fleet, in late February 1943, moving his headquarters to Malta on the eve of the HUSKY landings. The invasion was covered by Force H, now under Admiral Algernon Willis, who commanded the fleet carriers *Indomitable* and *Formidable*, the battleships *Nelson*, *Rodney*, *Warspite* and *Valiant*, four cruisers and eighteen destroyers. This task force proceeded to the Ionian Sea southeast of Sicily, where it was in position to deal with any sortie by the Italian battle fleet. South of Sardinia was a distant reserve force with the modern battleships *King George V* and *Howe*, along with two cruisers and six destroyers. (The *Howe*, commissioned in August 1942, was the final ship of the 'King George V' class and a very recent addition to the fleet.) Unlike TORCH and the (later) September 1943 landing on the Italian mainland (AVALANCHE), no escort carriers were involved. This was partly because local enemy air bases in Sardinia and Sicily had been neutralised by land-based air attacks, and partly because Malta could now be used during the landings as an unsinkable aircraft carrier, along with bases in Tunisia.

In Sicily, as in the invasion of North Africa, the Axis submarine force was unable to interfere, as a result of the Allied achievement of surprise and the deployment of powerful A/S forces. The Germans had sent nine more U-boats to the Mediterranean in November and December 1942, and a further eight arrived in the first six months of 1943. Taking into account losses and earlier arrivals, there were seventeen German submarines in the Mediterranean in June 1943, mostly based at Toulon and La Spezia. In the event they did not attack the initial landings in Sicily, as they had been deployed further west, off Algeria (where they had isolated successes against some of the invasion convoys in transit). The Italians still had forty-five boats in service, from what had once been the world's second largest submarine fleet. Some of them were nearer the approaches to Sicily than the U-boats, but they had little success, and four of them were sunk.

More surprising, for both sides, was the ineffective response of the Luftwaffe to Operation HUSKY. The assault convoys were sailing in seas around Malta, where Allied convoys had been repeated devastated by German and Italian bombers the year before. Allied planners expected heavy air attacks and significant naval losses; as Admiral Cunningham put it, 'To one who had fought through the Mediterranean campaign from the beginning it appeared almost magical that great fleets of ships could remain anchored on the enemy's coast, within 40 miles of his main aerodromes, with only such slight losses from air attack as were incurred.'[9]

Not all enemy air attacks could be intercepted. The destroyer USS *Maddox*, on A/S patrol on her own off the American beachhead on the first day of the invasion, was bombed by a Ju 88. She sank with two-thirds of her crew after her magazine exploded, the first major American warship sunk in the Mediterranean.[10] Other aircraft sank a brightly lit British hospital ship off the eastern beaches. The fleet carrier *Indomitable*, operating with the *Formidable* in the central Mediterranean, was torpedoed by an enemy medium bomber in an evening attack, a week after the landing.[11] The damage was serious; and the carrier would be under repair in America for the better part of a year. But in general Axis air attacks were no more than an irritant.

Most significantly, HUSKY was the first full-scale use by the Allies of their new war-winning amphibious technologies; it marked an important milestone in the history of Allied sea power. The landings in Sicily were a far cry from the Lofoten raid or the invasion of Madagascar. Even Operation TORCH in Morocco and Algeria, although a very big operation, was amateurish by comparison, and involved many elements of hurried improvisation.

The scale of the HUSKY landings was larger than TORCH, and the invading troops, in the final version of the plan, were concentrated in a much smaller area. Two armies landed side by side on the south coast of Sicily, the Seventh Army with three American infantry divisions, and the Eighth Army with four divisions (three British and one Canadian). As with TORCH, these formations were skilfully concentrated from several widely different directions. The amphibious part of the plan was one of unprecedented complexity, which was laid out by the British admiral Bertram Ramsay.

The geography of the Mediterranean and its normally calm seas meant that HUSKY combined ship-to-shore operations and shore-to-shore ones. The former involved no fewer than sixty-four deep-draught attack transports (APAs or LSIs), each carrying a load of landing craft. Two of the American divisions, one blooded in Algeria and Tunisia and the other fresh from the US, arrived off southern Sicily from Oran and Algiers in these attack transports. Most of the British Empire forces arrived in the same way, two British divisions and an independent brigade coming from Port Said in Egypt, and the Canadian division directly from the UK. The assault troops were landed in 40-foot landing craft

(LCAs and LCVPs) lowered from the attack transports as they stood about 10 miles offshore.

Other divisions went from shore to shore, carried all the way by landing craft on a relatively short voyage – 300 miles – within the Mediterranean. The third American assault division was transported from Bizerta and Tunis and the final British division came from Sfax (in Tunisia) and Malta. Some men and equipment were moved aboard British-built LCTs, but most were carried by brand-new American LSTs, LCIs and LCTs which had been ferried across the Atlantic. The British LSTs and LCIs were often manned by crews from warships under repair in American yards; they had sailed in flotillas via Bermuda in the course of the spring. The three prototype British LSTs used in TORCH were now supplemented by 141 of the mass-produced American version. One of the most important additions to the inventory for HUSKY turned out to be the new American amphibious truck, the DUKW.[12] Admiral Mountbatten watched the convoys assembling south of Malta on 9 July and was thoroughly impressed: 'I have been 27 years at sea, and I have never seen a sight like it in my life. It was like the Spithead Review multiplied by twenty. There was just a forest of masts in every direction, as far as the eye could see.'[13]

D-Day for Operation HUSKY was 10 July 1943. The British and Canadians landed on the southeastern coast of Sicily, the Americans about 25 miles to the west, on the south coast, either side of the port of Gela. The British beach areas were code-named ACID and BARK, the American ones CENT, DIME and JOSS. Each area had its own naval support group, initially with cruisers and destroyers. The Eastern Naval Task Force was commanded by Admiral Bertram Ramsay RN and the Western Naval Task Force (TF 80) by Admiral Kent Hewitt USN. Each admiral flew his flag in a specially appointed command ship, not a battleship or a cruiser but a converted merchantman. Space for staff personnel and communications equipment, rather than guns and armour, was now the most important feature.

The first wave of landings included 160,000 Allied troops, 14,000 vehicles, 600 tanks and 1,800 artillery pieces. The invaders were coming in against German and Italian troops and aircraft and not (as in Morocco and Algeria) just the Vichy French forces. Unlike the future landings in Normandy in 1944, those on Sicily took place at night; the first troops were scheduled to come ashore at 2.45 a.m.

The Axis, reeling from the rapid and unexpected collapse in North Africa and imperilled by defeat in Russia, had done little to prepare the defence of Sicily and its southern coast. There were beach defences, but they were not effectively manned. Fortunately for the attacking force, the Axis garrison put up little more than token resistance in the landing areas. Some of the coastal batteries opened fire, but it was half-hearted and soon suppressed. The invading troops did not face forewarned German formations, as they would less than two months later when they came ashore at Salerno (on mainland Italy).

The defending Italian troops in southern Sicily, with the many local reservists, pulled quickly back. The best of Italy's soldiers had been lost on distant battlefields. The most resistance developed in the American sector north of Gela, on the morning of the 10th. Counter-attacks by German and Italian tanks and aircraft over the next two days were broken up, partly by the supporting fire of the big American cruisers *Savannah* and *Boise*, each mounting fifteen 6-inch guns. The level of support was unprecedented compared to earlier landings either in the Atlantic or the Pacific, and it would be a feature of all future Allied landings.

The land campaign on Sicily went ahead rapidly, under the leadership of General Montgomery and General Patton, thanks to the rapid build-up and support of the Allied ground forces. The vital supply port of Augusta was captured by the British on the third day. Airfields were quickly established ashore. The follow-on forces comprised two British infantry divisions and, on the American side, an armoured division and an infantry division. Five weeks later – by 17 August – the Sicilian campaign was over. The Germans did successfully evacuate their two divisions across the narrow Strait of Messina to the mainland, where they would provide a reinforcement to their comrades who would soon be embattled there. Allied naval forces might have done more to interfere with this evacuation, but the Messina crossing point was hard to approach and well protected by enemy artillery and aircraft at the critical moment.

In June 1943, two weeks before the invasion of Sicily, Mussolini made his last major speech, to the Directory of the Fascist Party; it was later broadcast to the nation. His theme was 'the urgent tasks of the hour'. The Allies had to attempt an invasion of the Continent, he said, but that would fail; after that they would have no more cards to play. The enemy might be able to disembark troops, but that would not be the same as 'penetration [*penetrazione*]' or successful 'invasion':

> If the enemy tries to disembark it is most likely that he will be ground to a halt at what sailors call the 'waterline' [*bagnasciuga*], the line in the sand where the sea ends and dry land begins. If by any chance they penetrate any further, our reserve forces – which exist – will fall on those that have been able to disembark, and destroy them to the last man. So it can be said that they will have occupied part of our fatherland, but they will do so after having been laid out dead, not standing up.[14]

The Italian dictator did not boast about the ability of his navy and air force to stop the invaders at sea *before* they came ashore. But he was also wholly wrong about the resistance on land. Hopelessly compromised, even in the eyes of his senior colleagues, Mussolini would be forced from office two weeks after the *penetrazione* of Operation HUSKY.

HUSKY demonstrated the continuing inability of the Axis to prevent large-scale amphibious invasions or even to make them prohibitively costly. The Allies themselves expected much higher losses. The invasion of Sicily is now sometimes seen as unsuccessful, a 'bitter victory', partly due to the escape of the German garrison.[15] In reality Operation HUSKY was a stunning demonstration of British and American sea/air power, and a mastery of amphibious warfare on the largest scale. Despite missed opportunities by the British and American armies, losses of personnel and landing craft were so low that the Allied planners could immediately turn to the next jump, onto the mainland.

Accounts of the summer and autumn of 1943 in the Mediterranean tend to concentrate on Sicily and neglect Sardinia and Corsica. Neither of these islands was in the end defended, although Sardinia had been of much importance as an Axis air and naval base in the battles of 1940–42. After the defeat in North Africa the Germans had stiffened the Italian garrison of Sardinia with two understrength divisions, but these were withdrawn at the beginning of October, a month after the Italian government surrendered and the Allies invaded mainland Italy. The arrival of small Allied light naval forces enabled a quick takeover. Corsica, too, came under Allied control. Hitler, his armies now under great pressure on the mainland, decided that the French island could not be held; the German troops there were shipped 70 miles to Livorno.[16]

THE SURRENDER OF THE ITALIAN FLEET

The successful invasion of Sicily led to the fall of Mussolini. On the night of 24/25 July the Fascist Grand Council voted to restore the full powers of Vittorio Emanuele III. The indecisive 'little king' finally acted on the following day, Sunday, 25 July. Mussolini was dismissed and detained. Marshal Pietro Badoglio, seventy-one years old and formerly one of Fascist Italy's leading generals, was chosen to head the new government. The leadership of the Regia Marina changed too. Admiral Raffaele de Courten took over the main posts on 27 July, replacing both Mussolini as Minister of the Navy and Admiral Riccardi as the Italian Navy Chief of Staff. De Courten had commanded cruiser divisions during the war, and in March 1943 he had become Riccardi's deputy. A few ships had their overtly Fascist names replaced; notably, the battleship *Littorio* became the *Italia*.

The fighting in Sicily continued until 17 August. The new Italian government publicly undertook to continue the fight against the Allies alongside Germany. But behind the scenes the King and Badoglio began attempts to leave the war, a series of events later described as 'one of the saddest and most humiliating chapters in Italian history'.[17] The King was indecisive and no hero; Badoglio was inert and inflexible. The leaders of the armed forces of Fascist Italy were naturally loath to go over to the side of the British enemy or betray their German comrades in arms, and they furthermore had an exaggerated sense of their own achievements and abilities. All dreaded intervention by the Third Reich, but none seemed capable of making preparations to meet it. Hitler and his high command, for their part, had few illusions; they began to move 'reinforcement' troops into Italy and drafted an occupation plan, Operation AXIS (ACHSE).

After preliminary talks in Lisbon and Madrid an Italian Army staff officer representing the new government and high command was secretly flown to Allied-occupied Sicily at the end of August. On the afternoon of 3 September – for the British the fourth anniversary of the start of World War II – he accepted secret terms, dressed up as an armistice but in fact a surrender.[18] When the 'armistice' took force Italian forces were to cease 'all hostile activity'. Promised undertakings on the Italian side included 'Immediate transfer of the Italian Fleet and Italian aircraft to such points as may be designated by the Allied Commander in Chief [Eisenhower]', where they were to be subject to disarmament. It was agreed that the armistice would be announced literally on the eve of the full-scale Allied invasion of the Italian mainland. The Allied side did not reveal when and where this would happen. The details had to be kept secret to ensure military surprise.[19]

While they waited, the King and his advisers confined knowledge of the 'armistice' and its terms to a small circle of very senior leaders. Admiral de Courten knew about the general terms at least by 3 September. Three days later he learned that the Allies had specified that once the armistice had been announced the main Italian fleet was to proceed from La Spezia to the Allied-held port of Bône in eastern Algeria. But among those kept in ignorance was Admiral Carlo Bergamini, the commander of the Naval Battle Force (*Forza Navali da Battaglia*) at La Spezia. Bergamini, who had been an operational commander of heavy ship divisions throughout the war, believed that he was organising a 'sacrificial' naval operation against the imminent Allied invasion.[20] In reality the Allied landing was scheduled to take place in the early hours of Thursday, 9 September; the landing area for Operation AVALANCHE was at Salerno, south of Naples. On Wednesday evening the armistice was publicly announced by Eisenhower in a broadcast from Algiers. After an hour and a half, and a secret and angry Allied ultimatum, Marshal Badoglio spoke on Italian radio. The country, he announced, was giving up a struggle against overwhelming odds. Italian forces were immediately to cease fighting against the British and Americans, but they were 'to react to eventual attacks from any other source'. The armistice was evidently a complete surprise to Admiral Bergamini, who was furious about having been kept in the dark. However, after a heated long-distance telephone conversation with the Supermarina, Bergamini was persuaded not to scuttle his ships but to observe the armistice and put to sea. He had not at this time been told that the survival of the fleet was needed to secure the best terms from the Allies. All he knew was that he was to proceed to La Maddalena in Sardinia (Italian territory); it was not intimated that his ultimate destination was Bône (an Allied port).

Fearing arrest by the Germans, the King, Badoglio and members of the high command fled Rome early on Thursday morning (the 9th). The original intention had been to make their way by sea to La Maddalena. Instead, they drove to Pescara, on the Adriatic coast, where they embarked aboard the brand-new corvette *Baionetta*, bound for Brindisi – on the heel of the Italian 'boot'. Admiral de Courten travelled with the King's party.

The Italian Army had been given virtually no instructions. It was overcome in its barracks and disarmed in the next few days by a relatively small number of German troops. No organised resistance took place. The fate of the Regia Marina was different. The Naval Battle Force, the *Roma*, to *Vittorio Veneto* and to *Italia* (formerly the *Littorio*), along with the light cruisers *Eugenio di Savoia*, *Duca d'Aosta* and *Montecuccoli*, and a screen of eight destroyers, completed its departure from La Spezia at 3.40 a.m. on Thursday, 9 September. Some hours had been lost trying to gain information about the surrender arrangements and to agree a course of action among the fleet's officers. The light cruisers *Abruzzi*, *Garibaldi* and *Attilio Regolo* sailed from nearby Genoa. In overall command was Bergamini, flying his flag in the *Roma*.

The rapidly assembled fleet followed a course to the southwest, which would have taken it west of Corsica and Sardinia; reports from shadowing Allied planes at first indicated that they were making for Bône. At midday on Thursday, however, Bergamini turned east between Corsica and Sardinia, towards La Maddalena; the reasons for his fatal decision remain a matter of historical dispute. The change of course aroused some alarm on the Allied side as the Italian ships were now headed in the general direction of the Salerno beachhead. Then, at 2.24 p.m., Bergamini received a signal from the Supermarina's temporary transmitter outside Rome, warning him that German forces had already taken control of La Maddalena, and instructing him to proceed to Bône. He turned back to the west.

The course of the Naval Battle Force put it in easy range of Luftwaffe aircraft operating from the French south coast. The delay in departing La Spezia and the detour to La Maddalena meant that the Italian ships transited this danger zone in broad daylight and lingered there. Just after 3.45 p.m., when the Battle

Force was still off the north coast of Sardinia, German planes hit the *Roma* with two large precision-guided bombs.

This, the first use of such a weapon against a major warship, began a new era in sea/air warfare. As already mentioned, in connection with the Battle of the Atlantic, the Luftwaffe had secretly developed air-launched anti-shipping guided missiles. There were actually two types: the Fritz X (or FX 1400) was designed to attack large armoured ships, the Henschel Hs 293 was for use against convoys. The Fritz X was a big guided bomb – the '1400' in FX 1400 stood for its overall weight in kilograms (equal to 3,000 lb). It was dropped from high altitude – 20,000 feet – to help armour penetration, and to keep the launch aircraft safely above AA fire. Control surfaces on the bomb's fins allowed an operator in the launch aircraft to guide it to the target by radio control. In contrast, the Henschel Hs 293 was a small pilotless glider, rocket-boosted on launch from a bomber, which then glided to its target; the warhead was slightly larger than that of the Fritz X but with less penetrative power against armour. Units of the Luftwaffe's elite bomber group, KG 100, were trained to use these weapons; the initial carrier aircraft was the twin-engined Dornier Do 217.

The first Fritz X had actually been dropped some weeks earlier, on 21 July, on Augusta; this Sicilian port had just been captured by the Allies and was important for the supply of the HUSKY invasion. The first use of guided weapons against a warship at sea had come at the end of August with two attacks on British escort ships off the northwestern tip of Spain; the second attack sank the sloop *Egret* and damaged a destroyer. On 9 September it was eleven Dorniers from III./KG 100 which successfully attacked the fleet of Germany's erstwhile ally. The two Fritz X bombs hit the *Roma* six minutes apart and caused a fire; this eventually ignited her forward magazine and set off a devastating explosion. Some twenty-five minutes after the second hit the big ship broke in two and sank with 1,253 of her crew, including Admiral Bergamini and all his staff. A third Fritz X hit the *Italia* forty minutes later but caused only limited damage.

The rest of the Italian fleet continued under the command of Admiral Romeo Oliva, who was aboard the cruiser *Eugenio di Savoia*. Responding to belated but now explicit instructions from the Supermarina, Oliva turned south for Bône at 8.00 p.m.; he was also told the agreed arrangements for his ships – to fly black pennants and to train their guns fore and aft. After sailing through the night the Battle Force sighted waiting British ships off Cap de Garde near Bône, at 7.45 on Saturday morning. These were the battleships *Warspite* and *Valiant* and seven destroyers. Oliva's ships fell in behind the British and followed the *Warspite* to the east. As the strange convoy steamed past Bizerta in the afternoon Eisenhower and Cunningham came out aboard a British destroyer to look them over. The British admiral later recalled the moment: 'To see my wildest hopes brought to fruition, and my former flagship . . . leading her erstwhile opponents into captivity, filled me with the deepest emotion and lives with me still.'[21] Proceeding on through the Sicilian narrows, waters fought over so bitterly in the preceding three years, the convoy reached Malta on Sunday, 11 September. At about 10.00 a.m. the *Vittoria Veneto*, the *Italia* and the *Eugenio di Savoia* entered the Grand Harbour.

The other Italian ships were dispersed around the island's many inlets. They were joined by vessels that had made their way directly from Taranto on 9–10 September. These included the smaller battleships *Caio Duilio* and *Andrea Doria*, and the cruisers *Cadorna* and *Pompeo Magno*. In command was Admiral Da Zara, who passed, en route, a squadron of Allied cruisers rushing a British division to occupy Taranto. Admiral Cunningham, too, had now arrived in Malta. Da Zara came ashore to pay his respects, and Cunningham sent home his impressions: 'a nice enough man who spoke English well but felt his position terribly . . . There was little spirit left in this poor man.' On the 11th Cunningham made his most famous signal to the Admiralty: 'Be pleased to inform their Lordships that the Italian Battle Fleet now lies at anchor under the guns of the fortress of Malta.'[22]

Even the battleship *Giulio Cesare*, which had been serving as a training ship in Venice, was able to make her way down the Adriatic to arrive at Malta on the 13th. Indeed, except for the – very serious – loss of the *Roma*, the surrender of the major units of the Italian Navy had proceeded quite smoothly. The Regia Marina was now out of the war, although some vessels performed escort duties after the Badoglio government declared war on Germany in October 1943. The final development in this saga, set with powerful symbolism, took place in Malta at the end of September 1943. This was the signature of a full armistice by General Eisenhower and Marshal Badoglio. The ceremony took place aboard the battleship *Nelson*, moored in the Grand Harbour at Valletta.

The Germans still controlled, in occupied Italy, the badly damaged heavy cruisers *Bolzano* and *Gorizia*, the unfinished carrier *Aquila*, two old destroyers and some fleet torpedo boats; they played no further role in the fighting. The battleships *Vittorio Veneto* and *Italia* spent the rest of the war in the Great Salt Lake of the Suez Canal (they were scrapped at La Spezia in the early 1950s). After the war the Soviets received as reparations the battleship *Giulio Cesare* (which became the *Novorossiisk*), and the light cruiser *Duca D'Aosta* (renamed the *Kerch*). The French received two of the scout cruisers. The Greeks were awarded the light cruiser *Eugenio di Savoia*; this was in compensation for the old cruiser *Elli*, which had been illegally torpedoed by an Italian submarine in August 1940, two months before the outbreak of the Italian–Greek War.

THE INVASION OF MAINLAND ITALY

A landing on the Italian mainland had in principle been agreed by the Allied leaders in May 1943, but the actual operational planning took place very quickly, from mid-July. There was only a short pause between the end of the land campaign in Sicily (17 August) and the beginning of fighting on the mainland. On 3 September a British corps crossed the narrow Strait of Messina into Calabria (Operation BAYTOWN), and on 9 September the main British and American force came ashore in the Bay of Salerno, about 30 miles south of Naples (Operation AVALANCHE).

The Italian surrender meant that there would be no serious threat to the expedition from Axis surface ships, although the Allied leaders could not know that when the operation was being planned. The Naval Covering Force (Force H) under Admiral Willis RN sailed around the west coast of Sicily into the Tyrrhenian Sea. It was made up of essentially the same ships as for HUSKY: the battleships *Nelson*, *Rodney*, *Warspite* and *Valiant* and the fleet carriers *Formidable* and *Illustrious*, four cruisers and twenty destroyers. This task force could have dealt with Admiral Bergamini had he actually come out to fight; his sortie would indeed have been 'sacrificial'. The surrender of the surviving Italian submarine fleet – thirty-three boats reached Allied ports – also reduced the underwater threat to the invasion. Three U-boats attempted to operate in the Salerno area, but they caused only minor damage.

The German air danger was greater, and it determined the choice of the Bay of Salerno as the main landing area. A beachhead nearer Rome might have promised the immediate capture of the capital, but Salerno was the point furthest north which could be covered by Allied fighter planes from Sicily. Additional cover for the landing was provided by Admiral Philip Vian's Force V, composed of the British light carrier *Unicorn*, and four escort carriers – the *Attacker*, the *Battler*, the *Hunter* and the *Stalker* – which sailed through the Strait of Messina and into the Tyrrhenian Sea west of Salerno. The carriers had on board 106 new Seafire fighters, but this tactical experiment was not wholly successful. The Seafire, a navalised Spitfire, was a first-rate air fighter but had shortcomings as a carrier plane, partly because of its fragile undercarriage. The situation off Salerno, with slow escort carriers operating in windless conditions and with inexperienced pilots, was not a happy one. Over three days (9–12 September) thirty-two of the Seafires were written off in carrier landing accidents.[23]

Luftwaffe Focke-Wulf Fw 190s and Messerschmidt Bf 109s, operating as fighter-bombers, were used to some effect against ships off Salerno. At the other end of the technical scale were specialised anti-shipping weapons including the Fritz X guided bomb, the 1.5-ton monster that had sunk the *Roma*. On 12 September the *Savannah* was hit by a Fritz X; the American cruiser had provided gunfire support for the troops on Sicily, and was now doing the same at Salerno. Two days later another guided bomb struck the new cruiser HMS *Uganda*, and three days after that, on the 16th, the grand old battleship *Warspite* was hit. All three vessels could be repaired. In the case of the *Warspite* the bomb went right through the ship and out of the bottom of the hull. ('Those rocket bombs are the devil,' Cunningham wrote, 'and they are very, very dangerous.')[24] Seemingly indestructible, the veteran of Jutland, as well as Narvik, Calabria, Cape Matapan, Crete and Ceylon would be back at sea in time for the Normandy landing.

The Allied amphibious landings were built on the capabilities developed in North Africa and Sicily. Operation BAYTOWN was a shore-to-shore feint and met little resistance; operations in Calabria continued a week later when the British 1st Airborne Division was ferried by sea to Taranto from Bizerta. Operation AVALANCHE was another big Allied amphibious operation, strategically the most important so far, but actually mounted by a relatively small force on a wide front. Three infantry divisions, two British and one American, landed on D-Day; the British had embarked in Tripoli and Bizerta, the Americans in Oran. The shipping involved comprised twenty-four attack transports, twenty-eight LSTs and 250 assorted landing craft. In order to achieve surprise the landing was made before dawn with no preliminary naval bombardment.

Unlike any previous landing, there were some German ground forces covering the landing area. In the days that followed more were rapidly brought forward by Field Marshal Albert Kesselring, who now controlled the defence of central and southern Italy. Fierce land battles were fought, in which gunfire support of troops ashore played an important part.[25] For the Allies the fighting did not go well at first, and on 13–14 September serious thought was given to a withdrawal. But the arrival of reinforcements – some dropped by parachute – allowed the invaders to secure their position by 18 September, and the German forces pulled back. Salerno was important because it led to the capture two weeks later (on 1 October) of Naples – the first major port in mainland Europe to be taken by the Allies.

In October, with the main enemy fleet surrendered and southern Italy in Allied hands, the famous Force H was disbanded; during the month five battleships and two fleet carriers were sent home to the United Kingdom. Admiral Andrew Cunningham, who had commanded the whole Mediterranean Fleet, now moved to London as First Sea Lord, following Admiral Pound's severe illness and retirement. By October 1943, the Allies held all of southern Italy upto a front line just north of Naples, but their advance on land soon slowed. Their ground forces were limited, despite the inflow of follow-on divisions, and the terrain was rough and favoured the defenders. There was one attempt to turn the German GOTHIC line in January 1944 by landing two divisions in the Anzio–Nettuno area southwest of Rome in Operation SHINGLE. German naval forces could do very little to interfere with the Anzio landings, but the Luftwaffe was still dangerous. The AA cruiser HMS *Spartan* was sunk off Anzio by an Hs 293 glider bomb (not a Fritz X) at sunset on 29 January 1944. The *Spartan* had only been commissioned six months earlier, but fires aboard her could not be extinguished. She was the only warship larger than a destroyer to fall victim to an Hs 293.

Although the Germans could not drive the enemy landing force back into the sea they were able to contain the beachhead. The best Allied troops were regrouping for the cross-Channel landing and the defending German troops were well led and tenacious, fighting in terrain favourable to the defence. It took five months before their defences south of Rome collapsed. Despite Allied control of the sea and the long coastline it was not possible to outflank the defensive line of the Wehrmacht. Even after the loss of Rome (on 4 June 1944), Kesselring was able to withdraw his armies to a new position on the Arno. Naval forces played no significant part in the last year and a half of the Italian campaign.

A little-remembered shipping war continued in the Mediterranean even after the Allies took control of Sicily, Sardinia and southern Italy. To make up for the loss of the Italian Navy, the German Naval War Staff ordered another twenty-seven U-boats into the Mediterranean between September 1943 and May 1944. Fourteen made their way through the heavy defences at Gibraltar; seven were sunk, and six more turned back. The new Type XXIII U-boat was designed to be broken down into sections and transported by rail to the Mediterranean and elsewhere, but none of these electro-boats were actually deployed in the south. The older boats that did reach the Mediterranean were vulnerable to Allied ships and aircraft, operating in superior numbers and with advanced technology. Moreover, the U-boats' main base at Toulon did not have bomb-proof shelters like those on the Atlantic coast, and the submarines there suffered significant loses in 1944 from AAF attacks. The Germans scuttled two boats in Toulon as the naval port was about to be captured after the Operation DRAGOON landing on 15 August 1944 (see below); a third was wrecked. The last two U-boats in the Mediterranean, the *U 565* and *U 596*, were sunk in September 1944, as a result of an AAF bombing raid on Skaramagkas, near Athens.

Total Allied losses to U-boats in the Mediterranean after May 1943 were relatively low, including some forty-three merchant ships totalling 218,000 tons. This was an average of three ships a month (17,000 tons), with no losses at all after May 1944.[26] The light cruiser HMS *Penelope*, on which C.S. Forester's novel *The Ship* was based, was sunk by the *U 230* west of Naples in February 1944. She was the last major British (or Allied) warship lost in the Mediterranean. All told, however, the cost of victory had been heavy. By the end of the war the Royal Navy would have lost – from all causes – a battleship, two fleet carriers, sixteen cruisers, fifty-seven destroyers and forty-five submarines in what Correlli Barnett called the 'blue waters' of the Mediterranean (see p. 117).

Luftwaffe bombers were also active in the Mediterranean, attacking a number of Allied convoys, with a major effort in November 1943. One of the most dramatic moments in the sea/air war came in the following month with a surprise night raid by 105 Ju 88s on Bari, serving as a major supply port, in southeastern Italy. Two ammunition ships blew up, and leaking fuel caught fire. Altogether twenty-eight merchant ships were sunk or destroyed in the chain of explosions and fires. Some were relatively small coasters, but there were seven Liberty or 'Fort' type cargo ships; over 1,000 crew members and civilians died. A Luftwaffe effort against the convoys at sea had occasional success, despite the presence of land-based Allied fighters. In April 1944 Luftwaffe planes from southern France attacked the huge convoy UGS.38 (eighty-one ships) off Algiers. They sank an American destroyer and four merchant ships. Ammunition aboard the Liberty ship *Paul Hamilton* exploded after she was hit by an aerial torpedo; she went down with all 600 men on board, mostly AAF personnel in transit. Normally, however, the air attacks had only a nuisance value, accounting for one or two ships a month. The last occurred in June and July 1944; no ships were sunk.

But on balance the great waterway was now open with frequent large KMS and UGS convoys from Britain and the US.[27] A number of British capital ships also passed through the Mediterranean, on the way to the Eastern Fleet.

OPERATION DRAGOON IN THE SOUTH OF FRANCE

In addition to features of Italian geography, a major reason for the slow progress of Allied ground forces in Italy after Salerno was that troops and shipping were being concentrated for the cross-Channel invasion of northwestern France (Operation ROUNDUP/OVERLORD). The overall plan was that the cross-Channel invasion would be supported by a second landing in the south of France. There would be both a sledgehammer and an anvil, and ANVIL was the original code name of the southern invasion. In January 1944 the scope of the planned cross-Channel assault in the north was nearly doubled in size; it was increased from three to five assault divisions, and was to be mounted on a wider front.[28] Expansion demanded a large increase of shipping (especially landing craft) and support warships, which meant – in turn – that Operation ANVIL was delayed. Nevertheless, the American planners were insistent, after D-Day in Normandy (6 June 1944), on the need to acquire further large French ports, especially

Marseille in the Mediterranean. Cherbourg in Normandy had been for a number of weeks after the invasion the main port in Allied hands, and it had limited shipping capacity.

Operation ANVIL was renamed Operation DRAGOON in late July 1944, and it was actually mounted on 15 August. By this time the Americans and British had broken out of the Normandy beachhead, and the liberation of Paris was only a week away. Three veteran American divisions from Italy made the initial landings, having embarked in Naples aboard twenty-seven attack transports, seventy-seven LSTs and nearly 400 smaller landing craft. The follow-on forces, setting out from Taranto and Oran, were made up of seven French divisions – a mixture of veterans of the Italian campaign and newly raised troops from Algeria.

The naval side of DRAGOON was commanded by the American admiral Kent Hewitt. As with Sicily, Salerno and Anzio, the approaching landings met no serious opposition from German naval forces. Unlike the landing in northern France, the distance from Allied airfields to the DRAGOON beachhead was considerable, although some forward air bases on Corsica had been in use since November 1943. As a result, the naval covering forces included seven British and two American escort carriers, operating from Malta with 220 fighters on board. By this time, however, the Luftwaffe anti-shipping forces in the south of France had been much depleted by the demands of other fronts. The remaining eighty German aircraft, withdrawn to inland bases, mounted missions for the first week of the southern invasion. An LST was hit by a bomber-launched Hs 293 glider bomb on DRAGOON D-Day and had to be scuttled, but that was the only major loss.

Like Normandy (and unlike Salerno), the amphibious landings in the south of France were mounted in daylight. H-Hour on 15 August was 8.00 a.m. There were considerable German coastal defences, including 340mm batteries around Marseille and Toulon. Allied heavy gunfire support was provided by five elderly battleships, the British *Ramillies*, the French *Lorraine* and the American *Nevada*, *Texas* and *Arkansas*; the *Nevada* was a Pearl Harbor survivor. This was the only operation by American big-gun ships in the Mediterranean, and the first appearance there of a capital ship of the US Navy since the fleet carrier *Wasp* in early 1942.

The Allied troops which came ashore after the DRAGOON landings were largely unopposed by the Wehrmacht, which had been broken in France by the Normandy campaign. Weak German ground forces quickly retreated north up the Rhône valley. Marseille and Toulon were both captured on D+14 (28 August). From the middle of September 1944 both the big southern French ports were ready to accept reinforcements and supplies. Successive waves of arriving troops moved far to the north to form the right flank of the Allied armies advancing across the Rhine into Germany. By the end of the war in Europe over 900,000 personnel and over 4 million tons of supplies had been brought in through Marseille, Toulon and Port de Bouc.[29]

The end of the sea/air war in the Mediterranean was not marked by dramatic action. The Allied navies and air forces had been in command of these waters for eighteen months. From the beginning of 1943 the USAAF had played a significant role in the sea/air campaign for which it is not often given credit, and in 1944 most of the amphibious 'lift' and many of the assault troops were provided by the Americans. But in maritime terms the Mediterranean victory had been that of the Royal Navy. The cost in men and ships had been high, and the scale of fighting second only to the Battle of the Atlantic.[30]

CHAPTER 17

THE SUBMARINE WAR IN THE PACIFIC AND INDIAN OCEANS

CONVOY BATTLE OFF FORMOSA, 21 SEPTEMBER 1943

The Pescadores Islands lie between Formosa (now Taiwan) and the Chinese mainland. Makō in the Pescadores was the transit port from which the Japanese convoy sailed north, on the evening of 20 September 1943. A five-day trip across the East China Sea was planned, ending on the northern tip of Kyūshū at Moji – wartime Japan's busiest port; the distance of the voyage was some 1,000 miles.

By Atlantic standards the convoy was very small and the escort smaller still. There were five vessels – the tankers *Shōyō Maru* and *Ogura Maru No. 1*, and three cargo ships, including the *Argun Maru*. Protecting them was the *Shiriya*, a 15,000-ton naval oiler.[1] The *Shiriya* had been completed back in 1922 and was capable of only 12 knots, but 5.5-inch guns were mounted fore and aft; her crew numbered 150. Captain Nakao Hachiro, who had taken over the *Shiriya* the month before, was a regular naval officer; he was now in charge of the whole convoy. Some patrol planes provided cover overhead, as the convoy was still within range of the Formosa airfields.

On 1 September 1943 USS *Trigger*, a fleet submarine of the 'Gato' class (the main American wartime type), had departed Pearl Harbor on her sixth combat patrol. Commissioned in January 1942, she had just completed a major refit. She also had a new CO; Lt Commander Robert 'Dusty' Dornin was a member of the Annapolis class of 1935, and a hero of football games against West Point, who had served aboard the *Gudgeon* when she made the first ever American submarine patrol into Japanese home waters in the dark days of December 1941. Later he had become an expert in the use of the Torpedo Data Computer (TDC). Now aged thirty-one, Dornin had become one of the youngest American officers to be given a submarine command.

The East China Sea, above Formosa, was some 5,000 miles from the main American submarine base at Pearl Harbor. The *Trigger* spent two weeks sailing on the surface across the Central Pacific to reach her patrol area, stopping briefly at Johnston Island to top up her fuel and water.

The American 'fleet submarines' were half as big again as the German Type IX U-boats, and twice the size of the Type VIIs. They were built from the middle of the 1930s and intended not for commerce-raiding – which the US had legally foresworn – but to provide distant support for the capital ships in the expected mid-Pacific naval battle. Four big diesel motors provided power to keep up with the US battle line and engage the Japanese fleet. Their armament comprised six torpedo tubes fitted forward, and four aft, as well as a deck gun. By the submarine standards of the time, the fleet boats were quite habitable, with air conditioning and other creature comforts for the wartime crew of about sixty. These features would make the fleet submarines very effective – in their unexpected role as long-range hunters of merchant ships.

West of Okinawa, in bright moonlight early on 18 September, Lt Commander Dornin sank his first ship. The target was one of the new 6,400-ton Type 'A' cargo ships, steaming on its own. The *Yowa Maru* went down in two minutes, followed by a huge explosion as her boilers blew up.

Three days later, on the afternoon of the 21st, the *Trigger* sighted Captain Nakao's convoy off the northern point of Formosa; this was some 250 miles southwest of the first sinking. The convoy was zig-zagging at 8 knots; from what could be seen by the Americans, it was arrayed in two columns, three tanker-type ships to starboard (unknown to Dornin, the leading ship was the *Shiriya*), and three cargo ships to port. The presence of a patrol plane kept the *Trigger* at periscope depth and, running submerged on her batteries, the boat fell behind the convoy. As dusk fell Dornin ordered the *Trigger* to the surface and started the diesels, giving a high speed – for a submarine – of nearly 20 knots. He was able to re-locate the convoy by radar, and at 8,000 yards his lookouts made visual contact.

Maintaining formation, and no longer zig-zagging, Captain Nakao was now leading his convoy to the east. Dornin attacked from the starboard (southern) side, against the column of tankers. The *Shiriya* was probably not equipped with radar, and the Japanese lookouts failed to sight the low silhouette of the *Trigger* in the evening darkness. It was a classic night surface attack along the lines developed by Admiral Dönitz for his U-boats, although the American boat had the additional advantage of centimetric SJ radar. Dornin controlled the attack from the 'conning tower' compartment amidships, using the TDC; he was also able to follow the situation on an experimental Plan Position Indicator (PPI) radar display, an electronic map connected to the radar. Lieutenant Edward

Beach, Dornin's 'exec' (executive officer), stood on the open bridge above, alongside the lookouts; he exchanged information with the CO from his vantage point. (After the war Beach became a well-known submariner and author.)

At 8.56 p.m. Dornin fired three Mark XIV torpedoes from the forward tubes toward the *Shiriya*. The range was some 1,600 yards. Two torpedoes hit, only seconds apart. Dornin's later report described the scene: 'Flames shot five hundred feet into the air, lighting up the whole area as bright as day. All six ships could plainly be seen.' The *Shiriya* was carrying aviation fuel, and the effect of the torpedo hits was devastating:

Members of her crew in various stages of dress (most in white uniforms) could be seen running forward ahead of the rapidly spreading flames. She was still driving ahead, a brilliantly blazing funeral pyre. The men in the bow manned the bow gun and fired three or four times, but she was soon burning through her length. The flames were yellow-red, evidently from burning aviation fuel.[2]

Dornin launched the three torpedoes from the remaining forward tubes at the second tanker, the *Shōyō Maru*. She was hit and caught fire moments later. The cargo ship *Argun Maru* in the port column was hit by one of the first six torpedoes, and she broke in half and sank almost immediately; the radar operator on the *Trigger* saw the 'pip' disappear from his PPI display.

The *Trigger* was now visible to the Japanese by the light of fiercely burning tankers. Dornin fired four 'fish' (torpedos) from his stern tubes against the tanker *Ogura Maru No.1*, the final one 'down the throat' as the Japanese freighter turned to ram him. He was then able to crash dive to safety. About an hour later, torpedo tubes reloaded, the submarine re-surfaced. Dornin expended his last torpedo in an unsuccessful attack on one of the cargo ships and then withdrew. Four hours after the initial attack a glow visible astern and beyond the horizon flared up, evidently the explosion of the *Shōyō Maru*. The crew were allowed on deck, one by one, to witness the burning ships astern. The *Trigger* then began the long voyage back across the Pacific to the forward submarine base at Midway.

Captain Nakao was killed aboard the *Shiriya*; he was posthumously promoted to the rank of rear admiral. After two more successful war patrols Dornin was transferred to Washington to serve as an aide to Admiral King. The *Trigger* was lost in March 1945, on her twelfth patrol and under her fourth captain. Japanese ships and aircraft sank the submarine in the East China Sea, and there were no survivors.

THE AMERICAN CAMPAIGN AGAINST JAPANESE SHIPPING

The September 1943 patrol of the *Trigger* came at a turning point in the US Navy's campaign against Japanese merchant vessels. Lt Commander Dornin claimed to have sunk six vessels, totalling 44,700 tons. Japanese records available after the war corrected the figures to four ships and 27,000 tons; the discrepancy was typical of wartime reports. Nevertheless, even the smaller total made this the third most successful American submarine patrol since the start of the war. For the Japanese, a number of developments over the past year had begun to transform the American submarine from an irritant to an existential threat. No fewer than twenty-five submarines departed Pearl Harbor on war patrols in September 1943.

When they made their fatal decision in 1941 to begin the Pacific war, the leaders of Imperial Japan took into account – at least superficially – the shipping demands of a conflict with Britain and the United States. The strategic aim of the thrust into Southeast Asia was to gain access to the resources of the region, especially oil, rubber, bauxite and other minerals necessary for the conduct of modern war; these materials in turn had to be transported by sea to the home islands. This was in addition to the need to supply an army of over 1 million men in China and the Manchukuo puppet state. And even without that, shipping was crucial for the Japanese economy. This was noted in a post-war American survey: 'No major power in the world was more dependent on ocean shipping than Japan. Her entire economy in peace, and even more so in war, depended upon shipping to provide the basic materials for industry and to fill out the supply of staples required to feed and clothe her population.'[3]

One of the fundamental features of Japanese modernisation and economic development in the twentieth century had been the creation of a world class shipping fleet, and a strong shipbuilding industry. In December 1941 Japan possessed the third largest merchant marine in the world, with some 6.5 million tons of sea-going shipping. Much of it was modern, having been built, partly with state subsidies, in the 1930s.

The war with America and Britain certainly brought problems. Primarily this was the result of the Imperial Army and Navy taking over for their own uses much of the civilian tonnage, and not returning it. In contrast, at least for the first eighteen months after December 1941, Allied action was a relatively small factor in limiting Japanese strategic/economic shipping capacity. Front-line/operational convoys also took few losses; the conquest of the British, Dutch and American colonies, with big Japanese convoys steaming to Thailand, Malaya, the Philippines and the Netherlands Indies, was achieved at low cost, including that of Japanese merchant ships sunk. As Table 17.1 shows, combat losses up to the middle of 1942 were about 380,000 tons, on average only about twenty ships a month. This was more than made up for by Allied ships captured in Southeast Asia.

As the Pacific war progressed, however, a growing number of Japanese merchant ships were being sunk by enemy forces. Indeed, a blockade of Japan – economic

Table 17.1. Japanese Merchant Ship Losses, 1941–45

Year/ quarter	By submarine	By other causes	Total combat losses	Non-combat losses	Total losses
1941/iv	32,000	17,000	49,000	7,000	55,000
1942/i–ii	240,000	90,000	329,000	27,000	356,000
1942/iii–iv	372,000	183,000	555,000	66,000	622,000
1943/i–ii	558,000	138,000	696,000	31,000	727,000
1943/iii–iv	754,000	215.000	970,000	68,000	1,038,000
1944/i–ii	1,140,000	557,000	1,697,000	71,000	1,768,000
1944/iii–iv	1,248,000	748,000	1,997,000	58,000	2,055,000
1945/i–iii	587,000	1,716,000	2,303,000	117,000	2,420,000
Total	4,932,000	3,665,000	8,597,000	446,000	9,042,000

Source: Parillo, *Merchant Marine*, pp. 243–4.
Notes: Table gives tonnage loss and includes only vessels over 500 tons. Average size of Japanese merchant ships in the table was 2,800 tons (Cohen, *Japan's Economy*, pp. 265–6).

warfare – was a way in which both the Americans and the British had long envisaged that a war with Japan would be fought. They did not expect before 1939 to fight a submarine war against civilian shipping; unrestricted attacks had been made illegal by international treaty. Both countries embarked on large cruiser (surface ship) programmes, and both envisaged the use of forward bases like Hong Kong and Manila as blockade bases.

The Pacific conflict actually developed along very different lines. This was partly due to the spectacular initial Japanese successes which severely weakened the Americans and the British; these in turn allowed creation of a defensive perimeter and the elimination of any enemy bases remotely near the home islands.[4] There was no Allied cruiser campaign comparable to Admiral Raeder's Kreuzerkrieg, with raiding battleships, cruisers and auxiliary cruisers/raiders (although Churchill at least did very briefly in 1941 speak of the *Prince of Wales* and the *Repulse* playing in the Pacific the role of the *Scharnhorst* and the *Gneisenau* in the Atlantic). The war against 'ordinary' economic/strategic Japanese shipping was largely carried out by American submarines, although some front-line/operational shipping was subject to air attacks from the second half of 1942.

The actual pattern over the course of the whole Pacific war is shown in Table 17.1. In 1942 the Japanese merchant fleet suffered relatively low losses from all types of enemy action, including submarines. They amounted to about 20,000 tons of merchant shipping (equivalent to about seven vessels) a month over the whole Pacific in the first three quarters of 1942. After that the curve of losses turned sharply upward, rising to 100,000–150,000 tons (twenty-four to thirty-six ships) a month in the last three quarters of 1943, and then to 200,000 tons (forty-eight ships) a month in 1944.[5]

The statistics also show that compared to Allied losses in the Battle of the Atlantic a high proportion of Japanese shipping losses were caused by forces other than submarines; the biggest element was air attack. American planes would in the end sink 840 Japanese merchant ships, totalling 2,815,000 tons.[6] As Table 17.1 shows, non-submarine-caused Japanese losses quadrupled in 1944 compared to 1943. US Navy carrier task forces became able to operate much more freely over the western Pacific. The biggest single loss came in a carrier raid on the main mid-ocean base at Truk in February 1944, when 200,000 tons of Japanese shipping were sunk.[7] Meanwhile, the Japanese expended shipping in 1943–44 while attempting to reinforce their garrisons in the Solomons, New Guinea, the Marianas and the Philippines; this brought their transports and cargo ships within range of Allied land- or carrier-based aircraft.

The most important weapons deployed against Japanese shipping, however, were the American submarines, which until 1945 caused losses which were always double those of aircraft and surface ships. There had been no long-term American plans or training for a *submarine* war against shipping. The United States had signed the 1930 London Treaty, which greatly restricted such operations; in any event convoy and technical advances such as sonar were thought to have weakened the potential of undersea attack. Only in the autumn of 1940 did it become clear that Germany's U-boats were still a very effective weapon. In addition, the pre-war US Navy (like the Japanese one) was dominated by advocates of a traditional decisive naval battle, and submarines were envisaged as a supporting force for the battle fleet. Nevertheless, both admirals King and Nimitz had extensive experience in submarines, and in December 1941 Nimitz chose to formally assume command of the Pacific Fleet on the deck of the submarine USS *Grayling* – amidst the shattered surface fleet at Pearl Harbor.

President Woodrow Wilson had taken the US to war in 1917 largely in protest against the 'unrestricted' U-boat campaign of Imperial Germany, and as recently as September 1941 President Roosevelt had condemned the 'rattlesnakes of the Atlantic'. A few hours after Pearl Harbor, Admiral Stark in Washington issued an instruction: 'Execute unrestricted air and submarine warfare against Japan'. US Navy submarines could now attack merchant ships without warning, and had no obligation to secure the safety of their passengers and crew. The submarine *Swordfish* carried out the first successful American attack, on the 8,700-ton cargo liner *Atsutasan Maru* off Hainan Island on 16 December 1941.[8]

After a period of experimentation in the 1920s, the peacetime US Navy had commissioned about forty large, fast, fleet-support submarines (from the mid-1930s). During the Pacific war, 200 more 'fleet' submarines were commissioned, of the new 'Gato' (SS-212) class and two slightly modified sub-classes. These 1,525-ton boats could make 21 knots on the surface and 9 knots submerged. Unlike the other naval powers, the Americans did not, in wartime, build any medium-sized or coastal submarines; in the first year and a half of the war they did, however, use in combat some 906-ton 'S' class boats completed in the early 1920s. The large US Navy submarines would inevitably be available in smaller numbers than German U-boats, which were half their size. American shipyards never reached the German target of twenty boats a month – they averaged six a month in the peak year of 1943; two-thirds were produced in New England by the Electric Boat Company and the Portsmouth Navy Yard.

Table 17.2 lays out the size and losses of the American and Japanese submarine forces; Table 17.3 shows the American submarine force's Pacific operations, targeted against both warships and merchantmen. In December 1941 much of American submarine force was concentrated in the Philippines. Operations there, and later in the Netherlands Indies, were a dismal failure. With inexperienced and over-cautious commanders and crews, the twenty-eight submarines

Table 17.2. US and Japanese Submarine Forces, 1941–45

Year/	United States		Japan	
quarter	Cmsnd	Lost	Cmsnd	Lost
Pre-war	111		63	
1941/iv	4	2	0	1
1942/i–ii	16	4	8	6
1942/iii–iv	17	2	12	11
1943/i–ii	27	6	14	8
1943/iii–iv	47	8	12	19
1944/i–ii	20	8	12	36
1944/iii–iv	39	12	8	18
1945/i–iii	30	7	8	26
Total war-built	200	49	74	125

Source: Mor/4, p. 188; Alden, *Fleet Submarine*, pp. 252–74; Blair, *Silent Victory*, pp. 991–2; Polmar/Carpenter, *Submarines*, pp. 153–5.
Notes: 'Cmsnd' denotes submarines commissioned in this period (these only became operational 3–6 months after commissioning). 'Lost' includes both pre-war and war-built boats. US figures are global, but few submarines were deployed outside the Pacific. Of the 111 boats in commission in the USN in 1941, 65 were small or medium-sized boats commissioned in World War I or the early 1920s. Not included are 23 IJN transport submarines completed in 1944–45.

Table 17.3. US Submarine Patrols in the Pacific, 1941–45

Year/quarter	Pearl Harbor	Australia	Philippines/Java	Alaska
1941/iv	11	0	43	0
1942/i–ii	55	52	20	11
1942/iii–iv	58	76	0	28
1943/i–ii	85	49	0	20
1943/iii–iv	124	61	0	16
1944/i–ii	160	71	0	0
1944/iii–iv	188	100	0	0
1945/i–iii	151	7	0	0

Source: Blair, *Silent Victory*, pp. 901–83.
Notes: Patrols are cruises by individual submarines. 'Pearl Harbor' includes forward bases in the Central Pacific. 'Australia' is Fremantle and Brisbane. 'Alaska' is Dutch Harbor.

of the US Asiatic Fleet – fleet submarines and some older S-boats – sank no enemy warships and only six merchant ships over two months. The Japanese invasions proceeded without any serious opposition from the sea.[9]

The active American submarine force was withdrawn to Australia, to Fremantle (near Perth) and Brisbane, on the western and eastern coasts respectively, as well as to Pearl Harbor. When the vast Pacific region was divided into two overall commands in the spring of 1942 this would create some organisational confusion. The boats in Australia would come under General Douglas MacArthur's South West Pacific Area (from 1943 the Seventh Fleet) and those at Pearl Harbor under Admiral Chester Nimitz. (A smaller force was assembled for the defence of Alaska.) The US Navy submarines had little impact at the battles of the Coral Sea or Midway; a considerable number were, however, concentrated for the latter action in June 1942, and the *Nautilus* was able to reach the centre of the Japanese Mobile Force. Although codebreaking provided much advance information about Japanese ship movements, in 1942 the US Navy achieved considerably less than the Japanese against big warships. The only major sinkings were the heavy cruiser *Kako* sunk by the *S-44* off New Britain, in August (after the Battle of Savo Island), and the small light cruiser *Tenryū*, sunk by the *Albacore* off New Guinea in December.

Patrols were sent into the waters off Japan and in Southeast Asia. As Table 17.1 shows, the Japanese were losing only 40,000–50,000 tons a month to submarines in the second half of 1942, equivalent to fourteen to eighteen merchant ships. This was at a time when the U-boats in the Atlantic were sinking 530,000 tons a month, and ten times as many ships.

In the following year, 1943, the situation improved from the American point of view. The US Navy was no longer on the strategic defensive in 1943, and more and more submarines were being commissioned. The number of submarine patrols from Pearl Harbor and Australia increased to 185 in the second half of 1943 (compared to 134 in the second half of the previous year). Leadership of the submarine campaign in the Pacific was consolidated from January 1943 under Admiral Charles Lockwood as COMSUBPAC (following the death of his predecessor in a plane crash); Lockwod was subordinate to Admiral Nimitz. But American submarines were still sinking only about 100,000 tons of merchant shipping (equivalent to about thirty-five vessels) a month during the first three quarters of the year. Only one major Japanese warship was sunk in the whole course of 1943, the escort carrier *Chūyō*, torpedoed with very heavy loss of life by the *Sailfish* off Japan in December.

A major, but not exclusive, factor in the limited success of the American submarine fleet was what has been called the 'great torpedo scandal'. The problem was a complex technical one, involving the control and detonation of the torpedoes. It was not unlike the problem the Kriegsmarine encountered off Norway in 1940. The American Mark XIV torpedo sometimes ran too deep, passing under the target ship, and both the (secretly developed) magnetic and contact 'exploders' (pistols) malfunctioned, exploding prematurely or not at all. The 'scandal' was how long it took the US Navy to recognise the problem. As it happened, it was the *Trigger*, again, which played a key role. On her fifth patrol in June 1943 (this time not under the command of Dornin) she fired six torpedoes at the large aircraft carrier *Hiyō* as she departed Tokyo Bay. Her CO claimed a probable sinking, but Ultra decrypts revealed that the carrier had survived and only one torpedo had caused serious damage. This was the last straw for Nimitz and Lockwood who – nineteen months into the war – finally ordered the abandoning of the magnetic exploder. But a technical problem continued with the conventional *contact* exploder, which sometimes malfunctioned when the torpedo hit the target head-on at a 90° angle. Only in September 1943 was this problem isolated and a modified contact exploder fitted.[10]

In other respects the American submarines were well equipped. As well as the steam-driven Mark XIV, recovered examples of the German G7e electric torpedo were rapidly copied by Westinghouse and put into wide service as the Mark XVIII. This weapon was slower and had shorter range, but it did not leave a tell-tale wake. Powerful electronic equipment included both the 1.5m SD radar, which gave a warning of nearby enemy A/S aircraft, and also from the autumn of 1942 the excellent 10cm SJ surface-search radar – used for night attacks. Development of VHF radio made possible secure voice radio communications between submarines operating together as a 'wolfpack', which became increasingly frequent in 1944.[11]

The ability to decrypt a number of Japanese Navy and Army codes provided the US Navy submarine force with vital information about the movement of Japanese warships, convoys and troopships. Vital to the remarkable success of the submarines were the 'fleet radio units' at Pearl Harbor and Melbourne (FRUPAC and FRUMEL), which collaborated with the signals intelligence organisation in Washington and with the British Far East Combined Bureau (FECB) in the Indian Ocean Area.

Another development of late 1943 was the belated formation of the Japanese shipping protection force. Unlike the British in 1940–41, the Imperial Navy had failed to create a co-ordinated A/S organisation. This was partly because – unlike the British – its leaders had not experienced very large-scale A/S warfare in World War I. More fundamentally there was a general emphasis in the Japanese Navy on offensive and decisive battle. Nevertheless, the Japanese Army and the civilian shipping organisation were concerned about growing losses. In the command crisis which followed the death of Admiral Yamamoto, it was accepted that more attention needed to be paid to commerce protection. In November 1943 the Maritime Escort Command (*Kaijō Goei Sōtai*) was established under Admiral Oikawa Koshirō.[12] This was theoretically at the same administrative level as the Combined Fleet and the China Area fleet; Oikawa had been Minister of the Navy in 1940–41, and was actually senior in rank to the new C-in-C of the Combined Fleet, Admiral Koga. In reality, however, Oikawa had relatively few ships and aircraft at his disposal.

The Japanese Navy began the war with sixty-nine destroyers and had lost thirty-eight of them by the autumn of 1943; four out of seventeen war-built destroyers had also been sunk by that time. Two types of 1,200-ton escort destroyer (the 'Matsu' and 'Tachibana' class) were ordered for the Navy, but only about thirty of these vessels were completed, half in 1945 – far too late. The first vessel, the *Matsu,* was laid down in August 1943 and completed in April 1944; she only became operational in July. The Japanese Navy did build a considerable number of *kaibōkan* ('sea-going defence ships'), escort vessels of about 900 tons, powered by diesel or steam turbine and capable of 16–20 knots. These were roughly comparable to the British 'Flower'- and 'Castle' class corvettes. Four Type 'A' kaibōkan were built as prototypes before the war, but the first of a wartime class (Type 'B') was not completed until May 1943, and there were only fourteen of them. It was only in October 1943 that work began on numerically much larger groups (types 'C' and 'D') using prefabricated construction. Some 115 vessels were eventually built, but they were mostly completed in late 1944 and 1945. The Japanese did put five escort carriers into service and organise a special A/S naval air group, the 901st NAG. The carriers seldom engaged in shipping escort operations, and many of the land-based aircraft trained in the

A/S role were expended on other missions in the defence of the Philippines and Formosa in late 1944.

A/S equipment was not given a high priority. At the outbreak of the war the Imperial Navy relied on imported technology, much of it dating back to World War I. A few dozen Type 93 echo-ranging sonar sets were in service, but the main device was the hydrophone, a passive listening device. Both sonar and radar lagged behind, although the Germans did provide some technical assistance. The convoy system was not well developed, as it was believed to slow excessively the flow of shipping; latterly convoys of up to twenty merchant ships were assembled, but nothing on the scale of the forty-to-eighty-ship convoys of the Allies in the Atlantic.

Whatever the shortcomings of the Japanese A/S forces, the ships and aircraft of the Imperial Navy did succeed, over the war as a whole, in destroying a considerable number of American submarines. Altogether forty-eight US boats were lost in the Pacific, the greatest number (twenty) in 1944.[13] Most of those sunk were operating on the strategic/economic shipping route up the China coast from Southeast Asia to Japan. (The Formosa leg of this route is where the *Trigger* operated in late 1943.) Of these, nine American submarines were lost in the South China Sea.

The other way for the Japanese to deal with the submarine attacks, and the growing demand for shipping, was to accelerate production of replacement cargo ships and tankers. Construction of merchant ships had been allowed to decline in the last years before the war, as the private shipyards were used to build warships. Like the British in 1940, the Japanese had been able to capture or salvage a large amount of shipping in the first stages of the war; in the case of Japan this came to a total of 708,000 tons in 1941–42. Japanese emergency merchant ship construction was also successful, although it began to expand only in the autumn of 1942, with the laying out of new shipyards, and the development of a range of standard shipping types. The 6,500-ton, 450-foot Type '2A' cargo ship was not unlike the Liberty ship. In scale the building programme was similar to that of the UK, with 1,094,000 tons in the fiscal year (FY) 1943 and 1,590,000 tons in FY 1944 (to March 1945); production had been only 362,000 tons in FY 1942.[14] But it was in no way on the scale of the American programme. For the Allies, global construction of cargo ships and tankers had outpaced losses in the autumn of 1942. The Japanese, in contrast, were building one ship for every three sunk.

The year 1944 was the most successful for the American submarine force. Ultra intelligence remained a major advantage, and there were now a larger number of American submarines (often deployed in wolfpacks) and fully working torpedoes. In the final months of 1944, bases were captured in the western Pacific and northern Australia which were much closer to Japanese shipping lanes; the most important was at Guam.

Major Japanese warships were sunk in 1944. Compared to their limited role in the battles of the Coral Sea and Midway, and the fighting around Guadalcanal, American submarines played a decisive role in the great June 1944 Battle of the Philippine Sea. They sank the *Shōkaku* and the *Taihō*, two of three big Japanese carriers present. Involvement in the Battle of Leyte Gulf in October was less decisive but still significant. As the Combined Fleet moved into position to defend the Philippines against invasion, two heavy cruisers were torpedoed and sunk, including the *Atago*, the flagship of the Japanese admiral commanding the main force.[15]

General warship attrition also grew. In 1944, outside the major battles, American submarines sank two fleet carriers, three escort carriers, the (British-built) fast battleship *Kongō*, and seven more cruisers. This remarkable change was partly due to the Japanese shortage of fast escorts. One of the fleet carriers was the largest that had ever been built for any navy, the 62,000-ton *Shinano*. She had been constructed at Yokosuka using the hull of a 'Yamato' class battleship and in November 1944 was being transferred from Tokyo Bay to the relative safety of Kure (the Tokyo area was for the first time under threat of air attack). The submarine *Archerfish* hit her with four torpedoes in a night attack. The huge carrier had not completed fitting out, and the damage control systems were not fully working. Some 1,400 of the 2,500 men on board were drowned when the ship rolled over and sank by the stern.[16]

Meanwhile, by the second half of 1944 American submarines were sinking a monthly average of about 200,000 tons of Japanese merchant shipping (comparable to about seventy vessels). The critical tankers were targeted, reducing the supply of fuel from Southeast Asia, but even the trade across the Yellow Sea to Manchukuo and the rest of occupied China was interrupted. Codebreaking also allowed targeted attacks on front-line/operational convoys which were hurrying Japanese Army troops from China to the islands of the western Pacific to deal with expected American advances and invasions there. An important episode was the April–May 1944 interception of the large TAKE ('Bamboo') No. 1 convoy, which was transporting two Japanese Army divisions south from Shanghai to the Philippines and western New Guinea. Four troopships were sunk, and several thousand veteran soldiers lost; the surviving reinforcements were diverted to nearer destinations. This disaster contributed to the collapse of plans to defend New Guinea.

The innovation of the Maritime Escort Command was abandoned in view of the huge pressure on the ships and aircraft of the Combined Fleet. Admiral Oikawa moved to take over the Naval General Staff in August 1944 (after the resignation of General Tōjō), and the Maritime Escort Command was subordinated to the Combined Fleet.

The last months of 1944 and 1945 brought strategic changes that greatly affected the shipping war. The American capture of bases in the Philippines after the fighting of October–December 1944 fatally threatened the arterial supply line from Southeast Asia through the Formosa Strait and Luzon Strait to the home islands. (It was arguably this potential threat that had led Japan to attack the United States in the first place, back in December 1941, when the country embarked on the Southern Operation.)[17] Meanwhile the Americans established air bases within range of Japan. The Mariana Islands had been captured in June–July 1944, and a strategic bombing force of B-29s began to operate from there against Japan in November; later, in April 1945, bases for shorter-range bombers began to be developed on Okinawa.[18] In April 1945 the AAF began a campaign, Operation STARVATION, to block Japanese ports using mines dropped by B-29s. The mines caused a great deal of damage to the remnants of the Japanese merchant fleet, sinking 241 ships totalling 567,000 tons.[19]

US Navy submarines had less impact in 1945, because the surviving ships of the Japanese merchant fleet remained in harbour. In the first three months of 1945 losses of merchant ships to submarines averaged only 70,000 tons a month. A group of submarines did break into the Sea of Japan, using a new FM sonar to get through the defensive minefields in the Tsushima Strait. This was in June 1945 and it was the first time such operations had been attempted since late 1943; they now threatened the last Japanese links to the Asian mainland through the ports of eastern Korea.

THE JAPANESE FAILURE IN THE SHIPPING WAR

The Allies had even longer 'exposed' maritime supply lines than did the Japanese, across the Pacific and the Indian Ocean. The Japanese Navy, however, failed to cut these Allied shipping routes, mounting no effort comparable to the German U-boat campaigns of the two world wars. The war leadership in Tokyo did indeed carry out or plan operations to sever or threaten some sea arteries. The capture of Rangoon in March 1942 cut the Allied shipping route to China via the Burma Road. Admiral Nagumo's carrier raid against Ceylon in the spring of 1942 put the whole Indian Ocean region in danger. Plans were developed in the summer of 1942 – before Midway – for advances towards the Solomons, Fiji and Samoa which would block the supply route to Australia. But only a minimal attempt was made to mount a sustained attack on enemy shipping, let alone anything like the 'tonnage war' of Admiral Dönitz.

Table 17.4. Allied Merchant Ship Losses in the Pacific and Indian Oceans, 1941–45

Year/ quarter	(1) Pacific (all causes)	(2) Indian O. (all causes)	(3) E. Pacific (Jap. s/m)	(4) Philip./NI (Jap. s/m)	(5) Australia (Jap. s/m)	(6) SW Pac. (Jap. s/m)	(7) Indian O. (Jap. s/m)
1941/iv	432,000	1,000	41,000	5,000	0	0	0
1942/i–ii	498,000	419,000	11,000	79,000	14,000	12,000	200,000
1942/iii–iv	50,000	305,000	3,000	0	19,000	38,000	104,000
1943/i–ii	105,000	217,000	0	0	50,000	57,000	41,000
1943/iii–iv	28,000	269,000	0	0	0	8,000	90,000
1944/i–ii	0	215,000	7,000	0	0	0	102,000
1944/iii–iv	58,000	108,000	7,000	0	0	0	11,000
1945/i–ii	49,000	7,000	0	0	0	0	0
Total	1,219,000	1,542,000	69,000	83,000	82,000	114,000	548,000

Source: Rosk/1, p. 618; ibid./2, p. 486; ibid./3.1, p. 389; Rohwer, *Axis Submarine Successes*, pp. 259–91.
Notes: The first two columns (from Roskill) give losses in tonnage from enemy action *of all types*, including German and Italian action, as well as Japanese action. The third to seventh columns (from Rohwer) give losses caused by Japanese submarines. Figures are rounded to the nearest thousand.

Allied merchant shipping losses in the Indian Ocean and the Pacific over the whole war are laid out in Table 17.4. Much the worst period for the Allies was the winter of 1941–42, when well over 1 million tons were lost. This comprised the many ships sunk or captured as a result of the Japanese advance into Southeast Asia; as already mentioned, the Japanese were able to add 700,000 tons to their own shipping fleet as a result of their attack. After that, however, Allied losses at the hands of the Imperial Navy from all causes were small. The greatest impact was achieved in the Indian Ocean. There, between January 1942 and November 1944 (thirty-five months), Japanese submarines, based mostly at Penang in Malaya, destroyed nearly 550,000 tons of Allied shipping (ninety-eight vessels). In relative terms, however, this was only what the U-boats sank in the Atlantic in an average *month* in 1942. By 1943–44 the monthly rate of sinkings caused by *Japanese* submarines even in the Indian Ocean had fallen to 10,000 tons, equivalent to three ships every two months. The Imperial Navy was now substantially less successful than the growing force of U-boats from the MONSUN ('Monsoon' submarine group now operating in the region).[20]

Meanwhile, in the Pacific Ocean, the main naval theatre, Allied merchant ship losses were even lower. After the fall of the Philippines and the Netherlands Indies in the spring of 1942 and up to the end of the war, Japanese submarines accounted for only 225,000 tons of Allied merchant shipping (forty-one vessels) in the Pacific. As Table 17.4 shows, most of these vessels were sunk off the coast of eastern Australia or in support of the Solomons campaign in the autumn of 1942 and the spring of 1943; even then the number of sinkings was little more than a dozen merchant ships. Most remarkably, in the *eastern* Pacific – east of the International Date Line – Japanese submarines sank in the course of the whole war just fourteen merchant ships, only three of them off the coast of Canada or the US. (In contrast U-boats accounted for 397 Allied merchant ships – nearly 2 million tons – off the US East Coast in the first six months of 1942.) In November 1942, Admiral King remarked to a group of reporters (off the record) that Japanese submarines were not attacking merchant ships, and he hoped America's luck would hold: 'We're knocking on wood.'[21] Indeed, so limited was the threat in the eastern Pacific that in 1943 the US Navy was able to discontinue the convoy system.

At the end of 1943 Japanese submarine crews began systematic attacks on survivors from Allied merchant ships, machine-gunning lifeboats or even taking survivors aboard and murdering them. Although all the known atrocities of this type were perpetrated in the Indian Ocean, and only four Japanese submarines were involved, it appears to have been an action authorised from above. An operational order dated 20 March 1943 and issued by Admiral Mito Hisashi, commander of the 1st Submarine Squadron and serving at Truk, stated the following. 'Do not stop with sinking of enemy ships and cargoes; at the same time carry out the complete destruction of the crews of the enemy ships. If possible seize part of the crew and endeavour to secure information about the enemy.'[22]

The extreme contrast between the Japanese and the German naval strategy had several different causes. These in practice applied mainly to the submarine force, but they were also reflected in minimal use by the Japanese of surface raiders and long-range maritime aviation. Japanese naval doctrine was certainly a factor. The leaders of the Imperial Navy concentrated on preparing for a great set-piece battle in the Central Pacific. Submarines were to play an important part in this battle, as scouts and as a force that could wear down the enemy fleet. Commerce raiding – even the Tonnagekrieg – was a secondary task (and a less honourable one), and this value system was true for surface ships as well as for submarines.

In addition, the overall geographical situation was different for the two biggest maritime theatres; the strategic tasks of the German and Japanese navies were not the same. The Allied North Atlantic shipping route was vital to maintaining the population of Britain, one of the three main alliance partners. From 1942 it was important, too, for concentrating armies and air forces for an eventual invasion of the European Continent. Essentially, Germany was attempting to block that route. The German Navy and the Luftwaffe also possessed forward bases in northwestern France and Norway, and from these positions the distance to the Western Approaches of the British Isles was not great.

In contrast, the shipping routes across the Indian Ocean and the Pacific were not critical to the wartime survival of any of the three major Allied states.[23] Australia was exposed, but self-sustaining in terms of food. The transpacific route was important for supporting any offensive against Japan. But from the Japanese point of view such an offensive was best countered not by a campaign of attrition but by the decisive engagement of the battle fleet; this was a critical asset which Nazi Germany did not possess but which the Japanese Empire did.

Unlike the situation in the Atlantic, Allied shipping and ports in the Pacific and the Indian Ocean were well beyond the range of Japanese aviation, and at a very long distance from naval/submarine bases in the home islands, the mandates and even captured territories like Rabaul, Singapore or Penang. Meanwhile the north–south shipping route up the US Pacific coast could not be regarded as crucial to the American economy.[24]

Submarines would be much the most important Japanese anti-shipping weapon, but potentially there were other possibilities. In the Kreuzerkrieg Nazi Germany sent a dozen auxiliary cruisers (raiders) to operate in the distant oceans, but the Japanese made no comparable effort. They did deploy two new 10,000-ton cargo liners, the *Hōkoku Maru* and the *Aikoku Maru*, comprehensively outfitted as raiders. These vessels made two joint sorties into the eastern Pacific in the first month of the war, and sank two American cargo ships. After that they transferred to the Indian Ocean, but there, too, they sank or captured only a handful of ships.[25] The German raiders *Thor* and *Michel*, based in Japan, accounted for more shipping in the Indian Ocean in 1943 than did their counterparts in the Imperial Navy.

The Japanese also made very little use their big conventional warships for oceanic anti-shipping operations – in contrast to the Kriegsmarine (with, most successfully, the *Scharnhorst*, the *Gneisenau* and the *Admiral Hipper* in the Atlantic, the *Admiral Graf Spee* and the *Admiral Scheer* in the global sea lanes). There were no such cruiser raids in the Pacific, and only one brief sweep into the Indian Ocean, late in the war. One of the worst war crimes committed by the Imperial Navy was perpetrated during this operation. Commanded by Admiral Sakonjū Naomasa, the cruisers *Aoba*, *Chikuma* and *Tone* emerged through the Sunda Strait (between Sumatra and Java) in March 1944. The unescorted British MV *Behar*, bound from Melbourne to Bombay, had the misfortune to run into the *Tone* about 1,500 miles southwest of Java. The *Behar* was quickly sunk, but 100 survivors were picked up. Admiral Sakonjū (aboard the *Aoba*) signalled that only a handful of prisoners were to be kept for purposes of intelligence-gathering and the rest were to be 'disposed of'. In the following week the Japanese cruiser squadron returned to Batavia (now Jakarta), where about thirty prisoners were put ashore. On the night the *Tone* left Batavia for Singapore the remaining sixty-nine survivors – forty of them Indians or Goans – were taken up on deck and beheaded.[26] The *Behar* was the last merchant ship to be destroyed by an Axis surface raider – warship or auxiliary – during World War II. As well as being a despicable war crime, the event marked the end of an era in naval operations.

For the Japanese Navy the major anti-shipping weapon available was the submarine, although Japan's undersea fleet was not very large, nor was its construction programme ambitious. Until 1938 the Japanese had to work within a treaty limit of 52,600 tons, and like the Americans they opted for a small number of large 'cruiser' boats. Even in December 1941 the Imperial Navy possessed only sixty-three operational submarines, including forty-eight of the first class (*I*) type and fifteen of the second class (*Ro*) type.[27] Although another twenty-nine boats were under construction in 1941, Table 17.2 shows that the building programme only allowed the Japanese to maintain the submarine fleet at pre-war strength. Additional submarines were delivered in early 1944, but combat losses increased even more.

The Japanese built a variety of submarines before and during the war. Most were large and fast (up to 24 knots), and some were fitted with a hangar and catapult for scouting aircraft (rapidly assembled on the submarine's deck). The little planes proved of slight value as scouts; they are best remembered for setting off some forest fires in the northwestern US in late 1942. Moreover, the size of the 'I-boats' (larger even than the American 'fleet' boats) and long diving time (and noisy machinery) made them vulnerable to attack by enemy aircraft, surface ships and submarines. The Americans from the late 1930s constructed only one type of submarine and in much larger numbers; the Germans also concentrated until 1944 on two basic types.

The Imperial Navy wasted effort on eccentric, single-purpose projects. The two-man 46-ton 'Type A' midget submarine was designed before the war to be transported to the decisive battle in a carrier ship. Armed with two torpedoes, and powered by an electric motor, it was capable of a short burst of high speed. In the end the best-known use of the type was the attempt by six Type A boats to creep into Pearl Harbor on 7 December 1941 (having been piggybacked to Hawaii aboard conventional submarines).[28] Two further co-ordinated attacks were attempted six months later at the end of May 1942, against warships at Diego Suarez (Madagascar) and Sydney (Australia). The second attempt failed to hit the cruiser *Chicago*, but at Diego Suarez the old battleship HMS *Ramillies* was torpedoed and seriously damaged, along with a British tanker. In the desperate months of 1944–45, the Japanese Navy – like the Kriegsmarine – returned to the midget concept to protect their coasts. The *Kōryū* was a 60-ton submarine with two torpedoes and a crew of five. The prototype was complete by January 1945, and some 540 were planned by the autumn of 1945, but none saw service; the *Kairyū* was a smaller two-man boat.

At the other extreme, the Japanese developed a handful of huge submarine cruisers, of which the largest type, the 'I-400' class, was some 400 feet long and displaced 3,530 tons. This project was apparently supported by Admiral Yamamoto, who in early 1942 proposed production of eighteen very large submarines with global range, capable of mounting air attacks on North America, including the US East Coast cities.[29] The first 'boat' was laid down in Kure in January 1943, launched a year later, and commissioned at the very end of 1944. Changing wartime priorities meant that only six vessels were begun. They were each to carry three advanced twin-float strike aircraft, and the first of these planes was produced in the autumn of 1944. Two somewhat smaller 2,620-ton submarines, able to launch two strike aircraft, were completed about the same time. A plan was devised in 1945 for an attack on the Panama Canal, but this was altered to a strike against the American fleet anchorage at Ulithi. The *I-400* put to sea in July with three other large submarines and a total of ten aircraft, but the war ended before they could launch their attack; the *I-400* surrendered at sea to an American destroyer on 22 August, a week after the capitulation.

Somewhat more sensibly, in the autumn of 1943 the Imperial Navy ordered development of a submarine with high submerged speed, like the German Type XXI electro-boat. With large batteries and a streamlined hull, submarines of the 1,070-ton 'ST' class were intended to be capable of a burst of 19 knots under water. In the event the first unit, the *I-201*, was not laid down until March 1944 and was completed only in February 1945. Six more boats were launched, but only two were completed; like the German Type XXI, none saw operational service.

The Japanese organised most of their submarines under the Combined Fleet as the Sixth Fleet; this was formed in November 1940. The C-in-C of the Sixth Fleet – the Japanese equivalent of Karl Dönitz – was Admiral Shimizu Mizumi until March 1942, when he was replaced by Prince Komatsu Teruhisa. The limited number of submarines that were available at the start of the war operated in close co-ordination with the rest of the Combined Fleet. Some twenty-five submarines were concentrated around the Hawaiian Islands in December 1941, to follow up the surprise air strike; in the event they achieved nothing of importance. Another submarine flotilla was deployed to protect the landings in Thailand and northern Indochina; one boat made a sighting report which helped initiate the successful air attack on the *Prince of Wales* and the *Repulse*. Submarines were later committed to the Battle of Midway and to a series of actions in the South Pacific. As mentioned in a previous chapter (p. 234), they had early successes in this primary role, rather more than the Americans, sinking the *Yorktown* at Midway and the *Wasp* in the Solomons. USS *Juneau* was also sunk, and two other cruisers, USS *Chester* and HMAS *Hobart*, were seriously damaged.

After that the achievements of the Sixth Fleet, against both warships and merchant vessels, was much reduced. The over-ambitious expansion of the Japanese 'defensive' perimeter, followed by the loss of the strategic naval initiative at Midway, meant that from late 1942 a number of boats were assigned to the task of ferrying supplies to isolated and embattled island garrisons. The construction programme was altered to incorporate two types of purpose-built transport/supply submarine.[30] Symptomatic of the highly dysfunctional inter-service relations, the Japanese *Army* embarked on its own transport submarine programme in 1943; two dozen small submarines were built, each able to carry 40 tons of cargo.

Admiral Takagi Takeo, a younger and more energetic commander, was appointed in place of Komatsu in June 1943. Although Takagi had served in submarines in the 1920s, his recent service had been with surface ships; he commanded the fleet which won the Battle of the Java Sea in February 1942, and was the senior officer at the Battle of the Coral Sea. As the American counter-offensive in the Central Pacific developed in the autumn of 1943 and 1944 the Japanese submarine fleet was concentrated in a defensive role.[31] These missions were costly because of better American A/S techniques – developed in the Atlantic. They also failed to interfere to any serious extent with the landings in the Gilberts, the Marshalls, the Marianas, the Palau Islands and the Philippines. A submarine did sink the escort carrier *Liscome Bay* in November 1943 off Makin Atoll, but six of the nine boats deployed to the Gilberts were lost. Few resources were available to defend the Marshalls, where Kwajalein Atoll had been the main forward Japanese submarine base.

The first half of 1944 was without doubt the worst period for the Japanese submarine service. The Sixth Fleet flagship, the depot ship *Heian Maru*, was lost during the great American carrier raid on Truk in February 1944, as was the former flagship, the training cruiser *Katori*. In May 1944 an escort group led by the destroyer escort USS *England* rolled up a defensive patrol line of ten submarines east of the Admiralty Islands, sinking five boats. Admiral Takagi unwisely set up his new headquarters on Saipan, expecting the American offensive to develop not there but north of New Guinea. When the Americans unexpectedly came ashore on Saipan itself on 15 June, Takagi and his staff had to flee their headquarters at Garapan town on the west coast, and hide in the hills inland. A submarine sent to rescue them was sunk. Takagi sent out his last radio message on 4 July, and then evidently killed himself. Altogether the Japanese lost thirty-six boats in the first half of 1944. While American submarines sank two fleet carriers in the decisive Battle of the Philippine Sea, their Japanese equivalents failed to damage a single American ship.

The only new submarine weapon put into active service during the closing phase of the war was the *Kaiten*. This was a large *manned* torpedo. Significantly, there was high-level support for this suicide weapon – an analogy with the kamikaze plane. Development of the Kaiten began in February 1944, some months before the naval situation at sea actually became desperate. It was fundamentally an anti-warship weapon rather than a weapon for destroying merchant ships. Nearly 50 feet long, the Kaiten Type 1 was much too large to be fitted in a conventional submarine torpedo tube; it was normally carried on the deck.

The first simultaneous Kaiten attack took place on 20 November 1944: two I-boats carried Kaiten to attack the new American fleet anchorage at Ulithi, and a third attempted to strike against Palau. Four of the five Kaiten launched against Ulithi achieved no result, but the fifth sank USS *Mississinewa*, a 25,000-ton oiler. A second mass attack in January 1945 failed, and smaller attacks were successfully fended off by American A/S forces. The only other Kaiten success was the sinking of the destroyer escort USS *Underhill*; she went down two weeks before the war ended, as she escorted a convoy from Okinawa to the Philippines.

By August 1945 the Japanese submarine force had been reduced to twenty-two operational large and medium boats.[32] Its last action was a conventional one, the sinking of the heavy cruiser *Indianapolis* by the *I-58*, using a spread of six normal torpedoes. The attack took place on the night of 29/30 July 1945, a week before Hiroshima. The cruiser – the flagship of Admiral Spruance for a large part of the war – was steaming west to Leyte in the Philippines, after ferrying atomic bomb components to the Marianas. She was sailing unescorted and not zig-zagging. Two torpedoes hit, and the *Indianapolis* capsized in twelve minutes. Some 300 men went down with the ship. Her non-arrival in Leyte was not noted; over the next three days a further 550 more men perished in the shark-infested waters before a friendly aircraft chanced upon the survivors. It was surely an unnecessary tragedy. But on the other hand it was significant that the *Indianapolis* was the first major American combat ship to be sunk by a Japanese submarine since the escort carrier *Liscome Bay* in November 1943.

CHAPTER 18

THE US NAVY'S DRIVE ACROSS THE CENTRAL PACIFIC

November 1943–June 1944

AIR RAIDS ON RABAUL, 5 AND 11 NOVEMBER 1943

American aircraft carriers carried out two big attacks on the Japanese base at Rabaul on New Britain in early November 1943. With these raids began a new era in the history of the Pacific war. Nearly two years had passed since Pearl Harbor, a year since the turning point at Guadalcanal.

The first attempted American carrier attack on Rabaul, in February 1942, has already been described.[1] The *Lexington* task force had had to abandon its mission, although 'Butch' O'Hare achieved a remarkable air battle success. Since then, reinforced.and defended by powerful Japanese naval, air and land forces, Rabaul had become a strategic point for both sides in the Pacific sea/air war. The port and the airfield complex had occasionally been bombed, from high altitude, by small numbers of AAF heavy bombers flying from eastern New Guinea, but until the autumn of 1943 they were beyond range of effective direct attack.

The Americans now held the initiative. In the background were two major operations planned for November 1943. The first was in the South Pacific, and began at dawn on Monday, 1 November, when a Marine division came ashore on the west coast of Bougainville. This advance was itself a grave threat to Rabaul; American-held airfields on Bougainville, the largest island in the Solomons. would be little more than 200 miles away – a short range for bombers and their escorting fighters.[2] The second November operation was in the Central Pacific and scheduled for the 20th. Even more ambitious than the Bougainville landing, Operation GALVANIC involved the invasion of Tarawa and Makin in the Gilbert Islands. These would be the first major amphibious assaults of the Central Pacific campaign.

Both sides were strengthening their forces. Bill Halsey was Commander, South Pacific Area (COMSOPAC), with his headquarters ashore on Guadalcanal;

he was subordinate to Admiral Nimitz in Hawaii. Under Halsey was a carrier task force he planned to use to neutralise Japanese air bases in the Bougainville area. Task Force 38, built around the *Saratoga* and the new light carrier *Princeton*, was commanded by Admiral Ted Sherman. In late October Nimitz agreed to lend Halsey another group of carriers from the Central Pacific. Admiral Alfred 'Monty' Montgomery's Task Group 50.3 comprised the brand-new carriers *Essex*, *Bunker Hill* and *Independence*; they arrived at Epiritu Santo, south of Guadalcanal, on 5 November.

Admiral Koga Mineichi had taken over as C-in-C of the Combined Fleet after the death of Yamamoto in April 1943. He decided to send reinforcements south from Truk to Rabaul, where Admiral Kusaka Jinichi was now commander of the Southeast Area Fleet and the Eleventh Air Fleet.[3] This measure was triggered by a series of AAF attacks on Rabaul during October and early sightings of US naval movements near Bougainville. On 30 October the carriers *Shōkaku*, *Zuikaku* and *Zuihō* departed from Truk, under orders to fly off most of their air groups to land bases at Rabaul. This mission was given the code name Operation RO.

Meanwhile Kusaka had hastily despatched a battle group from his fleet in Rabaul to attack the American landing force at Bougainville. His hope was to repeat the success of Admiral Mikawa at Savo Island after the Guadalcanal landing. The Battle of Empress Augusta Bay, on the west coast of Bougainville, took place on the night of 1/2 November. The heavy cruisers *Haguro* and *Myōkō*, two light cruisers and six destroyers engaged four new American light cruisers and eight destroyers. The outcome was inconclusive, but the Japanese failed to interfere with the landing and Kusaka's squadron suffered heavier losses than the Americans.[4] Kusaka returned to Rabaul early the following morning, only to be caught up in another big strike by about forty AAF B-25 Mitchell bombers from New Guinea. This produced some dramatic and much-published low-level photographs of the *Haguro* and other vessels under attack. However, the AAF planes caused little damage, and they suffered heavy losses at the hands of the reinforced Rabaul fighter force. The *Haguro* and the *Myōkō*, which had been damaged in the cruiser battle in Empress Augusta Bay, departed for Truk on the 3rd; they played no further part in events.

In response to the American landings on Bougainville and the battle in Empress Augusta Bay, Admiral Koga ordered a large force of powerful surface ships to sail south from Truk. On 3 November, Admiral Kurita Takeo, who had replaced Admiral Kondō as Second Fleet commander in August, set out. Kurita flew his flag in the *Atago*; he was followed by the *Chikuma*, the *Chōkai*, the *Maya*, the *Mogami*, the *Suzuya* and the *Takao* – altogether half the Imperial Navy's surviving heavy cruisers. Also in the battle group were the new light cruiser *Noshiro* and four destroyers.

Radio intercepts, followed by air reconnaissance, had given Admiral Halsey warning of Kurita's movements.[5] He made the daring decision to mount a pre-emptive raid on Rabaul by sending in Sherman's *Saratoga* and *Princeton*. On the morning of Friday, 5 November, the two carriers launched a surprise air attack on Rabaul's Simpson Harbour, with twenty-two SBD Dauntless dive bombers and twenty-three TBF Avenger torpedo planes, covered closely by fifty-two of the new Grumman F6F Hellcat fighters. Kurita's cruiser force had sailed into the harbour only three hours earlier.

Captain Hara Tameichi, commander of a destroyer division, gave an account of the aftermath (he had been able to take his flagship, the *Shigure*, out to sea):

> We returned to harbour around 1000 and I was stunned at what had happened in less than an hour . . . What a disgrace!
>
> Flagship *Atago* was burning, and her sisters *Maya* and *Takao* were damaged. These three heavy cruisers, each packing the firepower of a squadron of destroyers, were disabled in one raid . . . Also damaged were heavy cruisers *Mogami* and *Chikuma*, and light cruisers *Agano* and *Noshiro*, as well as destroyers *Fujinami* and *Amagiri*. I rubbed my eyes and wondered if this could be real.
>
> It was all too real. At Rabaul headquarters the ordinarily mild Kusaka was furious. He bellowed imprecations at everyone.[6]

The attackers did not sink any Japanese ships, but they crippled the *Maya* and damaged three other heavy cruisers. The captain of Kurita's flagship was among those killed. Any thought of using the heavy cruisers against the Bougainville landing had to be abandoned.

A second carrier attack followed six days later, on Thursday (the 11th), mounted from two different directions. Planes from Sherman's Task Force 34, the *Saratoga* and *Princeton*, struck first, followed an hour later by planes from Montgomery's Task Group 50.3, *Essex*, *Bunker Hill* and *Independence*. In addition to Hellcats and Avengers, the second wave included two dozen of the new Curtiss SB2C Helldiver, a big dive bomber making its combat debut. One of the officers on the *Bunker Hill* later described the attack:

> We were 160 miles southeast of Rabaul when we launched, after an all-night, high-speed approach . . . At 0645 an early-bird scout had reported us to [Admiral] Kusaka and the attack by '*Sara*' and *Princeton* had alarmed him further . . . [W]hen at 0830 our planes roared past Cape St George [the southern tip of New Ireland] they collided with 68 'Zekes'. Dodging fighters and flak, the Americans struck through a film of rain at what they could see

in the harbour and channel, *Essex* planes at 0905 followed by those of *Bunker Hill* and *Independence*.[7]

By this time fewer shipping targets remained at Rabaul. Most of Kurita's cruisers had set off north towards Truk, a number of them in a damaged state. But an Avenger succeeded in putting a torpedo into the new light cruiser *Agano*.[8]

This time the Japanese did engage the American carriers. Sherman's task force was protected by storm clouds, but a heavily escorted counter-strike of about forty dive bombers and torpedo planes flew out against Montgomery's task group in the early afternoon of Thursday. The outcome of this air battle was highly significant; the Japanese reached the American task force, but they were unable to break through to the carriers and suffered heavy losses at the hands of the defending American fighters.

The Rabaul events weakened the detached Japanese air groups so badly that their 'mother' carriers could not be deployed against the invasion of the Gilberts (Tarawa) two weeks later. Serious damage had been inflicted on the Combined Fleet's cruiser force. The raids demonstrated the vulnerability of Rabaul as a forward fleet base, and the Japanese Navy had to fall back on Truk, over 950 miles to the north. But the really striking feature of November 1943 was the first deployment, in strength, of a new generation of American ships and combat aircraft. These would dominate the Pacific Ocean for the next two years.

THE US NAVY IN THE PACIFIC

American strategy in the Pacific was now radically changed by growing strength in warships and naval aircraft. The costly actions of 1942, at the Coral Sea, at Midway and in the Solomons, had been fought by the pre-war US Navy. Losses, especially of carriers, had been very high. The *Lexington*, the *Yorktown*, the *Hornet* and the *Wasp* had been sunk. The pre-war 'Yorktown' class *Enterprise* was the most active survivor of the pre-war carrier fleet; the veteran *Saratoga* would have only limited involvement in the main fighting after February 1944.[9] Now new and powerful ships and aircraft were becoming available. The 'Essex' and 'Independence' class were the 'fast carriers' which, more than other weapons, would win the naval war in the Pacific.[10]

The carriers of the 'Essex' (CV-9) class were now by far the most powerful warships in the world. At 27,000 tons, they were half as large again (by displacement) as the 'Yorktown' class. Their typical air group in 1944 was forty-two fighters, thirty-six dive bombers and twenty torpedo planes.

They were built in very large numbers for ships of their size. The first three (CV-9, 10 and 11) were ordered just after the shock of the French defeat in June

Table 18.1. Aircraft Carriers Operating in Pacific and Indian Oceans, 1943–45

	US			Japan			Britain		
	CV	CVL	CVE	CV	CVL	CVE	CV	CVL	CVE
Jan 1943	2	0	3	4	2	3	1	0	0
Nov 1943	6	5	8	4	2	4	0	0	1
Jun 1944	7	8	6	5	4	4	1	0	2
Oct 1944	9	8	18	2	3	2	3	0	5
Apr 1945	12	8	18	0	0	1	5	0	7

Notes: CV = fleet carrier, CVL = light carrier, CVE = escort carrier. Only vessels actually engaged in operations in the Pacific and Indian oceans are included, not training ships and aircraft transports. British vessels were mostly deployed in the Indian Ocean.

1940.[11] After a slow start production was greatly accelerated; the *Essex* herself was originally scheduled for commissioning in March 1944, but entered service fifteen months earlier (and arrived at Pearl Harbor, after working up, in early June 1943). Supported by Carl Vinson, Chairman of the House Naval Affairs Committee, ten more of the class were programmed within the Two Ocean Navy Act of July 1940. Of these ten, eight were actually ordered in September 1940, and four of these (CV-16, 17, 18 and 19) had joined the fleet by the time of the Battle of the Philippine Sea in June 1944, bringing the operational total to seven.[12] The final two vessels of the Two Ocean programme (CV-20 and 21) were ordered in December 1941, and one (the *Bennington*, CV-20) was ready before the end of the war. Ten more 'Essex' class carriers were ordered in August 1942, but only the *Bon Homme Richard* (CV-31) and the *Shangri-La* (CV-38) actually saw combat, in the summer of 1945.[13]

None of the 'Essex' class were lost in combat, although the *Bunker Hill* and the *Franklin* were very badly damaged by air attack in 1945 and were never operational carriers after the war. Others contributed to the active strength of the US Navy in the Cold War, fitted with angled decks and steam catapults, and carrying jets. Some of them operated off Vietnam against another Asian enemy, twenty-five years after the Japanese defeat.[14]

To supplement as quickly as possible its fast carrier force, the US Navy also embarked on a programme to commission the light carriers (CVLs) of the 'Independence' class. The programme had first been considered in the autumn of 1941, but was pushed forward after Pearl Harbor. These vessels were built using the hulls and machinery – already under construction – of 'Cleveland' class light cruisers; these cruisers were large vessels of 12,000 tons and 600 feet in length. The *Independence* (CVL-22) was originally laid down in May 1941 as the cruiser *Amsterdam* (CL-59). All nine CVLs were built at Camden, NJ, and all were commissioned in 1943. Although their displacement was less than half that of the 'Essex' class, and with a narrow flight deck some 200 feet shorter, they could steam at nearly 32 knots, operate with the big fleet carriers, and carry an air group of thirty-five planes of the latest type.[15]

A large number of escort carriers (CVEs) were now joining the Pacific Fleet. In addition to eleven 'Bogue' class CVEs commissioned in 1942 and early 1943, there were four of the larger and faster 'Sangamon' class. Meanwhile in June 1942 the American industrialist Henry Kaiser, who had built several new shipyards for Liberty cargo ships, offered to mass-produce very quickly fifty escort carriers to a new design. Kaiser won support from President Roosevelt himself, overcoming the initial opposition of the Navy. Some nineteen Kaiser-built 'Casablanca' class (7,800-ton) escort carriers were commissioned in the second half of 1943, and twenty-nine more in the first half of 1944.[16] Although all these 'jeep carrier' types were too slow and too poorly protected to operate together with the main fleet, they could play a direct air-support role in the island invasions, freeing the 'fast' fleet carriers and light carriers for high-speed action against the Japanese fleet. The huge fleet that invaded Saipan in June 1944 included seven fleet carriers and eight light carriers, and also seven 'Casablanca' class carriers in two 'carrier support units' and four more CVEs in the 'fuelling group' (operating as aircraft ferries).

The number of combat aircraft in the US Navy increased very rapidly, from 3,191 in the middle of 1942, to 8,696 in 1943, and 22,116 in 1944.[17] The Rabaul raids were, as mentioned, the first major combat operations of two new aircraft types, the Grumman F6F Hellcat and Curtiss SB2C Helldiver. The Hellcat was certainly the most important naval fighter plane of World War II and a central element in the American Pacific victory. The big fighter was not as manoeuvrable as the 1943 version of the Zero (the A6M5), but it flew about 30 knots faster, could out-dive it, and was more strongly constructed. The F6F was not, as is sometimes claimed, designed in response to the Zero; the specifications were worked out before the US Navy had much experience with the Japanese fighter.[18] But Grumman achieved the remarkable feat of progressing from the Hellcat's first flight test in June 1942, to delivery to naval fighter squadrons six months later, and to combat action at Marcus Island eight months after that. The Hellcat was the only operational American fighter plane of the war (AAF or Navy) which had not been test-flown before Pearl Harbor. Grumman, based on its earlier experience building naval aircraft, and with rapidly enlarged plants on Long Island, was able to produce as many as 600 Hellcats a month.

The other new American aircraft in the Rabaul raid, flying from the *Bunker Hill*, was the SB2C Helldiver. This new Curtiss dive bomber was a replacement for the Douglas SBD Dauntless, which had been so important at Midway. The Helldiver was a much larger aircraft, with nearly twice the weight and twice the engine power. Nearly 7,000 SB2Cs were eventually built. They complemented 9,800 Grumman TBF torpedo bombers, which had first been used at Midway.

The shipbuilding programme also meant that the US Navy stayed well ahead of the Japanese in big-gun ships. Six new fast battleships had been deployed to the Pacific by the end of 1943. Two even bigger post-treaty 'Iowa' class ships – the *Iowa* and the *New Jersey* – were commissioned in the spring and summer of 1943 and arrived in the Pacific in January 1944. Displacing 45,000 tons and nearly 900 feet long, they were capable of 33 knots. Two more of this class would arrive a year later. Smaller surface combat ships – cruisers and destroyers – also became available in very large quantities.

Meanwhile, strategic choices needed to be made. At the highest level there was an uneasy compromise in early 1943 between the American Pacific build-up and the 'Germany First' grand strategy which had been agreed earlier by the Allies. In January 1943 the Casablanca/SYMBOL Conference between the war leaders of Britain and the US formally gave priority to operations in Europe and North Africa. But, although many details were left unclear, a further advance of the American forces in the Pacific was also accepted.

The long-term – and inevitably inflexible – construction programme of major warships was an essential element explaining the strong interest of the US Navy in the Pacific. This is a factor which was, and is, often ignored by critics of American strategy. The shipyards had for many months been building a very large ocean-going battle fleet that could not effectively be used in European waters, especially after the beginning of 1943, when the German and Italian surface fleets had ceased to be significant opponents.

Another strategic debate, *within* the Pacific theatre, was also influenced by the imminent naval build-up. This was about whether the advance against Japan should be concentrated in the South Pacific or in the Central Pacific. Looking ahead to operations in 1943, General MacArthur urged an advance to Luzon in the Philippines from the South Pacific, moving through New Guinea and then north to Mindanao. Priority would be given to his South West Pacific Area (SWPA). In contrast, the US Navy, and especially Admiral King in Washington, wanted a direct advance across the Central Pacific.

There had been some logic behind the establishment of two top-level headquarters in the Pacific in the spring of 1942. Pearl Harbor and Brisbane were 4,700 miles apart. In addition – with the highly significant exceptions of the Pearl Harbor raid and the Battle of Midway – the Pacific fighting had begun in 1942 south of the equator, and an American central thrust would not be possible (even after Midway) until the fleet had been built up, presumably in 1943 and 1944.[19]

Complex technical issues were involved in these planning discussions, as well as inter-service, political and personal ones. The southern variant involved moving through and beyond Rabaul and the Bismarck Archipelago (New

Britain and New Ireland, the so-called Bismarcks Barrier) and driving west along the coast of New Guinea, with the basic support provided by land-based (US Army) air power. Any US Navy carriers that *were* committed to such a campaign would have to operate close to enemy air bases and as a result would face considerable risk. In favour of the South Pacific was the fact that most of the fighting in 1942 and early 1943 had taken place there; a complex of bases had already been set up south of the equator.

The Central Pacific route, in contrast, involved numerous small islands and much longer distances. Each 'island-hop' would be beyond the range of land-based air support – or in some cases even beyond the range of air reconnaissance. But the central route also allowed greater flexibility. It was the direction with which the senior leaders of the US Navy had become intimately familiar from the inter-war ORANGE plans (and war games) for a conflict with Japan. And, above all, it was the theatre that would make best use of the new battle fleet that was rapidly nearing completion in American shipyards.

There also was a political issue about the importance of the 'liberation' of the Philippines from enemy occupation, and the extent to which this conflicted with a more direct means of forcing a Japanese surrender.[20] In addition, inter-service rivalry also played no small part, the issue being essentially whether the US Army or the US Navy would run the war against Japan, with the Supreme Commander being either a general or an admiral. Very strong personalities were involved, notably Ernest King versus Douglas MacArthur.[21] The unwillingness of the President to force the issue meant acceptance of a compromise.

A Pacific strategy planning conference for US forces, held in Washington in March 1943, accepted a compromise strategy, dispersing the effort across the great ocean. It approved the continuation of MacArthur's advance in New Guinea and Admiral Halsey's operations up the western Solomons. But it also opened new fronts, approving operations in the North Pacific to re-capture Attu and Kiska in the Aleutians (which were US territory) and in the Central Pacific against the Gilbert Islands and the Marshall Islands. The top-level TRIDENT Conference, held in Washington two months later, in May 1943, approved an advance even further west across the Central Pacific, against both the Marshalls and the eastern Caroline Islands. The Carolines lay 1,000 miles west of the Marshalls and were the location of Truk (now Chuuk), the main Japanese naval base in the Central Pacific.

In June 1943 the American Joint Chiefs of Staff (JCS) in Washington developed further the compromise two-pronged advance. General MacArthur's forces in the SWPA would now bypass Rabaul and advance along the north coast of New Guinea. The Central Pacific advance would begin about 15 November 1943.[22] At the top-level first Quebec Conference (code-named QUADRANT) in

August 1943 – still three months before the beginning of the first actual Central Pacific invasion (at Tarawa in the Gilberts) – the decision to circumvent Rabaul was confirmed, with MacArthur's forces ordered to proceed across the Bismarck Sea, west of New Britain and New Ireland and seize the strategic Admiralty Islands (about 375 miles WNW of Rabaul). Most significantly it was decided at QUADRANT that in the Central Pacific the Mariana Islands (Guam, Saipan and Tinian) would be the next objective, after the planned capture of the Gilberts, the Marshalls and the eastern Carolines (including Truk).

The Central Pacific offensive did indeed begin in the Gilberts in November 1943, with the assault on Tarawa. Although this landing was unexpectedly costly in terms of Marine casualties, the campaign continued. At the SEXTANT Conference in Cairo in late November and December 1943 the supreme military planners urged a flexible strategic approach but still envisaged the seizure of Truk in July 1944, followed by the Marianas in October.

Relatively few American casualties were suffered in January 1944 during the capture of the Marshalls (notably Kwajalein Atoll), and the following month elements of the carrier fleet mounted highly successful raids against the Truk naval base and even against Japanese airfields in the Marianas. Meanwhile, even though MacArthur was not given all the resources he had demanded for the SWPA, his forces were able to make a more rapid advance than had been expected along the north coast of New Guinea.[23] A final compromise was worked out by the JCS in March 1944, which allowed both the southern and central advances to continue. Most remarkably, Truk would now be bypassed. The Philippines were kept as a medium-term objective, but in the short term priority was given to an attack on the Marianas, moved forward to June. Admiral King had become increasingly interested in the Marianas, which would block the main north–south route from Japan to Truk and Rabaul. He now had the support in the JCS of General 'Hap' Arnold, head of the US Army Air Force. Arnold wanted the Marianas as a second base (after western China) from which to mount air attacks on Japan, using the new AAF strategic bomber, the Boeing B-29 Superfortress.[24] The revised schedule for later operations set the invasion of the Palaus (western Carolines) for mid-September 1944, that of Mindanao (in the southern Philippines) would follow in mid-November, and then either Luzon or Formosa in mid-February 1945.

Classic military theory stresses a concentration of effort, and this was certainly the accepted view of the American armed services. In Europe General Marshall and the US Army planners based their strategic arguments on this principle, with their single-minded emphasis on a cross-Channel landing. They criticised Churchill and the British for dispersing the Allied effort into the Mediterranean. In contrast, in the Pacific, which was in most respects an all-

American theatre, the leaders of the US military establishment themselves failed to concentrate their advance. Division of effort greatly increased shipping requirements. On the other hand, the twin-track approach did have significant advantages. It kept the Japanese off balance and compelled them to spread their thinner resources along a very long strategic perimeter. This would prove to be of great value when the climax of the Pacific war came in May and June 1944.

The command structure in the Pacific had been laid out in 1942. Admiral Nimitz – CINCPAC – remained ashore at his headquarters in Oahu's Makalapa Crater. His Pacific Ocean Area command was divided into three zonal commands – North Pacific, Central Pacific and South Pacific. It was the Central Pacific that became the most important sector for Nimitz at the end of 1943 and into 1944. The South Pacific, latterly under Bill Halsey, had been the most active command after the invasion of Guadalcanal in August 1942. By the end of 1943, however, fighting south of the equator was mainly in the New Guinea area and came under General MacArthur's SWPA. The North Pacific, meanwhile, was only briefly important in the first half of 1943, during operations to re-capture the Aleutians.

On 5 August 1943 Admiral Raymond Spruance was given the most important sea-going post, under Nimitz, as commander of the Central Pacific Force; in April 1944 this would become the Fifth Fleet. Spruance had risen rapidly to senior command, making his name during the victory at Midway. He had replaced Admiral Halsey when the latter fell ill shortly before the June 1942 battle, and he then assumed tactical command of the whole American fleet at Midway after Admiral Fletcher's flagship was damaged. Spruance was not an 'aviator'; he had been CO of the battleship *Mississippi* in the late 1930s, and when the war in the Pacific broke out he was commander of a division of four heavy cruisers. He had taught at the Naval War College and probably possessed the broadest intellectual vision of any of the US Navy operational commanders. His strengths included methodical planning and sound judgement, which he had demonstrated as chief of staff to Admiral Nimitz from June 1942 to August 1943. Two important sub-commands were set up under Spruance that August. The first was the Fast Carrier Force under Admiral Charles 'Baldy' Pownall, and the second was V Amphibious Force ('V 'Phib') under Admiral Kelly Turner; V 'Phib provided amphibious 'lift' and a corps of Marines for the first operations in the Central Pacific.[25]

THE JAPANESE COMBINED FLEET

For the Imperial Navy the situation at the end of 1943 was far less favourable than that of its American counterpart. The Japanese naval armament programme, apparently so impressive pre-war, had little depth. Four fleet carriers – the *Shōkaku* and the *Zuikaku*, and the converted liners *Hiyō* and *Junyō* – had survived the 1942 fighting; this was more than had been the case for the American Pacific Fleet.[26] But only one new fleet carrier, the *Taihō* (laid down in July 1941), was scheduled for completion before the middle of 1944. Two light carriers had survived 1942, and at the start of 1943 work began at Yokosuka to convert two fast seaplane tenders, the *Chiyoda* and the *Chitose*, into light carriers; these were rushed into service by the end of 1943.[27] So worried were the Japanese after Midway, especially about air reconnaissance, that they converted two old battleships, the *Ise* and *Hyūga*, into hybrid or 'hermaphrodite' carriers, replacing the two rear turrets with seaplane catapults; a similar conversion was applied to the cruiser *Mogami*. The hull and machinery of the *Shinano*, the third 'Yamato' class super-battleship (laid down at Yokosuka in May 1940), was taken in hand for conversion to a giant 62,000-ton carrier, but her planned completion date was 1945. The Japanese did begin in the second half of 1942 an ambitious programme of medium-sized 'Katsuragi' class carriers, a simplified version of the *Hiryū* and *Sōryū*, which had fought at Midway. Only three would be completed in the last months of 1944; in the end none would be used operationally, and one was sunk by a submarine.

A more positive aspect for the sea/air war was the production of aircraft, where output was more flexible than for shipbuilding. Japan also had the advantage that unlike Germany – its aircraft plants did not come under bombing attack until the last months of the war. Production of Japanese naval aircraft went from 4,454 in 1942 to 9,965 in 1943, and would rise to 14,178 in 1944 – although this was considerably below the targets set.[28] This was matched by expanded and shortened aircrew training schemes.

The Japanese industry had some successes (more so than the British) at producing a new generation of naval aircraft in 1943–44. The Aichi D3A/VAL dive bomber was superseded by the Yokosuka D4Y Suisei ('Comet'), and Nakajima replaced their B5N/KATE torpedo bomber with the B6N Tenzan ('Heavenly Mountain'). Both the D4Y and the B6N (known to the Allies more prosaically by the code names JUDY and JILL) were considerably faster than the types they replaced. They had longer range than their American equivalents, which potentially gave them a considerable tactical advantage.

Less successful, however, was the development of fighter aircraft and twin-engined bombers. Fighters were critical for keeping air superiority over fleets and islands, and escorting formations of attack planes and bombers; the long-range Mitsubishi A6M2 or 'Zero' (Reisen) had given the Japanese a critical advantage in 1941–42. The Zero fighter, designed by Horikoshi Jirō, had shown itself superior to all Allied fighters in the Pacific, but success bred over-confidence. The Zero accounted for the largest part of Japanese naval combat aircraft production during the war; some 1,700 were built by Mitsubishi and Nakajima in 1942, 3,400 in 1943, and 3,500 in 1944. Very large numbers of A6Ms served on carriers and in land-based naval air groups in 1944. The design of the A6M was truly remarkable, but it was a light-weight fighter, with only a 1,000hp, 28-litre engine. The A6M5, the version rushed into service in large numbers in the autumn of 1943, was only slightly faster than its predecessors. All variants were now inferior to the US Navy Hellcats and Corsairs, as well as to the US Army Lockheed P-38 Lightnings and Republic P-47 Thunderbolts. For the last two years of the war the Japanese Navy would fight its crucial air battles with a qualitative and quantitative disadvantage in terms of equipment. At Mitsubishi, Horikoshi was undertaking leisurely development of a carrier-fighter replacement for the A6M Zero, the A7M Reppu ('Hurricane'). This was test flown only in May 1944 and never entered service.

The situation with respect to land-based twin-engined bombers was, if anything, worse. The long-range but vulnerable Mitsubishi G4M/BETTY remained the main land-based attack plane and was kept in production at two Mitsubishi plants until the end of the war, with 2,400 built in 1941–45.[29] Despite its spectacular success against the *Prince of Wales* and the *Repulse* in December 1941, the G4M had proved to be extremely vulnerable to fighters and anti-aircraft guns even in 1942. Its replacement, the Yokosuka P1Y Ginga ('Milky Way'), code-named FRANCES, was delayed by technical problems and entered service only in late 1944.

As important as the declining relative quality of aircraft were the inadequate training and experience of replacement Japanese aircrew. The relatively small cohort of pre-war pilots had been well trained, and in December 1941 had the significant advantage of operational flying experience in China. The naval pilot training scheme was accelerated in early 1943, and the period of training was reduced from ten months to six. Unlike in American procedure, veteran pilots were not posted home to give the flying schools the benefit of their knowledge about wartime conditions. Piloting any high-performance aircraft was a challenge, but carrier landing and over-sea navigation required special skill and training time. There were also a number of occasions in which skilled carrier aircrew were lost after emergency posting to shore bases; examples were Yamamoto's April 1943 I-GŌ operations in the South Pacific (see above, p. 242) and Koga's October 1943 RO operation to reinforce Rabaul (pp. 245, 371).

As for surface warships, there were no battleships nearing completion after the giant *Musashi* (the sister ship of the *Yamato*) was completed in August 1942. No new heavy cruisers were under construction in the shipyards, and only five lightly armed light cruisers, and of these one would not be completed until November 1944. Two fast battleships and four heavy cruisers had been lost in combat in 1942. The *Mutsu* (armed with 16-inch guns and, with the *Nagato*, the largest of the ten pre-war battleships) was sunk in a non-combat magazine explosion at Hashirajima in June 1943, with the loss of 1,100 men. The surface fleet had lost many smaller units in the Solomons, including the destroyers required to escort the heavy ships. This had serious implications, as the American submarine threat was growing due to codebreaking successes and technical improvements in torpedoes.

In Tokyo, Admiral Nagano Osami remained as Chief of the Naval General Staff. In the Combined Fleet, Admiral Koga Mineichi was appointed as the new C-in-C, after the April 1943 air ambush over Bougainville in which Admiral Yamamoto was killed and his chief of staff, Admiral Ugaki Matome, wounded. Koga took Yamamoto's place aboard the Combined Fleet flagship *Musashi* at Truk, although the change was not made public for six weeks. Koga was fifty-seven years old, a year younger than his predecessor. He had held senior commands in the Imperial Navy, as Vice Chief of the Naval General Staff in 1936 and commander of the main heavy cruiser force (the Second Fleet) in 1939. In September 1941 he became C-in-C of the China Area Fleet (where he led the naval side of the capture of Hong Kong), and from November 1942 he was commander of the important Yokosuka Naval District. Koga was evidently an able and energetic officer, and had been close to Yamamoto and Ugaki, but he had limited operational experience with carrier aviation.[30] His chief of staff was Fukudome Shigeru, an effective planner who had worked with Yamamoto, but he was also not an aviator.

As a consequence of the events of 1942, the Combined Fleet had been reorganised. Under Yamamoto the surviving aircraft carriers had, after Midway, been concentrated in a new Third Fleet, commanded initially by Admiral Nagumo and from November 1942 by Ozawa Jisaburō. Admiral Ozawa was a capable officer and had led his forces successfully in the battles for the Netherlands Indies. He had not been involved in the battles at Midway and in the Solomons; as result he bore no responsibility for the setbacks there. The removal in August 1943 of the more senior Admiral Kondō Nobutake as commander of the Second Fleet (the fast battleships and heavy cruisers) resolved an anomaly of rank and increased Ozawa's authority; he was well senior to Kondō's successor, Admiral Kurita Takeo.

Koga's appointment was soon followed – on 1 June 1943 – by radical plans to develop the Imperial Navy's land-based aviation. A new naval command, the First Air Fleet (*First Kōkū Kantai*), was created;[31] Admiral Kakuta Kakuji was put in charge at a special ceremony involving the Emperor himself. Kakuta had taken part in early carrier operations in the Philippines, the Bay of Bengal and the Aleutians. He then commanded a carrier force in the October 1942 Battle of Santa Cruz, and his planes operated from land bases in the Solomons in 1943.

The First Air Fleet was – in theory – the embodiment of sea/air warfare. The Imperial Navy was rebuilding a powerful force of land-based aircraft. It was intended to defend the perimeter of Japan's conquests, through a specially constructed network of island air bases. Originally the force consisted of only one air flotilla but the plan, based on the growing output of the aircraft industry, was to have a future strength of as many as 1,600 planes.

As with the Allies, Japanese strategy in 1943–44 worked at several levels. The Imperial Army did not play a major part in the Pacific in 1942, although it did despatch a small number of ground troops to the Solomons and New Guinea. The considerable air strength of the Japanese Army was not committed to the Central Pacific until after the fall of the Marianas in June 1944 (and even then only in small numbers). The generals were still focused on the fighting taking place on Asian mainland (and the continuing confrontation with the USSR). For them, the main effort in 1944 would be committed to ground offensives in China and against Northeast India (from Burma).

Nevertheless, in the autumn of 1943 the leaders of the Japanese Army and Navy came together, effectively for the first time since 1942, to consider the state of the war effort and the measures which needed to be taken. In the global conflict one of the country's Axis partners – Italy – had just been knocked out of the war. This development opened the Mediterranean–Suez Canal–Indian Ocean shipping route, and would also free up Allied warships, planes and army formations for the war with Japan. Meanwhile the prospect of an outright German victory in Europe now seemed remote. In the Asia-Pacific war the Allies were making progress in New Guinea and the Solomons and were likely to launch offensives elsewhere on the Japanese perimeter. As result of the staff discussions in Tokyo an 'absolute national defence zone' was laid out, in late September, running from Burma to the Kurile Islands. In the South and Central Pacific this zone was bounded by Timor and the Banda Sea (northwest of Australia), western New Guinea, the Carolines (with the Palau group and Truk), the Marianas and the Bonins. Territory beyond the zone – the Marshalls, the Gilberts, the western Solomons and eastern New Guinea and New Britain (including Rabaul) – was to be contested only to slow the pace of the American counter-attack and to inflict losses. (This strategic re-think, it should be noted, came *before* the American landings in Bougainville, Tarawa and Kwajalein.)

However, for five months the delineation of the main line of defence was not followed by significant concrete 'joint' inter-service action. It was only when an unexpected and hugely successful US carrier raid on the Truk naval base in February 1944 revealed the weakness of the Combined Fleet that the Japanese Army decided to send troops from the Asian continent to defend the threatened islands of the Central Pacific.

As for Admiral Koga, he had set out his position in an order issued on 23 May 1943, when he took command of the Combined Fleet: 'We defend what is ours and the task of meeting and striking the enemy must be the prerogative of the Imperial Navy. We shall defend ourselves to the last breath and shall totally destroy the enemy.'[32] In August and September 1943 the admiral had already had his staff prepare a series of operations for dealing with individual approaches to Japanese-held territories, across both the Pacific and the Indian Ocean. For the Pacific, nine so-called 'Z' operations were established, with forward bases and deployment positions. These involved the engagement of the enemy fleet by carrier task forces, land-based naval aircraft and submarines, participation in decisive battles and pursuit of defeated remnants.[33] The Combined Fleet would operate from its main base at Truk in the Carolines, as it had in the Solomons in 1942.

AMPHIBIOUS ADVANCE: THE ALEUTIANS, GILBERTS, MARSHALLS, MARIANAS AND PALAUS

There were two distinct elements involved in the war-winning military campaign that the United States fought in the Pacific in 1943–44. One, better known, was a series of sea/air battles between large fleets. The other, made possible by command of the seas and to some extent overshadowed, was the development of American amphibious warfare; Table 18.2 gives an overview of this.

The first major Allied landings outside the South Pacific were at Attu and Kiska in the Aleutians. These islands had been seized and garrisoned by the Japanese Army in June 1942, at the time of the Battle of Midway, as a northern anchor of their defensive perimeter. With an objective some 2,500 miles NNW of Hawaii, the Allied Aleutian counter-attack was literally a sideshow. The Aleutians lay at latitude 53°N, and they were very different from the tropical islands of the main Pacific campaigns. Their occupation would have made sense to the Japanese only if the Battle of Midway had been a victory. It was not possible to fortify them, and hard to supply them; after nine months there was still no local airstrip.

Attu was invaded on 11 May 1943; the terrain was a mountainous, treeless tundra measuring 35 miles from east to west and 20 miles from north to south. In overall command was Admiral Thomas Kinkaid. The 7th Division of the US Army had embarked at San Francisco, and the invasion force was carried by four attack transports This was not an assault landing; the first wave came ashore unopposed, in thick fog. For the first time, battleship gunnery support for the troops ashore was available. The *Idaho* and two Pearl Harbor survivors, the *Pennsylvania* and the *Nevada*, stood by, along with seven cruisers; they were not required. Only about 2,500 Japanese were on the island, including less than two battalions of infantry. However, the terrain was rugged and the raw

Table 18.2. Major US Amphibious Operations in the Pacific, 1942–45

Date	Initial objective	Operation code name	US formations
Aug 1942	Solomons/Guadalcanal	WATCHTOWER	1 MD (+Am, 25 ID, 2 MD)
May 1943	Aleutians/Attu	LANDCRAB	7 ID
Jun 1943	Solomons/New Georgia	TOENAILS	43 ID (+25, 37 ID)
Nov 1943	Solomons/Bougainville	CHERRYBLOSSOM	3 MD, 37 ID (+Am ID)
Nov 1943	Gilberts/Tarawa	GALVANIC	2 MD
Nov 1943	Gilberts/Makin	GALVANIC	27 ID
Jan 1944	Marshalls/Kwajalein	FLINTLOCK	4 MD, 7 ID
Feb 1944	Marshalls/Eniwetok	CATCHPOLE	106 IR, 22 MR
Feb 1944	Admiralties/Los Negros	BREWER	1 CD
Apr 1944	New Guinea/Hollandia	RECKLESS	24, 41 ID
Jun 1944	Marianas/Saipan	FORAGER	2, 4 MD, 27 ID
Jul 1944	Marianas/Guam	FORAGER	3 MD, 77 ID
Jul 1944	Marianas/Tinian	FORAGER	2, 4 MD
Sept 1944	NI/Morotai	TRADEWIND	31 ID
Sept 1944	Palau/Peliliu	STALEMATE I	1 MD (+81 ID)
Oct 1944	Philippines/Leyte	KING II	7, 24, 37, 40, 43 ID, 1 CD (+32, 77 ID, 11 AD)
Jan 1945	Philippines/Luzon	MIKE	6, 25, 37, 40, 43 ID (+24, 32, 33, 38 ID, 1 CD, 11 AD)
Feb 1945	Bonins/Iwo Jima	DETACHMENT	3, 4, 5 MD
Apr 1945	Ryūkyūs/Okinawa	ICEBERG	7, 96 ID, 1, 6 MD (+27, 77, 81 ID)

Notes: Only major formations are itemised. 'Follow-on' forces, after initial assault, in brackets.
MD = USMC div., ID = USA inf. div. (Am ID is Americal), AD = USA airborne div., CD = USA cav. div.

American troops inexperienced; it took nearly three weeks to gain control of the island, and American losses were relatively high.

At this stage of the war the Japanese high command were still prepared to cut their losses. Kiska – 200 miles *east* of Attu – had an Imperial Army garrison of over 5,000 men, but it had now been outflanked. This island was now secretly evacuated. In late July 1943 a force of warships crept in under cover of dense fog and took off every last soldier. Two weeks later a large American and Canadian force – 35,000 troops and nearly a hundred ships – arrived to invade Kiska and found the place deserted.

With hindsight the most significant aspect of these events would be the conduct of the Japanese Army garrison on Attu. Air-dropped leaflets calling on them to surrender were ignored. Eighteen days after the initial landing the commander, Colonel Yamasaki Yasuyo, led a suicidal mass bayonet attack – what the Americans called a 'banzai charge'. Of the whole garrison, only twenty-nine Japanese would be taken prisoner. The Tokyo government's propaganda began to speak of the defenders of Attu as *gyokusai* ('a shattered jewel'); they died rather than suffer dishonour. This anticipated the way the next stage of the 'island war' would be conducted, and indeed the wholesale suicide tactics of the last ten months of the conflict.

The Central Pacific campaign began with Tarawa Atoll, which lay 3,500 miles to the south of Attu, in the Gilbert Islands (now Kiribati). The Gilberts, part of a British colony, had been occupied by Japan in December 1941. The American force was under the overall command of Admiral Kelly Turner. The invasion, which began on 20 November 1943 – two weeks after the air attacks on Rabaul – was code-named Operation GALVANIC. The Southern Attack Force, carrying the larger Marine force for Tarawa Atoll, embarked in New Zealand and the New Hebrides (Vanuatu) in sixteen transports. The Northern Attack Force, carrying part of the US Army's 27th Division and intended for the much less heavily defended Makin Atoll, sailed from Hawaii in six transports.

The invasion of Tarawa was also the first American amphibious 'assault'. In contrast to Guadalcanal, Attu or Bougainville, it was a landing from the sea directly against a heavily defended enemy position.[34] The tiny objective of Betio island was the site of the only operational airfield on the Tarawa Atoll (and in the Gilberts as a whole). Measuring less than 300 acres, the island was packed with 2,600 Japanese naval infantry and 1,700 Japanese construction troops (plus about 500 Korean labourers) protected by log and concrete bunkers. The attacking American troops were more experienced and better trained than those on Attu; the 2nd Marine Division had fought on Guadalcanal. The Japanese had built most of their defences on the seaward (southern) side of Betio, not realising that the enemy would be able to mount an attack from the shallow lagoon (northern) side, using their new amphibious tractors ('amtracs' or LVTs).[35]

The American naval bombardment on the morning of the invasion was delivered by the battleships *Colorado*, *Maryland* and *Tennessee*, four cruiser and a number of destroyers. The shelling was intense but lasted only two and a half hours; the length of the air bombardment from supporting carriers was even shorter. Many more of the defenders survived than had been expected. Intelligence also misjudged the tidal conditions, and the 'reef', a coral apron stretching 750 yards offshore, was too shallow to allow passage of conventional landing craft. In the landing, carried out in the early morning, the amtracs were able to get ashore, but they suffered heavy losses and mechanical breakdowns as they travelled back and forth from the beaches. Conventional landing craft carrying reinforcements and supplies could not get beyond the edge of the reef, and the Marines had to wade ashore or shelter behind a pier jutting out into the lagoon. The senior commanders offshore and the gun-aimers on support ships had poor communications with the units fighting for the beachhead. The total US deaths in three days of the assault at Tarawa, mostly on Betio, were 1,009 men. This was a figure comparable to half the Marine and US Army losses on Guadalcanal over a *six-month* period from August 1942 to February 1943. Nevertheless, the Japanese garrison was destroyed almost to a man; of over 3,600 combatants, only seventeen were taken prisoner.[36]

US Army troops – rather than Marines – carried out the other landing on the Gilberts, at Makin Atoll, 125 miles to the north of Tarawa. The 27th Infantry Division made slow progress against a very small 300-man garrison; three days were needed to secure the main island, Butaritari. But the GIs suffered only sixty-four men killed.

Two months later, on 31 January 1944, Admiral Turner mounted his next attack, on the Marshall Islands (Operation FLINTLOCK). The Marshalls are the most extensive island group in Micronesia. The distance from Eniwetok Atoll at the northwestern corner of the Marshalls to Mili Atoll in the southeast is some 750 miles. Admiral Nimitz overrode the strong reservations of both admirals Spruance and Turner, and ordered a concentration of force against the centrally located Kwajalein Atoll. This meant bypassing the Japanese-occupied atolls – and bomber airfields – of Wotje and Maloelap to the east, and Jaluit to the south.

The main objective on Kwajalein Atoll was the airfields, built on two tiny islets – not unlike Betio on Tarawa. One – from which US-held Wake Atoll had been attacked in December 1941 – was in the north on Roi (adjacent to the garrison island of Namur). The other was on Kwajalein Island, 45 miles away across the lagoon, in the southern arc of Kwajalein Atoll. The Northern Attack Force struck Roi–Namur, under the command of Admiral Richard Conolly, who had distinguished himself in the invasion of Sicily and at Salerno. The main landing force left San Diego eighteen days before the invasion and sailed west across the Pacific via the Hawaiian Islands. Eight attack transports carried the new 4th Marine Division. The Southern Attack Force sailed from Pearl Harbor on 22 January, with Kwajalein Island as its objective. Twelve attack transports carried the US Army's 7th Division; elements of the division had stumbled through the Attu battle, but the troops had gained experience in the Aleutians and then undertook extensive training on Oahu. The attached Fire-Support Group comprised four battleships, three heavy cruisers and destroyers.

The Americans demonstrated an impressive ability to learn from the mistakes of Tarawa. Intelligence about the target and enemy tactics was now better, the communications system more extensive (with well-equipped command ships and robust portable radios ashore), and the troops were better trained. As at Tarawa, the invading troops transferred from their attack transports to amtracs (LVTs) which had been brought up by LSTs, but the amphibious tractors were used much more effectively than at Tarawa and they were supported by a tank version, the LVT(A). Rapid re-supply of the beachhead was implemented. Air support was better than at Tarawa, with three escort carriers for each landing.

Most important was artillery; the landings on Kwajalein Island were supported by a preliminary bombardment lasting two days, with battleships and cruisers lying only 2,000 yards off the beaches, and even closer support being laid on by destroyers and LCI gunboats.[37] Artillery fire at Roi–Namur was provided by three battleships, five cruisers and destroyers.

American losses in each of the island assaults (Kwajalein Island and Roi–Namur) were less than 200 killed, a fifth of the losses at Tarawa; the objectives were secure within three days. For the Japanese, however, the cost was just as devastating as in the Gilberts. Their troops killed at Roi–Namur numbered over 3,400 and at Kwajalein Island over 4,900; only 265 survived as prisoners, of whom 165 were Korean labourers.

The capture of Kwajalein had been unexpectedly easy for the Americans; it was followed two weeks later by a jump further north in the Marshalls, to Eniwetok Atoll (now Eniwetak), using uncommitted Army and Marine reserves. Eniwetok was the nearest place in the Marshalls to the Marianas, and it boasted a superb natural harbour. The Japanese garrison consisted mainly of an Army brigade (2,500 men), which had arrived from Manchuria only in the previous month. The soldiers had not had time to fortify the three small islets; in what was to be the last major American assault on a coral atoll, they were wiped out, in the naval bombardment or in brief battles. Within two weeks the 'Seabees' (naval construction battalions, or CBs) had laid out two airfields for fighters of the air-defence force and for long-range US Navy PB4Y Liberators.[38]

More important than air bases, the Americans gained in the Marshalls two large natural fleet anchorages. These were at Eniwetok and at Majuro Atoll; the latter lay 300 miles southeast of Kwajalein and had been undefended. Both places were quickly equipped with defences; a fleet of supply and service ships rapidly arrived to transform them into busy forward bases. Organised as mobile Service Squadrons (ServRons) 4 and 10, the unique floating bases would play a vital part in keeping the growing task forces ready for action, even when deployed more than halfway across the great ocean. The Pacific Fleet would now use Majuro and Eniwetok, rather than Pearl Harbor (2,750 miles to the east), as the starting point for its decisive carrier operations in the Central Pacific over the next nine months.

The loss of the Marshalls, although outside the September 1943 'absolute national defence zone', was a heavy and symbolic defeat for the Japanese. The Gilberts had been captured British territory; the Marshalls, in contrast, had been part of the *nanyō*, the pre-war Japanese Pacific Empire. The landings showed that the invaders could not be stopped at the water's edge, and that anything in range of their massive naval artillery would be destroyed. In addition the other garrisoned islands in the Marshalls – Wotje, Maloelap, Jaluit and

Mili – were simply bypassed. The exposed airfields were neutralised by bombing; as Morison put it, 'an airfield from which planes cannot operate is as harmless as a tennis court'. As Forrest Sherman, then Nimitz's deputy chief of staff, memorably put it: 'We shall let them wither on the vine'. The bypassed islands literally starved; on Wotje (for example) only a third of the garrison of over 3,000 men survived to surrender in September 1945.[39]

The largest of the island-hopping invasions of the Central Pacific was the attack on the Mariana Islands, Operation FORAGER. In terms of the land fighting this was different from earlier operations. The island objectives – Saipan, Tinian and Guam – were much larger in land area than coral atolls like Tarawa or Kwajalein. Saipan, the first objective, is some 12 miles from north to south, and 5 miles from east to west, with a 1,500-foot hill in the middle. Unlike any of the islands attacked before, the Marianas had a sizeable civilian population, including Japanese settlers. The landings also came after the Japanese Army had finally begun to despatch major forces to the Central Pacific. The Marianas (and Truk) were defended by the new Japanese Thirty-First Army, formed in February 1944 under General Obata Hideyoshi. Fortunately for the Americans, their submarines had been able to sink or detour a number of the transport ships attempting to bring in these Japanese troops.

The Northern Attack Force of Admiral Spruance's Fifth Fleet was tasked to take Saipan and nearby Tinian; in command – again – was Admiral Kelly Turner. Three divisions departed from the Hawaiian Islands in late May after completing their training there. Some thirty-seven troop transports and eleven cargo ships carried the 2nd and 4th Marine Divisions, with the US Army's 27th Division intended as a floating reserve; American ground forces in the Northern Attack Force totalled 71,000 men. At Eniwetok, now a jumping-off base for the next operation, the first-wave Marines transferred from assault transports to LSTs loaded with amtracs; the LSTs would carry them on the slow six-day final leg to Saipan. Just before dawn on 15 June 1944 the amtracs were launched offshore through the bow doors of the LSTs, and the men of the Marine divisions drove across the southwestern coast of Saipan.

The new Japanese 43rd Division had arrived on Saipan from Japan in May 1944. Its commander was General Saitō Yoshitsugo; under him there were also several independent Army battalions, and the total strength was 30,000 men, a much larger force than the Americans had expected. On the other hand, the Marine landing force had no difficulty establishing a deep perimeter and bringing in their artillery. Once again the Americans showed that it was impossible to prevent them coming ashore. Serious bombardment had begun on 14 May (D-1), with a support force including the old battleships *California*, *Colorado*, *Idaho*, *Maryland*, *Mississippi*, *New Mexico* and *Pennsylvania*, eleven cruisers and twenty-six destroyers. But there were many more targets that had to be engaged and suppressed than on the atolls. And the advancing troops came up against Japanese field fortifications and considerable artillery. Given the level of resistance and the arrival of intelligence that a major Japanese naval force was advancing towards the Marianas (see below, p. 402), Admiral Spruance postponed the planned invasion of Guam and ordered that his reserve (the 27th Infantry Division) be landed on Saipan. Transports and support ships were then ordered to a safer position east of the islands.[40]

In the end the three divisions of the V Amphibious Force were able to push the Japanese back to the northern part of Saipan, although there was a famous explosion of inter-service rivalry. The Marine general who was commanding the corps removed the Army general leading the 27th Division, on the grounds that the latter's forces were not moving rapidly enough. The bespectacled General H.M. 'Howlin' Mad' Smith had been one of the chief organisers of USMC amphibious forces, but this was his first Pacific combat command and his decisions went down badly with the US Army leadership in Washington.[41]

With or without the intervention of General Smith, the Japanese concluded that the battle was lost. The Japanese launched a fruitless banzai charge, the largest of the war, on 7 July, involving 3,000 soldiers and sailors. During all the fighting on Saipan some 30,000 Japanese troops were killed or committed suicide, along with several thousand civilians, in uniquely ghastly circumstances. Only some 900 Japanese troops surrendered. After ordering the fatal charge, General Saitō committed hara-kiri. Among the number of senior officers who died on Saipan was Admiral Nagumo, who shot himself on 6 July. The commander of the Japanese carriers at Pearl Harbor and at Midway, he had in March 1944 been made C-in-C of the Central Pacific Area Fleet; his headquarters were in what would turn out to be the Saipan death-trap. Also among the dead was Nagumo's current chief of staff, Admiral Yano Hideo; in 1943–44 Yano had been in charge of naval intelligence in his capacity as head of the Intelligence Bureau (*Jōhō Kyoku*) of the Naval General Staff. In addition, as already mentioned, the staff of the Japanese Navy's submarine force, the Sixth Fleet, had died on Saipan along with their commander, Admiral Takagi.[42] For the Americans, Saipan was the costliest ground operation thus far in the Pacific, a four-week battle against a large, entrenched Japanese Army force. Nearly 3,000 Marines and soldiers were killed – three times the number killed at Tarawa and twice that killed in the six-month Guadalcanal campaign.

Tinian, the smallest and flattest of the major Mariana Islands, was attacked on 24 July (D+41) in a shore-to-shore landing by the 2nd and 4th Marine Divisions from Saipan. Thanks to a prolonged bombardment and a well-chosen landing beach, resistance was effectively crushed within a week. The island was about to be converted by the Americans into the largest airfield in the world. Tinian would become the base from which the nuclear strikes against Hiroshima and Nagasaki would be launched in August 1945.

The Southern Attack Force under Admiral Conolly carried out the invasion of Guam. The island was a former American possession that had been captured by the Japanese from a tiny US Marine garrison in December 1941; it was somewhat larger than Saipan and lay 120 miles to the south. The 1944 landing was originally scheduled for 18 June (D+3 on Saipan), but did not actually occur until 21 July (D+36, and three days before the Tinian landing). The III Amphibious Force comprised the 3rd Marine Division, which had fought on Bougainville, another Marine brigade, and the Army's 77th Division. The Marines had embarked at Guadalcanal and were in position for an early attack, but they were pulled back to Eniwetok when the first landing date was abandoned. There they had awaited completion of the Saipan ground battle and the arrival of a reserve force from Hawaii, the 77th Division.

The resistance of the Japanese defenders on Guam had been worn down by a four-week, closely targeted bombardment, mainly by naval artillery. The garrison was smaller than on Saipan, and American losses were only about half as large. On 10 August, after three weeks of fighting, Guam was declared secure. Total Japanese killed on the island were about 18,000, with about 1,000 POWs. General Obata, commander of the whole Thirty-First Army, committed ritual suicide there on 11 August.

The saga of amphibious operations for the small islands of the Central Pacific ended with the battle for the Palau group, between Truk and the Philippine island of Mindanao. This operation began on 15 September 1944, four weeks after the end of the Guam battle; it was assigned the ill-omened code name STALEMATE I.[43] The Americans were not interested in the most important islands of the group (Kororo and Babelthuap), but in a nearby anchorage and in the much smaller island of Peleliu, with its airfield. The amphibious-assault phase progressed easily, employing the techniques of earlier landings. Five battleships, nine cruisers and fourteen destroyers bombarded Peleliu for three days, taking turns with air strikes launched from a dozen escort carriers. The men of the veteran 1st Marine Division came ashore in amtracs, supported by tanks.

The Japanese Army, however, had also learned lessons over the last months, and the reinforced regiment of 5,000 soldiers had dug into a substantial limestone ridge north of the airfield. They were to some extent protected from direct naval fire, and they did not bring the battle to a quick conclusion by mounting a banzai charge. An operation expected to last three or four days actually dragged on for two months. Organised Japanese resistance ended only on

25 November, and the fighting cost the US Marines 1,500 men, more than at Tarawa.

Peleliu was a mistake for the Americans in several respects. Earlier successes had bred over-confidence. The technique of amphibious assault seemed to have been mastered, and the island was expected to be quickly overrun, like Kwajalein or Eniwetok in the Marshalls. Peleliu anticipated Japanese tactics that would be employed in 1945, in more famous operations at Iwo Jima and Okinawa. And the capture of the island proved, with hindsight, to be unnecessary. The American command had belatedly decided to speed up their Philippines campaign, but the expedition for Peleliu was already at sea. As things turned out the anchorage was not needed for the American fleet. The excellent harbour at Ulithi, 400 miles to the northeast, would be occupied without a fight in late September (a week after the Peleliu landings), and it served as the major fleet base in the last months of the Pacific war.

SEA/AIR BATTLES IN THE CENTRAL PACIFIC

From September 1943 to March 1944, the US Navy developed the Fast Carrier Force which within a few months would give it complete victory in the western Pacific. In the summer and autumn of 1943, powerful ships and aircraft joined the fleet, and many more were in the pipeline. Elements of the growing sea/air fleet, originally operating from Pearl Harbor, began with raids on Marcus Island, the Gilberts, Wake and Rabaul in the summer and autumn of 1943. They then provided distant cover and support for the landings in the Gilberts (November 1943) and the Marshalls (January 1944).

The Fast Carrier Force was originally Task Force (TF) 50. It was re-designated as Task Force 58 on 6 January 1944, and as such it would go on to be the most powerful single naval force of World War II and surely one of the most famous fleets in naval history.[44] By the time of the invasion of the Marshall Islands in February 1944, TF 58 (then commanded by Admiral Marc Mitscher, and operating within Spruance's Central Pacific Force) included four task *groups*, each comprising one or two 'Essex' class fleet carriers and one or two 'Independence' class light carriers. The composition at this time of Task Group 58.2 (under Admiral 'Monty' Montgomery) was typical: three carriers, three fast battleships, a light cruiser and seven destroyers. TG 58.2 was bigger than the American fleet at Midway or the British Mediterranean Fleet in 1940–42, and there were three more task groups just like it.

As for the Japanese main carrier fleet, the Battle of Santa Cruz (near Guadalcanal) in October 1942 had effectively been the last engagement it fought for twenty months. This was partly because its air groups were flown ashore on several occasions to operate (unsuccessfully) from land bases, and partly because the expanse of the Pacific and the pace of the American raids made it difficult for Japanese carriers to engage them. Admiral Koga was eager to fight the Americans, and he committed a significant naval force to the north at the time of the American invasion of Attu in the Aleutians in May 1943. Extensive manoeuvres were also carried out by the Combined Fleet in home waters in May and June 1943.[45] And twice in the autumn of 1943 major warships were sent forward from Truk to anchorage at Eniwetok in the Marshalls, when American carriers raided Wake and the Gilberts. None of these expeditions resulted in a fleet encounter.

In the end, Japanese resistance to the American landings in the Gilberts and the Marshalls took the form of small-scale air and submarine attacks, rather than the use of the big surface ships of the Combined Fleet. When the Americans landed at Tarawa and Makin in late November 1943 the Japanese launched attacks by Navy twin-engined bombers flying from island bases in the Marshalls. The impact was reduced by the earlier diversion of a large number of Japanese planes to defend Rabaul. On the evening of 22 November 1943 (D+2 of the Gilberts operation), three fast carriers in one of the TF 50 task groups were steaming 30 miles west of Tarawa when they were attacked by a squadron of torpedo bombers flying at very low level. The new light carrier *Independence* was hit by a torpedo and had to be sent back to the West Coast for repairs; she would be out of the war for eight months. 'Butch' O'Hare was killed four nights later while flying an early night-fighter mission from the *Enterprise* to protect the carrier task force.[46]

The Japanese had more success at dawn on 24 November. Because the US Army troops on Makin Atoll advanced slowly, US Navy support ships had had to remain in the area. Three escort carriers were operating about 20 miles southwest of Butaritari when one of them, the *Liscome Bay* (the first of fifty 'Casablanca' class ships to enter service), was torpedoed by the submarine *I-75*. The torpedo set off an explosion, evidently in a weapons store; the fiercely burning ship went down a few minutes later. Among those who died were the admiral commanding the escort carrier group, the ship's captain and over 600 personnel. Fortunately for the Americans, the Japanese had no further successes. Six of the nine Japanese submarines that had been rushed to the Gilberts were sunk, an unsustainable loss rate. As already mentioned, the Japanese underseas fleet was unable to respond at all to the invasion of the Marshalls two months later.

The Japanese Navy's land-based bombers had been active in the Marshalls in early December 1943, when two fast-carrier task groups from Task Force 50 raided Kwajalein Atoll, in preparation for the landings there. The new *Lexington* was torpedoed after a skilful Japanese night attack on 4/5 December 1943. Only a few crew members were killed, however, and the damage was quickly repaired. Admiral 'Baldy' Pownall, the commander of the Fast Carrier Force, was criticised for the conduct of this operation, and after discussions at Pearl Harbor Nimitz replaced him with Admiral Marc 'Pete' Mitscher. Mitscher would turn out to be the most effective leader of the growing fast-carrier task forces until the end of the war. He was an aviation pioneer who had taken part in the US Navy's NC-4 transatlantic flight expedition in 1919; in 1941–42 he commanded the carrier *Hornet* during the Tokyo raid and at the Battle of Midway.

From about the time of the November 1943 raid on Rabaul, the fast-moving American fast carriers constantly kept on the offensive. The Japanese were on the back foot, never able to consolidate a defensive position, let alone take the offensive. From February 1944 Spruance's Central Pacific Force could use its new forward base at Majuro in the southeastern Marshalls. Lying in the heart of the Central Pacific, Majuro was 2,300 miles west of Pearl Harbor, and 2,100 miles north of Nouméa (which had been the forward base for the Guadalcanal fighting). From Majuro three of the four task groups sortied for Operation HAILSTONE, the first carrier raid against Truk Atoll in the Carolines. The strike was carried out on 17–18 February 1944, timed to support the landing on Eniwetok.

Truk had been the main base of the Japanese Combined Fleet in the Central Pacific. The Japanese realised at the start of 1944 that the big atoll had become exposed to attack by long-range land-based bombers and even carriers, and they now risked few of their remaining big ships there. The super-battleship *Musashi* (Admiral Koga's flagship) was the last major warship to depart Truk – for Japan – on 10 February 1944, along with a new light cruiser, and four destroyers. When the American planes arrived over the base a week later they found only a few damaged warships, but a large number of merchant ships. Two submarine tenders, seventeen cargo ships and six tankers were sunk by aircraft in the anchorage, as well as a light cruiser, two auxiliary cruisers and three destroyers which had been able to put to sea. More important was the big air battle, in which 250 of the 365 Japanese aircraft on hand were destroyed in the air or on the Truk airfields.[47] Admiral Spruance actually cruised right around the atoll in his flagship, the new 33-knot battleship *New Jersey*, accompanied by her sister ship the *Iowa*, two heavy cruisers and four destroyers; they sank another light cruiser and three destroyers. American submarines stationed around Truk sank the cruiser *Agano* (damaged at Rabaul in November 1943), a submarine and three merchant ships.

Only seventeen American planes were shot down during the Truk raid, about half what the Japanese lost in the surprise attack on Pearl Harbor. Counter-attacks against the American fleet were feeble, although the new fleet carrier *Intrepid* was forced to return to the US for repairs after being damaged in a night attack by a torpedo plane (a G4M/BETTY) flying from the major Japanese air base at Tinian in the Marianas. Although the Japanese lost no major warships, the Truk raid was of great importance, humiliating the Japanese Navy and leading to the (belated) transfer of Japanese Army divisions to the Central Pacific.[48]

After the Truk raid Admiral Mitscher continued westward to raid the Mariana Islands. He parted company with Spruance and the battleships, refuelled at sea and sailed on with two of his task groups. This was the first time that the Marianas had come under attack. Aside from yielding invaluable reconnaissance photos of the island chain, the carrier force badly damaged the leading elements of Admiral Kakuta's land-based First Air Fleet, which had just begun to deploy from the Japanese mainland. Some 170 aircraft were destroyed on the ground, and new airfield facilities on Tinian, Saipan, Guam and nearby Rota were badly damaged, for the loss of six American planes.

The remarkable feature of these operations was that the American carrier commanders were no longer afraid to operate within range of shore-based enemy aviation. The historian Clark Reynolds was not exaggerating when he concluded that the raids on Truk and the Marianas in February 1944 by TF 58 'revolutionised naval air warfare'. Samuel Eliot Morison made the same point: 'The strike on Truk demonstrated a virtual revolution in naval warfare; the aircraft carrier emerged as the capital ship of the future, with unlimited potentialities.'[49]

At the end of March 1944, Spruance carried out yet another long-range naval raid to the west from Majuro. Operation DESECRATE was targeted against the Japanese bases in the Palau islands in the western Carolines; much of the Combined Fleet had first withdrawn here when Truk was abandoned. The operation was intended partly to support General MacArthur's landings to the south at Hollandia in New Guinea (which would take place on 22 April).[50] A large number of merchant ships were sunk by air attacks in the Palaus, but the warships of the Combined Fleet had already withdrawn to points further west.

The death of Admiral Koga was one unexpected result of the Palau raid. The C-in-C of the Combined Fleet had witnessed the air raids first-hand from on shore, and then received incorrect reports of the imminent arrival of an American task force. He hurriedly decided to evacuate his headquarters from the Palaus to Davao on Mindanao in the southern Philippines. On the night of 31 March/1 April two giant four-engined Kawanishi H8K/EMILY flying boats departed from Palau to make the 600-mile flight due west to Davao. Koga's plane disappeared in a violent storm somewhere between Palau and Davao; no wreckage was ever found. The second H8K, carrying part of Koga's headquarters group, was buffeted by the same storm, and the flight crew decided to change their destination to Manila. The plane ran short of fuel and crash-landed in the sea near Cebu Island in the central Philippines. There the thirteen survivors, including Admiral Fukudome (Koga's chief of staff), fell into the hands of an American-led Filipino guerrilla force. Under threats of reprisals against the local population on Cebu, the survivors were handed over to occupying Japanese troops. The Filipino guerrillas, however, also captured a number of secret documents, and these were transported to Australia by submarine; they included the outline of current Combined Fleet doctrine, which became known as the 'Z' operations.[51]

The new C-in-C of the Combined Fleet, as of April 1944 and until the end of the war, was Admiral Toyoda Soemu. The third officer to hold this post during the war, Toyoda was rather different from his predecessors Yamamoto and Koga, not to mention Admiral Tōgō Heihachirō in the Russo-Japanese War. Toyoda raised his flag on the *Ōyodo*, a handsome new light cruiser, but she was a far cry from the super-battleships *Yamato* and *Musashi* which had served his predecessors. Moreover, the *Ōyodo* was tied up in harbour in Japan, either at Hashirajima in the Inland Sea or close to the centre of political power in Tokyo Bay. Indeed, in late September 1944 – on the eve of the Battle of Leyte Gulf – Toyoda would move the headquarters of the Combined Fleet ashore to an underground bunker on the grounds of Keiō University in Hiyoshi, on the southwestern outskirts of the Japanese capital.

Admiral Toyoda had commanded, consecutively, two of the Navy's fleets during the Sino-Japanese War. In April 1944, however, he was nearly sixty and had been serving in posts ashore for the past five years. He became head of the Imperial Japanese Navy Technical Department (*Kansei Hombu*) in October 1939, where he oversaw shipbuilding. After that he served as commander of Kure Naval District, as a member of the Supreme War Council (*Gunji Sangiin*) and finally as commander of the Yokosuka Naval District. He had no recent sea time, and no direct aviation experience.

Even before Admiral Koga's sudden death, the overall command of the Imperial Navy had been further shaken up. A month earlier, in late February 1944, General Tōjō Hideki was in the process of achieving an unprecedented concentration of power in his own hands. Prompted by Imperial dissatisfaction at various military setbacks, he had taken over the post of Chief of the Army General Staff from Field Marshal Sugiyama Hajime; at the same time he kept his own positions as the Emperor's Prime Minister, Minister of War and Minister of Munitions. Tōjō also achieved the removal of the long-serving Admiral Nagano as Chief of the Naval General Staff (NGS) and replaced him with the Minister of the Navy, Admiral Shimada Shigetarō (who also kept his cabinet post). Shimada was already regarded by many senior Japanese officers as a pliant and ineffectual tool of the general – some called him 'Tōjō's Geisha'.

The February 1944 shake-up in Tokyo came at the same time as organisational changes in the Combined Fleet, although these had been brought about by Admiral Koga. The First Fleet (First *Kantai*), the battleship squadron which had been the steel heart of the pre-war Imperial Navy, was finally disbanded. Most of the battleships had spent the war tied up at Hashirajima, vainly awaiting the Pacific Jutland. Their last commander, Admiral Nagumo, was moved to his fatal post on Saipan. The main battle force now took the form of a newly created First Mobile Fleet (First *Kidō Kantai*).[52] This First Mobile Fleet brought under one command both elements of the 'decisive battle forces'; these were the Second Fleet (formerly Admiral Kondō's cruiser force, but now including the battleships) and Admiral Ozawa's Third Fleet (with the aircraft carriers). Ozawa was now also the commander of the First Mobile Fleet and held a position (under Toyoda) comparable to that of Admiral Spruance (under Nimitz). The commander of the Second Fleet was still Admiral Kurita. Some ocean-going combat units did not come under Ozawa's control and remained directly under the Combined Fleet. These were the land-based naval air groups of Admiral Kakuta's First Air Fleet, the submarines of the Sixth Fleet under Admiral Takagi, and the escorts of Admiral Oikawa's Maritime Escort Command.

In the two months available between the death of Admiral Koga and the beginning of a full-scale and decisive fleet action – in the Marianas – there was little that could be done by the Imperial Navy. Toyoda evidently hoped that he would have more time to make preparations. In his despatch issued to senior commanders on 4 May 1944, when taking command of the Combined Fleet, Toyoda referred to the 'unprecedented opportunity' of a decisive battle, but he suggested that this battle would take place in the *autumn* (of 1944).

In reality Toyoda's plans were little different from Koga's 'Z' operations of 1943, which in turn were fundamentally the same as pre-war plans for a 'decisive' ambush battle against the advancing American fleet. Indeed, all of these had much in common with the experience of the Combined Fleet when fighting the Russian Navy in the summer of 1905. The day before his despatch to his commanders, Toyoda had issued Combined Fleet Order No. 76, outlining the so-called 'A' operation (A-GŌ).[53] As the enemy invasion fleet approached its objective – wherever that might be – it would be attacked by land-based aircraft and by the carrier planes of the First Mobile Fleet, which would be deployed at the crucial point. The submarine force would also play an important role. The attackers would begin by knocking out the American carriers, and then destroying the enemy transport force. The plans assumed that the Imperial Navy would somehow have the initiative, and that a decisive victory begun with the crippling of the enemy carrier forces would be followed by attacks on the enemy invasion fleet and pursuit of retreating enemy remnants.

The order was symptomatic of an organisation which had lost touch with reality.

THE BATTLE OF THE PHILIPPINE SEA, JUNE 1944

The Philippine Sea lies between the Philippines and the Marianas. The Battle of the Philippine Sea was fought in mid-June 1944; the Japanese know it, perhaps more appropriately, as the Battle of the Marianas. Whatever the name, the sea/air battle was the biggest of World War II. It was more significant even than the better-known Battle of Leyte Gulf, part of which took place in the same waters four months later.

The amphibious side of the invasion of the Marianas, Operation FORAGER, has already been described (see p. 389–91). As well as landing troops on the strategically positioned islands, the US Navy hoped the operation would finally bring the Combined Fleet out to fight, although there was no certainty this would happen; the Japanese Navy had not responded to earlier invasions in 1943 and early 1944, the Marianas were now some distance from Japanese naval bases and fuel sources, and the American fleet was now substantially stronger than its opponent.

The Japanese Navy laboured under fundamental weaknesses. First of all, its forces were now considerably weaker in quantity and quality than those of the Americans. Second, they were constantly put off balance by the pace of the American advance, and now that they had lost the initiative they did not know where the enemy would strike. The A-GŌ plan was not specifically about the defence of the Marianas, and the Japanese originally expected the Americans to strike in the Palau group, which lay nearly 1,000 miles to the southwest of the Marianas. As already mentioned, the headquarters of the shore-based air force (Admiral Kakuta's First Air Fleet) was based on Tinian, near Saipan. The headquarters of the whole submarine force (Admiral Takagi's Sixth Fleet), as well as that of Admiral Nagumo's small Central Pacific Area Fleet, were on Saipan. Rather than being a forward base for a decisive battle, both islands would very soon be literally in the front line.

Then, in the weeks before the actual Marianas invasion, there was yet another diversion. The Imperial Navy took the decision to re-deploy major surface and air forces to recapture the island of Biak, off the northwestern tip of New Guinea, which had been invaded by the Americans on 27 May 1944.[54] The counter-attack by the Japanese was code-named Operation KON ('Tidal Wave'). They were perhaps influenced by a degree of wishful thinking, as this southern theatre was closer to the new Combined Fleet surface-ship base at Tawi Tawi – in the Sulu Archipelago between the Philippines and the Netherlands Indies. On 10 June the super-battleships *Yamato* and *Musashi*, three heavy cruisers, a light cruiser and three destroyers departed from Tawi Tawi to the south to cover the counter-landing force (which comprised two cruisers, three destroyers and a transport) tasked to reinforce the Biak area, in an operation comparable to the 'Tokyo Express' of 1942. Perhaps more important, several hundred land-based planes from the Marianas and the Palaus were sent south to bolster the defence west of New Guinea, and they did not return for the decisive battle (one factor being the spread of malaria among their crews).

As a result of all this, the Japanese were in no position to intercept the American fleet before it effected the first landing in the Marianas, at Saipan, on Thursday, 15 June 1944. (The Japanese did carry out two daring very long-range reconnaissance flights from Truk to Majuro using a single high-speed Nakajima C6N/MYRT reconnaissance plane; they knew the Americans had left port but did not know their destination.) The first real warning of a direct danger had been a surprise mass sweep against airfields on Saipan and Tinian by 200 F6F Hellcat fighters from TF 58 carriers on the afternoon of Sunday, 11 June. Even this, however, did not convince the Japanese that invasion was necessarily imminent; it could be just a diversionary attack or a repetition of the February 1944 raid.

Admiral Ozawa took the main body of the First Mobile Fleet to sea from the Tawi Tawi anchorage as a precautionary measure at mid-morning on Tuesday. Within a couple of days, as the fleet sailed north into the Philippines, it became clear that enemy operations in the Marianas were more than a raid. On the morning of Thursday, 15 June, Admiral Toyoda in Tokyo ordered implementation of plan A-GŌ and issued a Nelsonian order: 'The fate of the Empire rests on this one battle. Every man is expected to do his utmost.'[55]

Meanwhile, the naval air groups of Admiral Kakuta's First Air Fleet, operating from land bases in the Marianas, were not able effectively to counter the air strikes, ambush the approaching enemy fleet, or even provide safe bases into which carrier-based aircraft could shuttle. Kakuta's air strength, already weakened by transfers to the south, was rapidly thinned out further. A succession of American carrier strikes from 11 June damaged all the airfields in the Marianas and the western Carolines. Some 110 Japanese aircraft were destroyed in the Marianas, as were the better part of 140 potential reinforcement planes transiting south from Japan via Iwo Jima in the Bonin Islands.

The general planning assumption of the Japanese had been that – wherever the decisive battle took place – the carriers of Ozawa's First Mobile Fleet would not be committed until a *third* of the American carriers had been put out of action by land-based attacks.[56] Moreover, the tactical plan envisaged long-range strikes from task groups positioned well beyond the range of American carrier planes. Japanese attack planes (and fighter escorts) had more endurance than their US Navy counterparts, but in addition they would also – in theory – attack

American ships and then fly on to land at bases in the Marianas, before refuelling, rearming and shuttling back to the carriers. At the critical moment Admiral Kakuta made fatally exaggerated claims for the successes of his land-based planes, and he did not reveal his own high losses or the extreme difficulty of using, for the shuttle raids, the air bases on Tinian, Rota and Guam (not to mention Saipan itself, where the main airfield would be taken on 18 June).

Ozawa's ships now passed through the central Philippines and exited east into the Philippine Sea in the early evening of Thursday (the 15th), through the San Bernardino Strait between the islands of Luzon and Samar. This was the same route that another Japanese battle group, under Admiral Kurita, would famously take in October 1944, during the Leyte Gulf battle. Early on Friday evening the main fleet was rejoined by the battle group detached for Operation KON, and all the ships began refuelling from a tanker unit in the middle of the Philippine Sea.

The largest battle fleet the Imperial Navy would ever assemble was now deployed into the formations in which it would fight the battle of 19–20 June.[57] Unlike most previous Pacific battles, and certainly unlike Midway or Leyte Gulf, the overall Japanese warship deployment was one extended column of ships pointed directly northeast towards the enemy – an unexpected simplicity that would confuse the Americans.

Ozawa's First Mobile Fleet was divided into three task groups. The Vanguard Force (the *Zeian Butai*) comprised the light carriers *Chitose*, *Chiyoda* and *Zuihō*, as well as the bulk of the Navy's surviving big surface ships – the super-battleships *Yamato* and *Musashi*, the fast battleships *Kongō* and *Haruna*, eight heavy cruisers, a new light cruiser and eight destroyers.[58] This task group was commanded by Admiral Kurita, commander of the Second Fleet, flying his flag in the cruiser *Atago*. The three light carriers were converted from fast naval auxiliaries; the *Zuihō* had fought in the 1942 Battle of Santa Cruz, and the *Chitose* and *Chiyoda* had been converted during 1943; each of the three ships could carry about thirty planes.

Some 100 miles astern were the two main carrier task groups. The 'A' (*Kō*) Group was centred on the fleet carriers *Shōkaku*, *Taihō* and *Zuikaku*, escorted by two heavy cruisers, a light cruiser and seven destroyers. The *Shōkaku* and *Zuikaku* were the last survivors of the Pearl Harbor raid. The *Taihō* was a brand-new armoured fleet carrier and the proud flagship of Admiral Ozawa.

The 'B' (*Otsu*) Group comprised the carriers *Hiyō*, *Junyō* and *Ryūhō*, escorted by the battleship *Nagato*, two heavy cruisers and eight destroyers. The *Hiyō* and *Junyō* had fought in the closing battles of the Guadalcanal campaign; with them was the light carrier *Ryūhō*, another former naval auxiliary, converted in 1942.[59]

The US Navy, for its part, now deployed a fleet that was much stronger than that of its opponent, both on paper and in practice. The carrier battles of 1942 had been fought with at most two or three carriers on the American side (at Midway and the Eastern Solomons). This time there were seven fleet carriers, and eight fast light carriers. They were organised into four task groups, operating more closely together (about 12 miles apart) than at Midway, where there had been two separate task forces. The basic elements were TG 58.1 (the fleet carriers *Hornet* and *Yorktown*, the light carriers *Belleau Wood* and *Bataan*), TG 58.2 (the fleet carriers *Bunker Hill* and *Wasp*, the light carriers *Cabot* and *Monterey*), TG 58.3 (the fleet carriers *Enterprise* and *Lexington*, the light carriers *San Jacinto* and *Princeton*) and TG 58.4 (the fleet carrier *Essex*, the light carriers *Langley* and *Cowpens*).[60] Remarkably, of these fifteen aircraft carriers all except the *Enterprise* had entered service since the Guadalcanal campaign. During the battle each task group was surrounded by a screen of three or four cruisers and a dozen destroyers. Unlike Midway or the battles around Guadalcanal, the Americans did not have any land-based tactical aircraft within range, although some long-range patrol planes did take part.

For this battle a separate Task Group 58.7 had been created under the command of Admiral Willis A. Lee, with the most modern and powerful battleship fleet assembled thus far anywhere in World War II. This comprised the brand-new 33-knot *Iowa* and *New Jersey*, the modern *Alabama*, *Indiana*, *North Carolina*, *South Dakota* and *Washington*,[61] as well as a screen of four heavy cruisers and fourteen destroyers. In the battle Admiral Spruance deployed TG 58.7 to the west of carrier task groups; Lee's mission was to mask them against attacks from the air (using the powerful AA batteries of the battleship), and also against possible surface attack.

As if this front-line strength was not enough, Admiral Spruance had at his disposal a separate fleet, Task Force 52, under the overall command of Admiral Kelly Turner. Tasked with providing close support for the Saipan invasion, it included many older and slower, but still formidable warships, among them seven battleships of the World War I era, eight escort carriers, eleven cruisers and thirty-nine destroyers. They would not play a large part in the coming fleet battle, but did come under limited attack from Japanese land-based planes.

The Americans had also deployed a large number of fleet submarines, in the battle role for which they had originally been designed. Strategically positioned in the Central and western Pacific were nineteen boats from Pearl Harbor and seven from the Seventh Fleet in Australia. Unlike the battles of 1942, American submarines would play a most significant role in the Philippine Sea action, both performing a vital long-range reconnaissance function and attacking the Japanese fleet; in the latter role they were now equipped with reliable torpedoes.

The submarines provided early warning of the movement of the Japanese fleet, including the passage of Ozawa's main force through the San Bernardino Strait on Thursday afternoon and the return (east of Mindanao) of the battle group sent on the abortive sortie toward Biak.

Late on Saturday evening (at 9.15 p.m.), 17 June, the approaching Japanese fleet was definitely sighted by the submarine *Cavalla* about 700 miles west of Saipan. This was nearly halfway across the Philippine Sea, but still well beyond the range of American carrier planes, even though the latter were now flying from ships that were operating west of the Marianas. Late on Sunday (the 18th) American DF did get a fix from a radio transmission 355 miles to the WSW of TF 58. Mitscher, the carrier task force commander, urged Spruance to throw his forces further forward during the night of 18/19 June, in order to put the carriers in position for an early launch against this target on Monday morning. Admiral Spruance, however, took the view that information about the position of the Japanese fleet forces was still too limited, and at 8.00 p.m. he made the critical decision to pull back to the east. This retreat had the advantage of lengthening the range for the Japanese, and bringing TF 58 closer to the beachhead at Saipan, where American troops had now been ashore for the better part of four days. This new position would also limit the possibility of a Japanese manoeuvre, around the north or south flank of the American task force, to attack the fleet or the beachhead area.

It is sometimes suggested that Spruance's decisions were influenced by the documents for the 'Z' operations, which had fallen into American hands as a result of Admiral Fukudome's plane crash on the night of 31 March–1 April. After considerable delay in getting these papers out of the Japanese-occupied Philippines, examined in Australia and fully translated at Pearl Harbor, a copy had been flown out to Spruance's flagship on 8 June. In reality they provided no more than an outline of general Japanese Navy doctrine and intentions, which was to respond to an enemy sortie without delay and, in close co-operation with land-based aircraft and submarines, to destroy the enemy carriers and invasion transports.[62] Admiral Spruance and his staff had already been aware of this.

The great sea/air battle commenced before dawn on Monday, 19 June. The Japanese fleet launched scout planes and then four consecutive air strikes. What the Americans later called Raid I departed from the three light carriers of the Vanguard Force from about 8.30 a.m. It included about sixty-five attacking planes, most of them A6M/ZEKE fighters, each armed with a 250kg (550lb) bomb and tasked with the 'special attack' role of putting the flight decks of the American carriers out of action.[63] There were also a handful of B6N/JILL torpedo planes. The incoming strike was picked up by American radar at 10.00 a.m. at a range of 150 miles and intercepted by radar-directed Hellcat fighters of the combat air patrol (CAP). The strike force was made up of the least well-trained Japanese pilots, and the heavily loaded fighter-bombers could not manoeuvre well. Raid I did not get beyond Admiral Lee's screening battleship force (TG 58.7), on station west of the carriers. One plane did hit the battleship *South Dakota* with a bomb and caused minor damage. Only twenty Japanese aircraft made it back to their ships.

The main strike, Raid II, was launched from further away by Ozawa's A Group – the three big fleet carriers – with 128 planes. It included eighty 'proper' naval attack planes (as distinct from the fighter-bombers of Raid I). Detected far out by radar at 11.07 a.m., the raid was broken up by the CAP. Only a handful of aircraft reached the carrier task groups, at about noon; two carriers in TG 58.2 had near misses from D4Y/JUDY dive bombers, and the *Enterprise* in TG 58.3 narrowly avoided a torpedo dropped by a B6N/JILL. Japanese losses were again devastating; 97 planes out of 128 failed to return. The forty-seven planes in Raid III, from the B Group, were mostly misdirected to a spurious target, and those that did succeed in approaching the American carriers at about 1.20 p.m. failed to press home their attacks; most of these planes, however, survived. The incoming final wave, Raid IV, included eighty-two planes, mainly from B Group, as well as some from the *Zuikaku*. Also misdirected, the few planes that reached the task force achieved nothing. Only nine of the eighty-two returned to their carriers; many more were destroyed or badly damaged trying to carry out the shuttle flight to land on Guam airfields.

Altogether on that Monday 373 planes had been launched from the Mobile Fleet on search missions or strikes. Only 130 returned. During the same day as many as fifty land-based planes were shot down. Neither carrier-based planes nor land-based ones seriously damaged any American ships; meanwhile TF 58 carriers lost only eighteen fighters, a dozen in air-to-air combat.

The whole sea/air battle on 19 June became known to the Americans as the 'Great Marianas Turkey Shoot'. The extreme imbalance of losses had a number of causes. The US Navy radar-controlled fighter-direction system was now very efficient, and the Navy's pilots, while sometimes inexperienced in air-to-air combat, had been through a very thorough training programme. The Americans had many more fighters, and F6F Hellcat was much superior to the A6M/ZEKE. Experienced Japanese carrier aircrew had been lost in early battles. Although the air groups of the big carriers of the A Group had had six months' training, those of B Group and the Vanguard Force had had only two or three months. When the Japanese carriers spent a month at Tawi Tawi they had been unable to conduct any flying training, even to gain deck-landing experience. The American submarine threat kept the carriers in harbour, and the primitive anchorage did not have an airstrip. As for the aircrew of the land-based First Air

Fleet, their operational training had been cut short by Admiral Kakuta from mid-1943.[64]

The air battle on that Monday morning was remarkable, and not just for the 'turkey shoot' of Japanese aircraft. More aircraft than ever before were concentrated by the two sides, but neither Japanese nor American planes succeeded in sinking or causing serious damage to *any* enemy ships. The crews of the Japanese strike aircraft were poorly trained and inexperienced. The Americans, for their part, did not launch any attack strikes, partly because they did not know the location of the Japanese fleet and partly because they concentrated on air-defence operations. Attack aircraft were kept in the carrier hangar decks or flown off to orbit well away from the defensive air battle, to allow the Hellcats of the CAP the fullest freedom to take off and land.

However the First Mobile Fleet faced acute danger from another direction altogether. The submarine *Albacore* had found the A Group early on Monday morning, and at 8.10 a.m. she succeeded in hitting the *Taihō* with a torpedo. At first the big carrier was able to continue operating normally, but damage control by the raw crew was poor, and at 2.32 p.m. leaking fumes from ruptured aviation petrol tanks set off a huge explosion, followed by a devastating fire; use of flammable unrefined fuel oil in the ship's boilers may also have been a factor. Admiral Ozawa had to leave the stricken ship, and she sank at 4.28 p.m. Meanwhile, that morning at 11.22 the submarine *Cavalla* had succeeded in hitting the *Shōkaku* with three torpedoes. At 12.10 the carrier suffered a secondary explosion similar to that aboard the *Taihō*; she sank with heavy loss of life at 2.01 p.m.

The explanation for the success of these submarine attacks includes the growing quality of the American submarine force and, on the Japanese side, poor A/S technique and a relatively weak destroyer screen. It was some time before admirals Spruance and Mitscher learned of this propitious turn of events, and the carrier sinkings came too late to affect their decisions and operations on that Monday. However, without the submarine attacks the Battle of the Philippine Sea might have ended as an inconclusive draw, at least in terms of warship losses. Instead it would be transformed into a swingeing combined-arms victory, although not one achieved solely by American flyers.

In contrast to the situation in 1942, Japanese submarines had no successes in the Battle of the Philippine Sea and suffered heavy losses; thirteen boats were sunk. The reasons for this poor showing included better American A/S procedures, the achievement of strategic surprise (landing in the Marianas rather than where the Japanese expected), and earlier losses to the Japanese undersea fleet.[65] Japanese submarines had been deployed further south, covering the Palaus, and a number were lost in May when their patrol line was overrun by the A/S sweep of USS *England* and her DE group.

The final phase of the battle came on Tuesday, 20 June, and was something of an anti-climax. Admiral Ozawa had transferred his flag to the cruiser *Haguro*, from where he was not able to stay abreast of the rapidly developing situation – the losses suffered by his attacking air groups, the likelihood of Japanese reinforcement land-based aircraft arriving, and the actual level of damage inflicted on the American fleet. His own surface fleet had suffered no harm – with the very significant exceptions of the *Taihō* and the *Shōkaku*. Neither Ozawa nor Admiral Toyoda at Combined Fleet headquarters seemed to have thought at this point that the battle was definitely lost. In any event the three elements of the Mobile Fleet turned together to the northwest with plans to carry out necessary refuelling from their tanker group. At 1.00 p.m. on Tuesday Ozawa was finally able to transfer his flag to the *Zuikaku*, and it became clear to him that the air strength of his seven surviving carriers amounted to only 100 operational planes. His scout planes did locate TF 58 at 5.15 that afternoon some 380 miles to the east; he launched a small strike of seven torpedo planes, but with no effect.

Admiral Mitscher had not ordered a carrier search on Monday night (19th/20th), although radar-equipped planes were available on his carriers and five Martin PBM Mariner flying boats were now operating out of an anchorage at Saipan. There was also no full-scale search on Tuesday morning. Although the two fleets were now only 325 miles apart, it was not until 4.00 on Tuesday *afternoon* that Admiral Spruance first received a scouting report from an American aircraft giving the position of the Japanese carriers. The hour was quite late, and the Japanese ships were far away. Nevertheless, he and Mitscher agreed to launch a mass attack to the west by 216 planes from three of his task groups. The striking force was made up of seventy-seven dive bombers and fifty-four torpedo bombers, escorted by eighty-five fighters. The attackers arrived over the First Mobile Fleet at 6.40 p.m., just as the sun was about to set in the west; hastily organised attacks began and continued until 7.30.

The three elements of the Japanese fleet were closer together than they had been on Monday, but despite a very large number of targets the American planes succeeded only in sinking (with a torpedo) the liner-carrier *Hiyō*, as well as two refuelling tankers; the carrier went down two hours after the torpedo hit, after another secondary explosion. A few other ships received minor damage, including the carriers *Junyō* and *Chiyoda*, as well as the battleship *Haruna* and a cruiser. Japanese air losses were very heavy. At the end of the fighting on Tuesday the First Mobile Fleet had been reduced to thirty-five carrier aircraft, compared to 430 the day before.[66]

The sea/air battle was not wholly one-sided. The Americans lost a large number of planes, short of fuel, during the return flight and in attempted night landings when they arrived back at TF 58. To aid the recovery Mitscher accepted the risk from enemy submarines and used searchlights as beacons, in addition to normal night landing lights. Nevertheless, eighty aircraft were lost when they crashed or were ditched; this was in addition to twenty American fighters and strike aircraft lost during the attack itself.[67]

Some senior American naval officers – especially the 'aviators' – were not satisfied with the outcome of the battle. Spruance, a number of them argued, was a non-aviator who had been too cautious. Some time passed before it became known that three Japanese carriers had actually been sunk, but even so six more had escaped. By pushing west, the aviators argued, Spruance and Mitscher could have destroyed the entire striking force of the Japanese Navy and perhaps shortened the war. It was claimed that Spruance had exaggerated the danger of a breakthrough to Saipan by the Japanese fleet, and that even if this had been achieved there would have been few targets to attack; the Japanese ships, moreover, had little fuel and they could have been readily dealt with. Comparisons were even made, then and later, with the Battle of Jutland in 1916, in which a superior British fleet let a weaker German one escape and, in the process, suffered higher losses.[68]

Spruance could have conducted the battle differently, but historians need to consider the outcome as well as the admiral's decisions. If Midway had been for the US Navy the decisive *defensive* battle of the Pacific war, the Philippine Sea was the decisive *offensive* battle. Unlike Jutland, the larger fleet suffered much lower losses – indeed no losses at all of ships. Unlike Jutland the outcome resolved a larger strategic issue (control of the Marianas). The main combat element of the Japanese Navy – the carrier air groups – had been destroyed. The landing in Saipan had been secured. There was even a direct *political* consequence when General Tōjō was forced to resign as head of the Japanese government after the fall of Saipan. This had been a crushing Japanese defeat, and an overwhelming American victory. It was achieved by Raymond Spruance, and it marked the culmination of a stunningly successful sea/air campaign conducted by him in the Central Pacific.

STALEMATE: THE ROYAL NAVY IN THE INDIAN OCEAN, APRIL 1942–AUGUST 1945

The naval forces of the British Empire took a relatively small part in the war in the Pacific in 1942, 1943 and 1944. This was true despite the fact that much of the fighting took place in the British Solomon Islands Protectorate (Guadalcanal), Australian Papua and the British Gilbert and Ellice Islands (Tarawa). The defence of the dominions of Australia and New Zealand in the South Pacific was effectively handed over to the United States at the beginning of 1942. A handful of British, Australian and New Zealand cruisers and destroyers operated in the Pacific; the only big ship was HMS *Victorious*, which arrived when US Navy carrier availability was at its lowest point, after the Guadalcanal battles. She was based at Nouméa (Nouvelle-Calédonie) alongside USS *Saratoga* from May to July 1943. As it happened this was also an inactive period for Japanese fleet activity, and the *Victorious* was not required for active combat operations. In November 1943, however, at the inter-Allied SEXTANT Conference in Cairo it was agreed in principle that the Royal Navy would send a carrier force to operate in the Pacific; the details remained to be clarified.[69]

The British did have a fleet in the Indian Ocean, but the naval war there was in sharp contrast to the accelerating advance of American forces in the South and Central Pacific. This is not the place to go into the full complexities of the 'other' war (p. 312), fought against Japan by Britain and the US, outside the Pacific in Southeast Asia,[70] but the basic story is that the Japanese Army had succeeded in rapidly overrunning British Empire forces in Burma in the spring of 1942, and blocking the only significant land–sea route between China and the outside world – effectively from the Burmese port of Rangoon (now Yangon). The terrain and limited road system of Burma and Northeast India (Assam) made an Allied recovery from within that region difficult. The British and Americans had other global priorities, and few ground or air forces to deploy in Southeast Asia. In any event they disagreed about the strategy to be followed there.[71]

The months from summer 1942 to the end of 1944 were a period of frustrating inaction in Southeast Asia, with numerous plans but few successful offensive operations.[72] As mentioned in Chapter 15 (p. 312), British planners did in 1942 draft a project, Operation ANAKIM, for recapturing Burma. This involved thrusts from several directions, including a landing on the coast of the Bay of Bengal, during the campaigning season of the coming winter (November 1942 to April 1943).[73] These plans initially came to nothing, but then the global situation of the Allies improved, and ANAKIM was revived by the British and Americans at the January 1943 Casablanca/SYMBOL Conference. It would be an enterprise that might be carried out in the winter of 1943–44. But five months later, at the Washington/TRIDENT Conference in May 1943, ANAKIM was dropped as unrealistic, at least as a full-scale operation to recapture Burma.

One reason these various schemes fell through was the weakness of Allied – British – naval forces in the Indian Ocean. Disasters in Southeast Asia – the loss of the *Prince of Wales* and the *Repulse*, the fall of Singapore, the naval defeats in the Netherlands Indies – were followed by the Japanese carrier raid on Ceylon in April 1942. Admiral James Somerville, the experienced and successful commander of Force H at Gibraltar in 1940–42, had taken over command of the Eastern Fleet in March 1942. The surviving ships of Somerville's command withdrew from Trincomalee in Ceylon to a safer base at Kilindini in East Africa (near Mombasa in Kenya). From there, in the months that followed, some of these vessels – especially two fleet carriers and a number of destroyers – were transferred to other theatres.[74] Somerville's big ships were reduced to three old battleships when his last carrier (the *Illustrious*) departed in January 1943, and even those three were redeployed or sent home in the months that followed. There was some build-up of RAF land-based strength on Ceylon, but not enough to guarantee full security against Japanese raids, and the aircraft involved lacked the range to support operations on the far side of the Bay of Bengal.

Fortunately for Somerville, the Japanese Navy did not after April 1942 mount a large-scale active threat in the Indian Ocean, and in September of 1943 he was able to move his (still weak) Eastern Fleet and its headquarters back to Ceylon. The main task of the Eastern Fleet was combating German and Japanese submarines in the Indian Ocean; U-boats were the greater problem, and a number of them had been redeployed to these waters when the Atlantic became too dangerous. Somerville had at his disposal a growing number of his own submarines, although few shipping targets were to be found in the Bay of Bengal.[75] Nevertheless, in January 1944 the British submarine *Tally-Ho* achieved the first combat success of the Eastern Fleet, when it sank the old Japanese light cruiser *Kuma* off the Malayan port of Penang.

For military, political, imperial and strategic-diplomatic reasons, the British, and especially Prime Minister Churchill, did not wish to appear passive in Southeast Asia. At the end of August 1943 Lord Louis Mountbatten – now an (acting) full admiral at age forty-three – was appointed Supreme Commander of a new Southeast Asia Command (SEAC), with its headquarters in Delhi. 'Dickie' Mountbatten was related to the British royal family, and Churchill backed him as an energetic leader, an officer with top-level experience, to become head of Combined Operations. It was hoped that he had the prestige and ability to co-ordinate the forces of the Empire, the US and China in this theatre. Mountbatten was not, in the end, able to achieve much in military terms, and even in his own professional sphere of the Royal Navy he and Admiral Somerville became ensnared in prolonged controversies. (As Arthur Marder wryly put it, 'Not having the Japanese to fight, the Admirals fought one another.'[76]) Somerville came to resent the advancement of a much younger man, but there were also issues of principle regarding the degree of centralisation imposed on the three local Cs-in-C (for the Army, Navy and RAF). Admiral Andrew Cunningham fully shared the sentiments of his close friend Somerville, and he made his influence felt when he became First Sea Lord in October 1943.

The Japanese Navy, meanwhile, had taken little active interest in the Indian Ocean since the April 1942 Nagumo raid, but the evident danger of a British offensive was growing by the summer and autumn of 1943. The Axis had lost North Africa and Sicily, and a naval officer of the stature of Lord Mountbatten had been appointed to a new Southeast Asia Command. When the new C-in-C of the Combined Fleet, Admiral Koga, devised his overall strategy in the summer of 1943 there were four interception zones in the Indian Ocean, for what were called 'Y' counter-attack operations using the ships and aircraft of the Japanese Navy; these paralleled the seven zones in the Pacific (for 'Z' operations).

In lieu of ANAKIM, various smaller Allied operations were projected in the SEAC era. The first was Operation BUCCANEER, the capture of the Andaman Islands, which lay about 350 miles out in the Bay of Bengal, off southwestern Burma. This plan dated back to the spring of 1943, and was dusted off by Mountbatten at the Cairo/SEXTANT Conference in November 1943. It fell through due to demands for resources in other global theatres, especially the Mediterranean. Most of the amphibious shipping that had been assembled in the Indian Ocean was sent back to Europe at the beginning of January 1944.[77]

Another operation, an invasion of the extreme northeast tip of Sumatra, had also been proposed in the spring of 1943. It was revived in early 1944, under the code name CULVERIN, and it had the strong support of the Prime Minister, the civilians in the British War Cabinet and Admiral Mountbatten. By this time, however, the Sumatra landing was strongly opposed by the British Chiefs of Staff (especially Admiral Cunningham); the military planners were now looking at operations in the Pacific as opposed to the Bay of Bengal, especially for the ships of the Royal Navy.

It was, indeed, not until the beginning of 1944 that the Admiralty could start reinforcing the Eastern Fleet. The Mediterranean route was open, and Mussolini's fleet had surrendered (although it took some time to prepare war-weary British ships for the Far East). Increasing numbers of American-built naval aircraft were becoming available to boost the striking power and air defence of British carriers. The Atlantic situation was also better, with the sinking of the *Scharnhorst* in December 1943, and serious damage inflicted on the *Tirpitz* in September 1943 and April 1944. Three modernised big-gun ships arrived in Ceylon in January 1944: the battle cruiser *Renown*, which was the sister ship of the *Repulse*, and the battleships *Queen Elizabeth* and *Valiant*, which had been the victims of the Italian limpet mine attack in Alexandria in December 1941. With them returned the carrier *Illustrious*, now equipped with modern aircraft, big American-supplied Corsair fighters and British monoplane Barracuda torpedo planes.

There was concern in Somerville's headquarters in Colombo when a large part of the Japanese fleet was suddenly re-based from the Central Pacific to Singapore in late February 1944. This was, in fact, the result of the successful American carrier raids on the bases in Rabaul and Truk. By early 1944 Admiral

Koga and his successor Admiral Toyoda expected to deal with any threat in the Indian Ocean not with the main body of the Combined Fleet, but rather by the transfer of land-based naval bomber units. (The Japanese did, however, attempt one cruiser raid into the Indian Ocean in March 1944, described in the previous chapter.) In the background was a final rash offensive by the Japanese Army launched from northern Burma towards Assam in India at the end of March 1944. This led to major defensive victories by British Empire ground forces at Kohima and Imphal (from April to June 1944), and the precipitate retreat of the fatally weakened Japanese invasion force. It was the largest defeat suffered by the Imperial Army thus far in the war.[78]

In April 1944, after twenty-eight months, the Eastern Fleet finally mounted a successful offensive, albeit on a small scale. Operation COCKPIT took place in the Bay of Bengal, a carrier air strike against Japanese installations on the island of Sabang. The objective lay just off the northwestern tip of Sumatra, by the northern entrance to the Malacca Strait. Sabang had an important airfield and a radar station, as well as harbour facilities and oil tanks. The raid was partly intended to divert Japanese naval forces at the time of General MacArthur's invasion of Hollandia in New Guinea.[79] Admiral Somerville commanded two task groups with a uniquely inter-Allied mix of British, American, French, Dutch and New Zealand ships; it was much the largest force that the Eastern Fleet had put into combat. The strike group comprised the fleet carriers HMS *Illustrious* and USS *Saratoga* (the big American ship being on loan from Admiral Nimitz). Accompanying the carriers were the *Renown*, a British cruiser and six destroyers. The second, support, task group included three battleships; Somerville himself was with this force, flying his flag in the *Queen Elizabeth*; the two other battleships were the *Valiant* and the French *Richelieu*. With them were four cruisers and nine destroyers. The Sabang raid was by its nature a trial run, and there was a single British attack, mounted by forty-six strike aircraft.

A more ambitious air attack (Operation TRANSOM) came a month later, on 17 May 1944. Planes from the *Saratoga* and the *Illustrious* struck oil installations and port facilities at Surabaya. The target was on Java, much further from Trincomalee, and close to the heart of Japanese power in the former Dutch East Indies. The operation had involved a long advance voyage with a refuelling stop at Port Exmouth in northwestern Australia. With MacArthur's landing at Biak on the eastern flank of the Dutch East Indies coming only ten days later (27 May 1944), it is not surprising that the Japanese Navy precipitately reinforced this area (Operation KON).

The last major air strike under Somerville's command (Operation CRIMSON) occurred in late July 1944, a month after the Japanese defeat at the Battle of the

Philippine Sea. The target was again Sabang, but the attack was significant for being an all-British air operation, mounted by the carriers *Illustrious* and *Victorious*. The air strike was followed by a battleship bombardment delivered by four big-gun ships.

In August 1944 Admiral Bruce Fraser arrived to take over from Somerville as C-in-C of the Eastern Fleet. Somerville's replacement had been on the cards since January 1944, partly because he was required as an influential 'fighting admiral' to head the British Admiralty Delegation (BAD) in Washington. The transfer of major ships to the Eastern Fleet had continued. The *Victorious* and the *Indomitable* joined the *Illustrious* in July 1944, and the first new battleship since the *Prince of Wales* in 1941 arrived in the form of the *Howe* in August. With the transfer of big ships from the Home Fleet, one participant described Trincomalee as 'Scapa Flow in technicolour'.[80] By this time, however, the decision had been taken to mount the main activity of the Royal Navy in the Pacific (rather than the Indian Ocean), with a major base at Sydney in eastern Australia. In late November Admiral Fraser's command became the British Pacific Fleet, and the Eastern Fleet ceased to exist. The most powerful warships left Ceylon for Sydney in December 1944.

Operations in the Bay of Bengal were left to a new East Indies Fleet, still based in Ceylon. These were older and smaller vessels, and the main air component was provided by half a dozen British escort carriers. By this time the Japanese naval forces in Southeast Asia had been reduced to a handful of ships and aircraft, all effectively cut off from Japan. There was a surprising spurt of British success in the last months of the fighting. In May 1945 the mission of the heavy cruiser *Haguro* to re-supply the Andaman Islands was revealed by Ultra, and the ship was ambushed and sunk in the Malacca Strait by a flotilla of British destroyers. It was seen on the British side as revenge for the Battle of the Java Sea in 1942, in which the *Haguro* had played a prominent part. In June the submarine *Trenchant* torpedoed and sank another heavy cruiser, the *Ashigara*, in the Bangka Strait off southern Sumatra. And at the very end of July 1945 two midget submarines, *XE-1* and *XE-3*, penetrated into Singapore harbour and set off limpet mines to immobilise the heavy cruiser *Takao* at her moorings in Johore Strait, on the north side of Singapore Island.[81]

By 1945, reinforced British Empire ground forces were able to successfully advance into Burma from the north, under General William 'Bill' Slim. They captured the inland centre of Mandalay in March. The East Indies Fleet executed long-delayed but small-scale operations on the Arakan coast of northwestern Burma, sometimes meeting resistance, more often after the Japanese ground forces had pulled out. A major landing at Rangoon, now code-named Operation DRACULA, was finally carried out on 1 May 1945, covered by six escort carriers.

The main pressure had been from Slim's armies to the north, however, and the Japanese Army had already abandoned the city.

* * *

In the fourth period of World War II, from January 1943 to June 1944, the Allies had won victory after victory. The home territories of Germany and Japan were not yet directly threatened by Allied offensives; Japan was not even under air bombardment. The Allies were still rolling back some of the initial conquests of Germany and Japan, and there were static areas like China, Southeast Asia and even northwestern Europe. Yet steady advances had been achieved, with few setbacks. Fascist Italy was knocked out of the war. From the summer of 1943 the Red Army never lost the initiative, although it was still fighting to liberate territory deep within Soviet borders. The cross-Channel attack and the resumption of ground war in Western Europe remained the great challenge of the war.

Before November 1942 the ground and air forces of the United States had seen little action against the European Axis powers. In 1943–44 the commitment greatly increased, with American soldiers now fighting in North Africa, Sicily and mainland Italy, and – especially in the first half of 1944 – being transported in large numbers to the United Kingdom in preparation for the cross-Channel invasion. Many USAAF fighter and bomber groups were also despatched across the Atlantic, for operations over the Mediterranean and in northwestern Europe. Contrary to initial Allied – and Japanese – strategic expectations, the US also continued to commit ground, air and – especially – naval forces to offensives in the South and Central Pacific in 1943–44. While 1942 had seemed a year of desperate defence against Japan, 1943–44 had been a time of uninterrupted advance.

The leadership of the Axis navies was not a decisive factor, but changes during this period of the war had been symptomatic. The traditionally minded Admiral Raeder was removed as head of the Kriegsmarine, replaced by the U-boat advocate Dönitz, as the fourth period began, in January 1943. Admiral Yamamoto was killed, and replaced as C-in-C of the Combined Fleet by Koga – who also died in the line of duty – and then by Toyoda. Admiral Iachino, the Italian battle fleet commander, was replaced in the spring of 1943; his successor, Bergamini, perished in September aboard the *Roma*.

On the Allied side, the poor health of Admiral Pound finally led to his retirement as First Sea Lord in September 1943; his replacement, Andrew Cunningham, was an officer with the most successful combat career of any of the national fleet commanders. The Labour politician A.V. Alexander remained as civilian head of the Royal Navy – First Lord of the Admiralty – although Churchill as Prime Minister and Minister of Defence kept a strong proprietary interest. The Navy in which there was less major change at the top was that of the US. Secretary of the Navy Knox died in April 1944 and was replaced by the more effective James Forrestal; both men, however, had an administrative/political role rather than an operational one. Admiral King remained as CNO/COMINCH and as a strong advocate of the US Navy and the Pacific war among the top-level decision-makers in Washington and at Allied conferences. Admiral Nimitz, ashore at Pearl Harbor, had great success as CINCPAC. Of the sea-going admirals the most important in this period was surely Raymond Spruance.[82] In the Atlantic, Admiral Fraser, the C-in-C of the British Home Fleet, conducted operations which eliminated or gravely damaged the last of the German battleships. Fraser would soon be ordered to take command in the Pacific. A different kind of operational success, comparable in its results, can be ascribed to the Royal Navy's Admiral Bert Ramsay, who planned and led the decisive Mediterranean amphibious operations.

The fleet actions of 1942 had worn down the pre-war strength of ships and aircraft on both sides. One feature of the following eighteen months – from January 1943 to June 1944 – was that the Axis powers suffered continuing heavy losses and could put very few replacements into service. The only new big-gun capital ship in any of the Axis navies was the ill-fated *Roma*; the only other major ships commissioned by the Italians were two more small cruisers. The Kriegsmarine received no new heavy ships, and on Hitler's orders some of the existing units were reduced to a training role. The Japanese brought into service one new full-size carrier (the *Taihō*), two light carriers and two light cruisers.

In contrast, the Americans and British suffered very low losses in this fourth period and were able to commission a great many large modern warships as their shipbuilding programmes reached their full potential. This was especially true for the United States, with the results that have been detailed in this chapter. The Royal Navy expanded on a much smaller scale in terms of major warships, but it did commission a fifth fleet carrier (the *Indefatigable*) and two new battleships (the *Howe* and the *Anson*), as well as eight light cruisers. Numerically most important had been the introduction of the Allied escort carriers. Too slow and too vulnerable to take part in fleet battles, they provided invaluable air support for shipping protection and amphibious operations.

The smaller escort ships were still a priority in the eighteen months from the start of 1943. They now reached the Allied fleets in very large numbers, especially when the destroyer escort (DE) programme finally came on stream. The Japanese, with their decisive-battle orientation, had concentrated their limited efforts on developing their battle fleet and did not begin to turn their efforts to building escorts until late 1943 or early 1944. The two surviving major Axis states were very different. The Japanese never made any serious attempt to assemble sea or air forces to attack Allied supply routes in the Pacific. The Germans, in contrast, devoted their naval production almost exclusively to submarines, and 1943 saw large increases in U-boat completions, as well as the preliminary introduction of innovations like acoustically guided torpedoes and the snorkel. The end of the period (mid-1944) saw the Germans beginning a fundamental transition to high-speed U-boats – which they would never be able to follow through.

In what had become increasingly a sea/air war, the Allies overwhelmed their enemies in 1943–44 in terms of availability and quality of aircraft and trained naval aircrew. The Germans and the Italians still did not develop even land-based anti-shipping aircraft in any quantity. Potentially their most significant development was the introduction of two types of anti-ship guided missiles (the Henschel Hs 293 and the Fritz X), but these were used only on a small scale. The Japanese Navy manufactured many aircraft for service from carriers and land bases. On the other hand, they had still not introduced, by mid-1944, replacements for their first generation of wartime aircraft, and the island-based defence strategy using land-based naval aviation proved to be very unrealistic. The Americans and British not only built far more aircraft, but also brought into service new types which gave them a clear qualitative superiority. The F6F Hellcat and F4U Corsair, serving with the US Navy and Marines and the Royal Navy, and the British Seafire, now provided air defence over Allied task forces; even the Fleet Air Arm now had modern strike aircraft. Also extremely important was the provision of land-based radar-equipped four-engined bombers for the A/S war.

Neither the Germans nor the Japanese had been able to develop a major amphibious capability, and they now had no hope of taking the initiative in this area, or even of preparing counter-landings. Satisfactory co-operation between the various services could not be achieved even in defence of coastal and island territories. Again, the Americans and British now devoted huge resources to deploying amphibious vessels of all shapes and sizes, from ocean-going 'combat loaders' (attack transports) and LSTs, to thousands of craft for landing troops and vehicles, even under hostile gunfire. How many of these vessels were available in the various theatres of war now determined Allied global strategy.

Backing this up was massive construction of Liberty ships, as well as emergency tankers. While it should not be forgotten that the tonnage of the pre-war British Merchant Navy had provided an incomparable shipping reserve from the outbreak of the war, the end of 1942 did see merchant ship construction overtake losses. Then in the course of 1943 and 1944 the quantity of 'merchant' shipbuilding, especially in the United States, greatly increased. Crucially, it gave the western Allies the continuing ability to run a network of huge strategic/

economic convoys, ferry troops and supplies long distances and support great amphibious expeditions. In this respect the opening of the shipping route through the Mediterranean was an event of great importance.

The Allied naval victory in 1943–44 was most obvious in the Mediterranean, where the Italian fleet surrendered and came fully under Allied control. The Luftwaffe, along with a few U-boats, remained the only impediment to Allied domination of the Mediterranean Sea. In the Atlantic the few surviving large German surface ships were now discounted by Hitler; they served as a weak 'fleet in being' in northern Norway, especially after the sinking of the *Scharnhorst* and the damaging of the *Tirpitz*. The Japanese battle fleet, especially the carrier force, had been much larger and more effective than its German or Italian equivalents. Japanese shore-based air units were better than their Italian equivalent although, in this period of the war, they achieved no more success than the Luftwaffe. Nevertheless, when the Combined Fleet finally committed itself – after eighteen months – to a full-scale sea/air engagement to defend the Marianas it suffered clear defeat.

As well as defeating the enemy fleets in battle, the Allies also won the shipping war. The defeat of the U-boats is appropriately dated from the decision by Admiral Dönitz to withdraw his submarines from the central Atlantic in May 1943. This is often explained by single factors like codebreaking successes or the extension of the range of some A/S aircraft, but the largely British victory had much broader and deeper roots. Fortunately for the Americans, they never met any similar submarine challenge in the Pacific. This complex victory, defeat of the enemy battle fleets and defeat of enemy submarines, meant that the British and Americans had won effective command of the seas and could move supplies and troops globally. Meanwhile by 1943 and early 1944 the US Navy passed a different, victorious, turning point in its own war fought by submarines and aircraft against enemy shipping in the Pacific. The Japanese had failed to develop A/S forces on anything like the scale or capability of the Allies in the Atlantic.

Last, and certainly not least, in the fourth period the British and Americans demonstrated a mastery of long-range amphibious warfare. The invasion of Sicily (Operation HUSKY) in July 1943 was the first 'mature' large-scale amphibious operation, combining mass, range and special technologies, and engaging an enemy with at least a degree of combat motivation in a semi-continental theatre. The invasion of the Marshall Islands (Kwajalein Atoll) in February 1944 demonstrated for the first time American mastery of a different kind of amphibious operation, a long-range *assault* against a very heavily (and fanatically) defended position.

The Battle of the Philippine Sea in June 1944 makes a fitting end to the fourth period. If, territorially, their victory was still far from complete, if the strategic bombing war had not delivered the results that some of its advocates had promised, the western Allies had already succeeded in defeating the navies of their enemies, and in reducing their strength to a level of near impotence. That success was a pre-condition for the overall defeat of the Axis.

PART V

COMMANDING THE SEAS, DEFEATING THE AXIS

JUNE 1944–AUGUST 1945

The roll call of the battles of this fleet reads like a sign post around the globe – on the road to final victory: North Africa, Sicily, Italy, Normandy, and Southern France; the Coral Sea, Midway, Guadalcanal, and the Solomons; Tarawa, Saipan, Guam, the Philippine Sea, Leyte Gulf; Iwo Jima and Okinawa. Nothing which the enemy held on any coast was safe from its attack.

President Harry S. Truman, US Navy Day Speech, 27 October 1945

CHAPTER 19

THE INVASION OF FRANCE AND THE DEFEAT OF THE THIRD REICH

NORMANDY ASSAULT FORCE G, 5–6 JUNE 1944

During Monday, 5 June 1944, World War II's largest, most complex and most important maritime operation – NEPTUNE – began. The objective ran for 50 miles along the Normandy coast, divided (from west to east) into areas code-named UTAH, OMAHA, GOLD, JUNO and SWORD.[1] The initial assault in each of these five areas would be fought by one Allied infantry division, or its equivalent.

The GOLD area was assigned to the British 50th (Northumbrian) Division. Assault Force G – for GOLD – departed from the Solent, near Southampton. The great number of vessels making up Force G were of widely different types and speeds: landing craft and towed barges; minesweepers; ocean-going transport ships; cruisers and destroyers. Because of this, they left port in eighteen convoys at different times throughout the 5th, starting at 9.45 a.m. The eight big transport ships, with the bulk of the assault infantry for GOLD, were among the last to depart, at about 7.30 in the evening.[2]

All the Force G convoys sailed past the Needles, landmark chalk stacks at the western end of the Isle of Wight, and then east along the island's Channel coast. One soldier, Alexander Baron, recalled this beginning:

> A few of the men stood listlessly at the rails, watching the Needles slowly drop back and become indiscernible in the dusk. There was a strange, flat feeling, a sensation as of living suspended between two planets, as the ship crawled with maddening slowness across the grey, bleak sea, against the grey, bleak, evening sky. There was no shore to be seen, only the walls of purple dusk creeping in from the farthest limits of the sea; no sound to be heard but the thudding of the engines below decks . . .[3]

Force G had a relatively short crossing to GOLD. The assault convoys for UTAH, OMAHA, JUNO and SWORD – Assault Groups 'U', 'O', 'J' and 'S' – had to set out from ports further east and west. Most of the ships for all five landing areas passed through a rendezvous zone nicknamed 'Piccadilly Circus', south of the Isle of Wight, and then 60 miles down the so-called 'Spout' towards Normandy, through ten swept and buoyed channels. A very large force of sweepers had cleared a passage through the enemy's large mid-Channel minefield on the night of 5/6 June, the biggest such operation of the whole war.

The assault convoys had extensive air cover, and the flanks of the Spout were covered by many warships. Perhaps the most remarkable feature of the Channel crossing was that so few German attacks took place. Allied planners had decided on a night crossing and a dawn landing to avoid air attacks and obtain tactical surprise. Indeed, because Operation NEPTUNE as a whole achieved surprise and the Luftwaffe had been so weakened in previous battles, there were no air attacks at all. No U-boats patrolled the Channel; as for the handful of small Kriegsmarine surface vessels, the Force G channels lay in the centre of the Spout, and the ships in the channels were shielded from any attacks. German torpedo boats from Le Havre mounted a small dawn sortie against the warships covering Force S on the eastern flank but, even there, none of the transport ships were affected.

Before and after the Channel crossing, Force G was organised into three naval groups. G1 and G2 each transported a brigade (three battalions) of infantrymen, embarked on four ocean-going transport ships and between sixty and seventy big tank landing craft (LCTs). G1, with the *Empire Arquebus*, *Empire Crossbow*, *Empire Spearhead* and HMS *Glenroy*, carried the 231st Brigade. Aboard G2, with the *Empire Halberd*, *Empire Lance*, *Empire Mace* and *Empire Rapier*, was the 69th Brigade. The *Glenroy* had been one of the very first Royal Navy landing ships. Aboard her were twenty-three assault landing craft (LCAs); each 9-ton LCA could carry a platoon of infantry, about thirty troops. The other seven transports were brand-new, civilian-manned 'C1' class cargo ships received from the US in the previous few months; they each carried between sixteen and eighteen LCAs. The other element of G1 and G2, the sixty to seventy LCTs, were much bigger than the LCAs; they were 600-ton sea-going vessels, about 190 feet long. The load of an LCT was up to nine tanks or other vehicles; some LCTs had been modified as fire-support vessels.

The third group (G3), which would assemble off the invasion area a few hours after the other two, carried the two brigades of the 50th Division's reserve, the 56th Brigade and 151st Brigade. These men would begin to come ashore after the first landing, when the neighbourhood of the beachheads could be expected to be relatively secure; they were to advance 'through' the first wave of infantry and push inland. They were crammed into the sea-going workhorses of the

Allied amphibious war, the American-built infantry landing vessels – LCI(L)s; vehicles and other equipment were stowed aboard the tank landing ships (LSTs). Altogether in G3 there were twenty-one American- or Canadian-manned LCI(L) s, twenty-nine US Navy LSTs and a dozen more LCTs.

During the early hours of the morning Allied heavy bombers, first British and then, in the final ten minutes before H-Hour, American, dropped bombs into the coastal area which was to be attacked. A Fire-Support Group of four light cruisers, a gunboat and thirteen destroyers stood by to support GOLD, and at 5.30 a.m. the ships opened fire on previously identified targets – strongpoints and coastal guns. The first salvoes were delivered by the cruiser *Ajax*, veteran of the *Graf Spee* battle.

Shortly after dawn, having reached a position about 7 miles offshore, the transports lowered their LCAs. Troops climbed down scrambling nets and into the LCAs to begin the final two-hour passage to the shore. The morning was grey and cold; it was raining and there was a considerable swell. At GOLD, as in other areas, the initial assault was carried out by battle-hardened troops. The 50th Division had fought in the Mediterranean; the first-wave 231st Brigade had landed in Sicily and southern Italy in 1943, and the 69th Brigade had taken part in the Battle of El Alamein and the invasion of Sicily.

Months of reconnaissance had given the invading forces a good knowledge of the terrain and the defences. Elements of two German divisions were deployed near the GOLD beaches, and the physical coastal defences were a considerable factor. A variety of steel and wooden obstacles, many with German Army anti-vehicle mines attached, were a recent development; they had been put in place from February 1944 and were designed to block and damage approaching landing craft.

The Allied troops had to be carried as far up the beach as possible while they were in the relative safety of their LCAs. They could then debark and 'get forward' into cover on dry land. The assaults were timed to begin after dawn, when the tide was low – but rising – and the German defensive obstacles were above the water and visible. The lead elements – engineers – were supposed to clear the obstacles to provide safe channels through which the LCAs and LCTs, and follow-on vessels, could pass. Covering the GOLD beaches were around twenty German field guns (under 100mm), as well as the same number of larger guns (up to 122mm), half a dozen of these in casemated batteries. Many of the guns were positioned to fire not out to sea, but laterally across the beaches.[4] Allied aircraft and naval vessels would bombard the German guns, and special equipment was deployed to cut a path through the beach obstacles. Tanks would be landed first to support the infantry. The rough seas on 6 June meant that 'Duplex Drive' (DD) tanks fitted with flotation equipment could not be sent ahead to support the infantry as they landed.

H-Hour at GOLD was 7.25 a.m. Dennis Bowen (not yet nineteen years of age) landed on the KING beach of GOLD with the 5th Battalion of the East Yorkshire Regiment (231st Brigade):

> We were told in the LCA to 'get your bayonets on'. When the front of the LCA went down and I saw the beach it hit me that this was double serious. I was halfway down the craft and the first few off jumped into fairly shallow water, but with the swell going up and down we jumped into deeper water just above our knees . . . We were under fire as we landed. On the beach was a Sherman tank burning and every NCO was shouting 'get forward, get forward!'[5]

The land battle at GOLD, on 6 June and the first days that followed, progressed without unexpected difficulties. Some attacking elements were held up for a few hours by local German strongpoints, but others were able to move inland. Fortunately the terrain behind the GOLD beaches was low-lying and sandy. The exit inland did not involve heavy combat, although traffic was congested. The reserve brigades of the 50th Division came ashore at midday. They were followed in the later afternoon by part of Assault Group 'L', which had passed through the Dover Strait with the lead elements of the 7th Armoured Division and the 51st (Highland) Division. By the end of the day nearly 25,000 British troops had come ashore at GOLD (part of a total of 128,000 Allied troops landed on 6 June in the five areas). Losses – killed and wounded – to the 50th Division and supporting units on D-Day had been about 400 men.[6] (By contrast, the American V Corps at OMAHA suffered losses of about 3,000.)

The most ambitious first-day tactical objectives of the D-Day planners were not reached. But on the second day the British troops ashore at GOLD linked up with the Canadians to their left at JUNO; on the third day came the first contact with the Americans on their right at OMAHA. By Thursday, 8 June, the 56th Brigade had advanced 8 miles inland, to the town of Bayeux, with its important road junction.

THE INVASION OF FRANCE: OPERATION NEPTUNE

Detailed consideration of the cross-Channel expedition began in early 1943, when the British general Frederick Morgan was put in charge of a planning staff in London. Morgan's post was designated as COSSAC – Chief of Staff to the 'Supreme Allied Commander' (although no such 'commander' had yet been appointed). The western Allies were busy with the Mediterranean campaign, but at the TRIDENT Conference in Washington in May 1943 a target date of 1 May 1944 was set.

The COSSAC planners (COSSAC was both an individual – General Morgan – and an organisation) came to the conclusion that the Seine Bay was the best landing area, rather than the Pas-de-Calais to the east, with its shorter crossing. Histories of D-Day planning sometime forget the maritime advantages of the chosen landing area. The Seine Bay allowed assault convoys to depart from a large number of British ports at the eastern and western ends of the Channel and to converge in the centre. Landing in the Pas-de-Calais would have meant movement of the eastern assault forces through the Dover Strait, observed by German spotters and under long-range artillery fire. Shipping in the Seine Bay was also protected from westerly winds by the Cotentin Peninsula.

In the early versions of the plan the availability of landing craft limited the proposed initial assault force to a total of three divisions and a landing area 20 miles wide. Most of the warship force supporting the landings would have been British. The intention was to mount a simultaneous but smaller diversionary operation in the south of France (originally code-named ANVIL); by this time – the middle of 1943 – the Allies were in a reasonably strong position in the western Mediterranean.[7]

By January 1944, the first four operationally successful large-scale amphibious operations against the European Axis powers had been completed (Morocco/Algeria, Sicily, southern Italy, Anzio/Nettuno). The Allies had begun more concrete preparation for NEPTUNE.[8] In October 1943 Admiral Bertram Ramsay had joined the COSSAC staff as Allied Naval Commander, Expeditionary Force (ANCXF). (Admiral Andrew Cunningham had held a similar post at the time of the TORCH landings in North Africa.) Ramsay, formally still on the retired list, had organised the Dunkirk evacuation. As the tide of war turned he had served under Admiral Cunningham as deputy naval commander for Operation TORCH, and then as commander of the 'Eastern' (British) naval task force during the Sicily invasion. Ramsay became – perhaps even more than Kelly Turner in the US Navy – the world's leading expert on naval operations of this type. Unlike some of his naval colleagues, Ramsay was a firm believer in 'combined operations', involving close co-operation with the other services and with the Americans.

The American general Dwight D. Eisenhower was named Supreme Commander of the Allied Expeditionary Force in early December 1943; the commander of Eisenhower's ground forces was the British general Bernard Montgomery. Eisenhower and Montgomery agreed that the initial assault force for the cross-Channel invasion had to be strengthened, and the breadth of the landing zone extended from 20 to 50 miles, to increase the chances of seizing the port of Cherbourg. It was at this time, in the late winter of 1943–44, that UTAH and GOLD were added as invasion areas. In the end, as we have seen, five divisions were committed to the seaborne assault landing – as well as three airborne divisions.

The expansion of the cross-Channel assault forces had important consequences. Many more landing vessels and support ships were required. The target date was pushed back to 31 May 1944 to take advantage of another month's production of landing craft. The proposed simultaneous landings in southern France were now postponed to free up amphibious shipping. Also, what had been conceived as a largely British naval operation now required additional support from the US Navy. This was finally agreed by Admiral King in Washington as late as 15 April. Three outdated battleships were committed: the *Arkansas* and the *Texas*, and the Pearl Harbor survivor *Nevada*. Also available were three heavy cruisers, the *Augusta*, and the *Tuscaloosa* and the brand-new 'Baltimore' class *Quincy*. More important for direct fire support at UTAH and OMAHA on D-Day would be two dozen American destroyers. Nevertheless, of 1,213 combatant ships involved, 79 per cent (about 960 vessels) were British, and 16.5 per cent (about 200) American.[9] The Allied naval effort was immense, nearly 7,000 combatant and transport vessels, including 4,000 landing vessels, half of which would cross the Channel under their own power, with the other half towed or carried aboard larger ships. Large naval screening forces were assigned to protect the transit route, with destroyers and MTBs covering both flanks, especially the western side. Beyond Land's End in Cornwall three escort carriers and ten anti-submarine escort groups, supported by Allied maritime patrol aircraft, were to stand guard against the U-boats.

As for the Germans, their thinking regarding the defence of the coastline of Western Europe was based largely on ground forces, and to some extent on the Luftwaffe. Admiral Theodor Krancke had since April 1943 been C-in-C of Navy Group West (with his headquarters in the Bois de Boulogne in Paris). In 1940–41 he had commanded the heavy cruiser *Admiral Scheer* in the Kriegsmarine's most successful oceanic raiding expedition. Now the surface striking forces at his disposal were extremely weak: three operational destroyers based on the Biscay coast, and five modern fleet torpedo boats and thirty-four MTBs (S-boats) based in the Channel.

Although the *Atlantikwall* had featured prominently in German propaganda, it had developed slowly. Defensive preparation along the French coast was accelerated by Hitler's Directive No. 51 of November 1943, which was concerned mainly with ground forces; shortly afterwards Field Marshal Rommel took over the task of preparing coastal defences. It was only in the late winter of 1943–44 that extensive beach obstacles began to be put in place.

The months of preparation complete, the great invasion could begin. The final date set for NEPTUNE was 5 June 1944. The weather began to worsen on Saturday, 3 June, and early on the 4th, based on forecasts, General Eisenhower decided to put off the assault for a day. Although the local weather was even worse during the 4th, the prediction of the meteorologists in the afternoon was that the weather would be better in two days' time. Early the following morning (the 5th), the general made the weighty decision that the operation would go ahead on the 6th. Most of the invasion armada had stayed snug in harbour, but part of the UTAH force, which had the longest approach time (from ports in the West Country), had sailed on the evening of the 3rd and failed to receive the postponement signal. The troops aboard had to spend extra hours in rough seas, a special problem for the men aboard the (smaller and less seaworthy) LCTs.

The German defences were not on the alert, and in this respect the brisk weather helped the Allies. Surface patrols had been kept in harbour on the night of 5/6 June, and there was no air surveillance over the Channel. The Germans did not see Allied minesweepers operating close to the French coast before dark on the evening of the 5th. As had been the case in the invasion of Sicily in 1943, enemy inaction bred a sense of unreality. 'As our forces approached the French coast without a murmur from the enemy or from their own radio', Admiral Ramsay later recalled, 'the realization that . . . almost complete tactical surprise had been achieved slowly dawned.' Such a situation 'had always seemed extremely unlikely'.[10] This was the final refutation of Hitler's boast in February 1941 that German forces would decisively block any attempt to land forces on the Continent.

The Allies placed exaggerated hopes on attacks by heavy bombers to 'soften up' the defending forces, but the bombs had little effect on D-Day, either on the coastal batteries or on enemy troops in the assault areas; they fell well inland. On the German side some fleet torpedo boats sortied from Le Havre, but although they fired a barrage of torpedoes and sank a new Norwegian-manned destroyer, they quickly withdrew. British heavy ships were stationed on the eastern flank to engage the heavy coastal batteries between the Orne river and Le Havre, and these were for the most part effectively neutralised.

Events on the beaches varied considerably across the five assault areas. Historians (and film-makers) have tended to concentrate on OMAHA, and on the period after the landing craft beached. OMAHA certainly turned out to be the most difficult. This was partly because of the terrain, and partly because of the unexpected presence behind the beaches of a quantity of effective German troops. It was also partly because of American planning decisions (including a long – 12-mile – approach by landing craft, and only a short preliminary naval bombardment). Of thirty-two DD tanks (amphibious Shermans) launched at 6,000 yards, twenty-seven foundered.[11] The other American landing, at UTAH, went much better, despite strong currents that pushed the initial assault force over a mile from its target beach. The British landings at GOLD and SWORD, and the Canadian landing at JUNO were also less difficult. Although fierce battles took place, all the beach areas – including OMAHA – were secured by the end of 6 June. Fire support of the eight American and three British destroyers off OMAHA was vital. In the next few days the advance was not as rapid as the planners had hoped, but the invading groups established a continuous front and thrust inland.

In this war of sea/air battles the most surprising feature – both for Allied commanders and for historians – was the weakness of attacks by the Luftwaffe against the invasion fleet during and after D-Day; this certainly contrasted with events at Salerno or Anzio. Allied fighters based in England – and very quickly in northern France – were able to install a stout shield over the battlefield. The Luftwaffe fighter force had been weakened in recent air battles over the Reich, and the damage to airfields and ground communications in France, made it much harder than expected to bring in reinforcement aircraft.

Having done nothing to block the initial landing, the Luftwaffe could do little to slow the transit of reinforcements across the Channel or the unloading activities on the French coast. Night raids by individual low-flying German aircraft were mounted on a considerable scale, but had limited effect. The bombers made use of a new weapon, held back for the invasion, the air-dropped pressure mine. Lying on the bottom in shallow water, it was triggered by changes of water pressure as a ship passed over it. The British quickly developed effective countermeasures. Among the Luftwaffe formations that suffered heavy losses over Normandy were KG 26 and KG 30, anti-shipping units, still flying the same bomber, the Junkers Ju 88, with which they had played such a big part in 1939–40.

Less surprising was the German Navy's continued failure as the battle progressed. Allied sea power had already defeated Germany in the Atlantic and the Channel. The negligible surface forces remaining – a handful of destroyers, fleet torpedo boats and S-boats – based on either side of the assault area, at Cherbourg (to the west), and Le Havre (to the east), could achieve little in the face of powerful Allied screening groups. On the night of 8/9 June three destroyers and a fleet torpedo boat sortied from Brest, but they were ambushed by a British destroyer flotilla and two ships were sunk. The potential of German MTBs had been demonstrated in a night attack in April 1944. Nine S-boats from Cherbourg fell upon an American LST convoy during an invasion rehearsal off the Devon coast at Slapton Sands. Two of the landing ships were sunk and two damaged, and nearly 1,000 American soldiers and sailors died. During the actual invasion two months later the S-boats accounted for a few Allied ships, but the German force was quickly worn down. On the night of 14/15 June (D+8) a heavy raid by Allied bombers sank three torpedo boats, 10 S-boats and numerous small craft in Le Havre.

The Germans had designated thirty-five U-boats – the LANDWIRT ('Farmer') group – as an anti-invasion force, but they achieved almost nothing. After the initial landing some nineteen of the boats were deployed to form a screen off the

French Biscay coast to guard against a second landing which never came. The nine boats, equipped with the new snorkel device and thus able to cruise continuously submerged, took station south of the Isle of Wight, and seven non-snorkel boats were at the western entrance to the Channel. These were effectively neutralised by Allied A/S forces.[12] Least effective of all were the German naval 'special forces' which became operational in the Channel in early July. These consisted of 'small battle units' (*Kleinkampfverbände* or *K-Verbände*) – midget submarines of the Marder type and explosive motorboats inspired by Italian successes in the Mediterranean.

Mines proved to be the most effective weapon against invasion shipping, accounting for 80 per cent of Allied losses.[13] In a little-recalled episode, five American destroyers were lost after striking mines off UTAH on 6–8 June. On 23 June, the light cruiser *Scylla*, flagship of the Eastern Task Force commander (Admiral Vian) was mined; although towed home, she would never be repaired.

The events of the land campaign in Normandy in the following weeks and months are well known. In the first ten days, 279,000 British and Canadian troops and 278,000 Americans were brought ashore, along with a total of 81,000 vehicles.[14] A severe storm on 19–22 June, with unexpected northeasterly winds, caused damage in the crowded beach areas and among unseaworthy tows in the mid-Channel. It wrecked the ingeniously designed artificial harbour, MULBERRY, off the OMAHA landing area. The second MULBERRY, half-finished at Arromanches, was also damaged but it continued to provide some shelter. So too did the five GOOSEBERRY (block ship) breakwaters at the five landing areas.

Fortunately the flow of supplies could be maintained. In the event only about a third of British stores came through the MULBERRY; half came across the beaches (sheltered by the GOOSEBERRY breakwaters), and the remainder through two small ports.[15] In addition, the Americans captured the important port of Cherbourg at the top of the Cotentin Peninsula on 26 June, with the support of a heavy naval bombardment by three American battleships and four cruisers; the place had been garrisoned by 21,000 German troops. Two days later, an outraged Hitler ordered the dismissal of General Friedrich Dollmann, commander of the Seventh Army in Normandy. It took three months for Allied engineers fully to make good the German demolition work at Cherbourg and to remove scuttled ships, but they had had the valuable experience of clearing Naples harbour.

Allied troops poured in through a constant cross-Channel ferry service, and now these ground forces contained a larger American component. By the end of the campaign in Normandy, in late August, 830,000 British Empire troops had been landed, and half as many Americans again (1.2 million). Also ashore were a total of 440,000 Allied vehicles and 3.1 million tons of stores.[16]

The Wehrmacht did not commit all its forces to the Normandy campaign, because its commanders expected a second landing in the Pas-de-Calais area, and this in turn was partly thanks to Allied 'deception' (Operation FORTITUDE). The German defenders attempted to contain the Normandy bridgehead, but concentrated on the eastern, British–Canadian, sector. Seven weeks after the original invasion, on 25 July, the Americans began an armoured breakout (Operation COBRA) from the western sector. With that, the German position in northern France began to collapse; after another month, on 25 August, Paris was liberated. This was roughly on the time-scale planned before D-Day, although the campaign developed quite differently from what had been expected; the original plan had been to secure the line of the Loire, before advancing east. Meanwhile on 15 August the amphibious invasion of southern France (Operation DRAGOON) was successfully carried out against limited German resistance.

After the end of the Normandy campaign there were only limited naval operations in Western European waters. Nevertheless, maritime factors were still extremely important. The build-up and supply of the Allied armies in the west – especially the all-important US Army – and their continued advance towards the Reich were dependent on maritime transport and on the availability of large deep-water ports.

While on D-Day and in the early weeks of the campaign the ground forces deployed in Normandy had been about the same size for the US and the British Empire, in the months that followed the American share became much larger. By the end of June the British and the Americans had each transported the equivalent of fifteen to sixteen divisions across the Channel, and the number for the British/Canadian armies would never be more than twenty. There were nine more American divisions in Britain, awaiting movement to the Continent, but only six more British or Canadian ones, and their top limit had been reached. The United States now had as many divisions again in the build-up pipeline, and the number of divisions committed to OVERLORD up to the end of the war would be sixty-one.[17] One indication of this is the number of convoys from North America, shown in Table 19.1.

Ports and maritime supply 'throughput' were crucial elements in the eventual Allied land victory in Western Europe. Cherbourg, in the original Normandy 'lodgement' area, was of vital importance, although the port was not fully functional until late September. The original Allied plan – before D-Day – had been to capture and develop supply and reinforcement ports in Brittany (Brest) and on the Biscay coast (Bordeaux, Saint-Nazaire). The Germans, however, as part of Hitler's strategy of creating 'fortress' strongpoints, held out in the western coastal ports, in some cases doing so until the end of the war. In any event the American breakout, when it came in late July, turned mainly east towards Paris

Table 19.1. Troop Movements across the Atlantic (Eastbound), June–December 1944

Month	Convoys	Personnel
Jun	14	126,700
Jul	19	171,700
Aug	15	169,300
Sept	17	99,100
Oct	15	173,500
Nov	13	176,900
Dec	18	150,000
Total	111	1,067,200

Source: Rosk/3.2, p. 431.
Notes: 'Personnel' includes all services.

to take advantage of the German collapse in Normandy, rather than west to consolidate supply lines. A secondary American thrust *was* directed to the west, but a month of hard fighting, and another big naval bombardment, were required to secure Brest (the garrison surrendered on 19 September). The port was in a much damaged state and now a long way from the front line; Allied engineers – with other urgent priorities – did not hurry to repair it.

The Canadian Army, advancing east up the French coast from the Normandy lodgement area, took Le Havre after a short siege on 12 September. In that port (and in nearby Rouen) considerable time was also required to make good German sabotage, but this was achieved. Contrary to original plans, many of the American reinforcement divisions would debark through this 'British' port complex. The German Army was able to hold a position on the Rhine–Meuse–Scheldt delta just north of Antwerp, so the big Dutch ports of Rotterdam and Amsterdam were still unavailable to the Allies as supply ports. Bremen and Hamburg, the other great European ports, were in the Reich itself and even further away. They would not be in Allied hands until the last days of the war.

From this point of view, the capture in late August 1944 of Marseille, Toulon and smaller Mediterranean ports in a relatively undamaged state after Operation DRAGOON was important for supplying the armies; they also served as an arrival route for American reinforcements (see Table 19.2).[18] These troops eventually operated at the southern end of the Allied line; they crossed the Rhine into Germany with the Sixth Army Group.

General Montgomery's failure to secure the approaches to Antwerp turned out to be a most serious oversight. The big Belgian port on the Scheldt river was captured on 6 September with the help of the local resistance, its port facilities largely intact. Unfortunately the lower Scheldt remained under German control, and as a result access to the port from the sea was still blocked. The Scheldt

Table 19.2. Allied Divisions Disembarked in France, 1944–45

	1944			1945		Total
	Jun	Jul–Sept	Oct–Dec	Jan–Mar	Apr–May	
Channel beaches						
British/Canadian	12	2	0	0	0	14
US	10	12	1	0	0	23
French	0	1	0	0	0	1
Polish	0	1	0	0	0	1
Channel ports						
British/Canadian	0	0	1	0	0	1
US	0	6	8	12	0	26
French	0	1	0	0	0	1
South of France						
British/Canadian	0	0	0	2	0	2
US	0	3	6	0	0	9
French	0	5	1	0	0	6
Total	22	31	17	14	0	84

Notes: Divisions deployed against Germany in northwest Europe in 1944–45 were nearly all sent across French beaches or through French ports. The Channel ports used for major troop movements were Cherbourg and Le Havre; in the south of France Marseille was the port of entry. The British 52nd Division, the only formation not sent through France, debarked in Ostend (Belgium) in October 1944. The US 17th Division was deployed by air in December 1944.

campaign was fought in September and October, involving shore-to-shore landing operations, and it was not until the end of November that Antwerp was open for Allied shipping. The city was the object of heavy attack by German V1 flying bombs and V2 ballistic missiles up to the end of March 1945; the accuracy and reliability of the V-weapons were poor, and the port continued to function.[19] The last major German counter-offensive in the west, the 'Battle of the Bulge', began in the Belgian Ardennes in mid-December 1944. The fighting was well inland, so naval forces played no combat role. Nevertheless, Antwerp was the major objective of the Panzer attack, which was halted before the end of the month. After the western Allies regained the initiative in January they began preparing for a crossing of the Rhine, which took place in early April 1945 and in part used naval landing craft transported by road.

The all-important flow of reinforcements across French beaches and then through French ports during these last nine months went largely unchallenged by the German naval or air forces. The *U 486*, a snorkel-equipped Type VIIC operating from Norway, did succeed in torpedoing the big troopship *Léopoldville* just off Cherbourg on Christmas Eve, 1944. During the crisis in the Ardennes reinforcements had been ordered to the Continent; two regiments of the American 66th Division had embarked in the *Léopoldville* at Southampton. About 760 American soldiers died in the cold waters of the Channel after a badly handled rescue operation. (The *U 486* executed a lethal cruise in the

Channel; she also sank two British frigates with acoustic torpedoes, and another cargo ship.) But this kind of setback for the Allies was very rare.

THE END OF THE BATTLE OF THE ATLANTIC, JUNE 1944–MAY 1945

It is misleading to use the term 'Battle of the *Atlantic*' to describe the U-boat war in these last months of the fighting, at least from the autumn of 1944. Few enemy submarines were operating in the open ocean. The Kriegsmarine had lost effective use of the French ports, a very significant setback. The snorkel U-boats at sea were mostly lurking in British coastal waters, where they could survive but could not destroy Allied shipping on any scale. This was a distinct phase of the U-boat war, but one that was irrelevant in strategic terms.

Table 19.3 shows how little U-boat activity was taking place in the North Atlantic in the last year of the war; only one or two Allied merchant ships were sunk each month. Allied losses in the inshore waters of the United Kingdom were larger than before, and the figure of 233,000 tons includes losses resulting from both U-boat torpedo attacks and mines. In UK waters only 139,000 tons (fifty-six ships) had been lost in the eighteen months *before* July 1944 (a third in the month of the cross-Channel invasion). In the last year of the war only a handful of Allied merchant ships were lost in distant seas – the Mediterranean, the South Atlantic or the Indian Ocean.

Allied A/S warfare in the last year of the war, as in the eighteen months before that, was a campaign in which aircraft played a most important role. A

Table 19.3. The Battle of the Atlantic, June 1944–May 1945

Year/ quarter	N. Atlantic tonnage lost	N. Atlantic ships lost	UK waters tonnage lost	UK waters ships lost	U-boats oper.	U-boats t&t	U-boats lost
1944/iii	38,000	6	95,000	23	188	246	75
1944/iv	13,000	4	96,000	23	141	260	31
1945/i	85,000	13	179,000	54	144	281	64
1945/ii	37,000	6	54,000	16	166	263	72
Total	174,000	29	233,000	116			
Total (all theatres)	838,000	184					242

Source: Rosk/3.2, pp. 456, 464, 478–9.
Notes: Losses are for Allied and neutral countries' merchant ships due to enemy action *of all types*, not just due to U-boats. Tonnage is GRT. U-boat numbers are total for German Navy (all theatres) at the start of each quarter; 'oper.' is operational U-boats, 't&t' is units involved in training and trials. U-boat figures include losses from all causes and in all theatres. U-boats lost does not include vessels surrendered or sunk at the end of the war.

total of sixty-eight U-boats were destroyed at sea by shore-based aircraft, compared to seventy-seven sunk by surface ships. Meanwhile, the number of British and Canadian purpose-built escort ships in the critical North Atlantic theatre continued to grow. By the start of January 1945 there were 144 frigates (destroyer escorts) and 324 corvettes (120 of them Canadian). The Allies had continued to improve their A/S technique, notably with the Squid mortar integrated with advanced sonar.

The Kriegsmarine made belated attempts to catch up. As already mentioned, a programme to develop greatly improved submarines, the Type XXI and the smaller Type XXIII, had begun in mid-1943 (see p. 322). The advanced design of the electro-boat was combined with new shipbuilding techniques, especially prefabrication. The new submarines were made up of eight sections, each built at an efficient and dispersed inland site; only a short period of final assembly would take place in the shipyards vulnerable to bombing. In the longer term it was planned that even this final stage would take place in a hardened facility invulnerable to Allied air attacks. The most elaborate of these centres was eventually located on the Weser river on the outskirts of Bremen, but there were also facilities at Hamburg, Kiel and Danzig. A production rate of forty boats a month was anticipated. The British were able to follow the development of the Type XXI programme, thanks partly to air reconnaissance and the decryption of reports from the Japanese embassy in Berlin, and there was considerable alarm on the Allied side.

Fortunately for the Allies, the Type XXI turned out to be the least successful of Hitler's 'miracle weapons'. The jet fighters, flying bombs and rockets at least made it into limited active service. Development of the submarine took longer than promised, and the design had many technical shortcomings, partly because it had been rushed into series production without a prototype.[20] Even if a few dozen had been put into service and teething problems resolved, the electro-boat would certainly not have made a great impact on the sea war. For all its speed, it would still not have been able to locate and home in on convoys in the open Atlantic.[21]

By the middle of 1944 the northern convoy route to Russia could still be an extremely difficult and unpleasant one, but this was due to the weather; it was now relatively safe for Allied merchant ships. There were few losses in JW convoys, and a number of U-boats were sunk. Axis aircraft and surface ships no longer presented serious danger.

Unfinished business remained in the form of the crippled *Tirpitz*, the sister ship of the *Bismarck*. In September 1944 another major attack was mounted, this time by the RAF with Lancaster bombers. The only other British heavy bomber attack on the giant battleship had been an unsuccessful raid on Trondheim by a small number of four-engined Lancasters and Halifaxes in April 1942.[22] Now the *Tirpitz* was moored on the Altafjord, and the attackers did not come directly from Britain but staged through a Soviet airfield near Arkhangelsk. The crews were from No. 9 and 617 squadrons, the latter being the famous 'Dam Busters', and their planes mostly carried one 12,000lb Tallboy bomb each. Although they had to bomb through a German smoke screen, the Lancasters achieved one direct hit on the forward part of the big ship. None of the German crew were killed, but the *Tirpitz* was no longer operationally seaworthy. Full repairs, including fitting of a new bow, were expected to take nine months.

In mid-October 1944, the *Tirpitz* was moved 150 miles down the coast from the Altafjord to near Tromsø, where another Lancaster raid struck the stationary ship off the island of Håkøya at the end of the month. One near-miss aft rendered the ship immobile. Operation CATECHISM, yet another Lancaster raid, followed on the morning of 12 November. The first bombs fell at 9.41 a.m., and there were a number of hits and near-misses, causing the battleship to list to port. Ten minutes later a magazine exploded, turret 'Caesar' was blown into the air and the big ship turned turtle, taking over half the crew of 1,700 men to their deaths.

Some 590,000 tons of supplies were despatched from North America to northern Russia between January and May 1945, although this was somewhat less (on a monthly basis) than in 1944. The Pacific remained the major route to Russia in this same period (730,000 tons from North America). A change in the supply system came with the opening of the Black Sea strait in January 1945. The Germans had been driven out of the Balkans in the autumn of 1944, and in February 1945 Turkey declared war on Germany. The route through the strait rapidly overtook the Persian Corridor. The first Allied supply ships were despatched in January 1945, and in the period to May the total was 520,000 tons; by comparison less than 50,000 tons were sent through the Persian Gulf in the same months. The Fourth Protocol of Lend-Lease aid to Russia ran from July 1944 to June 1945; deliveries before the end of the war in Europe exceeded the commitment of 5.7 million tons.[23] Allied control of the seas and enormous shipping capacity allowed both a build-up of ground forces and supplies in Western Europe, and the continued shipment of military and economic aid to the USSR.

FINALE IN THE BALTIC

While the western Allies were advancing from Normandy to the Rhine, the Red Army was driving forward through Belarus, the Baltic region and Poland. The naval events in the Baltic and the Black Sea in the second half of 1944 have already been described in Chapter 7 (see pp. 149–53). The last Axis naval forces had been cleared from the Black Sea in August 1944, after the Red Army overran, in succession, Romania and Bulgaria. The conquest of Estonia and the Finnish surrender in September 1944 gave the Soviet naval forces access to the open Baltic.

The Balkans and most of the Baltic region, Poland and Hungary had been lost. Even so, Hitler ordered the German Army to hold on to a bridgehead in northwestern Latvia, which was known as the Courland pocket. This outpost of the Reich was supplied by sea through the small ports of Libau (now Liepāja) and Windau (now Ventspils). Admiral Dönitz repeatedly argued the importance of holding the eastern Baltic littoral, especially to permit the training of the new Type XXI U-boat fleet, and this probably did influence the decision. Nevertheless, it was not the only reason for Hitler's last-ditch strategy, which had gone well beyond the rational; the Führer also hoped to keep Courland as a bridgehead for the moment when the Wehrmacht would be able to resume the offensive.

In early January 1945 the Red Army launched another big offensive across western Poland towards Germany proper. The right wing of this tidal wave was directed down the Vistula river to the Baltic. On 26 January Soviet troops reached the sea near Elbing (now Elbląg), cutting the land connection between the province of East Prussia and the rest of the Reich. East Prussia was a core German territory (perhaps *the* core German territory), and Hitler would never have given it up without a fight. The Wehrmacht at first held on to Pomerania, the belt of coastal territory running from Danzig (now Gdańsk) to Stettin (now Szczecin), but soon only besieged enclaves at Danzig and Kolberg (now Kołobrzeg) remained.

The Soviet fleet, previously bottled up around Leningrad, now operated submarines, coastal forces and aircraft in the open Baltic, threatening German supply missions (and evacuation shipping) to and from the besieged eastern ports. What is surprising is that the Kriegsmarine, including heavy ships, was able to operate effectively for so long within range of Soviet airfields. For three or four months the Germans carried out a very large-scale evacuation of East Prussia and other ports on the Baltic. Altogether some 2.2 million civilians and service personnel were sent westward by sea. Some famously tragic events ensued, notably the sinking of the liner MV *Wilhelm Gustloff* by the Soviet submarine *S-13* on 30 January, and that of the smaller MV *Goya* by the *L-3* on 16 April 1945. These were the worst maritime disasters of the war, with over 9,000 killed aboard the *Gustloff* and over 7,000 aboard the *Goya*. The evacuation route was also endangered by highly effective RAF aerial minelaying along the Baltic coast as far east as Gotenhafen (Gdynia, near Danzig).

These months in the Baltic saw the end of what was left of the Kriegsmarine. The *Admiral Hipper* was hit by an RAF bomb while in a floating dock at the Germaniawerft shipyard in Kiel on 3 April; the heavy cruiser suffered three more direct hits during another British RAF raid on the night of 9/10 April, which devastated her superstructure. The same night the *Admiral Scheer* was hit by a number of heavy bombs at the nearby Deutsche Werke and capsized. Most of her crew had been sent ashore into bomb shelters, so losses were light. Further east the German crews did what they could to put the other big ships out of operation to prevent them from falling intact into Soviet hands. The long-decommissioned battleship *Gneisenau* was sunk upright in shallow water, as a blockship across the entrance to Gotenhafen in late March, the day before the Russians arrived; she had never been fully repaired after being hit by an RAF bomb in Kiel in February 1942. As the Red Army took Stettin on 26 April the uncompleted aircraft carrier *Graf Zeppelin* – symbol of the failure of German sea/air power – was sunk in shallow water there. Thirty miles to the north, in the sea canal near Swinemünde (Świnoujście), the same fate was met by the heavy cruiser *Lützow* on 26 April. Under her original name, *Deutschland*, she had been the first of the 'pocket battleships'. Never a lucky ship, her hull had been badly damaged ten days earlier by a near-miss – a Tallboy super-heavy bomb dropped by 617 Squadron. Nevertheless, the *Lützow* ended the war in Soviet hands and superficially intact. In Kiel the heavy cruiser *Admiral Hipper* was further damaged in a heavy RAF bombing attack during the night of 2/3 May. She was scuttled by her crew early in the morning. The only survivor of the large cruisers was the *Hipper*'s sister ship, the *Prinz Eugen*. She had been in Swinemünde when the *Lützow* was hit, and she made her way to the relative safety of Copenhagen, along with the last light cruiser, the *Nürnberg*.

THE SURRENDER OF THE THIRD REICH

Admiral Karl Dönitz had stood loyally by the Führer in the last year of the war. Hitler, in turn, valued his naval commander, and increasingly so. In Hitler's eyes, Dönitz bore no obvious responsibility for the collapse of the German Army on the Eastern Front, or even for the failed defence against the Allied invasion of France. Göring, once the second man in the Reich, was now in disgrace. His once-vaunted Luftwaffe had lost the battle for the skies, and proved unable to prevent the bombing by day and night of German cities. The German Army was compromised by repeated defeat on the battlefield, but above all by the attempt on 20 July 1944, led by Army officers, to assassinate Hitler at his East Prussian headquarters and to overthrow the Nazi government in Berlin. The Kriegsmarine had almost no involvement in this conspiracy. And Dönitz and the naval high command unswervingly supported Hitler through these events. On 21 July 1944 Dönitz issued a proclamation to the Navy: 'Holy wrath and extravagant fury fill us over the criminal attempt which might have cost the life of our beloved Führer.' The 'insane, small clique of generals' were the tools of Germany's enemies. The death of the Führer would have doomed the German people to defeat and enslavement. 'We will deal with these traitors appropriately. The Navy stands true to its oath, in proven loyalty to the Führer, unconditional in readiness for battle ... Destroy ruthlessly anyone who reveals himself as a traitor. Long live our Führer, Adolf Hitler.'[24]

Earlier in the war Hitler and his naval leaders had met infrequently. The Führer's residence was mainly at the Wehrmacht headquarters at Rastenburg in East Prussia; the KORALLE naval command centre remained in the outskirts of Berlin at Bernau. When Hitler began to spend more time in the capital he met Admiral Dönitz more frequently. By February, March and early April 1945 they talked together several times a week.

In March 1945 most of the Kriegsmarine headquarters staff had been moved to Plön, a county town just south of Kiel. Dönitz and a small core staff remained at KORALLE until 19 April, three days after the final Soviet offensive on Berlin began. The admiral attended an event to mark Hitler's birthday in the Reich Chancellery bunker on the 20th. He was told he was to take overall command of the defence of the northern territories of the Reich; it was a moment when the advance of the Russians and western Allies seemed likely to cut Greater Germany in half. After this last meeting with his Führer, Dönitz departed for Plön.

Events now moved very rapidly. Hitler decided to meet his fate in Berlin. When confronted with the choice of successor, he rejected Göring and Himmler (the head of the SS). On the night of 28/29 April he drafted his 'Political Testament', which included details of who was to replace him. Admiral Dönitz would be head of a new government as *Reichspräsident*, as well as Minister of War; he would retain his position as C-in-C of the German Navy. During the night of 30 April Dönitz received a message from Martin Bormann in Berlin, administrative head of the Nazi party; Hitler was dead, and the admiral was ordered to take over as national leader.

In the chaos of these last days British and Russian forces came towards one another in northern Germany, and constant air attacks were mounted against the encircled enemy forces and territory. In 1940 Norway had been among the first countries conquered by Hitler's Wehrmacht and, ironically, it was one of the last refuges for the embattled operational German forces, even as the territory of the Third Reich itself was being overrun.[25] A few of the electro-boats actually put to sea in these last days. The Type XXI *U 2511* – commissioned in Hamburg in September 1944 – sortied from Bergen on the evening of 30 April, bound for the Caribbean. Its captain, Adalbert Schnee, was a relatively senior commander (a *Korvettenkapitän*) for a U-boat; he had served on the staff at U-boat HQ for two years. Schnee received a recall order on 4 May and returned to base.

Shortly before midnight on 7 May the *U 2336*, another of the Kriegsmarine's new-technology submarines (the small Type XXIII), attacked coastal convoy EN.591 in the Firth of Forth near Edinburgh; the 2,878-ton SS *Avondale Park* was the last ship to be sunk by a U-boat.

The RAF was supporting the northern wing of the Allied advance, Field Marshal Montgomery's 21st Army Group. During these last days RAF aircraft mounted heavy attacks in the western Baltic to prevent U-boats and other vessels transferring from Germany to bases in Norway with the aim of continuing the struggle. The *U 534*, sailing north through shallow water in the Kattegat on 5 May, sank after being damaged by a Coastal Command Liberator operating from Britain; the Type IXC was raised in the 1990s and is now on display (somewhat deconstructed) in Liverpool. Altogether twenty-seven U-boats were sunk by British aircraft in these waters between 1 April and the end of the war.[26]

The most tragic event of these weeks came with the sinking of two merchant ships in the Bay of Lübeck on Thursday, 3 May. The town of Lübeck itself had been liberated by the British Army on the previous day, but several vessels were anchored on the north side of the bay off Neustadt, a small port still controlled by the Germans. These had been identified by the British as troopships, perhaps vessels attempting to effect the transfer of Germans, including SS leaders, to Norway. There were actually four ships, hastily assembled by the SS to accommodate prisoners evacuated from the Neuengamme concentration camp near Hamburg. Rocket-firing RAF fighter-bombers mounted several attacks, sinking two of the ships with many prisoners aboard. The *Cap Arcona* was a large liner of 27,561 tons; the *Thielbek* a much smaller vessel but also packed with prisoners. The *Cap Arcona* caught fire and settled on her side in shallow water; the *Thielbek* capsized and sank in a few minutes. The death toll of the prisoners, trapped below decks or drowned in the cold water of the bays is estimated to have been about 7,000. It was one of the worst maritime tragedies in history, doubly terrible as it was caused by Allied action and took place within a few hours of the end of the fighting.

The day before, on the 2nd, Dönitz had driven north from Plön to Flensburg on the Danish border, where his government was installed at the German Naval Academy in nearby Mürwik. He then sent Admiral von Friedeburg to negotiate with Field Marshal Montgomery at his 21st Army Group headquarters near Lüneburg (about 60 miles south of Plön). After some attempted negotiation, Dönitz's representatives signed, at 6.30 p.m. on 4 May, the surrender of all forces in the Netherlands, northwestern Germany and Denmark, including all naval vessels, effective at 8.00 a.m. on 5 May.

Between 1 and 4 May many U-boats in German ports were scuttled. The largest group were sunk in Gelting Bay near Flensburg. (Some of these were sunk on receipt of the code word *REGENBOGEN* ('Rainbow'), although it is not clear whether this was issued with the approval of Dönitz.[27]) The Type XXI *U 2540* was one such scuttled U-boat: raised in 1957, and commissioned in the West German Navy as the *Wilhelm Bauer*, she is now a museum ship at Bremerhaven.

After the final surrender, the U-boats at sea began to put into Allied ports. In a procedure laid down by the victors, these vessels flew the black flag. The *U 249* arrived at Portland in Dorset on 9 May, and twenty-eight more boats followed, mostly sailing into other UK ports; four more surrendered at Portsmouth, New Hampshire, in the US. A larger number of surviving boats were transferred from Norwegian ports. Many of these boats were scuttled by the British off Northern Ireland in an operation code-named DEADLIGHT.[28]

The zombie government led by Karl Dönitz was of some use to the Allies in effecting the surrender of German forces, and it continued a shadow existence in Flensburg for two more weeks. On 23 May the admiral and his team were summoned to the MV *Patria*, a passenger ship of the Hamburg America Line, where a British–American liaison group had made their headquarters. There they were arrested.

CHAPTER 20

THE PHILIPPINES, OKINAWA, AND THE DEFEAT OF IMPERIAL JAPAN

THE SEA/AIR BATTLE OFF FORMOSA, 12–14 OCTOBER 1944

Task Force 38, the battle force of the American Third Fleet, assembled in the Philippine Sea on the evening of 7 October 1944, with Admiral Bill Halsey flying his flag in the fast battleship *New Jersey*. The fleet he commanded was even more powerful than the one which had fought the June battle in the Marianas. All four fast-carrier task groups were assembled for this operation, with an unprecedented strength comprising the *Enterprise*, eight 'Essex' class fleet carriers (including the new *Hancock* and *Franklin*) and eight light carriers. Total air strength was immense: some 1,060 aircraft, comprising 570 fighters and 490 strike aircraft. Accompanying the carriers were six fast battleships and a screen of fourteen cruisers and fifty-eight destroyers. One of the task groups had sortied from Manus Island in the Admiralties on 24 September, the other three had left Manus and Ulithi (in the western Carolines) on 4–6 October.

After refuelling at sea on 8 October, TF 38 began launching air attacks on Okinawa (in the Ryūkyū Islands) and northern Luzon (in the Philippines) on 9 and 10 October. The Okinawa strike was of much symbolic importance; US Navy planes were attacking the Japanese homeland for the first time.[1]

For the past year Japanese naval planning had been largely based on the rapid deployment of land-based fighters and bombers through a network of island bases. This strategy had not worked in the defence of the Marianas in June and July 1944, but there was no alternative, in view of the weak carrier strength of the Combined Fleet. The approaching enemy was now operating within range of major air bases on the Japanese mainland itself, and some headway had been made towards making up the aircraft losses suffered in the Marianas. The best trained was the 'T' Attack Force (*T-Kōgeki Butai*) designed to operate at night or in bad weather (the 'T' was for *taifū* – 'typhoon'). A drastic innovation – for the Imperial Navy –was co-operation with the air regiments of the Japanese Army, especially in fighter defence of airfields but also with the provision of a number of fast bombers.

The Japanese did have reasonably good intelligence about American naval strength, and they knew by the first days of October that a major enemy force was at sea. Admiral Toyoda Soemu, the Combined Fleet C-in-C, was in Formosa (now Taiwan); he was flying home from an inspection trip to the Philippines. Cut off from his headquarters outside Tokyo, Toyoda authorised his chief of staff, Admiral Kusaka Ryūnosuke, to decide upon a response. On the Tuesday morning, 10 October, Kusaka sent out an attack alert for two variants of the SHŌ ('Victory') battle plan. SHŌ 1 was designed as a response to an attack on the Philippines, SHŌ 2 as an attack on the Ryūkyū–Formosa area. Air strikes on the American fleet, mainly by naval aircraft, were to be mounted from bases on the mainland, Formosa and the Philippines, and without the major involvement of Combined Fleet ships. One consequence was that the planes and crews of new carrier groups training in Japan were transferred to shore bases and assigned to immediate action.[2]

A planned two days of American air strikes against Formosa began on Thursday, 12 October. Situated between Okinawa and the Philippines, the big island covered the Japanese shipping route from Southeast Asia and was also operationally vital to Japan as a staging point for planes coming south from the home islands. The American fleet did not achieve tactical surprise. Hundreds of enemy fighters were in the air when the first strike arrived, but they were not enough. Altogether 1,378 sorties by American carrier planes were flown on the 12th, wrecking Japanese air bases and destroying many aircraft in the air and on the ground.

Formosa – along with the Ryūkyūs and southern Kyūshū – was defended by the Second Air Fleet (Second *Kōkū Kantai*), formed after the catastrophe in the Marianas.[3] The air fleet commander, Admiral Fukudome Shigeru, had been chief of staff of the Combined Fleet under admirals Yamamoto and Koga, but he had limited aviation experience. Fukudome been able to put about 230 fighters into the air over Formosa, and he had been confident of some success. He witnessed events above his main base at Takao (now Kaohsiung) in southern Formosa:

> As I watched from my command post, a terrific aerial combat began directly above my head. Our interceptors swooped down in great force at the invading enemy planes ... In a matter of moments, one after another, planes were seen falling down, enveloped in flames. 'Well done! Well done! A tremendous success!' I clapped my hands. Alas! To my sudden disappoint-

> ment, a closer watch revealed that all those shot down were *our* fighters, and all those proudly circling above our heads were enemy planes! Our fighters were nothing but so many eggs thrown at the stone wall of the indomitable enemy formation.[4]

The first Japanese counter-attack to find and attack the ships of TF 38 was made on this day, by about 100 planes flying in daylight. They reported hitting two carriers, but in reality achieved nothing.

Friday, the 13th, saw more heavy American air strikes over Formosa, now meeting little opposition. The Japanese did not attempt big daylight operations over the sea. On Friday evening, however, about thirty planes of the T Attack Force were despatched, some equipped with radar. American ships were located in the evening and some came under attack. None of the carriers suffered serious damage, although the *Franklin* in TG 38.4 was lucky to avoid a hit. An aerial torpedo did strike the new heavy cruiser USS *Canberra* in TG 38.1. She was heavily damaged and had to be taken in tow. Ever aggressive, Admiral Halsey decided to continue strikes against Formosa for a third day (Saturday), partly in the hope that the crippled *Canberra* might act as a bait to lure out the Japanese fleet.

Something like 400 daylight sorties were launched by the Japanese from various points on Saturday, now including planes transferred ashore from the carrier force. They were not able to locate the American task groups. Another T Attack Force strike of thirty torpedo planes was launched, and in the evening some of them found TG 38.1 again, this time crippling the new light cruiser *Houston*. Very unusually, the torpedo was apparently dropped by an Army bomber operating as part of the T Attack Force.[5] Two cruisers had now been heavily damaged near the Japanese-held coast, and they had to be towed to safety at a very slow speed of about 4 knots. The *Houston* took a second air torpedo hit on Monday afternoon, from bombers launched as part of a daylight strike of 100 planes from Formosa. Fortunately the sea was calm and the two ships eventually reached the safety of Ulithi; from there they would return to the US for major repairs. On Sunday, 15 October, Halsey launched no more strikes against Formosa, and prepared to refuel his task groups in turn, while awaiting a chance to strike any Japanese ships that joined the battle. On the 17th, after no enemy fleet sortie had developed, he turned his attention to the Philippines.

The sea/air battle off Formosa is often passed over quickly by naval historians, because no Japanese ships were involved and no American ships lost; it was also overshadowed by the great battles that took place two weeks later. And yet it involved some of the heaviest air fighting of the war.

It had a deep effect on the Battle of Leyte Gulf, for oddly contradictory reasons. Very heavy losses were suffered by the Japanese air units based at

Formosa, Kyūshū and the Philippines, which fatally weakened them in the coming action in the Philippines. The air battle over Formosa and the attacks on TF 38 resulted in the destruction of 550–600 Japanese aircraft, mostly from the Imperial Navy. American combat losses of some seventy-six aircraft on 12–16 October were substantial but nowhere near as heavy.[6]

At the same time reports were accepted by the Japanese which hugely exaggerated the damage inflicted on the American fleet. The crews of the attacking planes, some inexperienced flyers, some from the Japanese Army, some operating in the darkness, made grossly overstated claims. Formation commanders, who should have known better, took the claims at face value or even embroidered them. All this was symptomatic of a dysfunctional war leadership, but it should be borne in mind that this was an emotionally charged moment: the American fleet was violating for the first time the home waters of Imperial Japan. An official communiqué of 16 October claimed that huge losses had been suffered by the American fleet: eleven carriers, two battleships and three cruisers sunk, and eight carriers, two battleships and four cruisers damaged. The government in Tokyo, for some days at least, accepted these figures uncritically.[7] A radio and press campaign was mounted at home, and patriotic mass meetings were held, one in Tokyo's Hibiya Park. The Emperor issued a rescript on 19 October, after meeting the chiefs of staff of the Army and Navy. He praised the conduct of sailors and soldiers in the battle: 'Our army and air forces, operating in close collaboration, counter-attacked the enemy fleet and heavily blasted it in a heroic fight. We deeply appreciate their achievement.'[8]

There does seem to have been a genuine – and bizarre – moment of collective national relief in Japan. Then, on 20 October, four US Army divisions landed on the island of Leyte in the central Philippines.

STRATEGY AND PLANS

In the months between the American capture of the Marianas in June–August 1944 and the sea/air battle with Japanese forces off Formosa in October the two sides had developed their plans for the next stage of the Pacific war.

With the Battle of the Philippine Sea in June 1944 and the capture of the Marianas the decisive offensive battle of the war with the Japanese Navy had been won. This victory and the arrival of more and more warships meant that the US Navy now controlled the Pacific high seas. By the late autumn the Americans could strike with carrier air raids wherever they wanted on the western rim of the great ocean, with the – temporary – exception of mainland Japan.

Strategic decisions for the Pacific were de facto made by the US Joint Chiefs of Staff (JCS) in Washington, although there was consultation with the British. The

JCS was balanced between the Army and the Navy, and included admirals Leahy and King, and generals Marshall and Arnold. The Pacific Ocean region was still divided by the US military forces into two independent theatres, the Pacific Ocean Area (POA) under Admiral Nimitz, based ashore in Hawaii, and the South West Pacific Area (SWPA) under General MacArthur in Brisbane, Australia. Each of the theatres had a 'joint' structure with subordinate commanders and forces (Army, Army Air Force, Navy and Marines), although the POA was dominated by the Navy and SWPA by the Army. The SWPA had its own naval force, kept small in 1942, 1943 and even early 1944; this was the Seventh Fleet, now under Admiral Thomas Kinkaid.

In the POA of Admiral Nimitz a unique 'platoon' system was introduced in 1944 to cope with the unbroken series of carrier raids and amphibious invasions; the ships remained in action, but the commander and his staff rotated, and some designations were changed. Admiral Spruance, the first commander of the Fifth Fleet, was substituted in late August 1944 by Admiral Halsey, and the main Pacific battle fleet was re-designated as the Third Fleet. With this change the designation of the main task force was changed from TF 58 to TF 38. (Spruance in turn would relieve Halsey from January to May 1945, and the designation would again be changed; Halsey took over from May 1945 to the end of the war.)

The build-up of overwhelming American strength relative to Japan permitted great flexibility. The Marianas were fully secured by August 1944, and the battle for New Guinea was complete; the next step was evidently the southern and central Philippines. There was a lengthy debate in 1944 within the leadership of the US military as to whether the main intermediate objective of the Pacific forces – before the final objective of the Japanese home islands – should be Formosa or Luzon (the latter the most important of the Philippine islands and located in the north of the archipelago). Essentially, Admiral King and the Navy favoured Formosa, while General MacArthur favoured Luzon (in part for political reasons). This debate was resolved in favour of Luzon in late October 1944, but as late as the beginning of the inter-Allied second Quebec Conference (code-named OCTAGON) in mid-September 1944, the Allied leaders were still considering a measured advance towards the Philippines from the south. There would be preliminary landings on Yap in the western Carolines and at Mindanao in the southern Philippines, and only after that, in December 1944, a landing on Leyte in the central Philippines. This restricted pace would give time for the steady construction of a chain of airfields from which the US Army Air Force could support each successive stage of the advance north.

At this point, however, an important contribution to the strategic planning was made by Admiral Halsey. In early September 1944 Halsey had been leading the carriers of Task Force 38 on raids against Japanese positions, including the Philippines. An energetic and aggressive commander, Halsey considered that the light Japanese air resistance encountered by his planes suggested that the progress into the Philippines should be considerably speeded up. He proposed to Admiral Nimitz on 13 September 1944 that the intermediate stages be cancelled and a jump be made immediately into the central Philippines at Leyte. This change was rapidly approved by Nimitz and General MacArthur's SWPA headquarters in Australia, and then by the Allied leaders at Quebec. The Leyte landing (Operation KING II) was now re-scheduled for 20 October. An immediate consequence of this decision was the rapid expansion of Admiral Kinkaid's Seventh Fleet, which along with extensive amphibious forces, was now supported by a large number of escort carriers, cruisers and destroyers, as well as a detachment of most of the older American battleships.

One aspect of the planning for this hastily accelerated operation was the role of the American battle fleet, which had not been involved in a major action against the Japanese fleet since the Battle of the Philippine Sea in June, and was liable to be involved in a full-scale engagement in the Philippines. It was felt by some senior officers, including Admiral King in Washington and Admiral Halsey at sea with the Third Fleet, that the task at hand demanded clearer definition; Halsey in particular was preoccupied with winning a decisive victory over the Combined Fleet. Much of Admiral Ozawa's warship fleet had escaped at the end of the June 1944 Battle of the Philippine Sea, as a result – it was argued – of Admiral Spruance putting priority on the defence of the landing force at Saipan rather than on an all-out counter-attack against the Japanese carriers. In any event Admiral Nimitz issued Halsey with instructions for the battle which specified that 'In case opportunity for destruction of major portion of the enemy fleet is offered or can be created, such destruction becomes the *primary task*.'[9]

The raids mounted by Halsey's carriers on Formosa and the northern Philippines, as outlined in the first section of this chapter, were part of these wide-ranging operations. After the momentous sea/air battle off Formosa most of the Fast Carrier Force had been repositioned to operate close to the northern and central Philippines, in preparation for the landing.

Japanese naval command arrangements had changed over the course of the war, and were now not so different from those of the Americans, although on a smaller scale. Like Admiral Nimitz, the C-in-C of the Combined Fleet was now based ashore, normally at his headquarters near Tokyo. Admiral Toyoda had survived in post despite the defeat of the Combined Fleet in the Battle of the Philippine Sea. As had also been the case in the June battle, it was one of Toyoda's subordinates, Admiral Ozawa, who commanded the main sea-going force, the First Mobile Fleet; the parallel was now with Admiral Halsey and the Third

Fleet. Under Ozawa were various tactical divisions, the most important of which was Admiral Kurita's Second Fleet, designated operationally as the 1st Attack Force. This had a parallel with Admiral Mitscher in Task Force 38, although by October 1944 the main Japanese force was made up of big-gun surface ships, while the American one consisted of aircraft carriers.

The breathtaking pace of the American advance put the Japanese high command in a difficult position. Even in 1942 the Imperial Navy could not defend every position gained, and by 1944 the correlation of forces was very much less favourable. No longer capable of mounting offensive operations, the Japanese had to prepare a range of defensive contingency plans, although in each case there was a hope to transform a defensive battle into a decisive victory, followed by the pursuit and destruction of the fleeing attackers. The proposed 'Z' operations of 1943 and the variant A-GŌ plans of spring 1944 were followed after the fall of the Marianas by Operation SHŌ ('Victory'). As already mentioned, SHŌ had four variants – for the Philippines, for Formosa and the Ryūkyūs, for central Japan (Honshū), and for northern Japan (Hokkaidō).

The Japanese battle fleet available for these defensive battles was similar to the one which had fought in the Philippine Sea, but it had fewer fleet carriers and far fewer carrier aircraft. In the first two and a half years of the war the carriers had been de facto the main force of the Imperial Navy. Most of the Japanese battleships – seven of them – had been held in reserve.[10] However, after June 1944 and the Philippine Sea defeat, Admiral Kurita's battleships and heavy cruisers were the strongest force surviving. They became the main striking force of the Combined Fleet, with the weakened carrier force for the moment useful as little more than bait. Organisation of a coherent operation was made more difficult by the dispersal of the fleet. The battleships and cruisers were based at Lingga Roads near Singapore, where they had access to fuel oil from Sumatra. The surviving carriers were based at home in the Inland Sea, where they could best carry out the training of their air groups.

Four land-based naval 'air fleets' mapped onto the variants of the SHŌ plan. The First Air Fleet, rebuilt after the Marianas battle, was based in the Philippines, the Second in Formosa, the Ryūkyūs and southern Kyūshū, the Third in central Japan on Honshū, and the Twelfth in northern Japan on Hokkaidō.

The American attack, wherever it came, would have to be contested – as in the Marianas in June 1944 – using both the land-based air groups and the First Mobile Fleet. In the case of the warship fleet the emphasis, in the short term at least, would have to be the battleships and cruisers of Kurita's Second Fleet, although under the overall command of Ozawa. By August 1944 it had been decided that the emphasis would be on attacking the enemy landings – wherever they occurred – as soon as possible after they took place. Considerable effort was made between August and October at the Second Fleet base at Lingga Roads to prepare for this action.

Admiral Toyoda, the C-in-C of the Combined Fleet, provided post-war US Navy interviewers with an account – probably truthful – of his strategic intention for the Combined Fleet:

> Since without the participation of our Combined Fleet there was no possibility of land-based forces in the Philippines having any chance against your forces at all, it was decided to send the whole fleet, taking the gamble. If things went well we might obtain unexpectedly good results; but if the worst should happen, there was a chance that we would lose the entire fleet; but I felt that that chance had to be taken . . . Should we lose the Philippines operations, even though the fleet should be left, the shipping lane to the south would be completely cut off so that the fleet, if it should come back to Japanese waters, could not obtain its fuel supply. If it should remain in southern waters, it could not receive supplies of ammunition and arms. There would be no sense in saving the fleet at the expense of the Philippines.[11]

THE BATTLE OF LEYTE GULF

The climactic sea/air encounter between the US Navy and the Imperial Japanese Navy which took place in the Philippines in October 1944 is known as the Battle of Leyte Gulf. The name is somewhat misleading, as the fighting did not take place in that body of water; nevertheless, the gulf was certainly the eye of the storm. The battle consisted of four actions fought hundreds of miles apart, but concentrated in time on Wednesday the 25th and Thursday, 26 October.

The American planners had, after much discussion, decided to make their first landing in the Philippines in the central part of the archipelago, the Visayan Islands. Leyte, which lies in the eastern Visayas, is a heavily forested island, mountainous in parts; much larger than Saipan (and about the same size as Crete), Leyte had a pre-war population of nearly 1 million people. Taking the island would in the end require a conventional ground-forces campaign, involving six US Army divisions and lasting over two months, until the end of December. Elements of four divisions, organised as the Sixth Army and operationally subordinate to General MacArthur, were landed on the east coast of Leyte near the main town, Tacloban, on Friday, 20 October. Unlike in many other Pacific island battles, US Marine formations would not take part.

The first two divisions of the invasion force had left Oahu on 15 September. Their original objective had been Yap in the western Carolines, but that operation was cancelled. They then proceeded via Eniwetok to Manus in the

Admiralties, where they joined forces with two more US Army divisions which had been fighting in New Guinea. The huge armada of 518 ocean-going transports and support ships, including forty attack transports, ten big LSDs and 151 LSTs arrived in Leyte Gulf without incident.[12]

The Japanese Army had not prepared strong coastal fortifications on Leyte. The original intention was to concentrate the defence of the Philippines further north, on the main island of Luzon. The thinly spread division on Leyte in late October at first offered little resistance to the invaders. A squadron of veteran American battleships, with smaller ships, was assembled within Admiral Kinkaid's Seventh Fleet (also subordinate to MacArthur) to provide gunfire support, but they proved to be unnecessary – at least for that function. The American GIs moved inland quickly and overran a number of air bases, although the rainy weather made it difficult to exploit them quickly for use by the AAF.

The air strikes by Halsey's Third Fleet in the week before the invasion, especially on Formosa, but also on Luzon, had done much to dislocate the Japanese defences. The potential of the land-based First and Second Air Fleets had been greatly reduced, as had the air strength of carriers and air groups which were training in home waters. The First Mobile Fleet was still divided, with the carriers in the home islands and Kurita's battleships and cruisers at Lingga Roads near Singapore.

Evidence of a likely landing became available to the Japanese on Tuesday, 17 October, when reports were received of small enemy landings on the approaches to Leyte Gulf. In the early morning of 18 October, Admiral Kurita took a large squadron of battleships and cruisers, designated as the 1st Attack Force, to sea from Lingga Roads;[13] his destination was a forward anchorage at Brunei in Borneo. At 11.10 p.m. he received a signal from Kusaka, Toyoda's chief of staff in Tokyo, outlining operations in the now likely event of a landing on Leyte. The 1st Attack Force was to advance through the San Bernardino Strait and destroy the enemy at the Tacloban anchorage on a to be determined in the future, but designated as 'X-Day'. The carrier force would sortie from Japan and lure the enemy fleet to the north. Land-based aircraft would deal with the American carriers, while the submarine force would destroy damaged American ships and attack troop convoys. On the morning of 21 October, X-Day was specified as dawn on Wednesday, 25 October.

Kurita had a good war record. He led the cruiser raid into the Bay of Bengal in 1942, and fought creditably as a cruiser commander in the Solomons, before replacing Admiral Kondō in mid-1943 as Second Fleet commander. He had commanded the Vanguard Force of the First Mobile Fleet in the Battle of the Philippine Sea, directly subordinate to Admiral Ozawa. Now, in October 1944 Kurita was in command of the main striking force of the First Mobile Fleet. He was still nominally subordinate to its C-in-C, but Ozawa was several hundred miles away to the northeast, with the remnants of the Japanese carrier force.

Kurita sortied from Brunei on the afternoon of Sunday, 22 October. He again flew his flag in the heavy cruiser *Atago*, as he had in the Battle of the Philippine Sea. Admiral Ugaki Matome commanded the core 'division' of this force, Sentai 1, with the battleships *Yamato*, *Musashi* and *Nagato*. The rest of the 1st Attack Force was made up of the fast battleships *Kongō* and *Haruna* (Sentai 3), nine more heavy cruisers, two new light cruisers and nineteen destroyers.

As had happened during the Battle of the Philippine Sea, a large force of American fleet submarines was positioned at strategic choke points in the western Pacific to provide intelligence about Japanese fleet movements and mount attacks; altogether some twenty-four boats were on station. Early on Monday morning (the 23rd) the American submarines *Darter* and *Dace* reported the position of Kurita's approaching battle fleet off the island of Palawan, north of Borneo, and they also mounted highly successful attacks. Their torpedoes sank Admiral Kurita's flagship, the *Atago*, and a second heavy cruiser, the *Maya*; another heavy cruiser, the *Takao*, was damaged so badly that she had to return to base. Admiral Kurita had to swim for his life from the sinking *Atago* and was picked up by a destroyer; he transferred his flag to the *Yamato*.

Despite these losses, Kurita's force entered the Sibuyan Sea – between Luzon and the Visayas – at dawn on Tuesday the 24th. The Japanese warships were located by American scout planes, and a series of full-scale air strikes ensued. The four big attacks that day in the Sibuyan Sea were mounted by three of Halsey's task groups, with planes from the *Enterprise*, four 'Essex' class fleet carriers (the *Essex*, the *Intrepid*, the *Lexington* and the *Franklin*) and the light carrier *Cabot*.[14] The swarm of TBM Avenger torpedo planes and SB2C Helldiver dive bombers damaged a number of ships. Another of Kurita's heavy cruisers, this time the *Myōkō*, had to be sent back to base, reducing the total to six: the *Chikuma*, the *Chōkai*, the *Haguro*, the *Kumano*, the *Suzuya* and the *Tone*. The main air attack, however, ended up being concentrated on the super-battleship *Musashi*.

The 1st Attack Force had no carriers and as a result no fighter cover to break up the American air strikes. The force of land-based fighters in the Philippines had been weakened in American air strikes or by transfers to Formosa. Those planes available were deployed offensively, searching out to the east for the US task forces in the Philippine Sea. Combined Fleet headquarters also hoped that Ozawa's carrier decoy force would lure away the American planes. Although retrofitted with a large number of light AA guns – in the case of the *Musashi* 130 25mm guns – the defensive fire of Kurita's ships did not prove very effective. All told, only eighteen American planes were lost during the strikes in the Sibuyan Sea.

The 64,000-ton *Musashi* was torpedoed at 10.29 a.m. by an Avenger from the *Intrepid* and then subjected to repeated strikes by more Avengers and Helldivers. By 3.25 p.m., after having been hit by no fewer than nineteen torpedoes and seventeen bombs, the battleship's speed had been reduced to 6 knots, and she had been left behind by Admiral Kurita. At 7.36 p.m. the great ship capsized, going down with 1,000 men, nearly half her complement.[15]

From the American point of view the Japanese central force seemed to have been stopped. The attacking fliers made exaggerated reports of their successes and indeed, late in the afternoon, the weakened 1st Attack Force had reversed course. Under the weight of the air attack, Kurita turned to the west to lengthen the range of the enemy strikes. Shortly afterwards, however, he received a direct order from Admiral Toyoda at Combined Fleet headquarters in Tokyo to continue: 'With confidence in heavenly guidance, the entire force will attack!'[16] The 1st Attack Force resumed its advance.

Meanwhile, a second, smaller task group, composed of the old battleships *Yamashiro* and *Fusō* supported by the heavy cruiser *Mogami* and four destroyers, had been sent towards Leyte Gulf from Brunei by a southerly route. This detachment was commanded by Admiral Nishimura Shōji, flying his flag in the *Yamashiro*.[17] Nishimura was under Kurita's overall command, and the intention was that he would join up with the central force on X-Day to take part in the massacre of American transports in Leyte Gulf. The decision to set up this mission had been made only on the evening of the 21st. Nishimura's force was also sighted by American scout planes, but unlike the fleet in the Sibuyan Sea it did not come under heavy air attack on Tuesday. The fatal encounter would occur in the Surigao Strait in the early hours of Wednesday (the night of 24/25 October).

The Battle of Surigao Strait, the southwestern entrance to Leyte Gulf (between Leyte and the Dinagat Islands), was something of a throwback. On both sides the heavy ships dated from the era of World War I. The *Fusō* and the *Yamashiro* were commissioned in 1915 and 1917 respectively, equivalent to Jellicoe's *Iron Duke* 'super-dreadnought' flagship at Jutland. They were confronted in the Surigao Strait by an American battleship fleet including the *Mississippi* and five survivors of Pearl Harbor – the *California*, the *Maryland*, the *Pennsylvania, the Tennessee* and the *West Virginia*, all of which had been commissioned between 1916 and 1923.[18] They were under the command of Admiral Jesse B. Oldendorf, flying his flag in the heavy cruiser *Louisville*. Oldendorf was also in charge of the bulk of the major warships in Admiral Kinkaid's Seventh Fleet; these included seven other cruisers (including the Australian-manned 'County' class *Shropshire*) and twenty-eight destroyers.

Historians sometimes maintain that during this night encounter Oldendorf's battleships successfully carried out the classic battleship manoeuvre of 'crossing the T'; this involves a column of ships passing at right angles in front of an enemy column, enabling all its guns to fire broadside, while the enemy can only bring their forward guns to bear. In fact the American battleships hardly moved, and it would be more correct to say that they pummelled the Japanese from ahead as they advanced up the narrow strait.[19] A mass night attack by American PT boats (MTBs) at the entrance to the Surigao Strait achieved no results – demonstrating the limitations of the 'mosquito boats'. The American destroyer flotillas were much more effective. The destroyer *Melvin* evidently inflicted two fatal torpedo hits on the *Fusō* at 3.09 a.m., and the Japanese vessel sank at 3.45, before the American battleships opened fire. Somewhat later, at 4.11 a.m., the *Newcomb* finished off the *Yamashiro*, after she had been battered by radar-controlled battleship fire. There were only a handful of survivors from each battleship.[20] The American ships suffered no damage from chaotic Japanese return fire.

The surviving Japanese ships gave up the attempt to break into Leyte Gulf, but as they retreated to the south in the darkness they stumbled upon another advancing Japanese squadron, this one commanded by Admiral Shima Kiyohide and including the heavy cruisers *Nachi* and *Ashigara*, light cruiser *Abukuma*, and five destroyers. In the confusion the *Nachi* collided with the damaged *Mogami*. The Shima force was able to withdraw to the west, but not the damaged *Mogami*; after being shelled by pursuing cruisers and attacked by enemy planes she sank the following morning.[21]

So far the great battle in the Philippines seemed to be progressing very favourably from the American point of view. Two major forces of Japanese surface ships attempting to attack the landing area in Leyte Gulf had been beaten off with very heavy losses. The third and fourth parts of the battle, however, which developed on 25 and 26 October, would prove far more controversial.

On Tuesday, 24 October, Admiral Halsey had used the carriers of his TF 38 to attack the battleships and cruisers in the Sibuyan Sea which threatened the invasion forces. This one-sided battle had been on the whole successful, but the Japanese land-based naval air groups were certainly not harmless. On Tuesday morning the light carrier *Princeton* was conducting air strikes against Japanese land targets in the Philippines with Sherman's TG 38.3, stationed east of Luzon. At 10.00 a.m. a single Japanese dive bomber appeared and hit the vessel with one 250kg (440lb) bomb; the series of fires and explosions resulting from this eventually destroyed her. The main explosion caused heavy loss of life aboard the light cruiser USS *Birmingham*, which lay alongside with her crew helping fight the fire. The *Princeton* sank at 5.50 p.m.; she was the only American fast carrier built in wartime to be sunk.

That same Tuesday, Admiral Halsey was very concerned with the Japanese carriers, which had still not been located. These enemy ships represented a considerable threat to his own forces (especially in view of the longer range of Japanese carrier planes and their theoretical ability to shuttle through the Philippines' land bases). More fundamentally, the American admiral, known to the American public as 'Bull' Halsey, was an offensively minded officer. He very much wanted to achieve a decisive victory over the enemy fleet, which he identified with the Japanese carrier force. As it happened, Halsey's scout planes finally sighted the carrier force to the northeast at 4.40 on Tuesday afternoon, as his strike aircraft were returning from their successful attacks on the Sibuyan Sea. Halsey ordered the three carrier task groups on hand to move rapidly north to confront the enemy. They expected a rapid dash through the night to put the American ships in a position to mount decisive strikes the following morning. With hindsight, critics of Halsey have used the term 'Bull's Run' to describe his manoeuvre on the night of 24/25 October.[22]

In June, Spruance had kept Mitscher's fast carriers back to protect the forces engaged in the invasion of Saipan, and to prevent the sudden appearance of an enemy task force on one of his flanks. He had done this even though a considerable force of escort carriers, older battleships and cruisers was available in the Saipan area in the form of TF 52. Halsey's position in October was similar, but his assumptions were that the 'central force' in the Sibuyan Sea had been heavily damaged and driven off, and that Admiral Kinkaid's Seventh Fleet, with its escort carriers, older battleships, cruisers and destroyers, could deal with any minor threat that remained. Based aboard the fast battleship *New Jersey*, Halsey believed he could safely head off in pursuit of the enemy to the north, keeping to the time-honoured operational principle of not dividing his fleet – which included both carriers and fast battleships.

The perspective of Admiral Kinkaid in the Seventh Fleet was different. He was based, along with the senior US Army general Walter Krueger, aboard the amphibious command ship USS *Wasatch* (a converted merchant ship). Multiple Japanese threats were evident, and there were an amphibious force and troops ashore to protect. American command arrangements meant Kinkaid could not readily communicate with Halsey; he was subordinate to MacArthur, Halsey was subordinate to Nimitz. Kinkaid had been able to halt and destroy the Japanese Southern Force in the Surigao Strait with his own powerful fleet of surface ships. As far as he knew, the centre force had been stopped too, and in any event he also believed (from information received indirectly) that Halsey had formed and deployed a force of fast battleships and cruisers, designated as Task Force 34, to patrol the exit into the Philippine Sea from the San Bernardino Strait. Unfortunately the actual situation was very different. At 6.45, shortly after dawn on the morning of Wednesday, 25 October, a Japanese armada was suddenly sighted by the lookouts of the escort carriers on station off the coast of

Samar, the large island just northeast of Leyte, and directly to the north of the entrance to Leyte Gulf. Admiral Kurita had arrived aboard the super-battleship *Yamato*, leading his 1st Attack Force.

Kinkaid had under his command in the Seventh Fleet an escort-carrier (CVE) group (Task Group 71.4) with an impressive total of sixteen vessels, mostly of the 'Casablanca' class. The mission of the CVEs was to provide local air cover, A/S patrols and support for ground troops. They were organised into three 'task units', the northernmost of which, nearest the San Bernardino Strait, was Task Unit 71.4.3, known as 'Taffy 3'.

Operating some 35 miles off the coast of Samar and covering the northern approaches to Leyte Gulf, Taffy 3 was commanded by the very able Admiral Clifton Sprague, and consisted of six escort carriers, the *Fanshaw Bay*, the *Kalinin Bay*, the *Kitkun Bay*, the *Gambier Bay*, the *St. Lo* and the *White Plains*;[23] they were protected by a small screen of three destroyers and four destroyer escorts.

It was an A/S plane from Taffy 2 that had first sighted the approaching Japanese fleet that morning. The 1st Striking Force had passed through San Bernardino Strait during the night, some seven hours behind Kurita's original schedule, as a result of the submarine and air attacks of the previous days; his final approach south along the coast of Samar should have been made under cover of darkness. Nevertheless, the immediate Japanese advantage seemed great, even after the losses of the previous day. Kurita still commanded four battleships (one with 18-inch guns), six heavy cruisers, two light cruisers and eleven destroyers. The CVEs of Taffy 3 attempted to pull out of the way at their slow maximum speed of 17.5 knots. Their defensive gunnery armament against surface ships was one 5-inch gun, and they had virtually no armour.

Admiral Kurita, with no air or radio intelligence to go on, did not know what he was facing, indeed whether it was actually an American fleet stronger than his own. He was now operating in the area from which, on the previous day, one of the American fast-carrier groups had launched strikes against him in the Sibuyan Sea. Aiming to make maximum use of the surprise that had been achieved, Kurita ordered a 'general attack', rather than keeping close control of his forces; the result was that the ensuing thrust was poorly co-ordinated.

The lunge of the Japanese 1st Striking Force would turn out to be one of the most dramatic naval encounters of the whole of World War II. The small American escort launched a courageous counter-attack. The destroyers *Hoel* and *Johnston*, and the DE *Samuel B. Roberts* were sunk, but some confusion was caused among the Japanese. Nevertheless, the *Gambier Bay*, the CVE nearest the Japanese cruisers, suffered the first of several hits at 8.20 a.m., and capsized at 9.07.

The situation was indeed threatening, with a powerful force of heavy ships engaging weakly armed CVEs and a weak destroyer screen. Kinkaid did have the battleship force which had won the Battle of Surigao Strait during the previous night, but they were a hundred miles away and these ships had expended much of their armour-piercing ammunition. At 9.11 a.m., after an engagement lasting two hours, Kurita turned to the north to assess what remained for him a very confused situation. At 12.30 p.m., coming under increasing air attack he decided to give up any attempt to proceed on to the Tacloban anchorage in Leyte Gulf, and turned back north to retrace his steps through the San Bernardino Strait.

The six-hour Battle off Samar raises two related questions. The first concerned whose fault it was that Admiral Kurita's fleet of battleships and cruisers could approach the entrance to Leyte Gulf without being spotted or attacked; the second is why Kurita decided to turn around when the chance to inflict major damage to the invader's fleet was apparently within his grasp. The questions are perhaps best considered in reverse order.

Kurita's advantage was not as overwhelming as is often depicted. This was not like HMS *Glorious* and the German battleships off Narvik in 1940. Each of CVEs carried about sixteen fighters and twelve torpedo bombers. The total air strength of the three CVE task units in Task Group 71.4, all within close range of Kurita's fleet, amounted to 298 fighters and 209 torpedo bombers at the start of the battle.[24] In addition Taffy 1 and Taffy 2 (Task Units 71.4.1 and 71.4.2) were some distance to the south, and not under immediate threat of direct attack by the guns of the Japanese surface ships. Three of Kurita's heavy cruisers, first the *Suzuya*, and then the *Chōkai* and the *Chikuma*, were immobilised by air attack from the CVEs and would eventually sink.

Furthermore, in the course of the morning Kurita learned of the complete destruction of Nishimura's battleship detachment in the Surigao Strait and received (inaccurate) air reports suggesting that another large American carrier force was assembling to the north of his position. This would be a more honourable target for Kurita's big ships than transports in Leyte Gulf which had probably already been unloaded. Moreover, this new American force could potentially cut his line of retreat. Meanwhile his destroyers were beginning to run out of fuel, and further operations at high speed would put his whole fleet at risk. A continuation of the charge into Leyte Gulf could have seen the complete destruction of the main fleet of the Japanese Navy.[25]

In the event, Kurita was able to withdraw safely through the San Bernardino Strait late on Wednesday afternoon – the enemy carrier force having turned out to be a phantom. A final American air attack was made on Thursday morning in the Sibuyan Sea, during which a light cruiser was sunk, but the rest of the force returned safely to Brunei on 28 October.

The second – not unrelated – question is whose responsibility it was that Kurita was able to surprise the CVEs off Samar. This naturally raised most controversy in the US Navy. Halsey and Kinkaid were involved in an unseemly battle of memoirs in the early post-war years, and Halsey – who died in 1959 – never admitted responsibility.[26] Admiral Nimitz, in Hawaii, made every effort to dampen down controversy within his command after what had been, overall, an undoubted victory. On the other hand, he was certainly aware that things had gone wrong. As he confidentially wrote to Admiral King in Washington, three days after the battle, 'That the San Bernardino detachment of the Japanese Fleet . . . did not completely destroy all of the escort carriers . . . is nothing short of a special dispensation from the Lord Almighty'.[27] Halsey had set off on 'Bull's Run' without protecting the exit from the San Bernardino Strait. Kinkaid was sometimes criticised for not taking steps to patrol these waters with ships or aircraft from his own Seventh Feet, but there had been communication confusion that made him believe Halsey had left a covering force (Task Force 34). As a result, Kinkaid took no action and did not request help from Halsey's Third Fleet on Tuesday. Nimitz himself could be criticised for his original directive to Halsey to make the destruction of the enemy fleet the primary task – rather than protection of the invasion force.

The fourth part of the Battle of Leyte Gulf saw the destruction of Ozawa's decoy carrier force, officially designated by the Japanese as the 'Mobile Force Main Body', far out in the Philippine Sea. Surigao Strait had been an untimely reincarnation of Jutland. The action which the Americans call the Battle off Cape Engaño was an equally odd version of the carrier versus carrier battles that had begun two years earlier, in May 1942, in the Coral Sea. Both were peculiar variations on the theme, the result of one side being so much stronger than the other.

What Spanish explorers called *Cabo Engaño* ('Cape Deception') is just off the northeastern tip of Luzon, but the battle itself was fought nearly 250 miles further out in the Philippine Sea. The name of the cape, at least, was appropriate, because Admiral Halsey had fallen for a clever deception. The Mobile Force Main Body had departed the Inland Sea under Admiral Ozawa at midnight on 20–21 October (Friday/Saturday). The *Zuikaku*, Ozawa's flagship, was the only fleet carrier in the force; the big ship was a veteran of the Pearl Harbor attack, the 1942 Indian Ocean raid and the battles of the Coral Sea and the Philippine Sea. There were also three light carriers, which were conversions of fast naval auxiliaries, the *Chitose*, the *Chiyoda* and the *Zuihō*. All four ships had fought in the Battle of the Philippine Sea.[28] Making up the numbers were the 'hermaphrodites', *Ise* and *Hyūga*, two more old super-dreadnoughts (like the *Fusō* and the *Yamashiro*), but modified after Midway to handle and launch long-range reconnaissance seaplanes from the after part of the ship, while keeping four of their six main-gun twin turrets. They were only capable of 23 knots and did not actually carry any aircraft in October 1944.

Late on Tuesday morning (24th) Ozawa launched the largest strike he could from his carriers, but it consisted of only thirty-four fighters, twenty-eight dive bombers and six torpedo planes. These attacked Sherman's TG 38.3 through cloudy skies. Fifteen planes were shot down, but most of the remainder landed on air bases in the Philippines, and only three returned to the carriers. No damage was caused to the American fleet. Ozawa's carrier force was now not just weak, but an empty shell. The remaining strike force on board comprised exactly five aircraft – four dive bombers and a torpedo plane. They could certainly not launch any attacks against the pursuing Americans. Defensive fighter strength consisted of only twenty-four Zero fighters, and as a result of this the air battles over the Japanese carrier fleet would be completely one-sided.

The air strikes by TF 38 began early on the morning of Wednesday (the 25th), at about the same time that the battleships and cruisers of Kurita's 1st Striking Force – 550 miles to the south – were approaching Taffy 3 off Samar. The first wave of attacking US Navy planes sank the light carrier *Chitose* and damaged the *Zuikaku* sufficiently to force Ozawa to transfer his flag to the cruiser *Ōyodo*. A further five strikes arriving through the course of the day sank the three surviving Japanese carriers and a destroyer.

Halsey had organised his fast battleships into Admiral Lee's Task Force 34 to pursue and finish off Ozawa's carrier fleet, but it now had to be recalled to deal with Kurita and the crisis off Samar. Nimitz sent what became later a famous signal to Halsey, 'Where is Task Force 34?' Like Kinkaid, Nimitz had believed TF 34 was on station off the San Bernardino Strait. The supposedly meaningless 'padding' words sent with the coded message, 'the world wonders', appeared (not illogically) to be a reprimand; it certainly threw Halsey into a rage. Late on Wednesday morning the battleships were recalled from their pursuit of the remnants of Ozawa's fleet and sent to support Kinkaid, but by then the crisis in the south had been resolved. Shuffling east and then west, Admiral Lee's powerful task force of six fast battleships and a number of cruisers and destroyers did not engage enemy warships in any part of these Philippine battles.

The *Ise* and the *Hyūga* escaped serious damage; this was quite remarkable, given the decoy role of the 'weird sisters', their slow speed and the strength of the American air attack. Admiral Ozawa and the *Ōyodo* also survived the battle, reaching a safe anchorage off Japan at midday on Friday.

Taking into account all four parts of the Battle of Leyte Gulf (and adding the earlier sea/air battle off Formosa), a few conclusions can be made. First of all, it was a great victory for Admiral Halsey and the men of the US Navy and a great defeat for the Japanese. Despite this, two distinguished military historians in an important book on military 'misfortune' included this October battle: 'the Battle of Leyte Gulf is most certainly a case of military failure [for the US].'[29]

But imperfection is not the same as failure, and it is certainly not the same as defeat.

The problem at Leyte Gulf is normally seen as Halsey's falling for the Japanese lure, dashing off in pursuit and failing to protect the northern approaches to Leyte Gulf. This is true, and Halsey was probably fortunate that the losses among the escort carriers were not higher than they were. Nevertheless, a more important criticism concerns the fundamental flaw in the American command structure, for which no one in the Pacific naval forces of the United States bore direct responsibility: there was no overall commander for the Third and Seventh fleets. This situation went back to the division of the Pacific theatre in early 1942 between Nimitz and MacArthur. This geographical split was at least understandable in 1942 – although still strategically unfortunate – when the rear bases and combat areas were so far apart, in Australia and Hawaii. But by the autumn of 1944 the two prongs of the American transpacific advance had come together, and all naval operations in the western Pacific should have been under one command, probably with a commander-in-chief nearer than Hawaii. What kept the inadequate system in place was inertia, the previous success of American operations, inter-service rivalry, and an unwillingness of the President – in very poor health and with bigger problems on his mind – to confront the issue.

Far more criticism, both at an operational and a political level, can be aimed at the Japanese. They certainly lost the battle, despite some clever footwork. Admiral Toyoda's battle plan was foolhardy, with no chance of success, certainly with the forces available. As in the Marianas with the Battle of the Philippine Sea, a major reason for the defeat of the Japanese was the failure of the land-based naval air groups to provide the support that was expected.

The second conclusion, following on from the above, concerns the relative importance of the October 1944 Battle of Leyte Gulf compared to the June 1944 Battle of the Philippine Sea.[30] Much more has been written about Leyte Gulf than the June battle, partly because of the dramatic events in October and the fact that for the Japanese this was their *last* full-scale naval battle. Their warship losses on 22–26 October were indeed heavier than in the Battle of the Philippine Sea: three battleships, four aircraft carriers, six heavy cruisers and three light cruisers, compared to three fleet carriers in June. Losses of Japanese land-based aircraft were higher in October, especially if the Formosa battles are included. On the other hand, losses by the Japanese of trained carrier aircraft and crews were much higher in June – in the famous 'turkey shoot'. The overall forces involved in the Battle of the Philippine Sea were numerically not much smaller than at Leyte Gulf, and on the Japanese side the carrier force and the number of carrier-borne aircraft were much larger in June than in October. The Philippines were, in strategic terms, also probably a less important objective than the Marianas, despite the post-war quote from Admiral Toyoda cited in the previous section (see p. 446). And the last battle is not necessarily the decisive one.

The battle for Leyte island did not end on 25 October. The ground campaign continued to the end of December. Attempts by the Japanese to reinforce Leyte from the west were like the 'Tokyo Express' runs into Guadalcanal. American air strikes were mounted to the west of the island, but the better part of three more Japanese divisions were shipped into Leyte from Luzon and China. Nevertheless, the US Army finally landed another division on the west coast in early December and ended effective Japanese resistance. These battles led to the loss of the Japanese escort carrier *Shinyō* (torpedoed by a submarine) and two more heavy cruisers in the Manila Bay area, the *Nachi* on 5 November and the *Kumano* on 25 November; the wreck of the *Nachi* yielded an especially valuable haul of documents for US naval intelligence.

Meanwhile, in November the surviving heavy ships of the 1st Attack Force attempted to make their way from Brunei back to the home islands. The (British-built) battleship *Kongō* was torpedoed and sunk by the submarine USS *Sealion* while sailing north through the Formosa Strait in company with the *Yamato*, the *Nagato* and the light cruiser *Yahagi* on the night of 20/21 November. However, the battleship *Haruna*, sailing together with the carrier *Junyō*, successfully ran the submarine gauntlet home to Japan in early December.

Wednesday, 25 October, had been the climax of the Battle of Leyte Gulf, but the day marked the beginning of something more tragic and desperate. At 7.40 a.m., as the Battle off Samar was raging 30 miles to the north, a Japanese pilot flying from an airfield on Luzon crashed his bomb-carrying A6M/ZEKE fighter into the escort carrier USS *Santee*. This was the first organised Japanese suicide air attack. This bizarre form of warfare – along with other types of suicide attack – would henceforth be a central feature of the final ten months of the Pacific sea/air war.

The *Santee* had been operating southeast of the entrance to Leyte Gulf as part of the Taffy 1 escort carrier unit. Sixteen crew members were killed and a serious fire started, but it was brought under control. All the same, the objective of the attack had been achieved: the carrier could no longer operate her aircraft. Remarkably, the *Santee* was hit a few minutes later by a torpedo from the submarine *I-56*, but she survived that as well.[31] At 10.51 a.m. a second CVE was less fortunate. Another Zero crashed into the *St. Lo*, which was part of Taffy 3 and had just escaped the big guns of Admiral Kurita's attack force. Petrol and munitions were ignited, and she sank about half an hour later.

The initiative for this drastic new 'tactic' came from the middle echelons of the Japanese naval command. The prime mover was Admiral Ōnishi Takijirō, who had just been appointed commander of the First Air Fleet in the

Philippines.[32] Unlike most of the other admirals of the Imperial Navy, the fifty-four-year-old Ōnishi had long experience in aviation. In 1941–42 he had been chief of staff of the Eleventh Air Fleet, the headquarters for land-based naval aviation that was so important in the conquest of Southeast Asia and the Philippines. After February 1942 he spent two and a half years in Tokyo organising the development and production of naval aircraft.

Ōnishi had been caught up in the Formosa air battle while en route from Japan to his new command, but he finally reached the Philippines on 17 October. Two days later he drove from Manila to the base of the battered 201st Naval Air Group at Mabalacat in central Luzon. There, during a meeting of the air group commanders, the forceful Ōnishi outlined the overall counter-attack which the Imperial Navy planned to put into effect to deal with an invasion of the Philippines. He also, and evidently on his own initiative, proposed that Zero fighters carrying 250kg (550lb) bombs be crash-dived into the flight decks of American carriers to prevent them – at the critical moment of the battle – from operating their aircraft.[33] The senior leaders of the air group agreed, and ready volunteers came forward from the ranks of the pilots.

Cultural factors were certainly involved in this extraordinary development. As one of the most perceptive western accounts described the Mabalacat meeting, 'The decision to adopt organised suicide tactics had been made in a matter of minutes, though the psychological groundwork had been laid during many centuries.'[34] In any event, the first unit was formed the following day, 20 October. The initial *Tokubetsu Kōgekitai* (abbreviated to *Tokkōtai*) or 'Special Attack Unit' was given the name *Shinpū* after the 'divine wind', the storm at sea which was said to have saved Japan from invasion by Mongol fleets in 1274 and 1281. An alternative transliteration, better known in the west, is 'kamikaze'.[35]

The Imperial Navy was not, however, forced into this solely by the Leyte invasion, or even by the fall of the Marianas. Heroic-suicidal feats were part of Japanese naval tradition, notably the attempt to sink blockships off Port Arthur (now Lüshunkou) during the Russo-Japanese War, and the midget submarine attack on Pearl Harbor. The development of suicide weapons had certainly begun before the autumn of 1944. The Naval General Staff approved the development of the Kaiten manned torpedo (built around the Type 93 oxygen-driven torpedo) in February 1944. The *Ōka* rocket-propelled aircraft, essentially a manned bomb, was approved by the Navy in August 1944, and the first ten were completed by the end of September – before the invasion of the Philippines. For the Navy's leaders there was a cold-blooded practical and rational element. In the face of far superior American air power, kamikaze attacks were no more costly to the attackers than conventional attacks would have been, and they caused much more widespread damage (at least against unarmoured ships).

Technically, with their dispersed approach the kamikazes were also a counter to very effective Allied radar air-defence systems.[36] There was even a kind of *strategic* 'logic' to the use of the kamikazes: they were intended to make the cost of fighting so high for the Americans that they would accept a form of war termination which permitted survival of Japan's imperial political system and perhaps even the retention of some or all of its overseas empire.

The enthusiastic response of young fliers to calls for self-immolation, both in October 1944 and later months, are harder to explain than the decision of their superiors (although easier to excuse). In addition to powerful cultural factors, there came into play a toxic mix of peer pressure and education/propaganda imposed by the extreme nationalists of the later Meiji state.

LUZON, IWO JIMA, OKINAWA

The last three campaigns in the Pacific war, on the approaches to Japan, were different from one another. In each case, however relentless, American advances faced bitter Japanese resistance. Of the three, the Luzon campaign is probably the least well known. Luzon was the most important of the islands in the Philippines, and after a long debate within the American armed services – lasting through much of 1944 – it had been chosen rather than Formosa as a major objective. The resistance of Japanese ground forces on Luzon was reduced by the earlier decision – made in early October – to transfer troops south to defend Leyte. By November American control of the seas made it impossible to bring in Imperial Army reinforcements to Luzon from China and Japan.

The Luzon campaign, like the battle on Leyte, was run by the US Army; Marine Corps involvement was minimal. Four Army divisions were chosen for the invasion. Two came from Bougainville and New Britain, and the other two from western New Guinea. Troop movements by sea began in mid-December and the invasion force came together at the Leyte anchorage, now a forward base. The huge transport convoy, Task Force 77, departed from Leyte on 4–5 January, and the four divisions came ashore on 9 January 1945 at Lingayen Gulf, northwest of Manila. This was the same large bay where the Japanese had landed in December 1941.

There was no effective interference to the Luzon landings by Japanese naval warships or submarines. The very last surface battle of the Pacific war was, however, fought on the night of 7/8 January, when the old destroyer *Hinoki* sortied out of Manila Bay to be sunk in unequal combat with four American destroyers. Some midget submarines operated from Japanese shore bases in the central Philippines, but they also achieved nothing; they were similar to the boats used at Pearl Harbor, Sydney and Madagascar.

Kamikaze air attacks now became a significant factor, however. These mostly involved aircraft of the Japanese Navy, and they began their attack as Task Force 77 made its way through the Surigao Strait and up the west side of the Philippines. The escort carrier *Ommaney Bay* was crashed at long range by a twin-engined suicide bomber while crossing the Sulu Sea on 4 January; she was so badly damaged that she had to be sunk. The threat became even more dangerous in the confines of Lingayen Gulf, where US warships were concentrated to support the landings. Saturday, 6 January, three days before the troops came ashore, was much the worst day. The kamikazes were now better prepared than they had been at Leyte, and dozens of them came in at low level from nearby airfields. Conventional AA fire was ineffective, and fighter cover provided by a dozen escort carriers could not intercept all the attackers. At noon the battleship *New Mexico*, part of the Fire Support Unit, was hit on her navigation bridge. Some thirty men were killed, including the CO of the battleship (Captain Robert W. Fleming) and the British general Herbert Lumsden, who was attached to General MacArthur's SWPA headquarters. Lumsden, who had commanded a corps at El Alamein, was the most senior British Army officer to be killed in action – anywhere – in World War II. Admiral Bruce Fraser, who sank the *Scharnhorst* and was now C-in-C of the new British Pacific Fleet, was standing near Lumsden and narrowly escaped death. Also hit were the battleship *California*, three cruisers and three destroyers; none were sunk. Fortunately for the invaders, the Japanese only had enough aircraft in the Philippines for one burst of attacks, and there was no serious air interference with the actual amphibious operation. More important, the landings of the four American divisions met no opposition from enemy ground forces; the Japanese Army under General Yamashita did not attempt to fight at Lingayen, preferring to drag out the campaign in less accessible rural areas of eastern Luzon.

One other tragic episode of the Luzon campaign involved the Imperial Navy. The Japanese Army did not want to hold the densely populated city of Manila, but Admiral Iwabuchi Sanji, head of the naval base forces in Manila port, with 15,000 sailors under his command, persisted in fighting for the city. The battle, which lasted for six weeks, until 3 March, took a very high toll on Filipino civilians; the total killed has been put at 100,000. Iwabuchi had commanded the battleship *Kirishima*, sunk off Guadalcanal in 1942; he committed suicide in the final stages of the battle.

The campaign in 1945 on Luzon and other islands of the Philippines was fought by the four US Army divisions landed at Lingayen Gulf, along with several more divisions brought in as reinforcements. No more major contested amphibious landings took place. Seen from a modern perspective and in strictly military terms, the campaign in the Philippines did not bring the defeat of Japan any closer. It did, however, avenge a defeat for MacArthur and the US Army in 1941–42, and it liberated a region for which the United States bore political responsibility; the latter factor would have been even more telling had the war continued – as originally expected – into 1946 or 1947.

American control of Luzon also meant control of the Luzon Strait between the Philippines and Formosa. This had the effect of further restricting the route for Japanese shipping up the China coast from Southeast Asia to Japan (although it was still possible to pass through the narrower strait between Formosa and the Chinese mainland). On the night of 9/10 January Admiral Halsey took the whole Third Fleet, with fourteen carriers and eight fast battleships, through the Luzon Strait to raid the coast of the South China Sea (west of the Philippines). The operation demonstrated the range and freedom of movement of American carrier task groups and the extreme weakness of the Japanese naval power at sea and in the air. After supporting, from the west of Luzon, the landings at Lingayen, and mounting another series of air strikes on Formosa, Halsey crossed the South China Sea to raid ports and airfields in Indochina, and then Hainan and Hong Kong. Many Japanese merchant ships were sunk. After the ten-day raid the Third Fleet passed back through the Luzon Strait and into the open Pacific on 20 January.[37]

By the time the Battle of Manila ended in March 1945 the Japanese homeland itself, rather than Formosa or the Philippines, had become the main target of American sea/air operations. Admiral Spruance replaced Halsey in a planned rotation on 26 January, after the latter's return from the South China Sea, and the Third Fleet was again re-designated as the Fifth Fleet. Admiral Mitscher took over from Admiral John McCain in command of the Fast Carrier Force, now again Task Force 58.

Leaving his base at Ulithi, Mitscher mounted the first carrier strikes against the Tokyo area of central Honshū (the Kantō Plain) on 16–17 February 1945. His massive force now included nine 'Essex' class fleet carriers (with the new *Bennington* and *Randolph*) and five light carriers. A fifth task group had been organised for radar-equipped night-fighters, with the pre-war *Saratoga* and *Enterprise*. In view of the kamikaze danger and the relative lack of enemy warship targets, the aircraft mix of the fleet carriers had been altered to include fewer torpedo planes and more fighters; three-quarters of the total were now Hellcats and Corsairs. The AAF had begun high-altitude B-29 Superfortress raids on the Tokyo area from the Marianas in late November 1944. These, however, had so far been relatively small in scale and were still ineffective at the time of the spectacular Navy raid. Although the weather was poor, Task Force 38 mounted 638 strike sorties at low level, including attacks on airfields and industrial targets, and fought successful dogfights with enemy interceptors.

The carrier raids on the Tokyo area were partly intended to reduce Japanese resistance to the invasion of Iwo Jima, which began on 19 February. The volcanic island was 750 miles south of Tokyo, in what are known in the West as the Bonin Islands.[38] The Bonins were valuable to both sides as air bases. They had played a strategic role in Japanese preparation for the Battle of the Philippine Sea, because air reinforcements for the Marianas could be ferried through them. The exposed Bonins had been raided several times by American carrier task forces; in the September 1944 attack a TBM Avenger from the light carrier *San Jacinto* flown by twenty-year-old Lieutenant (JG) George H.W. Bush, the future American President, was hit by AA fire over the Bonins; he was saved by a 'life-guard' submarine after having to parachute into the ocean. Iwo Jima had also been identified by the American planners as a base for long-range AAF P-51 escort fighters and as an emergency landing field for B-29 heavy bombers based in the Marianas.

In contrast to the Philippines, the invasion of Iwo Jima (Operation DETACHMENT) was organised by Admiral Nimitz rather than General MacArthur. The landing force consisted of three Marine divisions, not troops from the US Army. The 4th and 5th Marine Divisions were transported from Hawaii, the 3rd from Guam. The amphibious armada, again commanded by Kelly Turner, approached Iwo from Saipan. James Forrestal, the Secretary of the Navy, was aboard Turner's flagship as an observer.

Harassment of the landing force by Japanese aircraft had limited effect, as Iwo was 750 miles from the nearest air bases on the mainland. Nevertheless, the Japanese Third Air Fleet did rapidly organise a kamikaze force, recruiting pilots who had been in training for carrier operations. The carrier *Saratoga* had to be sent home to the West Coast after being badly damaged by three kamikaze strikes on the afternoon of 21 February, and that evening the escort carrier *Bismarck Sea* was sunk after being crashed by one suicide plane. After that the threat diminished. Attempts at attack by six Japanese submarines had little effect, and three were sunk by escorts or A/S carriers.

Iwo Jima was famously one of the most bitterly fought landing operations, as the small volcanic island (about half the area of Manhattan) had been heavily fortified. A preliminary naval gunfire bombardment by heavy ships began on 16 February, followed by a landing on the 19th. A month passed before Iwo Jima was completely secured. Nearly the entire Japanese Army garrison of 21,000 men were killed; American deaths, mostly among Marines, were 6,800.

In early February – two weeks before the Iwo landings – Admiral Ugaki Matome had been appointed commander of the Fifth Air Fleet. His task was to defend the southwestern part of Japan proper, the island of Kyūshū. It was the nearest point to the Ryūkyū Islands, where the next American attack was expected. Ugaki had been commander of Kurita's battleships at the battles of the Philippine Sea and Leyte Gulf, but he had previously served under Admiral Yamamoto as his chief of staff; he was a key planner of the Pearl Harbor and Midway operations, as well as of the sea/air operations in the Solomons in early 1943. Although lacking a specialist aviation background he was now entrusted with a large number of land-based naval air squadrons. Above all his task was to organise kamikaze attacks.

Along with organising mass kamikaze attacks for defending the Ryūkyū Islands and Kyūshū, Ugaki also oversaw plans for a very long-range strike using highly trained aircrew. Operation TAN ('Red Heart') involved eighteen of the new twin-engined P1Y/FRANCES bombers, flying a 1,550-mile one-way mission from the tip of Kyūshū to Ulithi. Partly due to bad weather the raiders arrived after dark on 11 March; only one of them succeeded in crashing the flight deck of a carrier, the new *Randolph*, and that ship suffered relatively minor damage (although she would be under repair for nearly a month). The rest of Task Force 58 was able to put to sea from Ulithi three days later, on 14 March, for another grand raid on Japan.

This time the fast carriers targeted not the Tokyo area but airfields on Kyūshū and the remnants of the Imperial Navy in the Inland Sea. On 19 March carrier planes attacked Kure, damaging the battleship *Ise* and burning out the light carrier *Ryūhō*, a veteran of the Philippine Sea battle. These operations involved a high level of risk for the Americans, as their carriers steamed only 50 miles off the coast. Conventional bombers (not kamikazes) from Ugaki's Fifth Air Fleet damaged two fleet carriers in TG 58.2, the *Franklin* and the *Wasp*. A solitary dive bomber appeared out of the low clouds about the *Franklin*, the task group flagship, and hit her with one 250kg bomb. Secondary explosions of fuel and munitions in the carrier's hangar and flight decks caused devastating damage and eventually led to the deaths of 807 members of her crew. This was the largest loss of personnel on an American warship since the *Arizona* at Pearl Harbor.[39] The *Franklin* was rebuilt after the war, but she was never used in operational service again. Over 100 crewmen were killed aboard the *Wasp* after one bomb hit, but she was able to continue flight operations before being sent home for repairs.

Two days later Task Force 58 was the object of the first attempted use of the Ōka ('Cherry Blossom') rocket aircraft. With its 1,200kg (2,646lb) warhead, 'this little horror' (as Morison aptly described it) seemed a powerful weapon.[40] It had a glide range of 20 miles from its launcher aircraft and a terminal dive speed of about 575 mph. The formation of G4M/BETTY twin-engined bombers, slowed by their heavy load, were unable to avoid the US Navy interceptors. All eighteen launcher aircraft were shot down some 60 miles away from American carriers; none were able to launch their human missiles. In later weeks a few more ships would be damaged in Ōka attacks; the only destruction of a US warship came on 12 April, off Okinawa, when the 'radar picket' destroyer *Mannert L. Abele* was hit and sank in five minutes; five of six launcher aircraft had been shot down by the CAP.

The final major Pacific amphibious operation was code-named ICEBERG and was directed against Okinawa and nearby islands in the Ryūkyū island group. Okinawa was ten times the size of Saipan, and about 70 miles from one end to the other. American possession of the islands would fully cut Japan off from the resources of the south and provide air bases to support the planned invasion of southwestern Japan proper. American troops came ashore on Okinawa on 1 April 1945, Easter Sunday, five weeks before the end of the war in Europe. The scale of the American operation was huge, especially considering the distances involved from home bases. Two US Army divisions came from Leyte, where they had been involved in the long land battle there. The other two formations were the 1st and 6th Marine Divisions, veterans from Guam and Peleliu. Another Army division was shipped to Okinawa after the initial landing. The strength of American naval gunfire made the commander of the Japanese Thirty-Second Army decide not to contest the beaches with his two divisions, but to fight to the death from entrenched positions inland. The ground battle for Okinawa lasted for nearly three months; organised resistance by the Japanese on the ground only finished on 22 June.

The Japanese Navy could do little to interfere with the preliminary bombardment or the arrival of the first wave of landings. But the most striking feature of the Okinawa campaign was the scale of kamikaze operations; it was, like Guadalcanal, a Verdun of the sea/air war. The Japanese armed forces had formally agreed to use 'special' tactics in a comprehensive and co-ordinated way, very different from the first experiments at Leyte. This was formally recorded in a top-level Army–Navy agreement of 5 February 1945. Admiral Ugaki's Fifth Air Fleet would also co-ordinate the operations of the neighbouring Third and Tenth Air Fleets, and the Imperial Army's Sixth Air Army (Sixth *Kōkūgun*). Altogether 1,900 kamikazes were launched against American forces during the Okinawa campaign, 1,465 in the mass KIKUSUI ('Floating Chrysanthemum') operations.[41] The largest number of launches was on 6–7 April (KIKUSUI II) with 230 Navy planes and 125 from the Army. The American press only released news of the kamikaze attacks on 12 April, six months after they had begun off Leyte Gulf; the information had been suppressed to avoid undermining morale on the home front.[42] KIKUSUI II and III (185 and 165 launches, respectively, mostly naval aircraft) presented the heaviest danger; they were launched on 12–13 and 16 April. The four organised KIKUSUI attacks in May were on a smaller scale. In June, the last big attack (KIKUSUI X on 21–22 June) involved 'only' forty-five suicide planes.

The *Bunker Hill*, Admiral Mitscher's flagship, and one of the first of the 'Essex' class carriers, was crashed nearly simultaneously by two kamikazes on 11 May. In the resulting explosions of fuel and munitions she lost nearly 400 of her crew, mostly from smoke inhalation. Mitscher and his staff had to transfer to a destroyer, and then move to the *Enterprise*. The *Bunker Hill* needed to return to the US; she would not see service as an operational carrier again.

The Okinawa campaign lasted twelve weeks. Thanks to the kamikazes, it was the most lethal campaign fought by the US Navy during World War II. Some thirty vessels were lost and 4,900 sailors were counted as dead or missing, a number only slightly less than that of US Army troops killed in the ground battle.[43] The American fleet air defence with its radar system was highly effective against organised concentrated conventional attacks, but it had great difficulty with dispersed and low-flying kamikazes.

Nevertheless, the effect of the kamikaze campaign off Okinawa is often exaggerated. Despite spectacular photographs of incoming kamikazes and burning aircraft carriers, no large American warship – fleet carrier, battleship or cruiser – was sunk during the Okinawa campaign by a kamikaze. Three escort carriers were sunk by kamikazes earlier, but none off Okinawa. The main victims this time were the 'radar picket' destroyers posted out to sea to give early warning of approaching strikes.

After the war, Ukagi's chief of staff, Admiral Yokoi Toshiyuki, wrote a critical analysis of the practical shortcomings of the campaign (not to mention the moral ones), which he claimed he had disapproved of from the beginning. In his view, employing suicide tactics was an inefficient use of highly trained manpower. Even carrying a 250kg bomb a kamikaze plane would not normally be able to sink a ship, and certainly not an armoured one. Given the one-way nature of the attacks, the commanders in headquarters ashore were not able accurately to gauge the result.[44] This last factor was certainly important, as a constant tendency to exaggerate success meant that a ghastly but ineffective tactic was continued; Admiral Ugaki's diary, for example, is full of wishful thinking. Although the Fifth Air Fleet attempted to use its very fast C6N/MYRT reconnaissance planes to locate targets, and some elite fighter units to clear the way for the kamikazes, the strikes were never well co-ordinated.

The suicide mission of the super-battleship *Yamato* was a spectacular example of the kamikaze spirit. The Germans in November 1918 issued an order for a final sortie of their High Seas Fleet (which provoked a mutiny), and the Italians in 1943 talked about a 'sacrificial' mission. The Imperial Japanese Navy actually carried out such a 'death ride'. On the afternoon of 6 April (D+5 of Operation ICEBERG) the *Yamato* sortied from the Tokuyama depot in the Inland

Sea where she had taken on fuel for her one-way trip to Okinawa. Escorted by the new light cruiser *Yahagi* and eight destroyers, she emerged from the Bungo Strait just before midnight. Admiral Itō Seiichi was in command of Operation TEN-ICHI; he had been Vice Chief of the Naval General Staff in Tokyo from September 1941 to December 1944, when he replaced Admiral Kurita in the rump of the Second Fleet.

There was no military logic behind the *Yamato* sortie. At best it was a *demonstration* of surface-ship activity – probably intended more than anything else to save face before the Imperial Army. If the sortie was supposed to be co-ordinated with kamikaze air strikes it did not work out. Friday, 6 April, had been one of the worst days off Okinawa for kamikaze attacks – three US Navy destroyers were sunk. However, the 7th, the day *Yamato* made her suicide run, saw relatively little Japanese air activity. Radio intercepts and air reconnaissance gave the Americans detailed advance warning of the sortie. The *Yamato* was hit by the first bomb at 12.40 p.m. She eventually took eleven torpedo hits, rolled over, and sank in a huge explosion. The column of smoke could be seen from distant Kyūshū. Admiral Itō had retired to his cabin and went down with the ship. Some survivors (including Itō's chief of staff) were rescued by the destroyers, but 2,498 men of the *Yamato* were killed. The *Yahagi*, along with five of the destroyers, was also sunk. Her captain, Hara Tameichi, a veteran of many Pacific destroyer battles, lived to write his memoirs;[45] he spent hours in the water before being picked up by a friendly ship.

The loss of the *Yamato* was the effective end of the Combined Fleet. Admiral Toyoda remained the central figure in the Imperial Navy, but from May 1945 he did so as head of the Naval General Staff, replacing Admiral Oikawa Koshirō. Admiral Ozawa, Vice Chief of the NGS since December 1944, took over the nominal Combined Fleet and the Maritime Escort Command, but he probably had more to do with the latter organisation. With kamikaze attacks now the centre of the activities of the Imperial Navy, Admiral Ōnishi became Vice Chief of the NGS.

Another feature of the Okinawa campaign was the arrival in the main Pacific combat zone, near Japan, of the ships and aircraft of the British Pacific Fleet (BPF). They operated as Task Force 57 within Admiral Spruance's Fifth Fleet. On 26 March, six days before American troops landed on Okinawa, British carrier planes carried out air strikes against the Sakishima Islands; part of the Ryūkyūs, these islands were 175 miles southwest of Okinawa and on the air route for Japanese attack planes staging north from Formosa.

The creation of the BPF had come about after sharp debate among the Allies and within the British war leadership. The wartime idea of a strong British naval presence in the war against Japan dated back to November–December 1943 and the Cairo/SEXTANT Conference. At that meeting the British and Americans agreed that their main effort in the war against Japan would be in the Pacific (rather than the Indian Ocean). This was at a time when the American carrier campaign in the Central Pacific was just beginning, and the fleet was still based at Pearl Harbor. Meanwhile General MacArthur and the forces of the South West Pacific Area (SWPA) command were beginning their campaign along the north-central coast of New Guinea (see pp. 248–9). In early 1944 one proposal was that British forces might operate in the SWPA, in what the planners called a 'middle road' between the Central Pacific and the Indian Ocean.

Prime Minister Churchill regarded the Indian Ocean and Southeast Asia as politically the most important place for British (Imperial) naval operations. The British Chiefs of Staff Committee, led by General Alan Brooke, saw the situation from the more narrowly military-operational perspective. They were concerned with what would bring the war in the Far East to an end most quickly while maintaining Britain's status as a global military power. They also realised that in the short term – certainly before Germany was defeated – the only force which Britain could deploy against Japan would be the Royal Navy. Numerous new and powerful ships were now on hand, which had little purpose in European waters. Admiral Cunningham, the First Sea Lord, was strongly committed to Pacific operations, partly because of his big fleet outlook and partly because of a desire to assure a strong place for the Royal Navy in the expected competition for post-war funding. The plan for a British fleet in the Pacific was revived in September 1944 at the Quebec/OCTAGON Conference with a personal offer from the Prime Minister to President Roosevelt. This was accepted without any consultation involving Admiral King; according to Churchill the President intervened 'to say that the British Fleet was no sooner offered than accepted'.[46]

Admiral Bruce Fraser was the C-in-C of the BPF. He was a highly experienced officer, having served as Third Sea Lord and then in the Home Fleet. He had been Churchill's first choice to replace Pound as First Sea Lord in mid-1943 but he had declined the post, citing Andrew Cunningham's higher standing in the fleet; he had then gone on to oversee the sinking of the *Scharnhorst* in December 1943. Although a gunnery officer, he had aviation experience as captain of the carrier *Glorious* in the 1930s. Fraser was based ashore in Sydney and was not in direct control of the combat operations of the BPF. He had many organisational tasks in Australia, and as a full admiral he would have outranked American commanders to whom the units of the BPF would be subordinate (effectively as a task group of the US Navy's Fifth/Third Fleet). His subordinate, Admiral Bernard Rawlings, was the actual commander of the fleet off Japan, with the famous Admiral Philip Vian commanding the carrier force.

In late January 1945 the BPF had mounted preliminary operations against oil refineries near Palembang at the southern end of Sumatra. The raid was launched from a force which included four British fleet carriers and a modern battleship, all en route from Trincomalee in Ceylon to their new main base at Sydney. When it was fully assembled in waters off Japan the British Pacific Fleet exceeded – as a battle fleet – anything the Royal Navy had deployed in the earlier years of the war. Rawlings flew his flag in the battleship *King George V*, which was accompanied by a sister ship, the *Howe*. Admiral Vian's carriers were the *Illustrious*, the *Indomitable*, the *Indefatigable* and the *Victorious*. The air groups of the four carriers totalled 154 fighters and sixty-five Grumman Avenger strike aircraft.[47]

Deployment of a British fleet in Japanese home waters involved huge logistical challenges. Sydney was 12,500 miles from the UK, and the forward base at Manus in the Admiralty Islands lay 2,000 miles from Sydney. As Admiral Fraser put it in his post-war despatch: 'The distances involved are similar to those of a fleet based in Alexandria, and with advanced anchorages at Gibraltar and the Azores, attacking the North American coast between Labrador and Nova Scotia.'[48] The Royal Navy did not have the extensive 'fleet train' of supply and repair ships developed by the Americans, but the US Navy was generous in its support.

The British carriers had steel-armoured flight decks and enclosed hangar decks, which provided rather better protection against a hit by a kamikaze than did the wooden decks of the American carriers. The British reinforcements proved more welcome to the US Navy than originally expected, as a number of the American fleet carriers had to return to base after being damaged by Japanese aircraft in the Okinawa campaign or off Japan. On the other hand, the British armoured carriers could not simple shrug off enemy air attack. The *Illustrious* suffered such serious damage from a near miss on 6 April 1945 that she was knocked out of the war, having to return to Sydney and then all the way back to Britain for lengthy structural repairs.

After the end of the Okinawa campaign the American carriers continued pounding what was left of the Imperial Navy. Most of the enemy warships were immobilised by lack of fuel and tied up in the Inland Sea. The first in this wave of attacks by Helldivers, Hellcats and Corsairs began on 24 July – two weeks before the bombing of Hiroshima. It saw the sinking of the former flagship of the Combined Fleet, the light cruiser *Ōyodo*, as well as a newly completed 'Unryū' class fleet carrier, the *Amagi*; both warships capsized. Badly damaged were the 'hermaphrodite' battleships *Ise* and *Hyūga*, the last of the fast battleships, the *Haruna*, as well as the heavy cruisers *Tone* and *Aoba*.[49] All were sunk upright in shallow water, with their superstructures sticking out of the sea. Four days later the raiders returned and damaged another incomplete 'Unryū' class ship, the *Katsuragi*. Mitscher had been reluctant to send his aircrew in against heavy AA fire for a target which no longer represented a serious military threat. In fact losses in these July raids were heavy, including 133 American aircrew. (By way of contrast, the Japanese lost only fifty-five fliers in the 1941 attack on Pearl Harbor.)

The British Pacific Fleet took part in raids on the Tokyo area, but it was not involved in the late July strikes against the Japanese fleet. The force was now designated as Task Force 37 and consisted of the carrier *Victorious*, as well as the *Formidable* and the new *Implacable*, with the *King George V*, six cruisers and fifteen destroyers.

The last surviving big-gun vessel of the Imperial Navy was the battleship *Nagato*, which ended the war moored off the Yokosuka naval base, near Tokyo. Admiral Yamamoto's flagship in 1941, she was immobilised by lack of fuel; she was now employed as an AA platform, and was damaged during a carrier raid on 18 July. The strength of the once mighty Imperial Japanese Navy at the end of the war, in terms of undamaged ships in home waters, was three light cruisers, twenty-seven destroyers and fifty submarines.[50]

THE SURRENDER OF IMPERIAL JAPAN

After the April sortie of the *Yamato* no major Japanese surface ships put to sea, even on suicide missions. Still, individual leaders of the Imperial Navy took a significant part in the politics of these final months of the war. General Tōjō had resigned as the Emperor's Prime Minister in July 1944 after the fall of Saipan. His successor, an ineffective and poorly informed general, Koiso Kuniaki, presided for seven months over worse defeats. Then at the beginning of April 1945, with the Americans ashore on Okinawa, the seventy-seven-year-old Admiral Suzuki Kantarō – a veteran of Tsushima – was appointed Prime Minister. Also among the 'big six' top leaders in the new Supreme Council for the Direction of the War (*Saikō Sensō Shidō Kaigi*) were Admiral Toyoda (now Chief of the Naval General Staff) and Admiral Yonai Mitsumasa (Minister of the Navy). Suzuki and Yonai were broadly in favour of bringing the war to an end, if satisfactory terms could be agreed. Toyoda and the two Army generals on the Supreme Council, Umezu Yoshijirō and Anami Korechika, preferred to fight on, accepting invasion.

The new cabinet faced insoluble problems. The Russians announced in April 1945 that they would not renew their 1941 neutrality treaty with Japan. Nazi Germany surrendered in May. Okinawa fell in June, completely severing the shipping route to the south and threatening Kyūshū. On 26 July the governments of the US, Britain and China issued the Potsdam Declaration from their victorious conference in Berlin. They demanded that Japan accept unconditional surrender or face 'prompt and utter destruction'. Then came the atomic bombing of Hiroshima on 6 August, followed three days later by the Soviet invasion of Manchuria and the second nuclear attack, on Nagasaki.

Foreign Minister Tōgō and Admiral Suzuki now pressed for the acceptance of the Potsdam Declaration, even though its terms demanded removal from government of all those responsible for the wars of conquest ('self-willed militaristic advisers whose unintelligent calculations have brought the Empire of Japan to the threshold of annihilation'), as well as the trial of war criminals, complete disarmament of Japan, and occupation of the country by Allied forces.[51] The opposition of the two senior Army generals and Admiral Toyoda was finally overcome, at the last minute, by the intervention of the Emperor. At 12.00 noon on 15 August an Imperial rescript was broadcast, announcing an end to the fighting – although without using the words 'defeat' or 'surrender'.

The two flag officers most identified with the horror of the kamikazes responded to the end of the war in a similar way. Admirals Ugaki and Ōnishi had begun the war from very different professional perspectives, the first as a big-gun traditionalist, the second as a pioneering naval aviator. Ugaki was now commander of the land-based Fifth Air Fleet, his headquarters located in a cave near the Ōita air base in eastern Kyūshū. Early on the morning of 15 August the admiral ordered preparation of a small and final suicide strike by D4Y/JUDY dive bombers, in which he intended to take a direct part. He heard the Imperial rescript at midday, but ignored it. In the afternoon a formation of eleven dive bombers took off for the west, with Admiral Ugaki sitting in the rear seat of one of them. A final 'diving on target' signal was transmitted by the little attack group in the evening; in reality Ugaki failed to engage any American ships and crashed somewhere near Okinawa.

Meanwhile, Admiral Ōnishi, still Vice Chief of the Naval General Staff, was at his quarters in Tokyo. He had been appointed in May; in August his fanatical advice had been that certain victory could be achieved if only 20 million Japanese gave up their lives in a 'special attack' effort.[52] In the early hours of the 16th, shortly after Ugaki disappeared on his futile air mission, Ōnishi committed hara-kiri. Refusing a *coup de grâce* after his ritual disembowelment, he lingered in agony until the evening. Admiral Toyoda, for his part, finally accepted defeat, remaining as head of the NGS until that organisation was liquidated in October. He was imprisoned by the Allies, tried for war crimes and acquitted; he died of a heart attack in 1957.

The Red Army entered the war with Japan on 9 August 1945. The big offensive in Manchuria was a significant factor behind the decision of the Japanese government to surrender. The naval side of these events was not so important, but it deserves mention. Before 1941 the Soviet Pacific Fleet had been built up, at least in terms of aircraft, coastal artillery, MTBs and submarines. After the German invasion in 1941 tens of thousands of Pacific Fleet sailors had been transferred to the European front, mostly to serve in the ground forces, but in

1944–45 naval strength in Siberia began to be increased again. At Yalta in February 1945 the USSR secretly agreed to enter the war in the Far East, a development welcomed by the American planners, who expected to have to carry out an invasion of Japan against stiff resistance.

Admiral King agreed to a secret build-up of Russian naval forces. This involved transfer of ships and training Soviet naval personnel, and was known as Project HULA. The Soviet Pacific Fleet would receive 180 small warships, including thirty 1,400-ton frigates, sixty minesweepers, thirty LCI(L)s and fifty-six small sub-chasers.[53] The base for Project HULA was set up at Cold Bay in southwestern Alaska, 80 miles east of Dutch Harbor. From mid-April 1945 thousands of naval personnel from the neutral USSR were brought to Cold Harbor aboard merchant ships returning from Siberia. The first American-supplied vessels, some minesweepers, departed for naval bases in the USSR at the end of May.

Atomic bombs and the sudden Japanese capitulation changed Allied calculations. Nevertheless, small Soviet naval operations took place in northwestern Korea, southern Sakhalin and the Kurile Islands. These began on 12 August and continued after the Japanese agreement to surrender on 15 August. The larger new Soviet-built warships – two light cruisers and eleven destroyers – did not take part, although some submarines put to sea as a covering force.

Poor communications and over-zealous Japanese troops meant broken-backed fighting continued for weeks. The Soviet forces as a whole lost 12,000 men killed in the three-week war with Japan, with losses of the Soviet Pacific Fleet numbering 900.[54] The heaviest fighting took place on 18–23 August, with the invasion of the island of Shimushu (now Shumshu), the most northerly of the Kuriles, lying next to the Kamchatka Peninsula. This involved a shore-to-shore invasion from Petropavlovsk on Kamchatka, with numerous small warships including American-supplied LCI(L)s. Shimushu (and neighbouring Paramushiru – now Paramushir) was defended by the Imperial Army's 91st Division, and about 500 Russian servicemen were killed before resistance was overcome.

On the twentieth anniversary of the 1945 victory the Russian naval forces in the Soviet Far East were awarded the Red Banner (*Krasnoznamennyi*) honorific for their wartime service. What was now the Red Banner Pacific Fleet had in the meantime become one of the most powerful Soviet fleets, with large modern submarines, surface ships and squadrons of jet bombers. In reality the Pacific Fleet had only fought skirmishes against defeated enemy forces in August 1945; its role, however, would have been considerably greater if an Allied invasion of Japan had actually been mounted in the autumn of 1945.

The first of hundreds of ships of the American Third Fleet entered Sagami Bay, to the west of Tokyo Bay and overlooked by Mount Fuji, on Monday,

27 August. The following day an advance party of the 11th Airborne Division was flown into the Atsugi naval air base, west of Tokyo. On the 30th, General MacArthur arrived at Atsugi, and a Marine regiment came ashore at Yokosuka, in Tokyo Bay itself. Steps were taken to assure the security of the bay; an American newsreel showed the Stars and Stripes being raised over the wrecked *Nagato* off Yokosuka. USS *Missouri* and a number of other ships moved into Tokyo Bay. The British presence included the *King George V*, the *Duke of York* and the carrier *Indefatigable*.

The brief surrender ceremony on the morning of 2 September was presided over by General MacArthur on behalf of the Allies. This caused considerable annoyance in the higher ranks of the US Navy, but the admirals were gratified that the surrender ceremony would be staged aboard one of their warships. The surrender document was signed on the veranda deck of USS *Missouri*, now anchored in Tokyo Bay. General MacArthur signed for the Allies, Admiral Nimitz signed for the United States; Admiral Fraser of the BPF signed for the United Kingdom. The *Missouri* was the third of the 'Iowa' class battleships, and the flagship of Admiral Halsey's Third Fleet. She had only entered active service in January 1945, but she bore the name of President Truman's home state (and had been launched by his daughter).[55] MacArthur and the Japanese delegation, including General Umezu, were ferried out to the *Missouri* aboard American destroyers. Admiral Tomioka Sadatoshi represented the Imperial Navy. A huge fly-past by US Navy and AAF aircraft was carried out as a show of force.

The end of the war was a prolonged affair. Occupation troops began to land in Japan on 2 September, and the surrender of bypassed islands and garrisons commenced at the same time. On 2 September the cruiser USS *Portland* accepted the surrender of the garrison of Truk in the Carolines. On 3 September General Yamashita in the Philippines formally surrendered his command. As already mentioned, on the 6th a British task force took the surrender of the Japanese garrison of Rabaul, in a ceremony held on the flight deck of the new light carrier HMS *Glory*. The cruiser HMS *Sussex* passed through the Strait of Malacca after a channel had been swept through the minefields there. Aboard her, on 5 September, Admiral Cedric Holland – who had conducted the less successful negotiations with the French at Mers el-Kébir in July 1940 – oversaw the surrender of the Singapore garrison by a Japanese general and Admiral Fukudome. A week later, in a larger formal ceremony in Singapore's City Hall, Lord Mountbatten took the surrender of all Japanese forces in Southeast Asia.

* * *

The fifth and final period of World War II at sea ran from June 1944 to August 1945. In overall terms the two surviving Axis powers suffered total military defeat. It was a time of deliverance, the liberation of territory in Europe and Asia from Axis occupation. It was certainly a time of the final destruction of all the armed forces of Germany and Japan. The Red Army broke the back of the remaining German ground forces in the western USSR, and then pushed rapidly into Poland and the Balkans in late 1944, before moving on to Berlin and Vienna. In August 1945 the Russians invaded Manchuria.

The United States and Britain finally carried out their long-time commitment to a 'continental' grand strategy, deploying massive ground and air forces to fight a triumphant campaign in northwestern Europe. For Britain it was a last gasp, but an ultimately victorious effort. American ground forces were engaged overseas on a larger scale than ever before, especially in northwestern Europe but also in the Philippines and Okinawa; preparations were being made to fight in Japan itself. Meanwhile, the strategic air power of Britain and the United States was finally achieving a degree of the effect, against both Germany and the Japanese mainland, that its adherents had prematurely claimed; the ultimate element were the atomic bombs.

In terms of the sea/air war, victory had already been won by the end of June 1944. The German and Italian battle fleets had been defeated. The effective striking power of the Imperial Japanese Navy had been destroyed in the Philippine Sea in June 1944. The later Battle of Leyte Gulf, in October 1944, was geographically wider in scale and involved more American warships. But it was essentially a gesture on the part of the Imperial Navy, a 'banzai charge' on the operational level. Afterwards the last, now redundant, Axis giants were picked off from the air. The *Tirpitz* was sunk in November 1944, as she lay hidden in a Norwegian fjord; the *Yamato* went down in April 1945 off Kyūshū in another pointless suicide operation. The destruction of fleet remnants at Kiel, Swinemünde, Gotenhafen and Kure – old battleships, carriers and cruisers – no doubt jogged memories of events which had occurred only a few years earlier, but those events now seemed to come from a completely different era of naval warfare.

Meanwhile, by June 1944, the British and American maritime forces had also been victorious in the Battle of the Atlantic. In this fifth phase of the war the U-boat threat was not seriously revived. Despite Allied fears, the high-speed German submarines never entered service, and the 'inshore' snorkel-equipped U-boat campaign proved to be of only very limited importance. The Allies continued to enjoy unhindered use of global shipping arteries across the Atlantic, to northern Russia and to the Persian Gulf and even the Black Sea. An enormous pool of merchant shipping had been assembled. Above all, huge armies from the United States and the British Empire were supported and reinforced in the western part of mainland Europe, without any naval challenge from the enemy. The Japanese submarine fleet was even less effective. In the war against Japan, the Allied shipping arteries now reached – unhindered – to the western Pacific. Massive mobile/floating fleet bases were set up at Ulithi, Manus and Guam, able to support operations against the Japanese home islands.

At the same time, the anti-shipping war of the American submarine fleet reached an unprecedented scale, as Japanese shipping protection continued to be ineffective. The campaign was geographically capped by the capture of Luzon in January 1945, which largely cut the north–south shipping routes along the China coast. Japanese shipping links with any point on the Asian mainland, even with northern China and Korea (and with the undefeated Japanese armies there), were close to completely severed. Even coastal trade within the Japanese main islands was becoming impossible. Whether Japan could have been brought to formal surrender by maritime blockade alone, rather than by invasion or the use of the atomic bombs, is a debatable point. Without such a surrender the blockade certainly could have led to mass starvation on an unprecedented scale.

Control of the sea meant Allied amphibious warfare could be conducted on an ever larger scale in the last year of the war. In the Pacific long leaps continued, into the Philippines, into Iwo Jima and into Okinawa; the expeditionary forces grew larger and larger with each operation. The greatest maritime achievement of the war, however, was in Europe – the cross-Channel invasion of June 1944. The Normandy landing involved only a short voyage, but heavy fighting took place with defending ground troops on some of the beaches. Nevertheless, Operation NEPTUNE itself met only slight opposition from enemy aircraft, surface ships and submarines. Allied technology – vast flotillas of beaching craft and artificial harbours – sustained the logistic effort across the Channel until several major ports were captured and cleared. The second invasion of France, Operation DRAGOON, was mounted in the south in August without significant opposition.

Also vital was the transoceanic build-up of American and British Empire ground and air forces in Britain before June 1944, and the continued ferrying of follow-on divisions into the captured ports in France *after* the Normandy invasion – until Germany could be crushed by armies from the west as well as from the east. The Kriegsmarine and the Luftwaffe could also do nothing to prevent this, in the face of overwhelming Allied sea/air power. The same was true of the Japanese Army and Navy in the Philippines and Okinawa, despite even more fanatical last-ditch fighting. The Japanese had not been able to prevent any of the numerous American amphibious invasions in late 1942 and 1943–44. In 1944–45 – after the Marianas – they did not even attempt to stop the Americans coming ashore. Naval warfare took the form of suicide attacks by Japanese aircraft and ships, in an attempt to save military 'honour' and make the invaders pay the highest possible price.

CONCLUSION

THE COMMANDED SEA

How did the war for the oceans affect the outcome of the global conflict? A strong case can be made that the war for the Atlantic was considerably more important than the war for the Pacific. This ranking might well seem to run against common sense. After all, the United States committed to the Pacific fighting the overwhelming share of the largest battle fleet ever built, as well as much of its military aviation, and perhaps half of its amphibious forces. The Japanese surface fleet and naval air force were much larger than those of any of the continental European powers. In the European/Atlantic war, large-scale battles involving heavy warships and aircraft were rare and sometimes indecisive. The largest – the pursuit and destruction of the battleship *Bismarck* – involved just two big ships on the German side. There were three full-scale fleet actions in the Pacific – Midway, the Philippine Sea and Leyte Gulf – battles which involved the main strength of two very large navies. Three more major naval actions took place involving capital ships – battleships and/or aircraft carriers – on both sides.[1] There can be no doubt that the war between the Americans and the Japanese will always be a most important chapter in any history of navies or sea warfare.

And yet from the point of view of 'grand strategy' – and from the perspective of the 1940s – Nazi Germany was far more dangerous for the Allied cause than was Imperial Japan. Hitler might have been able to knock Britain out of the war, by invasion or by forcing the government in London – after blockade or bombing – to conclude a negotiated peace. With Britain out of the war, a challenge to German/Axis hegemony in Europe and the Mediterranean would have been extremely difficult.[2] Also, in the Pacific the maritime war lasted a shorter time. Japan only began to fight Britain and the United States in December 1941; this was eighteen months after the Third Reich had achieved direct or indirect control of most of continental Europe and North Africa. As is evident from several chapters of this book, I share the view of a number of naval historians that the Battle of the Atlantic was never such a 'near-run thing' as it is often depicted – Britain never faced an actual supply crisis. But successfully maintaining Allied control of the Atlantic required immense and decisive effort.

My intention is certainly not to belittle the American contribution, both before and after December 1941. The industrial power and massed armed forces of the United States were essential to mount any effective counter-attack against Germany in the west. However, this counter-attack could only be achieved with the existence of bases on the periphery of continental Europe that could be held and supplied. Control of these bases demanded the ability of the Allies to use the transatlantic routes for their own purposes and to deny such use to the Axis.

In contrast, the east–west transpacific route was, in the war years, of little *economic* importance to either side (although the north–south shipping routes along the coast of China from Southeast Asia did have great significance for Japan).[3] Japan, despite its large population, was in the 1940s also much weaker – economically, technically and militarily – than Germany. It was evident, too, that once Germany and Italy were defeated, Japan would have no chance to hold out against a heavily armed global super-coalition comprising the British Empire, the US, the USSR and – often forgotten – China.

Thanks to the successful efforts of Admiral King, the United States arguably devoted too much of its naval, air and logistical resources to defeating Japan. In terms of its major warships it actually fought a 'one-ocean' war. Nazi Germany was the most important opponent of the Allies, and this is not just the opinion of one historian. It was also the view of Prime Minister Churchill and President Roosevelt in 1942 and early 1943. This 'Germany First' grand strategy was shared by all three of the British service chiefs, by the leadership of the US Army and, at one critical moment, even by an American Chief of Naval Operations, Admiral Harold Stark.[4]

A corollary to this emphasis on the Atlantic is a second argument. This is that the contribution of the British Empire to the Allied victory in the maritime war – especially in the Atlantic and the Mediterranean – deserves more credit than it is often accorded today. There is no doubt that the outcome of the war, despite the defeat of Nazi Germany, Fascist Italy and Imperial Japan, was in all but the short term a severe setback for Britain. The factors involved were very wide-ranging; they included the economic burden of victory, the inability to maintain control of Imperial possessions in the face of growing demands for independence among subject peoples, and the implications of the development of nuclear weapons. The Royal Navy, in particular, never recovered from the losses suffered at the hands of the Germans and Japanese, nor caught up with the astonishing warship construction programmes of its great American ally. By the 1950s the British Merchant Navy and civilian shipbuilding industry were in steep decline (ironically, caused by Japanese post-war competition).

But to project that weakness back before 1944–45 is misleading. As the historian Stephen Roskill put it, the British were – by 1942 – 'trying to fight a five-ocean war with, at best, a two-ocean Navy'.[5] The Royal Navy was indeed able to play only a very limited part in the war against Japan. But it was the dominant Allied warship force in the North and South Atlantic, the Mediterranean and the Indian Ocean through most or all of World War II. The British Merchant Navy, with its huge pre-war tonnage and its access to London-based trade systems and global ports, made a unique contribution, first to Allied survival, and then to Allied victory. Royal Navy carrier-based aviation was a singular weakness – compared to that of the US and Japan – but the Royal Air Force by mid war had deployed highly effective long-range anti-submarine squadrons, and British experts pioneered amphibious warfare and convoy defence, as well as anti-submarine and anti-aircraft weaponry. The British, at least until 1943–44, were world leaders in the development of electronic equipment and of codebreaking.

Finally, there is the nature of the whole conflict of 1939–45 to consider. 'Because World War II was in truth worldwide, it was basically a naval war.' Admiral Chester Nimitz set out this assessment in his foreword to a general history published in 1961.[6] The German-American admiral from Texas has – with justification – been rated the most successful naval commander of that war, as C-in-C of the American Pacific Fleet. This was true despite the fact that he was an administrator and strategist (under Admiral King in Washington) and did not take a direct part in combat operations. His aim in 1961 was probably to maintain the importance of the US Navy in the minds of the American public and gain leverage in the inter-service struggles of the Cold War (he had also served post-war in Washington as Chief of Naval Operations).

At one level Nimitz was surely going too far. This is not really the old question of 'Who won the war?' argued between veterans and supporters of one or other branch of military service, or between historians of different countries. But sea power, *along with* land power and air power, was crucial in the European and the Asian struggle. World War II was different from World War I which, despite some modern 'globalist' thinking, was fundamentally a European land war (but a war which one side won because it controlled world resources). World War II was indeed a 'worldwide war', a war of continents. Sea power was not exclusively important. As the great naval thinker Admiral Herbert Richmond put it: 'Sea power did not win the war itself: it *enabled* the war to be won.'[7] His concept of sea power as a *process* – 'the power of using the sea for one's own purpose and depriving the enemy of its use' – certainly must have great bearing.

One of the attractions of Richmond's thinking is his broad view of strategy: 'the command of the sea . . . had been secured by the combined action of the land, sea, and air forces directed against the armed forces of the enemy. The *commanded sea* was now a safe bridge across which the allied land forces could move into whichever of the enemy or enemy-occupied territories should be selected.'[8] Britain, whose power was then based on a global empire, could not have survived had it not kept the ability to control and use the sea – and had it not continued to be able to deprive the Germans of the ability to mount an invasion with their superior land and air forces. For all its economic and demographic power, the United States, its shores situated between 3,000 and 5,000 miles from the combat theatres, could not have projected effective military power had it not been able to master the sea routes (not least by a vast effort to build cargo ships and amphibious vessels). Russia could not have survived if Britain had been knocked out of the war, or if the United States had been unable to make an effective contribution.[9] The remarkable military capabilities of Germany and Japan could not have been contained, and eventually crushed, without Allied command of the seas.

ENDNOTES

The following abbreviations are used in the Endnotes, including the first citation, to make them as compact as possible, as well as in the Bibliography. For example, 'Mor/12, pp. 415–29' is an abbreviation of Samuel Eliot Morison, *History of United States Naval Operations in World War II*, vol. 12. Fuller details of sources which have been abbreviated are given in the Bibliography.

CHSWW	*Cambridge History of the Second World War*
CMH	US Army Center of Military History [website]
CWP	Gilbert, *Churchill War Papers*
C&R	Kimball, *Churchill and Roosevelt*
DRZW	*Das Deutsche Reich und der Zweite Weltkrieg* [multi-volume official history]
GSWW	*Germany and the Second World War* [multi-volume official history]
Hins	Hinsley, *British Intelligence in the Second World War* [multi-volume official history]
HUSMCO	*History of US Marine Corps Operations in World War II* [multi-volume official history]
JC Report	*Investigation of the Pearl Harbor Attack*
JNMSL	Joint Army–Navy Assessment Committee. 'Japanese Naval and Merchant Shipping Losses during World War II by All Causes'
KTB/SKL	Rahn, *Kriegstagebuch der Seekriegsleitung*
LOKH	Wagner, *Lagevorträge der Oberbefehlshabers der Kriegsmarine vor Hitler*
M&ME	*The Mediterranean and Middle East* [multi-volume official history]
Mor	Morison, *History of United States Naval Operations in World War II* [multi-volume official history]
NHHC	Naval History and Heritage Command of the US Navy [website]
NINH	*New Interpretations in Naval History* [series]
PHA	*Hearings before the Joint Committee on the Pearl Harbor Attack*
PHP	Goldstein/Dillon, *Pearl Harbor Papers*
RA/VO	*Russkii arkhiv/Velikaia Otechestvennaia* [series]
RM	MacArthur, *Reports of General MacArthur*
Rosk	Roskill, *The War at Sea*
SWW	Churchill, *Second World War*
USAWWII	*United States Army in World War II* [multi-volume official history]
USNA	Evans/Grossnick, *United States Naval Aviation*
USSBS	*United States Strategic Bombing Survey*
WAJ	*War against Japan* [multi-volume official history]

INTRODUCTION

1. Simpson, *Cunningham Papers*/2, p. 38 [10 May 1945].
2. Rosk/2, p. 317.
3. Domarus, *Hitler Reden*/4, p. 1,668.
4. Rosk/2, p. 317.
5. Richmond, *Statesmen and Sea Power*, pp. ix, 330–1; Halpern, *Keyes Papers*/3, p. 251 [29 June 1942]. Admiral Sir Herbert Richmond (1871–1946) held a range of senior commands and staff posts in the RN (he was at one point the captain of HMS *Dreadnought*). Richmond also vigorously promoted the study of naval history as a part of officer training. He was critical of the notion that the big decisive battle was the object of naval war, and in World War I was a leading advocate of the introduction of convoys. His readiness to criticise the Admiralty led to his premature retirement in 1931. After this he taught at Cambridge University and was master of a college there. *Statesmen and Sea Power* was a version of his Ford Lectures, delivered at Oxford in 1943–44. The book was concerned with the 'manner in which the statesmen of this country have dealt with this matter of sea power during the last three and a half to four centuries', from 1559 to the 'German wars'. Richmond took a broad view of the political and economic context of naval history and produced lucid prose. One biographer described him as 'a man with the capacity to explain both the navy to the nation and nation to the navy: to the mutual advantage of each' (Schurman, *Education*, p. 146).
6. Kennedy, *Rise and Fall of British Naval Mastery*, p. 305. 'Sea/air' was not a common usage in the war years. However, the British organised a 'Joint Sea/Air War Committee', involving the RAF and the RN, in the immediate post-1945 period. The American admiral Ernest King spoke of 'sea–air power' in his memoirs (*Fleet Admiral King*, p. 257), as did Hanson Baldwin, the doyen of American war correspondents, in the description of the 'sea–air battle' at Okinawa (*Sea Fights*, p. 297). Stephen Roskill used the term 'sea–air organisation' in his history of the RN (Rosk/2, p. 83). My colleague Phillips O'Brien used 'air–sea power' in yet another sense – as an antonym to 'land power' in *How the War Was Won* (pp. 14–15, 484–7).

   Roskill brought out the institutional side of this, expressing an intention to cover the war at sea 'from a two-service angle' (Rosk/2, p. xv); by 'services' he meant the RN and the RAF. Roskill's four volumes constitute a magnificent achievement, but his biographer is correct to point out that the work was essentially about the navy (Gough, *Historical Dreadnoughts*, p. 134). The research teams behind some of the other post-war multi-volume British official histories, notably those covering grand strategy, the campaigns in the Mediterranean, the war against Japan, and British intelligence, were actually more successful than Roskill in bringing off a 'joint' multi-service approach. They are also in contrast to the American official histories, which were essentially written on behalf of four separate services.

CHAPTER 1 THE TWILIGHT WAR, SEPTEMBER 1939–APRIL 1940

1. Caulfield, *Night*, p. 150; Cain, *Electra*, p. 18. It was claimed in October 2017 that the wreck of the *Athenia* had been discovered, lying in 650 feet of water.
2. *KTB/SKL*, Bd 1, pp. 15-E–17-E.
3. 'Pre-dreadnought' is a term used for older and smaller battleships completed before HMS *Dreadnought* (1906). Typically they had four main guns in two turrets (compared to ten main guns in five turrets for the *Dreadnought*).
4. When these ships entered service they were considerably heavier than their declared tonnage. The 'standard' displacement of the *Scharnhorst* class was 34,800 tons, not 26,000; the 'standard' displacement of the *Panzerschiffe* was 11,700 tons, not 10,000 (*Conway's 1922–1946*, pp. 225, 227; Hins/1, pp. 505–7).
5. For a fuller discussion of the Washington and London naval treaties see the discussion on the RN in the next section.
6. The incomplete fourth ship was sold to the USSR in 1940, and the fifth never entered service.

7. Although the Allies later used these tonnage figures to describe the U-boat classes, the vessels were actually heavier. Surface displacement of a mid-war Type VII was about 750 tons, that of a mid-war Type IX nearly 1,100 tons.
8. *Conway's 1922–1946*, p. 220; Maiolo, *Royal Navy*, p. 74.
9. *GSWW*/1, p. 479, ibid./2, pp. 64–5. The fleet strength envisaged by the Z-Plan was not, as is sometimes suggested, wholly unrealistic. The enlarged Kriegsmarine would have been smaller than the actual future British, American and Japanese wartime navies, and smaller than the planned strength of the Soviet Navy. In World War I the German Navy had operated twenty-five modern capital ships, and forty-four armoured and light cruisers (not to mention obsolete ships). In 1914 Germany had 132 destroyers, and it completed another 112 during the war. Actual German U-boat construction for the 1939–45 war would be more than five times the 239 envisaged in the Z-Plan.
10. Although often referred to as 'battle cruisers', the *Scharnhorst* and the *Gneisenau* were officially categorised as *Schlachtschiffe* ('battleships'). The *Wilhelm Gustloff* was sunk by a Soviet submarine in the Baltic in 1945 while taking part in the evacuation of East Prussia; it was one of the worst-ever disasters in maritime history.
11. *GSWW*/2, p. 156.
12. The French Navy will be discussed in Chapter 4.
13. Barnett, *Engage*, pp. 51–2; Marder, *Dardanelles to Oran*, p. 110. For a sympathetic recent biography of Pound see Brodhurst, *Anchor*.
14. Kennedy, *British Naval Mastery*, pp. 267–97; Barnett, *Engage*, p. 16. I prefer the re-interpretation by George Peden, *Arms/Economics*, and his chapter in Rodger et al., *Strategy and the Sea*, pp. 148–58, as well as Edgerton, *Warfare State*. Important general overviews of the readiness of the RN for World War II are Marder, *Dardanelles to Oran*, pp. 33–63, and Rodger, '*The Royal Navy in the Era of the Two World Wars: Was It Fit for Purpose?*'.
15. For strong criticism of the Washington and London treaties see Barnett, *Engage*, pp. 22, 24, and Kennedy, *British Naval Mastery*, pp. 275–7.
16. The shipyards that were closed were Beardmore in Glasgow and Palmers near Newcastle (the latter closure the impetus for the famous Jarrow March of 1936). The Portsmouth and Devonport naval dockyards, which had been important for battleship building before 1918, were largely used for repairs and refits during the inter-war years.
17. *Conway's 1922–1946*, pp. 11–12.
18. Germany was not a signatory of the Washington and London treaties, but construction of the *Bismarck* (although not its excess tonnage) was legal within the terms of the Anglo-German Naval Agreement.
19. The British did later undertake the – pointless – construction of the 44,500-ton *Vanguard*, making use of four spare 15-inch-gun turrets. Laid down on the Clyde in October 1941, the big ship was commissioned in August 1946.
20. Dual-purpose naval guns could be used against both surface targets and aircraft.
21. This very important topic is covered by Till, *Air Power*, and Buckley, *Trade Defence*.
22. There is much to criticise – with hindsight – about decisions made by British politicians in 1918 and subsequent decades. Nevertheless, unlike the US and Japan, the British Isles *were* faced with a real threat of air attack, and the priority given to long-range bombers (as a deterrent force) and to high-quality land-based interceptor fighters (for actual air defence) is understandable.
23. The FAA was actually formed in 1924 as a sub-organisation of the RAF; the term is often used to denote just the post-1937 arrangements.
24. In the 1920s the USN and IJN each built two small carriers and two large capital ship conversions. The RN also had in commission three smaller carriers: a converted liner (*Argus*, commissioned in 1918), a converted battleship (*Eagle*, 1924), and the first ship designed from the keel up as a carrier (*Hermes*, 1924).
25. In the later 1930s the USN commissioned the *Yorktown* (September 1937), the *Enterprise* (May 1938) and the *Wasp* (April 1940), and the IJN the smaller *Sōryū* (December 1937) and *Hiryū* (July 1939). In 1939 the RN would lay down two more fleet carriers (*Indefatigable* and *Implacable*), and a light carrier (*Unicorn*); the USN began one fleet carrier and the IJN two (in addition to a number of conversions). In the event, due to

more urgent wartime priorities the RN ships were not completed until 1943–44. The RN lost two of its four operational fast fleet carriers in the first nine months of the war. The neutral American and Japanese were not losing carriers then, but they would certainly 'catch up' in losses during 1942. By December of 1942 the RN would actually have five fleet carriers, the USN three, and the IJN one. In 1943–44 the USN finally raced ahead of the RN, when a large number of new fleet carriers entered service.

26. Till, *Air Power*, pp. 96–7; Rosk/1, p. 31; ibid./2, p. 415; *USNA*/2, p. 91; Peattie, *Sunburst*, p. 29. It should be noted, however, that the figure of 410 British aircraft does not include those in RAF Coastal Command.
27. The relatively small size of RN carrier air groups in 1939–40 was based partly on the limited overall number of carrier aircraft available, and also on the RN practice of limiting the air group of individual carriers to planes that could actually fit on the closed hangar deck (below the fight deck). The USN, in contrast, used both the hangar deck and the flight deck for aircraft parking, greatly increasing capacity (and speed of launch and recovery). The *Ark Royal* had two hangar decks and a theoretical capacity of seventy-five aircraft, but the new 'Illustrious' class armoured carriers had only one hangar deck. Later in the war the FAA adopted USN practice and larger air groups were carried.
28. The Fairey Albacore biplane and the later Fairey Barracuda monoplane were torpedo bombers that were capable of steep diving attacks. Neither was used much in this role.
29. 'Navalised' versions of RAF aircraft had some additional equipment, including arrestor hooks. The Sea Hurricane and the early versions of the Seafire (a 'navalised' Spitfire) – both available in 1941–42 – did not have folding wings; as a result the number that could be carried on each carrier was limited.
30. Wartime developments in the FAA are dealt with in chapters 6, 8 and 18.
31. The Fairey Barracuda torpedo bomber entered service in 1943 and the Fairey Firefly (two-seat) fighter in 1944. A remarkable failure was the Blackburn Firebrand single-seat carrier fighter, a project which commenced in the summer of 1940. The RN was fortunate that from 1943 onwards most of its carrier aircraft – fighters and torpedo planes – were supplied by the US under Lend-Lease.
32. Pre-war, the USN was not allowed long-range landplanes, and the US Army Air Corps took little interest in coastal patrol. The IJN did develop landplanes for reconnaissance and offensive strikes, but paid no attention to trade defence.
33. The Blackburn Botha twin-engined torpedo bomber and Saunders-Roe Lerwick flying boat were both technical failures. The Bristol Beaufort twin-engined torpedo bomber entered service, in relatively small numbers, in the spring of 1940.
34. *Geschichte des Zweiten Weltkrieges*, p. 684.
35. The early period of the U-boat war, from September 1939 to December 1941 is more fully covered in Chapter 5.
36. A *Geschwader* (like KG 26 or KG 30) was roughly equivalent to an RAF group. Each Geschwader was (confusingly for English-speakers) made up of several *Gruppen* (e.g. II./KG 30 was the second Gruppe of KG 30). Each Gruppe usually included several squadrons (*Staffeln*).
37. In the film the *Graf Spee* was represented by the 'Des Moines' class heavy cruiser USS *Salem*.
38. Millington-Drake, *Drama*, p. 163, italics in original.
39. Despatch: 'River Plate Battle', p. 2,760.
40. Ibid., p. 2,764.

CHAPTER 2 NORWAY: A COSTLY VICTORY

1. Haarr, *Invasion*, pp. 144–5.
2. Hubatsch, *Weserübung*, p. 99.
3. Ismay, *Memoirs*, pp. 118–19.
4. *CWP*/1, pp. 883–4.

5. *GSWW/2*, p. 280.
6. Designated in the 1920s as the Atlantic Fleet, it was renamed in 1932 after the Invergordon Mutiny.
7. Hins/1, p. 122 [6 April].
8. Koop, *Scharnhorst Class*, p. 41. The time, 5.22 a.m., would be 4.22 a.m. according to British reckoning.
9. From the subtitle of the 1966 book by J.L. Moulton, *The Norwegian Campaign of 1940: A Study of Warfare in Three Dimensions.*
10. The battleships *Nelson* and *Barham* were being repaired after war damage, the battle cruiser *Hood* was refitting, and the *Queen Elizabeth* was completing her full-scale modernisation. The *Malaya* was in the Mediterranean; and the four remaining 'Revenge' class ships had been detached to protect shipping – especially troop convoys from Canada and Australia – against German raiders.
11. Brown, *Norway*, pp. 144–6.
12. The three other RN carriers were also unavailable; the *Eagle* had been escorting troop convoys in the Indian Ocean and was undergoing emergency repairs in Singapore; the *Hermes* was in West Africa taking part in anti-raider patrols; the *Argus* was serving as a training carrier.
13. *GSWW/2*, p. 211.
14. Reynolds, *In Command*, p. 126.
15. Barnett, *Engage*, p. 119–39. For recent assessments of Churchill's role in Norway see Bell, *Churchill*, pp. 328–33, and Kiszely, *Anatomy*, pp. 285–8.
16. Maund, *Assault*, p. 40.
17. See Levy, 'Inglorious End'.

CHAPTER 3 THE DEFENCE OF THE BRITISH ISLES

1. 'Gun Buster' [Richard Austin], *Return*, p. 220. The 'unrelieved funereal black' of the sky over Dunkirk came from burning oil tanks.
2. Gardner, *Evacuation*, Table 3c; Ellis, *France and Flanders*, p. 239. Originally prepared in 1949 as an RN in-house 'staff history', *Evacuation* gives extensive details.
3. Rosk/1, p. 603.
4. Gardner, *Evacuation*, p. 124.
5. Ibid., p. 183. Tennant was the basis for the naval officer played by Kenneth Branagh in the 2017 film *Dunkirk*.
6. Divine, *Nine Days*, pp. 183–4 [W.H. Simmons of tug *Servia*]. See also Gardner, *Evacuation*, pp. 89–90.
7. Ellis, *France and Flanders*, p. 243.
8. 'Gun Buster', *Return*, p. 253.
9. Ellis, *France and Flanders*, pp. 19, 327.
10. In his authoritative discussion of German decisions at Dunkirk, Karl-Heinz Frieser stresses Hitler's desire to assert his authority over the German Army leadership (*Legend*, pp. 291–314).
11. *GSWW/2*, pp. 291, 293.
12. About 28,000 British non-combat troops ('useless mouths') had been withdrawn in the preceding days from Channel ports in northeastern France and Belgium, when the extent of the crisis became evident, and with it the implications for cross-Channel supply. These are not usually counted as part of the emergency DYNAMO evacuation.
13. The implications of this desperate situation for the French Navy are discussed in Chapter 4.
14. Crabb, *Tragedy*, pp. 1–4, 235, 240–4, 247. Jonathan Fenby, *The Sinking of the Lancastria: Britain's Greatest Maritime Disaster and Churchill's Cover-Up* (London, 2006).
15. Klee, *Dokumente*, pp. 298–300 [30 June]. This concept was similar to that of the later Allied Operation RANKIN of May 1943, which was a plan for dealing with a sudden German collapse in late 1943 or 1944.
16. Ibid., pp. 301–2 [30 June, 2 July]; Hubatsch, *Hitlers Weisungen*, pp. 61–5 [16 July].

17. Small-scale attacks on coastal shipping and ports – the *Kanalkampf* – began on 10 July and lasted for four weeks.
18. *GSWW*/2, p. 218; Collier, *Defence*, p. 440; Barnett, *Engage*, pp. 214, 228–9; *M&ME*/1, p. 156. The British apparently were not aware of the extent of damage to the *Scharnhorst* and the *Gneisenau*, and they wrongly believed that the new battleship *Bismarck* was ready for action.
19. *LOKH*, pp. 108–9 [11 July]; Halder, *Kriegstagebuch*/2, pp. 48–9 [31 July].
20. Klee, *Dokumente*, p. 305.
21. Regarding the finality of the decision made at the 31 July conference, I agree here with argument of the Walter Ansel: '*Sea Lion* was dead! Everybody high up knew it, or thought he did' (*Hitler Confronts*, p. 191).
22. Hubatsch, *Hitlers Weisungen*, pp. 65–6 [1 Aug.].
23. In October 1917 the Germans did land an army division on the Baltic islands of Dago (Hiiumaa) and Oesel (Saaremaa), supported by much of the High Seas Fleet. But that was carried out against crumbling Russian opposition and was not regarded as an important precedent.
24. Klee, *Dokumente*, p. 343.
25. There was no landing area 'A' in the narrow final plan insisted upon by the Navy. In the original Army broad-front version, area 'A' had been at Deal, north of Dover.
26. The Allied invasion of North Africa in November 1942 was not really comparable to SEA LION; the initial landing comprised the equivalent of five divisions moving very long distances against weak (Vichy French) resistance; Sicily and Normandy were more like SEA LION, with a mix of shore-to-shore and ship-to-shore elements. ('Shore-to-shore' normally means that the troops land at their destination from the vessels in which they embarked in a friendly port; 'ship-to-shore' means that the troops are carried on larger transport ships from which they transfer, usually near the invasion beach, into smaller craft.)
27. On the development of British–American preparations for amphibious landings see chapters 13 and 16.
28. These preparations are detailed by Peter Schenk in *Invasion of England 1940* based on extensive use of the German archives. However, Schenk's conclusion (pp. 357–8), that the middle-echelon command had in about eight weeks put a viable invasion force together – only to have it thwarted by a lack of imagination on the part of the Kriegsmarine leadership – is unconvincing.
29. Collier, *Defence*, p. 221.
30. Cited in Wheatley, *Sea Lion*, p. 105. It is impossible to agree with the statement of Peter Schenk that 'the development of most of amphibious technology, be it landing craft, submersible tanks or artificial harbours, stems from Sealion' (*Invasion*, p. 358). There is no evidence of the Allies copying German efforts.
31. Grinnell-Milne, *Silent Victory*, Map 1. The Nore was the historic term used for the RN command in the Thames estuary, north of Chatham.
32. Collier, *Defence*, p. 227.
33. Admiral Richmond did single out, in his wartime lectures, the weakness of British 'flotilla forces' in the 'narrow seas' at the time of the 1940 invasion threat (*Statesmen*, pp. 309–10). As for the use of the RAF, the historian John Buckley has correctly emphasised the limitations of Bomber Command as an anti-invasion force in 1940 (*Trade Defence*, pp. 189–93).
34. Ansel, *Hitler Confronts*, p. 315.
35. *CWP*/2, p. 828 [17 Sept.].
36. Ibid., p. 1,045 [5 Nov.].
37. Dakar and the Mediterranean are discussed in detail in Chapter 4 (pp. 72–3), and Chapter 6, respectively.
38. This was also the view of the 1957 official history: see Collier, *Defence*, p. 430. If the question is 'Who won the Battle of Britain?', then RAF Fighter Command won it; the 'battle' was an air campaign. But if the question is 'Why did Germany not invade Britain?', then the answer may be different.
39. *CWP*/2, p. 247 [4 June].

40. Longmate, *Island Fortress*, p. 267. Wheatley's account made similar conclusions: 'Sea power, or rather the lack of it [by the Germans] was the underlying difficulty, which . . . could not be mastered.' This applied both to the landing and to subsequent supply by sea (*Sea Lion*, pp. 129–30).
41. Hubatsch, *Hitlers Weisungen*, pp. 67–71 [12 Nov.]; Warlimont, *Inside*, pp. 116–17. A counterfactual might be proposed, in which the Wehrmacht decided to make *methodical* preparation for a spring 1941 invasion. A proper fleet of landing craft would be prepared, and crews and troops would be trained and exercised over the winter. All three services would be ordered to make the invasion of Britain a task of the highest priority. But such a decision would have involved a major political shift and a fundamental change in organisational relationships within the Wehrmacht. In any event, the German invaders would have had to confront, in the spring of 1941, a RN that was still greatly superior, as well as much stronger British land and air defences. The invasion of Russia would have to be put back for a year. (Arguably this scenario is what Stalin himself actually expected in the spring of 1941, but that is another story.)
42. Ciano, *Diary*, p. 415 [18–21 Jan.].
43. *LOKH*, p. 356 [13 Feb.], italics in original.

CHAPTER 4 THE BITTER FATE OF THE FRENCH NAVY

1. The *Dunkerque* and the *Strasbourg* are often described as 'battle cruisers', but the French classified them as *navires de ligne*.
2. Jordan/Dumas, *French Battleships*, p. 82.
3. Lasterle, 'Gensoul', p. 844.
4. Under the Washington Treaty there was no limit to the quantity of cruisers, destroyers and submarines any signatory could have, but individual ships had to conform to internationally agreed (qualitative) size limits.
5. Clark, *Calculated Risk*, pp. 108, 110.
6. *CWP/2*, p. 474; Simpson, *Somerville Papers*, p. 110 [4 July].
7. On the Battle of Punta Stilo see Chapter 6 (pp. 111–15).
8. The French breakthrough task force originally also included the cruiser *Gloire*, but she suffered a mechanical breakdown and ended up in Casablanca.
9. Auphan/Mordal, *Marine Française*, p. 238.
10. The invasion of Madagascar, Operation IRONCLAD, is described in Chapter 13 (pp. 278–9).
11. Treatment of Operation TORCH has been one of the more complicated aspects of organising this book. The transoceanic invasion was outlined in the introduction, because it is an especially important example of the use of sea power. The French side of TORCH, including the politics involved, is covered here, in a chapter about the French Navy before and after the 1940 armistice and Mers el-Kébir. Chapter 12 briefly considers the relationship between the invasion in the context of the Battle of the Atlantic (p. XX), while Chapter 13 looks at TORCH as an important stage in the development of Allied amphibious capability (pp. 282–5).
12. Auphan/Mordal, *Marine Française*, pp. 346–7.
13. Ibid., p. 370.
14. Ibid., pp. 289, 380.
15. Buffetaut, 'Marine Française', pp. 18–19.
16. The American response in discussed further in Chapter 8 (pp. 159–60).

CHAPTER 5 THE BATTLE OF THE ATLANTIC, ROUND ONE, JUNE 1940–DECEMBER 1941

1. 'Commander, U-boats' in German was *Befehlshaber der U-Boote*, with the abbreviation *BdU*. For the sake of clarity the name of the shore headquarters will be translated as 'U-boat HQ'.
2. Blair, *U-boat War/1*, p. 198.

3. Hessler, *U-boat War*/I.1, pp. 52–3 [20 Oct.], italics in original.
4. Hague, *Allied Convoy System*, pp. 127, 134.
5. GRT stands for gross register tonnage and is a measure of the internal volume of a merchant ship in 'register tons' (100 cubic feet). It is not the same as displacement, which is used to measure the size of a warship by indicating how many tons of water it displaces.
6. Slaven, *Shipbuilding*, p. 126.
7. Ibid., pp. 22, 126; Behrens, *Merchant Shipping*, p. 22; Lane, *Ships*, p. 66.
8. Hancock/Gowing, *War Economy*, p. 175. These figures are GRT-equivalent tonnage, an approximation based on deadweight tonnage (DWT) converted at the ratio 1.3:1. GRT is based on volume, DWT on weight that can be carried.
9. Hubatsch, *Hitlers Weisungen*, pp. 100–3 [6 Feb.]; Domarus, *Hitler Reden*/4, p. 1,668 [24 Feb.].
10. There is strong similarity here, I would argue, with Air Marshal Arthur Harris and his conception of the task of RAF Bomber Command.
11. It was not necessary to decrypt enemy radio transmissions to obtain valuable information from them. Direction finding (DF) involved obtaining a bearing on a radio transmitter. If two receivers (on shore stations or ships) were involved, it was possible to calculate by triangulation – with varying degrees of accuracy – the location of the transmitting enemy naval unit. The U-boats attempted to counter this technique by keeping their messages very short.
12. The Canadian Pacific liner, completed in 1932, had been one of the largest and fastest vessels available to the British. She was by far the largest vessel sunk by U-boats during the war. As a fast troopship, the *Empress of Britain* had carried as many as 3,000 troops on each trip to the Middle East; but on this occasion she was homeward bound from Suez, with only her crew and a few passengers on board.
13. Corum, *Luftwaffe*, p. 280.
14. Mor/1, p. xi. The most complete (and readable) chronological survey can be found in the two volumes of Clay Blair, *Hitler's U-boat War*.
15. To be even more concrete, in human terms losses of British merchant seamen were about 500 in 1939, 5,800 in 1940 and 7,000 in 1941 (Behrens, *Merchant Shipping*, p. 181). These figures do not include 'lascars', crew members hired in British India and elsewhere in the Empire, who formed more than a quarter of pre-war merchant ship crews.
16. The most readily available statistics do not break down cause of loss by geographical region.
17. *C&R*/1, pp. 103–4 [7 Dec. 1940]; *CWP*/3, pp. 315–17 [6 Mar. 1941], pp. 552–4 [27 Apr. 1941].
18. *Statistical Digest*, p. 135. What became the vitally important 'Liberty ship' programme will be discussed more fully in Chapter 10.
19. Howarth/Law, *Battle of the Atlantic*, p. 275. Philip Goodhart, in *Fifty Ships that Saved the World*, admitted the limited military effectiveness of the 'Towns', but rightly stressed their symbolic value.
20. The weak state of RAF Coastal Command at the start of the war was outlined in Chapter 1 (p. 20).
21. ASV is the abbreviation for 'airborne surface vessel'. It was long claimed that the first sinking of a U-boat by a Coastal Command aircraft operating alone occurred on 30 November 1941 off Saint-Nazaire. In fact the boat in question (the *U 206*) seems to have struck a mine. The actual first sinking probably took place as late as 7 July 1942, when the *U 502* was sunk by an RAF Wellington bomber in the Bay of Biscay.
22. Later radar developments are touched on in Chapter 12 (p. 259).
23. Codes and cyphers (ciphers) are technically different, but to avoid too much jargon both will be referred to in this book as 'codes'. The word 'decode' is also used rather than the more correct 'decrypt' or 'decypher'.
24. Hinsley/Stripp, *Codebreakers*, p. 6. Hinsley's extended counterfactual argument runs as follows: (1) Ultra provided indispensable help in 1941, and again in 1942 and 1943; (2) without it, the cross-Channel invasion would have been delayed until 1946; and (3) by this time the Germans would have developed more advanced weapons (pp. 11–13).

A version of the case about the role of Ultra in later 1941 was made by Werner Rahn in the German official history. He cited the work of another major naval historian, Jürgen Rohwer, who, on the basis of complicated calculations of tonnage sunk per Atlantic U-boat, contended that nearly 1.5 million tons of shipping were saved by Ultra in the second half of 1941 (*GSWW*/6, p. 368). Rohwer's calculations factor out the departure of U-boats to other fronts, but they are still speculative. In any event in his main text Rahn attributes the decline in U-boat success to 'the successful use of the convoy system' and 'withdrawal of boats from the main area of operations' (p. 367). For a fuller refutation of the primacy of Ultra see Gardner, *Decoding*, pp. 172–7.

25. Behrens, *Merchant Shipping*, p. 188.
26. Milner, *Battle of the Atlantic*, p. 66. The point about the crisis being exaggerated in traditional accounts is not a new one. See for example Blair, *U-boat War*/1, pp. 418–27, and Gardner, 'First Turning Point', in Till, *Seapower*, pp. 109–23.
27. *GSWW*/6, p. 431.
28. The *Prinz Eugen* was launched at Kiel in August 1938 and assigned a ship name used in the Austro-Hungarian Navy; Austria had been annexed by Germany in the previous March. Prince Eugene of Savoy (1663–1736) was a famous general of the Austrian Empire. There were also four surviving German light cruisers, but they were not used for long-range Atlantic operations; they risked structural damage in heavy seas.
29. Raeder, *Struggle*, pp. 209–12.
30. See Chapter 6 for a description of the contemporaneous Mediterranean battles. The new armoured carrier *Illustrious* had been badly damaged there in January 1941.
31. In the end the *Repulse* never engaged the *Bismarck*, as she was detached on 25 May to refuel in Newfoundland. On 24 May, after the *Hood* was sunk, the *Rodney* was ordered to join the *Bismarck* pursuit, and she took part in the final destruction of the German battleship.
32. At very long range, plunging shells strike the target from near the vertical, so horizontal protection on the armoured deck is critically important. Vertical side-armour is more important at close and medium range where the trajectory of shell is nearer the horizontal.
33. Müllenheim-Rechberg, *Battleship Bismarck*, p. 109.
34. A subsequent expedition in 2015 led by the late Paul Allen (co-founder of Microsoft) and David Mearns recovered a ship's bell from the *Hood*. This relic was put on exhibition in the National Museum of the RN in Portsmouth in May 2016, the seventy-fifth anniversary of May 1941.
35. German heavy ships had as their main secondary armament 5.9-inch (150mm) anti-ship guns, which could not be used effectively against aircraft. New American and British heavy ships mounted 4.5- or 5-inch secondary guns, 'dual-purpose' weapons usable against surface ships or aircraft. To make a comparison, when the battleship USS *Washington* deployed to the Pacific in late 1942, her AA armament included ten 5-inch dual-purpose guns on either beam, as well as eight 40mm.
36. See Chapter 12 (pp. 264–9) for the 1942 Russian convoys.
37. On the loss of the *Prince of Wales* and the *Repulse* see Chapter 9 (pp. 187–8).

CHAPTER 6 THE STRUGGLE FOR THE MEDITERRANEAN

1. Simpson, *Somerville Papers*, p. 212 [*c*. 20 Dec.]. This statement was made later, in November 1940, following another indecisive engagement, at Cape Spartivento; it did, however, express the long-term RN doctrine.
2. 'Calabria 1940', rather than 'Punta Stilo', is the British battle honour. In any event the 'battle' also involved Italian air attacks which took place far from Calabria, at either end of the Mediterranean.
3. J.P. Parker quoted in Smith, *Action Imminent*, p. 67.
4. Cunningham, *Odyssey*, p. 262.
5. Simpson, *Cunningham Papers*/1, p. 111 [13 July]; Macintyre, *Fighting Admiral*, p. 75.
6. Simpson, *Cunningham Papers*/1, p. 109 [13 July]. There had been an exchange of fire between groups of capital ships at Mers el-Kébir, but this was surely a bombardment rather than a sea battle.

7. Italy had treaty tonnage available for new construction due to disposal of out-of-date ships.
8. The four older ships, built before Fascism, were named after (1) the unifier of Italy (Cavour); (2) Julius Caesar; (3) a Roman general (Gaius Duilius); and (4) a Genoese admiral of the 1500s (Andrea Doria). *Littorio* is the Italian-language version of *Lictor*, in Roman times the bodyguard-cum-standard-bearer who carried the *fasces*. The term was widely used by the Fascist regime; after the overthrow of Mussolini in 1943 the ship *Littorio* became the *Italia*. Vittorio Veneto was the place where the Italian Army won a final battle against Austria-Hungary in late 1918. The third ship of the 'Littorio' class, completed in 1942, would be the *Roma*; and fourth (unfinished) vessel was the *Impero* ('Empire').
9. Ciano, *Diary*, p. 370 [13 July].
10. Barnett, *Engage*, p. 165. Elsewhere Barnett contrasted a 'blue water' strategy with a 'grey water' strategy of Atlantic convoy escort (p. 250). Barnett's arguments are thought-provoking but not always clear. He conflated: (1) the historical 'continental' and 'maritime' strategies of Britain; (2) Mahanian and non-Mahanian concepts of naval strategy (decisive battle versus trade protection); and (3) inter-Allied strategic debates of 1943–44 (cross-Channel versus attack on the Italian 'underbelly').
11. *LOKH*, p. 136 [6 Sept.]. The September 1940 argument was partly based on Raeder's uneasiness about the pending Russian campaign, but that does not make his views illogical.
12. The most powerful battleships, the *Nelson* and the *Rodney* and the new *King George V* and *Prince of Wales*, were retained in the Home Fleet. They made their first appearance (only in the western Mediterranean) in late 1941. One of the Navy's three battle cruisers (the *Hood* or the *Renown*) usually operated from Gibraltar with Force H, where their high speed was also needed for raider-hunting operations in the Atlantic. Three of the four unmodernised and slow 'R' class battleships served for a time in the Mediterranean (the *Ramillies* and the *Royal Sovereign* at Alexandria, and the *Resolution* at Gibraltar with Force H), but they were soon removed to serve as Atlantic convoy escorts.
13. The AA cruisers were small (4,200-ton) 'C' class cruisers, converted in the 1930s and now equipped with from eight to ten 4-inch dual-purpose (anti-ship and anti-aircraft) guns.
14. The battleships *South Dakota* and *Washington* engaged the *Hiei* and the *Kirishima* in a night battle off Guadalcanal; both Japanese ships were seriously damaged and soon sank.
15. Simpson, *Somerville Papers*, p. 206 [7 Dec.]; Simpson, *Cunningham Papers*/1, p. 218 [30 Dec.].
16. Campioni would be executed after a show trial by the Fascist puppet government of northern Italy in May 1944. As governor of the Dodecanese Islands in the Aegean, he had refused to take his forces over to the Wehrmacht after the Italian surrender to the Allies.
17. There were compelling reasons – historic, geostrategic, logistical, diplomatic, ideological and economic – why Nazi Germany decided to concentrate its forces in Russia rather than in the Mediterranean. The invasion of Russia would eventually be lethal for Germany, but that does not mean there was a less unrealistic alternative.
18. The Junkers Ju 87 Stuka and Ju 88 were completely different aircraft. Both were equipped for dive bombing, but the smaller single-engined Ju 87 had a steeper dive and was capable of more accurate bombing, although it normally only carried one 500kg bomb or smaller. The Ju 87 had shorter range than a Ju 88 and was more vulnerable to defending fighters.
19. Hins/1, pp. 384–5.
20. An unarmoured carrier like the *Ark Royal* or one of the American 'Yorktown' class would probably have been sunk by this attack. On the other hand the USN ships, at least, were designed to carry more fighters, and these might have been a more effective means of defence than an armoured deck and an enclosed hangar. The wooden decks of the American carrier were also relatively easy to repair. The damaged *Illustrious* would be out of action for the better part of a year, as would be her sister ships, the *Formidable*, and the *Indomitable* after bomb hits in 1941 and 1942. The *Illustrious* suffered serious structural damage from a near miss by a kamikaze off Okinawa in 1945 and was not operational

again. On the other hand, the *Formidable*, the *Indefatigable* and the *Victorious* all survived kamikaze strikes in 1945 with little damage.

21. The Fairey Albacore torpedo bomber had just entered service, but it was a slow biplane little different from the Swordfish.
22. Pack, *Cunningham*, p. 177; Simpson, *Cunningham Papers*/1, p. 415 [28 May].
23. In terms of complexity and scale the only parallel was with the Guadalcanal campaign, which lasted for a shorter period (from August 1942 to January 1943).
24. The Axis air attacks concentrated on the airfields and, to a lesser extent, the naval base. Civilian deaths as a result of air raids between June 1940 and December 1943 were relatively low, at 1,486.
25. Italian losses in the *Oceania* and the *Neptunia* have been given as 5,000 men (Hocking, *Disasters*/2, pp. 499, 520), but Bragadin maintained they were under 400 (*Italian Navy*, p. 131).
26. Naval-History.Net, 'Campaign Summaries of World War 2: British Submarines at War (Part 1 of 2 – 1939–42)'; online at http://www.naval-history.net/WW2CampaignsBritishSubs.htm (accessed 17 February 2019).
27. *M&ME*/2, p. 281.
28. Sadkovich, *Italian Navy*, p. 197; Ciano, *Diary*, p. 463.
29. See Chapter 14 (p. 291) for operations in 1942.
30. Brown, *Royal Navy and Mediterranean*/1, p. 81; Bragadin, *Italian Navy*, p. 356.
31. Sadkovich, *Italian Navy*, p. 344.
32. *M&ME*/1, p. 246; ibid./2, p. 223; Behrens, *Merchant Shipping*, p. 309.
33. The crews of the Italian submarines were not well trained, and the boats in the Mediterranean tended to wait, passive and submerged, in pre-assigned zones (Bagnasco, *Submarines*, pp. 27, 130–7).
34. Turner, *Filming History*, p. 58.
35. *Nuatatori*, strictly speaking, translates as 'swimmers' rather than 'divers'. The British sometimes used the term 'limpeteer' for these daring Italian frogmen.
36. Simpson, *Cunningham Papers*/1, p. 180 [16 Jan. 1942].
37. Ibid., p. 554.

CHAPTER 7 DEFENDING THE MOTHERLAND: THE EMBATTLED SOVIET NAVY, JUNE 1941–DECEMBER 1944

1. 'Tallinn' is the Estonian-language spelling. The Russian-language spelling is 'Tallin'. The long-term Soviet intention was to build a full-scale naval base at Paldiski, some 30 miles west of Tallinn. The honorific title 'Red Banner' was awarded in 1928 for the heroic action of Baltic Fleet personnel in the revolution and civil war.
2. Russian surnames, place names and ship names are transliterated using the Library of Congress system but with the apostrophes (for 'soft signs') omitted (e.g. *Maksim Gorkii*, not *Maksim Gor'kii*). Full transliteration is used in references to printed sources in notes and bibliography.
3. Panteleev, *Morskoi front*, pp. 138–9.
4. Zubkov, *Tallinskii proryv*, p. 371. This book is an exhaustive study of the disaster.
5. 'Corvette' is used here for the Russian term *storozhevaia korabl*, sometimes translated as 'guard ship'. Those available at the start of the war were twin-screw, turbine-powered vessels, 235 feet in length.
6. Rohwer/Monomakh, *Fleet*, p. 103; Spasskii, *Istoriia*/4, p. 254.
7. Kalashnikov, *Krasnaia armiia*, p. 161; Rohwer/Monomakh, *Fleet*, pp. 136–7.
8. The Berlin raid by naval aircraft from Saaremaa on 7–8 August preceded another raid by long-range army bombers which was launched from a base near Leningrad on 10–11 August.
9. The author travelled to Leningrad in the 1970s aboard the *Baltika* (formerly the *Viacheslav Molotov*), sister ship of the *Iosif Stalin*.
10. In 1948 the *Avrora* was raised and comprehensively rebuilt; from 1960 she has been an iconic museum ship in the centre of Leningrad/Saint Petersburg.
11. Achkasov et al., *Boevoi put'*, p. 553.

12. Kalashnikov, *Krasnaia armiia*, p. 161; Rohwer/Monomakh, *Fleet*, pp. 137.
13. Rohwer/Monomakh, *Fleet*, pp. 137–8.
14. The famous battles for the Arctic convoys are discussed more fully in Chapter 12 (pp. 264–9).
15. *RA/VO*/5(4), pp. 65–6 [31 Mar. 1944].
16. Krivosheev, *Poteri*, p. 388. It is not clear if these figures include personnel of naval brigades fighting alongside the Red Army; probably they do not.
17. The accurate 'skip-bombing' technique was developed by the Americans in the Pacific in 1943, using A-20s and other aircraft. A low-flying plane bounced its bomb off the surface of the sea and into the target ship.
18. Krivosheev, *Poteri*, p. 499. These figures apparently refer primarily to *German* ships rather than those of other Axis states.
19. The *L-16* was sunk off Hawaii by a Japanese submarine, which mistook it for an American boat; Japan and the USSR were not, of course, at war.
20. Rohwer/Hümmelchen, *Chronology*, p. 298. In February and March 1949 the battleship *Giulio Cesare* and the light cruiser *Emanuele Filiberto Duca D'Aosta* were taken over by the USSR as war reparations. They were renamed the *Novorossiisk* and the *Kerch*. Six Italian destroyers were also transferred.
21. Ruge, *Opponents*, pp. 162, 167.
22. Rohwer/Monomakh, *Fleet*, p. 261.
23. Polmar/Noot, *Submarines*, p. 34.
24. *RA/VO*/5(3), p. 221.
25. Klaus Schmider has pointed out that Eltigen was the only Allied amphibious operation that was actually defeated in World War II (personal correspondence).
26. Ruge, *Opponents*, p. 102. At the end of the fighting in August 1944, the Black Sea Fleet included eleven medium submarines and eighteen small ones; only sixteen of the total were operational (Platonov, *Korabli*/3, p. 17; Polmar/Noot, *Submarines*, p. 125). A further six small submarines were transferred from other fleets to the Black Sea during the summer of 1944, but they arrived too late to take part in combat operations.
27. Tsvetkov, *Krasnyi Kavkaz*, pp. 245–6.
28. Ruge, *Opponents*, p. 29; Polmar/Noot, *Submarines*, pp. 104–6.
29. For the new U-boats see Chapter 19 (p. 432).
30. In January 1943, partly as a result of the failure of an attack by two German cruisers against a lightly escorted British convoy in the Barents Sea (and also because of the Stalingrad crisis), a furious Hitler had replaced Admiral Raeder with Admiral Dönitz and declared that large surface ships were useless. These events are described in Chapter 15 (pp. 307–9).
31. In an overview of the activities of the Baltic Fleet, written on 20 December 1944, Admiral Kuznetsov was sharply critical of the failure to mount more than small-scale air attacks on the *Admiral Scheer* on 23 November; it was a day on which flying conditions had been favourable (*RA/VO*/10, p. 344).
32. Rohwer/Monomakh, *Fleet*, p. 171; *RA/VO*/5(4), p. 66 [31 Mar.].
33. Ruge, *Opponents*, p. 50. Soviet operations along the Baltic coast of Germany in 1945 are described in Chapter 19 (434).

CHAPTER 8 AN UNDECLARED NAVAL WAR: THE NEUTRAL US AND THE AXIS THREAT

1. The USN adopted its later famous 'task force' system in February 1941, based on British experience in 1939–40. The aim was to allow flexibility and permit task force commanders to focus flexibly on operations rather than routine administrative functions. Decimals were used to indicate sub-organisation; Task Unit 4.1.3 was part of Task Force 4, the 'Support Force' of the Atlantic Fleet. Task *groups* were nested within task forces, for example Task Group 1.3 (part of Task Force 1), which is referred to at the end of this chapter.
2. Morgan/Taylor, *Logs*, p. 146.
3. Ibid., p. 147.

4. Topp, *Odyssey*, pp. 1–18.
5. All USN ships had a unique designation including a type and a sequential number. This system is helpful to historians if the same name was used twice, or if a ship was renamed. DD stood for destroyer; DD-605, commissioned in 1942, was the second *Caldwell*.
6. A second 'South Dakota' class was completed twenty years later. The *Washington* (BB-47) of the 'Colorado' class had been launched and was about 75 per cent complete when work stopped.
7. The London Naval Treaty terms were more complex than those of the 1922 Washington Treaty. In 1930 the RN was permitted roughly the same overall tonnage as the USN, but with fewer heavy cruisers and more light cruisers. The United States built only eight light cruisers in the late 1920s and 1930, compared to twenty built by Britain.
8. This legislation authorised a long programme, but funding was approved on an annual basis. The fiscal year (FY) was not the same as the calendar year. The US FY 1935, for example, ran from 1 July 1934 to 30 June 1935. The definition of 'under age' depended on type: for battleships it was twenty-six years since completion, for carriers and cruisers twenty years, for destroyers sixteen years.
9. *Conway's 1922–1946*, p. 88. Production of the other 'standard' USN wartime destroyer, the 2,050-ton 'Fletcher' class, did not begin until later; the first units only entered active service in late 1942, and eventually 175 were completed.
10. Ibid., pp. 89. The evolution of US naval construction in wartime will be discussed later, especially in Chapter 18 (pp. 373–6).
11. For further discussion of of USN aviation see pp. 208–9, 373–5.
12. The USN designation system included type and manufacturer and, for the further aircraft of that type by the same manufacturer, a sequential number. The PBY was the first 'PB' (patrol bomber) design built by Consolidated Aircraft Corporation ('Y'). The PB4Y of 1942 was the third Consolidated patrol bomber design to be used (the B-24 Liberator in USN service).
13. *USNA/2*, p. 93.
14. NHHC, 'Budget of the US Navy: 1794 to 2014'; online at https://www.history.navy.mil/research/library/online-reading-room/title-list-alphabetically/b/budget-of-the-us-navy-1794-to-2004.html (accessed 17 February 2019).
15. University of Virginia [UVA] – Miller Center – Presidential Speeches, 'April 2, 1917: Address to Congress Requesting a Declaration of War Against Germany'; online at https://millercenter.org/the-presidency/presidential-speeches/april-2-1917-address-congress-requesting-declaration-war (accessed 17 February 2019).
16. At this stage the USN preferred to draw its personnel from voluntary enlistment and was able to continue to do so.
17. Hall, *Supply*, p. 180; Hancock/Gowing, *War Economy*, p. 258. The huge programme of Allied merchant ship construction is discussed further in Chapter 12 (pp. 251–3, 262).
18. University of Virginia [UVA] – Miller Center – Presidential Speeches, 'May 27, 1941: Fireside Chat 17: On An Unlimited National Emergency'; online at https://millercenter.org/the-presidency/presidential-speeches/may-27-1941-fireside-chat-17-unlimited-national-emergency (accessed 17 February 2019). Linking Hitler's plans for 'world domination' with the war in China reflected the apparent belief of the American government that Japanese aggression in China was incited by Nazi Germany. This was not actually the case.
19. The Chief of Naval Operations was (and still is) based in Washington and responsible for the administration of the Navy as a whole. The post of 'C-in-C, US Fleet', which existed until February 1941, was the operational head of Navy, based with most of the fleet on the West Coast (or at Hawaii).
20. This is not the place to judge overall American foreign policy in this period. Arguably, however, a clear 'Germany First' decision might have led to a more conciliatory foreign policy towards Japan in the medium term, at least until Germany had been eliminated as a threat. On the other hand, a confrontation with Japan may have been seen by the administration as a 'back door' to war with Germany, given the terms of the Tripartite Pact. Plan Dog preceded the entry of the USSR into the war; in addition, Admiral Stark

did not anticipate that war with Japan would begin in the way that it did, with Pearl Harbor leaving America in a greatly weakened position in the Pacific.

21. British and American policy with respect to Japan is discussed more fully in Chapter 9 (pp. 174, 178, 181–2).
22. Although Denmark had been occupied it was allowed nominal independence under the Third Reich; there was no government-in-exile. From this point of view Demark was regarded as friendly to the Axis.
23. *CWP*/3, p. 1,081 [19 Aug. 1941].
24. University of Virginia [UVA] – Miller Center – Presidential Speeches, 'September 11, 1941: Fireside Chat 18: On The Greer Incident'; online at https://millercenter.org/the-presidency/presidential-speeches/september-11-1941-fireside-chat-18-greer-incident (accessed 17 February 2019).

CHAPTER 9 JAPAN ATTACKS BRITAIN AND AMERICA, DECEMBER 1941–APRIL 1942

1. *PHP*, pp. 159–60.
2. As with the USN designation system, the first letter indicated the type, and the last the manufacturer (e.g. Nakajima, Aichi and Mitsubishi). The B5N, D3A and A6M would later be code-named KATE, VAL and ZEKE by the Allies.
3. Okumiya/Horikoshi, *Zero*, pp. 45–7; Toland, *Rising Sun*, p. 214.
4. The 'level' bombers were B5N torpedo planes flying in formation at 5,000 feet and carrying very heavy bombs.
5. Spiller, *Survivors*, p. 24.
6. Smith/Meehl, *War Stories*, p. 41; Prange et al., *December 7*, pp. 145, 472.
7. Elsewhere I have argued that World War II effectively began in July 1937 (*World War II*, pp. 6–7). The present book mainly covers the maritime war *after* September 1939.
8. The Japanese were particularly concerned about supplies reaching China by sea via Hong Kong, Hanoi and Rangoon.
9. Drea, *Essays*, pp. 19–25; Lai, *Shanghai and Nanjing*, pp. 20, 59–63; Evans/Peattie, *Kaigun*, pp. 450–1.
10. Lai, *Shanghai and Nanjing*, pp. 41–4; Peattie, *Sunburst*, pp. 102–28. The memoir of the naval fighter pilot Sakai Saburo includes an account of fighting over China from May 1938 to October 1939 (*Samurai!*, pp. 27–34). In 1941–42 Sakai took part in the air war over the Philippines, the Netherlands Indies, New Guinea and Guadalcanal, and was probably the IJN's most successful surviving fighter pilot.
11. Only the two 12-inch-gun ships did not take part in World War II.
12. In accordance with the Washington Treaty the battle cruiser *Hiei* was partially disarmed in 1929 and reclassified as a training ship. She was both rearmed and modernised in the late 1930s (completed January 1940), and became an active fast battleship.
13. The treaty only covered the area to meridian of longitude 110°E, so the British could legally develop a new base at Singapore.
14. As already noted, the Washington Treaty did not limit the number of cruisers that a navy could possess, but it did set a maximum size (10,000 tons and 8-inch guns).
15. Six large 'light' (6-inch-gun) cruisers were laid down in 1931–35, and when Japan left the treaty system in 1935 they were retrofitted or completed with 8-inch guns in place of 6-inch guns. This meant the Japan actually began the Pacific war with eighteen heavy cruisers.
16. Details of the Japanese submarine fleet and its wartime operation are given in Chapter 17 (pp. 362–9).
17. The *Sōryū* was laid down in violation of the 1922 Washington Treaty, although she was commissioned after Japan had left the treaty system.
18. Kennedy, *Great Powers*, p. 257; Harrison, *Economics of World War II*, p. 3; Cohen, *Japan's Economy*, p. 246.
19. Ike, *Japan's Decision*, p. 106 [21 July]. There were a number of meetings of the Liaison Conference. It was notionally a body for co-ordinating the actions of the government and

the leaders of the armed services. The most important members of the Emperor's government took part, including the Prime Minister, the Foreign Minister and the ministers for the Army and the Navy (who were both military officers); the military were directly represented by the chiefs of the general staffs of the two armed services.

20. Meanwhile, the southern German Pacific colonies, notably northeastern New Guinea and the western Solomon Islands, came under the British Empire. The Gilbert Islands, south of the Marshalls, were already a British protectorate before 1914, as were the eastern and central Solomons. This situation was important for the naval events of 1942–43.
21. The Combined Fleet was the major sea-going command of the Imperial Navy and incorporated all naval forces in the Pacific, but not those of the small China Area Fleet. By early 1941 the forces of the Combined Fleet were organised in six numbered warship fleets and two 'air fleets'.
22. Unlike the Liaison Conferences, the Emperor formally presided at the (rare) Imperial Conferences.
23. Ike, *Japan's Decision*, pp. 138–9 [6 Sept.]. Admiral Nagano presumably meant the battle could not be taken to the American mainland.
24. Ibid., p. 140 [6 Sept.].
25. *RM*/2.1, p. 18.
26. *PHP*, pp. 115–18 [7 Jan. 1941].
27. *JC Report*, p. 253.
28. Ibid., p. 262.
29. *PHA*/39, p. 321.
30. Also lost in the attack were 100 Marines, 200 soldiers and sixty-eight civilians.
31. Mawdsley, *December*, p. 176.
32. Formosa is now Taiwan. The Pescadores (now the Penghu Islands) were a small island group between Formosa and the mainland; an important Japanese naval base (Makō) was located there.
33. *CWP*/3, p. 1,426; *The Times*, 20 Nov., 3 Dec.
34. The time in Malaya was eighteen hours ahead of Hawaii, so 8 December was the first day of the war.
35. Mawdsley, *December*, p. 60.
36. *Rikkō* was the abbreviation of *rikujō kōgeki-ki*. Naval air group (NAG) is a translation of the Japanese term *kōkūtai*. A NAG typically comprised about ninety bombers. During the war the Allies gave the G3M the code name NELL and the G4M the code name BETTY.
37. Halpern, *Keyes Papers*/3, p. 243 [26 Jan.]. The comment was by Admiral Alexander Ramsay (not to be confused with Admiral Bertram Ramsay).
38. The first Allied reaction to the landing at Rabaul was a planned (but cancelled) strike by a USN carrier task force against enemy ships in the harbour. This had significant implications, and is described at the beginning of Chapter 10.
39. This 'army' was equivalent to a corps in western forces.
40. The Type 93 torpedo was installed in heavy cruisers in 1935–38, but many destroyers carried the older Type 90, a 24-inch torpedo with conventional propulsion.
41. The first purpose-built aircraft carrier of the Royal Netherlands Navy, acquired in 1948 (the former HMS *Venerable*), was named the *Karel Doorman*.
42. The *Kaga* did not take part in the Indian Ocean raid; she had run aground some weeks previously and now required repairs in Japan.
43. *WAJ*/2, pp. 115, 127.
44. Marder, *Friends/Enemies*/2, pp. 94–5.
45. Ibid., pp. 116–18; Prados, *Decoded*, pp. 282–3; Stuart, 'Air Raid'.
46. Ibid.; Simpson, *Somerville Papers*, p. 408 [10 June 1942].
47. This statement is alleged to have been made informally after dinner during a visit to Washington in March 1946. The source was the Canadian ambassador, Lester Pearson (Tomlinson, *Moment*, pp. 21–2, 200). The version in Churchill's *History* described the situation in less dramatic terms (*SWW*/4, p. 164).

48. Admiral Yamamoto and the staff of the Combined Fleet had also advocated the capture of Ceylon, but they had no troops of their own to commit to such an operation. This is still a fascinating counterfactual. We cannot say how a naval defeat or even a small landing would have affected the political situation in India.
49. Lundstrom, *Campaign*, p. 205.
50. Richmond, *Statesmen*, p. 328.
51. The British raiding strategy will be discussed in Chapter 13, along with the development of amphibious warfare.

CHAPTER 10 THE PACIFIC IN THE BALANCE: FROM CARRIER RAIDS TO MIDWAY

1. This British-developed technology, which became important in the Pacific air war in a later period, was known as IFF ('Identification Friend or Foe'). Allied aircraft would be fitted with electronic transponders to distinguish them from those of the enemy.
2. The pilots of the *Lexington* fighter squadron, VF-2, were ashore, transitioning to new aircraft. VF-3 was normally assigned to the *Saratoga* (CV-3), but that ship had been damaged by a Japanese submarine.
3. Mor/3, p. 267. Good accounts of the 20 February air battle are Lundstrom, *First Team*, pp. 88–108, and Tagaya, *Rikko Units*, pp. 35–7.
4. Johnston, *Queen*, pp. 60–1. Stanley Johnston was a war correspondent for the *Chicago Tribune*.
5. Ibid., p. 60.
6. CMH, 'Medal of Honor Recipients, World War II: O'Hare, Edward Henry'; online at https://history.army.mil/moh/wwII-m-s.html#OHARE (accessed 17 February 2019).
7. The Central Pacific–South Pacific split would be at the heart of strategic planning discussions for both the Americans and the Japanese from early 1942 to late 1944. The equator forms a convenient geographical dividing line. The South Pacific included the island supply route from the Panama Canal to Australia, and also the route west towards the Philippines via the Solomon Islands and northern New Guinea. The Central Pacific was the West Coast–Hawaii–Mariana Islands axis. Japanese bases in the Caroline Islands (notably Truk) acted as a hub which could support operations north and south of the equator. The North Pacific, which might be seen as the Alaska–northern Japan axis (Aleutian Islands–Kurile Islands), turned out to be less important, mainly for climatic reasons.
8. Prange et al., *Miracle*, p. 23; Agawa, *Admiral*, p. 297. As mentioned in Chapter 9, the C-in-C of the Combined Fleet had used the threat of resignation in November 1941 to ensure he was given a sufficient carrier force for the Pearl Harbor attack.
9. The Germans, Italians and Japanese did on 18 January 1942 sign an agreement about operational zones in the Indian Ocean, divided at longitude 70°E. This was a tactical agreement of very limited practical consequence.
10. *C&R*/1, pp. 399–402 [9 Mar.].
11. On the development of US strategy in the Pacific later in 1942 and 1943 see Chapter 11 (pp. 227–8, 248–9).
12. On USN developments in the North Atlantic, see Chapter 8 (pp. 165–9).
13. Perry, *Views*, p. 78.
14. Frank, 'Winners'. The best-known admiral who was chosen was Bill Halsey. Raymond Spruance, who won the Pacific war in 1943–44 as C-in-C of the battle fleet, was also not on the admirals' list; he was a relatively unknown flag officer in February 1942.
15. Aviation buffs may question this point. My basic argument would be that aircraft of the IJN had better range, but American aircraft could sustain more damage, and the USN developed effective air-combat tactics to deal with the best of the Japanese fighters, the A6M Zero. In the second half of 1943 new USN types would become significantly superior to their Japanese opponents (including the A6M), but even in 1941–42 available aircraft could hold their own.
16. Interestingly, the British naval test pilot Eric Brown, who flew a very large number of wartime aircraft evaluated the SBD-5 and judged it 'from the performance standpoint . . .

a very mediocre aeroplane'. In contrast he found the Grumman F4F 'one of the finest shipboard aeroplanes ever created' (Brown, *Wings*, pp. 51–2, 59).

17. For an outline of this important but complex technical question see the article by Norman Friedman in Gardiner, *Eclipse*, pp. 37–52.
18. Some of the Japanese fleet carriers in 1942 were smaller. The *Hiryū* and the *Sōryū* carried only fifty-four planes at Midway.
19. Buell, *Master*, p. 196.
20. *Thirty Seconds over Tokyo* is the title of a book about the raid written by one of the B-25 pilots, Ted Lawson, and published in 1943. The book was made into an MGM film in 1944.
21. One of the fullest recent accounts of the Coral Sea argues that 'Had the invasion troops got through to Port Moresby, they would have almost certainly overwhelmed the smaller, poorly trained Australian garrison' (Lundstrom, *Admiral*, p. 203). For a similar opinion from the Australian side see McCarthy, *South-West Pacific Area*, p. 82.
22. The Pacific codebreaking effort in the first half of 1942 is described in detail in Parker, *Advantage*.
23. Two destroyers had been sunk off Wake in December by Marine land-based aircraft.
24. IJN ships were traditionally organised into tactical units termed 'divisions' (*sentai*). Sentai 1–3 were the battleships, Sentai 4–8 the heavy cruisers.
25. Mor/4, p. 42.
26. Strictly speaking, the encounter between HMS *Hermes* and the six carriers of the Mobile Force off Tricomalee in April 1942 was a carrier battle, but the British carrier was incapable of offensive action.
27. Buell, *Master*, p. 200. Fletcher was also criticised for not mounting further strikes by the *Yorktown* on the afternoon of 8 May; see the defence of Fletcher by John Lundstrom (*Admiral*, pp. 201–3.)
28. The Main Body included Sentai 1, with the super-battleship *Yamato* and the two 16-inch-gun ships, *Nagato* and *Mutsu*. Sentai 3, with the 'Kongo' class fast battleships, was split between the Mobile Force and the Second Fleet. Sentai 2, with the four older (14-inch-gun) battleships, departed Japan on 29 May as a cover force for the Aleutian invasion, but saw no action.
29. It has been argued that had the Japanese organisational procedures been more flexible the undamaged *Zuikaku* would have been provided with an ad hoc air group to take part in Operation MI (Parshall/Tully, *Sword*, pp. 65–6).
30. This operation (AL) is normally described as a 'diversion' (to confuse the Americans and support Operation MI). It was actually an operation in its own right. The NGS regarded the Aleutians as strategically important to protect the approaches to Japan and to block potential American-Soviet co-operation (Prange et al., *Miracle*, pp. 23–4; Parshall/Tully, *Sword*, pp. 37, 43–8).
31. Buell, *Master*, pp. 200–2; Love et al., *Chiefs*, p. 150.
32. Of the other fleet carriers, the *Saratoga* was under repair from a submarine torpedo hit suffered in January, and the *Wasp* was still in the Atlantic Fleet. The *Ranger* was considered unsuitable for Pacific operations.
33. The most important consequence of the Dutch Harbor raid was the capture of a flyable A6M Zero fighter which was damaged by ground fire during the 4 June raid. Unable to return to the carrier *Ryūjō*, the pilot attempted a forced landing on a small Aleutian island, but was killed in the process. The slightly damaged machine was recovered in July, moved to the US and quickly repaired and tested; much was learned about the strengths and weaknesses of the type.
34. Dates in the following section will be based on the date on the *eastern* side of the International Date Line (longitude 180°), which is where Midway Atoll is located and where the main events of the battle took place.
35. An earlier Japanese float-plane sighting would not necessarily have prevented the (very successful) American first strike. It might, however, have enabled an effective Japanese counter-strike which could have damaged or sunk American carriers. This would have meant that even if the American first strike had been as successful as it was, the overall outcome of the battle might have been a draw.

In the worst case (for the Americans), the Japanese carriers that actually came under attack from TF 16 and TF 17 dive bombers at about 10.20–10.30 a.m. would have been less vulnerable to damage; only the aircraft that had returned from the Midway strike, with fuel and munitions exhausted, would have been aboard. A combination of greater damage to the American carriers and less damage to the Japanese ones could, indeed, have led to a Japanese victory at Midway.

36. Ugaki, *Victory*, p. 142 [8 June].
37. Parshall/Tully, *Sword*, pp. 229–31, 438; Fuchida/Okumiya, *Midway*, pp. 155–6. Fuchida also led the strike on Pearl Harbor. Parshall and Tully compellingly contradict Fuchida.
38. Holmes, *Secrets*, p. 103.
39. Ballard/Archibold, *Return*, pp. 158–80.
40. Churchill, *World Crisis*/3, p. 106.
41. The Japanese certainly did not lose their entire carrier fleet at Midway. By the autumn they were able to operate two fleet carriers (*Shōkaku* and *Zuikaku*), two 24,150-ton auxiliary carriers (*Junyō* and *Hiyō*), two light carriers (*Ryūjō* and *Zuihō*) and three escort carriers. The loss of carrier *aircrew* was not as catastrophic as is sometimes suggested, as many of these men survived the sinking of their ships. Loss of trained maintenance personnel was perhaps more important. See arguments regarding these points by John Prados, and by Parshall and Tully (Prados, *Combined Fleet*, pp. 337–8; Parshall/Tully, *Sword*, pp. 416–17).
42. The *Saratoga*, having completed her repairs, just missed the Midway battle. The *Wasp* departed Norfolk, Virginia, for the Pacific on 6 June.
43. Ugaki, *Victory*, p. 155 [7 June].
44. An extensive 'What if?' can be found in a recent book by Dallas Isom (*Inquest*, pp. 269–93). See also the comments by Richard Overy (*Allies*, pp. 43–4).
45. The historians Jonathan Parshall and Anthony Tully argue that the Japanese landing force would have been too weak to overcome the garrison and improvised fortifications at Midway (*Sword*, pp. 487–90). It is questionable, however, whether the atoll could actually have been held if the American fleet had been defeated and the Combined Fleet was intact.
46. Morison, *Strategy*, p. 46. The titles of influential books reflect this perception of Midway, for example, Incredible Victory by Walter Lord and Miracle at Midway by Gordon Prange et al.
47. The failure of the Japanese submarines has been blamed partly on the incompetence of Admiral Komatsu Teruhisa, the overall commander of the force (the Sixth Fleet); he was a cousin of the Empress (Parshall/Tully, *Sword*, p. 97; Bergamini, *Conspiracy*, p. 123). There were also mechanical problems with the submarines (Polmar/Carpenter, *Submarines*, pp. 23–6). In any event the command of the Combined Fleet had not been informed that the submarine patrol line had not reached its assigned position in time.
48. Prados, *Combined Fleet*, p. 305.
49. Potter, *Nimitz*, p. 98.
50. Mor/4, p. 158. See the defence of Fletcher at Midway in Lundstrom, *Admiral*, p. 301.

CHAPTER 11 THE SOUTH PACIFIC: THE AMERICAN OFFENSIVES AT GUADALCANAL, THE SOLOMONS AND NEW GUINEA, AUGUST 1942–MAY 1944

1. Tregaskis, *Guadalcanal Diary*, pp. 31–2.
2. Mor/5, p. 37.
3. O'Connor, *Japanese Navy*, p. 83 [Ohmae].
4. Mor/5, p. 63.
5. Readers expecting a straightforward chronology may wonder why this chapter jumps ahead to events in the Pacific that began in August 1942 – and came to a climax in November 1942 – before discussing events in the 'European' theatre in the first half of the year. My sense is that the clearest approach is to continue the Pacific strand developed in the previous two chapters. Nevertheless, the reader needs to keep in mind that the war was being fought simultaneously in different places: it was a global war.

6. The original initial objectives had been: (1) Tulagi, where the Japanese set up a seaplane base in May; and (2) the unoccupied Santa Cruz Islands, east of the Solomons.
7. This was also true of Norway in 1940, but the duration of that campaign was shorter and the forces and stakes involved were much smaller.
8. Whether or not the USMC was part of the USN leads to a certain amount of hair splitting. An authoritative contemporary survey noted that 'the Marine Corps is not an integral part of the Navy, but is a part of the Naval Establishment, and . . . only the Secretary of the Navy as the Deputy of the President has authority to give direct orders to the Commandant of the Corps' (Furer, *Administration*, p. 548). The USMC is still administered by the Navy Department.
9. One of the surprising features of 1941–45 was the complete absence of USMC formations from the European (and 'Mediterranean') theatres. This was true despite an American strategy centred on amphibious landings in German-occupied Europe.
10. D+11 was the eleventh day after the initial landing; the day of the landing would be 'D-Day'. Allied planners and later historians have used this terminology to indicate time since the start of an operation.
11. Frank, *Guadalcanal*, p. 613. American naval losses in the Battle of Guadalcanal were nearly three times as high as ground-force losses.
12. Ibid., p. 121; O'Connor, *Japanese Navy*, p. 85 [Ohmae]. See also Dull, *Japanese Navy*, pp. 193–4. Another Japanese cruiser force had suffered very heavy damage off Midway in June, including the loss of the *Mikuma*.
13. Morison, *Two-Ocean War*, p. 183. The 2013 biography by John Lundstrom (*Black Shoe Carrier Admiral*) is a defence of Fletcher. From October 1943 until the end of the war the admiral was commander of the relatively inactive North Pacific Area (one of the three area commands under Admiral Nimitz).
14. Tonga, a British protectorate east of Fiji, was used by the USN as a forward base.
15. Hughes, *Halsey*, p. 176; Potter, *Nimitz*, p. 198.
16. Altogether 175 destroyers of the 'Fletcher' (DD-445) class would be commissioned, the second largest destroyer class ever built (if the four-stackers built for World War I are counted as one class). Displacing 2,100 tons and with a length of 377 feet, the Fletchers were substantially larger than the preceding 'Benson/Gleaves' class (1,630 tons, 348 feet). Armament (five 5-inch guns, ten torpedo tubes) was similar, but they carried more fuel and had deck space for more AA guns and electronics. The lead ship was laid down in November 1941; she was named after the uncle of Frank Jack Fletcher. The late-war 'Allen M. Sumner' (DD-692) class were built on the same hull but had three twin-gun turrets (rather than five single-gun turrets); seventy vessels of this class were commissioned from January 1944 onwards.
17. Among the ratings lost aboard the *Juneau* were the five Sullivan brothers from Iowa, who had been allowed to serve together. The tragedy of an Irish-American family became the subject of *The Fighting Sullivans*, a feature film released in February 1944; a new destroyer (DD-537) was named USS *The Sullivans*. It was reported in March 2018 that the wreck of the *Juneau* had been discovered at a depth of 14,000 feet by an expedition led by Paul Allen in the research ship *Petrel*.
18. Only two of the six American fast battleships were available at Guadalcanal on 14–15 November. The *North Carolina*, torpedoed in September, was under repair. Of the 'South Dakota' class, the new *Indiana* arrived in the Solomons later that month, after the big battle, the *Massachusetts* was operating off North Africa as part of Operation TORCH, and the *Alabama*, commissoned in August, was still working up.
19. The Mark 3 main gunnery radar of the *Washington* was based on the British Type 284.
20. Frank, *Guadalcanal*, pp. 601, 610. Cruiser losses include the Australian cruiser *Canberra*.
21. The following two sections of the chapter cover the period *after* December 1942, which is the general end-point of Part III of this book. The current section covers events in 1943 in the central and northern Solomons. The final section, on New Guinea, even takes in developments in 1944. The intention is to follow events in the South Pacific through to their logical conclusion. This approach allows concentrated coverage of the Central Pacific campaign in chapters 18 and 20.

22. On the eastern side of the Solomons chain are Alite, Finuana and Choiseul.
23. The Battle of the Bismarck Sea is covered in the next section.
24. Symonds, *World War II*, p. 411.
25. Admiral Koga's activities as C-in-C, Combined Fleet, will be dealt with mainly in Chapter 18 (pp. 282–4, 393–6).
26. American and Canadian forces landed on Attu in the Aleutians on 11 May. Allied moves against Attu and Kiska Islands are covered in Chapter 18 (pp. XX–XX).
27. Morison, *Two-Ocean War*, pp. 278–9; Gough, *Dreadnoughts*, pp. 56–7; Mor/6, pp. 180–91.
28. The 'second phase' of Japanese grand strategy, it will be recalled, had begun in about March 1942, after the initial conquest of the 'southern resource zone'.
29. Empress Augusta had been the wife of Kaiser Wilhelm I. Bougainville (unlike the rest of the Solomons) was a German colony until 1919. The unlikely local names came from the more than thirty years (1884–1919) during which northern Papua and New Britain were parts of a German protectorate. The Bismarck Sea (and the Bismarck Archipelago) were named after the German Chancellor of that era; at that time New Britain was known as Neupommern ('New Pomerania').
30. The last surface engagement of the Solomons campaign would be the Battle of Cape St George, fought northwest of Bougainville on 24–25 November. A squadron of destroyers commanded by Captain Arleigh Burke intercepted a Japanese destroyer force which had brought reinforcements from Rabaul. There were five destroyers on either side; three Japanese destroyers were sunk, and Burke's force suffered no losses.
31. With hindsight, the Japanese were lucky to avoid natural disaster at Rabaul; they had positioned a major naval base and complex of airfields in a place subject to volcanic activity. The town would be destroyed by another eruption in 1994.
32. In March 1943, at about the time the offensives northwest of Guadalcanal in the central Solomons began, Admiral King set up global fleet commands. Even numbers were assigned to the Atlantic/European theatres and odd numbers to the Pacific. All ships operating under the overall command of MacArthur ('MacArthur's Navy') in the SWPA became the Seventh Fleet, and all ships operating under the overall command of Nimitz in the South Pacific became the Third Fleet. The Fifth Fleet was Nimitz's main force, operating from Pearl Harbor.
33. For operations in the Aleutians see Chapter 18 (pp. 384–6).
34. The *Australia* and the *Shropshire* were 'County'class heavy cruisers, the second vessel having been despatched by the Admiralty as a replacement for the *Canberra* (lost at Savo Island).
35. There are actually two straits, Vitiaz and Dampier, separated by a small volcanic island.
36. Manus would at the end of 1944 become the main forward base of the British Pacific Fleet. More recently it has been in the news as a site used by the Australian government for detaining illegal immigrants from Southeast Asia.
37. An area fleet (*kōmen kantai*) was a large regional command of the Japanese Navy, which might contain several surface and/or air fleets. The operations of the British Eastern Fleet in the Indian Ocean are outlined in Chapter 18 (pp. 406–12).
38. The air strikes in the Marianas (11 June), the subsequent American landing on Saipan on (15 June), and the Battle of the Philippine Sea (19–20 June) are covered in Chapter 18 (pp. 389–91, 398–406).

CHAPTER 12 THE BATTLE OF THE ATLANTIC, ROUND TWO, JANUARY–DECEMBER 1942

1. Bethlehem-Fairfield was built by a subsidiary of Bethlehem Steel in the Fairfield district of south Baltimore. Operations began in 1941. The yard was originally laid out with thirteen slipways.
2. Roosevelt, *Public Papers . . . Roosevelt*/1941, pp. 397–8 [27 Sept.].
3. The (standard) displacement tonnage of a Liberty ship was 14,300 tons. Gross register tonnage (GRT), a measure of internal volume, was 7,176 tons. The weight that could be carried ('deadweight') was 10,800 tons.

4. The prototype of the Liberty ship was not the *Patrick Henry* but the British *Ocean Vanguard*. Laid down on 14 April, the *Ocean Vanguard* was launched by Todd-California on 16 August, six weeks before Liberty Fleet Day.
5. Domarus, *Hitler Reden*/4, p. 1,939 [8 Nov.].
6. German bombers were, however, important against the Arctic convoys to Russia (see next section), and losses caused by them were included in the 'Atlantic' statistics.
7. Losses in UK home waters were much reduced in 1942 (215,000 tons, ninety-one ships); this was about a quarter the level of 1941. The short-range British air and sea A/S defences were now formidable.
8. Mor/1, p. 413; Gannon, *Drumbeat*, p. 240.
9. Mor/1, pp. 154–5.
10. Ibid., pp. 200–1.
11. In their thoughtful study of the battle the historians Eliot Cohen and John Gooch make this 'failure to learn' the most important factor (Cohen/Gooch, *Misfortunes*, pp. 59–94). See also Brown, *U-boat Assault*, pp. xi–xv, 12–17, 181–4.
12. Blair, *U-boat War*/1, pp. 749–53. Blair's argument is that over the nine months new construction made up for transfers to the Pacific. However, there was a dip in operational destroyer numbers in the Atlantic in early 1942, as twenty-six newly commissioned vessels required time to work up.
13. Slessor, *Central Blue*, p. 491; Love et al., *Chiefs*, p. 137. The 512-page biography of King by Thomas Buell confines the unsuccessful 1942 defence of the Atlantic seaboard to ten pages (*Master*, pp. 282–91); treatment in King's own memoirs is also minimal (King/Whitehill, *King*, pp. 236–50).
14. Kahn, *Seizing*, p. 245. This is not the place to go into details but, among other measures, the M4 machine was equipped with a fourth rotor, which greatly increased the complexity of its cyphers. Final success in breaking into TRITON/SHARK took place in 1943 (see pp. 311, 313).
15. Centimetric radar used a much shorter wavelength, measured in centimetres rather than metres. The 268M ship-borne radar was based on the 1.5m ASV Mk II radar (designed for aircraft), while the much superior Type 271 (widely introduced in 1942) had a 10cm wavelength; it was capable of longer range and sharper resolution.
16. An American destroyer escort (DE) programme was sidetracked by the need to build landing craft, and these vessels would begin active service in the American and British navies only in the middle of 1943.
17. Rosk/1, p. 602; ibid./2, p. 474.
18. Buckley, *Trade Defence*, p. 138; Milner 'Battle', pp. 58–9; Bell, 'Air Power'. Buckley and Milner make a good critical case, but Bell's argument, which exonerates Churchill from the delay in providing aircraft, seems convincing.
19. Hague, *Convoy System*, pp. 127–8, 134–5. Losses to *westbound* convoys and among ships sailing independently in either direction added a great deal to Allied losses. Figures for merchant ships that had become detached from their convoys (or were stragglers) are harder to find in tabular form; on an annual basis they could in some cases be as high as those actually lost 'in convoy' (Hague, *Convoy System*, pp. 115–18).
20. Blair, *U-boat War*/2, p. 65.
21. Augsburg in Bavaria manufactured U-boat machinery. On the ineffectiveness of the bomber campaign in 1941–42 see Rössler, *U-boat*, pp. 248–9. USAAF daylight attacks on the shipyards did not begin in any strength until 1943.
22. There were also U-boat bunkers in Germany and at Bergen and Trondheim in Norway, although these were less heavily attacked.
23. Leighton/Coakley, *Logistics*/1, p. 741, ibid./2, p. 842.
24. Hall, *Supply*, p. 425.
25. *Statistical Digest*, p. 174.
26. Smith, *Conflict*, pp. 2, 78–80.
27. Hins/2, p. 476.
28. The two raids, in the Lofoten Islands, are covered in Chapter 13 (pp. 271–3).

29. Unlike many other major convoy designations, the northern Russian ones (PQ and QP, and later JW and RA) were not based on geographical points.
30. The wreck of the *Edinburgh* lay in the southern Barents Sea at a depth of 800 feet. She had 465 ingots of gold aboard, which had been despatched by the Soviet government to pay for Allied supplies. Most of the bullion was recovered in the 1980s by British salvage divers.
31. Mor/1, p. 179.
32. On the Soviet Northern Fleet see also Chapter 7 (pp. 147–9). The total number of vessels for PQ.17 excludes three small British 'rescue ships'.
33. The *King George V* was under repair, having rammed and sunk a British destroyer in May. As described in Chapter 11 (p. 240), in November the USS *Washington* would play a decisive role on the other side of the globe in the naval Battle of Guadalcanal.
34. The *Lützow* had dropped out, having run aground while threading her way through a narrow channel in the Lofoten Islands.
35. Barnett, *Engage*, p. 718.
36. Irving, *Destruction*, p. 301.
37. Irving, *Destruction*, pp. 207–8; Despatch: 'Convoys to North Russia', p. 5,146; Rosk/2, pp. 139–42; Hins/2, p. 222; *GSWW*/6, p. 455.
38. *C&R*/1, p. 602.
39. Developments on the Arctic convoy route in 1943–44 are discussed in Chapter 15 (pp. 316–21).
40. Mottar, *Persian Corridor*, p. 481.
41. Ibid., p. 482. Two important works in Russian, especially about the Pacific shipping route, are Paperno, *Lend-liz*, and Suprun, *Lend-liz*.

CHAPTER 13 BRITAIN AND THE BEGINNINGS OF AMPHIBIOUS OPERATIONS IN EUROPE, MARCH 1941–DECEMBER 1942

1. Despatch: 'Lofoten Islands', p. 3,686.
2. Rosk/1, p. 342.
3. *CWP*/3, p. 41.
4. For details see Kahn, *Seizing*, pp. 154–61; Hins/1, p. 337. Martin Gilbert states, probably incorrectly, that seizing the code materials was the actual purpose of CLAYMORE (*CWP*/3, p. 2, note 2).
5. The terms 'joint' and 'combined' are ambivalent and are used, in connection with the military history of World War II, in a number of quite different ways. See Mor/2, p. 23.
6. There was even a – completely unrealistic – view that Britain could create secret armies on the Continent. For these secret armies the 'detonator' for self-liberation would – at some point in the future – be a landing by relatively small British forces, led by mobile/armoured columns.
7. The Zeebrugge raid was an amphibious attack intended to block the entrance to a Belgian port, mainly to prevent its use by U-boats.
8. Mountbatten's father was Prince Louis of Battenberg in Hesse, Germany, who had served in the RN and held the post of First Sea Lord in 1914 (alongside Winston Churchill). His mother (Princess Viktoria of Hesse) was a grand-daughter of Queen Victoria, and sister of the Empress of Russia. The family name was anglicised from Battenberg to Mountbatten in 1917, amidst wartime anti-German fervour. In the 1930s the younger Mountbatten had been very close to the Prince of Wales, briefly King Edward VIII.
9. The LCI – and LCI(L) – was designated as a landing 'craft' rather than a landing 'ship', apparently because it was originally intended to be moved in segments across the oceans from America to foreign theatres of operation and assembled there. For the British, the term LCI avoided confusion with the LSI, which was an even larger vessel able to carry numerous landing craft. The American designation for an LSI was APA.
10. Tank size increased rapidly during the war. On the American side the 15-ton Light Tank M3 or M5 (Stuart) was replaced by the Medium 35-ton Medium Tank M4 (Sherman).
11. An ingenious system of ballast tanks allowed the LST to convert from sea-going to beaching mode. The LSTs were not intended to take part in the initial assault on an enemy

beachhead, as they would be vulnerable to enemy artillery fire. They would be brought in as soon as possible in the second echelon, after the landing area had been secured.

12. Although the amphibious truck was often known as a 'Duck', the DUKW acronym came about by chance, from the General Motors nomenclature system. 'D' stood for 1942, 'U' for utility, 'K' for all-wheel drive, and 'W' for twin rear axles. GM designated the 1941 standard (non-amphibious) truck as the CCKW.
13. Hall, *Supply*, pp. 424–5. The figure quoted was ostensibly for landing 'craft', but larger types (landing 'ships') were presumably included in it. Overall US naval construction was, by tonnage, nearly four times that of the UK.
14. These paragraphs only outline the variety of this important group of vessels. From 1943 a number of landing craft were fitted with artillery pieces and rockets to provide close support during assault landings. The Americans also operated a number of fast transports (APDs), converted from destroyers and destroyer escorts to carry four LCVPs. The LSD and LSM were built in quantity but only entered service towards the end of the war; the 'landing ship, dock' (LSD) (built in the US to a British specification) was about 460 feet long, and had an inner well from which smaller landing craft could be floated out through a stern door; the 'landing ship (medium)' (LSM), used in 1944–45 and only by the USN, was a 200-foot vessel halfway in size between an LCT and an LST.
15. Rosk/2, pp. 170, 173.
16. Despatch: 'Diego Suarez', p. 1,616.
17. The term 'super-raid' was used by the Canadian historian Brian Villa, and it is a useful term to distinguish large-scale attacks like Dieppe from earlier and smaller Commando raids like those on the Lofotens (Villa, *Unauthorised Action*, pp. 232–3).
18. *GS*/3.2, p. 621n.
19. Rosk/2, p. 250.
20. Villa, *Unauthorized Action*, p. 239.
21. The long-range shipping aspects of TORCH were covered in Chapter 12 (pp. XX–XX). The discussion here is about the operational/tactical features of the landings themselves.
22. The military situation at the eastern end of the North African front – in Egypt – was still not clear in August and September 1942. The Battle of El Alamein began on 23 October and would throw Rommel back in a headlong retreat, but the Allied planners could not have anticipated this two months earlier.
23. The Mediterranean convoy battles in the summer of 1942 are described in the next chapter.
24. Dwight D. Eisenhower Presidential Library, Museum & Boyhood Home, 'Interview with Thomas T. Handy on November 6, 1972 for Dwight D. Eisenhower Library', p. 70; online at https://eisenhower.archives.gov/research/oral_histories/oral_history_transcripts/handy_thomas_486.pdf (accessed 17 February 2019). General Handy replaced Eisenhower in Washington in charge of the Operations Division of Marshall's staff. I am indebted to Steven Kepher for bringing this quotation to my attention.
25. Coakley/Leighton, *Global Logistics*/1, p. 455. See the more positive assessment by Barnett in *Engage*, pp. 539–40.
26. The delay in the cross-Channel landing will be discussed further in Chapter 19 (see pp. 422–3). Briefly, it could be argued that it was the July 1942 *decision* to invade North Africa (rather than the actual carrying out of the invasion), which put ROUNDUP back to 1944. Another general factor was the deployment of large forces to the Pacific in 1942–43, which diverted necessary American ground, naval and air forces. Lack of experience by British and American ground troops may also have meant that a 1943 cross-Channel landing was never feasible.
27. For the campaigns in Sicily and mainland Italy see Chapter 16 (pp. 334–9, 344–6).

CHAPTER 14 THE MEDITERRANEAN: THE BRITISH REGAIN THE INITIATIVE, JANUARY 1942–NOVEMBER 1942

1. MW stood for 'Malta Westward'. The first convoy so designated was MW.3 in November 1940. The last, MW.32, sailed from Alexandria in June 1943.

2. The introduction of the Bristol Beaufighter marked a radical improvement in the capability of the RAF in the sea/air war (the machine was also used as a night-fighter over the UK). The first examples flew into Malta in the spring of 1941, and many later served with Coastal Command. This powerfully armed, twin-engined aircraft had a maximum speed of 320 mph; its range of 1,500 miles was far superior to that of the Hurricane and Spitfire interceptors. The Beaufighter Mk IC was adapted for a maritime ('coastal') role, and the Mk VIC, in service from the spring of 1943, could carry a torpedo.
3. Hins/2, p. 347.
4. Although this March 1942 action is sometimes referred to as the Second Battle of Sirte, the RN battle honour is 'Sirte', and the text follows this. The First Battle of Sirte was an inconclusive engagement fought in December 1941.
5. Bush, *Bless our Ship*, pp. 229–30.
6. Despatch: 'Battle of Sirte', p. 4,380.
7. *CWP*/2, p. 589.
8. Cunningham, *Odyssey*, p. 455.
9. Hague, *Convoy System*, pp. 195–6; Behrens, *Merchant Shipping*, p. 309.
10. Somerville's activities in the Eastern Fleet are described in chapters 9 (pp. 192–5) and 18 (pp. 407–11).
11. The Kriegsmarine did operate one captured (British-built) Greek destroyer as the *Hermes*, in the Mediterranean in 1942–43, but only in the convoy-escort role.
12. Genoa was within bombing range of France. The hull of the *Impero* was towed away for safety to Brindisi on the Adriatic in early June 1940, and she was never completed.
13. Rosk/1, p. 601, ibid./2, p. 472, ibid./3.1, pp. 379–81; *M&ME*/3, p. 411.
14. Sadkovich, *Italian Navy*, pp. 189, 239–40, 266–7, 286.
15. Three old American battleships and two American escort carriers would briefly operate in the Mediterranean in August 1944, during the invasion of southern France.
16. Whitehall and the Admiralty were critical of the failure of the convoy and Harwood's apparent dithering. The historian Correlli Barnett later criticised Harwood as 'a novice of a C-in-C in his first crisis of command', who lacked Cunningham's 'iron grasp' (Barnett, *Engage*, pp. 509–13). Harwood remained as C-in-C, Levant until June 1943, but after that he was not given any significant commands.
17. Officially the covering force was divided into a number of task groups, all under Admiral Syfret's overall command, as Force F; but for the sake of continuity it is usually referred to Force H.
18. Despatch: 'Mediterranean Convoy Operations', p. 4,505; Brown, *Carrier Operations*, pp. 76–8; Friedman, *Fighters*, p. 114.
19. *GSWW*/6, p. 720n.
20. Ibid., pp. 834–5; Sadkovich, *Italian Navy*, pp. 343–4.
21. *M&ME*/3, p. 327, ibid./4, p. 210. These figures give losses on the Libyan convoy route *and* elsewhere in the Mediterranean.
22. *GSWW*/6, p. 837, following Santoni.
23. Creveld, *Supplying War*, p. 199.
24. Simpson, *Cunningham Papers*/2, p. 85 [30 Mar. 1943].
25. In some respects, of course, the war had been 'global' since 1939. On the other hand, the two elements, the Sino-Japanese War and the European war (Britain and France against Germany), had not been directly connected.
26. Roskill, *Strategy of Sea Power*, p. 177.
27. Richmond, *Statesmen*, p. 330.

CHAPTER 15 THE BATTLE OF THE ATLANTIC, ROUND THREE, JANUARY 1943–MAY 1944

1. *GSWW*/6, p. 458.
2. Ross, *Blindfold Games*, p. 167.
3. Despatch: 'Convoys to North Russia, 1942', p. 5,154.
4. *GSWW*/6, pp. 464–5.

5. Ibid., pp. 348, 391. Regarding the of number of operational boats at the start of 1943, note the very minor difference (212 versus 213) between this source and Table 15.1 (based on Roskill).
6. Behrens, *Shipping*, p. 336 [1 Mar. 1943]. Plans for the abortive Operation ANAKIM are also noted in Chapter 18 (p. 407).
7. Harry Hinsley's account in the official history tactfully and cautiously claims a central role for signals intelligence in the March 1943 events (Hins/2, pp. 548–9). An extreme – and distorted – version of this was depicted in the 2001 film *Enigma*, based on the Robert Harris novel; the book and the film are largely based on the March 1943 crisis.
8. Rosk/2, p. 450. The Liberator was not used by RAF Bomber Command in its main campaign of night raids in Europe. Of the new British-built RAF types, no Avro Lancasters were provided to Coastal Command during the war, and only a few Handley Page Halifaxes. More four-engined bombers could certainly have been provided for A/S duties.
9. Ibid., p. 274.
10. Hague, *Convoy System*, pp. 128, 135. Losses for merchant ships that had become detached from their convoys (or were stragglers) are harder to find in tabular form; on an annual basis they could in some cases be as high as those actually lost 'in convoy' (ibid., pp. 115–18).
11. For the Axis convoy crisis in the Mediterranean see Chapter 16 (pp. 330–3).
12. Padfield, *Dönitz*, p. 299.
13. The Soviets were eager for deliveries to northern Russia to continue. Their reasons included the relative proximity of the ports in northern Russia to the fighting front and the nature of some of the equipment now being delivered (under the Third Protocol of Lend-Lease). This equipment included bulky items like railway engines, which could not readily be handled in Persia or the Far East.
14. Doenitz, *Memoirs*, p. 376; Salewski, *Seekriegsleitung*/2, p. 335.
15. Hins/3.1, p. 266.
16. *LOKH*, p. 565 [1–3 Jan. 1944].
17. The *Victorious* was the only modern British fleet carrier available in the Atlantic in early April 1944. The *Illustrious* was in the Indian Ocean, the *Formidable* and the *Indomitable* were refitting, and the *Indefatigable* was still working up.
18. The April 1944 Sabang raid by the carrier *Illustrious* is discussed further in Chapter 18 (p. 410).
19. Mottar, *Persian Corridor*, pp. 481–2.
20. Ibid., p. 481.
21. The scale of these shipments should be kept in perspective. Each of the weekly fifty-ship transatlantic convoys carried 500,000 tons of cargo.
22. Padfield, *Dönitz*, pp. 322–6.
23. Hellmuth Walter was a German engineer who pioneered a closed-cycle engine which used hydrogen peroxide as a fuel. The engine did not require an external source of oxygen; in theory this allowed the development of true submarines which would not need to surface and could operate at high speed while submerged. Although Admiral Dönitz supported Walter, and British intelligence feared deployment of German Walter boats, in practice the system turned out to be highly complex and dangerously volatile; it never got beyond the prototype stage. Early post-war attempts by the RN to harness the technology were also unsuccessful.
24. The outcome of the programme for the Type XXI and Type XXIII electro-boats is described in Chapter 19 (p. 432).
25. Blair, *U-boat War*/2, pp. 313–15, describes the serious shortcomings of the wartime snorkel.
26. Luftwaffe operations against convoys in the Mediterranean in 1943–44 are covered in Chapter 16 (p. 347).
27. It was in the spring of 1943 that numbered 'fleet' headquarters were created by the USN, with odd numbers assigned to the Pacific and even numbers to the Atlantic. The Second Fleet was the main Atlantic Fleet, the Fourth Fleet and the Eighth Fleet were the forces in the South Atlantic and the Mediterranean, respectively; the Twelfth Fleet was the former 'Naval Forces, Europe', based in the UK (Furer, *Administration*, p. 186).

28. Elliott, *Escort Ships*, p. 57.
29. The British also built two dozen very basic convoy-protection vessels known as MAC (merchant aircraft carrier) ships. Based on bulk carriers and tankers fitted with flight decks, they were civilian-manned, flew the Red Ensign and carried cargo as well as three to four Swordfish biplanes. The first, MV *Empire MacAlpine*, entered service in mid-1943 after the submarine threat had abated; their aircraft never sank a U-boat, but they may well have deterred attacks.
30. Most of the American vessels in this class were named after geographical sounds (large ocean inlets); the lead American ship (CVE-9) was named after Bogue Sound in North Carolina.
31. The first two of these carriers were of the 'Bogue' class, named after Card Sound (CVE-11) and Core Sound (CVE-13). The third (CVE-29) was named after the Santee river in South Carolina; she was a converted naval oiler, and such vessels were named after rivers.
32. This 'Bogue' class escort carrier (CVE-21) was named after Block Island Sound. The *Guadalcanal* (CVE-60), unusually for an Atlantic CVE, was of the 'Casablanca' class; like some sister ships, she was named after a recent (1942) battle; most of the class were named after bays on the American coastline.
33. The periods detailed here (January to May 1943, and June 1943 to May 1944) do not fit exactly into normal three-month 'quarters' (as in Table 15.1). The reason for this periodisation is that May 1943 was the turning point in the Battle of the Atlantic, and in June 1944 and afterwards there were unusually high losses, related to the Normandy invasion. The second period is more than twice as long as the first, so the rate of *monthly* losses was much lower. Nearly all the losses in the North Atlantic, the South Atlantic and the Indian Ocean from June 1943 to May 1944 were caused by U-boats rather than aircraft or surface ships (or Japanese submarines). In the Mediterranean about half of shipping losses were caused by air attack in this period.
34. Buell, *Master*, p. 199; Farago, *Tenth Fleet*, p. 245.
35. Ellis, *Victory*/1, p. 29; Ruppenthal, *Logistical Support*/1, pp. 231–2, 237, 258.

CHAPTER 16 THE MEDITERRANEAN: THE ALLIES GAIN CONTROL, NOVEMBER 1942–AUGUST 1944

1. Hins/2, pp. 494–5.
2. The 830-ton *KT 1* (*Kriegstransporter 1*), built in Genoa that year, was the first of a 1941 programme of small emergency cargo ships, designed by Deutsche Werft.
3. Cocchia, *Convogli*, pp. 321–6. Cocchia would undergo three years of treatment for his burns. In 1960–63, as an admiral, he was in charge of the Italian Navy's Historical Branch.
4. *LOKH*, p. 428 [17 Nov.]. Raeder's assessment was drafted before the extent of Rommel's retreat across Libya and the pace of the Allied build-up in Algeria were clear. The 'Panzer Army' was the *Deutsch-Italienische Panzerarmee* (formerly *Panzerarmee Afrika*), commanded by Field Marshal Erwin Rommel.
5. *M&ME*/4, p. 400.
6. Sadkovich, *Italian Navy*, p. 343; *M&ME*/4, p. 407. There was also some movement of personnel and supplies by air, but this traffic was increasingly endangered by Allied fighter planes.
7. *DRZW*/8, p. 1,109.
8. Mor/10, p. 250.
9. Despatch: 'Invasion of Sicily', p. 2,080.
10. A replacement 'Sumner' class *Maddox* would be at the centre of the 1964 Gulf of Tonkin incident, at the start of direct US involvement in Vietnam.
11. The *Indomitable* was apparently torpedoed by a Regia Aeronautica SM.79 (Dunning, *Courage*, p. 259; Rohwer/Hümmelchen, *Chronology*, p. 223), although the historian J. David Brown credited it to a Luftwaffe Ju 88 (*Carrier Operations*, p. 85).
12. The origins and development of the LST, the LCI and the DUKW were outlined in Chapter 13 (pp. 275–7).
13. Fergusson, *Maze*, p. 240.

14. Susmel/Susmel, *Opera omnia*/31, p. 96 [24 June]. This is sometimes known to critics of Mussolini as his *discorso del bagnasciuga* ('waterline speech') – not a compelling call for action but a symptom of the dictator's confusion and military/maritime ignorance. He had mixed up the waterline (*bagnasciuga*) of a ship with the tidal waterline (*battigia*) of a beach.
15. D'Este, *Bitter Victory: The Battle for Sicily.*
16. The contribution of the revived French Navy in these events was mentioned at the end of Chapter 4 (p. 78).
17. Aga Rossi, *A Nation Collapses*, p. 130.
18. The continuing denial of 'surrender' was still evident in a prominent post-war history of the Regia Marina. Marc' Antonio Bragadin argued that the polite treatment accorded by the British to Admiral Da Zara when he arrived at Malta demonstrated that 'the Allied military leaders did not consider the Italian ships as belonging to a fleet which had surrendered to a victor' (*Italian Navy*, p. 319).
19. A British corps crossed the Strait of Messina onto the Calabrian mainland on 3 September, but both the Allies and the Italians realised that the main invasion would have to come further north; see the next section of this chapter.
20. Much was made of 'sacrificial mission' by Bragadin (*Italian Navy*, pp. 308–9), but how real the intent and preparations were is open to question. The naval response to the invasion of Sicily had certainly been feeble.
21. Cunningham, *Odyssey*, p. 563.
22. Simpson, *Cunningham Papers*/2, p. 128.
23. For the story of Force V see Brown, *Carrier Operations*/1, pp. 84, 86–7.
24. Simpson, *Cunningham Papers*/2, p. 130.
25. Naval historians suggest that gunfire from the warships saved the day at Salerno; the verdict of the US Army official history is more measured (Blumenson, *Salerno to Cassino*, pp. 118–22, 145).
26. Mor/10, p. 364.
27. The first 'slow' convoy in the KMS series that went right through from Gibraltar to Alexandria was KMS.19X (17–26 May 1943); the last was KMS.64, which arrived in Port Said on 22 November 1944. There was also a 'fast' KMF series, effectively beginning as a through route with KMF.22, which arrived in Port Said on 29 August 1943; KMF.36 reached Port Said on 19 November 1944. The first American UGS through-convoy was UGS.9 (seventy-nine merchant ships) which departed New York on 28 May 1943 and arrived in Port Said on 23 June; the final convoy, UGS.95 departed Hampton Roads on 28 May 1945. This information details only eastbound convoys.
28. This section breaks with strict chronology to follow the logic of geography; it takes the Mediterranean campaign beyond the spring of 1944 to its logical conclusion. For the planning and logistics of the 6 June 1944 landing in Normandy see Chapter 19 (pp. 422–8).
29. Morison, *Two-Ocean War*, p. 419.
30. Vincent O'Hara's account of the Mediterranean campaign is a valuable one, but he is incorrect to suggest that American forces played *the* major role in Mediterranean or that the USN was the dominant sea power there in May 1945 (*Struggle*, pp. xvi, 261–2).

CHAPTER 17 THE SUBMARINE WAR IN THE PACIFIC AND INDIAN OCEANS

1. The American submarine report for late 21 September gave a total of six ships, but another source, based on Japanese records, listed, in addition to the *Shiriya*, seven rather than five merchant ships departing Makō on the 20th. Imperial Japanese Navy Page, 'IJN *Shiriya*: Tabular Record of Movement'; online at http://www.combinedfleet.com/Shiriya_t.htm (accessed 17 February 2019); NHHC, 'Trigger I (SS-237)'; online at https://www.history.navy.mil/research/histories/ship-histories/danfs/t/trigger-i.html (accessed 17 February 2019); US Navy Office of Naval Records and History, Ships' Histories Section, Navy Department, 'History of USS *Trigger* (SS 237)'; online at http://www.scribd.com/doc/176268145/SS-237-Trigger-Part1 (accessed 17 February 2019).

2. Beach, *Salt and Steel*, pp. 149–54.
3. *USSBS/9*, p. 1.
4. The only foreign bases near Japan were in Siberia, but the Russians were neutral and their fleet was still small and had limited access to the open sea.
5. The published source for Japanese losses by month (Parillo, *Merchant Marine*, pp. 243–4) gives tonnage lost but not the number of ships. The total loss of 8.6 million tons (ships over 500 tons) was for 3,032 ships, so the average size of a ship was about 2,800 tons (Cohen, *Japan's Economy*, pp. 265–6). The average size of individual *Allied* merchant ships lost due to enemy action (in all theatres) was larger, about 4,200 tons (Rosk/3.2, p. 479).
6. JNMSL, p. vii. This includes 640,000 tons by the AAF directly, 1,609,000 tons by USN aircraft (mostly carrier-based), and 567,000 tons by aerial mines dropped by AAF aircraft in 1945. In addition, a small number of ships were sunk by the aircraft of America's allies.
7. The Truk raid is described in Chapter 18 (pp. 394–5).
8. The *Atsutasan Maru* had been requisitioned from the Mitsui Co. by the Japanese Army in 1941 and was serving as a troop transport/flak ship in the invasion of Thailand.
9. The failure of the US Asiatic Fleet submarines is candidly described in Blair, *Victory*, pp. 127–204.
10. The *Trigger* sailed on her sixth patrol to Formosa that month with unmodified contact exploders; Dornin would report five 'duds' during his two attacks.
11. The USN decided not to fit a snorkel to their wartime submarines. Homing torpedoes like the German acoustic T5 'escort-killer' were not deployed until the very end of the war (Alden, *Fleet Submarine*, p. 91).
12. Alternative translations have been used for this organisation, including 'Grand Escort Command' (Mor/8, p. 14), 'Shipping Convoy Headquarters' (Hayashi/Coox, *Kogun*, p. 82), or 'Maritime Traffic Protection Headquarters' (Marder, *Old Friends*/2, p. 377).
13. Four more USN submarines were lost in accidents outside hostile waters. Of the forty-eight lost on combat operations, three were lost due to grounding.
14. Cohen, *Japan's Economy*, p. 267. The programme contrasts with the extraordinary post-war boom, when Japanese shipyards came to dominate the world industry. By the end of the 1950s production, by tonnage, equalled peak Japanese wartime levels, and by 1968 it had reached 9.1 million tons (2,929 vessels) in one year (Chida/Davies, *Japanese Shipping and Shipbuilding Industries*, p. 202).
15. The battles of the Philippine Sea and Leyte Gulf are covered in chapters 18 (pp. 398–406) and 20 (pp. 446–57), respectively.
16. The second fleet carrier sunk in 1944 was the new *Unryū*, torpedoed in December 1944 in the East China Sea by USS *Redfish*. She was rushing *Ōhka* kamikaze aircraft from Kure to Manila.
17. The Japanese government in 1941 was most concerned about gaining control of the resources of the British and Dutch colonies in Southeast Asia. The US-controlled Philippines did not possess the same key resources as Malaya or the Dutch East Indies, but ships and aircraft based there had the potential to choke off Japanese shipping.
18. The campaign to capture the Marianas is covered in Chapter 18 (pp. 389–91, 398–406), and the campaign in the Philippines and Okinawa in Chapter 20 (pp. 446–60, 464–6).
19. JNMSL, p. vii. The figure for AAF minelaying was not accompanied by dates, but the B-29 minelaying campaign began only at the end of March 1945.
20. The greater success of the German submarines in the Indian Ocean is indicated by the figures in Table 17.4. The tonnage sunk by Japanese submarines (column 7) can be compared to losses from 'all causes' (column 2). After the middle of 1942 the difference is largely explained by U-boat operations. The figures in columns 2 and 7 are not, however, directly comparable, as they come from different sources.
21. Perry, *'Dear Bart'*, p. 110.
22. See Marder, *Old Friends*/2, pp. 254–8. The timing of Admiral Mito's order suggests it may have been a response to reported Allied actions against survivors of the Japanese convoy destroyed in the Bismarck Sea a few days earlier.
23. The fourth ally, China, was in a different position as far as shipping was concerned; but relieving the supply problems of Chungking (Chongqing) would have required a very

large amphibious operation. American strategy, at least in 1943, had as an objective the opening of a supply route to the southwestern coast of China, through the South China Sea.

24. One of the best-informed books on Japanese submarines argues that they should have been concentrated on blocking the shipping artery to Hawaii (Boyd/Yoshida, *Japanese Submarine Force*, pp. 189–90). It is difficult to see how such a campaign could have been sustained.
25. The *Hōkoku Maru* was destroyed off the Cocos Islands (northwest of Australia) in November 1942, in a duel with an armed Dutch tanker and an Indian corvette.
26. For the MV *Behar* atrocity Admiral Sakonjū was tried by the British in Hong Kong in 1947–48 and hanged; he had maintained that the order not to keep prisoners came from a higher naval authority.
27. Western sources sometimes refer to all Japanese submarines as 'I-boats' after the style of 'U-boats', but this is not technically inaccurate. The 'I' prefix was only used for the large 'cruiser' boats.
28. The British X-craft, used successfully against the *Tirpitz* in 1943, was the nearest equivalent to the Type A, but the X-craft was never intended for open-sea operations. XE1 and XE3 damaged the heavy cruiser *Takao* at Singapore in the last days of the war, on 31 July 1945.
29. Polmar/Carpenter, *Submarines*, pp. 54–5, 111–15; *Conway's 1922–1946*, p. 203.
30. The first transport submarine (*I 361*) was laid down at Kure in February 1943 and commissioned in May 1944. The 1,440-ton boats of her class could carry 22 tons of cargo and 110 troops.
31. The Central Pacific campaign as a whole is the subject of Chapter 18.
32. Polmar/Carpenter, *Submarines*, p. 63. This figure excludes non-operational high speed boats, transport submarines, and four former German U-boats based at Singapore and Java.

CHAPTER 18 THE US NAVY'S DRIVE ACROSS THE CENTRAL PACIFIC, NOVEMBER 1943–JUNE 1944

1. For the February 1942 raid on Rabaul see the beginning of Chapter 10 (pp. 201–3).
2. Details of the 1943 Solomon Islands operations, including the advance on Bougainville, were given in Chapter 11 (pp. 241–5).
3. Kusaka Jinichi is not to be confused with his cousin, Kusaka Ryūnosuke, who was the planner of the Hawaii and Midway operations.
4. The Battle of Empress Augusta Bay was also discussed in Chapter 11 (pp. 244–5).
5. Kurita's force was sighted by a long-range patrol plane at noon on 4 November while approaching Rabaul from the west. However, on the 3rd, Nimitz had been able to warn Halsey about the planned movement, based on a radio intercept; as a result Halsey had time to put his carriers in position. John Prados cited the Rabaul raids as a key example of the use of radio intelligence at the operational level (Prados, *Combined Fleet*, pp. 512, 728; Prados, *Islands*, pp. 335).
6. Hara, *Captain*, pp. 244–5.
7. Mor/6, pp. 331–2. This account was written by Commander James Shaw, who wrote the first draft of this Morison volume. ZEKE was the Allied code name for the A6M Zero fighter.
8. On the following day the unlucky *Agano* was torpedoed by an American submarine. The cruiser then had to be towed north to Truk for temporary repairs; another submarine would sink her as she left Truk in February 1944.
9. The *Saratoga* operated with the British in the Indian Ocean in the summer of 1944. She returned briefly in 1945 to cover the invasion of Iwo Jima in 1945, before being badly damaged by a kamikaze.
10. Speed was a crucial factor in the Pacific naval battles. The fast carriers of the 'Essex' and 'Independence' class were capable of a sustained speed in combat of about 32 knots; they could cover 440 miles in twelve hours, along with their cruiser and destroy screen. In contrast, the escort carriers (CVEs) could only make 16–18 knots.

11. Hull numbers are given here, as names were changed during construction. CV-10 was originally named *Bon Homme Richard* but entered service as the *Yorktown* [II]. The original name was eventually assigned to CV-31, laid down in February 1943.
12. Five of the first seven 'Essex' class carriers to be operational would be with the fleet at the Battle of the Philippine Sea in June 1944. The *Intrepid* (CV-11) was absent, undergoing repairs after damage suffered in the Marshalls, and the *Hancock* (CV-19) was still working up in the Caribbean.
13. For reasons that are not easy to explain, another *eight* 'Essex' class ships were ordered in August 1944.
14. The *Lexington* would remain in commission as a training carrier until 1991 and is now a museum ship. Also preserved are the *Hornet*, the *Intrepid* and the *Yorktown*.
15. The new 'Essex'- and 'Independence' class ships continued the USN's policy of naming carriers after battles or earlier American warships. Five of them would eventually be named after carriers lost in 1942: the new *Yorktown*, *Lexington*, *Hornet*, *Wasp* and *Langley*. The *Cabot*, the *Essex*, the *Franklin*, the *Hancock*, the *Independence*, the *Intrepid* and the *Randolph* (along with the *Hornet* and the *Wasp*) perpetuated the names of sailing warships which fought against the RN in the War of Independence or the War of 1812. Others commemorated American land battles, mostly those fought against Britain in the Revolutionary War (the *Bennington*, the *Bunker Hill*, the *Cowpens*, the *Princeton* and the *Ticonderoga* – along with the *Lexington* and the *Yorktown*). Four more were named after land battles against other enemies – Mexico (the *Monterey* and the *San Jacinto*), Germany in 1918 (the *Belleau Wood*) and Japan in 1942 (the *Bataan*).
16. All the 'Casablanca' class ships served in the USN, mostly in the Pacific. Despite original intentions they did not operate with the RN, which received additional 'Bogue' class vessels instead.
17. *USNA/2*, p. 92. This is a global total, but most of these aircraft were in the Pacific. USMC aircraft are included. Date is 1 July of the given year.
18. The Grumman F6F was originally ordered as an improved F4F Wildcat, a back-up in case there were problems with the new fighter initially favoured by the USN, the Vought F4U Corsair. Grumman, on its own initiative, developed the F6F into a very different aircraft from the F4F, and it was eventually fitted with the same huge 2,000-hp engine as the Corsair, the (42-litre) Pratt and Whitney R-2800. In the middle years of the war the Corsair mainly flew from American land bases (and with the RN), and the Hellcat became the standard USN carrier fighter (Friedman, *Fighters*, pp. 133–41).
19. There is a parallel here with the strategy in Europe, where a cross-Channel invasion was not feasible before – at the earliest – the spring of 1943. This meant that the initial American operations were mounted elsewhere, i.e. North Africa.
20. The longer-term objective of the Allied advance was still unclear. In 1943 the intermediate objective was (roughly) the Celebes Sea, which is bounded by Mindanao, Borneo and Celebes (Sulawesi). At the Cairo/SEXTANT Conference in late November and December 1943 the strategic goal was moved north to the Formosa–China Coast–Luzon triangle.
21. MacArthur was only a theatre commander, while King was C-in-C (and Chief of Staff) of the USN. General George Marshall was Chief of Staff of the Army; MacArthur was the same age as Marshall, but in some repects senior to him, having served as (an unusually young) Chief of Staff in 1930–35. MacArthur was a hero of World War I and had strong support among the American public (rightly or wrongly) after his defence of the Philippines in 1941–42. He also enjoyed political support in the Republican Party. Marshall had difficult relations with MacArthur and generally gave first priority to the war in Europe (which was definitely an 'Army' war), but he also wished to maintain the status of the US Army in the war against Japan.
22. The June 1943 Joint Chiefs of Staff plan was based on a campaign starting in the Marshalls, but in July the initial objective was changed to the Gilberts.
23. See Chapter 11 (pp. 245–50) for the New Guinea campaign.
24. The B-29 first flew in September 1942. It had an operational range of 3,250 miles (compared to 2,100 miles for the B-24 Liberator) and a bomb load of 20,000 pounds (compared to 8,000 pounds).

25. The same structure was applied to other USN theatres. III 'Phib operated in the Solomons under Halsey's Third Fleet, and VII 'Phib with the Seventh Fleet under General MacArthur.
26. See Table 18.1 for comparative carrier strength.
27. A distinction is made here between wartime 'light' carriers and 'escort' carriers. Both were conversions and had limited aircraft capacity, but the former were capable of a speed which allowed them to operate with the main fleet; they generally had better protection and compartmentalisation.
28. *Interrogation of Japanese Officials*/1, p. 202. Production is by Japanese fiscal year, e.g. '1942' is April 1942 to March 1943.
29. Francillon, *Japanese Aircraft*, p. 386. Annual medium bomber production for the IJN was 465 (1942), 959 (1943) and 1,436 (1944); these was were mainly G4Ms (*Interrogation of Japanese Officials*/1, p. 204).
30. Koga is a little-discussed commander in histories of the Pacific war, certainly in contrast to his predecessor, Yamamoto. He never actually led the Combined Fleet in battle. However, the historian John Prados seems correct in his rehabilitation of Koga as an energetic and innovative C-in-C (*Combined Fleet*, pp. 484–9).
31. A comparable organisation existed in the winter of 1941–42 during the invasion of Malaya and the Philippines. This was the Eleventh Air Fleet (Eleventh Kōkū Kantai) created in January 1941. The aircraft carriers that raided Pearl Harbor with Nagumo's Mobile Force were also known as the First Air Fleet, but it was disbanded after Midway. Prados argues that the initiative for the 1943 First Air Fleet came from Koga and the Combined Fleet staff, rather than Admiral Nagano and the Naval General Staff. He also assigns an important role to Captain Fuchida Mitsuo (*Combined Fleet*, p. 539–40).
32. Ibid. p. 486.
33. Ibid., p. 487. The designation may have been based on the international maritime signal flag 'Z', which Admiral Tōgō Heihachirō raised as an 'order execute' at the Battle of Tsushima in 1905.
34. The invasion of Guadalcanal involved an initial pitched battle for Tulagi Island, but no fighting took place on the main island of Guadalcanal in the early days.
35. Designed for the US Marine Corps before the war, the LVT ('landing vehicle, tracked') was an ingenious piece of automotive technology, propelled on land or water by cleated tracks. The early versions were able to carry 2 tons of supplies or twenty-four men. Although invaluable for mobility, the basic LVT was vulnerable; made of steel but not armoured, it had no roof.
36. Some 500 Korean labourers had also been present, working on the Tarawa fortifications; of these only 129 survived.
37. The basic LCI (landing craft, infantry) was a 160-foot sea-going vessel; it was readily adapted as a platform for 40mm guns. The LST (landing ship, tank) was a 330-foot tank landing vessel.
38. Eniwetok Atoll is now most famous for the first H-bomb test, carried out in 1954. Bikini Atoll, also in the Marshalls and 200 miles to the east of Eniwetok, would be the site of the 1946 A-bomb test. Among the target ships at Bikini would be the veteran carrier USS *Saratoga*, the Japanese battleship *Nagato* and the captured German heavy cruiser *Prinz Eugen*.
39. Mor/7, p. 307; Smith, *Coral*, p. 104; Peattie, *Nan'yō*, p. 305.
40. The decisive naval Battle of the Philippine Sea, fought on 19–20 June, is covered in the final section of this chapter.
41. The US Army, used to operating with larger formations, tended to employ more systematic tactics and questioned the ability of Marine generals to handle large combined-arms operations. The USMC stressed aggressive (and costly) forward movement to destroy enemy forces as rapidly as possible. General Smith advised: 'Hit quickly, hit hard and keep right on hitting. Give the enemy no rest, no opportunity to consolidate his forces and hit back at you' (*Coral*, p. 17).
42. The foolhardy transfer of these Japanese headquarters to Saipan (and nearby Tinian) was presumably based partly on the previous existence of military facilities there (both islands

had been pre-war Japanese territory). It was also not expected that the Marianas would be the first objective of the next American advance; Truk and the Palaus were thought to be under more immediate threat. (The death on Tinian of Admiral Kakuta and the First Air Fleet command will be described in the penultimate section of this chapter.)

43. The Palau group of islands are usually considered to be part of the Carolines, although they lie well to the west. The Carolines were, sequentially, a Spanish colony, briefly a German one, a Japanese mandate and, after 1945, an American trusteeship. Palau became a tiny independent republic in 1982, separating from the rest of the Carolines, which became the Federated States of Micronesia (including Truk and Yap). Operation STALEMATE II would have been the invasion of Yap; it was cancelled after the September 1944 decision to attack Leyte.
44. The Fast Carrier Force had been designated as TF 50 during the invasion of the Gilberts. During the period from August 1944 to April 1945 it would be redesignated as TF 38, when the Fifth Fleet (under Spruance) became the Third Fleet (under Halsey). Command of the fast carriers themselves remained with Admiral Marc Mitscher until late October 1944, when he was replaced by Admiral John S. McCain Sr (grandfather of the late Senator John McCain). Mitscher, in turn, resumed command of the carriers in late January 1945, and the designation TF 58 came back into use.
45. Prados, *Combined Fleet*, pp. 476–8. Prados speculates that the May–June 1943 operations may have been an offensive sweep, which was put off by the loss of the battleship *Mutsu* in an accidental explosion on 8 June and the torpedoing of the carrier *Hiyō* off Yokosuka two days later. More likely these activities were intended by Koga, the new C-in-C, as preparation for future campaigns.
46. For the February 1942 air battle of Rabaul, in which O'Hare became a national hero, see the beginning of Chapter 10.
47. Rohwer/Hümmelchen, *Chronology*, p. 261.
48. Admiral Nagumo's removal from command of the First Fleet in February 1944 (and transfer to the new Central Pacific Area Fleet) may have been connected with these events.
49. Reynolds, *Fast Carriers*, p. 141; Mor/7, p. 332.
50. On the important Hollandia operation see Chapter 11 (p. 249).
51. This episode is dealt with in detail in Bradsher, 'Story', and Layton, *I Was There*, pp. 484–5. The nature of the 'Z' operations (or plans), which dated from the summer of 1943, has already been discussed. An evaluation of the importance of this intelligence coup for the Battle of the Philippine Sea will be given in the next section of this chapter.
52. The First Mobile Fleet should not be confused with the First Air Fleet.
53. The translation of Toyoda's Order No. 76 of 3 May 1944 (*Campaigns of the Pacific War*, pp. 226–31) is not fully clear, in terms of the geographical options and the formations involved. The 'Task Force' evidently refers to Ozawa's First Mobile Fleet, the 'Base Air Force' to elements of Kakuta's First Air Fleet, and the 'raiding attacks' to the operations by submarines of Takagi's Sixth Fleet (also referred to as the 'Advanced Expeditionary Force' or *Senken Butai*).
54. The background to the Biak operation was given in Chapter 11 (pp. 249–50).
55. Mor/8, p. 231. Another translation is given in Admiral Ugaki's diary: 'The rise and fall of the empire depends on this one battle, so everyone is expected to exert further efforts' (*Fading Victory*, p. 400). Nelson's original signal, hoisted on the morning of Trafalgar in 1805, was 'England expects that every man will do his duty'.
56. Ugaki, *Fading Victory*, p. 402; Mor/8, p. 207.
57. The Philippine Sea battle involved the entire first-line carrier strength of the Imperial Navy, nine vessels. (The old *Hōshō* and four surviving escort carriers did not take part.) Four old and slow Japanese battleships were absent: the *Fusō* and the *Yamashiro* had largely been removed from front-line duties; the *Ise* and the *Hyūga* were still working up in Japan. The only heavy cruisers not taking part in Operation A-GŌ were the *Aoba*, which had been committed to the abortive Biak operation, and the *Nachi* and the *Ashigara*, which were covering the northern approaches to Japan.
58. The Vanguard Force is sometimes labelled as 'Group C' or 'CarDiv 3'. The deployment of the Japanese forces before the Battle of the Philippine Sea was the opposite of that at

Midway. In 1942, at Midway, the carriers of the Mobile Force (Kidō Butai) formed the vanguard, and the heavy battleships were grouped in the 'main body', about 200 miles astern.

59. The A Group is often labelled as 'Group A' or 'CarDiv 1', B Group as Group B or 'CarDiv2'.
60. The USN actually had five more fleet carriers in commission. Of the pre-war ships, the *Saratoga* was refitting after operating with the British Eastern Fleet, and the *Ranger* was in the Atlantic. Of the 'Essex' class, the *Intrepid* was under repair after suffering a torpedo hit off Truk in February 1944, and the *Hancock* and the *Ticonderoga* were still working up. There was also another light carrier; the *Independence* was completing repairs after torpedo damage in the 1943 Gilberts operation.
61. The eighth new 16-inch-gun battleship, the *Massachusetts*, was refitting in Puget Sound, Washington.
62. Bradsher, 'Story', and Layton, *I Was There*, pp. 484–5. The affair also showed the limits of intelligence sharing. The raw documents were available in Brisbane on 20 May and took nearly three weeks to reach the operational commander in the Central Pacific.
63. The fighter-bomber strike of Raid I anticipated the better-known kamikaze strikes during the Battle of Leyte Gulf in October 1944; these also were intended to put the flight decks of the American carriers out of action at a critical moment. See the published diary of Ugaki Matome, commander of Sentai 1 in the Vanguard Force; in his comments on Raid I, 'special attack' seems to have been mistranslated as 'suicide attack'(*Fading Victory*, p. 421). Captain Jo Eiichirō, captain of the *Chiyoda*, one of the carriers in the Vanguard Force, had been arguing for the use of suicide attacks since 1943. Unlike the Leyte attacks, however, Raid I in the Battle of the Philippine Sea did not explicitly involve one-way suicide missions.
64. Mor/8, pp. 319–20. The details of overall Japanese air losses in the Battle of the Philippines Sea and their causes are complicated. An assessment of losses suffered by Japanese planes operating from the carriers and land bases on 19 June was made by the Americans soon after the war. It included 366 destroyed in the air by USN fighters (surely an over-estimate), seventeen destroyed on the ground (on Marianas airfields) and nineteen shot down by the AA guns of the fleet. The same source estimated that only about forty aircraft penetrated the US fighter defence (*Campaigns of the Pacific War*, p. 214). It certainly seems the case that most of the attacking planes had been engaged 50–60 miles distant from TF 58 (Friedman, *Fighters*, pp. 124–6). A number of aircraft in Raid II from the A Group were hit by friendly fire as they passed over the Vanguard Force. In view of the low standard of training and long over-water flights involved, there must have been numerous non-combat ('operational') losses on the Japanese side. In addition, a few aircraft aboard the *Taihō* and the *Shōkaku* went down with those ships in the afternoon of the 19th.
65. Prados, *Combined Fleet*, pp. 563–5.
66. Mor/8, p. 301.
67. Ibid., p. 321. Many of the returning planes ditched near American warships; the sea was flat calm and their crews were often rescued.
68. Clark Reynolds made the Jutland analogy in *Fast Carriers*, pp. 204–10. Other well-informed critics of Spruance's decision not to advance to the west on the night of 18/19 June and launch an air strike the following morning include his biographer Thomas Buell (*Warrior*, pp. 26–80), as well as William Y'Blood (*Red Sun*, pp. 204–11) and Ronald Spector (*Eagle*, p. 312). Samuel Eliot Morison's measured discussion comes out in favour of Spruance (Mor/8, pp. 313–19, Morison, *Two-Ocean War*, pp. 344–5). The British naval historian Eric Grove described the Philippine Sea as 'one of the most decisive fleet actions of all time' (*Fleet to Fleet*, p. 145).
69. For the British Pacific Fleet in 1945 see Chapter 20 (pp. 466–8).
70. There was, of course, a third major theatre, one which made the greatest demands on the manpower of the Japanese Army. This was the fighting in eastern and central China with the armies of Chiang Kai-shek.
71. The Americans saw significant potential in the Chinese Army, if it could be properly supplied through northern and central Burma; as a result that was where they wanted

any offensive operations concentrated. The British took a less rosy view of Chinese potential – and as an imperial power they had a more antagonistic relationship with the Chinese Nationalists. They were, in any event, more interested in the southern part of Southeast Asia, and their former possessions in Malaya and Singapore.

72. In a book published in 2017 (*Eastern Waters*), Andrew Boyd correctly stressed the neglected subject of the importance of Japan in British naval strategy in the later 1930s, arguably as a 'linchpin of victory'. His suggestion that the RN played a substantial positive role in the Indian Ocean in 1942–44 is, however, difficult to accept.
73. The period from May to October/November of each year was considered to be a time when the weather ruled out amphibious operations against the west coast of Burma. The name 'Anakim' came from a race of giants described in the Old Testament.
74. On the early British defeats at the hands of the Japanese Navy see Chapter 9 (pp. 185–95).
75. See Chapter 17 (pp. 362–5) for Axis submarine operations in the Indian Ocean.
76. Marder, *Old Friends*/2, p. 327.
77. This shipping was required in the short term to support the landing at Anzio in central Italy. The invasion of France, projected for May 1944, also promised to demand an even larger amount of amphibious 'lift'.
78. Kohima and Imphal had no direct connection with the naval war. Nevertheless, those defeats greatly weakened the Japanese Burma Area Army, forcing its retreat in northern central Burma at the end of the monsoon period in November 1944 and allowing naval landings by British Empire forces against limited opposition in the spring and summer of 1945.
79. On Hollandia see Chapter 11 (p. 249).
80. Brown, *Carrier Operations*/1, p. 112.
81. The *Takao* was no longer operational before this attack, having been torpedoed by an American submarine at the beginning of the Battle of Leyte Gulf. The July 1945 mission was, however, a very dangerous one, and two of the British submariners were awarded the Victoria Cross.
82. Bill Halsey had been a better-known fleet commander in 1942, and in late 1944 would again be prominent. In our fourth period (January 1943 to June 1944), however, he was serving ashore in what was then a secondary theatre, the South Pacific Area.

CHAPTER 19 THE INVASION OF FRANCE AND THE DEFEAT OF THE THIRD REICH

1. Although the assault areas are often described as 'beaches' (e.g. 'GOLD beach' or 'OMAHA beach'), troops came ashore some distance from one another in each assault area, and the term used at the time was 'area'. The western three-quarters of the GOLD area were unsuitable for an amphibious landing; the 'beaches' to be assaulted within GOLD were code-named JIG and KING; they were separated from one another by 1,000 yards.
2. Brown, *Invasion*, Section 1 [*Landing*], pp. 97–9, Section 1 [Appendices], pp. 102–4.
3. Baron, *From the City*, p. 132.
4. Holborn, *D-Day Landing*, pp. 48–55; Trew, *Gold Beach*, pp. 16–17, 20–3.
5. Holborn, *Gold Beach*, pp. 132–3.
6. Ellis, *Victory*/1, p. 223, Holborn, *D-Day Landing*, p. 194.
7. The execution of Operation ANVIL, later renamed DRAGOON, was discussed with other late-war Mediterranean operations in Chapter 16 (pp. 347–9).
8. Anzio was not successful in the exploitation phase, but three infantry divisions and an armoured division were successfully put ashore in the initial period.
9. Ellis, *Victory*/1, pp. 67–8, 507.
10. Brown, *Invasion*, Section 1 [*Landing*], p. 86.
11. Lewis, *Omaha Beach*, pp. 291–307.
12. Hessler, *U-boat War*/3, pp. 67–82; Blair, *U-boat War*/2, pp. 53–89.
13. Brown, *Invasion*, Section 2 [*Campaign*], p. 4.
14. Ellis, *Victory*/1, p. 264.
15. Ibid., p. 479.

16. Ibid., p. 478.
17. Ibid., p. 308.
18. The invasion of southern France in August 1944, Operation DRAGOON, was described in Chapter 16 (pp. 347–9).
19. The V2 campaign is usually associated with attacks on Britain, but in fact more missiles landed on Antwerp than on London.
20. Blair, *U-boat War*/1, pp. x–xi, and Tooze, *Wages*, pp. 612–18, describe the shortcomings of the actual Type XXI design and failures in the mass production programme.
21. There was a second electro-boat class, the Type XXIII, but it was a small 230-ton coastal vessel; only 114 feet long, the Type XXIII had a small armament of two torpedoes. It was at least actually used operationally, albeit on a small scale. The first unit – the *U 2324* – sortied from Kristiansand in Norway in January 1945 and five others undertook operational missions, sinking a few small merchant ships in British coastal waters.
22. One of the Halifaxes was damaged during the April 1942 *Tirpitz* raid and crash-landed on a frozen lake in Norway; the plane later fell through the ice, intact. The remains were raised by divers in 1973; considerably the worse for wear, they serve as a unique exhibition at the RAF Museum in London.
23. Coakley/Leighton, *Logistics*/2, p. 681.
24. Padfield, *Dönitz*, p. 373. One naval officer took part in the planning and implementation of the attempted coup – and was hanged after its failure. This was Berthold von Stauffenberg, the elder brother of the army colonel who carried the bomb into Hitler's conference room. But this von Stauffenberg had been an expert in international law and not a career naval officer; he had joined the Navy as a legal advisor in 1939.
25. Equally ironically, one of the other last hold-out areas for the German Army and Luftwaffe in the south were the annexed Czech lands.
26. Rosk/3.2, pp. 301, 467–9.
27. Padfield, *Dönitz*, pp. 419–20.
28. Two boats, the *U 530* and *U 977*, made their way to Argentina, where they arrived in July. The long cruise of the *U 977* was all the more remarkable because she was a small Type VII.

CHAPTER 20 THE PHILIPPINES, OKINAWA, AND THE DEFEAT OF IMPERIAL JAPAN

1. Although Okinawa (the largest island of the Ryūkyū group) lies 400 miles southwest of Kyūshū, it was a prefecture of Japan proper. The Doolittle carrier raid on Japan in April 1942 had been mounted by Army bombers, and they did not land back aboard the *Hornet*.
2. The historian John Prados argues that this 'air-only SHŌ' was a fundamental mistake of the naval command and greatly affected the later Battle of the Philippines (*Storm*, pp. 125–31). Two other variants of the defence plan existed: SHŌ 3 for the defence of the Japanese mainland, and SHŌ 4 for Hokkaidō and for the Kurile Islands in the north.
3. As mentioned in the previous chapter, a Kōkū Kantai was roughly comparable to an RAF Coastal Command 'Group', although in theory it was more mobile (more like a German Fliegerkorps).
4. O'Connor, *Japanese Navy*, p. 104. Fukudome was the admiral who had been captured (along with important documents) by American-led guerrillas in early April 1944, when his flying boat crashed in the Philippines; he was subsequently handed over by the guerrillas to the Japanese Army.
5. Imperial Japanese Navy, online at http://www.combinedfleet.com (accessed 17 February 2019). The Army aircraft was a new type of twin-engined bomber, a Mitsubishi Ki-67/PEGGY. USS *Houston* carried the name of a cruiser sunk in the 1942 Battle of Sunda Strait; USS *Canberra* was named after the Australian ship sunk at Savo Island.
6. Mor/12, pp. 94, 106.
7. Ibid., p. 108. Admiral Fukudome blamed Captain Kuno Shūzō, the commander of the T Attack Force, for accepting these exaggerated claims, and passing them directly to the NGS and IGHQ (O'Connor, *Japanese Navy*, pp. 104–5). Secret internal correspondence indicated that the claims were taken seriously, at least for a time, by the government. Even

naval specialists – Fukudome among them – believed that serious damage must have been caused to the US carrier fleet, although they accepted that the aircrew claims were probably inflated (Drea, *Essays*, p. 136; Ugaki, *Fading Victory*, p. 120–1; Prados, *Storm*, pp. 147–51).

8. Hoyt, *Japan's War*, p. 373. The Emperor also stressed the increasingly serious war situation and urged closer co-operation between the Army and Navy.
9. Reynolds, *Fast Carriers*, p. 256, italics in original.
10. The Japanese battleship fleet did sortie at the time of the Midway operation, but it never got near the fighting. One of the two biggest pre-war ships, the *Mutsu*, was lost after a non-combat magazine explosion in home waters in June 1943, which left seven battleships inactive in Japan. Four additional 'fast' battleships – modernised battle cruisers – were very active in the early campaigns; during this fighting the *Hiei* and the *Kirishima* were lost off Guadalcanal.
11. *Campaigns of the Pacific War*, p. 281.
12. Cannon, *Leyte*, pp. 40–2. An LSD was a 'landing ship dock', a 17-knot, 4,000-ton ship with a well-deck for carrying and launching landing craft.
13. The First Mobile Fleet was divided into two major elements. The designation '1st Attack Force' is my translation of '1st *Yugeki Butai*' (which is sometimes abbreviated as 1-YB). Other sources translate this as the '1st Diversionary Attack Force' or the '1st Raiding Force' (Lacroix/Wells, *Japanese Cruisers*, p. 353); both of these versions, while not incorrect, seem misleading. In practice, in the Battle of Leyte Gulf, Kurita's task group was the *opposite* of a 'diversionary' or decoy force; other task groups were deployed to divert attention from it. The Kurita task group is often assigned the title 'Central Force' in American accounts, which is at least geographically appropriate.

    Meanwhile, the smaller carrier force which was actually supposed to provide the diversion or decoy at Leyte bore the designation 'Mobile Force [*sic*] Main Body' (*Kidō Butai Hontai*) (sometimes abbreviated as KdMB). The C-in-C of the whole First Mobile Fleet, Admiral Ozawa, was located with this force.
14. The fourth carrier group, Admiral McCain's TG 38.1, with the *Hancock*, the *Hornet*, the *Wasp* and two light carriers, had left the area. It had been ordered to retire to Ulithi to regroup on the evening of 22 October.
15. The wreck was located in March 2015 at a depth of about 3,300 feet by the exploration vessel *Octopus*, in an expedition sponsored by Paul Allen.
16. *Campaigns of the Pacific War*, p. 301.
17. The Nishimura task group was officially designated as Force 3 (*Butai 3*) of Kurita's 1st Attack Force. (Force 1 and Force 2 of the 1st Attack Force were the two elements of the main Kurita task group in the Sibuyan Sea.) The Americans called the Nishimura task group the Southern Force.
18. The only other surviving Pearl Harbor battleship was the *Nevada*, which was refitting after supporting the Allied landings in France. The *Mississippi* had been in the Atlantic in December 1941.
19. Vego, *Leyte*, p. 266.
20. The wrecks of the *Fusō* and the *Yamashiro* were located in November 2017 at a depth of 650 feet by the exploration vesssel *Petrel*, in an expedition sponsored by Paul Allen.
21. The Shima task group was formally designated as the 2nd Attack Force (abbreviated as 2-YB), and its movements had not been properly co-ordinated with the Nishimura force.
22. Wheeler, *Kinkaid*, p. 482. 'Bull' was a nickname cultivated by the American press (the admiral was normally known as Bill Halsey). Bull Run, of course, was a famous Civil War battle.
23. The numerous CVEs were mostly named after minor bodies of water on the American coastline. But some – like the big carriers – were named after American military victories. These names extended over better than a century and a half. CVE-66 was named after the 1776 Battle of White Plains. CVE-63, the *St. Lo*, was named after the July 1944 Battle of Saint-Lô, fought during the Normandy breakout; she had originally been named USS *Midway*.

24. No doubt the figure of 209 'torpedo bombers' overstates Admiral Sprague's capability. The Grumman TBF Avenger (built by General Motors as the TBM) was designed as a torpedo bomber, but training and equipment of the TBF/TBM planes on the CVEs were oriented more towards ground support and glide-bombing attacks.
25. The problem of fuel was stressed by Arthur Marder in his explanation of Kurita's decision (*Old Friends*/2, p. 380). A careful analysis of (or apology for) Kurita and his decision was made by Itō Masanori, one of the best-known contemporary Japanese commentators on naval affairs. It includes an account of a post-war interview with the admiral (*End*, pp. 165–79).
26. For Morison's summary, highly critical of Halsey, see Mor/12, pp. 193–7, 293–6.
27. Potter, *Nimitz*, p. 343.
28. The fleet carrier *Junyō* did not join other units in the First Mobile Fleet. Her air group had been detached to land bases at the time of the Formosa air battle in early October, and she was assigned to transport special supplies to Brunei and Manila.
29. Cohen/Gooch, *Military Misfortunes*, p. 243.
30. The names of the two battles are misleading. The June battle ('Philippine Sea') was essentially a battle for the Marianas – and Japanese historians know it as this. The October battles ('Leyte Gulf') were actually a battle for the Philippines as a whole. The carrier-versus-carrier action in October was fought in the Philippine Sea (well to the east of Cape Engaño). For a brief period the US Navy called it the 'Second Battle of the Philippine Sea'.
31. The surprising survival of USS *Santee* had several causes. Most of her air group had already been launched, so she was less vulnerable to secondary explosions of fuel and munitions. She was one of four USN CVEs converted from fleet oilers (hence her 'river' name, after the Santee river in South Carolina), and ships of that class were larger than other escort carriers. Her crew was experienced; their battle service went back to Operation TORCH in North Africa.
32. The timing of the start of the kamikaze campaign seems to have been confused by Japanese propaganda. The Japanese radio announced on 20 October that a suicide attack had been made five days earlier (and four days before Ōnishi's Mabalacat meeting) by Admiral Arima Masafumi, the commander of the 26th Air Flotilla. Arima had apparently flown from Luzon aboard a G4M/BETTY. His target on 15 October was the carriers of TG 38.4, which were carrying out air strikes against the Philippines. It is uncertain whether Arima's flight had actually been an intentional suicide mission or whether – more likely – this was a conventional strike from which a senior officer did not return. Arima had been the captain of the carrier *Shōkaku* during the 1942 battles around Guadalcanal (Ugaki, *Fading Victory*, p. 382; Prados, *Storm*, pp. 157–8).
33. It will be recalled that a similar 'special' tactic had been planned four months earlier in the Battle of the Philippine Sea with the Zero fighter-bombers operating from the light carriers of the Vanguard Force. It had *not* been intended, however, that these planes would actually be crashed into enemy ships.
34. Morris, *Nobility*, p. 283. Another thoughtful survey is Hill, 'Kamikaze'.
35. This book will mainly use the term 'kamikaze', which is familiar to western readers. *Tokkō* ('special attack unit') was the term officially used by the Japanese Navy and in the national press, but it is a euphemism. 'Suicide attack' certainly describes the essence of the act, but fundamentally misses its purpose. As one career naval officer put it to his men: 'Our mission is suicidal and it is. But I wish to emphasize that suicide is not the objective. The objective is victory' (Hara, *Destroyer Captain*, p. 284).
36. Friedman, *Fighters*, pp. 150–4.
37. The raid was partly intended to catch the 'hermaphrodite' battleships *Ise* and *Hyūga* which had been withdrawn to Southeast Asia after the Leyte Gulf battle. These ships had limited combat power, and Halsey was here taking his search for 'decisive battle' well beyond the point of diminishing returns. In any event, the two old battleships, loaded with raw materials, safely made the passage from Singapore to the home islands, through a heavy submarine barrage, in the middle of February 1945.
38. Strictly speaking, Iwo Jima is in the Volcano Islands. Sources, however, often refer to the whole island chain south of Tokyo (the Nanpō Islands) as the Bonins.

39. The *Franklin* was not the last occasion in World War II when the crew of a large American warship would suffer very heavy loss of life. As recounted in Chapter 17 (p. 369), some 880 men would be lost from the cruiser *Indianapolis* when she was torpedoed by a Japanese submarine on 30 July 1945.
40. Mor/14, p. 224.
41. An account by Ugaki's Chief of Staff gives the figure of 700 aircraft lost off Okinawa, but this may refer just to the Fifth Air Fleet (O'Connor, *Japanese Navy*, p. 134).
42. Dower, *War*, p. 52; *WAJ*/4, p. 93.
43. Appleman, *Okinawa*, p. 445.
44. O'Connor, *Japanese Navy*, p. 130 [Yokoi].
45. Hara, *Destroyer Captain*.
46. *SWW*/6, pp. 134–7.
47. Brown, *Carrier Operations*/1, p. 131. The *Formidable* replaced the *Illustrious* on 14 April.
48. Marder, *Old Friends*/2, p. 419.
49. There was an irony in the survival of the *Haruna* to this late date. In the desperate days of December 1941 the US press had announced that she had been sunk off the Philippines by a B-17.
50. Fukui, *Vessels*, p. xi. In addition, three destroyers and four submarines survived outside Japanese home waters. The fleet carrier *Junyō*, torpedoed by a submarine in December 1944, ended the war in dockyard hands at Sasebo. The only surviving large warship in operational condition was probably the new light cruiser *Sakawa*, under camouflage at Maizuru on the north coast of Honshū.
51. Butow, *Decision*, p. 243.
52. Ibid., p. 205.
53. Russell, *Project Hula*, pp. 39–40.
54. Krivosheev, *Poteri*, pp. 309, 392.
55. Since 1999 the battleship *Missouri* has been preserved as a museum ship at Pearl Harbor.

CONCLUSION THE COMMANDED SEA

1. The battles of the Eastern Solomons, Guadalcanal and Santa Cruz were the other Pacific events. Leyte Gulf actually involved three separate large-scale actions.
2. Limitation of space does not permit discussion of the role of the USSR in this 'hypothetical'. However, with Nazi Germany fighting – after the defeat of Britain – a one-front ground/air war in the East, the Soviet position would surely have been precarious.
3. The main transpacific 'economic' route in 1941–45 was actually the little-discussed Lend-Lease supply line from the US West Coast to Vladivostok in Siberia. But since the USSR was neutral in the Asia-Pacific war until August 1945 it need not be brought into these comparisons.
4. This was discussed more fully in Chapter 8 (p. 165). Stark made the case for 'Germany First' in the now well-known Plan Dog memorandum of December 1940. That was, to be sure, written before Russia entered the war and before Pearl Harbor. But Stark's arguments convincingly stress the unchanging strategic priority of Europe and the Atlantic.
5. Rosk/2, p. 238.
6. Potter/Nimitz, *Great Sea War*, p. v.
7. Richmond, *Statesmen*, p. 336 (my emphasis).
8. Ibid., p. 332 (my emphasis). Richmond was here writing specifically about the Atlantic and the Mediterranean in the autumn of 1943, but his judgement could also be applied to the Pacific.
9. The corollary is also true: the United States would not have been able to make an effective contribution if the USSR had not survived.

BIBLIOGRAPHY

The range of publications on the sea war of 1939–45 is immense; this list is selective. Among other sources, it includes all material referred to in abbreviated form in the notes; the list is a single alphabetical one to allow readers to follow these references up quickly. Also listed are other sources that have been most useful for this book; there is a preference for material which appeared soon after the war, and also for the most recent publications. Dates in square brackets given at the end of some entries indicate the earliest known date of publication, if a later edition or reprint has been cited.

BOOKS AND ARTICLES

Abazzia, Patrick. *Mr. Roosevelt's Navy: The Private War of the US Atlantic Fleet, 1939–1942* (Annapolis, 1976).

Achkasov, V.I. et al. *Boevoi put' Sovetskogo Voenno-morskogo flota* (Moscow, 1988).

Aga Rossi, Elena. *A Nation Collapses: The Italian Surrender of September 1943* (Cambridge, 2000) [1993].

Agawa, Hiroyuki. *The Reluctant Admiral: Yamamoto and the Imperial Navy* (Tokyo, 1979).

Alden, John D. *The Fleet Submarine in the US Navy: A Design and Construction History* (London, 1979).

—— *US Submarine Attacks during World War II: Including Allied Submarine Attacks in the Pacific Theatre* (Annapolis, 1989).

Alfaro-Zaforteza, Carlos, Marcus Faulkner and Alan James. *European Navies and the Conduct of War* (London, 2013).

Ansel, Walter. *Hitler Confronts England* (Durham NC, 1960).

—— *Hitler and the Middle Sea* (Durham NC, 1972).

Appleman, Roy E. et al. *Okinawa: The Last Battle* [*USAWWII*] (Washington, 1947).

Aristov, A.P. et al. (eds). *Flagmany* (Moscow, 1991).

Asada Sadao. *From Mahan to Pearl Harbor: The Imperial Japanese Navy and the United States* (Annapolis, 2006).

Aselius, Gunnar. *The Rise and Fall of the Soviet Navy in the Baltic, 1921–1941* (London, 2005).

Assmann, Kurt. *Deutsche Schicksaljahre* (Wiesbaden, 1953).

Auphan, Paul and Jacques Mordal. *La Marine Française dans la Seconde Guerre Mondiale* (Paris, 1976) [1959].

Baer, George W. *One Hundred Years of Sea Power: The US Navy, 1890–1990* (Stanford, 1994).

Bagnasco, Erminio. *Submarines of World War II* (Annapolis, 1977).

Bagnasco, Erminio and Augusto de Toro. *The Littorio Class: Italy's Last and Largest Battleships 1937–1948* (Barnsley, 2011).

Baldwin, Hanson. *Sea Fights and Shipwrecks* (Garden City, 1955).

Ball, Simon. *The Bitter Sea: The Struggle for Mastery in the Mediterranean 1935–1949* (London, 2009).
—— 'The Mediterranean and North Africa, 1940–1944', in *CHSWW/1*, pp. 358–88.
Ballantine, Duncan S. *US Naval Logistics in the Second World War* (Princeton, 1946).
Ballard, Robert D. and Rick Archbold. *Return to Midway* (London, 1999).
Barnett, Correlli. *Engage the Enemy More Closely: The Royal Navy in the Second World War* (London, 1991).
Baron, Alexander. *From the City, from the Plough* (London, 1948).
Bath, Alan Harris. *Tracking the Axis Enemy: The Triumph of Anglo-American Naval Intelligence* (Lawrence KS, 1998).
Baugh, David A. 'Richmond and the Object of Sea Power', in James Goldrick and John B. Hattendorff (eds), *Mahan is Not Enough: The Proceedings of a Conference on the Works of Sir Julian Corbett and Admiral Sir Herbert Richmond* (Newport, 1993), pp. 13–38.
Beach, Edward L. *Salt and Steel: Reflections of a Submariner* (Annapolis, 1999).
Behrens, Catherine B.A. *Merchant Shipping and the Demands of War* (London, 1955).
Bekker, Cajus. *Hitler's Naval War* (London, 1978) [1971].
Bell, Christopher M. *The Royal Navy, Seapower and Strategy between the Wars* (London, 2000).
—— *Churchill and Sea Power* (Oxford, 2013).
—— 'Air Power and the Battle of the Atlantic: Very Long Range Aircraft and the Delay in Closing the Atlantic "Air Gap" ', *Journal of Military History*, 79:3 (2015), pp. 691–719.
Bennett, G.H. and Roy Bennett. *Hitler's Admirals* (Annapolis, 1994).
Bercuson, David J. and Holger H. Herwig. *The Destruction of the Bismarck* (London, 2002).
Berezhnoi, S.S. *Korabli i suda VMF SSSR, 1928–1945: Spravochnik* (Moscow, 1988).
—— *Flot SSSR: Korabli i suda lendliza: Spravochnik* (St Petersburg, 1994).
Bergamini, John. *Japan's Imperial Conspiracy* (London, 1971).
Bird, Keith. *Erich Raeder: Admiral of the Third Reich* (Annapolis, 2006).
Bischof, Gunther and Robert L. Dupont. *The Pacific War Revisited* (Baton Rouge, 1997).
Blair, Clay. *Silent Victory: The US Submarine War against Japan* (Philadelphia, 1975).
—— *Hitler's U-boat War* (2 vols, London, 2000) [1996–98].
Blumenson, Martin. *Salerno to Cassino* [*USAWWII*] (Washington, 1993) [1967].
Bollinger, Martin J. *From the Revolution to the Cold War: A History of the Soviet Merchant Fleet from 1917 to 1950* (Windsor, 2012).
Boyd, Andrew. *The Royal Navy in Eastern Waters: Linchpin of Victory, 1935–1942* (Barnsley, 2017).
Boyd, Carl and Yoshida Akihiko. *The Japanese Submarine Force and World War II* (Shrewsbury, 1996).
Bradford, James C. *Quarterdeck and Bridge: Two Centuries of American Naval Leaders* (Annapolis, 1997).
Bradsher, Greg. 'The "Z Plan" Story: Japan's 1944 Naval Battle Strategy Drifts into US Hands', *Prologue*, 37:3 (2005).
Bragadin, Marc' Antonio. *The Italian Navy in World War II* (Annapolis, 1957).
Brescia, Maurizio. *Mussolini's Navy: A Reference Guide to the Regia Marina, 1930–1945* (Annapolis, 2012).
Brodhurst, Robin. *Churchill's Anchor: Admiral of the Fleet Sir Dudley Pound* (London, 2000).
Brower, Charles F. *Defeating Japan: The Joint Chiefs of Staff and Strategy in the Pacific War, 1943–1945* (New York, 2012).
Brown, David [J.D.], *Carrier Operations in World War II* (2 vols, London, 1974) [1968].
Brown, David [J.D.] (ed.). *Invasion Europe* (London, 1994).
—— *Naval Operations of the Campaign in Norway, April–June 1940* (London, 2000) [1950].
—— *The Royal Navy and the Mediterranean* (2 vols, London, 2002) [1952, 1957].
—— *The Road to Oran: Anglo-French Naval Relations*, September 1939–July 1940 (London, 2006).
Brown, David K. *Nelson to Vanguard, Warship Design and Development, 1923–1945* (London, 2000).
—— *Atlantic Escorts: Ships, Weapons and Tactics in World War II* (Barnsley, 2007).

Brown, Eric. *Wings of the Navy: Flying Allied Carrier Aircraft of World War Two* (Annapolis, 1987) [1980].
Brown, Ken. *U-boat Assault on America: Why the US was Unprepared for War in the Atlantic* (Barnsley, 2017).
Buckley, John. *The RAF and Trade Defence 1919–1945: Constant Endeavour* (Keele, 1995).
Budiansky, Stephen. *Battle of Wits: The Complete Story of Codebreaking in World War II* (London, 2001).
Buell, Thomas. *The Quiet Warrior: A Biography of Admiral Raymond A. Spruance* (Boston, 1974). *Master of Sea Power: A Biography of Fleet Admiral Ernest J. King* (Annapolis, 1995) [1980].
Buffetaut, Yves. 'Marine Française, 1943–45', *Marines*, special no. 2, May 1995.
Bush, Edward. *Bless Our Ship* (London, 1958).
Butow, Robert. *Japan's Decision to Surrender* (Stanford, 1954).
Bykofsky, Joseph and Harold Larson. *The Transportation Corps: Operations Overseas* [USAWWII] (Washington, 1990) [1957].
Cain, T.J. *HMS Electra* (London, 1976) [1959].
The Campaigns of the Pacific War [USSBS] (New York, 1969) [1946].
Cannon, M. Hamlin. *Leyte: The Return to the Philippines* [*USAWWII*] (New York, 1993) [1953].
Carlson, Elliot. *Joe Rochefort's War: The Odyssey of the Codebreaker Who Outwitted Yamamoto at Midway* (Annapolis, 2011).
Carroll, Francis M. *Athenia Torpedoed: The U-boat Attack that Ignited the Battle of the Atlantic* (Annapolis, 2012).
Caulfield, Max. *A Night of Terror: The Story of the Athenia Affair* (London, 1962) [1958].
Chaplin, Philip. 'What Happened to the Royal Marines', *United States Naval Institute Proceedings*, 75:10 (1949), pp. 1,177–9.
Chida Tomohei and Peter N. Davies. *The Japanese Shipping and Shipbuilding Industries: A History of Their Modern Growth* (London, 1990).
Churchill, Winston. *The World Crisis* (6 vols, New York, 1923–31).
——. *The Second World War* (5 vols, London, 1948–54).
Ciano, Galeazzo. *Diary 1937–1943* (London, 2002) [1947].
Claasen, Adam R.A. *Hitler's Northern War: The Luftwaffe's Ill-Fated Campaign, 1940–1945* (Lawrence KS, 2001).
Clark, Mark. *Calculated Risk: His Personal Story of the War in North Africa and Italy* (London, 1951).
Clayton, Andrew. *Three Republics, One Navy: A Naval History of France 1870–1999* (Solihull, 2014).
Coakley, Robert W. and Richard M. Leighton. *Global Logistics and Strategy* (2 vols, Washington, 1995) [1955–68].
Cocchia, Aldo. *Convogli: Un marinaio in guerra 1940–1942* (Milan, 2004).
Cohen, Eliot A. and John Gooch. *Military Misfortunes: The Anatomy of Failure in War* (New York, 1991).
Cohen, Jerome B. *Japan's Economy in War and Reconstruction* (London, 1949).
Collier, Basil. *The Defence of the United Kingdom* (London, 1957).
Conway's All the World's Fighting Ships, 1922–1946 (Greenwich, 1980).
Corum, James S. *The Luftwaffe: Creating the Operational Air War, 1918–40* (Lawrence KS, 1999).
Coutau-Bégarie, Hervé and Claude Huan. *Darlan* (Paris, 1989).
Cowman, Ian. *Dominion or Decline: Anglo-American Naval Relations in the Pacific, 1937–1941* (Oxford, 1996).
Crabb, Brian. *The Forgotten Tragedy: The Story of the Sinking of HMT Lancastria* (Donington, 2002).
—— *Operation Pedestal: The Story of Convoy WS21S in August 1942* (Donington, 2014).
Craven, W.F. and J.L. Cate. *The Army Air Forces in World War II* (5 vols, Chicago, 1948–53).
Cressman, Robert J. *The Official Chronology of the US Navy in World War II* (Annapolis, 2005).

Creveld, Martin van. *Supplying War: Logistics from Wallenstein to Patton* (Cambridge, 1977).
Cumming, Anthony J. *The Royal Navy and the Battle of Britain* (Annapolis, 2010).
Cunningham, Andrew. *A Sailor's Odyssey* (London, 1951).
Cutler, Thomas J. *The Battle of Leyte Gulf: 23–26 October 1944* (New York, 1994).
Davidson, Joel R. *The Unsinkable Fleet: The Politics of US Navy Expansion in World War II* (Annapolis, 1996).
Derry, T.K. *The Campaign in Norway* (London, 1952).
Das Deutsche Reich und der Zweite Weltkrieg (13 vols, Stuttgart, 1979–2008).
D'Este, Carlo. *Bitter Victory: The Battle for Sicily, July–August 1943* (New York, 1988).
Divine, David. *The Nine Days of Dunkirk* (London, 1959).
Doenitz, Karl. *Memoirs: Ten Years and Twenty Days* (London, 1990) [1958].
Domarus, Max. *Hitler: Reden und Proklamationen 1932–1945* (4 vols, Leonberg, 1988) [1973].
Donovan, Peter and John Mack. *Code Breaking in the Pacific* (Cham, 2014).
Doughty, Martin. *Merchant Shipping and War: A Study in Defence Planning in the Twentieth Century* (London, 1982).
Douglas, W.A.B. et al. *The Official Operational History of the Royal Canadian Navy in the Second World War, 1939–1943* (2 vols, St Catharines ON, 2002–07).
Dower, John. *War Without Mercy: Race and Power in the Pacific War* (London, 1986).
Drea, Edward J. *In the Service of the Emperor: Essays on the Imperial Japanese Army* (Lincoln NE, 1998).
Dulin, Robert O. and William H. Garzke. *Battleships: United States Battleships in World War II* (London, 1976).
Dull, Paul. *A Battle History of the Imperial Japanese Navy, 1941–1945* (Cambridge, 1978).
Dunning, Chris, *Courage Alone: The Italian Air Force 1940–1943* (Manchester, 2009).
Dyer, George Carroll. *The Amphibians Came to Conquer: The Story of Admiral Richmond Kelly Turner* (2 vols, Washington, 1971).
Edgerton, David. *Warfare State: Britain, 1920–1970* (Cambridge, 2006).
—— *Britain's War Machine: Weapons, Resources, and Experts in the Second World War* (London, 2011).
Ehlers, Robert, *The Mediterranean Air War: Airpower and Allied Victory in World War II* (Lawrence KS, 2015).
Elliott, Peter. *Allied Escort Ships of World War II: A Complete Survey* (London, 1977).
Ellis, L.F. *The War in France and Flanders, 1939–1940* (London, 1953).
—— *Victory in the West* (2 vols, London, 1962–68).
Evans, David C. and Mark R. Peattie. *Kaigun: Strategy, Tactics, and Technology in the Imperial Japanese Navy, 1887–1941* (Annapolis, 1997).
Evans, Mark L. and Roy A. Grossnick. *United States Naval Aviation, 1910–2010* (2 vols, Washington, 2015).
Farago, Ladislas. *The Tenth Fleet* (New York, 1962).
Faulkner, Marcus. *War at Sea: A Naval Atlas 1939–1945* (Barnsley, 2012).
Fergusson, Bernard. *The Watery Maze: The Story of Combined Operations* (London, 1961).
Ferris, John. 'Intelligence', in *CHSWW/1*, pp. 637–63.
Field, James A. *The Japanese at Leyte Gulf: The Shō Operation* (Princeton, 1947).
Ford, Douglas. *The Pacific War: Clash of Empires in World War II* (London, 2011).
Ford, Jack. 'The Forlorn Ally: The Netherlands East Indies in 1942', *War & Society*, 11: 1 (1993), pp. 105–27.
Francillon, René J. *Japanese Aircraft of the Pacific War* (London, 1979).
Frank, Richard, *Guadalcanal: The Definitive Account of the Landmark Battle* (New York, 1990).
—— *Downfall: The End of the Imperial Japanese Empire* (London, 1999).
—— 'Ending the Pacific War: "No Alternative to Annihilation" ', in Daniel Marston (ed.), *The Pacific War Companion: From Pearl Harbor to Hiroshima* (Oxford, 2005).
—— 'Picking Winners', *Naval History*, 25:3 (2011), p. 25.
Franklin, George D. *Britain's Anti-Submarine Capability, 1919–1939* (London, 2003).
Friedman, Norman. *Naval Radar* (Greenwich, 1981).
—— *US Aircraft Carriers: An Illustrated Design History* (London, 1983).

—— *US Destroyers: An Illustrated Design History* (London, 1983).
—— *US Cruisers: An Illustrated Design History* (London, 1985).
—— *US Battleships: An Illustrated Design History* (London, 1986).
—— *British Carrier Aviation: The Evolution of the Ships and Their Aircraft* (London, 1988).
—— *US Amphibious Ships and Craft: An Illustrated Design History* (Annapolis, 2002).
—— *British Destroyers and Frigates: The Second World War and After* (London, 2006).
—— *British Cruisers: Two World Wars and After* (Barnsley, 2011).
—— *The British Battleship, 1906–1946* (Barnsley, 2015).
—— *Fighters over the Fleet: Naval Air Defence from Biplanes to the Cold War* (Barnsley, 2016).
Frieser, Karl-Heinz. *The Blitzkrieg Legend: The Campaign in the West, 1940* (Annapolis, 2005).
Fuchida Mitsuo and Okumiya Masatake. *Midway:The Battle that Doomed Japan* (London, 1957).
Fukui Shuzuo. *Japanese Naval Vessels at the End of World War II* (London, 1992).
Furer, Julius A. *Administration of the Navy Department in World War II* (Washington, 1959).
Gamble, Bruce. *Target: Rabaul: The Allied Siege of Japan's Most Infamous Stronghold, March 1943–August 1945* (Minneapolis, 2013).
Gannon, Michael. *Operation Drumbeat: The Dramatic True Story of Germany's First U-boat Attacks along the American Coast in World War II* (New York, 1990).
Garand, George W. and Truman R. Strobridge. *Western Pacific Operations* [*HUSMCO*] (Washington, 1971).
Gardiner, Robert (ed.). *The Eclipse of the Big Gun: The Warship 1906–45* (London, 1992).
—— *The Golden Age of Shipping: The Classic Merchant Ship, 1900–1960* (London, 1994).
Gardner, W.J.R. *Decoding History: The Battle of the Atlantic and Ultra* (Annapolis, 1999).
—— (ed.). *The Evacuation from Dunkirk: 'Operation Dynamo'* (London, 2010) [1949].
Garland, Albert N. and Howard McGaw Smyth. *Sicily and the Surrender of Italy* [*USAWWII*] (Washington, 1993) [1963].
Garzke, William H. and Robert O. Dulin. *Battleships: Axis and Neutral Battleships in World War II* (Annapolis, 1985).
Germany and the Second World War (13 vols, Oxford, 1990–).
Geschichte des Zweiten Weltkrieges 1939–1945 (Würzburg, 1960).
Gilbert, Martin (ed.). *The Churchill War Papers* (3 vols, London, 1993–2000).
Glantz, David M. *Soviet Operational and Tactical Combat in Manchuria, 1945: August Storm* (London, 2003).
Goldstein, Donald M. and Katherine V. Dillon (eds). *The Pearl Harbor Papers: Inside the Japanese Plans* (Washington, 1993).
—— *The Pacific War Papers: Japanese Documents of World War II* (Washington, 2004).
Gooch, John. *Mussolini and His Generals: The Armed Forces and Fascist Foreign Policy, 1922–1940* (Cambridge, 2007).
Goodhart, Philip. *Fifty Ships that Saved the World: The Foundation of the Anglo-American Alliance* (London, 1965).
Gordon, G.A.H. *British Seapower and Procurement between the Wars: A Reappraisal of Rearmament* (Basingstoke, 1988).
Gough, Barry M. *Historical Dreadnoughts: Arthur Marder, Stephen Roskill and Battles for Naval History* (Barnsley, 2010).
Goulter, Christina J.M. *A Forgotten Offensive: Royal Air Force Coastal Command's Anti-Shipping Campaign, 1940–45* (London, 1995).
Goulter, Christina, Andrew Gordon and Gary Sheffield. 'The Royal Navy Did Not Win the "Battle of Britain": But We Need a Holistic View of Britain's Defences in 1940', *RUSI Journal*, 151:5 (2006), pp. 66–7.
Grand Strategy (6 vols, London, 1956–76).
Greene, Jack and Alessandro Massignani. *The Naval War in the Mediterranean 1940–1943* (Chatham, 1999).
Gretton, Peter. *Convoy Escort Commander* (London, 1964).
Grier, Howard D. *Hitler, Dönitz and the Baltic Sea: The Third Reich's Last Hope, 1944–45* (Annapolis, 2007).

Grinnell-Milne, Duncan. *The Silent Victory* (London, 1958).
Grooss, Poul. *The Naval War in the Baltic*, 1939–1945 (Barnsley, 2017) [2014].
Grove, Eric. *Fleet to Fleet Encounters: Tsushima: Jutland: Philippine Sea* (London, 1991).
—— *The Price of Disobedience: The Battle of the River Plate Reconsidered* (Thrupp, 2000).
Grove, Eric (ed.). *The Defeat of the Enemy Attack upon Shipping, 1939–1945* (Aldershot, 1997) [1957].
Gun Buster [Richard Austin]. *Return From Dunkirk* (London, 1940).
Haarr, Geirr, *The German Invasion of Norway: April 1940* (Barnsley, 2009).
—— *The Gathering Storm: The Naval War in Northern Europe, September 1939–April 1940* (Barnsley, 2014).
Hagan, Kenneth. *This People's Navy: The Making of American Sea Power* (New York, 1991).
Hague, Arnold. *The Allied Convoy System 1939–1945: Its Organization, Defence and Operation* (St Catherines ON, 2000).
Halder, F. *Kriegstagebuch: Tägliche Aufzeichnungen des Chefs des Generalstabes des Heeres, 1939–1942* (3 vols, Stuttgart, 1965).
Hall, H. Duncan. *North American Supply* (London, 1955).
Halpern, Paul G. *The Keyes Papers* (3 vols, London, 1972–81).
Hamer, David. *Bombers versus Battleships: The Struggle between Ships and Aircraft for the Control of the Surface of the Sea* (London, 1998).
Hancock, W.K. and M.M. Gowing. *British War Economy* (London, 1949).
Hara Tameichi. *Japanese Destroyer Captain* (New York, 1961).
Hardesty, Von and Ilya Grinberg. *Red Phoenix Rising: The Soviet Air Force in World War II* (Lawrence KS, 2012).
Harrison, Gordon A. *Cross-Channel Attack* [*USAWWII*] (Washington, 1951).
Harrison, Mark (ed.). *The Economics of World War II: Six Powers in International Comparison* (Cambridge, 1998).
Hashimoto Mochitsura. *Sunk: The Story of the Japanese Submarine Fleet, 1941–1945* (London, 1954).
Haslop, Dennis. *Britain, Germany and the Battle of the Atlantic: A Comparative Study* (London, 2013).
Hayashi Saburo and Alvin D. Coox. *Kogun: Japanese Army in the Pacific War* (Westport CT, 1978).
Hayes, Grace Person. *The History of the Joint Chiefs of Staff in World War II: The War against Japan* (Annapolis, 1982).
Hearings before the Joint Committee on the Pearl Harbor Attack (39 parts, Washington, 1946).
Heinl, R.D. 'What Happened to the Royal Marines', *United States Naval Institute Proceedings*, 75:1 (1979), pp. 169–77.
Heinrichs, Waldo. 'The Role of the United States Navy', in Dorothy Borg and Okamoto Shumpei (eds), *Pearl Harbor as History: Japanese–American Relations, 1931–1941* (1973), pp. 197–224.
—— *Threshold of War: Franklin D. Roosevelt and American Entry into World War II* (New York, 1988).
Hendrie, Andrew W.A. *The Cinderella Service: Coastal Command 1939–1945* (Barnsley, 2006).
Herman, Arthur. *Freedom's Forge: How American Business Produced Victory in World War II* (New York, 2012).
Herwig, Holger H. *Politics of Frustration: The United States in German Naval Planning, 1889–1941* (Boston, 1976).
—— 'The Failure of German Sea Power, 1914–1945: Mahan, Tirpitz, and Raeder Reconsidered', *International History Review*, 10:1 (1988), pp. 68–105.
Hessler, Günter. *The U-boat War in the Atlantic, 1939–1945* (2 vols, London, 1989).
Hezlet, Arthur. *British and Allied Submarine Operations in World War II* (2 vols, Gosport, 2001).
Hill, Peter. 'Kamikaze, 1943–5', in Diego Gambetta (ed.), *Making Sense of Suicide Missions* (Oxford, 2005), pp. 1–42.
Hillgruber, Andreas. *Germany and the Two World Wars* (Cambridge MA, 1981).

Hinsley, F.H. et al. *British Intelligence in the Second World War: Its Influence on Strategy and Operations* (5 vols, London, 1979–90).
Hinsley, F.H. and Alan Stripp (eds). *Codebreakers: The Inside Story of Bletchley Park* (Oxford, 1993).
History of US Marine Corps Operations in World War II (5 vols, Washington, 1958–71).
Hobbs, David, *A Century of Carrier Aviation: The Evolution of Ships and Shipborne Aircraft* (Barnsley, 2009).
—— *The British Pacific Fleet: The Royal Navy's Most Powerful Strike Force* (Barnsley, 2011).
—— *British Aircraft Carriers: Design, Development and Service Histories* (Barnsley, 2014).
Hocking, Charles. *Dictionary of Disasters at Sea during the Age of Steam* (2 vols, London, 1969).
Holborn, Andrew. *The D-Day Landing on Gold Beach: 6 June 1944* (London, 2015).
Holmes, W.J. *Double-Edged Secrets. US Naval Intelligence Operations in the Pacific during the Second World War* (Annapolis, 1979).
Holwitt, Joel Ira. *Execute against Japan: The US Decision to Conduct Unrestricted Submarine Warfare* (College Station TX, 2009).
Hone, Thomas and Trent Hone. *Battle Line: The United States Navy, 1919–1939* (Annapolis, 2006).
Horie, Y. 'The Failure of the Japanese Convoy Escort', *United States Naval Institute Proceedings*, 82:10 (1956), pp. 1,073–81.
Hough, Frank O. et al. *Pearl Harbor to Guadalcanal* [*HUSMCO*] (Washington, 1958).
Howarth, Stephen and Derek Law (eds). *The Battle of the Atlantic 1939–1945: The 50th Anniversary International Naval Conference* (London, 1994).
Howe, George F. *Northwest Africa: Seizing the Initiative in the West* [*USAWWII*] (Washington, 1957).
Howse, Derek. *Radar at Sea: The Royal Navy in World War 2* (Basingstoke, 1993).
Hoyt, Edwin. *Japan's War: The Great Pacific Conflict, 1853–1952* (London, 1986).
Hubatsch, Walther. *Weserübung: Die Deutsche Besetzung von Dänemark und Norwegen 1940* (Göttingen, 1960).
Hubatsch, Walther (ed.). *Hitlers Weisungen für die Kriegführung 1939–1945: Dokumente des Oberkommandos der Wehrmacht* (Frankfurt, 1962).
Hughes, Thomas. *Admiral Bill Halsey: A Naval Life* (Cambridge MA, 2016).
Humble, Richard. *Fraser of North Cape* (London, 1983).
Hunt, Barry D. *Sailor-Scholar: Admiral Sir Herbert Richmond 1871–1946* (Waterloo ON, 1982).
Ike Nobutaka (ed.). *Japan's Decision for War: Records of the 1941 Policy Conferences* (Stanford, 1967).
Inoguchi Rikihei and Nakajima Tadashi. *Divine Wind: Japan's Kamikaze Force in World War II* (London, 1959).
Interrogation of Japanese Officials [USSBS] (2 vols, Washington, 1946).
Investigation of the Pearl Harbor Attack: Report of the Joint Committee on the Investigation of the Pearl Harbor Attack, Congress of the United States (Washington, 1946).
Irving, David, *The Destruction of Convoy PQ 17* (New York, 1968).
—— *Hitler's War* (2 vols, London, 1977).
Isby, David (ed.). *The Luftwaffe and the War at Sea 1939–45: As Seen by Officers of the Kriegsmarine and Luftwaffe* (London, 2005).
Isley, Jeter and Philip Crowl. *The US Marines and Amphibious War: Its Theory and Its Practice in the Pacific* (Princeton, 1951).
Ismay, Hasting. *Memoirs* (London, 1960).
Isom, Dallas W. *Midway Inquest: Why the Japanese Lost the Battle* (Bloomington, 2007).
Itō Masanori. *The End of the Imperial Japanese Navy* (London, 1963) [1956].
James, Brian. 'Pie in the Sky', *History Today*, 56:9 (2006), pp. 38–40.
James, D. Clayton. *The Years of MacArthur* (3 vols, London, 1970–85).
Johnston, Stanley. *Queen of the Flat-Tops: The USS Lexington and the Coral Sea Battle* (London, 1943).

Joint Army–Navy Assessment Committee. 'Japanese Naval and Merchant Shipping Losses during World War II by All Causes' (Washington, 1947).
Jordan, John and Robert Dumas. *French Battleships 1922–1956* (Barnsley, 2009).
Jordan, John and Jean Moulin. *French Cruisers 1922–1956* (Barnsley, 2013).
—— *French Destroyers: Torpilleurs d'Escadre and Contre-Torpilleurs, 1922–1956* (Barnsley, 2015).
Jordan, Roger. *The World's Merchant Fleets, 1939: The Particulars and Wartime Fates of 6,000 Ships* (London, 2006).
Kahn, David. *Seizing the Enigma: The Race to Break the German U-boat Codes, 1939–1943* (London, 1992).
Kalashnikov, K.A. et al. (eds). *Krasnaia armiia v iiune 1941 goda (statisticheskii sbornik)* (Tomsk, 2001).
Kapitanets, I.M. *Voina na more 1939–1945: Voenno-morskoi iskusstvo vo Vtoroi mirovoi i Velikoi Otechestvennoi voinakh* (Moscow, 2005).
Kennedy, Paul. *The Rise and Fall of British Naval Mastery* (Basingstoke, 1976).
—— *The Rise and Fall of the Great Powers: Economic Change and Military Conflict from 1500 to 2000* (London, 1989).
Kersaudy, François. *Norway 1940* (London, 1990).
Kieser, Egbert. *Hitler on the Doorstep: Operation 'Sea Lion': The German Plan to Invade Britain, 1940* (London, 1999) [1987].
Kimball, Warren F. (ed.). *Churchill and Roosevelt: The Complete Correspondence* (3 vols, Princeton, 1984).
King, Ernest J. and Walter M. Whitehill. *Fleet Admiral King: A Naval Record* (London, 1953).
Kiszely, John. *Anatomy of a Campaign: The British Fiasco in Norway* (Cambridge, 2017).
Klee, Karl. *Das Unternehmen Seelöwe: Die geplante deutsche Landung in England 1940* (Göttingen, 1958).
—— *Dokumente zum Unternehmen Seelöwe: Die geplante deutsche Landung in England 1940* (Göttingen, 1959).
Knox, Macgregor, *Mussolini Unleashed, 1939–1941: Politics and Strategy in Fascist Italy's Last War* (Cambridge, 1982).
—— *Hitler's Italian Allies: Royal Armed Forces, the Fascist Regime, and the War of 1940–43* (Cambridge, 2000).
Koburger, Charles W. *Steel Ships, Iron Crosses, and Refugees: The German Navy in the Baltic, 1939–1945* (New York, 1989).
Koop, Gerhard. *Battleships of the Scharnhorst Class: The Backbone of the German Surface Forces at the Outbreak of War* (London, 1999).
—— *Pocket Battleships of the Deutschland Class* (London, 2000).
Koop, Gerhard and Klaus-Peter Schmolke. *Battleships of the Bismarck Class: Bismarck and Tirpitz: Culmination and Finale of German Battleship Construction* (London, 1998).
—— *Heavy Cruisers of the Admiral Hipper Class: Admiral Hipper, Blücher, Prinz Eugen, Seydlitz, Lützow* (London, 2001).
—— *German Destroyers of World War II* (London, 2003).
Krivosheev, G.F. (ed.). *Rossiia i SSSR v voinakh XX veka: Poteri vooruzhennykh sil – Statisticheskoe issledovanie* (Moscow, 2001).
Krug, Hans-Joachim et al. *Reluctant Allies: German–Japanese Naval Relations in World War II* (Annapolis, 2001).
Kuehn, John T. 'The War in the Pacific, 1941–1945', in *CHSWW/1*, pp. 420–54.
Kuznetsov, N.G. *Kursom k pobede* (Moscow, 1989).
—— *Krutye povoroty: Iz zapisok admirala* (Moscow, 1997).
Lacey, Sharon Tosi. *Pacific Blitzkrieg: World War II in the Central Pacific* (Denton TX, 2013).
Lacroix, Eric and Linton Wells. *Japanese Cruisers of the Pacific War* (Annapolis, 1997).
Lai, Benjamin. *Shanghai and Nanjing 1937: Massacre on the Yangtze* (Oxford, 2017).
Lane, Frederic C. *Ships for Victory: A History of Shipbuilding under the US Maritime Commission in World War II* (Baltimore, 2001) [1951].
Lasterle, Philippe. 'Could Admiral Gensoul Have Averted the Tragedy of Mers el-Kebir?', *Journal of Military History*, 67:3 (2003), pp. 835–44.

Lavery, Brian. *Churchill's Navy: The Ships, Men and Organisation, 1939–1945* (London, 2006).
Layton, Edwin T. *And I Was There: Pearl Harbor and Midway – Breaking the Secrets* (New York, 1985).
Leighton, Richard M. and Robert W. Coakley. *Global Logistics and Strategy* [*USAWWII*] (2 vols, Washington, 1955–68).
Levy, James. 'The Inglorious End of the *Glorious*', *Mariner's Mirror*, 86:3 (2000), pp. 302–9.
—— *The Royal Navy's Home Fleet in World War II* (Basingstoke, 2003).
Lewin, Ronald. *The Other Ultra: Codes, Cipher and the Defeat of Japan* (London, 1982).
Lewis, Adrian R. *Omaha Beach: A Flawed Victory* (Chapel Hill, 2001).
Llewellyn-Jones, Malcolm. *Royal Navy and Anti-submarine Warfare, 1917–49* (London, 2006).
Llewellyn-Jones, Malcolm (ed.). *The Royal Navy and the Arctic Convoys: A Naval Staff History* (London, 2007).
—— *The Royal Navy and the Mediterranean Convoys: A Naval Staff History* (London, 2007) [1944, 1945, 1957].
Longmate, Norman. *Island Fortress: The Defence of Great Britain 1603–1945* (London, 2001).
Lord, Walter. *Incredible Victory: The Battle of Midway* (London, 1968) [1967].
Love, Robert W. 'Fighting a Global War', in Kenneth J. Hagan (ed.), *In Peace and War: Interpretations of American Naval History* (Westport CT, 1978), pp. 263–89.
—— *History of the US Navy* (2 vols, Harrisburg, 1993).
—— 'FDR as Commander in Chief', in Robert W. Love (ed.), *Pearl Harbor Revisited* (London, 1995), pp. 173–89.
Love, Robert W. (ed.). *Pearl Harbor Revisited* (London, 1995).
Love, Robert W. et al. *The Chiefs of Naval Operations* (Annapolis, 1980).
Loxton, Bruce. *The Shame of Savo: Anatomy of a Naval Disaster* (Annapolis, 1994).
Lüdde-Neurath, Walter. *Unconditional Surrender: A Memoir of the Last Days of the Third Reich and the Dönitz Administration* (London, 2010) [1964].
Lund, Paul and Harry Ludlam. *The Night of the U-boats* (London, 1973).
Lunde, Henrik O. *Hitler's Preemptive War: The Battle of Norway, 1940* (Havertown, 2009).
Lundstrom, John B. *The First South Pacific Campaign: Pacific Fleet strategy, December 1941–June 1942* (Annapolis, 1976).
—— *The First Team: Pacific Naval Air Combat from Pearl Harbor to Midway* (Annapolis, 1984).
— *Black Shoe Carrier Admiral: Frank Jack Fletcher at Coral Sea, Midway, and Guadalcanal* (Annapolis, 2006).
MacArthur, Douglas. *Reports of General MacArthur* (2 vols, Washington, 1994) [1950].
Macintyre, Donald. *Fighting Admiral: The Life of Admiral of the Fleet Sir James Somerville* (London, 1961).
Maiolo, Joseph, *The Royal Navy and Nazi Germany, 1933–39: A Study in Appeasement and the Origins of the Second World War* (London, 1998).
—— *Cry Havoc: The Arms Race and the Second World War, 1931–1941* (London, 2011).
Mallett, Robert. *The Italian Navy and Fascist Expansionism, 1935–1940* (London, 1998).
Marder, Arthur, J. *Portrait of an Admiral: The Life and Papers of Sir Herbert Richmond* (London, 1952).
—— *From the Dardanelles to Oran: Studies of the Royal Navy in War and Peace, 1915–1940* (London, 1974).
—— *Operation Menace: The Dakar Expedition and the Dudley North Affair* (London, 1976).
—— *Old Friends, New Enemies: The Royal Navy and the Imperial Japanese Navy* (2 vols, Oxford, 1981–90).
Marston, Daniel (ed.). *The Pacific War Companion: From Pearl Harbor to Hiroshima* (Oxford, 2005).
Matloff, Maurice. *Strategic Planning for Coalition Warfare* [*USAWWII*] (2 vols, Washington, 1959–90).
Maund, L.E.H. *Assault From the Sea* (London, 1949).
Mawdsley, Evan. *World War II: A New History* (Cambridge, 2009).

—— *December 1941: Twelve Days that Began a World War* (New Haven, 2011).
—— 'Naval Strategies in Collision: Britain, the US, and Japan at the Beginning of the Pacific War', *Global War Studies*, 11:1 (2014), pp. 8–40.
McBride, William M. *Technological Change and the United States Navy, 1865–1945* (Baltimore, 2000).
McCarthy, Dudley. *South-West Pacific Area – First Year: Kokoda to Wau, Australia in the War of 1939–1945* (Canberra, 1959).
McLachlan, Donald. *Room 39: A Study in Naval Intelligence* (New York, 1968).
The Mediterranean and Middle East (6 vols, London, 1954–88).
Meister, Jürg. *Der Seekrieg in den osteuropäischen Gewassern 1941–1945* (Munich, 1958).
Miller, Edward S. *War Plan Orange: The US Strategy to Defeat Japan, 1897–1945* (Annapolis, 1991).
Miller, John. *Guadalcanal: The First Offensive* [*USAWWII*] (Washington, 1948).
Miller, Michael. *Europe and the Maritime World: A Twentieth-Century History* (New York, 2012).
—— 'Sea Transport', in *CHSWW/3*, pp. 174–95.
Millington-Drake, Eugen (ed.). *The Drama of Graf Spee and the Battle of the River Plate: A Documentary Anthology, 1914–1964* (London, 1964).
Milner, Marc. *North Atlantic Run: The Royal Canadian Navy and the Battle of the Convoys* (Toronto, 1985).
—— 'The Battle of the Atlantic', in John Gooch (ed.), *Decisive Campaigns of the Second World War* (London, 1990), pp. 45–66.
—— *Canada's Navy: The First Century* (Toronto, 1999).
—— *Battle of the Atlantic* (Stroud, 2005).
—— 'The Atlantic War', in *CHSWW/1*, pp. 455–84.
Moore, George. *Building for Victory: The Warship Building Programmes of the Royal Navy, 1939–1945* (Gravesend, 2002).
Morgan, Daniel and Bruce Taylor. *U-boat Attack Logs: A Complete Record of Warship Sinkings from Original Sources 1939–1945* (Barnsley, 2011).
Morison, Samuel Eliot, *History of United States Naval Operations in World War II* (15 vols, London, 1948–62).
—— *American Contributions to the Strategy of World War II* (London, 1958).
—— *The Two-Ocean War: A Short History of the United States Navy in the Second World War* (Boston, 1963).
Morris, Ivan. *The Nobility of Failure: Tragic Heroes in the History of Japan* (London, 1975).
Morton, Louis, *Strategy and Command: The First Two Years* [*USAWW2*] (Washington, 1961).
Mottar, T.H. Vail. *The Persian Corridor and Aid to Russia* [*USAWW2*] (Washington, 1952).
Moulton, J.L. *The Norwegian Campaign of 1940: A Study of Warfare in Three Dimensions* (London, 1966).
Müllenheim-Rechberg, Burkhard von. *Battleship Bismarck, A Survivor's Story* (Annapolis, 1980).
Mulligan, Timothy. *Neither Sharks nor Wolves: The Men of Nazi Germany's U-boat Arm, 1939–1945* (London, 1999).
Neitzel, Soenke. *Der Einsatz der deutschen Luftwaffe über dem Atlantik und der Nordsee, 1939–1945* (Bonn, 1995).
—— 'Kriegsmarine and Luftwaffe Co-operation in the War against Britain 1939–1945', *War in History*, 10:4 (2003), pp. 448–63.
Nofi, Albert A. *To Train the Fleet for War: The US Navy Fleet Problems, 1923–1940* (Newport RI, 2010).
O'Brien, Phillips. *How the War Was Won: Air-Sea Power and Allied Victory in World War II* (Cambridge, 2015).
—— *The Second Most Powerful Man in the World: The Life of Admiral William D. Leahy, Roosevelt's Chief of Staff* (London, 2019).
O'Connor, Raymond (ed.). *The Japanese Navy in World War II: In the Words of Former Japanese Naval Officers* (Annapolis, 1969).

O'Hara, Vincent. *Struggle for the Middle Sea: The Great Navies at War in the Mediterranean 1940–1945* (London, 2009).
—— *Torch: North Africa and the Allied Path to victory* (Annapolis, 2015)
O'Hara, Vincent P. et al. (eds). *On Seas Contested: The Seven Great Navies of the Second World War* (Annapolis, 2010).
Oi Atsushi. 'Why Japan's Anti-Submarine Warfare Failed', *United States Naval Institute Proceedings*, 78:6 (1952), pp. 587–600.
Okumiya Masatake and Horikoshi Jiro. *Zero: The Story of the Japanese Navy Air Force 1937–1945* (London, 1957).
Overy, Richard, *Why the Allies Won* (London, 1995).
Pack, S.W.C. *Cunningham the Commander* (London, 1974).
—— *The Battle of Sirte* (London, 1975).
Padfield, Peter. *Dönitz: The Last Führer – Portrait of a Nazi War Leader* (London, 1984).
Panteleev, Iu.A. *Morskoi front* (Moscow, 1965).
Paperno, A.Kh. *Lend-liz: Tikhii okean* (Moscow, 1998).
Parillo, Mark P. *The Japanese Merchant Marine in World War II* (Annapolis, 1993).
Parker, Frederick D. *Priceless Advantage: US Navy Communications Intelligence and the Battles of Coral Sea, Midway, and the Aleutians* (Washington, 1993).
Parshall, Jonathan and Anthony Tully. *Shattered Sword: The Japanese Story of the Battle of Midway* (Dulles VA, 2005).
Patalano, Alessio. *Post-war Japan as a Sea Power: Imperial Legacy, Wartime Experience, and the Making of a Navy* (London, 2015).
Payton-Smith, D.J. *Oil: A Study of War-time Policy and Administration* (London, 1971).
Peattie, Mark R. *Nan'yō: The Rise and Fall of the Japanese in Micronesia, 1885–1945* (Honolulu, 1988).
—— *Sunburst: The Rise of the Japanese Naval Air Power, 1909–1941* (London, 2002).
Peden, G.A. *Arms, Economics, and British Strategy: From Dreadnoughts to Hydrogen Bombs* (Cambridge, 2007).
Perry, Glen C.H. *'Dear Bart': Washington Views of World War II* (Westport CT, 1982).
Platonov, A.V. *Sovetskie boevyi korabli, 1941–1945 gg.* (5 vols, Saint Petersburg, 1985).
Polmar, Norman and Dorr B. Carpenter. *Submarines of the Imperial Japanese Navy* (London, 1986).
Polmar, Norman and Jurrien Noot. *Submarines of the Russian and Soviet Navies, 1718–1990* (Annapolis, 1991).
Pope, Dudley. *73 North: The Battle of the Barents Sea* (London, 1958).
Porch, Douglas. *Hitler's Mediterranean Gamble: The North African and the Mediterranean Campaigns in World War II* (London, 2004).
Postan, Michael M. *British War Production* (London, 1952).
Potter, Elmer B. *Nimitz* (Annapolis, 1976).
—— *Bull Halsey* (Annapolis, 1985).
Potter, Elmer B. and Chester W. Nimitz (eds). *The Great Sea War: The Story of Naval Action in World War II* (London, 1961) [1960].
Prados, John. *Combined Fleet Decoded* (Annapolis, 2001) [1995].
—— *Islands of Destiny: The Solomons Campaign and the Eclipse of the Rising Sun* (New York, 2012).
—— *Storm over Leyte. The Philippine Invasion and the Destuction of the Japanese Navy* (New York, 2016).
Prange, Gordon. *At Dawn We Slept: The Untold Story of Pearl Harbor* (Harmondsworth, 1991) [1982].
Prange, Gordon et al. *Miracle at Midway* (London, 1983).
—— *December 7, 1941: The Day the Japanese Attacked Pearl Harbor* (London, 1988).
Price, Alfred. *Aircraft versus Submarine in Two World Wars* (Barnsley, 2007).
Prysor, Glyn. *Citizen Sailors: The Royal Navy in the Second World War* (London, 2011).
Rademacher, Cay. *Drei Tage im September: Die letzte Fahrt der Athenia 1939* (Hamburg, 2009).
Raeder, Erich. *The Struggle for the Sea* (London, 1959).
The RAF in Maritime War (8 vols, Air Historical Branch, 2010) [1947].

Rahn, W. 'German Naval Strategy and Armament during the Interwar Period', in Phillips O'Brien (ed.), *Technology and Naval Combat in the Twentieth Century and Beyond* (London, 2001), pp. 109–27.

Rahn, Werner and Gerhard Schreiber. *Kriegstagebuch der Seekriegsleitung, 1939–1945* (68 vols, Herford, 1988–97).

Raphaël-Leygues, Jacques and François Flohic. *Darlan* (Paris, 1986).

Ratcliff, R.A. *Delusions of Intelligence: Enigma, Ultra, and the End of Secure Ciphers* (Cambridge, 2006).

Redford, Duncan. 'The March 1943 Crisis in the Battle of the Atlantic: Myth and Reality', *History*, 92:305 (2007), pp. 64–83.

—— *A History of the Royal Navy: World War II* (London, 2014).

Remmelink, Willem, ed. *The Invasion of the Dutch East Indies* (Leiden, 2016).

Reynolds, Clark G. 'The Continental Strategy of Imperial Japan', *United States Naval Institute Proceedings*, 109:8 (1983), pp. 64–71.

—— *Admiral John H.Towers: The Struggle for Naval Air Supremacy* (Annapolis, 1991).

—— *The Fast Carriers: The Forging of an Air Navy* (Annapolis, 2013) [1968].

Reynolds, David. *In Command of History: Churchill Fighting and Writing the Second World War* (Penguin Books, 2005).

Richards, Denis and Hilary St George Saunders. *The Royal Air Force, 1939–1945* (3 vols, London, 1953–54).

Richmond, Herbert. *Amphibious Warfare in British History* (Exeter, 1941).

—— *Statesmen and Sea Power* (Oxford, 1946).

The Rise and Fall of the German Air Force, 1933–1945 (Kew, 2001) [1948].

Rodger, N.A.M. *The Admiralty* (Lavenham, 1979).

—— 'The Royal Navy in the Era of the Two World Wars: Was It Fit for Purpose?', *Mariner's Mirror*, 97:1 (2011), pp. 272–84.

Rodger, N.A.M. (ed.). *The Sea in History: The Modern World* (Martlesham, 2017).

Rodger, N.A.M. et al. (eds). *Strategy and the Sea: Essays in Honour of John B. Hattendorf* (Woodbridge, 2016).

Rohwer, Jürgen. *The Critical Convoy Battles of March 1943: The Battle for HX.229/SC122* (London, 1977) [1975].

—— *Allied Submarine Attacks of World War Two: European Theatre of Operations, 1939–1945* (London, 1997).

—— *Axis Submarine Successes 1939–1945: German, Italian and Japanese Submarine Successes, 1939–1945* (London, 1999).

Rohwer, Jürgen and Igor Amosov. 'Strange Parallels in Stalin's and Hitler's Naval Programmes', in *NINH* (2001), pp. 281–302.

Rohwer, Jürgen and Gerhard Hümmelchen. *Chronology of the War at Sea 1939–1945: The Naval History of World War Two* (London, 1992).

Rohwer, Jürgen and Mikhail S. Monomakh. *Stalin's Ocean-Going Fleet: Soviet Naval Strategy and Shipbuilding Programme, 1935–1953* (London, 2001).

Roosevelt, Franklin D. *The Public Papers and Addresses of Franklin D. Roosevelt* (13 vols, New York, 1938–50).

Roskill, Stephen, *The War at Sea* (3 vols, London, 1954–61).

—— *The Strategy of Sea Power: Its Development and Application* (London, 1962).

—— *Naval Policy between the Wars* (2 vols, London, 1968–76).

—— *Churchill and the Admirals* (London, 1977).

Ross, Alan. *Blindfold Games* (London, 1986).

Rössler, Eberhard. *The U-boat: The Evolution and Technical History of German Submarines* (London, 2001).

Ruge, Friedrich. *Sea Warfare 1939–1945: A German Viewpoint* (London, 1957).

—— *The Soviets as Naval Opponents, 1941–1945* (Cambridge, 1979).

Runyan, Timothy and Jan M. Copes (eds). *To Die Gallantly: The Battle of the Atlantic* (Boulder, 1994).

Ruppenthal, Roland G. *Logistical Support of the Armies* [*USAWWII*] (2 vols, Washington, 1995) [1953].

Russell, Richard A. *Project Hula: Secret Soviet–American Cooperation in the War Against Japan* (Washington, 1997).
Russkii arkhiv. Velikaia Otechestvennaia (14 vols, Moscow, 1993–2001).
Sadao Asada. 'The Japanese Navy and the United States', in Dorothy Borg and Okamoto Shumpei (eds), *Pearl Harbor as History: Japanese–American Relations, 1931–1941* (New York, 1973), pp. 225–26.
Sadkovich, James J. *The Italian Navy in World War II* (Westport CT, 1994).
Sadkovich, James J. (ed.). *Reevaluating Major Naval Combatants of World War II* (New York, 1990).
Sakai Saburo. *Samurai!* (New York, 1957).
Salewski, Michael. *Die deutsche Seekriegsleitung, 1935–1945* (3 vols, Frankfurt, 1970–75).
Samuelsen, Lennart. 'The Naval Dimension of the Soviet Five-Year Plans, 1925–1941', in *NINH* (1998), pp. 203–30.
Santoni, Alberto. *Ultra siegt im Mittelmeer: Die entscheidende Rolle der britischer Funkaufklärungen beim Kampf um den Nachschub für Nordafrika* (Koblenz, 1985).
Schenk, Peter. *The Invasion of England 1940: The Planning of Operation Sealion* (London, 1990) [1987].
Schofield, Brian B. *Operation Neptune* (London, 1977).
Schurman, D.M. *The Education of a Navy: The Development of British Naval Strategic Thought, 1867–1914* (London, 1965).
Shaw, Henry I. et al. *Central Pacific Drive* [*HUSMCO*] (Washington, 1966).
Simpson, Michael. *The Life of Admiral of the Fleet Andrew Cunningham: A Twentieth Cenury Naval Leader* (London, 2004).
Simpson, Michael (ed.). *The Somerville Papers* (London, 1995).
—— *The Cunningham Papers* (2 vols, Aldershot, 1999–2006).
Slaven, Anthony. *British Shipbuilding: A History, 1500–2010* (Lancaster, 2013).
Slessor, John. *The Central Blue: Recollections and Reflections* (London, 1956).
Smith, Holland M. Coral and Brass (London, 1958) [1947].
Smith, Kevin. *Conflict over Convoys: Anglo-American Logistics Diplomacy in the Second World War* (Cambridge, 1996).
Smith, Malcolm. *British Air Strategy between the Wars* (Oxford, 1984).
Smith, Michael. *The Emperor's Codes: Bletchley Park and the Breaking of Japan's Secret Ciphers* (London, 2002).
Smith, Peter. *Action Imminent: Three Studies of the Naval War in the Mediterranean Theatre during 1940* (London, 1980).
Smith, Rex Allan and Gerald A. Meehl. *Pacific War Stories: In the Words of Those Who Survived* (New York, 2004).
Spasskii, I.D. et al. *Istoriia otechestvennogo sudostroeniia*, vol. 4 (Saint Petersburg, 1996).
Spector, Ronald H. *Eagle against the Sun: The American War with Japan* (New York, 1985).
Spiller, Henry. *Pearl Harbor Survivors: An Oral History of 24 Servicemen* (Jefferson NC, 2002).
Statistical Digest of the War (London, 1951).
Steinert, Marlis G. *Capitulation 1945: The Story of the Dönitz Régime* (London, 1969) [1967].
Stern, Robert C. *Fire from the Sky: Surviving the Kamikaze Threat* (Annapolis, 2010).
—— *The US Navy and the War in Europe* (Barnsley, 2012).
Stoler, Mark A. *Allies and Adversaries: The Joint Chiefs of Staff, the Grand Alliance, and US Strategy in World War II* (Chapel Hill NC, 2000).
Stuart, Rob. 'Was the RCN Ever the Third Largest Navy', *Canadian Naval Review*, 5:3 (2009), pp. 4–9.
—— 'Air Raid Colombo, 5 April 1942: The Fully Expected Surprise Attack', *RCAF Journal*, 3:4 (2014), pp. 33–47.
Sullivan, Brian R. 'A Fleet in Being: The Rise and Fall of Italian Sea Power, 1861–1943', *International History Review*, 10:1 (1988), pp. 106–24.
Suprun, M.N. (ed.). *Lend-liz i Rossiia* (Arkhangelsk, 2006).
Susmel, E. and D. Susmel (eds). *Opera omnia di Benito Mussolini* (36 vols, Florence, 1952–63).

Swanborough, Gordon and Peter M. Bowers. *United States Navy Aircraft since 1911* (London, 1990).
Symonds, Craig L. *The Battle of Midway* (New York, 2011).
—— *Neptune: The Allied Invasion of Europe and the D-Day Landings* (Oxford, 2014).
—— 'For Want of a Nail: The Impact of Shipping on Grand Strategy in World War II', *Journal of Military History*, 18:3 (2017), pp. 657–66.
—— *World War II at Sea: A Global History* (New York, 2018).
Syrett, David. *The Defeat of the German U-boats: The Battle of the Atlantic* (Columbia SC, 1994).
Tagaya Osamu. *Mitsubishi Type 1 Rikko 'Betty' Units of World War 2* (Botley, 2001).
—— *Imperial Japanese Naval Aviator, 1937–45* (Botley, 2002).
Taylor, Theodore. *The Magnificent Mitscher* (New York, 1954).
Terraine, John. *The Right of the Line: The Royal Air Force in the European War, 1939–1945* (Sevenoaks, 1988).
Thetford, Owen. *Aircraft of the Royal Air Force since 1918* (London, 1988).
—— *British Naval Aircraft since 1912* (London, 1991)
Thomas, Martin. 'After Mers-el-Kébir: The Armed Neutrality of the Vichy French Navy, 1940–43', *English Historical Review*, 112:447 (1997), pp. 643–70.
Till, Geoffrey. *Air Power and the Royal Navy* (London, I979).
Till, Geoffrey (ed.). *Seapower: Theory and Practice* (Ilford, 1994).
Toland, John. *The Rising Sun: The Decline and Fall of the Japanese Empire, 1936–1945* (New York, 1970).
Tomblin, Barbara. *With Utmost Spirit: Allied Naval Operations in the Mediterranean, 1942–1945* (Lexington KY, 2004).
Tomlinson, Michael. *The Most Dangerous Moment: The Japanese Assault on Ceylon 1942* (London, 1979) [1976].
Tooze, Adam. *The Wages of Destruction: The Making and Breaking of the Nazi Economy* (London, 2006).
Topp, Erich. *The Odyssey of a U-boat Commander* (Westport CT, 1992).
Tregaskis, Richard. *Guadalcanal Diary* (London, 1943).
Trew, Simon. *Gold Beach (Battle Zone Normandy)* (Stroud, 2004).
Tsvetkov, I.F. *Gvardeiskii kreiser Krasnyi Kavkaz* (Leningrad, 1990).
Tully, Anthony P. *Battle of Surigao Strait* (Bloomington, 2009).
Turner, John. *Filming History* (London, 2001).
Tute, Warren. *The Deadly Stroke* (London, 1973).
Ugaki Matome. *Fading Victory: The Diary of Admiral Matome Ugaki, 1941–1943* (Pittsburgh, 1991).
United States Strategic Bombing Survey (10 vols, New York, 1976).
Vego, Milan. *The Battle for Leyte, 1944: Allied and Japanese Plans, Preparations, and Execution* (Annapolis, 2006).
Villa, Brian L. *Unauthorized Action: Mountbatten and the Dieppe Raid* (Oxford, 1994).
Wagner, Gerhard (ed.). *Lagevorträge der Oberbefehlshabers der Kriegsmarine vor Hitler, 1939–1945* (Munich, 1972).
Wallach, Jehuda L. 'The Sea Lion That Did Not Roar: Operation Sea Lion and its Limitations', in John B. Hattendorf and Malcolm H. Murfett (eds), *The Limitations of Military Power* (Basingstoke, 1990), pp. 173–202.
The War against Japan (5 vols, London, 1957–69).
Wardlow, Chester. *The Transportation Corps: Responsibilities, Organization, and Operations* [*USAWII*] (Washington, 1990) [1951].
Warlimont, Walter. *Inside Hitler's Headquarters 1939–45* (London, 1962).
Wheatley, Ronald. *Operation Sea Lion: German Plans Made by the German High Command under Adolf Hitler for the Invasion of England, 1939–1942* (Oxford, 1958).
Wheeler, Gerald E. *Kinkaid of the Seventh Fleet: A Biography of Admiral Thomas C. Kinkaid US Navy* (Washington, 1995).
Whitley, M.J. *German Coastal Forces of World War Two* (London, 1992).
Wildenberg, Thomas. *Gray Steel and Black Oil: Fast Tankers and Replenishment at Sea in the US Navy, 1912–1992* (Annapolis, 1996).

Willmott, H.P. *Empires in the Balance: Japanese and Allied Pacific Strategies to April 1942* (Annapolis, 1982).
—— *The Barrier and the Javelin: Japanese and Allied Pacific Strategies, February to June 1942* (Annapolis, 1983).
—— *Grave of a Dozen Schemes: British Naval Planning and the War against Japan, 1943–1945* (Shrewsbury, 1996).
—— *The Battle of Leyte Gulf: The Last Fleet Action* (Bloomington, 2015).
Winklareth, Robert I. *Naval Shipbuilders of the World: From the Age of Sail to the Present Day* (London, 2000).
Winton, John. *Ultra in the Pacific: How Breaking Japanese Codes and Ciphers Affected Naval Operations Against Japan, 1941–45* (Barnsley, 1993).
Wragg, David. *Total Germany: The Royal Navy's War against the Axis Powers 1939–1945* (Barnsley, 2015).
Y'Blood, William T. *Red Sun Setting: The Battle of the Philippine Sea* (Annapolis, 2003).
Zimm, Alan D. *Attack on Pearl Harbor: Strategy, Combat, Myths, Deceptions* (Havertown PA, 2011).
Zolotarev, V.A. and V.S. Shlomin. *Kak sozdavalas' voenno-morskaia moshch' Sovetskogo Soiuza* (2 vols, Moscow, 2004).
Zubkov, R.A. *Tallinskii proryv Krasnoznamennogo Baltiiskogo flota: Sobytiia, otsenki, uroki* (Moscow, 2012).

DESPATCHES

A number of important secret wartime despatches from British field commanders to London were published officially in the UK in the post-war years as supplements to the *London Gazette*. Although in some cases these have been censored or condensed, they contain a first-hand view of events, as well as a great deal of information. The despatches are available online at http://www.london-gazette.co.uk (accessed 18 February 2019). The number in parentheses is the Issue/Supplement number in the *Gazette* (Edition/London).

'River Plate Battle' (No. 37989)
'First and Second Battles of Narvik on 10th and 13th of April 1940 Respectively' (No. 38005)
'The Evacuation of the Allied Armies from Dunkirk and Neighbouring Beaches' (No. 38017)
'Raid on Military and Economic Objectives in the Lofoten Islands' (No. 38331)
'Sinking of the German Battleship *Bismarck* on 27th May, 1941' (No. 38098)
'The Capture of Diego Suarez' (No. 38225)
'The Battle of Sirte of 22nd March, 1942' (No. 38073)
'Mediterranean Convoy Operations' (No. 38377)
'Convoys to North Russia, 1942' (No. 39041)
'The Invasion of Sicily' (No. 38895)
'Operations in Connection with the Landings in the Gulf of Salerno on 9th September 1943' (No. 38899)
'The Assault Phase of the Normandy Landings' (No. 381110)
'The Contribution of the British Pacific Fleet to the Assault on Okinawa, 1945' (No. 38308)

A useful list of other relevant British despatches is available online at https://www.ibiblio.org/hyperwar/UN/UK/londongazette.html (accessed 18 February 2019).

ONLINE SOURCES

The internet is an invaluable resource, with more and more material becoming available. As with print material, only a very limited range of sources can be listed here.

Convoy Web Founded by the late Arnold Hague, features detailed material on the routes and composition of individual Allied convoys; see www.convoyweb.org.uk (accessed 18

February 2019). The expanded 2015 version of the database is not available online, but may be viewed at Guildhall Library, Aldermanbury, London EC2V 7HH.

Google Earth An especially valuable tool for anyone trying to follow the campaigns at sea and in coastal areas.

HyperWar Founded by the late Patrick Clancey as a 'Hypertext History of the Second World War', contains electronic versions of a number of important printed books, notably the multi-volume official histories of the US Navy, US Marine Corps, US Army and US Army Air Force (not all complete); see http://www.ibiblio.org/hyperwar (accessed 18 February 2019).

Imperial Japanese Navy Page Founded by Jonathan Parshall, includes highly detailed tabular records of movement for many Japanese warships; see http://www.combinedfleet.com (accessed 18 February 2019).

Naval History and Heritage Command of the US Navy Contains a huge amount of text, statistics and images; see https://www.history.navy.mil (accessed 18 February 2019). Among the source available on the NHHC site is the Dictionary of American Naval Fighting Ships (DANFS), which provides full histories of individual vessels; see https://www.history.navy.mil/research/histories/ship-histories/danfs.html (accessed 18 February 2019).

Naval-History.Net Founded by the late Gordon Smith, features details of the wartime operations of the Royal Navy, including warship histories: see http://www.naval-history.net (accessed 18 February 2019).

uboat.net Provides extensive information about individual German submarines, as well as details of Allied anti-submarine activities; see https://uboat.net (accessed 18 February 2019).

US Army Center of Military History Provides – among other things – online versions of the US Army 'Green Books', the published multi-volume official history of the Army in World War II, including material on grand strategy, logistics and amphibious operations; see https://history.army.mil (accessed 18 February 2019).

INDEX

Abe, Adm. Hiroaki 238–9
Abrial, Adm. Jean-Marie 77
Adachi, Gen Hatazō 247, 249
Addu Atoll 192
Admiralty Is. 249, 378
Aitape 249
Aleutian Is. 215–17, 229, 243, 377, 384–6
Alexander, A.V. 12, 412
Algeria xv–xviii, 64, 76, 283–4, 332, 348
Algiers xvi–xviii, 71, 76–7, 283
Allen, Paul 487n34, 497n17, 514n15, 514n20
Allied conferences
  Atlantic Conference (Aug. 1941) 165
  Casablanca/SYMBOL 312, 334, 376, 407
  Washington/TRIDENT 377, 407, 422
  Quebec I/QUADRANT 244, 377–8
  Cairo/SEXTANT 378, 407, 409, 466, 508n20
  Quebec II/OCTAGON 443, 467
  Yalta/ARGONAUT 471
  Potsdam/TERMINAL 469
Allied convoys
  convoy series
    HX 86
    JW 308
    KMF 505n27
    KMS 347
    MW 501n1
    PQ 266, 500n29
    SC 86
    TC 87
    UGS 347
    UT 327
    WS 87
  individual convoys (codenamed)
    COLLAR 120–1, 131
    EXCESS 123, 131
    HALBERD 131, 297
    HARPOON 292, 295–6
    HATS 119, 130–1
    PEDESTAL 208, 283, 294–7
    STONEAGE 297, 328
    SUBSTANCE 131
    VIGOROUS 292–4
  individual convoys (numbered)
    AT.10 263
    GM.2 131
    HG.76 95
    HX.1 86
    HX.79 83, 85
    HX.84 100
    HX.150 168
    HX.156 154–5
    HX.229 315
    HX.237 315
    HX.239 315
    JW.51A 308
    JW.51B 265, 307–8
    JW.52 316
    JW.53 316
    JW.54A 316, 318
    JW.54B 318
    JW.55A 318
    JW.55B 318
    JW.59 149
    MC.4 131
    ME.6 131
    MF.2 130
    MKS.30 323
    MW.5 131
    MW.10 286, 288–9
    MW.11 293
    MW.13 297
    ON.18 168
    ON.20 154

ON.154 260
ON.202 323, 326
ONS.5 315
ONS.18 326
ONS.92 260
PQ.13 266
PQ.14 266
PQ.15 266
PQ.16 266
PQ.17 265–9, 292, 302
PQ.18 269
QP.11 266
SC.1 86
SC.7 83–5,
SC.48 168
SC.94 260
SC.122 315
SC.129 315
SC.130 316
SL.1 87
SL.125 264
SL.139 323
SL.178 87
TMF.1 264
UGS.38 347
WS.1 87, 129
WS.124 168–9
WS.19Z 292–3
WS.21S 295
WS.33 87
Allied headquarters and staffs
ABDA 191, 205
CCS 244
COSSAC 422–3
SEAC 408–9
SHAEF 423
Allied landing vessels
APA 252, 278, 336, 500n9
APD 501n14
combat loader 275, 414
DD tanks 421, 425
DUKW 277, 284, 337, 501n12
LCA 275, 337, 420
LCI 248, 275–6, 278, 337, 388, 500n9, 509n37
LCM 275–6
LCP 275
LCT 248, 276–8, 337, 420
LCVP 275, 337
LSD 447, 501n14, 514n12
LSI 271, 275, 279, 281, 336,
LSM 501n14
LST 248, 276–8, 337, 500n11, 509n37
LVT (amtrac) 277, 386–7, 509n35
Allied military operations
ACROBAT 289
ANAKIM 312, 407
ANVIL 347–8, 423
AVALANCHE 335, 340, 345
BAYTOWN 344–5
BOLERO 263, 280, 327
BUCCANEER 409
CHARIOT 278
COBRA 428
CRUSADER 134, 289, 298
CULVERIN 409
DESECRATE 395
DETACHMENT 462
DRAGOON 78, 347–9, 428–9, 474
DYNAMO 47, 52
FLINTOCK 387
FORAGER 389, 398
FORTITUDE 428
GALVANIC 370, 386
GYMNAST 280
HAILSTONE 394
HUSKY 312, 334–7, 339, 415
ICEBERG 464
IRONCLAD 278–9
JUBILEE 280–2
KING II 444
NEPTUNE 419–20, 422–4, 474
OVERLORD 347, 428
RANKIN 483n15
RUTTER 280–1
ROUNDUP 263, 280, 285, 334, 347, 501n26
SHINGLE 345–6
SLEDGEHAMMER 280, 282
STALEMATE 391
STARVATION 362
TORCH xv–xix, 74, 76, 228, 263–4, 280, 282–5
WATCHTOWER 224, 227–8, 231
Allied shipbuilding 251–3, 262–3, 312, 414–15
see also British merchant fleet, shipbuilding; US merchant fleet, shipbuilding
Allied 'shipping crisis' (1943) 263
Allied strategy
amphibious operations 474
Atlantic A/S organisation 314–15
British–French strategy in 1939–40 21, 31
cross-Channel landing plans 279–80, 501n26, 473
deterrent strategy vs Japan (1941) 182, 186
'Germany First' 165, 205, 228, 376, 476, 491n20, 516n4
global command regions agreed 204
Mediterranean strategy (1943) 334

North Africa invasion (1942) 282–5
Pacific 376–7, 442–4, 508n20
see also Allied conferences; British strategy; US strategy
Altafjord 266–8, 317–20, 433
amphibious operations xvi, xx, 55, 197, 273–4, 303–4, 391, 423
follow-on forces xviii, 474
ship-to-shore 336, 484n26
shore-to-shore 58, 248–9, 276, 281, 336–7, 345, 390, 430, 471, 484n26, 484n62
Anami, Gen. Korechika 469
Åndalsnes 41–2
Andaman Is. 191, 409
Andrews, Adm. Adolphus 257
Anglo-German Naval Agreement 9–10
Ansel, Walter 61, 484n21
Antwerp 429–30, 513n19
Anzio 345–6, 512n8
Arakan coast 411
Arima, Adm. Masafumi 515n32
Arnold, Gen. Henry H. ('Hap') 378, 443
Atlantic, Battle of the 83–110, 154–6, 165–9, 307–27, 431–3
Attu 215, 377, 384–6, 393, 498n26
Augusta 338
Auphan, Adm. Gabriel 77
Axis Mediterranean convoys 126–9, 297–300, 328–34
Axis strategy 162–3
agreement on operational zones (1942) 494n9
see also German strategy; Japanese strategy; Tripartite Pact
Azores 63, 324

Badoglio, Marshal Pietro 111, 121, 339–41, 343
Balbo, Italo 117
Ballard, Robert 108, 220
Barbey, Adm. Daniel 248–9
Bari air raid 347
Barnett, Correlli 12–13, 117, 347, 481n15, 510n10, 501n25, 502n16
Baron, Alexander 419
Bataan 185
Bay of Bengal raid (1942) 191
Beach, Lt Edward 351–2
Behar atrocity 365–6, 507n26
Behrens, Catherine 98
Bell, Christopher 260, 483n15, 499n18
Benghazi 122, 126, 289, 300
Bergamini, Adm. Carlo 340–2
Bergen 30, 33, 37–8, 499n22
Betio 386–7
Bettica, Lt Cmdr Ener 329
Bey, Adm. Erich 318–19
Biak 249–50, 398–9
Bismarck Archipelago 188, 228, 244, 376–7
Bismarck pursuit (RHINE EXERCISE) 101–9
Bismarck Sea battle 242, 247, 506n22
Bismarcks barrier 249, 376–7
Bizerte 75, 126
Blackett, Patrick 313
Blair, Clay 486n14, 487n26, 499n12, 503n25, 506n9, 513n20
Bloody Ridge 231–2
Bône 328
Bonin Is. 399, 462, 515n38
Bora Bora 205
Bougainville 230, 241–2, 244–5, 370–2
Bowen, Dennis 422
Bowhill, Air Marshal Edward 97
Boyd, Andrew 512n72
Boyd, Carl 507n24
Boyington, Maj. Gregory ('Pappy') 242
Bragadin, Marc' Antonio 505n18, 505n20
Brest 64, 70, 78, 428–9
Brisbane 443
Britain
Chiefs of Staff (COS) 409
Combined Operations Headquarters (COHQ) 273–4
Inter-Service Training and Development Centre (ISTDC) 274
Joint Intelligence Committee 187
technical cooperation with US 165
see also British strategy
British Air Force *see* Royal Air Force
British codebreaking 477
Axis Mediterranean convoys 127–8, 328
Atlantic war 89, 97–8, 258–9, 313, 316, 486n24
Bletchley Park 45, 97
Cape Matapan battle 124
Far East Combined Bureau (FECB) 193, 212, 359
German commerce raiders 99
Government Code & Cypher School (GC&CS) *see* British codebreaking, Bletchley Park
Indian Ocean 193, 411
North Cape battle 318
PQ.17 267
Ultra 97
see also German Navy, communications systems; US codebreaking
British Expeditionary Force (1939–40) 21, 47, 86
British merchant fleet 12, 85–6, 196, 414–15, 477

British-controlled foreign-flag ships 80, 86
ship repair 93
shipbuilding 91, 93, 262, 477
see also Allied shipbuilding
shipping policy/import replacement 93
ships
Athenia 3–5, 480n1
Avondale Park 437
Behar 365–6, 507n25
Cyclops 255
Empire Arquebus 420
Empire Crossbow 420
Empire Halberd 420
Empire Lance 420
Empire Mace 420
Empire Rapier 420
Empire Spearhead 420
Empress of Britain 90, 486n12
Fiscus 84
Laconia 261
Léopoldville 430
Mauretania 129
Ocean Vanguard 499n4
Ocean Venture 252
Ocean Voice 252
Ohio 296–7
Queen Elizabeth 87, 327
Queen Mary 87, 263, 327
Waimarama 297
British military operations
AERIAL 53
CLAYMORE 271–21
CRUSADER 289, 298
DYNAMO 52–3
MENACE 72–3
see also Allied military operations
British Navy *see* Royal Navy
British strategy
assumes Mediterranean and Indian Ocean responsibility (1942) 205
detonator strategy (1940–41) 500n6
economic blockade of Germany (1939–40) 32
Mediterranean strategy 117–18, 334
raiding strategy (1940–42) 197, 269–74, 278–81
'super-raid' 280
Singapore strategy 185–7
strategy against Japan (1944–45) 467
see also Allied strategy
Brooke, Gen. Alan 467
Broome, Cmdr John ('Jackie') 267–9
Brown, Eric 494n16
Brown, Adm. Wilson 201
Bruneval raid 278
Buckley, John 484n33, 499n18
Buell, Thomas 210, 495n19, 499n13, 511n68
Bulge, Battle of the 430
Burge, Richard 171
Burke, Adm. Arleigh 498n30
Burma 407, 410–11
Burnett, Adm. R.L. 308
Bush, Capt. Eric 287
Bush, George H.W. 462

Calabria battle (Punta Stilo) 111–15, 487n2
Calabria invasion (1943) 344–5
Callaghan, Adm. Daniel 238–9
Campioni, Adm. Inigo 111, 113, 119–22, 488n16
Canada 44, 87, 94, 262, 281–2, 336–7, 385, 422, 425, 427, 429
see also Royal Canadian Navy
Canadian Army 24, 44, 87, 281–2, 336–7, 385, 422, 425, 427–9
Cape Engaño battle 454–5
Cape Esperance battle 233
Cape Gloucester landing 249
Cape Matapan battle 124
Cape St George battle 498n30
Cape Spada battle 119
Cape Spartivento battle 120–2
Carls, Adm. Rolf 310
Caroline Is. 177, 212, 227, 377–8, 383, 394, 472
Carpender, Adm. Arthur 248
Casablanca xvi-xviii, 75–6
Cavagnari, Adm. Domenico 111, 116–17
Cebu 395–6
Ceylon 191–5, 320, 408–9, 411, 494n48
Chamberlain, Neville 3, 12, 42, 69
Channel Dash (1942) 110
Chatham 13
Cherbourg 50, 423, 427–8
China 161–2, 164, 172–4, 186, 353, 383, 407–8, 476, 492n8, 506n23, 511n70, 511n71
see also Sino-Japanese War
Churchill, Winston 12–13, 33, 42, 61–2, 70–2, 90, 92, 162, 167, 186, 188, 194, 269, 273–4, 279–81, 312, 316, 354, 378, 408, 412, 467, 476, 483n15, 499n18
Ciano, Galeazzo 117, 128
Cocchia, Capt. Aldo 329, 504n3
Cohen, Eliot 455, 499n11, 515n29
Colombo 193, 409
combined operations *see* amphibious operations
Commandos 274
Conolly, Adm. Richard 387, 391

convoys
  economic/strategic vs front-line/ operational 302, 354
  see also Allied convoys; Axis Mediterranean convoys
Coral Sea battle 210–15, 495n21
Corregidor 185, 204
Corsica 78, 339
Corum, James 90–1
Courland 152, 434
Crete 124–6
Creveld, Martin van 300
Crimea 145–6, 150–1
Crutchley, Adm. Victor 225–6
Cunningham, Adm. Andrew xv–xvii, 67, 103, 111–15, 119–21, 123–5, 133–4, 284, 290, 300, 313, 333, 335–6, 342–3, 345, 408–9, 412, 423, 467

D-Day (6 June 1944) *see* Normandy invasion
Da Zara, Adm. Alberto 293, 343, 505n18
Dakar 67, 72–3, 78
Darlan, Adm. Jean-François 64–5, 68–71, 74–78
Darwin raid 189
D'Este, Carlo 505n15
de Courten, Adm. Raffaele 339–41
de Gaulle, Gen. Charles 71–2, 77
de Laborde, Adm. Jean 75–7
decisive-battle concept 156, 480n5
Denmark 31, 437, 492n22
Denmark Strait battle 103–5
Denning, Norman 97
destroyers-for-bases deal (1940) 94, 162
Diego Suarez 278–9, 366
Dieppe raid 280–2
Dönitz, Adm. Karl 4, 9–10, 83–5, 88–9, 97, 132, 152, 255, 257, 260–2, 278, 309–11, 315–16, 318–19, 321–2, 324, 332, 351, 412, 415, 434–8
Doolittle raid 210
Doorman, Adm. Karel 190, 493n41
Dornin, Lt Cmdr Robert 350–2, 358, 506n10
Douhet, Giulio 117
DRAGOON *see* France, southern invasion
Draemel, Adm. Milo F. 217
DRUMBEAT *see* Eastern seaboard U-boat campaign
Dutch East Indies *see* Netherlands Indies
Dunkirk 47–53
Durban 133, 169, 279

Eastern seaboard U-boat campaign (1942) 255–8, 364, 499n13
Eastern Solomons battle 235–6
Edgerton, David 481n14
Edwards, Capt. Heywood 155
Eisenhower, Gen. Dwight D. xv–xvi, xviii, 283, 334, 340, 342–3, 423–5, 501n24
El Alamein 300, 501n22
Eltigen landing (1943) 150, 490n25
Empress Augusta Bay battle 244–5, 371
English Channel 47
Enigma cypher machine *see also* German Navy, communications systems
Eniwetok 388, 509n38
Espiritu Santo 74, 227, 229

Fédala 75–6
Feodosiia 145–6
Fiji 201, 205, 229, 362
Finland 32–3, 149, 153
  Finnish ships
    Väinämöinen 153
Fleet Air Arm (RN)
  aircraft
    Albacore 124, 266, 482n28, 489n21
    Avenger 325, 468
    Barracuda 320, 409, 482n28
    Corsair 320, 409
    Firebrand 482n31
    Firefly 482n31
    Fulmar 120, 123, 131, 295
    Hellcat 320
    Martlet 20, 295, 320
    Sea Gladiator 19
    Sea Hurricane 269, 295, 482n29
    Seafire 414, 482n29
    Skua 19, 24, 37, 46
    Swordfish 19, 40, 46, 66–7, 106–7, 114, 120, 124, 325
  attack on the *Tirpitz* 320
  doctrine 106–7, 114
  re-equipment 320
  strength 18
  see also RAF, Coastal Command
Fleming, Capt. Robert W. 460
Fletcher, Adm. Frank Jack 209, 212–15, 217–23, 225, 229, 233, 235–6, 495n27, 496n50, 497n13
Forbes, Adm. Charles 34–5, 38–40, 60, 100
Forester, C.S. 288
Formosa 172, 378, 443
Formosa sea/air battle 439–42
Forrestal, James 413, 462
France
  armistice with Germany 64–5
  defeat in 1940 42–4, 50–1
  Free French government-in-exile 72
  Norway 43

Vichy government xv, xvii, xix, 69–70, 74, 76
see also French Navy
France, southern invasion (1944) 347–9, 423, 428–9, 474
Franco, Francisco 122
Frank, Richard 208, 233
Fraser, Adm. Bruce 318–20, 411, 413, 460, 467–8, 472
French Navy (*Marine Nationale*) 64–80
Alexandria squadron (1940–43) 67, 71, 77–8
Forces de Haute Mer 75
Force de Raid 64, 69
Free French Naval Forces (*FNFL*) 77
Jeune École 68, 75
pre-war developments 67–8
Toulon scuttling (1942) 76–7
warships 68
Algérie 76
Bretagne 64, 66, 71
Colbert 76
Dunkerque 8, 64–8, 71, 76, 116, 197, 485n1
Dupleix 76
Émile Bertin 42, 69, 78
Foch 76
Jean Bart 68, 70, 75, 78
Lorraine 67, 78, 348
Mogador 66
Primauguet 75
Provence 64, 66, 71, 77
Richelieu 67–68, 70–1, 73, 75, 78, 410
Strasbourg 8, 64, 66, 68, 71, 75–7, 485n1
Fricke, Adm. Kurt 310
Friedeburg, Adm. Hans-Georg von 437
Frieser, Karl-Heinz 483n10
Fuchida, Capt. Mitsuo 171, 193, 219, 496n37, 509n31
Fukudome, Adm. Shigeru 382, 396, 402, 440–1, 472, 513n4, 513n7

Gannon, Michael 255, 499n8
Gardner, W.J.R. 487n24, 487n26
Genda, Minoru 170
Gensoul, Adm. Marcel 64–7, 69
German Air Force *see* Luftwaffe
German codebreaking
Allied Naval Cypher No. 3 (Convoy code) 311
B-Dienst 258, 311
German merchant fleet 22
ships
Cap Arcona 437
Duisburg 128
Goya 434
Hamburg 272
KT 1 328–9
Odenwald 168
Patria 438
Rio de Janeiro 34
Robert Ley 11
Thielbak 437
Wilhelm Gustloff 434
German Navy (*Kriegsmarine*)
Baltic evacuation (1945) 434
Basis Nord 142
commerce raiders 99, 365
communications systems
Enigma cypher machine 5, 97, 258, 272
HEIMISCH/DOLPHIN 259
TRITON/SHARK 258–9, 291, 499n14
equipment and weapons
magnetic mine 23
radar 319
Seetakt 319
Flottenchef 23, 44, 46, 100, 267
KORALLE headquarters 322, 436
Kreuzerkrieg 6, 25, 28, 99–100, 254, 365
Naval War Staff (*Seekriegsleitung*) 11, 24, 26, 44, 46, 52, 55, 99, 101, 108, 118, 147, 267, 309–10
Navy Group Command East 23
Navy Group Command North 318
Navy Group Command South 310
Navy Group Command West 23, 424
Normandy 420, 426–7
pre-war developments 5–11
naval operations
BERLIN 100
CERBERUS (ZERBERUS) 110
DRUMBEAT (PAUKENSCHLAG) 255
HERCULES (HERKULES) 298
JUNO 44–6
OSTFRONT 318
REGENBOGEN (1942) 397
RHINE EXERCISE (RHEINÜBUNG) 101, 105–6, 108
RÖSSELSPRUNG (KNIGHT'S MOVE) 266–8
WESER EXERCISE (WESERÜBUNG) 29, 31, 33, 41–2
Versailles limits 7–8
Z-plan 10, 99, 481n9
see also German codebreaking; German Navy U-boat force; German Navy warships; Luftwaffe
German Navy U-boat force
in Indian Ocean 1942–44 363, 408, 431
inshore operations (1944–45) 473
in Mediterranean 132–3, 291, 333, 335, 344, 346

and Normandy 426–7
and North Africa invasion xviii, 264
operational zone in Atlantic extended (1941) 166
prize rules (1939–41) 4, 167
scuttling (REGELBOGEN) 437–8
strength in 1940–41 87–8
strength in 1942 254
surrender (DEADLIGHT) 438
tonnage war 89, 132, 262–3, 302
U-boats
U 1 9
U 21 23
U 27 10, 88
U 29 22
U 30 3–5, 23
U 37 10, 88
U 39 22
U 47 22, 85
U 48 83–4
U 52 23
U 69 167
U 73 296
U 81 132
U 85 255
U 99 84, 88
U 100 84, 95
U 110 5, 97
U 123 255
U 144 143
U 156 261
U 206 486n21
U 230 346
U 249 438
U 331 133
U 486 430–1
U 502 486n21
U 505 325
U 530 513n28
U 534 437
U 539 322
U 549 325
U 552 155
U 559 291
U 565 346
U 568 168
U 596 346
U 652 167
U 701 255
U 954 316
U 977 513n28
U 2324 513
U 2336 437
U 2511 436
U 2540 438
U-boat bunkers 261, 314
U-boat equipment and weapons
AA guns 315, 322, 326
G7e torpedo 358
Metox radar detector 254, 261, 314
Naxos U 322
snorkel 322, 414, 427, 431, 473, 503n25
T5/GNAT torpedo 323, 326, 414
U-boat types
Type VII 10, 88, 90, 94, 254–5, 322, 481n7
Type IX 10, 88, 322, 481n7
Type XIV 254
Type XVIII 322
Type XXI 322, 432, 434, 436, 513n20.
Type XXIII 322, 346, 432, 437, 513n2
withdrawal from North Atlantic (1943) 316
wolfpack tactics (*Rudeltaktik*) 89, 95, 256, 313–14, 322–3
wolfpacks (U-boat groups)
DELFIN (DOLPHIN) 264
HECHT (PIKE) 260
LANDWIRT (FARMER) 426
LEUTHEN 326
MONSUN (MONSOON) 363
MOSEL (MOSELLE) 315
STOSSTRUPP (SHOCK TROOP) 155
STREITAXT ('Battle-axe') 264
see also Dönitz, Adm. Karl; Atlantic, Battle of
German Navy warships
ship types
auxiliary cruisers (raiders) 99, 142
battleships 99
pocket battleship (Panzerschiffe) 8, 27, 30, 37, 435
MTBs (S-boats) 30, 52–3, 150, 296, 424–5
small battle units (*K-Verbände*) 427
supply ships 25, 100, 109, 255
ships
Admiral Graf Spee 8, 24–8, 482n37
Admiral Hipper 9, 29, 36–7, 61, 99–100, 307, 434–5
Admiral Scheer 8, 99–100, 143, 153, 168, 435, 490n31
Atlantis 99
Bismarck 9–10, 16, 99, 101–9, 481n18, 484n18
Deutschland 8, 24–5
see also German Navy warships, ships, *Lützow* (2)
Friedrich Eckoldt 308
Gneisenau 8, 23, 34. 36, 44–6, 99–101, 110, 435, 481n10
Graf Zeppelin 10, 435

Hermes 502n11
Komet 142
Krebs 272
Lützow (1) 142
Lützow (2) (ex-*Deutschland*) 30–1, 37, 99, 109, 153, 266–7, 307, 310, 317–18, 435, 500n34
Michel 99, 365
Nürnberg 435
Niobe 153
Pinguin 99
Prinz Eugen 9, 99, 100–1, 103–5, 109, 110, 152, 266, 435, 487n28, 509n38
Scharnhorst 8, 10, 23, 34, 36, 44–6, 99–101, 109–10, 307, 310, 317–19, 481n10
Schleswig-Holstein 21
T 18 153
Thor 365
Tirpitz 9–10, 99, 102, 143, 265–8, 278, 310, 317–20, 432–3
shipyards 9
see also German Navy U-boat force
German operations
AXIS (ACHSE) 341
BARBAROSSA 56
FELIX 122
ICE JAM (EISSTOSS) 152
MERCURY (MERKUR) 125
ICARUS (IKARUS) 44
PLATINUM FOX (PLATINFUCHS) 146
SEA LION (SEELÖWE) 53–63, 484n21, 485n40
German strategy
against Britain (1940–41) 53–5, 62–3, 79, 87
armed forces (Wehrmacht) high command (OKW) 54, 56, 57, 122
continentalist strategy 7
defence of Tunisia 331–2
invasion of Poland 21
invasion of Low Countries and France 50
invasion of Norway 29–31, 272–3
invasion of Soviet Union 55–7, 62, 135,142, 195
Mediterranean alternative 118, 122, 291
in Scandinavia (1939–40) 32
support for Italy 122
German-Soviet Non-Aggression Pact (1939) 55, 80, 142
Germany
begins World War II 21
declares war on US 183
inter-service rivalry 7, 10, 51, 55, 91, 310, 435–6
occupation of Italy 340–1
occupation of southern France (1942) 76
relations with Vichy France 72
surrender 437–8
see also German operations; German strategy
Ghormley, Adm. Robert 162, 229–30, 236, 238, 256
Gibraltar xv–xviii, 63, 66, 73, 112, 118, 122, 346
Gilbert, Martin 500n4
Gilbert Is. 244, 370, 377–8, 493n21
see also Tarawa
Godfroy, Adm. Réne-Émile 67, 78
Godt, Adm. Eberhard 310
Golovko, Adm. A.G. 142, 146, 148
Gooch, John 455, 499n11
GOOSEBERRY 427
Göring, Hermann 10, 51, 91, 310, 435–6
Gorshkov, Adm. Sergei 146
Gough, Barry 480n6
Greece 86, 121, 124
ships
Elli 343
Grove, Eric 511n68
Guadalcanal 224–42
Guadalcanal naval battle (Oct. 1942) 240
Guam 184, 378, 391–2
Guthrie, Woody 154

Halifax, Edward 33, 183
Halsey, Adm. William 209, 217, 236, 238, 240, 242, 370–2, 439, 441, 443–4, 450–1, 454–6, 461, 494n14, 507n5, 512n82, 514n22, 515n26, 515n37
Handy, Gen. Thomas 284, 501n24
Hangzhou Bay (1937) 173
Hanko 143, 153
Hara, Capt. Tameichi 372, 466
Harcourt, Adm. Cecil 328–9
Harstad 43–4, 46
Harwood, Adm. Henry 26–8, 290, 294, 502n16
Hashirajima 382, 396–7
Hawaiian Operation (Pearl Harbor) 169, 170–2, 179–84, 366, 492n20, 494n8, 498n32, 516n55
Hewitt, Adm. H. Kent 284, 337, 348
Higgins, Andrew 275
Hinsley, F.H. 98, 269, 486n24, 503n7
Hirohito 180, 382, 442, 470, 493n22, 514n8
Hiroshima 69
Hitler, Adolf xviii, 7–8, 10–11, 24, 33, 42, 50–1, 54, 57, 62–3, 72, 74, 87, 90, 98, 102, 108, 110, 118, 122, 151–2, 164, 166, 169, 183, 195, 253, 259,

265–9, 272, 274, 285, 291, 298, 307, 309–10, 318–19, 321, 331–2, 340, 413, 415, 424, 427–8, 432, 434–6
Hiyoshi 396
Holland, Capt. Cedric 65, 472
Holland, Adm. Lancelot 103–5, 121
Hollandia 249
Holmes, Wilfred ('Jasper') 220, 496n38
Horikoshi, Jirō 176, 380–1
Horton, Adm. Max 312
Hvalfjörður 167
Hyakutake, Gen Harukichi 232, 245

Iachino, Adm. Angelino 122, 124, 131, 287–8, 293–4, 334, 412
Iceland 44, 164, 167
Ichiki, Col. Kiyonao 231
Imamura, Gen. Hitoshi 190, 245
India 194, 205, 312, 383, 410, 486n15, 494n48
Indochina, French 74, 165, 173–4, 178, 182, 186–7, 461
Ingersoll, Adm. Royal 206, 257, 323
Inoue, Adm. Shigeyoshi 212, 214
Iran 270, 321
  see also Persian Gulf Lend-Lease route
Irving, David 269
Isom, Dallas 496n44
Italian Air Force (*Regia Aeronautica*) 117
  aircraft
    SM.79 19, 114, 131, 293
    SM.81 114
  torpedo bombers (*aerosiluranti*) 131, 293
Italian Army 341
Italian merchant fleet
  convoys
    M 43 299
  losses 127–9, 299
  ships
    Conte Rosso 127–8
    Neptunia 128
    Oceania 128
    Rex 160
    Victoria 298
Italian Navy (*Regia Marina*)
  Decima MAS 133
  equipment and weapons
    radar 117
    sonar 117
  fuel supply 117, 292
  Naval Battle Force 340
  Operation C3 298
  pre-war developments 116–17
  Supermarina 111, 335
  surrender (1943) 339–43
  see also Italian Navy warships
Italian Navy warships
  ship types
    aircraft carriers 117, 291, 343
    battleships 116–17, 291
    cruisers 116
    destroyers 116
    escorts 116
    MTBs 133
    submarines 132–4, 296
  ships
    Abruzzi 341
    Andrea Doria 117, 343
    Aquila 291, 343
    Attilio Regolo 291, 341
    Axum 296
    Baionetta 341
    Bande Nere 287
    Bartolomeo Celleoni 119
    Bolzano 397, 343
    Cadorna 343
    Caio Duilio 117, 120, 343
    Camicia Nera 329
    Conte di Cavour 111, 116, 120
    Da Barbiano 128
    Da Giussano 128
    Da Recco 329
    Duca d'Aosta 341, 343, 490n20
    Eugenio di Savoia 293, 330, 341–3
    Fiume 124
    Folgore 329
    Garibaldi 341
    Giulio Cesare 111, 343, 490n20
    Gorizia 287, 335, 343
    Imperio 291
    Littorio (Italia) 116, 120, 131, 287, 291, 294, 299, 330, 339, 341
    Lupo 329
    Montecuccoli 293, 330, 341
    Ms 16 296
    Ms 22 296
    Muzio Attendolo 297, 330
    Pola 124
    Pompeo Magno 343
    Roma 291, 330, 335, 341–2
    Trento 128, 287, 294
    Trieste 128, 334–5
    Vittorio Veneto 116, 120–1, 124, 131, 341, 343
    Zara 124
Italy
  armistice 339–41
  declares war on Allies 115–16
  declares war on Germany 343
  invasion of mainland 344–6
  and sea power 115
Itō, Masanori 515n25

Itō, Adm. Seiichi 466
Itō, Lt Cmdr Takuzo 203
Iumashev, Adm. I.S. 142
Iuzhnaia Ozereika 150
Iwabuchi, Adm. Sanji 460
Iwo Jima 399, 462, 515n38

Jaluit 387–8
Japan
air raids on 210, 378, 461–3, 468–9
blockade of 353–4, 361–2, 474, 506n3
diplomatic codes (PURPLE) 181
economic sanctions against (1941) 165, 182
economic weakness 172–3, 176–7
and French Indochina 74, 174
Imperial Conference 174, 178, 244, 493n22
Imperial General Headquarters (IGHQ) 215, 228, 240, 247
Liaison Conference 177, 492n19
mandated islands (*nanyō*) 177, 227, 365, 388, 493n20
naval treaty negotiations 174–6
and Netherlands Indies 173
and Soviet Union 178, 469
Tripartite Pact 163–4, 174, 179
see also Hirohito; Japanese strategy; Sino-Japanese war
Japan, Sea of 362
Japanese Army 188, 229
air army
Sixth 464
Attu 384
field armies
Sixteenth 189
Seventh 232, 245
Eighteenth 247, 249
Thirty-First 389, 391
Thirty-Second 464
Burma 407, 410
Ceylon 194
China 178, 188, 228
deployments to Pacific,1943–4 383, 395
divisions
2nd 189, 232
18th 185
38th 189, 232, 240
43rd 389
48th 189
51st 247
91st 471
Guadalcanal 229, 231
island-defence tactics (1944) 391–2
low interest in Pacific theatre (1942–44) 204, 228–9, 247, 383, 389, 395
Malaya 188
Marianas 389
Netherlands Indies 191, 229
New Guinea 211, 229, 245–9
Peliliu 391
Philippines 229
Soviet Russia 178, 188, 228
units
Ichiki Detachment 231
Kawaguchi Detachment 231
South Seas Detachment 211
Japanese merchant fleet
convoy system 350–2, 360
island supply 243, 302, 361, 457
TAKE no. 1 convoy 361
losses 353–5, 357–8
ship types
Type A 351
Type 2A 360
shipbuilding 360, 477
ships
Argun Maru 350, 352
Atsutasan Maru 355
Ogura Maru No. 1 350, 352
Shōyō Maru 350, 352
Yowa Maru 351
Japanese Navy
amphibious operations 173, 245
area fleets (*Hōmen Kantai*) 498n37
Central Pacific 390, 398
China 173, 243, 359, 382, 493n21
Southeast 371
Southwest 249
A/S capability 359–60, 404
competing views on naval strategy 1942 204
communications systems
JN-25 (AN-code) 181, 193
decisive battle doctrine 177, 179–80, 191, 243, 359, 384, 397, 399, 413
experience in China (1937–41) 172–3
equipment and weapons
radar 360, 441
Type 93 sonar 360
Type 93 torpedo 189–90, 243, 458, 493n40
Kaiten torpedo 369, 458
fleets
First 397
First Air (1941–42) 181, 509n31
First Air (1943) 382–3, 395, 397–9, 445, 457, 509n31, 510n53
First Mobile (Ozawa) 397, 399–400, 405, 444–5, 447, 510n53, 514n13
Vanguard Force (June 1944) 400, 402–3, 447, 510n58, 511n63, 511n64

A Group (June 1944) 400, 403–4, 511n59, 511n64
B Group (June 1944) 400, 403, 511n59
Second 178, 180, 182, 188, 215–16, 245, 371, 382, 397, 400, 445–6
1st Attack Force (Oct. 1944) 445, 447–9, 452, 514n13, 514n17
2nd Attack Force (Oct. 1944) 514n21
'Main Body' (Oct. 1944) 454, 514n13
Second Air 440, 445, 447
Third 382, 397
Third Air 445, 462, 464
Fourth 212
Fifth Air 462–5, 470
Sixth 367–8, 390, 397–8, 496n47, 510n53
Eighth 247–8
Tenth Air 464
Eleventh Air 188, 371, 458, 509n31
Twelfth Air 445
Combined Fleet 178–81, 204, 210, 212, 215–16, 243, 359, 361–2, 367, 371, 382, 384, 393, 395, 396–8, 410, 412, 415, 440, 445–6, 449, 466, 493n21
headquarters 382, 384, 394, 396, 440, 444
Main Body (June 1942) 215–16, 220
reorganisation 382, 397
Mobile Force (Kido Butai) 170, 180–1, 188–9, 191, 193, 204, 212, 215–8, 220–2, 454, 514n13
Maritime Escort Command 359, 361–2, 397, 466
Naval General Staff (NGS) 177–8, 180, 204, 215, 229, 243, 361, 382, 394, 466, 469–70, 495n30
operations
A-GŌ 397, 399
AL 495n30
C 191–2, 195
I-GO 242
KON 250, 398, 400, 410
May–June 1943 Koga operation 393, 510n45
MI 204, 220, 495n30
MO 211–3, 215, 229
RO 245, 371, 381
SHŌ 440, 445, 513N2
TAN 463
TEN-ICHI 466
Y 409
Z 384, 396, 402, 409, 509n33
pre-war plans 177
pre-war developments 174
shipbuilding programmes 379–80
SNLF (naval infantry) 225, 247
Tokyo Express 243, 302
war crimes 364, 366
see also Japanese Navy aviation; Japanese Navy warships
Japanese Navy aviation
air fleets
First (1941–42) 181, 509n31
First (1943) 382–3, 395, 397–9, 445, 457, 509n31, 510n53
Second 440, 445, 447
Third 445, 462, 464
Fifth 462–5, 470
Tenth 464
Eleventh 188, 371, 458, 509n31
Twelfth 445
air losses in China 173
aircraft
A6M/ZEKE 171, 176, 185, 192, 375, 380–1, 402–3, 457, 495n33
A7M/SAM 381
B5N/KATE 19, 171, 218, 220, 380, 492n4
B6N/JILL 380, 402–3
C6N/MYRT 399, 465
D3A/VAL 171, 193, 218, 220, 380
D4Y/JUDY 380, 403, 470
G3M/NELL 173, 187, 493
G4M/BETTY 187, 202, 225, 232–3, 242, 381, 395, 463, 493n36
H6K/MAVIS 201, 211
H8K/EMILY 216, 395
P1Y/FRANCES 381, 463
aircraft production 18, 380, 509n29
aircrew training 381, 403–4
A/S group 359
co-operation with Army aviation 440–1
equipment and weapons
airborne radar 441
rikkō (land-based attack aircraft) 187, 189, 233, 493n36, 509n29
T Attack Force 439–401
Japanese Navy warships
ship types
battleships 174–6, 445, 514n10
fleet carriers 176, 379–80
cruisers 175, 492n15
destroyers 175, 359
destroyer escorts 359
escorts (kaibōkan) 359
midget submarines 366–7, 459
submarines 175, 180, 216, 234, 362–9, 474

shipbuilding 174–6, 360, 379–80
ships
Agano 244, 372–3, 394, 507n8
Aikoku Maru 365
Akagi 170, 176, 181, 189, 191, 219
Amagi 468
Amagiri 243, 372,
Aoba 213, 363, 468
Ashigara 191, 411, 450, 510n57
Atago 237, 240, 361, 371–2, 400, 448
Chikuma 365, 371–2, 448, 453
Chitose 380, 400, 454–5
Chiyoda 380, 400, 405, 454–5, 511n63
Chōkai 225–6, 371, 448, 453
Chūyō 358
Fujinami 372,
Furutaka 233
Fusō 449–50, 454, 510n57, 514n20
Haguro 190–1, 244, 250 371, 405, 411, 448
Haruna 188, 238, 400, 405, 448, 457 468, 516n49
Hayate 184
Heian Maru 368
Hiei 181, 238–9, 492n12
Hinoki 457
Hiryū 176, 181, 184, 189, 191, 219–20, 222, 495n18
Hiyō 235, 237, 358, 380, 400, 405, 510n45
Hōkoku Maru 365, 507n25
Hōsho 173, 216, 510n57
Hyūga 380, 454–5, 468, 515n37
I-19 234
I-26 234
I-58 369
I-75 393
I-168 220, 222
I 201 367
I-400 367
Ise 380, 454–5, 468, 515n37
Jintsu 243
Junyō 216, 235, 237, 380, 400, 405, 457, 515n28, 516n50
Kaga 173, 176,181, 189, 222, 493n42
Kako 234, 357
Katori 368
Katsuragi 330, 468
Kikuzuki 213
Kinugasa 239
Kirishima 181, 238–40, 514n10
Kisaragi 184
Kongō 188, 237–8, 400, 448, 457
Kuma 408
Kumano 448, 457
Matsu 359
Maya 371–2, 448
Mogami 190, 220, 371–2, 380, 449–50
Musashi 176, 250, 381–2, 394, 398, 400, 448–9
Mutsu 382, 495n28, 510n45, 514n10
Myōkō 191, 213, 244, 250, 371, 448
Nachi 190–1, 450, 457, 510n57
Nagara 238, 240
Nagato 174, 382, 400, 448, 457. 469, 472, 509n28
Noshiro 250, 371–2
Ōyodo 396, 455, 468
Ryūhō 400, 463
Ryūjō 173, 191, 216, 234–5
Sakawa 516n50
Sendai 244–5
Shigure 372
Shinano 361, 380
Shinyö 457
Shiriya 350–2
Shōhō 211, 213
Shōkaku 176, 180–1, 191, 211, 213–15, 235, 237, 371, 400
Sōryū 171, 176, 181, 184, 189, 191, 219, 492n17
Suzuya 371, 448. 453
Taihō 380, 400, 404
Takao 240, 371–2, 411, 448, 512n28
Tenryū 357
Tone 365–6, 448, 468
Unryū 506n16
Yahagi 457, 466
Yamashiro 449–50, 454, 514n20
Yamato 176, 215, 237, 242, 250, 398, 400, 448, 452, 457, 465–6
Zuihō 216, 235, 237, 371, 400, 454
Zuikaku 176, 180–1, 191, 209, 211, 213–14, 235, 371, 380, 400, 403, 405, 454–5, 495n29
Japanese strategy
absolute national defence zone (1943) 244, 383, 388
strategic phases of war
first phase 204
second phase 204–5
third phase 244
see also Hawaiian operation; Southern operation
Japanese suicide operations 385–6
Saipan banzai charge 385
'shattered jewel' (*gyokusai*) concept 385
Yamato sortie 465–6
see also kamikaze air attacks
Java 189–91
Java Sea battle 189–91
Jellicoe, Adm. John 34, 221, 449

Johnstone, Stanley 203, 494n4
Joubert de la Ferté, Philip 97, 313
Juminda mine barrage 136
Jutland 406, 511n68

Kahn, David 258
Kaiser, Henry 252, 375
Kakuta, Adm. Kakuji 217, 382, 395, 397–400, 404, 426
kamikaze air attacks 457–60, 463–5, 515n32, 515n33, 515n35, 516n41
Kennedy, John F. 243–4
Kennedy, Paul xxi, 13, 481n15
Kerch 145–6, 150–1
Kernével 278
Kesselring, Field Marshal Albert 291, 298, 345–6
Keyes, Adm. Roger 274
Kidd, Adm. Isaac 183, 289
Kidō Butai (Mobile Force) *see* Japanese Navy, fleets
Kimmel, Adm. Husband 166, 182–3, 301
King, Adm. Ernest J. 164, 166, 169, 203, 206–10, 212, 214–15, 217, 222, 227, 235–6, 244, 256–8, 284, 290, 301, 314–15, 323, 326, 355, 364, 376–8, 424, 443–4, 467, 471, 476, 480n6, 499n13
Kinkaid, Adm. Thomas 217, 236, 248, 384, 443–4, 447, 449, 451–2, 454–5
Kirkenes 147, 149
Kiska 215, 384–5
Kiszely, John 483n15
Knox, Frank 162, 207–8, 413
Kokoda 246–7
Kolombangara 241, 243–4
Koga, Adm. Mineichi 243–5, 371, 382, 384, 393, 395–7, 409–10, 509n30, 509n31, 510n45
Kohima–Imphal battle 410, 512n78
Koiso, Gen. Kuniaki 469
Kola Inlet 146
Komatsu, (Prince) Adm. Teruhisa 367–8, 496n47
Kondō, Adm. Nobutake 180, 182, 188, 215, 220, 237, 240, 371, 382, 397
Konoe, Fumimaro 179
Kota Bharu landing 187
Kra Isthmus 187
Krancke, Adm. Theodor 100, 309, 424
Kretschmer, Otto 84, 95
Kristiansand 30, 37, 513n21
Kronshtadt 135–8, 142–4,151
Kula Gulf battle 243
Kummetz, Adm. Oskar 30, 46, 307–9, 318
Kuno, Capt. Shūzo 513n7
Kuril Islands 181, 383, 471, 494n7, 513n2
Kurita, Adm. Takeo 190, 220, 238, 245, 371–3, 382, 397, 400, 445, 447–9, 452–3, 455, 457, 466, 507n5, 514n13, 514n17, 515n25
Kusaka, Adm. Jinichi 245, 371–2
Kusaka, Adm. Ryūnosuke 181, 440, 447
Kuznetsov, Adm. Nikolai 135, 141–2, 146, 148, 490n31
Kwajalein 368, 378, 387–88
Kyūshū 462–3, 469

La Maddalena 335, 341
La Spezia 330, 335, 340, 363
Laconia incident 261
Lae 209, 246–7, 249
Land, Adm. Emory 251
Langsdorff, Capt. Hans 25–8
Laval, Pierre 74
Layton, Cmdr Edwin 212
Le Havre 429
Leahy, Adm. William 207, 443
Leathers, Frederick 115, 312
Lee, Adm. Willis ('Ching') 240, 401, 455, 477
Lemp, Fritz-Julius 4–5, 23, 97
Lend-Lease 148, 163–4, 260, 269–70, 320–1, 324, 433, 482n31, 503n13, 516n3
  see also Russian convoys
Leningrad 143–4, 151–2
Leygues, George 69
Leyte 443, 446
Leyte Gulf battle 446–57, 473
  see also Cape Engaño; Samar; Sibuyan Sea; Surigao Strait
Liberty Fleet Day 251
Liberty ships 164, 251–3, 414, 498n3, 499n4
  see also US merchant ships
Liepāja 143, 434
Lindemann, Capt. Ernst 102
Lingayen Gulf landings 185, 459–60
Lingga Roads 445–7
Liverpool 56, 83, 86–7, 90, 97
Lockwood, Adm. Charles 358
Lofoten raid 271–3
London Naval Treaty (1930) 9, 15–16, 31, 157–8, 175, 481n15, 481n18, 491n7
Lorient 88, 261, 278
Los Negros 249
Love, Robert 258, 499n13
Low, Adm. Francis 323, 326
Luftwaffe 10
  aircraft types
    Bf 109 19–20, 344
    Do 217 323, 342
    Fw 190 344
    Fw 200 90–1

He 111 19, 24, 39, 90, 323
He 177 323
Ju 87 19, 42, 48, 122, 197, 488n18
Ju 88 19, 24, 39, 90, 197, 261, 323, 426, 488n18
anti-shipping operations 24, 39–40, 90–1, 123, 125–6, 323
equipment and weapons
guided weapons
Fritz X 323, 342, 344–6, 414
Hs 293 323, 342, 346, 414
magnetic mines 66
pressure mines 426
formations 482n36
KG 26 24, 39, 266, 426
KG 30 24, 39, 266, 426
KG 40 323
KG 100 342
Luftflotte 4 291
StG 2 123
X. Fliegerkorps 24, 39, 122, 127, 131
Mediterranean (1944) 347
Normandy 420, 426
North Africa invasion xviii
Salerno 344–5
Sicily 341–2
Lumsden, Gen. Herbert 460
Lundstrom, John 194, 495n21, 495n27, 496n50, 497n13
Lunga Point 224, 230, 232, 236
Lütjens, Adm. Günther 34–6, 46, 100–9
Luzon 185, 376, 378, 443, 459–61
Lyttleton, Oliver 262

MacArthur, Gen. Douglas 185, 228, 244, 246, 248–9, 376–8, 443, 446–7, 456, 461, 472, 498n32, 508n21
McCain, Adm. John S. 461, 510n44, 514n14
McCarthy, Dudley 495n21
McCurdy, Russell 171–2
Madagascar 74, 278–9
Mahan, Capt. Alfred Thayer 156, 177
Majuro 388, 394
Makin 386–7, 393
Makō 350, 493n32
Malay Barrier 184, 186, 188–9, 191
Malaya 179, 187–8
Maloelap 387–8
Malta 114, 117, 123, 126–31, 133, 197, 289, 297–300, 302, 332, 335–7, 343
Malta convoys 111, 115, 130–1, 267, 283, 286–9, 292–7, 302, 328, 501n1
see also PEDESTAL convoy
Manila 179, 460
Manus 249, 439, 468, 498n36
Marcus 209–10, 392
Marder, Arthur 12, 408, 515n25
Mariana Is. 17, 227, 362, 378, 389–91, 395, 398–406, 415, 456–7, 461
see also Guam; Saipan; Tinian
Marseille 347–9, 429
Marshall, Gen. George 227, 244, 280, 378–9, 443, 508n21
Marshall Is. 177, 183, 209, 227, 244, 377–8, 383, 387–9, 393–4, 415, 493n20, 508n22
see also Kwajalein; Eniwetok; Majuro
Matapan battle 124
Mearns, David 105, 487n34
Meisel, Adm. Wilhelm 310
Mers el-Kébir 64–7, 70–1
Midway 215–23, 357, 367–8
Mikawa, Adm. Gunichi 225–6, 233, 239, 247–8
Mili 387, 389
Milne Bay 242, 247
Milner, Marc 499n18
Mindanao 376, 378, 443
mine warfare 23, 32–5, 56–7, 60–1, 66, 87, 90, 101, 110, 128, 135–7, 142–4, 152, 293, 333, 362, 420, 426–7, 431, 434, 472, 486n21, 506n6, 506n19
Mito, Adm. Hisashi 364
Mitscher, Adm. Marc ('Pete') 210, 392, 394–5, 402, 405–6, 461, 465, 468, 510n44
Montgomery, Adm. Alfred ('Monty') 371–3, 392
Montgomery, Gen. Bernard 338, 423, 429, 437
Monsarrat, Nicholas 94
Morgan, Gen. Frederick 422–3
Mori, CPO Jūzō 171
Morison, Samuel Eliot 91, 189, 221, 223, 236, 243, 255–6, 266, 289, 395, 463, 511n68, 515n26
Morocco xv–xviii, 75, 264, 280, 284–5
Morris, Ivan 458, 515n34
Mountbatten, Adm. Louis 274–5, 278, 282, 337, 408–9, 472, 500n8
MULBERRY harbour 427
Munda 241
Murmansk 146–7
Mussolini, Benito 115–16, 121, 128, 132, 183, 294, 298, 338–9, 505n14

Nakao, Capt. Hachiro 350–2
Nagano, Adm. Osami 177–80, 204, 221, 24[illegible] 382, 396
Nagumo, Adm. Chūichi 180–1, 189, 191, 193–4, 215, 217–20, 235, 237, 39[illegible] 397–8, 510n48

Namsos 40–2
Naples 126, 329–30, 345
Narvik 29, 32, 37–8, 43
Nelson, Horatio 119, 127, 188, 399, 510n55
NEPTUNE *see* Normandy invasion
Netherlands 42, 80, 86, 173, 437
Netherlands Indies 173, 178–9, 182, 188–91
  see also Southern Operation
Netherlands Navy 190–1, 493n41
  ships
    De Ruyter 190
    Gelderland 153
    Java 190
New Britain 245–6, 249, 377, 383, 498n29
New Caledonia *see* Nouvelle-Calédonie
New Georgia 241–3
New Guinea 211, 228, 245–50, 361, 377–8, 383, 398–9
New Ireland 249, 377
Nimitz, Adm. Chester 206–9, 212, 217, 222, 228, 234–6, 242, 301, 355, 358, 371, 379, 394, 387, 413, 443–4, 454–6, 462, 472, 477, 507n5
Nishimura, Adm. Shōji 449, 514n17
Noble, Adm. Percy 312
Normandy invasion 419–28, 474, 512n1
North Africa invasion xv–xix, 74–7, 228, 263–4, 280, 282–5, 334, 485n11
North Africa land campaign
  Egypt, Libya 121–2, 126, 130, 132, 289–90, 298–300, 309, 328, 331, 501n22
  Algeria, Tunisia 76, 331–3
North Cape battle (1943) 318–19
Northwest Europe land campaign (1944–45) 428–30
Norway 86–7, 98–9, 110, 146, 265–6, 269, 271–3, 280, 310, 415, 436–7
Norway invasion (1940) 29–46, 55–6, 79–80
Norwegian Navy 425
  ships
    Eidsvold 29
    Norge 29
Nouméa 74, 205, 229, 236
Nouvelle-Calédonie 74, 205, 229
Novorossiisk 150

Obata, Gen. Hideyoshi 9, 391
Odessa 145
O'Hara, Vincent 505n30
O'Hare, Edward ('Butch') 203, 393
Oikawa, Adm. Koshirō 179, 359, 361, 397, 466
Okinawa 362, 439, 464–8, 480n6
Oktiabrskii, Adm. F.S. 142, 144, 149–51
Oldendorf, Adm. Jesse 449
Oliva, Adm. Romeo 342
Ōmae, Capt. Toshikazu 226, 233
Ōmori, Adm. Sentarō 244
Ōnishi, Adm. Takijirō 457–8, 466, 470
Oran xvi–xviii, 66, 76, 283, 300, 333
Oslo 30–1, 41
OVERLORD *see* Normandy invasion
Overy, Richard 496n44
Ozawa, Adm. Jisaburō 181, 191, 382, 397, 399–400, 404–5, 444–5, 447–8, 454–5, 466

Pacific Lend-Lease route 270, 321, 516n3
Pacific Ocean Area (POA, US theatre command) 376, 379, 443
  see also Nimitz
Palau Is. 378, 383, 391, 395, 398–9, 510n42, 510n43
  see also Peliliu
Palembang raid (Sumatra) 467–8
Panteleev, Adm. Iurii 136–7
Pantelleria I. 274, 293
Papua 211–13, 215, 228–9, 246–8
Parker, J.P. 113, 487n3
Parshall, Jonathan 495n29, 496n37, 496n41, 496n45, 496n47
Pearl Harbor 207, 209, 212, 216, 357–9, 376, 388, 413, 467
Pearl Harbor raid *see* Hawaiian Operation
Pearson, Lester 493n47
Peden, George 481n14
PEDESTAL convoy 283, 294–7
Peleliu 391–2
Penang 363
Persian Gulf Lend-Lease route 270, 321, 334 433
Pescadores 350, 493n32
Pétain, Marshal Philippe 64, 69, 74–7
Petropavlovsk 270, 321
Petsamo–Kirkenes operation 149
Philippine Sea battle 361, 368–9, 398–406, 415–16, 442, 456–7, 473, 511n68, 515n30, 515n33
Philippines 227, 246, 361, 376–8, 395, 444,446, 461, 474
Philippines invasion (1941–42) 180, 182, 184–5, 204, 356
Philippines invasion (1944–45) 443–61
  see also Leyte; Leyte Gulf battle; Luzon invasion
Phillips, Adm. Tom 186–8
Plan Dog 165, 491n20, 516n4
  see also Stark, Adm. Harold
Plymouth 13
Poland 10–11, 21, 25, 43, 433–4
Polish Navy and merchant marine 21
  merchant ships

Batory 21
Pilsudski 21
warships
Gryf 21
Kujawiak 293
Orzel 34
Wicher 21
Port Lyautey xvi
Port Moresby 211–16, 228–9, 246, 303, 495n21
Portsmouth 13
Portugal 324
Potsdam Declaration 469–70
Pound, Adm. Dudley xvi, 12, 38, 60, 70–1, 267–8, 274, 412, 481n13
Pownall, Adm. Charles ('Baldy') 379, 394
Prados, John 222, 496n41, 507n5, 509n30, 509n31, 510n45, 513n2
Prien, Günther 22, 85, 95
Project HULA 471
Punta Stilo *see* Calabria battle

Rabaul 188, 201–3, 209, 211, 225, 227–34, 241–8, 370–3, 376–8, 381, 383, 472, 498n31, 507n5
Raeder, Adm. Erich 5–7, 10–11, 23–5, 33–4, 37, 44, 46, 55–6, 63, 72, 89, 99, 101–2, 108, 110, 118, 122, 132, 147, 196, 254, 266, 307, 309–10, 316, 331–2, 412, 488n11
Rahn, Werner 269, 487n24
Ramsay, Adm. Alexander 188, 493n37
Ramsay, Adm. Bertram 51, 284, 336–7, 413, 423, 425
Rangoon 362, 407, 411, 492n8
Rawlings, Adm. Bernard 467–8
Reynolds, Clark 395, 511n68
Riccardi, Adm. Arturo 121, 332, 339
Richardson, Adm. James 166
Richmond, Adm. Herbert xix, 172, 195, 301, 477–8, 480n5, 484n33, 516n8
River Plate battle 26–8
Rochefort, Capt. Joseph 212, 216, 223
Rohwer, Jürgen 487n24
Roi-Namur 387–8
Romania 144, 151, 292
Rommel, Erwin 122, 126, 289–90, 298, 331–2, 424
Roosevelt, Franklin D. 75, 94, 154, 158, 161–4, 166–7, 195, 205, 207–8, 210, 242–3, 251, 262, 280, 312, 375, 467, 476
Roskill, Stephen 243, 268, 272, 301, 477, 480n6
Ross, Alan 308
Rosyth 13, 60
Rota 395
Rouen 429
Royal Air Force (RAF)
aircraft types
Beaufighter 286, 502n2
Beaufort 96, 482n33
Blenheim 35, 96, 194
Botha 482n33
Catalina 20, 96, 106, 193–4, 269
Fortress 20
Halifax 109, 432–3, 503n8, 513n22
Hampden 40
Hudson 20, 96
Lancaster 432
Lerwick 482n33
Liberator 20, 96, 260, 313, 437, 503n8
Sunderland 20, 40, 84, 96
Wellington 40, 96, 294, 314, 486n21
Whitley 96
anti-invasion role 60, 62, 484n33, 484n38
Atlantic 'Air Gap' 260
attacks on U-boat bases 261, 314
attacks on U-boat shipyards 261, 314
Baltic minelaying campaign 434
in Battle of Atlantic 96–7, 106, 109, 260, 313–14
Biscay A/S offensives 260–1, 314–16, 324. 486n21
Ceylon 193–4
Coastal Command 18, 60, 96, 260–1, 313–14, 324
Dunkirk 49
equipment and weapons
air-dropped depth charges 260
ASV Mk I radar 97
ASV Mk II radar 106, 260, 261
ASV Mk III radar 260
centimetric radar 260, 313–14, 320
fighter direction 295
Leigh Light 261
rockets 325
groups
No. 15 96–7
No. 19 96
No. 201 286
Malaya 187
Malta 114, 125, 127–8, 130, 132
strategic bombing strategy 17, 194
Tirpitz attacks 432–3
Tunisia blockade 330, 332–3, 335
wartime role 477
Royal Australian Air Force 212
Royal Australian Navy 407
ships
Australia 225, 248, 498n34

Canberra 226
Hobart 368
Perth 190
Shropshire 248, 449, 498n34
Sydney 119
Royal Canadian Navy 95, 254, 258–9, 281, 302, 314–15, 324, 432
Royal Navy (RN) 476–7
Admiralty building 13
amphibious warfare 477
anti-invasion preparations (1940) 62–3
British Admiralty Delegation (Washington) 290, 312–13, 411
coastal forces 60
equipment and weapons
ASDIC (sonar) 84–5, 94, 355
ASV Mk IIN radar 106, 107
centimetric radar 499n15
FOXER 323
HF/DF 97, 259, 313, 316, 325
IFF 494n1
Type 79 radar 119
Type 271 259
Type 284 radar 103, 497n19
Type 286 radar 95, 97
Squid A/S mortar 432
fleet train 468
fleets
British Pacific 411, 466–9
East Indies (1944–45) 411
Eastern 186, 191–3, 407–11
Home 13, 34, 39, 59–60, 100, 102, 413, 488n12
Mediterranean 13, 127, 133–4, 286, 290, 294, 335, 345
Forces
H 66, 102, 112, 290, 335, 344–5, 488n12
K 128–9, 286, 328–9
Q 328–9
V 344, 505n23
Z 187–8
TF 37 469
TF 57 466
offensive doctrine 112
operations
COCKPIT 410
CRIMSON 410–11
DEADLIGHT 438
DRACULA 411–12
HATS 119, 130
GOODWOOD 320–1
MASCOT 320–1
RETRIBUTION 333
SOURCE 317
TITLE 317
TRANSOM 410
TUNGSTEN 319–20
Operational Intelligence Centre (OIC) 45, 97, 259
Operational Research (OR) 313
Singapore strategy 185
submarine operations
Mediterranean 127–8, 299
midget submarines 317, 411, 507n28, 512n81
Indian Ocean 408, 411
Western Approaches 96–7, 312
see also British codebreaking; Fleet Air Arm; Royal Navy warships
Royal Navy warships
ship types
aircraft carriers 16, 18, 468, 477, 481n25
amphibious vessels 275–7, 477
armed merchant cruisers 4–5, 23, 100
escort carriers 91, 163, 314, 320, 324–6, 348, 411, 413, 504n29
battleships 14, 16, 488n12
corvettes 60, 84, 94–5, 259, 313, 324
cruisers 14–6, 491n7
destroyers 15, 17, 324
destroyer escorts/frigates 91, 95, 259, 324
MTBs 60
submarines 127–8, 408, 411
X-craft 317, 411, 507n28
ships
Achates 308
Active 15
Afridi 17
Ajax 26–7, 421
Anson 269, 413
Archer 325
Argonaut 328–9
Argus 147, 293, 481n24, 483n12
Ark Royal 16, 18, 22, 24, 28, 40, 46, 66–7, 72, 102, 106–7, 112, 120–1, 123, 131–2, 482n27, 488n20
Attacker 252, 325, 344
Audacity 91, 324
Aurora 128, 328
Avenger 264, 269, 325
Baquachero 277
Barham 5, 22, 72–3, 119, 124–5, 131, 133
Battler 325, 344
Bayntun 324
Bedouin 293
Belfast 23, 319
Biter 314, 325
Bonaventure 132
Boxer 277
Breconshire 289

Bulolo 284
Cairo 293, 296–7
Calcutta 125
Calypso 132
Campbeltown 278
Cleopatra 286, 328
Cornwall 192–3
Cumberland 14, 26, 28
Dasher 325
Dido 286, 328
Dorsetshire 108, 192–3
Duke of York 267, 269, 318–19, 472
Glengyle 275
Glenroy 420
Glowworm 35–6
Eagle 68, 103, 112, 114, 292–3, 295–7, 481n24, 483n12
Edinburgh 266, 500n30
Egret 342
Electra 3
Emperor 320
Euryalus 286–7, 328
Exeter 26–7, 190
Fencer 320
Fiji 125
Formidable 18, 103, 124–5, 192, 321, 335–6, 344, 469, 488n20, 503n17, 516n47
Furious 18, 38–40, 103, 147, 295, 320–1
Galatea 133
Glory 245, 472
Gloucester 125
Gurkha 39
Hermes 67, 192–4, 481n24, 483n12
Hermione 294
Hood 24, 60, 66, 102–5, 107–8, 112, 121, 483n10, 487n34
Howe 335, 411, 413, 468
Hunter (DD) 38
Hunter (CVE) 344
Illustrious 18, 119–121, 123–5, 131, 163, 279, 320, 344, 408–11, 468, 510n20, 503n17, 516n47
Implacable 469, 481n25
Indefatigable 321 413, 468, 472, 481n25, 488n20, 503n17
Indomitable 18, 192, 279, 295–6, 335–6, 411, 468, 488n20, 503n17, 504n11
Jamaica 308, 318
Jervis 17
Jervis Bay 100
King George V 16, 102–4, 106–7, 335, 468–9, 472, 488n12, 500n33
Largs 284
Liverpool 293
London 267
Malaya 112, 114, 119, 163, 293, 483n10
Manchester 296–7
Manxman 130
Medway 299
Naiad 286
Nelson 14, 23, 60, 102, 131, 295, 335, 343–4, 483n10, 488n12
Neptune 113, 128
Newcastle 120, 294
Nigeria 296
Norfolk 267, 318–19
Onslow 308
P42 297
Partridge 293
Penelope 128, 286, 288, 346
Prince of Wales 16, 102–110, 131, 165, 186–7, 488n12
Princess Beatrix 271–2, 275, 281, 283
Queen Emma 271–2, 275, 281, 283
Queen Elizabeth 16, 103, 119, 129, 131, 133, 409–10, 483n10,
Quentin 329
Ramillies 112, 120–1, 192, 279, 348, 366, 488n12
Renown 16, 28, 35–6, 38–9, 44, 102, 120–1, 409–10, 488n12
Repulse 35, 39, 44, 102–3, 187, 487n31
Resolution 66, 72–3, 112, 192, 488n12
Revenge 60, 192
Rodney 14, 35, 39, 60, 102–3, 106–7, 131, 295, 335, 344, 487n31, 488n12
Royal Oak 22
Royal Sovereign 112, 114, 149, 192, 488n12
Scylla 427
Sheffield 39, 107, 308, 319
Somali 272
Southampton 18, 123
Spartan 325
Stalker 325, 344
Suffolk 39
Sussex 472
Tally-Ho 408
Trenchant 411
Trinidad 266
Uganda 345
Unicorn 33, 481n25
Upholder 127–8
Valiant 16, 35, 39, 46, 66, 103, 112, 11 121, 123–4, 131, 133, 335, 342, 344, 409–10
Vampire 194
Vanguard 481n20

Victorious, 18, 102–3, 106–7, 147, 208, 266–7, 295, 320, 407, 411, 468–9, 489n20, 503n17
*Warspite*16, 38–9, 103, 112–14, 119, 121, 124–5, 192, 342, 344–5
York 125
Royal New Zealand Navy 407
Achilles 26–7
Leander 243
Russell Is. 241
Russia *see* Soviet Union
Russian convoys 147, 264–70, 307–9, 316–21, 432–3, 516n3
Ryūkyū Is. 439–40, 462, 464, 466
see also Okinawa

Saaremaa (Ösel) 143, 153, 484n23
Sabang raids 410–11
Safi 16, 284
Saint-Nazaire 70, 278
Saipan 177, 368, 398, 509n42
Saipan invasion 389–90
see also Japanese Army, Marianas; Philippine Sea battle
Saitō, Gen. Yoshitsugo 389–90
Sakishima Is. 466
Sakonjū, Adm. Naomasa 365, 507n26
Salamaua 209, 246
Salerno 344–5
Samar, Battle off 451–4
Samoa 229
San Bernardino Strait 400, 447, 451–5
Santa Cruz battle 236–7
Sardinia 339
Savo Island 225–7
Scapa Flow 13, 22, 24, 34, 102
Schenk, Peter 484n28, 484n30
Schmider, Klaus 490n25
Schnee, Lt Cmdr Adalbert 436
Schurman, D.M. 480n5
Scott, Adm. Norman 233, 238–9
SEA LION
see German operations
sea power xix, 477, 480n5
sea/air war xxi, 480n6
Sevastopol 145–6, 151
Shaw, Cmdr James 507n7
Sherbrooke, Capt. Robert 308
Sherman, Adm. Forrest 389
Sherman, Adm. Frederick ('Ted') 202, 214, 371–3, 450, 455
Shima, Adm. Kiyohide 450
Shimada, Adm. Shigetarō 396
Shimizu, Adm. Mizumi 367
Shimushu invasion 471
Short, Gen.Walter 182–3
Shortland Is. 230
Sibuyan Sea 448–9
Sicily invasion 334–9, 415
Singapore 179, 185–6, 188, 195, 409, 411, 445, 472
Singora landing 187
Sino-Japanese War (1937–45) 172–4, 186, 188, 491n18
Sirte battle 286–9, 502n4
Skerki Bank 328–9
Slapton Sands 426
Slessor, Air Marshal John 313
Slim, Gen. William 411–12
Smart, Harley 172
Smith, Gen. Holland M. 390, 509n41
Smith, Kevin 263
Solomon Is. 224, 240–1, 243–5, 377, 383, 493n20
Somerville, Adm. James 51, 66, 70, 102, 112, 115, 120–1, 192–4, 290, 407–8, 410–11
South China Sea raid (1944) 461, 515n37
South of France invasion (1944)
see France, southern invasion
South West Pacific Area (SWPA, US theatre command) 376, 379, 443
see also MacArthur, Gen. Douglas
Southeast Asia campaign (1942–45) 407
Southeast Asia Command (SEAC) 408–9
Southern Operation (1941–42) 178–80, 185–91
Soviet Army Air Force (VVS) 141
Soviet-Japanese Neutrality Pact 469
Soviet merchant ships
Alev 136
Armeniia 145
Balkhash 137
Ella 137
Everita 137
Iosif Stalin 143
Krasnogvardeets 321
Vironia 136
Soviet Navy (*Voenno-morskoi flot*)
aircraft types
A–20 148
DB–3F 141
DB–3T 141, 143
MBR–2 141
PBY 148
Pe–2 153
amphibious operations 145, 150–1
fleets
Baltic 135–6, 138, 141, 143, 148, 151, 153, 434, 489n1
Black Sea 141, 144–6, 148–51, 490n26
Northern 146–9, 266–7

Pacific 141, 148, 470–1
Italian naval reparations 149, 490n20
Lend-Lease 148, 471
loss of three Black Sea destroyers (Oct. 1943) 150
Main Naval Staff 147, 151
naval aviation 139, 141, 147–8, 151, 153, 434
naval cooperation with Germany (1939–41) 142
naval infantry 144, 146–7, 490n16
personnel strength 148
pre-war developments 138–42
organisation 141, 147–8
pre-war purges 141–2
Project HULA 471
shipbuilding programme 140–1
submarine operations 143, 147, 149, 152–3
Tallinn convoy 135–8
see also Soviet Navy warships

Soviet Navy warships
ship types
battleships 139–41
cruisers 139–40
destroyers 140
MTBs 139
minesweepers
sub-chasers (*okhotniki*) 148
submarines 139–40
ships
Arkhangelsk (*Royal Sovereign*) 149
Avrora 144, 489n10
Besposhchadnyi 150
Chervona Ukraïna 145
Frunze 145
Gnevnyi 140, 143
Iakov Sverdlov 136–7
K-21 268
Kharkov 150
Kirov 136–7, 140, 143–4
Krasnyi Kavkaz 146, 149–50
Krasnyi Krym 146, 149–51
Kronshtadt 144
Kuibyshev 145
L-16 490n19
Maksim Gorkii 136, 140
Marat 136, 139, 144
Minsk 137
Moskva 144
Murmansk (*Milwaukee*) 149
Sevastopol 145
Sovetskaia Ukraina 145
Tashkent 145
Oktiabrskaia Revoliutsiia 136, 139, 144
Parizhskaia Kommuna 139, 144–5, 149
Shch-307 143
Skoryi 137
Sovetskaia Ukraina 145
Sovetskii Soiuz 140, 144
Sposobnyi 150
Voroshilov 149–51

Soviet Union
invaded by Germany 56–7
invasion of Finland 32
invasion of Manchuria (1945) 469–70
Stavka VGK 147, 150, 153
see also Soviet Navy

Special Operations Executive (SOE) 273
Spector, Ronald 511n68
Speer, Albert 310
Spitsbergen raid 317
Sprague, Adm. Clifton 452
Spruance, Adm. Raymond 217–8, 221–3, 235–6, 379, 387, 390, 394–5, 401–2, 405–6, 413, 443–4, 451, 461, 494n14, 511n68
Stalin, Joseph 135, 150, 316–7, 485n41
Stamsund 272
Stark, Adm. Harold 164–6, 182–3, 206–8, 257, 355, 476, 491n20, 516n4
Stauffenberg, Berthold von 513n24
Stepanov, Admiral G.A. 151
Stumpf, Reinhard 298
submarine warfare and international law 4, 26, 80, 161, 167, 261, 354–5, 364
Suez Canal 117–18, 126, 196, 290, 298, 383
Sullivan brothers 497n17
Sumatra 320, 409, 467
Sunda Strait battle 190–1
Surabaya 189–90
Surabaya raid (1944) 250, 410
Surigao Strait battle 449–50
Suursaari 138
Suzuki, Adm. Kantarō 469–70
Svolvær 272
Sweden 32–3, 267
Sydney 233, 366, 411, 467–8
Syfret, Adm. Neville 279, 291, 295

Tacloban 446
Takagi, Adm. Takeo 190, 212–13, 368, 390, 397–8
Tallinn-Kronshtadt convoy (Aug. 1941) 135–8, 143, 489n1
Tanaka, Adm. Raizō 234, 239–40
Taranto 343, 345
Taranto raid 119–20, 133–4,
Tarawa 378, 386–7
see also Gilbert Is.
Tassafaronga battle 234
Tawi Tawi 398–9, 403

Tennant, Adm. William 48, 52483n5
Thach, Lt Cmdr John 202–3
Thailand 182, 187–8
Tinian 177, 378, 389–91, 509n42
Tobruk 122, 126, 130, 289, 294, 298, 300
Tōgō, Adm. Heihachirō 396, 509n33
Tōgō Shigenori 470
Tōjō, Gen. Hideki 174, 186, 396, 406, 469
Tomioka, Adm. Sadatohi 472
Tonga 236, 497n14
Topp, Erich 155
TORCH
  see North Africa invasion
Toulon 75–8, 346, 348–9, 429
Tovey, Adm. John 60, 100–3, 106, 108, 113, 114, 267–9, 308, 318
Toyoda, Adm. Soemu 396–7, 399, 405, 410, 440, 444, 446, 449, 457, 466, 469–70
Tregaskis, Richard 224
Tributs, Adm. V.F. 135–7, 142
Trincomalee 193–4, 408, 411
Tripartite Pact 162–3, 165, 174, 179, 491n20
Tripoli 126, 300, 331
Trondheim 29–30, 41–2, 46, 317, 432–3, 499n22
Truk 212, 230, 355, 368, 373, 377–8, 383–4, 394–5, 472, 494n7
Truman, Harry 472
Tsushima 177, 509n33
Tulagi 211, 213, 224–5, 231, 497n6
Tully, Anthony 495n29, 496n37, 496n41, 496n45, 496n47
Tunisia 76, 126, 283, 285, 300, 328–33
Turner, John 133
Turner, Adm. R. Kelly 225, 230, 379, 386–7, 389, 401, 462

U-boats *see* German Navy U-boat force
Ugaki, Adm. Matome 219, 221, 242, 250, 448, 462–3, 470
Ulithi 392, 463
Ultra 97–8
  see also British codebreaking; US codebreaking
Umezu, Gen. Yoshijirō 469, 472
United States
  arsenal of democracy policy 163
  conscription 162
  declaration of war in 1917 161, 163
  economic sanctions against Japan 165, 174
  economic strength 176
  isolationism 161
  Joint Chiefs of Staff (JCS) 205, 377–8, 442–3
  Neutrality Acts 161
  Pearl Harbor investigation 180
  repairs British warships 123, 125
  Robin Moor incident 167
  shipyards 86, 93, 164, 251–3, 262, 312
  technical cooperation with Britain 165
  see also Allied strategy; Lend-Lease; US strategy
US Army
  divisions
    1st Cavalry 249
    7th 384, 387
    11th Airborne 472
    27th 386–7, 389–90
    66th 430
    77th 391
  field army
    Sixth 446
    Seventh 336
  see also US Army Air Force
US Army Air Force
  air minelaying campaign against Japan 362
  aircraft
    A-20 Boston/Havoc 247, 490n17
    B-17 Flying Fortress 169, 182, 185, 229, 332, 334, 516n49
    B-25 Mitchell 210, 247, 371
    B-24 Liberator 294, 314, 329–30, 332
    B-29 Superfortress 362, 378, 462, 508n24
    P-38 Lightning 242, 381
    P-39 Airacobra 242
    P-40 Warhawk 242
    P-47 Thunderbolt 381
    P-51 Mustang 462
  maritime patrol role 160, 258
  Naples air raid (Dec. 1942) 329–30
  New Guinea 377
  pre-war Pacific air strategy 185
  raids on Rabaul 370–1
  strategic bombing of Japan (1944–5) 378, 461
US codebreaking
  Atlantic battle (1943–44) 325
  Coral Sea 212
  FRUPAC 359
  FRUMEL 359
  Japanese diplomatic code (PURPLE) 181
  Midway 216
  New Guinea 249
  Pacific submarine war 358, 360
  Pearl Harbor 180–1
  Rabaul raid (1943) 372, 507n5
  see also British codebreaking; German Navy, communications systems; Japanese Navy, communications systems

US Marine Corps (USMC) 497n8
 divisions
  1st 230, 249, 249, 391, 464
  2nd 386, 389
  3rd 391, 462
  4th 387, 389, 462
  5th 462
  6th 464
 landing vessel development 275
 pre-war developments 230–1
US merchant fleet 86, 156
 shipbuilding xx, 86, 93, 163–4, 251–3, 262, 312
  see also Allied shipbuilding
 ships
  Adabelle Lykes 252
  America 169
  George F. Elliot 225
  James MacKay 253
  John C. Fremont 252
  Kentucky 293
  Louise Lykes 253
  Manhattan 169
  Patrick Henry 252
  Robin Moor 167
  Sinclair Superflame 252
  Star of Oregon 252
  Washington 168
 types
  C1 cargo ship 252, 420
  C2 cargo ship 252
  C3 cargo ship 252
  Liberty ship 252
 US Maritime Commission 252
 War Shipping Administration 262
US Navy
 amphibious forces
  III 'Phib 509n29
  V 'Phib 379
  VII 'Phib 248, 509n29
 Central Pacific Force 379, 392, 394
  see also Fifth Fleet
 command structure (1942) 205–8
 equipment and weapons
  AA systems 237, 487n35
  CXAM-1 radar 201–2
  FM sonar 362
  fighter direction 403, 459
  Mk XIV torpedo problems 358
  Mk XVIII torpedo 358
  Mk 3 FC 497n19
  PPI radar display 351–2
  SD radar 358
  SG radar 238
  SJ radar 351, 358
  Torpedo Data Computer (TDC) 350–1
  VHF radio (TBS) 358
 Fast Carrier Force 379, 392, 394, 444, 461, 510n44
 fleet train 388, 468, 474
 fleets
  Atlantic 166, 206, 257, 323, 503n27,
  Pacific 166, 206
  Asiatic 166
  Second 503n27
  Third 439, 443–4, 447, 454, 461, 471, 471–2, 498n32, 503n27, 510n44
  Fourth 503n27
  Fifth 379, 389, 443, 461, 498n32, 510n44
  Seventh 248, 357, 401, 443–4, 447, 449, 451–2, 498n32
  Eighth 503n27
  Tenth 323, 326
  Twelfth 503n27
 General Board 206–7
 hunter-killer A/S operations 325
 Neutrality Patrol 166
 North Pacific Force 248
 Pacific Ocean Area (POA) 376, 379, 443
  Central Pacific Area 379
  North Pacific Area 497n13
  South Pacific Area 229, 236, 370, 379, 512n82
 Patrol Force, US Fleet (1940–41) 166
 personnel 162
 platoon command system 443
 pre-war annual budget 160
 pre-war history 156
 pre-war operations in Atlantic 98–9, 165–9
 ship designation system 491n5, 491n12
 ship transfers from Pacific to Atlantic 1941 166
 sea frontiers
  Caribbean 255
  Eastern 255, 257
  Gulf 255
 Seabee (construction battalion, CB) 388
 Servron (service squadron) 388
 Southwest Pacific Force 248
  see also US Navy, fleets, Seventh
 task forces 490n1
  TF 1 168, 490n1
  TF 4 490n1
  TF 8 209
  TF 11 201–3, 209
  TF 16 210, 217–19, 222, 496n35
  TF 17 209, 212, 214, 217–22, 496n35
  TF 19 167
  TF 34 372, 451, 454–5
  TF 37 469

TF 38 371, 439, 441–5, 450, 455, 461, 510n44
TF 50 371, 392–3
TF 52 401, 451
TF 57 466
TF 58 392, 395, 399, 401–5, 443, 461, 463, 510n44, 511n64
TF 61 225, 235–6, 248
TF 71 452–3
TF 77 459–60
TF 80 337
task groups (fleet carriers)
TG 38.1/58.1 392, 401–2, 441, 514n14
TG 38.2/58.2 392, 401, 403, 463
TG 38.3/58.3 401, 450, 455
TG 38.4/58.4 401, 441, 515n32
task units (CVEs)
TU 71.4.3 (Taffy 3) 452, 457
warship programmes 93, 376, 413
Naval Act of 1916 156
Second Vinson Act (1938) 158, 177
Vinson-Trammel Act (1934) 158, 177
Vinson-Walsh Act (1940) 159
Two Ocean Navy Act 159–60, 177, 374
WAVES 323
see also US codebreaking; US Navy aviation; US Navy submarine force; US Navy warships
US Navy aviation 160, 208–9, 375
aircraft
F4F Wildcat 184, 202–3, 208, 232, 242, 495n16
F4U Corsair 242, 414, 508n18
F6F Hellcat 372, 375, 381, 403, 414, 508n18
PBM Mariner 405
PBY Catalina 160, 216–8, 221–2, 491n12
PB4Y Liberator 388, 491n12
SBD Dauntless 208, 232, 494n16
SB2C Helldiver 372, 375
TBD Devastator 19, 208, 218–9
TBF Avenger 233, 375, 515n24
aircraft strength 160, 375
US Navy submarine force 350–62, 415, 474
defence of Philippines (1941–42) 356–7
equipment and weapons
Mk XIV torpedo problems 358
Mk XVIII torpedo 358
Torpedo Data Computer (TDC) 350–1
VHF radio (TBS) 358
Philippine Sea battle 401–2, 404
unrestricted operations 355
submarines
Albacore 357, 404
Cavalla 402, 404
Dace 448
Darter 448
Grayling 207, 355
Gudgeon 350
Nautilus 222
Redfish 505n16
Roper 255
Sealion 457
Swordfish 355
Trigger 350–2, 358, 506n
wolfpacks 358
US Navy warships
ship types
battleships 156–9, 376
fleet carriers (CV) 157–9, 208–9, 373–4, 508n15
light carriers (CVL) 374–5
escort carriers (CVE) 324–5, 375, 504n30, 504n31, 504n32
cruisers 157–9, 491n7
destroyers 157–9, 491n9, 497n16
destroyer escorts (DE) 324, 413
MTBs (PT boats) 234, 450
attack transports 275
ships
Alabama 401
Arkansas 348, 424
Arizona 171–2, 183
Astoria 220–226
Atlanta 238–9
Augusta 165, 285, 424
Bataan 401
Belleau Wood 401
Bennington 374, 461
Birmingham 450
Bismarck Sea 462
Boise 338
Bon Homme Richard 374, 508n11
Bunker Hill 371–5, 401, 465
Cabot 401, 448
California 171, 389, 449, 460
Canberra (CA-70) 441
Chester 234
Chicago 226, 233, 366
Cleveland 245
Colorado 386, 389
Columbia 245
Cowpens 401
Denver 245
England 368, 404
Enterprise 158, 208, 209–10, 212–13, 217, 219–20, 225, 234–7, 239, 373, 393, 401, 403, 439, 448, 461, 465, 481n25
Essex 371–4, 401, 448
Fanshaw Bay 452

Fletcher 238
Franklin 374, 439, 441, 448, 463
Gambier Bay 452
Greer 167, 251
Hancock 439, 511n60, 514n14
Helena 239, 243
Hoel 452
Hornet (CV-8) 159, 209–10, 212–13, 217–18, 220, 234, 236–7
Hornet (CV-12) 401, 508n14, 514n14
Houston (CA-30) 190
Houston (CL-81) 441
Idaho 168, 389
Independence 371–4, 393
Indiana 401
Indianapolis 369, 391, 516n39
Intrepid 373, 394, 448–9, 508n14
Iowa 376, 394, 401
Johnston 452
Juneau 234, 239, 368, 497n17
Kalinin Bay 452
Kearny 168
Kitkun Bay 452
Langley 401
Lexington (CV-2) 157, 201–3, 209, 212, 214, 373
Lexington (CV-16) 374, 393, 401, 448, 508n14
Liscome Bay 368, 393
Long Island 209, 232
Louisville 449
Maddox 336
Mannert L. Abele 464
Maryland 171 386, 389, 449
Massachusetts 75
Melvin 450
Mississinewa 369
Mississippi 168, 389, 449
Missouri 159, 472, 516n55
Monterey 401
Montpelier 245
Mount Vernon 169
Nevada 171, 348, 384, 424
New Jersey 376, 394, 401, 439. 451
New Mexico 389, 460
Newcomb 450
North Carolina 234, 236, 240, 401
Northampton 217, 234
O'Bannon 238
Oklahoma 171
Omaha 168
Ommaney Bay 460
Panay 173
Pennsylvania 171, 384, 389, 449
Pensacola 158
Portland 239, 472
Princeton 371–2, 401, 450
PT-109 243
Quincy (CA-39) 169, 226
Quincy (CA-71) 424
Randolph 461, 463
Ranger 75, 169, 495n32
Reuben James 154–7, 168
S-44 357
Samuel B. Roberts 452
San Francisco 238–9
San Jacinto 401, 462
Santee 325, 457, 504n31, 515n31
Saratoga 157, 209, 225, 234–5, 371–3, 407, 410, 461–2, 507n9, 509n38
Savannah 338, 345
Shangri-La 374
South Dakota 236–7, 240, 401, 403
St. Lo 452, 457
Tennessee 171, 386, 449
Texas 348, 424
Tuscaloosa 168, 267, 424
Underhill 369
Vincennes 169, *226*
Wakefield 169
Wasatch 451
Washington 240, 267, 401, 487n35
Wasp (CV-7) 159, 221, 225, 234–6, 292, 481n25, 496n42
Wasp (CV-18) 401, 463, 514n14
West Point 169
West Virginia 171, 449
White Plains 452
Wichita 168, 267
Yorktown (CV-5) 158, 166, 209, 212–14, 217–23, 481n25, 495n27
Yorktown (CV-10) 401, 508n11, 508n14
US strategy
assumes overall command in Pacific (1942) 205
hemispheric defence 72, 162, 165
regional commands in Pacific (POA, SWPA) 205, 376
war plans
ORANGE 227, 377
Pacific planning conference (Mar. 1943) 377
RAINBOW 5 165
see also Allied strategy
US Strategic Bombing Survey 506n3
USSR *see* Soviet Union

Vaagso raid 272–3
Vandegrift, Gen. Arthur 230
Vella Gulf battle 243

Vella Lavella invasion 241, 244
Versailles treaty (1919) 7–10
Vestfjord 271
Vian, Adm. Philip 286–8, 293–4, 427, 467
Villa, Brian 282, 501n14, 501n20
Vinson, Carl 158–9, 374
Vitiaz Strait 249, 498n35
Vittorio Emanuele III 339
Vladimirskii, Adm. L.A. 150–1
Voroshilov, Marshal K.E. 135

Wake Atoll 184, 209, 392–3
Walter, Hellmuth 322, 503n23
Warburton-Lee, Capt. Bernard 37–8
Washington Naval Conference/Treaty (1922) 9, 14–6, 67–8, 116–7, 157–9, 174–6, 481n15, 481n18, 492n12, 492n14, 492n14
Wavell, Gen. Archibald 191
Wheatley, Ronald 485n40
Whitworth, Adm. William Jock 35, 38
Willis, Adm. Algernon 335, 344
Wilson, Woodrow 158, 161, 201
Wotje 387–9

Y'Blood, William 511n68
Yamaguchi, Adm. Tamon 219–20
Yamamoto, Adm. Isoroku 176, 179–81, 187, 204, 211–12, 215–16, 220–1, 237, 239, 242, 367, 382, 494n48,
Yamasaki, Col. Yasuyo 385
Yamashita, Gen. Tomoyuki 460, 472
Yano, Adm. Hideo 390
Yap 443, 446, 510n43
Yokoi, Adm. Toshiyuki 465
Yonai, Adm. Mitsumasa 469
Yoshida Akihiko 507n24

Z-Plan *see* German Navy
Zapasnik, Fred 155
Zhavoronkov, Gen. S.F. 148